UNIX® SYSTEM V RELEASE 4

D1405534

User's Reference Manual / System Administrator's Reference Manual

(Commands m-z)

◇

Intel Processors

◇

Published by Prentice Hall, Inc.
A Simon & Schuster Company
Englewood Cliffs, New Jersey 07632

IMPORTANT NOTE TO USERS

TRADEMARKS

10 9 8 7 6 5 4

ISBN 0-13-951328-0

UNIX
PRESS
A Prentice Hall Title

P R E N T I C E   H A L L

ORDERING INFORMATION

UNIX® SYSTEM V RELEASE 4 DOCUMENTATION

To order single copies of UNIX® SYSTEM V Release 4 documentation, please call (201) 767-5937.

ATTENTION DOCUMENTATION MANAGERS AND TRAINING DIRECTORS:

For bulk purchases in excess of 30 copies, please write to:

Corporate Sales
Prentice Hall
Englewood Cliffs, N.J. 07632

Or call: (201) 461-8441.

ATTENTION GOVERNMENT CUSTOMERS:

For GSA and other pricing information, please call (201) 767-5994.

Prentice-Hall International (UK) Limited, *London*
Prentice-Hall of Australia Pty. Limited, *Sydney*
Prentice-Hall Canada Inc., *Toronto*
Prentice-Hall Hispanoamericana, S.A., *Mexico*
Prentice-Hall of India Private Limited, *New Delhi*
Prentice-Hall of Japan, Inc., *Tokyo*
Simon & Schuster Asia Pte. Ltd., *Singapore*
Editora Prentice-Hall do Brasil, Ltda., *Rio de Janeiro*

Preface

UNIX System V Reference Manuals describe the interfaces and execution behavior of each System V component. The components of UNIX System V include the graphical user interface (GUI), Shell command line interface, application program interface (API) and Device Driver Interface / Driver Kernel Interface (DDI/DKI), as well as device special files, header files and other system files. The following table summarizes the general categories of manual pages:

Table 1: Manual Page Categories

Description	Section Reference
□ *Shell & Command Line Interface*	
— General Purpose Utilities	1
— Maintenance Utilities	1M
□ *Application Program Interface (API)*	
— UNIX System Calls	2
— C Language Libraries	3
□ *System Files & Devices*	
— System File Formats	4
— Miscellaneous Facilities	5
— Special Files (Devices)	7
□ *Device Driver Interface/Driver Kernel Interface (DDI/DKI)*	
— DDI/DKI Driver Data Definitions	D1
— DDI/DKI Driver Entry Point Routines	D2
— DDI/DKI Kernel Utility Routines	D3
— DDI/DKI Kernel Data Structures	D4
— DDI/DKI Kernel Defines	D5

Reference Manuals supply technical reference information that describes the source-code interfaces and run-time behavior of each component of System V on a component by component basis. As concise reference material, manual pages assume some familiarity with the information.

Organization of the Reference Manuals

Each section in a Reference Manual consists of a number of independent entries called "manual pages." A "Table of Contents" precedes each manual page section. Within each section, manual pages are arranged in alphabetical order based on the name of the component described by that manual page. Some manual pages may describe several commands, functions, or other type of system facility. In such cases, the manual page appears only once in a table of contents, alphabetized under its "primary" name, the name that appears at the upper corners of each manual page. For each Reference Manual, a "Permuted Index" of all manual pages for that manual is provided at the back of the book.

This latest edition of the UNIX System V Release 4 Reference Manuals has reorganized the reference manuals to make it easier to identify which manual contains a given manual page, and to locate the manual page within that manual. The new organization of the UNIX System V Reference Manuals

- includes all reference manual pages found in various Programmer's Guides in the Reference Manuals

- makes each manual page unique, rather than repeating it in different Reference Manuals

- sorts each section together, rather than breaking it out by subsection, for example, all of Section 1, including subsections 1C, 1F, 1M, and 1N

- precedes each section with its own table of contents

The set of UNIX System V Reference Manuals organizes the manual pages into volumes aligned with the different types of interfaces that make up UNIX System V Release 4. Manual pages for the same type of components are found in the same volume, and components of different types are found in separate volumes. For example, you will no longer find programming commands (**cc**, **make**, and so on) in the *Programmer's Reference Manual*. Those commands have been moved to join Section 1 commands in the *User's Reference Manual/System Administrator's Reference Manual*. At the same time, all Section 4, 5 and 7 manual pages, which describe various system files and special files (devices) and were previously located in the *Programmer's Reference Manual* or the *System Administrator's Reference Manual*, have been consolidated in a new, separate volume entitled *System Files and Devices Reference Manual*. The table on the following page lists the contents of the new complete set of Reference Manuals:

Table 2: The UNIX System V Release 4 Reference Manual Set

Reference Manual	Description	Sections
User's Reference Manual/ System Administrator's Reference Manual (Commands a – l and m – z)	General-Purpose User Commands	1
	Basic Networking Commands	1C
	Form and Menu Language Interpreter	1F
	System Maintenance Commands	1M
	Enhanced Networking Commands	1N
Programmer's Reference Manual: Operating System API	System Calls	2
	BSD System Compatibility Library	3
	Standard C Library	3C
	Executable and Linking Format Library	3E
	General-Purpose Library	3G
	Math Library	3M
	Networking Library	3N
	Standard I/O Library	3S
	Specialized Library	3X
Programmer's Reference Manual: Windowing System API	X Window System Library	3X11
	X Window System Toolkit	3Xt
	OPEN LOOK Intrinsics Toolkit	3W
System Files and Devices Reference Manual	System File Formats	4
	Miscellaneous Facilities	5
	Special Files (Devices)	7
Device Driver Interface/ Driver Kernel Interface Reference Manual	DDI/DKI Driver Data Definitions	D1
	DDI/DKI Driver Entry Point Routines	D2
	DDI/DKI Kernel Utility Routines	D3
	DDI/DKI Kernel Data Structures	D4
	DDI/DKI Kernel Defines	D5

Reference Manual Index

A "Permuted Index" for this reference manual is provided at the back. The Permuted Index is a list of keywords, alphabetized in the second of three columns, together with the context in which each keyword is found. The manual page that produced an entry is listed in the right column.

Entries are identified with their section numbers shown in parentheses. This is important because there is considerable duplication of names among the sections, arising principally from commands and functions that exist only to exercise a particular system call.

The index is produced by rotating the NAME section of each manual page to alphabetize each keyword in it. Words that cannot fit in the middle column are rotated into the left column. If the entry is still too long, some words are omitted, and their omission is indicated with a slash ("/").

Here is an example of some of the entries produced for the manual pages `rand`(3C), `sleep`(1), `sleep`(3), and `sleep`(3C):

Figure 1: Sample of a Permuted Index

generator	rand, srand simple random number	rand(3C)
srand simple	random number generator rand, ...	rand(3C)
rand, srand	simple random number generator	rand(3C)
interval	sleep suspend execution for an	sleep(1)
interval	sleep suspend execution for an	sleep(3)
interval	sleep suspend execution for an	sleep(3C)
generator rand,	srand simple random number	rand(3C)

Table of Contents

Introduction to the User's Reference Manual/System Administrator's Reference Manual

Section 1 – Commands a – l

Table of Contents   1

Table of Contents

Table of Contents

Table of Contents

Table of Contents

Section 1 – Commands m – z

Table of Contents

Table of Contents

Table of Contents

Table of Contents

Section 4 – File Formats

Table of Contents

Section 5 – Miscellaneous Facilities

Section 7 – Special Files

Permuted Index

Introduction

This reference manual describes the commands of the UNIX system. It contains individual manual pages that describe user and administrative commands. (For a general overview of the UNIX system, see the *Product Overview*.)

Note that not all commands described in this manual are available in every UNIX system. Some of the features require additional utilities that may not exist on your system.

Organization of this Reference Manual

This manual contains the following sections (sorted together, alphabetically):

Section	Component Type
1	Commands (User)
1C	Commands (Basic Networking)
1F	Commands (Form & Menu Language Interpreter (FMLI))
1M	Commands (Administration)
1N	Commands (Enhanced Networking)

Section 1 (*Commands, user*) describes programs intended to be invoked directly by the user or by command language procedures, as opposed to subroutines that are called by the user's programs. Commands usually are in the **/usr/bin** and **/usr/sbin** directories. In addition, some commands are in **/sbin**. These directories are searched automatically by the command interpreter called the *shell*. Also, UNIX systems often have a directory called **/usr/lbin** that contains local commands.

Section 1C (*Commands, basic networking*) contains commands that are used when files are exchanged with another computer system.

Section 1F (*Commands, forms and menus*) contains commands and programs that are used by the Form & Menu Interpreter (FMLI).

Section 1M (*Commands, system maintenance*) contains commands and programs that are used in administering a UNIX system.

Section 1N (*Commands, enhanced networking*) contains commands and programs that are used for enhanced networking.

Manual Page Format

All manual page entries use a common format, not all of whose parts always appear:

- The **NAME** section gives the name(s) of the entry and briefly states its purpose.

- The **SYNOPSIS** section summarizes the use of the command, program or function. A few conventions are used:

  - `Constant width typeface` strings are literals and are to be typed just as they appear.

  - *Italic* strings usually represent substitutable argument prototypes and functions.

  - Square brackets [ ] around an argument prototype indicate that the argument is optional. When an argument prototype is given as *name* or *file*, it typically refers to a file name.

  - Ellipses . . . are used to show that the previous argument prototype may be repeated.

  - For commands, an argument beginning with a minus − or plus + sign is often taken to be a flag argument, even if it appears in a position where a file name could appear. Therefore, it is unwise to have files whose names begin with − or +.

- The **DESCRIPTION** section describes the utility.

- The **EXAMPLE** section gives example(s) of usage, where appropriate.

- The **FILES** section gives the file names that are built into the program.

- The **SEE ALSO** section gives pointers to related information. Reference to manual pages with section numbers other than those in this book can be found in other reference manuals, as listed above.

- The **DIAGNOSTICS** section discusses the diagnostic indications that may be produced. Messages that are intended to be self-explanatory are not listed.

■ The **NOTES** section gives generally helpful hints about the use of the utility.

How to Get Started

This discussion provides the basic information you need to get started on the UNIX system: how to log in and log out, how to communicate through your terminal, and how to run a program. (See the *User's Guide* for a more complete introduction to the system.)

Logging In

You must connect to the UNIX system from a full-duplex ASCII terminal or the console monitor (on a PC). You must also have a valid login ID, which may be obtained (together with how to access your UNIX system) from the administrator of your system. Common terminal speeds are 1200, 2400, 4800 and 9600 baud. Some UNIX systems have different ways of accessing each available terminal speed, while other systems offer several speeds through a common access method. In the latter case, there is one "preferred" speed; if you access it from a terminal set to a different speed, you will be greeted by a string of meaningless characters. Keep hitting the BREAK, INTERRUPT, or ATTENTION key until the **login:** prompt appears.

Most terminals have a speed switch that should be set to the appropriate speed and a half-/full-duplex switch that should be set to full-duplex. When a connection has been established, the system displays **login:**. You respond by typing your login ID followed by the RETURN key. If you have a password, the system asks for it but will not print, or "echo," it on the screen. After you have logged in, the ENTER, RETURN, NEW-LINE, and LINE-FEED keys all have equivalent meanings.

Make sure you type your login name in lower-case letters. Typing upper-case letters causes the UNIX system to assume that your terminal can generate only upper-case letters, and it will treat all letters as upper-case for the remainder of your login session. The shell will print a **$** on your screen when you have logged in successfully.

When you log in, a message-of-the-day may greet you before you receive your prompt. For more information, consult the **login**(1) manual page, which discusses the login sequence in more detail, and the **stty**(1) manual page, which tells you how to describe your terminal to the system. The **profile**(4) manual page explains how to accomplish this last task automatically every time you log in.

Logging Out

To log out of your system type an end-of-file indication (ASCII EOT character, usually typed as CTRL-d) to the shell. The shell will terminate, and the **login:** message will appear again.

How to Communicate Through Your Terminal

When you type on your keyboard, your individual characters are being gathered and temporarily saved. Although they are echoed back to you (displayed on the screen), these characters will not be "seen" by a program until you press ENTER (or RETURN or NEW-LINE) as described above in "Logging In."

UNIX system terminal input/output is full duplex. It has full read-ahead, which means that you can type at any time, even while a program is displaying characters on the screen. Of course, if you type during output, your input characters will have output characters interspersed among them. In any case, whatever you type will be saved and interpreted in the correct sequence. There is a limit to the amount of read-ahead, but it is not likely to be exceeded.

The character @ cancels all the characters typed before it on a line, effectively deleting the line. (@ is called the "line kill" character.) The character # erases the last character typed. Successive uses of # will erase characters back to, but not beyond, the beginning of the line; @ and # can be typed as themselves by preceding them with \ (thus, to erase a \, you need two #s). These default erase and line kill characters can be changed; see the **stty**(1) manual page.

CTRL-s (also known as the ASCII DC3 character) is entered by pressing the CONTROL key and the alphabetic **s** simultaneously; it is used to stop temporarily screen output. It is useful with CRT terminals to prevent output from disappearing before it can be read. Output is resumed when a CTRL-q (also known as DC1) is pressed. Thus, if you had typed **cat** *yourfile* and the contents of *yourfile* were passing by on the screen more rapidly than you could read it, you would enter CTRL-s to freeze the output. Entering CTRL-q would allow the output to resume. The CTRL-s and CTRL-q characters are not passed to any other program when used in this manner. Also, there may be a scroll lock key on your keyboard that can be used to stop temporarily screen output.

The ASCII DEL (also called "rubout") character is not passed to programs but instead generates an interrupt signal, just like the BREAK, INTERRUPT, or ATTENTION signal. This signal generally causes whatever program you are running to terminate. It is typically used to stop a long printout to the screen that you do not want. Programs, however, can arrange either to ignore this signal altogether or to be notified and take a specific action when it happens (instead of being terminated). The editor **ed**(1), for example, catches interrupts and stops what it's doing, instead of terminating, so an interrupt can be used to halt an editor printout without losing the file being edited.

Besides adapting to the speed of the terminal, the UNIX system tries to be intelligent about whether you have a terminal with the NEW-LINE function, or whether it must be simulated with a CARRIAGE-RETURN and LINE-FEED pair. In the latter case, all *input* CARRIAGE-RETURN characters are changed to LINE-FEED characters (the standard line delimiter), and a CARRIAGE-RETURN and LINE-FEED pair is echoed to the terminal. If you get into the wrong mode, the **stty**(1) command will rescue you.

Tab characters are used freely in UNIX system source programs. If your terminal does not have the tab function, you can arrange to have tab characters changed into spaces during output, and echoed as spaces during input. Again, the **stty**(1) command will set or reset this mode. The system assumes that tabs are set every eight character positions. The **tabs**(1) command will set tab stops on your terminal, if that is possible.

How to Run a Program

When you have successfully logged into the UNIX system, a program called the shell is communicating with your terminal. The shell reads each line you type, splits the line into a command name and its arguments, and executes the command. A command is simply an executable program. Normally, the shell looks first in your current directory (see "The Current Directory" below) for the named program and, if none is there, then in system directories, such as **/usr/bin**. There is nothing special about system-provided commands except that they are kept in directories where the shell can find them. You can also keep commands in your own directories and instruct the shell to find them there. See the manual entry for **sh**(1), under the sub-heading "Parameter

Substitution," for the discussion of the **PATH** shell environmental variable.

The command name is the first word on an input line to the shell; the command and its arguments are separated from one another by space or tab characters.

When a program terminates, the shell will ordinarily regain control and give you back your prompt to show that it is ready for another command. The shell has many other capabilities, which are described in detail on the **sh**(1) manual page.

The Current Directory

The UNIX system has a file system arranged in a hierarchy of directories. When you received your login ID, the system administrator also created a directory for you (ordinarily with the same name as your login ID, and known as your login or home directory). When you log in, that directory becomes your current or working directory, and any file name you type is, by default, assumed to be in that directory. Because you are the owner of this directory, you have full permissions to read, write, alter, or remove its contents. Permissions to enter or change other directories and files will have been granted or denied to you by their respective owners or by the system administrator. To change the current directory, use the **cd** command (see the **cd**(1) manual page).

Pathnames

To refer to files or directories not in the current directory, you must use a pathname. Full pathnames begin with /, which is the name of the root directory of the whole file system. After the slash comes the name of each directory containing the next subdirectory (followed by a /), until finally the file or directory name is reached (for example, **/usr/ae/filex** refers to file **filex** in directory **ae**, while **ae** is itself a subdirectory of **usr**, and **usr** is a subdirectory of the root directory). Use the **pwd** command (see the **pwd**(1) manual page) to print the full pathname of the directory you are working in. See the introduction to section 2 in the *Programmer's Reference Manual: Operating System API* for a formal definition of *pathname*.

If your current directory contains subdirectories, the pathnames of their respective files begin with the name of the corresponding subdirectory (without a prefixed /). A pathname may be used anywhere a file name is required.

Important commands that affect files are **cp**, **mv**, and **rm**, which respectively copy, move (that is, rename), and remove files (see the **cp**(1), **mv**(1) and **rm**(1) manual pages). To find out the status of files or directories, use **ls** (see the **ls**(1) manual page). Use **mkdir** for making directories and **rmdir** for removing them (see the **mkdir**(1) and **rm**(1) manual pages).

Text Entry and Display

Almost all text is entered through an editor. Common examples of UNIX system editors are **ed**(1) and **vi**(1). The commands most often used to print text on a terminal are **cat**, **pr**, and **pg** (see the **cat**(1), **pr**(1) and **pg**(1) manual pages). The **cat** command displays the contents of ASCII text files on the screen, with no processing at all. The **pr** command paginates the text, supplies headings, and has a facility for multi-column output. The **pg** command displays text in successive portions no larger than your screen.

Writing a Program

Once you have entered the text of your program into a file with an editor, you are ready to give the file to the appropriate language processor. The processor will accept only files observing the correct naming conventions: all C programs must end with the suffix **.c**, and Fortran programs must end with **.f**. The output of the language processor will be left in a file named **a.out** in the current directory, unless you have invoked an option to save it in another file. (Use **mv** to rename **a.out**.) If the program is written in assembly language, you will probably need to load library subroutines with it (see the **ld**(1) manual page).

When you have completed this process without provoking any diagnostics, you may run the program by giving its name to the shell in response to the **$** prompt. Your programs can receive arguments from the command line just as system programs do; see the **exec**(2) manual page. For more information on writing and running programs, see the *Programmer's Guide: ANSI C and Programming Support Tools*.

Communicating with Others

Certain commands provide inter-user communication. Even if you do not plan to use them, it's helpful to learn something about them because someone else may try to contact you. **mail** or **mailx** (see the **mail**(1) and **mailx**(1) manual pages) will leave a message whose presence will be announced to another user when they next log in and at periodic intervals during the session. To communicate with another user currently logged in, use **write** (see the **write**(1) manual page). The corresponding entries in this manual also suggest how to respond to these commands if you are their target.

See the tutorials in the *User's Guide* for more information on communicating with others.

Section 1 – Commands m – z

NAME

m4 – macro processor

SYNOPSIS

m4 [*options*] [*files*]

DESCRIPTION

The **m4** command is a macro processor intended as a front end for C, assembler, and other languages. Each of the argument files is processed in order; if there are no files, or if a file name is –, the standard input is read. The processed text is written on the standard output.

The options and their effects are as follows:

-e   Operate interactively. Interrupts are ignored and the output is unbuffered.

-s   Enable line sync output for the C preprocessor (#line ...)

-B*int*   Change the size of the push-back and argument collection buffers from the default of 4,096.

-H*int*   Change the size of the symbol table hash array from the default of 199. The size should be prime.

-S*int*   Change the size of the call stack from the default of 100 slots. Macros take three slots, and non-macro arguments take one.

-T*int*   Change the size of the token buffer from the default of 512 bytes.

To be effective, the above flags must appear before any file names and before any -D or -U flags:

-D*name*[=*val*]   Defines *name* to *val* or to null in *val*'s absence.

-U*name*   undefines *name*.

Macro calls have the form:

name(arg1,arg2, . . ., argn)

The (must immediately follow the name of the macro. If the name of a defined macro is not followed by a (, it is deemed to be a call of that macro with no arguments. Potential macro names consist of alphanumeric characters and underscore (_), where the first character is not a digit.

Leading unquoted blanks, tabs, and new-lines are ignored while collecting arguments. Left and right single quotes are used to quote strings. The value of a quoted string is the string stripped of the quotes.

When a macro name is recognized, its arguments are collected by searching for a matching right parenthesis. If fewer arguments are supplied than are in the macro definition, the trailing arguments are taken to be null. Macro evaluation proceeds normally during the collection of the arguments, and any commas or right parentheses that happen to turn up within the value of a nested call are as effective as those in the original input text. After argument collection, the value of the macro is pushed back onto the input stream and rescanned.

m4 makes available the following built-in macros. These macros may be redefined, but once this is done the original meaning is lost. Their values are null unless otherwise stated.

define
the second argument is installed as the value of the macro whose name is the first argument. Each occurrence of $n in the replacement text, where n is a digit, is replaced by the n-th argument. Argument 0 is the name of the macro; missing arguments are replaced by the null string; $# is replaced by the number of arguments; $* is replaced by a list of all the arguments separated by commas; $@ is like $*, but each argument is quoted (with the current quotes).

undefine
removes the definition of the macro named in its argument.

defn
returns the quoted definition of its argument(s). It is useful for renaming macros, especially built-ins.

pushdef
like define, but saves any previous definition.

popdef
removes current definition of its argument(s), exposing the previous one, if any.

ifdef
if the first argument is defined, the value is the second argument, otherwise the third. If there is no third argument, the value is null. The word unix is predefined.

shift
returns all but its first argument. The other arguments are quoted and pushed back with commas in between. The quoting nullifies the effect of the extra scan that will subsequently be performed.

changequote
change quote symbols to the first and second arguments. The symbols may be up to five characters long. changequote without arguments restores the original values (that is, ` ´).

changecom
change left and right comment markers from the default # and new-line. With no arguments, the comment mechanism is effectively disabled. With one argument, the left marker becomes the argument and the right marker becomes new-line. With two arguments, both markers are affected. Comment markers may be up to five characters long.

divert
m4 maintains 10 output streams, numbered 0-9. The final output is the concatenation of the streams in numerical order; initially stream 0 is the current stream. The divert macro changes the current output stream to its (digit-string) argument. Output diverted to a stream other than 0 through 9 is discarded.

undivert
causes immediate output of text from diversions named as arguments, or all diversions if no argument. Text may be undiverted into another diversion. Undiverting discards the diverted text.

divnum
returns the value of the current output stream.

dnl	reads and discards characters up to and including the next newline.
ifelse	has three or more arguments. If the first argument is the same string as the second, then the value is the third argument. If not, and if there are more than four arguments, the process is repeated with arguments 4, 5, 6 and 7. Otherwise, the value is either the fourth string, or, if it is not present, null.
incr	returns the value of its argument incremented by 1. The value of the argument is calculated by interpreting an initial digit-string as a decimal number.
decr	returns the value of its argument decremented by 1.
eval	evaluates its argument as an arithmetic expression, using 32-bit arithmetic. Operators include +, −, *, /, %, ** (exponentiation), bitwise &, |, ^, and ~; relationals; parentheses. Octal and hex numbers may be specified as in C. The second argument specifies the radix for the result; the default is 10. The third argument may be used to specify the minimum number of digits in the result.
len	returns the number of characters in its argument.
index	returns the position in its first argument where the second argument begins (zero origin), or −1 if the second argument does not occur.
substr	returns a substring of its first argument. The second argument is a zero origin number selecting the first character; the third argument indicates the length of the substring. A missing third argument is taken to be large enough to extend to the end of the first string.
translit	transliterates the characters in its first argument from the set given by the second argument to the set given by the third. No abbreviations are permitted.
include	returns the contents of the file named in the argument.
sinclude	is identical to **include**, except that it says nothing if the file is inaccessible.
syscmd	executes the UNIX System command given in the first argument. No value is returned.
sysval	is the return code from the last call to **syscmd**.
maketemp	fills in a string of **XXXXX** in its argument with the current process ID.
m4exit	causes immediate exit from **m4**. Argument 1, if given, is the exit code; the default is 0.
m4wrap	argument 1 will be pushed back at final EOF; example: **m4wrap(`cleanup()´)**

errprint   prints its argument on the diagnostic output file.

dumpdef   prints current names and definitions, for the named items, or for all if no arguments are given.

traceon   with no arguments, turns on tracing for all macros (including built-ins). Otherwise, turns on tracing for named macros.

traceoff   turns off trace globally and for any macros specified. Macros specifically traced by **traceon** can be untraced only by specific calls to **traceoff**.

SEE ALSO

as(1), cc(1)

NAME

mach – display the processor type of the current host

SYNOPSIS

/usr/ucb/mach

DESCRIPTION

The mach command displays the processor-type of the current host.

SEE ALSO

arch(1)

machid(1), uname(1) in the *User's Reference Manual*
uname(2), sysinfo(2) in the *Programmer's Reference Manual*

NAME

machid – *get processor type truth value*

SYNOPSIS

machid [*option*]

DESCRIPTION

The **machid** command returns a value to indicate the computer processor, model, hard disk, and/or bus architecture.

The following are **machid** usages and the meaning of their return codes.

machid

Exit Code	Machine Type
0	Generic AT386 machine
1	Compaq 386
2	AT&T 6386 or 6386E
4	AT&T 6386/SX
5	AT&T 6386/25
6	AT&T 6386E/33
10	AT&T 6386E/33 Model S

machid -s

Exit Code	Meaning
0	Bootable Non-SCSI Hard Disk
1	Bootable SCSI Hard Disk

machid -e

Exit Code	Meaning
0	AT&T 6386E/33 Model S configured correctly
3	Not configured correctly

machid -p

Exit Code	Meaning
3	Machine has a 80386
4	Machine has a 80486

machid -a

Exit Code	Meaning
0	Machine uses an AT Bus Architecture
1	Machine uses an EISA Bus Architecture

SEE ALSO

sh(1), test(1), true(1), uname.

NOTES

This command supersedes the old machid family (**pdp11, u3b2, u3b5, u3b15, vax, 386, u370**) manual page which is obsolescent.

NAME

mail, rmail – read mail or send mail to users

SYNOPSIS

Sending mail:

mail [**-tw**] [**-m** *message_type*] *recipient* . . .

rmail [**-tw**] [**-m** *message_type*] *recipient* . . .

Reading mail:

mail [**-ehpPqr**] [**-f** *file*]

Forwarding mail:

mail **-F** *recipient* . . .

Debugging:

mail [**-x***debug_level*] [*other_mail_options*] *recipient* . . .

mail **-T** *mailsurr_file recipient* . . .

DESCRIPTION

A *recipient* is usually a user name recognized by **login**(1). When *recipients* are named, **mail** assumes a message is being sent (except in the case of the **-F** option). It reads from the standard input up to an end-of-file (CTRL-d) or, if reading from a terminal device, until it reads a line consisting of just a period. When either of those indicators is received, **mail** adds the *letter* to the *mailfile* for each *recipient*.

A *letter* is composed of some *header lines* followed by a blank line followed by the *message content*. The *header lines* section of the letter consists of one or more UNIX postmarks:

> **From** *sender date_and_time* [**remote from** *remote_system_name*]

followed by one or more standardized message header lines of the form:

> *keyword-name***:** [*printable text*]

where *keyword-name* is comprised of any printable, non-whitespace, characters other than colon (':'). A **Content-Length:** header line, indicating the number of bytes in the *message content* will always be present. A **Content-Type:** header line that describes the type of the *message content* (such as text, binary, multipart, etc.) will always be present unless the letter consists of only header lines with no message content. Header lines may be continued on the following line if that line starts with white space.

Sending mail:

The following command-line arguments affect SENDING mail:

-m   causes a **Message-Type:** line to be added to the message header with the value of *message_type*.

-t   causes a **To:** line to be added to the message header for each of the intended recipients.

-w   causes a letter to be sent to a remote recipient without waiting for the completion of the remote transfer program.

If a letter is found to be undeliverable, it is returned to the sender with diagnostics that indicate the location and nature of the failure. If **mail** is interrupted during input, the message is saved in the file **dead.letter** to allow editing and resending. **dead.letter** is always appended to, thus preserving any previous contents. The initial attempt to append to (or create) **dead.letter** will be in the current directory. If this fails, **dead.letter** will be appended to (or created in) the user's login directory. If the second attempt also fails, no **dead.letter** processing will be done.

rmail only permits the sending of mail; uucp(1C) uses **rmail** as a security precaution. Any application programs that generate mail messages should be sure to invoke **rmail** rather than **mail** for message transport and/or delivery.

If the local system has the Basic Networking Utilities installed, mail may be sent to a recipient on a remote system. There are numerous ways to address mail to recipients on remote systems depending on the transport mechanisms available to the local system. The two most prevalent addressing schemes are UUCP-style and Domain-style. With UUCP-style addressing, remote recipients are specified by prefixing the recipient name with the remote system name and an exclamation point (such as sysa!user). A series of system names separated by exclamation points can be used to direct a letter through an extended network (such as **sysa!sysb!sysc!user**). With Domain-style addressing, remote recipients are specified by appending an '**@**' and domain (and possibly sub-domain) information to the recipient name (such as **user@sf.att.com**). (The local System Administrator should be consulted for details on which addressing conventions are available on the local system.)

Reading Mail:
The following command-line arguments affect READING mail:

-e   causes mail not to be printed. An exit value of 0 is returned if the user has mail; otherwise, an exit value of 1 is returned.

-h   causes a window of headers to be initially displayed rather than the latest message. The display is followed by the '?' prompt.

-p   causes all messages to be printed without prompting for disposition.

-P   causes all messages to be printed with *all* header lines displayed, rather than the default selective header line display.

-q   causes **mail** to terminate after interrupts. Normally an interrupt causes only the termination of the message being printed.

-r   causes messages to be printed in first-in, first-out order.

-f *file*   causes **mail** to use *file* (such as **mbox**) instead of the default *mailfile*.

mail, unless otherwise influenced by command-line arguments, prints a user's mail messages in last-in, first-out order. The default mode for printing messages is to display only those header lines of immediate interest. These include, but are not limited to, the UNIX **From** and **>From** postmarks, **From:**, **Date:**, **Subject:**, and **Content-Length:** header lines, and any recipient header lines such as **To:**, **Cc:**, **Bcc:**, etc. After the header lines have been displayed, **mail** will display the contents (body) of the message only if it contains no unprintable characters. Otherwise, **mail** will issue a warning statement about the message having binary content and **not** display the content. (This may be overridden via the **p** command. See below.)

For each message, the user is prompted with a **?**, and a line is read from the standard input. The following commands are available to determine the disposition of the message:

#	Print the number of the current message.
–	Print previous message.
<new-line>, +, or n	Print the next message.
! *command*	Escape to the shell to do *command*.
a	Print message that arrived during the **mail** session.
d, or **dp**	Delete the current message and print the next message.
d *n*	Delete message number *n*. Do not go on to next message.
dq	Delete message and quit **mail**.
h	Display a window of headers around current message.
h *n*	Display a window of headers around message number *n*.
h a	Display headers of all messages in the user's *mailfile*.
h d	Display headers of messages scheduled for deletion.
m [*persons*]	Mail (and delete) the current message to the named *person(s)*.
n	Print message number *n*.
p	Print current message again, overriding any indications of binary (that is, unprintable) content.
P	Override default brief mode and print current message again, displaying all header lines.
q, or CTRL-D	Put undeleted mail back in the *mailfile* and quit **mail**.
r [*users*]	Reply to the sender, and other *user(s)*, then delete the message.
s [*files*]	Save message in the named *file(s)* (**mbox** is default) and delete the message.
u [*n*]	Undelete message number *n* (default is last read).
w [*files*]	Save message contents, without any header lines, in the named *files* (**mbox** is default) and delete the message.
x	Put all mail back in the *mailfile* unchanged and exit **mail**.
y [*files*]	Same as save.
?	Print a command summary.

When a user logs in, the presence of mail, if any, is usually indicated. Also, notification is made if new mail arrives while using **mail**.

The permissions of *mailfile* may be manipulated using **chmod** in two ways to alter the function of **mail**. The other permissions of the file may be read-write (0666), read-only (0664), or neither read nor write (0660) to allow different levels of privacy. If changed to other than the default (mode 0660), the file will be preserved even when empty to perpetuate the desired permissions. (The administrator may override this file preservation using the **DEL_EMPTY_MAILFILE** option of **mailcnfg**.)

The group id of the mailfile must be **mail** to allow new messages to be delivered, and the mailfile must be writable by group **mail**.

Forwarding mail:
The following command-line argument affects FORWARDING of mail:

    -F *recipients*   Causes all incoming mail to be forwarded to *recipients*. The mailbox must be empty.

The **-F** option causes the *mailfile* to contain a first line of:

    Forward to *recipient*. . .

Thereafter, all mail sent to the owner of the *mailfile* will be forwarded to each *recipient*.

An **Auto-Forwarded-From:** . . . line will be added to the forwarded message's header. This is especially useful in a multi-machine environment to forward all a person's mail to a single machine, and to keep the recipient informed if the mail has been forwarded.

Installation and removal of forwarding is done with the **-F** invocation option. To forward all your mail to **systema!user** enter:

    mail -F systema!user

To forward to more than one recipient enter:

    mail -F "user1,user2@att.com,systemc!systemd!user3"

Note that when more than one recipient is specified, the entire list should be enclosed in double quotes so that it may all be interpreted as the operand of the **-F** option. The list can be up to 1024 bytes; either commas or white space can be used to separate users.

If the first character of any forwarded-to recipient name is the pipe symbol ('|'), the remainder of the line will be interpreted as a command to pipe the current mail message to. The command, known as a *Personal Surrogate*, will be executed in the environment of the recipient of the message (that is, basename of the *mailfile*). For example, if the mailfile is **/var/mail/foo**, **foo** will be looked up in **/etc/passwd** to determine the correct userID, groupID, and **HOME** directory. The command's environment will be set to contain only **HOME**, **LOGNAME**, **TZ**, **PATH** (= **/usr/usr/bin:**), and **SHELL** (= **/usr/bin/sh**), and the command will execute in the recipient's **HOME** directory. If the message recipient cannot be found in **/etc/passwd**, the command will not be executed and a non-delivery notification with appropriate diagnostics will be sent to the message's originator.

After the pipe symbol, escaped double quotes should be used to have strings with embedded whitespace be considered as single arguments to the command being executed. No shell syntax or metacharacters may be used unless the command specified is **/usr/bin/sh**. For example,

    mail -F "|/bin/sh -c \"shell_command_line\""

will work, but is not advised since using double quotes and backslashes within the shell_command_line is difficult to do correctly and becomes tedious **very** quickly.

Certain %keywords are allowed within the piped-to command specification and will be textually substituted for *before* the command line is executed.

%R   Return path to the message originator.
%c   Value of the **Content-Type:** header line if present.
%S   Value of the **Subject:** header line if present.

If the command being piped to exits with any non-zero value, **mail** will assume that message delivery failed and will generate a non-delivery notification to the message's originator. It is allowable to forward mail to other recipients **and** pipe it to a command, as in

```
mail -F "carol,joe,|myvacationprog %R"
```

Two UNIX System facilities that use the forwarding of messages to commands are **notify**(1), which causes asynchronous notification of new mail, and **vacation**(1), which provides an auto-answer capability for messages when the recipient will be unavailable for an extended period of time.

To remove forwarding enter:

```
mail -F ""
```

The pair of double quotes is mandatory to set a NULL argument for the −F option.

In order for forwarding to work properly the *mailfile* should have **mail** as group ID, and the group permission should be read-write.

mail will exit with a return code of **0** if forwarding was successfully installed or removed.

Debugging:

The following command-line arguments cause **mail** to provide DEBUGGING information:

−T *mailsurr_file*   causes **mail** to display how it will parse and interpret the **mailsurr** file.

−x*debug_level*   causes **mail** to create a trace file containing debugging information.

The −T option requires an argument that will be taken as the pathname of a test **mailsurr** file. If NULL (as in −T ""), the system **mailsurr** file will be used. To use, type 'mail −T *test_file recipient*' and some trivial message (like "testing"), followed by a line with either just a dot ('.') or a CTRL-D. The result of using the −T option will be displayed on standard output and show the inputs and resulting transformations as **mailsurr** is processed by the **mail** command for the indicated recipient. Mail messages will never actually be sent or delivered when the −T option is used.

The **-x** option causes **mail** to create a file named **/tmp/MLDBG**_process_id_ that contains debugging information relating to how **mail** processed the current message. The absolute value of _debug_level_ controls the verboseness of the debug information. Zero implies no debugging. If _debug_level_ is greater than zero, the debug file will be retained **only** if **mail** encountered some problem while processing the message. If _debug_level_ is less than zero the debug file will always be retained. The _debug_level_ specified via **-x** overrides any specification of **DEBUG** in **/etc/mail/mailcnfg**. The information provided by the **-x** option is esoteric and is probably only useful to System Administrators. The output produced by the **-x** option is a superset of that provided by the **-T** option.

Delivery Notification

Several forms of notification are available for mail by including one of the following lines in the message header.

> **Transport-Options:** [/_options_]
> **Default-Options:** [/_options_]
> **>To:** _recipient_ [/_options_]

where the "/_options_" may be one or more of the following:

/delivery   Inform the sender that the message was successfully delivered to the _recipient_'s mailbox.

/nodelivery
        Do not inform the sender of successful deliveries.

/ignore   Do not inform the sender of unsuccessful deliveries.

/return   Inform the sender if mail delivery fails. Return the failed message to the sender.

/report   Same as **/return** except that the original message is not returned.

The default is **/nodelivery/return**. If contradictory options are used, the first will be recognized and later, conflicting, terms will be ignored.

FILES

dead.letter	unmailable text
/etc/passwd	to identify sender and locate recipients
/etc/mail/mailsurr	
	routing / name translation information
/etc/mail/mailcnfg	
	initialization information
$HOME/mbox	saved mail
$MAIL	variable containing path name of _mailfile_
/tmp/ma∗	temporary file
/tmp/MLDBG∗	debug trace file
/var/mail/∗**.lock**	lock for mail directory
/var/mail/:saved	directory for holding temp files to prevent loss of data in the event of a system crash.
/var/mail/_user_	incoming mail for _user_; that is, the _mailfile_

SEE ALSO

chmod(1), login(1), mailx(1), notify(1), write(1), vacation(1)

mail_pipe(1M), mailsurr(4), mailcnfg(4) in the *System Administrator's Reference Manual*
User's Guide

NOTES

The "Forward to recipient" feature may result in a loop. Local loops (messages sent to **usera**, which are forwarded to **userb**, which are forwarded to **usera**) will be detected immediately. Remote loops (mail sent to **sys1!usera1** which is forwarded to **sys2!userb**, which is forwarded to **sys1!usera**) will also be detected, but only after the message has exceeded the built-in hop count limit of 20. Both cases of forwarding loops will result in a non-delivery notification being sent to the message originator.

As a security precaution, the equivalent of a **chmod s+g** is performed on the *mailfile* whenever forwarding is activated via the **–F** option, and a **chmod s–g** is done when forwarding is removed via the **–F** option. If the setGID mode bit is not set when **mail** attempts to forward an incoming message to a command, the operation will fail and a non-delivery report with appropriate diagnostics will be sent to the message's originator.

The interpretation and resulting action taken because of the header lines described in the Delivery Notifications section above will only occur if this version of **mail** is installed on the system where the delivery (or failure) happens. Earlier versions of **mail** may not support any types of delivery notification.

Conditions sometimes result in a failure to remove a lock file.

After an interrupt, the next message may not be printed; printing may be forced by typing a **p**.

NAME

mail_pipe – invoke recipient command for incoming mail

SYNOPSIS

mail_pipe [**-x** *debug_level*] **-r** *recipient* **-R** *path_to_sender* **-c** *content_type*
-S *subject*

DESCRIPTION

When a new mail message arrives, the **mail** command first checks if the recipient's mailbox indicates that the message is to be forwarded elsewhere (to some other recipient or as the input to some command). If the message is to be piped into a recipient-specified command, **mail** invokes **mail_pipe** to do some validation and then execute the command in the context of the recipient.

Command-line arguments are:

-x *debug_level*   Turn on debugging for this invocation. See the description of the **-x** option for the **mail** command for details.

-r *recipient*   The recipient's login id.

-R *path_to_sender*   The return address to the message's originator.

-c *content_type*   The value of the **Content-Type:** header line in the message.

-S *subject*   The value of the **Subject:** header line in the message if present.

mail_pipe is installed as a setuid-to-root process, thus enabling itself to change it's user and group ids to that of the recipient as necessary.

When invoked, **mail_pipe** performs the following steps (if a step fails, the exit code is noted as [*N*]):

- Validate invocation arguments [**1**].
- Verify that recipient name is ≤ 14 characters long [**2**].
- Verify that the setgid flag for the recipient mailbox is set [**3**].
- Open **/var/mail/**recipient [**4**].
- Verify that recipient's mailbox starts with the string **Forward to** [**5**].
- Find pipe symbol indicating start of command string in recipient mailbox [**6**].
- Find entry for recipient in **/etc/passwd** [**7**].
- Set gid to recipient's gid [**8**].
- Set uid to recipient's uid [**9**].
- Change current directory to recipient's login directory [**10**].
- Allocate space to hold newly **exec**'ed environment for recipient command [**11**].
- Parse the recipient command, performing any %*keyword* expansions required. See the 'Forwarding mail' section of **mail**(1), for more information regarding %*keyword* substitutions [**12**].
- Execute recipient command [**13** if **exec** fails, otherwise exit code from recipient command itself].

FILES

`/etc/passwd`	to identify sender and locate recipients
`/var/mail/`*recipient*	incoming mail for *recipient*; that is, the mail file
`/tmp/MLDBG*`	debug trace file
`/usr/lib/mail/mail_pipe`	mail_pipe program

SEE ALSO

mail(1), notify(1), vacation(1)

NAME

     `mailalias` – translate mail alias names

SYNOPSIS

     `mailalias` [`-s`] [`-v`] *name* . . .

DESCRIPTION

     `mailalias` is called by `mail`. It places on the standard output a list of mail addresses corresponding to *name*. The mail addresses are found by performing the following steps:

1.   Look for a match in the user's local alias file `$HOME/lib/names`. If a line is found beginning with the word *name*, print the rest of the line on standard output and exit.

2.   Look for a match in the system-wide alias files, which are listed in the master path file `/etc/mail/namefiles`. If a line is found beginning with the word *name*, print the rest of the line on standard output and exit. If an alias file is a directory name *dir*, then search the file *dir/name*. By default, the file `/etc/mail/namefiles` lists the directory `/etc/mail/lists` and the file `/etc/mail/names`.

3.   Otherwise print *name* and exit.

The alias files may contain comments (lines beginning with `#`) and information lines of the form:

     name list-of-addresses

Tokens on these lines are separated by white-space. Lines may be continued by placing a backslash (\\) at the end of the line.

If the `-s` option is not specified and more than one name is being translated, each line of output will be prefixed with the name being translated.

The `-v` option causes debugging information to be written to standard output.

FILES

     `$HOME/lib/names`   private aliases
     `/etc/mail/namefiles`   list of files to search
     `/etc/mail/names`   standard file to search

SEE ALSO

     `uucp`(1), `mail`(1)
     `smtp`(1M), `smtpd`(1M), `smtpqer`(1M), `smtpsched`(1M), `tosmtp`(1M) in the *System Administrator's Reference Manual*

NAME

    `mailstats` – print statistics collected by sendmail

SYNOPSIS

    `/usr/ucb/mailstats` [*filename*]

DESCRIPTION

    `mailstats` prints out the statistics collected by the **sendmail** program on mailer usage. These statistics are collected if the file indicated by the **s** configuration option of **sendmail** exists. **mailstats** first prints the time that the statistics file was created and the last time it was modified. It will then print a table with one row for each mailer specified in the configuration file. The first column is the mailer number, followed by the symbolic name of the mailer. The next two columns refer to the number of messages received by *sendmail*, and the last two columns refer to messages sent by *sendmail*. The number of messages and their total size (in 1024 byte units) is given. No numbers are printed if no messages were sent (or received) for any mailer.

    You might want to add an entry to **/var/spool/cron/crontab/root** to reinitialize the statistics file once a night. Copy **/dev/null** into the statistics file or otherwise truncate it to reset the counters.

FILES

    `/var/spool/cron/crontab/root`
    `/dev/null`

SEE ALSO

    `sendmail`(1M)

NOTES

    `mailstats` should read the configuration file instead of having a hard-wired table mapping mailer numbers to names.

NAME

mailx – interactive message processing system

SYNOPSIS

mailx [*options*] [*name* . . .]

DESCRIPTION

The command **mailx** provides a comfortable, flexible environment for sending and receiving messages electronically. When reading mail, **mailx** provides commands to facilitate saving, deleting, and responding to messages. When sending mail, **mailx** allows editing, reviewing and other modification of the message as it is entered.

Many of the remote features of **mailx** work only if the Basic Networking Utilities are installed on your system.

Incoming mail is stored in a standard file for each user, called the **mailbox** for that user. When **mailx** is called to read messages, the **mailbox** is the default place to find them. As messages are read, they are marked to be moved to a secondary file for storage, unless specific action is taken, so that the messages need not be seen again. This secondary file is called the **mbox** and is normally located in the user's **HOME** directory [see **MBOX** (ENVIRONMENT VARIABLES) for a description of this file]. Messages can be saved in other secondary files named by the user. Messages remain in a secondary file until forcibly removed.

The user can access a secondary file by using the **–f** option of the **mailx** command. Messages in the secondary file can then be read or otherwise processed using the same COMMANDS as in the primary **mailbox**. This gives rise within these pages to the notion of a current **mailbox**.

On the command line, *options* start with a dash (–) and any other arguments are taken to be destinations (recipients). If no recipients are specified, **mailx** attempts to read messages from the **mailbox**. Command-line options are:

–d	Turn on debugging output.
–e	Test for presence of mail. **mailx** prints nothing and exits with a successful return code if there is mail to read.
–f [*filename*]	Read messages from *filename* instead of **mailbox**. If no *filename* is specified, the **mbox** is used.
–F	Record the message in a file named after the first recipient. Overrides the **record** variable, if set (see ENVIRONMENT VARIABLES).
–h *number*	The number of network "hops" made so far. This is provided for network software to avoid infinite delivery loops. This option and its argument is passed to the delivery program.
–H	Print header summary only.
–i	Ignore interrupts. See also **ignore** (ENVIRONMENT VARIABLES).

-I	Include the newsgroup and article-id header lines when printing mail messages. This option requires the **-f** option to be specified.
-n	Do not initialize from the system default *mailx.rc* file.
-N	Do not print initial header summary.
-r *address*	Use *address* as the return address when invoking the delivery program. All tilde commands are disabled. This option and its argument is passed to the delivery program.
-s *subject*	Set the Subject header field to *subject*.
-T *file*	Message-id and article-id header lines are recorded in *file* after the message is read. This option will also set the **-I** option.
-u *user*	Read *user*'s **mailbox**. This is only effective if *user*'s **mailbox** is not read protected.
-U	Convert **uucp** style addresses to internet standards. Overrides the **conv** environment variable.
-V	Print the **mailx** version number and exit.

When reading mail, **mailx** is in *command mode*. A header summary of the first several messages is displayed, followed by a prompt indicating **mailx** can accept regular commands (see COMMANDS below). When sending mail, **mailx** is in *input mode*. If no subject is specified on the command line, a prompt for the subject is printed. (A subject longer than 1024 characters causes **mailx** to print the message *mail: ERROR signal 10*; the mail will not be delivered.) As the message is typed, **mailx** reads the message and store it in a temporary file. Commands may be entered by beginning a line with the tilde (˜) escape character followed by a single command letter and optional arguments. See TILDE ESCAPES for a summary of these commands.

At any time, the behavior of **mailx** is governed by a set of *environment variables*. These are flags and valued parameters which are set and cleared via the **set** and **uns**et commands. See ENVIRONMENT VARIABLES below for a summary of these parameters.

Recipients listed on the command line may be of three types: login names, shell commands, or alias groups. Login names may be any network address, including mixed network addressing. If mail is found to be undeliverable, an attempt is made to return it to the sender's *mailbox*. If the recipient name begins with a pipe symbol (|), the rest of the name is taken to be a shell command to pipe the message through. This provides an automatic interface with any program that reads the standard input, such as **lp**(1) for recording outgoing mail on paper. Alias groups are set by the **alias** command (see COMMANDS below) and are lists of recipients of any type.

Regular commands are of the form

    [*command*] [*msglist*] [*arguments*]

If no command is specified in *command mode*, **print** is assumed. In *input mode*, commands are recognized by the escape character, and lines not treated as commands are taken as input for the message.

Each message is assigned a sequential number, and there is at any time the notion of a current message, marked by a right angle bracket (>) in the header summary. Many commands take an optional list of messages (*msglist*) to operate on. The default for *msglist* is the current message. A *msglist* is a list of message identifiers separated by spaces, which may include:

n	Message number **n**.
.	The current message.
^	The first undeleted message.
$	The last message.
*	All messages.
n–m	An inclusive range of message numbers.
user	All messages from **user**.
/string	All messages with **string** in the subject line (case ignored).
:c	All messages of type c, where c is one of:

d	deleted messages
n	new messages
o	old messages
r	read messages
u	unread messages

Note that the context of the command determines whether this type of message specification makes sense.

Other arguments are usually arbitrary strings whose usage depends on the command involved. File names, where expected, are expanded via the normal shell conventions [see **sh**(1)]. Special characters are recognized by certain commands and are documented with the commands below.

At start-up time, **mailx** tries to execute commands from the optional system-wide file (**/etc/mail/mailx.rc**) to initialize certain parameters, then from a private start-up file (**$HOME/.mailrc**) for personalized variables. With the exceptions noted below, regular commands are legal inside start-up files. The most common use of a start-up file is to set up initial display options and alias lists. The following commands are not legal in the start-up file: **!**, **C**opy, **edit**, **followup**, **F**ollowup, **hold**, **mail**, **pre**serve, **reply**, **R**eply, **shell**, and **visual**. An error in the start-up file causes the remaining lines in the file to be ignored. The **.mailrc** file is optional, and must be constructed locally.

COMMANDS

The following is a complete list of **mailx** commands:

! *shell-command*

Escape to the shell. See **SHELL** (ENVIRONMENT VARIABLES).

*comment*

Null command (comment). This may be useful in **.mailrc** files.

=   Print the current message number.

?   Prints a summary of commands.

alias *alias name ...*

group *alias name ...*

Declare an alias for the given names. The names are substituted when *alias* is used as a recipient. Useful in the **.mailrc** file.

alternates *name ...*

Declares a list of alternate names for your login. When responding to a message, these names are removed from the list of recipients for the response. With no arguments, **alternates** prints the current list of alternate names. See also **allnet** (ENVIRONMENT VARIABLES).

cd [*directory*]

chdir [*directory*]

Change directory. If *directory* is not specified, **$HOME** is used.

copy [*filename*]

copy [*msglist*] *filename*

Copy messages to the file without marking the messages as saved. Otherwise equivalent to the **save** command.

Copy [*msglist*]

Save the specified messages in a file whose name is derived from the author of the message to be saved, without marking the messages as saved. Otherwise equivalent to the **Save** command.

delete [*msglist*]

Delete messages from the **mailbox**. If **autoprint** is set, the next message after the last one deleted is printed (see ENVIRONMENT VARIABLES).

discard [*header-field* ...]

ignore [*header-field* ...]

Suppresses printing of the specified header fields when displaying messages on the screen. Examples of header fields to ignore are **status** and **cc**. The fields are included when the message is saved. The **Print** and **Type** commands override this command. If no header is specified, the current list of header fields being ignored will be printed. See also the **undiscard** and **unignore** commands.

dp [*msglist*]

dt [*msglist*]

Delete the specified messages from the **mailbox** and print the next message after the last one deleted. Roughly equivalent to a **delete** command followed by a **print** command.

echo *string* ...
>   Echo the given strings [like echo(1)].

edit [*msglist*]
>   Edit the given messages. The messages are placed in a temporary file and the **EDITOR** variable is used to get the name of the editor (see ENVIRON-MENT VARIABLES). Default editor is ed(1).

exit
xit   Exit from **mailx**, without changing the **mailbox**. No messages are saved in the **mbox** (see also quit).

file [*filename*]
folder [*filename*]
>   Quit from the current file of messages and read in the specified file. Several special characters are recognized when used as file names, with the following substitutions:
>
> | | |
> |---|---|
> | % | the current **mailbox**. |
> | %*user* | the **mailbox** for *user*. |
> | # | the previous file. |
> | & | the current **mbox**. |
>
>   Default file is the current **mailbox**.

folders
>   Print the names of the files in the directory set by the **folder** variable (see ENVIRONMENT VARIABLES).

followup [*message*]
>   Respond to a message, recording the response in a file whose name is derived from the author of the message. Overrides the **record** variable, if set. See also the Followup, Save, and Copy commands and **outfolder** (ENVIRONMENT VARIABLES).

Followup [*msglist*]
>   Respond to the first message in the *msglist*, sending the message to the author of each message in the *msglist*. The subject line is taken from the first message and the response is recorded in a file whose name is derived from the author of the first message. See also the followup, Save, and Copy commands and **outfolder** (ENVIRONMENT VARIABLES).

from [*msglist*]
>   Prints the header summary for the specified messages.

group *alias name* ...
alias *alias name* ...
>   Declare an alias for the given names. The names are substituted when *alias* is used as a recipient. Useful in the **.mailrc** file.

headers [*message*]
>   Prints the page of headers which includes the message specified. The **screen** variable sets the number of headers per page (see ENVIRONMENT VARIABLES). See also the **z** command.

help   Prints a summary of commands.

hold [*msglist*]
preserve [*msglist*]
        Holds the specified messages in the **mailbox**.

if *s* | *r*
*mail-command*s
else
*mail-command*s
endif   Conditional execution, where *s* executes following *mail-command*s, up to an
        else or endif, if the program is in *send* mode, and *r* causes the *mail-command*s to be executed only in *receive* mode. Useful in the **.mailrc** file.

ignore [*header-field* ...]
discard [*header-field* ...]
        Suppresses printing of the specified header fields when displaying messages on the screen. Examples of header fields to ignore are **status** and
        cc. All fields are included when the message is saved. The Print and
        Type commands override this command. If no header is specified, the
        current list of header fields being ignored will be printed. See also the
        undiscard and **unig**nore commands.

list   Prints all commands available. No explanation is given.

mail *name* ...
        Mail a message to the specified users.

Mail *name*
        Mail a message to the specified user and record a copy of it in a file
        named after that user.

mbox [*msglist*]
        Arrange for the given messages to end up in the standard **mbox** save file
        when **mailx** terminates normally. See **MBOX** (ENVIRONMENT VARIABLES)
        for a description of this file. See also the **exit** and **quit** commands.

next [*message*]
        Go to next message matching *message*. A *msglist* may be specified, but in
        this case the first valid message in the list is the only one used. This is
        useful for jumping to the next message from a specific user, since the
        name would be taken as a command in the absence of a real command.
        See the discussion of *msglist*s above for a description of possible message
        specifications.

pipe [*msglist*] [*shell-command*]
| [*msglist*] [*shell-command*]
        Pipe the message through the given *shell-command*. The message is treated
        as if it were read. If no arguments are given, the current message is piped
        through the command specified by the value of the **cmd** variable. If the
        page variable is set, a form feed character is inserted after each message
        (see ENVIRONMENT VARIABLES).

preserve [*msglist*]
hold [*msglist*]
> Preserve the specified messages in the **mailbox**.

Print [*msglist*]
Type [*msglist*]
> Print the specified messages on the screen, including all header fields.
> Overrides suppression of fields by the **ig**nore command.

print [*msglist*]
type [*msglist*]
> Print the specified messages. If **crt** is set, the messages longer than the
> number of lines specified by the **crt** variable are paged through the com-
> mand specified by the **PAGER** variable. The default command is **pg**(1) (see
> ENVIRONMENT VARIABLES).

quit   Exit from **mailx**, storing messages that were read in **mbox** and unread
> messages in the **mailbox**. Messages that have been explicitly saved in a
> file are deleted.

Reply [*msglist*]
Respond [*msglist*]
> Send a response to the author of each message in the *msglist*. The subject
> line is taken from the first message. If **record** is set to a file name, the
> response is saved at the end of that file (see ENVIRONMENT VARIABLES).

reply [*message*]
respond [*message*]
> Reply to the specified message, including all other recipients of the mes-
> sage. If **record** is set to a file name, the response is saved at the end of
> that file (see ENVIRONMENT VARIABLES).

Save [*msglist*]
> Save the specified messages in a file whose name is derived from the
> author of the first message. The name of the file is taken to be the
> author's name with all network addressing stripped off. See also the
> **C**opy, **followup**, and **F**ollowup commands and **outfolder** (ENVIRON-
> MENT VARIABLES).

save [*filename*]
save [*msglist*] *filename*
> Save the specified messages in the given file. The file is created if it does
> not exist. The file defaults to **mbox**. The message is deleted from the
> **mailbox** when **mailx** terminates unless **keepsave** is set (see also
> ENVIRONMENT VARIABLES and the **exit** and **quit** commands).

set
set *name*
set *name=string*
set *name=number*
> Define a variable called *name*. The variable may be given a null, string, or
> numeric value. **Set** by itself prints all defined variables and their values.

See ENVIRONMENT VARIABLES for detailed descriptions of the **mailx** variables.

shell Invoke an interactive shell [see also **SHELL** (ENVIRONMENT VARIABLES)].

size [*msglist*]
> Print the size in characters of the specified messages.

source *filename*
> Read commands from the given file and return to command mode.

top [*msglist*]
> Print the top few lines of the specified messages. If the **toplines** variable is set, it is taken as the number of lines to print (see ENVIRONMENT VARIABLES). The default is 5.

touch [*msglist*]
> Touch the specified messages. If any message in *msglist* is not specifically saved in a file, it is placed in the **mbox**, or the file specified in the **MBOX** environment variable, upon normal termination. See **exit** and **quit**.

Type [*msglist*]
Print [*msglist*]
> Print the specified messages on the screen, including all header fields. Overrides suppression of fields by the **ignore** command.

type [*msglist*]
print [*msglist*]
> Print the specified messages. If **crt** is set, the messages longer than the number of lines specified by the **crt** variable are paged through the command specified by the **PAGER** variable. The default command is **pg**(1) (see ENVIRONMENT VARIABLES).

undelete [*msglist*]
> Restore the specified deleted messages. Will only restore messages deleted in the current mail session. If **autoprint** is set, the last message of those restored is printed (see ENVIRONMENT VARIABLES).

undiscard *header-field* ...
unignore *header-field* ...
> Remove the specified header fields from the list being ignored.

unset *name* ...
> Causes the specified variables to be erased. If the variable was imported from the execution environment (for example, a shell variable) then it cannot be erased.

version
> Prints the current version.

visual [*msglist*]
> Edit the given messages with a screen editor. The messages are placed in

a temporary file and the **VISUAL** variable is used to get the name of the editor (see ENVIRONMENT VARIABLES).

write [*msglist*] *filename*
>Write the given messages on the specified file, minus the header and trailing blank line. Otherwise equivalent to the **save** command.

xit

exit   Exit from **mailx**, without changing the **mailbox**. No messages are saved in the **mbox** (see also **quit**).

z[+ | −]
>Scroll the header display forward or backward one screen–full. The number of headers displayed is set by the **screen** variable (see ENVIRON-MENT VARIABLES).

TILDE ESCAPES

The following commands may be entered only from *input mode*, by beginning a line with the tilde escape character (˜). See **escape** (ENVIRONMENT VARIABLES) for changing this special character.

~! *shell-command*
>Escape to the shell.

~.   Simulate end of file (terminate message input).

~: *mail-command*

~_ *mail-command*
>Perform the command-level request. Valid only when sending a message while reading mail.

~?   Print a summary of tilde escapes.

~A   Insert the autograph string **Sign** into the message (see ENVIRONMENT VARIABLES).

~a   Insert the autograph string **sign** into the message (see ENVIRONMENT VARIABLES).

~b *names* ...
>Add the *names* to the blind carbon copy (Bcc) list.

~c *names* ...
>Add the *names* to the carbon copy (Cc) list.

~d   Read in the **dead.letter** file. See **DEAD** (ENVIRONMENT VARIABLES) for a description of this file.

~e   Invoke the editor on the partial message. See also **EDITOR** (ENVIRON-MENT VARIABLES).

~f [*msglist*]
>Forward the specified messages. The messages are inserted into the message without alteration.

~h   Prompt for Subject line and To, Cc, and Bcc lists. If the field is displayed
            with an initial value, it may be edited as if you had just typed it.

~i *string*
            Insert the value of the named variable into the text of the message. For
            example, **~A** is equivalent to **Environment variables set and
            exported in the shell are also accessible by ~i.**

~m [*msglist*]
            Insert the specified messages into the letter, shifting the new text to the
            right one tab stop. Valid only when sending a message while reading
            mail.

~p   Print the message being entered.

~q   Quit from input mode by simulating an interrupt. If the body of the mes-
            sage is not null, the partial message is saved in **dead.letter**. See **DEAD**
            (ENVIRONMENT VARIABLES) for a description of this file.

~r *filename*
~< *filename*
~< *!shell-command*
            Read in the specified file. If the argument begins with an exclamation
            point (!), the rest of the string is taken as an arbitrary shell command and
            is executed, with the standard output inserted into the message.

~s *string* ...
            Set the subject line to *string*.

~t *names* ...
            Add the given *name*s to the To list.

~v   Invoke a preferred screen editor on the partial message. See also **VISUAL**
            (ENVIRONMENT VARIABLES).

~w *filename*
            Write the message into the given file, without the header.

~x   Exit as with ~q except the message is not saved in **dead.letter**.

~| *shell-command*
            Pipe the body of the message through the given *shell-command*. If the
            shell-command returns a successful exit status, the output of the command
            replaces the message.

ENVIRONMENT VARIABLES

The following are environment variables taken from the execution environment
and are not alterable within **mailx**.

HOME=*directory*
            The user's base of operations.

MAILRC=*filename*
            The name of the start-up file. Default is **$HOME/.mailrc**.

The following variables are internal **mailx** variables. They may be imported from the execution environment or set via the **set** command at any time. The **unset** command may be used to erase variables.

allnet
> All network names whose last component (login name) match are treated as identical. This causes the *msglist* message specifications to behave similarly. Default is **noallnet**. See also the **alternates** command and the **metoo** variable.

append
> Upon termination, append messages to the end of the **mbox** file instead of prepending them. Default is **noappend.**

askcc Prompt for the Cc list after the Subject is entered. Default is **noaskcc.**

askbcc
> Prompt for the Bcc list after the Subject is entered. Default is **noaskbcc.**

asksub
> Prompt for subject if it is not specified on the command line with the **-s** option. Enabled by default.

autoprint
> Enable automatic printing of messages after **delete** and **undelete** commands. Default is **noautoprint.**

bang Enable the special-casing of exclamation points (!) in shell escape command lines as in **vi**(1). Default is **nobang.**

cmd=*shell-command*
> Set the default command for the **pipe** command. No default value.

conv=*conversion*
> Convert uucp addresses to the specified address style. The only valid conversion now is **internet**, which uses domain-style addressing. Conversion is disabled by default. See also the **-U** command-line option.

crt=*number*
> Pipe messages having more than *number* lines through the command specified by the value of the **PAGER** variable [**pg**(1) by default]. Disabled by default.

DEAD=*filename*
> The name of the file in which to save partial letters in case of untimely interrupt. Default is **$HOME/dead.letter.**

debug Enable verbose diagnostics for debugging. Messages are not delivered. Default is **nodebug.**

dot Take a period on a line by itself during input from a terminal as end-of-file. Default is **nodot.**

EDITOR=*shell-command*
> The command to run when the **edit** or **~e** command is used. Default is **ed**(1).

escape=*c*

Substitute *c* for the ˜ escape character. Takes effect with next message sent.

folder=*directory*

The directory for saving standard mail files. User-specified file names beginning with a plus (+) are expanded by preceding the file name with this directory name to obtain the real file name. If *directory* does not start with a slash (/), **$HOME** is prepended to it. In order to use the plus (+) construct on a **mailx** command line, **folder** must be an exported **sh** environment variable. There is no default for the **folder** variable. See also **outfolder** below.

header

Enable printing of the header summary when entering **mailx**. Enabled by default.

hold   Preserve all messages that are read in the **mailbox** instead of putting them in the standard **mbox** save file. Default is **nohold**.

ignore

Ignore interrupts while entering messages. Handy for noisy dial-up lines. Default is **noignore**.

ignoreeof

Ignore end-of-file during message input. Input must be terminated by a period (.) on a line by itself or by the ~. command. Default is **noignoreeof**. See also **dot** above.

keep   When the **mailbox** is empty, truncate it to zero length instead of removing it. Disabled by default.

keepsave

Keep messages that have been saved in other files in the **mailbox** instead of deleting them. Default is **nokeepsave**.

MBOX=*filename*

The name of the file to save messages which have been read. The **xit** command overrides this function, as does saving the message explicitly in another file. Default is **$HOME/mbox**.

metoo   If your login appears as a recipient, do not delete it from the list. Default is **nometoo**.

LISTER=*shell-command*

The command (and options) to use when listing the contents of the **folder** directory. The default is **ls**(1).

onehop

When responding to a message that was originally sent to several recipients, the other recipient addresses are normally forced to be relative to the originating author's machine for the response. This flag disables alteration of the recipients' addresses, improving efficiency in a network where all machines can send directly to all other machines (for example, one hop away).

outfolder
> Causes the files used to record outgoing messages to be located in the directory specified by the **folder** variable unless the path name is absolute. Default is **nooutfolder**. See **folder** above and the Save, Copy, followup, and Followup commands.

page Used with the **pipe** command to insert a form feed after each message sent through the pipe. Default is **nopage**.

PAGER=*shell-command*
> The command to use as a filter for paginating output. This can also be used to specify the options to be used. Default is **pg**(1).

prompt=*string*
> Set the *command mode* prompt to *string*. Default is "**?** ".

quiet Refrain from printing the opening message and version when entering **mailx**. Default is **noquiet**.

record=*filename*
> Record all outgoing mail in *filename*. Disabled by default. See also **outfolder** above. If you have the **record** and **outfolder** variables set but the **folder** variable not set, messages are saved in +*filename* instead of *filename*.

save Enable saving of messages in **dead.letter** on interrupt or delivery error. See **DEAD** for a description of this file. Enabled by default.

screen=*number*
> Sets the number of lines in a screen–full of headers for the headers command. It must be a positive number.

sendmail=*shell-command*
> Alternate command for delivering messages. Default is **/usr/bin/rmail**.

sendwait
> Wait for background mailer to finish before returning. Default is **nosendwait**.

SHELL=*shell-command*
> The name of a preferred command interpreter. Default is **sh**(1).

showto
> When displaying the header summary and the message is from you, print the recipient's name instead of the author's name.

sign=*string*
> The variable inserted into the text of a message when the **~a** (autograph) command is given. No default [see also **~i** (TILDE ESCAPES)].

Sign=*string*
> The variable inserted into the text of a message when the **~A** command is given. No default [see also **~i** (TILDE ESCAPES)].

toplines=*number*
> The number of lines of header to print with the **top** command. Default is 5.

VISUAL=*shell-command*
> The name of a preferred screen editor. Default is **vi**(1).

FILES

`$HOME/.mailrc`	personal start-up file
`$HOME/mbox`	secondary storage file
`/var/mail/*`	post office directory
`/usr/share/lib/mailx/mailx.help*`	help message files
`/etc/mail/mailx.rc`	optional global start-up file
`/tmp/R[emqsx]*`	temporary files

SEE ALSO

ls(1), **mail**(1), **pg**(1)

NOTES

The **−h** and **−r** options can be used only if **mailx** is using a delivery program other than **/usr/bin/rmail**.

Where *shell-command* is shown as valid, arguments are not always allowed. Experimentation is recommended.

Internal variables imported from the execution environment cannot be **unset**.

The full internet addressing is not fully supported by **mailx**. The new standards need some time to settle down.

Attempts to send a message having a line consisting only of a "." are treated as the end of the message by **mail**(1) (the standard mail delivery program).

NAME

    make – maintain, update, and regenerate groups of programs

SYNOPSIS

    make [–**f** *makefile*] [–**eiknpqrst**] [*names*]

DESCRIPTION

    make allows the programmer to maintain, update, and regenerate groups of computer programs. **make** executes commands in *makefile* to update one or more target *names* (*names* are typically programs). If the –**f** option is not present, then **makefile**, **Makefile**, and the Source Code Control System (SCCS) files **s.makefile**, and **s.Makefile** are tried in order. If *makefile* is –, the standard input is taken. More than one –**f** *makefile* argument pair may appear.

    make updates a target only if its dependents are newer than the target. All prerequisite files of a target are added recursively to the list of targets. Missing files are deemed to be outdated.

    The following list of four directives can be included in *makefile* to extend the options provided by **make**. They are used in *makefile* as if they were targets:

    .DEFAULT: If a file must be made but there are no explicit commands or relevant built-in rules, the commands associated with the name **.DEFAULT** are used if it exists.

    .IGNORE: Same effect as the –**i** option.

    .PRECIOUS: Dependents of the **.PRECIOUS** entry will not be removed when quit or interrupt are hit.

    .SILENT: Same effect as the –**s** option.

    The options for **make** are listed below:

    –**e**   Environment variables override assignments within makefiles.

    –**f** *makefile*   Description filename (*makefile* is assumed to be the name of a description file).

    –**i**   Ignore error codes returned by invoked commands.

    –**k**   Abandon work on the current entry if it fails, but continue on other branches that do not depend on that entry.

    –**n**   No execute mode. Print commands, but do not execute them. Even command lines beginning with an **@** are printed.

    –**p**   Print out the complete set of macro definitions and target descriptions.

    –**q**   Question. **make** returns a zero or non-zero status code depending on whether or not the target file has been updated.

    –**r**   Do not use the built-in rules.

    –**s**   Silent mode. Do not print command lines before executing.

    –**t**   Touch the target files (causing them to be updated) rather than issue the usual commands.

Creating the makefile

The makefile invoked with the −f option is a carefully structured file of explicit instructions for updating and regenerating programs, and contains a sequence of entries that specify dependencies. The first line of an entry is a blank-separated, non-null list of targets, then a :, then a (possibly null) list of prerequisite files or dependencies. Text following a ; and all following lines that begin with a tab are shell commands to be executed to update the target. The first non-empty line that does not begin with a tab or # begins a new dependency or macro definition. Shell commands may be continued across lines with a backslash-new-line (\ new-line) sequence. Everything printed by make (except the initial tab) is passed directly to the shell as is. Thus,

```
echo a\
b
```

will produce

```
ab
```

exactly the same as the shell would.

Sharp (#) and new-line surround comments including contained \ new-line sequences.

The following makefile says that **pgm** depends on two files **a.o** and **b.o**, and that they in turn depend on their corresponding source files (**a.c** and **b.c**) and a common file **incl.h**:

```
pgm: a.o b.o
        cc a.o b.o −o pgm
a.o: incl.h a.c
        cc −c a.c
b.o: incl.h b.c
        cc −c b.c
```

Command lines are executed one at a time, each by its own shell. The **SHELL** environment variable can be used to specify which shell **make** should use to execute commands. The default is **/usr/bin/sh**. The first one or two characters in a command can be the following: @, −, @−, or −@. If @ is present, printing of the command is suppressed. If − is present, **make** ignores an error. A line is printed when it is executed unless the −s option is present, or the entry .SILENT: is included in *makefile*, or unless the initial character sequence contains a @. The −n option specifies printing without execution; however, if the command line has the string $(MAKE) in it, the line is always executed (see the discussion of the MAKEFLAGS macro in the "Environment" section below). The −t (touch) option updates the modified date of a file without executing any commands.

Commands returning non-zero status normally terminate **make**. If the −i option is present, if the entry .IGNORE: is included in *makefile*, or if the initial character sequence of the command contains −, the error is ignored. If the −k option is present, work is abandoned on the current entry, but continues on other branches that do not depend on that entry.

Interrupt and quit cause the target to be deleted unless the target is a dependent of the directive .PRECIOUS.

Environment

The environment is read by **make**. All variables are assumed to be macro definitions and are processed as such. The environment variables are processed before any makefile and after the internal rules; thus, macro assignments in a makefile override environment variables. The −e option causes the environment to override the macro assignments in a makefile. Suffixes and their associated rules in the makefile will override any identical suffixes in the built-in rules.

The **MAKEFLAGS** environment variable is processed by **make** as containing any legal input option (except −f and −p) defined for the command line. Further, upon invocation, **make** "invents" the variable if it is not in the environment, puts the current options into it, and passes it on to invocations of commands. Thus, **MAKEFLAGS** always contains the current input options. This feature proves very useful for "super-makes". In fact, as noted above, when the −n option is used, the command $(MAKE) is executed anyway; hence, one can perform a **make** −n recursively on a whole software system to see what would have been executed. This result is possible because the −n is put in **MAKEFLAGS** and passed to further invocations of $(MAKE). This usage is one way of debugging all of the makefiles for a software project without actually doing anything.

Include Files

If the string **include** appears as the first seven letters of a line in a *makefile*, and is followed by a blank or a tab, the rest of the line is assumed to be a filename and will be read by the current invocation, after substituting for any macros.

Macros

Entries of the form *string1* = *string2* are macro definitions. *string2* is defined as all characters up to a comment character or an unescaped new-line. Subsequent appearances of $(*string1*[:*subst1*=[*subst2*]]) are replaced by *string2*. The parentheses are optional if a single-character macro name is used and there is no substitute sequence. The optional :*subst1*=*subst2* is a substitute sequence. If it is specified, all non-overlapping occurrences of *subst1* in the named macro are replaced by *subst2*. Strings (for the purposes of this type of substitution) are delimited by blanks, tabs, new-line characters, and beginnings of lines. An example of the use of the substitute sequence is shown in the "Libraries" section below.

Internal Macros

There are five internally maintained macros that are useful for writing rules for building targets.

$*   The macro $* stands for the filename part of the current dependent with the suffix deleted. It is evaluated only for inference rules.

$@   The $@ macro stands for the full target name of the current target. It is evaluated only for explicitly named dependencies.

$<   The $< macro is only evaluated for inference rules or the .DEFAULT rule. It is the module that is outdated with respect to the target (the "manufactured" dependent file name). Thus, in the .c.o rule, the $< macro would evaluate to the `.c` file. An example for making optimized `.o` files from `.c` files is:

```
.c.o:
        cc -c -O $*.c
```

or:

```
.c.o:
        cc -c -O $<
```

$?**   The **$? macro is evaluated when explicit rules from the makefile are evaluated. It is the list of prerequisites that are outdated with respect to the target, and essentially those modules that must be rebuilt.

$%   The **$%** macro is only evaluated when the target is an archive library member of the form **lib(file.o)**. In this case, **$@** evaluates to **lib** and **$%** evaluates to the library member, **file.o**.

Four of the five macros can have alternative forms. When an upper case D or F is appended to any of the four macros, the meaning is changed to "directory part" for D and "file part" for F. Thus, **$(@D)** refers to the directory part of the string **$@**. If there is no directory part, `./` is generated. The only macro excluded from this alternative form is **$?**.

Suffixes

Certain names (for instance, those ending with `.o`) have inferable prerequisites such as `.c`, `.s`, etc. If no update commands for such a file appear in *makefile*, and if an inferable prerequisite exists, that prerequisite is compiled to make the target. In this case, **make** has inference rules that allow building files from other files by examining the suffixes and determining an appropriate inference rule to use. The current default inference rules are:

```
.c      .c~       .f      .f~     .s      .s~     .sh     .sh~    .C      .C~
.c.a    .c.o      .c~.a   .c~.c   .c~.o   .f.a    .f.o    .f~.a   .f~.f   .f~.o
.h~.h   .l.c      .l.o    .l~.c   .l~.l   .l~.o   .s.a    .s.o    .s~.a   .s~.o
.s~.s   .sh~.sh   .y.c    .y.o    .y~.c   .y~.o   .y~.y   .C.a    .C.o    .C~.a
.C~.C   .C~.o     .L.C    .L.o    .L~.C   .L~.L   .L~.o   .Y.C    .Y.o    .Y~.C
.Y~.o   .Y~.Y
```

The internal rules for **make** are contained in the source file **rules.c** for the **make** program. These rules can be locally modified. To print out the rules compiled into the **make** on any machine in a form suitable for recompilation, the following command is used:

```
make -pf - 2>/dev/null </dev/null
```

A tilde in the above rules refers to an SCCS file [see **sccsfile**(4)]. Thus, the rule `.c~.o` would transform an SCCS C source file into an object file (`.o`). Because the **s.** of the SCCS files is a prefix, it is incompatible with the **make** suffix point of view. Hence, the tilde is a way of changing any file reference into an SCCS file reference.

A rule with only one suffix (for example, `.c:`) is the definition of how to build x from x`.c`. In effect, the other suffix is null. This feature is useful for building targets from only one source file, for example, shell procedures and simple C programs.

Additional suffixes are given as the dependency list for **.SUFFIXES**. Order is significant: the first possible name for which both a file and a rule exist is inferred as a prerequisite. The default list is:

.SUFFIXES: .o .c .c~ .y .y~ .1 .1~ .s .s~ .sh .sh~ .h .h~ .f .f~ .C
.C~ .Y .Y~ .L .L~

Here again, the above command for printing the internal rules will display the list of suffixes implemented on the current machine. Multiple suffix lists accumulate; **.SUFFIXES:** with no dependencies clears the list of suffixes.

Inference Rules

The first example can be done more briefly.

```
pgm: a.o b.o
        cc a.o b.o -o pgm
a.o b.o: incl.h
```

This abbreviation is possible because **make** has a set of internal rules for building files. The user may add rules to this list by simply putting them in the *makefile*.

Certain macros are used by the default inference rules to permit the inclusion of optional matter in any resulting commands. For example, **CFLAGS**, **LFLAGS**, and **YFLAGS** are used for compiler options to **cc**(1), **lex**(1), and **yacc**(1), respectively. Again, the previous method for examining the current rules is recommended.

The inference of prerequisites can be controlled. The rule to create a file with suffix **.o** from a file with suffix **.c** is specified as an entry with **.c.o:** as the target and no dependents. Shell commands associated with the target define the rule for making a **.o** file from a **.c** file. Any target that has no slashes in it and starts with a dot is identified as a rule and not a true target.

Libraries

If a target or dependency name contains parentheses, it is assumed to be an archive library, the string within parentheses referring to a member within the library. Thus, **lib(file.o)** and **$(LIB)(file.o)** both refer to an archive library that contains **file.o**. (This example assumes the **LIB** macro has been previously defined.) The expression **$(LIB)(file1.o file2.o)** is not legal. Rules pertaining to archive libraries have the form **.XX.a** where the *XX* is the suffix from which the archive member is to be made. An unfortunate by-product of the current implementation requires the *XX* to be different from the suffix of the archive member. Thus, one cannot have **lib(file.o)** depend upon **file.o** explicitly. The most common use of the archive interface follows. Here, we assume the source files are all C type source:

```
lib: lib(file1.o) lib(file2.o) lib(file3.o)
        @echo lib is now up-to-date
.c.a:
        $(CC) -c $(CFLAGS) $<
        $(AR) $(ARFLAGS) $@ $*.o
        rm -f $*.o
```

In fact, the `.c.a` rule listed above is built into **make** and is unnecessary in this example. A more interesting, but more limited example of an archive library maintenance construction follows:

```
lib: lib(file1.o) lib(file2.o) lib(file3.o)
        $(CC) -c $(CFLAGS) $(?:.o=.c)
        $(AR) $(ARFLAGS) lib $?
        rm $?
        @echo lib is now up-to-date
.c.a:;
```

Here the substitution mode of the macro expansions is used. The `$?` list is defined to be the set of object filenames (inside `lib`) whose C source files are outdated. The substitution mode translates the `.o` to `.c`. (Unfortunately, one cannot as yet transform to `.c~`; however, this transformation may become possible in the future.) Also note the disabling of the `.c.a:` rule, which would have created each object file, one by one. This particular construct speeds up archive library maintenance considerably. This type of construct becomes very cumbersome if the archive library contains a mix of assembly programs and C programs.

FILES

[Mm]akefile and s.[Mm]akefile
/usr/bin/sh

SEE ALSO

cc(1), lex(1), yacc(1), printf(3S), sccsfile(4)

cd(1), sh(1) in the *User's Reference Manual*

See the "make" chapter in the *Programmer's Guide: ANSI C and Programming Support Tools*

NOTES

Some commands return non-zero status inappropriately; use −i or the − command line prefix to overcome the difficulty.

Filenames with the characters = : @ will not work. Commands that are directly executed by the shell, notably cd(1), are ineffectual across new-lines in **make**. The syntax `lib(file1.o  file2.o  file3.o)` is illegal. You cannot build `lib(file.o)` from `file.o`.

NAME

makedbm – make a Network Information Service (NIS) dbm file

SYNOPSIS

`/usr/sbin/makedbm` [-l] [-s] [-i *yp_input_file*] [-o *yp_output_name*]
  [-d *yp_domain_name*] [-m *yp_master_name*] *infile outfile*

`makedbm` [-u *dbmfilename*]

DESCRIPTION

The **makedbm** command takes *infile* and converts it to a pair of files in **dbm**(3) format, namely *outfile*.**pag** and *outfile*.**dir**. Each line of the input file is converted to
a single **dbm** record. All characters up to the first TAB or SPACE form the key, and
the rest of the line is the data. If a line ends with '\', then the data for that
record is continued on to the next line. It is left for NIS clients to interpret '**#**';
makedbm does not itself treat it as a comment character. *infile* can be '–', in which
case the standard input is read.

makedbm is meant to be used in generating **dbm** files for NIS and it generates a
special entry with the key *yp_last_modified*, which is the date of *infile* (or the
current time, if *infile* is '–').

The following options are available:

-l   Lowercase. Convert the keys of the given map to lower case, so that host
      name matches, for example, can work independent of upper or lower case
      distinctions.

-s   Secure map. Accept connections from secure NIS networks only.

-i *yp_input_file*
      Create a special entry with the key *yp_input_file*.

-o *yp_output_name*
      Create a special entry with the key *yp_output_name*.

-d *yp_domain_name*
      Create a special entry with the key *yp_domain_name*.

-m *yp_master_name*
      Create a special entry with the key *yp_master_name*. If no master host
      name is specified, *yp_master_name* will be set to the local host name.

-u *dbmfilename*
      Undo a **dbm** file. That is, print out a **dbm** file one entry per line, with a
      single space separating keys from values.

SEE ALSO

dbm(3)

NAME

makefsys – create a file system

SYNOPSIS

makefsys

DESCRIPTION

The makefsys command allows you to create a file system.

The command invokes a visual interface (the make task available through the sysadm command).

The initial prompt allows you to select the device on which to create the file system. After selecting the device, you are asked some further questions before the file system is created.

The identical function is available under the sysadm menu:

sysadm make

DIAGNOSTICS

The makefsys command exits with one of the following values:

0   Normal exit.

2   Invalid command syntax. A usage message is displayed.

7   The visual interface for this command is not available because it cannot invoke fmil. (The FMLI package is not installed or is corrupted.)

SEE ALSO

checkfsys(1M), labelit(1M), mkfs(1M), mountfsys(1M), sysadm(1M)

NAME

makekey – generate encryption key

SYNOPSIS

/usr/lib/makekey

DESCRIPTION

makekey improves the usefulness of encryption schemes depending on a key by increasing the amount of time required to search the key space. It attempts to read 8 bytes for its *key* (the first eight input bytes), then it attempts to read 2 bytes for its *salt* (the last two input bytes). The output depends on the input in a way intended to be difficult to compute (that is, to require a substantial fraction of a second).

The first eight input bytes (the *input key*) can be arbitrary ASCII characters. The last two (the *salt*) are best chosen from the set of digits, ., /, and upper- and lower-case letters. The salt characters are repeated as the first two characters of the output. The remaining 11 output characters are chosen from the same set as the salt and constitute the *output key*.

The transformation performed is essentially the following: the salt is used to select one of 4,096 cryptographic machines all based on the National Bureau of Standards DES algorithm, but broken in 4,096 different ways. Using the *input key* as key, a constant string is fed into the machine and recirculated a number of times. The 64 bits that come out are distributed into the 66 *output key* bits in the result.

makekey is intended for programs that perform encryption. Usually, its input and output will be pipes.

SEE ALSO

ed(1), crypt(1), vi(1)

passwd(4) in the *System Administrator's Reference Manual*

NOTES

makekey can produce different results depending upon whether the input is typed at the terminal or redirected from a file.

This command is provided with the Encryption Utilities, which is only available in the United States.

NAME

man – display reference manual pages; find reference pages by keyword

SYNOPSIS

/usr/ucb/man [–] [–t] [–M *path*] [–T *macro-package*] [[*section*] *title*. . .]
     title . . .
/usr/ucb/man [–M *path*] –k *keyword* . . .
/usr/ucb/man [–M *path*] –f *filename* . . .

DESCRIPTION

The **man** command displays information from the reference manuals. It can display complete manual pages that you select by *title*, or one-line summaries selected either by *keyword* (–k), or by the name of an associated file (–f).

A *section*, when given, applies to the *titles* that follow it on the command line (up to the next *section*, if any). **man** looks in the indicated section of the manual for those *titles*. *section* is either a digit (perhaps followed by a single letter indicating the type of manual page), or one of the words **new**, **local**, **old**, or **public**. If *section* is omitted, **man** searches all reference sections (giving preference to commands over functions) and prints the first manual page it finds. If no manual page is located, **man** prints an error message.

The reference page sources are typically located in the **/usr/share/man/man?** directories. Since these directories are optionally installed, they may not reside on your host; you may have to mount **/usr/share/man** from a host on which they do reside. If there are preformatted, up-to-date versions in corresponding **cat?** or **fmt?** directories, **man** simply displays or prints those versions. If the preformatted version of interest is out of date or missing, **man** reformats it prior to display. If directories for the preformatted versions are not provided, **man** reformats a page whenever it is requested; it uses a temporary file to store the formatted text during display.

If the standard output is not a terminal, or if the – flag is given, **man** pipes its output through **cat**. Otherwise, **man** pipes its output through **more** to handle paging and underlining on the screen.

The following options are available:

–t   **man** arranges for the specified manual pages to be **troff**ed to a suitable raster output device (see **troff** or **vtroff**). If both the – and –t flags are given, **man** updates the **troff**ed versions of each named *title* (if necessary), but does not display them.

–M *path*
    Change the search path for manual pages. *path* is a colon-separated list of directories that contain manual page directory subtrees. When used with the –k or –f options, the –M option must appear first. Each directory in the *path* is assumed to contain subdirectories of the form **man[1-81-p]**.

–T *macro-package*
    man uses *macro-package* rather than the standard –man macros defined in **/usr/ucblib/doctools/tmac/tmac.an** for formatting manual pages.

−k *keyword* ...

> **man** prints out one-line summaries from the **whatis** database (table of contents) that contain any of the given *keyword*s.

−f *filename* ...

> **man** attempts to locate manual pages related to any of the given *filename*s. It strips the leading pathname components from each *filename*, and then prints one-line summaries containing the resulting basename or names.

MANUAL PAGES

Manual pages are **troff** or **nroff** source files prepared with the **−man** macro package.

When formatting a manual page, **man** examines the first line to determine whether it requires special processing.

Preprocessing Manual Pages

If the first line is a string of the form:

> ´ \" 　*X*

where *X* is separated from the the the '"' by a single SPACE and consists of any combination of characters in the following list, **man** pipes its input to **troff** or **nroff** through the corresponding preprocessors.

e	**eqn**, or **neqn** for **nroff**
r	**refer**
t	**tbl**, and **col** for **nroff**

If **eqn** or **neqn** is invoked, it will automatically read the file /usr/ucblib/pub/eqnchar [see **eqnchar**(5)].

ENVIRONMENT

MANPATH	If set, its value overrides **/usr/share/man** as the default search path. The **−M** flag, in turn, overrides this value.
PAGER	A program to use for interactively delivering **man**'s output to the screen. If not set, 'more −s' (see **more**) is used.
TCAT	The name of the program to use to display **troff**ed manual pages. If not set, '**lp** −Ttroff' (see **lp**) is used.
TROFF	The name of the formatter to use when the **−t** flag is given. If not set, **troff** is used.

FILES

/usr/share/man	root of the standard manual page directory subtree
/usr/share/man/man?/*	unformatted manual entries
/usr/share/man/cat?/*	nroffed manual entries
/usr/share/man/fmt?/*	troffed manual entries
/usr/share/man/whatis	table of contents and keyword database
/usr/ucblib/doctools/tmac/man.macs	
	standard −man macro package
/usr/ucblib/pub/eqnchar	

SEE ALSO

apropos(1), cat(1), catman(1M), col(1), eqn(1), nroff(1), refer(1), tbl(1), troff(1), whatis(1), eqnchar(5)

col(1), lp(1), more(1) in the *User's Reference Manual*

NOTES

The manual is supposed to be reproducible either on a phototypesetter or on an ASCII terminal. However, on a terminal some information (indicated by font changes, for instance) is necessarily lost.

Some dumb terminals cannot process the vertical motions produced by the **e** (**eqn**(1)) preprocessing flag. To prevent garbled output on these terminals, when you use **e** also use **t**, to invoke **col**(1) implicitly. This workaround has the disadvantage of eliminating superscripts and subscripts — even on those terminals that can display them. CTRL-Q will clear a terminal that gets confused by **eqn**(1) output.

NAME

mapchan – Configure tty device mapping.

SYNOPSIS

mapchan [-ans] [-f *mapfile*] [*channels* . . .]

mapchan [-o] [-d] [*channel*]

DESCRIPTION

mapchan configures the mapping of information input and output of the UNIX system. The mapchan utility is intended for users of applications that employ languages other than English (character sets other than 7 bit ASCII).

mapchan translates codes sent by peripheral devices, such as terminals, to the internal character set used by the UNIX system. mapchan can also map codes in the internal character set to other codes for output to peripheral devices (such as terminals, printers, console screen, etc.). Note that PC keyboard configuration is accomplished through the mapkey(1) utility.

mapchan has several uses: to map a *channel* (-a or -s); to unmap a *channel* (–n and optionally -a); or to display the map on a *channel* (optionally -o,-d, *channels*).

mapchan with no options displays the map on the user's *channel*. The map displayed is suitable as input for mapchan.

The options are :

-a   When used alone, sets all *channels* given in the default file (/etc/default/mapchan) with the specified map. When used with –n, it refers to all *channels* given in the default file. Superuser maps or unmaps all *channels*, other users map only *channels* they own. The -a option can not be used with the -d, -o, or -s options.

-d   Causes the mapping table currently in use on the given device, *channel*, to be displayed in decimal instead of the default hexadecimal. An ASCII version is displayed on standard output. This output is suitable as an input file to mapchan for another *channel*. Mapped values are displayed. Identical pairs are not output. The –d option can not be used with -a, -f, –n, -o or -s options.

-f   Causes the current *channel* or list of channels to be mapped with *mapfile*. The -f option can not be used with -d, –n, -s, or -o options.

-n   Causes null mapping to be performed. All codes are input and output as received. Mapping is turned off for the user's *channel* or for other *channels*, if given. -a used with –n will turn mapping off for all *channels* given in the default file. This is the default mapping for all *channels* unless otherwise configured. The -n option can not be used with -d, -f, -o, or -s options.

-o   Causes the mapping table currently in use on the given device, *channel*, to be displayed in octal instead of the default hexadecimal. An ASCII version is displayed on standard output. This output is suitable as an input file to mapchan for another port. Mapped values are displayed. Identical pairs are not output. The –o option can not be used with -a, -d, -f, –n, or -s options.

-s   Sets the user's current *channel* with the *mapfile* given in the default file.
The **-s** option can not be used with any other option.

The user must own the *channel* in order to map it. The super-user can map any
channel. Read or write permission is required to display the map on a *channel*.

Each tty device *channel* (display adapter and video monitor on computer, parallel
port, serial port, etc.) can have a different map. When the UNIX system boots,
mapping is off for all *channels*.

mapchan is usually invoked in the **/etc/rc2** file. This file is executed when the
system enters the multiuser mode and sets up the default mapping for the system. Users can invoke **mapchan** when they log in by including a **mapchan** command line in their **.profile** or **.login** file. In addition, users can remap their
channel at any time by invoking **mapchan** from the command line. *channels* not
listed in the default file are not automatically mapped. *channels* are not changed
on logout. Whatever mapping was in place for the last user remains in effect for
the next user, unless they modify their **.profile** or **.login** file.

For example, the default file **/etc/default/mapchan** can obtain:

```
tty1
tty2    ibm
tty3    wy60.ger
lp      ibm
```

The default directory containing *mapfiles* is **/usr/lib/mapchan**. The default
directory containing *channel* files is **/dev**. Full pathnames may be used for *channels* or *mapfiles*. If a *channel* has no entry, or the entry field is blank, no mapping
is enabled on that *channel*. Additional *channels* added to the system (for example,
adding a serial or parallel port), are not automatically entered in the **mapchan**
default file. If mapping is required, the system administrator must make the
entries. The format of the *mapfiles* is documented in the **mapchan**(4) manual page.

Using a Mapped channel

The input information is assumed to be 7-or 8-bit codes sent by the peripheral
device. The device may make use of dead or compose keys to produce the codes.
If the device does not have dead or compose keys, these keys can be simulated
using **mapchan**.

One to one mapped characters are displayed when the key is pressed and the
mapped value is passed to the kernel.

Certain keys are designated as dead keys in the *mapfile*. Dead key sequences are
two keystrokes that produce a single mapped value that is passed to the kernel.
The dead key is usually a diacritical character, the second key is usually the letter
being modified. For example, the sequence **'e** could be mapped to the ASCII
value 0xE9, and displayed as **e'**.

One key is designated as the compose key in the *mapfile*. Compose key sequences
are composed of three keystrokes that produce a single mapped value that is
passed to the kernel. The compose key is usually a seldom used character or
CTRL-*letter* combination. The second key is usually the letter being modified.
The third key may be another character being combined, or a diacritical character.

For example, if @ is the compose key, the sequence @ c O could be mapped to the ASCII value 0xA9, and displayed as ©.

Characters are not echoed to the screen during a dead or compose sequence. The mapped character is echoed and passed to the kernel once the sequence is correctly completed.

Characters are always put through the input map, even when part of dead or compose sequences. The character is then checked for the internal value. The value may also be mapped on output. This should be kept mind when preparing map files.

The following conditions will cause an error during input:

1. non-recognized (not defined in the *mapfile*) dead or compose sequence.

2. restarting a compose sequence before completion by pressing the compose key in the middle of a dead or compose sequence (this is an error, but a new compose sequence is initiated).

If the *mapfile* contains the keyword **beep**, a bell sounds when either of the above conditions occurs. In either case, the characters are not echoed to the screen, or passed to the kernel.

In order to allow for character sequences sent to control the terminal (move the cursor, and so on) rather than to print characters on the screen, **mapchan** allows characters sequences to be specified as special sequences which are not passed through the normal mapping procedure. Two sections may be specified, one for each of the input (keyboard) and output (screen) controls.

Character Sets

The internal character set used is defined by the *mapfiles* used. By default, this is the ISO 8859/1 character set which is also known as dpANS X3.4.2 and ISO/TC97/SC2. It supports most of the Latin alphabet and can represent most European languages.

Several partial map files are provided as examples. They must be modified for use with specific peripheral devices. Consult your hardware manual for the codes needed to display the desired characters. Two map files are provided for use with the console device: **/usr/lib/mapchan/ibm** for systems with a standard PC character set ROM, and **/usr/lib/mapchan/iso** for systems with an optional ISO 8859/1 character set ROM.

Care should be taken that the **stty** settings [see **stty**(1M)] are correct for 8-bit terminals. The **/etc/gettydefs** file may require modifications to allow logging with the correct settings.

7-bit U.S ASCII (ANSI X3.4) should be used if no mapping is enabled on the *channel*.

FILES

/etc/default/mapchan
/usr/lib/mapchan/*

NOTES

Some non-U.S keyboards and display devices do not support characters commonly used by command shells and the C programming language. It is not recommended that these devices be used for system administration tasks.

Printers can be mapped, output only, and can either be sent 8-bit codes or one-to-many character strings using **mapchan**. Line printer spooler interface scripts can be used (**setuid root**) to change the output map on the printer when different maps are required (as in changing print wheels to display a different character set). See **lpadmin**(1M) and **lp**(7) for information on installing and administering interface scripts.

Not all terminals or printers can display all the characters that can be represented using this utility. Refer to the device's hardware manual for information on the capabilities of the peripheral device.

Use of *mapfiles* that specify a different internal character set per channel, or a set other than the 8-bit ISO 8859 set supplied by default can cause strange side effects. It is especially important to retain the 7-bit ASCII portion of the character set [see **ascii**(5)]. System utilities and many applications assume these values.

Media transported between machines with different internal code set mappings may not be portable as no mapping is performed on block devices, such as tape and floppy drives. However, **trchan** with an appropriate *mapfile* can be used to translate from one internal character set to another.

Do not set **ISTRIP** [see **stty**(1)] when using **mapchan**. This option causes the eighth bit to be stripped before mapping occurs.

SEE ALSO

lpadmin(1M), **mapkey**(1M), **mapchan**(4), **ascii**(5), **keyboard**(7), **lp**(7)
stty(1M) in the *User's Reference Manual*

NAME

mapkey, mapscrn, mapstr – configure monitor screen mapping

SYNOPSIS

mapkey [−doxV] [*datafile*]
mapscrn [−dg] [*datafile*]
mapstr [−dg] [*datafile*]

DESCRIPTION

mapscrn configures the output mapping of the virtual terminal screen on which it is invoked. mapkey and mapstr configure the mapping of the keyboard and string keys (e.g., function keys) of the virtual terminal. mapkey can only be run by the superuser.

mapscrn and mapstr function on a per-virtual terminal (VT) basis. Mapping on one VT does not affect any other VT. Setting the default for every VT can be done using the −g option.

If a file name is given on the argument line, the respective mapping table is configured from the contents of the input file. If no file is given, the default files in /usr/lib/keyboard and /usr/lib/console are used. The −d option causes the mapping table to be read from the kernel instead of written and an ASCII version to be displayed on the standard output. The format of the output is suitable for use as input files to mapscrn, mapkey, or mapstr.

The sum of the characters in the strings for mapstr (in the /usr/lib/keyboard/strings file) can be a maximum of 512.

mapkey, when downloading a mapping table, overwrites the default mapping table for all VTs (thus affecting all VTs using the default mapping table) unless the −V option is specified. In this case, only the VT in which mapkey −V was invoked is affected, and the VT will revert to using the default mapping table when it is closed or the user logs out.

When mapkey displays the mapping table being used, it is the default mapping table unless the −V option is specified. In this case, mapkey displays the mapping table in use on the VT in which mapkey −V was invoked.

Non-superusers can run mapkey and mapstr when the −d option is given.

With the −o or −x options, mapkey displays the mapping table in octal or hexadecimal, respectively.

FILES

/usr/lib/keyboard/*
/usr/lib/console/*

NOTES

There is no way to specify that the map utilities read their configuration tables from standard input.

SEE ALSO

keyboard(7), display(7)

NAME

maplocale – convert Release 4 locale information to different format

SYNOPSIS

maplocale -f *new_format* [-t *territory*] [-c *codeset*] *SVR4_locale_name*

DESCRIPTION

maplocale converts Release 4 locale information into a format suitable for use with applications that require a different locale format. Currently, only conversion to SCO UNIX/XENIX format is supported, therefore, *new_format* must be XENIX.

The *SVR4_locale_name* must be the name of a valid locale, which will be the name of one of the sub-directories in the /usr/lib/locale directory.

Release 4 locale names use the form *language*[_*territory*[.*codeset*]]. If the locale name does not have the optional *codeset* or *territory* parts the -t and -c options must be used to specify the territory and code set for the locale.

SCO Specific Information

The converted data files will be placed in the directory:

/usr/lib/lang/*language*/*territory*/*codeset*.

If an abbreviated Release 4 locale name is used, the file /etc/default/lang will be updated and a line of the following form added to it:

LANG=*language_territory.codeset*

EXAMPLE

To convert the Spanish locale which is stored in the ISO 8859-1 code set, use the command:

maplocale -fXENIX -tES -c88591 es

DIAGNOSTICS

All error messages should be self explanatory.

FILES

/usr/lib/locale
/usr/lib/lang
/etc/default/lang

NAME

mconnect – connect to SMTP mail server socket

SYNOPSIS

/usr/ucb/mconnect [-p *port*] [-r] [*hostname*]

DESCRIPTION

mconnect opens a connection to the mail server on a given host, so that it can be tested independently of all other mail software. If no host is given, the connection is made to the local host. Servers expect to speak the Simple Mail Transfer Protocol (SMTP) on this connection. Exit by typing the **quit** command. Typing EOF sends an end of file to the server. An interrupt closes the connection immediately and exits.

OPTIONS

-p *port*   Specify the port number instead of the default SMTP port (number 25) as the next argument.

-r   "Raw" mode: disable the default line buffering and input handling. This gives you a similar effect as **telnet** to port number 25, not very useful.

FILES

/usr/ucblib/sendmail.hf   help file for SMTP commands

SEE ALSO

sendmail(1M)

Postel, Jonathan B *Simple Mail Transfer Protocol*, RFC821 August 1982, SRI Network Information Center

NAME

mcs – manipulate the comment section of an object file

SYNOPSIS

mcs [–a *string*] [–c] [–d] [–n *name*] [–p] [–v] *file* . . .

DESCRIPTION

The **mcs** command is used to manipulate a section, by default the .comment section, in an ELF object file. It is used to add to, delete, print, and compress the contents of a section in an ELF object file, and only print the contents of a section in a COFF object file. **mcs** must be given one or more of the options described below. It applies each of the options in order to each file.

The following options are available.

–a *string*   Append *string* to the comment section of the object files. If *string* contains embedded blanks, it must be enclosed in quotation marks.

–c   Compress the contents of the comment section of the ELF object files. All duplicate entries are removed. The ordering of the remaining entries is not disturbed.

–d   Delete the contents of the comment section from the ELF object files. The section header for the comment section is also removed.

–n *name*   Specify the name of the comment section to access if other than .comment. By default, **mcs** deals with the section named .comment. This option can be used to specify another section.

–p   Print the contents of the comment section on the standard output. Each section printed is tagged by the name of the file from which it was extracted, using the format *filename* [*member_name*] : for archive files; and *filename* : for other files.

–v   Print, on standard error, the version number of **mcs**.

If the input file is an archive [see **ar**(4)], the archive is treated as a set of individual files. For example, if the –a option is specified, the string is appended to the comment section of each ELF object file in the archive; if the archive member is not an ELF object file, then it is left unchanged.

If **mcs** is executed on an archive file the archive symbol table will be removed, unless only the –p option has been specified. The archive symbol table must be restored by executing the **ar** command with the –s option before the archive can be linked by the **ld** command. **mcs** will produce appropriate warning messages when this situation arises.

EXAMPLES

```
mcs -p file      # Print file's comment section

mcs -a string file   # Append string to file's comment section
```

FILES

TMPDIR/**mcs***	temporary files
TMPDIR	usually **/var/tmp** but can be redefined by setting the environment variable **TMPDIR** [see **tempnam** in **tmpnam**(3S)].

SEE ALSO

ar(1), **as**(1), **cc**(1), **ld**(1), **tmpnam**(3S), **a.out**(4), **ar**(4)
See the "Object Files" chapter in *Programmer's Guide: ANSI C and Programming Support Tools*

NOTES

mcs cannot add to, delete or compress the contents of a section that is contained within a segment.

NAME

mesg – permit or deny messages

SYNOPSIS

mesg [–n] [–y]

DESCRIPTION

mesg with argument **–n** forbids messages via **write**(1) by revoking non-user write permission on the user's terminal. **mesg** with argument **–y** reinstates permission. All by itself, **mesg** reports the current state without changing it.

FILES

/dev/tty*

SEE ALSO

write(1)

DIAGNOSTICS

Exit status is 0 if messages are receivable, 1 if not, 2 on error.

NAME

message – put arguments on FMLI message line

SYNOPSIS

message [-t] [-b [*num*]] [-o] [-w] [*string*]
message [-f] [-b [*num*]] [-o] [-w] [*string*]
message [-p] [-b [*num*]] [-o] [-w] [*string*]

DESCRIPTION

The **message** command puts *string* out on the FMLI message line. If there is no
string, the *stdin* input to **message** will be used. The output of **message** has a
duration (length of time it remains on the message line). The default duration is
"transient": it or one of two other durations can be requested with the following
mutually-exclusive options:

-t   explicitly defines a message to have transient duration. Transient mes-
       sages remain on the message line only until the user presses another key
       or a **CHECKWORLD** occurs. The descriptors **itemmsg**, **fieldmsg**,
       invalidmsg, **choicemsg**, the default-if-not-defined value of **oninter-
       rupt**, and FMLI generated error messages (for example, from syntax
       errors) also output transient duration messages. Transient messages
       take precedence over both frame messages and permanent messages.

-f   defines a message to have "frame" duration. Frame messages remain on
       the message line as long as the frame in which they are defined is
       current. The descriptor **framemsg** also outputs a frame duration
       message. Frame messages take precedence over permanent messages.

-p   defines a message to have "permanent" duration. Permanent messages
       remain on the message line for the length of the FMLI session, unless
       explicitly replaced by another permanent message or temporarily super-
       seded by a transient message or frame message. A permanent message
       is not affected by navigating away from, or by closing, the frame which
       generated the permanent message. The descriptor **permanentmsg** also
       outputs a permanent duration message.

Messages displayed with **message -p** will replace (change the value of) any message currently displayed or stored via use of the **permanentmsg** descriptor. Like-
wise, **message -f** will replace any message currently displayed or stored via use
of the **framemsg** descriptor. If more than one message in a frame definition file is
specified with the **-p** option, the last one specified will be the permanent duration
message.

The *string* argument should always be the last argument. Other options available
with **message** are the following:

-b [*num*] rings the terminal bell *num* times, where *num* is an integer from 1 to
            10. The default value is 1. If the terminal has no bell, the screen will
            flash *num* times instead, if possible.

-o   forces **message** to duplicate its message to *stdout*.

-w   turns on the working indicator.

EXAMPLES

When a value entered in a field is invalid, ring the bell 3 times and then display **Invalid Entry: Try again!** on the message line:

        invalidmsg=`message -b 3 "Invalid Entry: Try again!"`

Display a message that tells the user what is being done:

        done=`message EDITOR has been set in your environment` close

Display a message on the message line and *stdout* for each field in a form (a pseudo-"field duration" message).

        fieldmsg="`message -o -f "Enter a filename."`"

Display a blank transient message (effect is to "remove" a permanent or frame duration message).

        done=`message ""` nop

NOTES

If **message** is coded more than once on a single line, it may appear that only the right-most instance is interpreted and displayed. Use **sleep**(1) between uses of **message** in this case, to display multiple messages.

message -f should not be used in a stand-alone backquoted expression or with the **init** descriptor because the frame is not yet current when these are evaluated.

In cases where `**message -f** "*string*"` is part of a stand-alone backquoted expression, the context for evaluation of the expression is the previously current frame. The previously current frame can be the frame that issued the **open** command for the frame containing the backquoted expression, or it can be a frame given as an argument when **fmli** was invoked. That is, the previously current frame is the one whose frame message will be modified.

Permanent duration messages are displayed when the user navigates to the command line.

SEE ALSO

sleep(1) in the *UNIX System V User's Reference Manual*

NAME

migration – move an archive from one set of volumes to another

SYNOPSIS

migration -B [-dlmotuvAENS] *bkjobid ofsname ofsdev ofslab descript*

DESCRIPTION

migration is invoked as a child process by **bkdaemon**(1M) to move an existing archive made by some other arbitrary method to a new set of volumes. The existing backup history log entry of the archive is updated to reflect the new volumes and destination information of the archive.

bkjobid is the job id assigned by **backup**(1M). *ofsdev* is the name of the UNIX raw (character) device on which the archive resides. *ofslab* is the volume label on the archive [see **labelit**(1M)]. *descript* is a description for a destination device in the form:

> *dgroup:dname:dchar:dlabels*

dgroup specifies a device group. **dname** specifies a device name. *dchars* specifies characteristics for the specified device and group (see **device.tab**(4) for a further description of device characteristics). *dlabels* specifies the media names for the media to be used for the archive.

Options

d*   Do not update the backup history log entry for the archive.

l*   Create a long form of the backup history log that includes a table-of-contents for the archive. This includes the data used to generate an *ls -l*-like listing of each file in the archive.

m*   Mount the originating filesystem read-only before starting the backup and remount it with its original permissions after completing the backup.

o   Permit the user to override media insertion requests (see **getvol**(1M) -o).

t*   Create a table of contents for the backup on additional media instead of in the backup history log.

u*   Unmount the originating filesystem before performing the backup and remount it with its original permissions after completing the backup.

v*   Validate the archive as it is written. A checksum is computed as the archive is being written; as each medium is completed, it is re-read and the checksum recomputed to verify that each block is readable and correct. If either check fails, the medium is considered unreadable. If **-A** has been specified, the archiving operation fails; otherwise, the operator is prompted to replace the failed medium.

A   Do not prompt the user for removable media operations (automated operation).

E*   Report an estimate of media usage for the archive; then perform the backup.

N*   Report an estimate of media usage for the archive; do not perform the backup.

S*   Generate a period (.) for every 100 (512 byte) blocks read-from or written-to the archive on the destination device.

User Interactions

The connection between an archiving method and **backup**(1M) is more complex than a simple fork/exec or pipe. **backup**(1M) is responsible for all interactions with the user, either directly, or through **bkoper**(1M). Therefore, **migration** neither reads from standard-input nor writes to standard-output or standard-error. A method library must be used [see **libbrmeth**(3)] to communicate reports (estimates, periods, status, and so on) to **backup**(1M).

DIAGNOSTICS

If **migration** successfully completes its task, it exits with a 0 status. If any of the parameters to **migration** are invalid, it exits with a 1 status. If any error occurs which causes **migration** to fail to complete *all* portions of its task, it exits with a 2 status.

Errors are reported if any of the following occur:

1.   **-t** is specified together with **-A.**

2.   **-A** is specified together with **-o.**

3.   **-t** is specified and the destination device does not support removable media.

4.   **-A** is specified and more than one removable medium is required.

5.   Unrecoverable errors occurred in trying to read or write the destination device.

6.   **-m** is specified and the originating filesystem could not be mounted read-only.

7.   **-m** is specified and the originating filesystem could not be unmounted.

8.   **-o** is not specified and insufficient media names are supplied in *descript*.

9.   **-u** is specified and the filesystem could not be unmounted.

10.   **-u** is specified and the filesystem could not be remounted.

FILES

/usr/oam/bkrs/tables/bkhist.tab
$TMP/filelist$$

SEE ALSO

awk(1), backup(1M), device.tab(4), getvol(1M), grep(1), labelit(1M), libbrmeth(3), ls(1), prtvtoc(1M), restore(1M), rsoper(1M), sed(1), time(2), urestore(1M)

NAME

　　mkdir – make directories

SYNOPSIS

　　mkdir [–m *mode*] [–p] *dirname* . . .

DESCRIPTION

　　mkdir creates the named directories in mode 777 (possibly altered by umask(1)).

Standard entries in a directory (for example, the files ., for the directory itself, and .., for its parent) are made automatically. mkdir cannot create these entries by name. Creation of a directory requires write permission in the parent directory.

The owner ID and group ID of the new directories are set to the process's real user ID and group ID, respectively.

Two options apply to mkdir:

–m　　This option allows users to specify the mode to be used for new directories. Choices for modes can be found in chmod(1).

–p　　With this option, mkdir creates dirname by creating all the non-existing parent directories first.

EXAMPLE

　　To create the subdirectory structure ltr/jd/jan, type:

```
mkdir -p ltr/jd/jan
```

SEE ALSO

　　sh(1), rm(1), umask(1)
　　intro(2), mkdir(2) in the *Programmer's Reference Manual*

DIAGNOSTICS

　　mkdir returns exit code 0 if all directories given in the command line were made successfully. Otherwise, it prints a diagnostic and returns non-zero.

NAME

mkfifo – make FIFO special file

SYNOPSIS

mkfifo path . . .

DESCRIPTION

mkfifo creates the FIFO special files named by its argument list. The arguments are taken sequentially, in the order specified; and each FIFO special file is either created completely or, in the case of an error or signal, not created at all.

For each *path* argument, the mkfifo command behaves as if the function mkfifo [see mkfifo(3C)] was called with the argument *path* set to *path* and the *mode* set to the bitwise inclusive OR of S_IRUSR, S_IWUSR, S_IRGRP, S_IWGRP, S_IROTH and S_IWOTH.

If errors are encountered in creating one of the special files, mkfifo writes a diagnostic message to the standard error and continues with the remaining arguments, if any.

SEE ALSO

mkfifo(3C) in the *Programmer's Reference Manual*

DIAGNOSTICS

mkfifo returns exit code 0 if all FIFO special files were created normally; otherwise it prints a diagnostic and returns a value greater than 0.

NAME

mkfs (generic) – construct a file system

SYNOPSIS

mkfs [–F *FSType*] [–v] [–m] [*current_options*] [–o *specific_options*] *special* [*operands*]

DESCRIPTION

mkfs constructs a file system by writing on the *special* file; *special* must be the first argument. The file system is created based on the *FSType, specific_options* and *operands* specified on the command line. mkfs waits 10 seconds before starting to construct the file system. During this time the command can be aborted by entering a delete (DEL).

operands are *FSType*-specific and the *FSType* specific manual page of mkfs should be consulted for a detailed description.

current_options are options supported by the s5-specific module of mkfs. Other *FSTypes* do not necessarily support these options. *specific_options* indicate suboptions specified in a comma-separated list of suboptions and/or keyword-attribute pairs for interpretation by the *FSType*-specific module of the command.

The options are:

–F   Specify the *FSType* to be constructed. The *FSType* should either be specified here or be determinable from /etc/vfstab by matching the *special* with an entry in the table.

–v   Echo the complete command line, but do not execute the command. The command line is generated by using the options and arguments provided by the user and adding to them information derived from /etc/vfstab. This option should be used to verify and validate the command line.

–m   Return the command line which was used to create the file system. The file system must already exist. This option provides a means of determining the command used in constructing the file system. It cannot be used with *current_options, specific_options*, or *operands*. It must be invoked by itself.

–o   Specify *FSType*-specific options.

NOTES

This command may not be supported for all *FSTypes*.

FILES

/etc/vfstab   list of default parameters for each file system

SEE ALSO

makefsys(1M), vfstab(4)

Manual pages for the *FSType*-specific modules of mkfs

NAME

mkfs (bfs) – construct a boot file system

SYNOPSIS

mkfs [–F bfs] *special blocks* [*inodes*]

DESCRIPTION

mkfs is used to create a boot file system, which is a contiguous flat file system, to hold the bootable programs and data files necessary for the boot procedure.

The argument *special* is the device special file that refers to the partition on which the file system is to be created. The *blocks* argument is used to specify the size of the file system. The block size is automatically 512 bytes.

The *inodes* argument specifies the number of files that the file system will hold.

NOTES

This file system is intended to hold the bootable files and data files for the boot procedure. Use as a general purpose file system is not recommended.

SEE ALSO

See the *System Administrator's Guide* for more information about the boot file system.

NAME

mkfs (s5) – construct an **s5** file system

SYNOPSIS

mkfs [**-F s5**] [*generic_options*] *special*
mkfs [**-F s5**] [*generic_options*] [**-b** *block_size*] *special blocks*[*:i-nodes*] [*gap blocks/cyl*]
mkfs [**-F s5**] [*generic_options*] [**-b** *block_size*] *special proto* [*gap blocks/cyl*]

DESCRIPTION

generic_options are options supported by the generic **mkfs** command.

mkfs constructs an **s5** file system by writing on the *special* file using the values found in the remaining arguments of the command line. **mkfs** builds a file system with a **root** directory and a **lost+found** directory.

The options are:

-F s5   Specifies an **s5**-FSType.

-b *blocksize*   Specifies the logical block size for the file system. The logical block size is the number of bytes read or written by the operating system in a single I/O operation. Valid values for *blocksize* are 512, 1024, and 2048. The default is 1024.

If the second argument to **mkfs** is a string of digits, the size of the file system is the value of *blocks* interpreted as a decimal number. This is the number of *physical* (512 byte) disk blocks the file system will occupy. If the number of i-nodes is not given, the default is approximately the number of *logical* blocks divided by 4. **mkfs** builds a file system with a single empty directory on it. The boot program block (block zero) is left uninitialized.

If the second argument is the name of a file that can be opened, **mkfs** assumes it to be a prototype file *proto*, and will take its directions from that file. The prototype file contains tokens separated by spaces or new-lines. A sample prototype specification follows (line numbers have been added to aid in the explanation):

```
 1.    /dev/rdsk/0s0
 2.    4872 110
 3.    d--777 3 1
 4.    usr   d--777 3 1
 5.          sh    ---755 3 1 /sbin/sh
 6.          ken   d--755 6 1
 7.                $
 8.          b0    b--644 3 1 0 0
 9.          c0    c--644 3 1 0 0
10.          slnk  l--777 2 2 /var/tmp
11.          $
12.    $
```

Line 1 in the example is the name of a file to be copied onto block zero as the bootstrap program.

Line 2 specifies the number of *physical* (512 byte) blocks the file system is to occupy and the number of i-nodes in the file system.

Lines 3-10 tell **mkfs** about files and directories to be included in this file system.

Line 3 specifies the root directory.

Lines 4-6 and 8-10 specify other directories and files.

Line 10 specifies the symbolic link **slnk** set up in **/usr** and containing **/var/tmp**.

The $ on line 7 tells **mkfs** to end the branch of the file system it is on, and continue from the next higher directory. The $ on lines 11 and 12 end the process, since no additional specifications follow.

File specifications give the mode, the user ID, the group ID, and the initial contents of the file. Valid syntax for the contents field depends on the first character of the mode.

The mode for a file is specified by a 6-character string. The first character specifies the type of the file. The character range is **-bcdl** to specify regular, block special, character special, directory, and symbolic link files respectively. The second character of the mode is either **u** or **-** to specify set-user-id mode or not. The third is **g** or **-** for the set-group-id mode. The rest of the mode is a 3 digit octal number giving the owner, group, and other read, write, execute permissions [see **chmod**(1)].

Two decimal number tokens come after the mode; they specify the user and group IDs of the owner of the file.

If the file is a regular file, the next token of the specification may be a path name whence the contents and size are copied. If the file is a block or character special file, two decimal numbers follow which give the major and minor device numbers. If the file is a directory, **mkfs** makes the entries . and .. and then reads a list of names and (recursively) file specifications for the entries in the directory. As noted above, the scan is terminated with the token **$**.

The *gap blocks/cyl* argument in both forms of the command specifies the rotational gap and the number of blocks/cylinder. If the *gap* and *blocks/cyl* are not specified or are considered illegal values a default value of gap size 10 and 162 blocks/cyl is used.

NOTES

With a prototype file there is no way to specify hard links.

The maximum number of i-nodes configurable is 65500.

FILES

/etc/vtoc/*

SEE ALSO

generic **mkfs**(1M), **dir**(4), **fs**(4)
chmod(1) in the *User's Reference Manual*

NAME

mkfs (ufs) – construct a **ufs** file system

SYNOPSIS

mkfs [–F ufs] –C [*generic_options*] *special*

mkfs [–F ufs] –C [*generic_options*] [–o *specific_options*] *special size*

DESCRIPTION

generic_options are options supported by the generic **mkfs** command.

mkfs constructs a file system by writing on the special file *special* unless the '–o N' flag has been specified. The numeric *size* specifies the number of sectors in the file system. **mkfs** builds a file system with a root directory and a **lost+found** directory [see **fsck**(1M)]. The number of inodes is calculated as a function of the file system size.

The options are:

–F ufs   Specifies the **ufs**-FSType.

–C   Create no more than 64K inodes. Ensures compatibility with the pre-Release 4 UNIX System. **diskadd** [see **diskadd**(1M)] calls **mkfs** with this option.

–o   Specify **ufs** file system specific options. The following options are available:

    N   Do not write the file system to the *special* file. This suboption gives all the information needed to create a file system but does not create it.

    nsect=*n*   The number of sectors per track on the disk. The default is **18**.

    ntrack=*n*   The number of tracks per cylinder on the disk. The default is **9**.

    bsize=*n*   The primary block size for files on the file system. It must be a power of two, currently selected from **4096** (the default) or **8192**.

    fragsize=*n* The fragment size for files on the file system. The **fragsize** represents the smallest amount of disk space that will be allocated to a file. It must be a power of two currently selected from the range **512** to **8192**. The default is **1024**.

    cgsize=*n*   The number of disk cylinders per cylinder group. This number must be in the range **1** to **32**. The default is **16**.

    free=*n*   The minimum percentage of free disk space allowed. Once the file system capacity reaches this threshold, only a privileged user is allowed to allocate disk blocks. The default value is **10%**.

rps=n The rotational speed of the disk, in revolutions per second. The default is **60**.

nbpi=n The number of bytes for which one inode block is allocated. This parameter is currently set at one inode block for every 2048 bytes.

opt=s|t   Space or time optimization preference; **s** specifies optimization for space, **t** specifies optimization for time. The default is **t**.

apc=n The number of alternates per cylinder (SCSI devices only). The default is **0**.

gap=n The expected time (in milliseconds) to service a transfer completion interrupt and initiate a new transfer on the same disk. It is used to decide how much rotational spacing to place between successive blocks in a file. The default is 4.

NOTES

The value of the **nbpi** operand in the output of **mkfs** **-m** is always 2048, even if the file system was created with some other value.

SEE ALSO

fsck(1M), generic **mkfs**(1M), **dir**(4), **fs**(4)

NAME

mkmsgs – create message files for use by **gettxt**

SYNOPSIS

mkmsgs [–o] [–i *locale*] *inputstrings msgfile*

DESCRIPTION

The **mkmsgs** utility is used to create a file of text strings that can be accessed using the text retrieval tools (see **gettxt**(1), **srchtxt**(1), **exstr**(1), and **gettxt**(3C)). It will take as input a file of text strings for a particular geographic locale (see **setlocale**(3C)) and create a file of text strings in a format that can be retrieved by both **gettxt**(1) and **gettxt**(3C). By using the –i option, you can install the created file under the **/usr/lib/locale/***locale***/LC_MESSAGES** directory (*locale* corresponds to the language in which the text strings are written).

inputstrings   the name of the file that contains the original text strings.

msgfile   the name of the output file where **mkmsgs** writes the strings in a format that is readable by **gettxt**(1) and **gettxt**(3C). The name of *msgfile* can be up to 14 characters in length, but may not contain either \0 (null) or the ASCII code for / (slash) or : (colon).

–i *locale*   install *msgfile* in the **/usr/lib/locale/***locale***/LC_MESSAGES** directory. Only someone who is super-user or a member of group **bin** can create or overwrite files in this directory. Directories under **/usr/lib/locale** will be created if they don't exist.

–o   overwrite *msgfile*, if it exists.

The input file contains a set of text strings for the particular geographic locale. Text strings are separated by a new-line character. Nongraphic characters must be represented as alphabetic escape sequences. Messages are transformed and copied sequentially from *inputstrings* to *msgfile*. To generate an empty message in *msgfile*, leave an empty line at the correct place in *inputstrings*.

Strings can be changed simply by editing the file *inputstrings*. New strings must be added only at the end of the file; then a new *msgfile* file must be created and installed in the correct place. If this procedure is not followed, the retrieval function will retrieve the wrong string and software compatibility will be broken.

EXAMPLES

The following example shows an input message source file **c.str**:

```
File %s:\t cannot be opened\n
%s: Bad directory\n
            .
            .
            .
write error\n
            .
            .
```

The following command uses the input strings from **c.str** to create text strings in the appropriate format in the file **ux** in the current directory:

```
mkmsgs c.str UX
```

The following command uses the input strings from **FR.str** to create text strings in the appropriate format in the file **UX** in the directory **/usr/lib/locale/french/LC_MESSAGES/UX**.

         mkmsgs -i french FR.str UX

These text strings would be accessed if you had set the environment variable **LC_MESSAGES=french** and then invoked one of the text retrieval tools listed at the beginning of the DESCRIPTION section.

FILES

    /usr/lib/locale/*locale*/LC_MESSAGES/*   message files created by **mkmsgs**(1M)

SEE ALSO

    exstr(1), **gettxt**(1), **srchtxt**(1)
    gettxt(3C), **setlocale**(3C) in the *Programmer's Reference Manual*

NAME

mknod – make a special file

SYNOPSIS

mknod *name* **b** | **c** *major minor*

mknod *name* **p**

DESCRIPTION

mknod makes a directory entry for a special file.

name is the special file to be created. The second argument is either **b**, to indicate a block-type special file, or **c**, to indicate a character-type. The last two arguments are numbers specifying the *major* and *minor* device numbers; these may be either decimal or octal. The assignment of major device numbers is specific to each system. You must be a privileged user to use this form of the command.

The second case is used to create a FIFO (named pipe).

NOTES

If mknod is used to create a device in a remote directory (Remote File Sharing), the major and minor device numbers are interpreted by the server.

SEE ALSO

mknod(2) in the *Programmer's Reference Manual*

NAME

mknod – make a special file

SYNOPSIS

mknod *name* **b** | **c** *major minor*
mknod *name* **p**
mknod *name* **m**
mknod *name* **s**

DESCRIPTION

mknod makes a directory entry for a special file.

In the first case, *name* is the special file to be created. The second argument is either **b** to indicate a block-type special file or **c** to indicate a character-type. The last two arguments are numbers specifying the *major* and *minor* device numbers; these may be either decimal or octal [see mknod(2) in the *Programmer's Reference Manual* for information on minor device number values]. The assignment of major device numbers is specific to each system. You must be the super-user to use this form of the command.

The second case is used to create a FIFO (named pipe).

The third case is used to create XENIX shared memory handles.

The fourth case is used to create XENIX semaphore handles.

NOTES

If mknod is used to create a device in a remote directory (Remote File Sharing), the major and minor device numbers are interpreted by the server.

SEE ALSO

mknod(2) in the *Programmer's Reference Manual*

NAME

mkpart – disk maintenance utility

SYNOPSIS

/etc/mkpart [-f *filename*] [-p *partition*] ... [-P *partition*] ... [-b]
[-B *filename*] [-A *sector*] ... [-V] [-v] [-i] [-x *file*]
[-t [vpa]] *device*

/etc/mkpart -F *interleave raw_device*

DESCRIPTION

mkpart will not be supported in a future release. See "NOTES" below.

This program allows the system administrator to display and modify the data structures that the disk driver uses to access disks. These structures describe the number, size, and type of the partitions, as well as the physical characteristics of the disk drive itself.

The user maintains a file of stanzas, each of which contains comments and parameters. The stanzas are of two varieties: those that describe disk partitions and disk devices. Stanzas may refer to other stanzas of the same type so that common device or partition types may be customized. By default, the stanza file is named /etc/partitions. The required parameter, *device,* specifies the device stanza for the disk to be used.

The following options may be used with mkpart:

-f *filename*　　specifies the partition and device specification stanza file. If not present, /etc/partitions is assumed.

-p *partition*　　removes a partition from the vtoc on the specified device. The *partition* is a stanza that indicates the partition to be removed by its partition number parameter; no comparisons are made by attribute. Note: Alternate partitions cannot be removed.

-P *partition*　　adds a partition to the vtoc on the specified device. *partition* is a stanza which contains and/or refers to other stanzas that contain all of the necessary parameters for a vtoc partition.

-b　　　　　　　causes only the boot program to be updated, unless other options are specified.

-B *filename*　　specifies a different boot program than the one given by the device stanza.

-A *sector*　　marks the specified sector as bad and assigns it an alternate if possible. *sector* is a zero-based absolute sector number from the beginning of the drive. To compute a sector number given cylinder, head, and (0-based) sector in track, the formula is cylinder * (sectors-per-track * heads-per-cylinder) + head * (sectors-per-track) + sector.

-V　　　　　　causes a complete surface-analysis pass to be run. This first writes a data pattern (currently 0xe5 in every byte) to each sector of the disk, then reads each sector. Any errors are noted and the bad sectors found are added to the alternates table if possible.

−v   causes a non-destructive surface-analysis pass to be run. This just reads every sector of the disk, noting bad sectors as above.

−i   initializes the VTOC on the drive to default values, clearing any existing partition and bad-sector information which may have existed. This is the only way to remove an alternate partition and can be used to re-initialize a drive which may have obsolete or incorrect VTOC data on it.

−x *file*   writes a complete *device* and partition stanza list for the specified *device* to file.
Note: The tags in the file are pseudo names used to identify the slice.

−t [*vpa*]   creates a listing of the current vtoc. The sub-parameters specify pieces to be printed: a - alternate sectors, **p** - *partitions*, and **v** - *vtoc* and related structures.

The *partitions* file is composed of blank-line-separated stanzas. (Blank lines have only tabs and spaces between new-lines). Commentary consists of all text between a '#' and a *new-line*. Stanzas begin with an identifier followed by a ':', and are followed by a comma-separated list of parameters. Each parameter has a keyword followed by an '=' followed by a value. The value may be a number, another stanza's name, a double quoted string, or a parenthesis-surrounded, comma-separated list of numbers or ranges of numbers, as appropriate for the keyword. Numbers may be written as decimal, octal, or hexadecimal constants in the form familiar to C programmers.

Device specification stanzas may contain the following parameters:

usedevice = *name*   causes the named stanza's parameters to be included in the device definition.

boot = *string*   indicates that the string is the filename of a bootstrap program to install on the disk.

device = *string*   gives the filename of the character special device for the disk.

heads = *number*   specifies the number of tracks per cylinder on the device.

cyls = *number*   is the number of cylinders on the disk.

sectors = *number*   is the number of sectors per track.

bpsec = *number*   is the number of bytes per sector.

dserial = *string*   is an arbitrary string which is recorded in the volume label. (Multibus systems only)

vtocsec = *number*   gives the sector number to use for the volume table of contents.
Note: for AT386 systems, this number must be 17.

altsec = *number*   is the sector to use for the alternate block table.

badsec = *number-list*   lists the known bad sectors. These are appended to any specified in the command line or found during surface analysis.

Partition stanzas may have the following parameters:

usepart = *name*   refers to another partition stanza.

partition = *number*   gives this partition's entry number in the vtoc.

tag = *tagname*   A partition tag specifies the purpose of the partition. The *tagnames* are reserved words which are presently used for identification purposes only:

> **BACKUP** means the entire disk.
> **ROOT** is a root file system partition.
> **BOOT** is a bootstrap partition.
> **SWAP** is a partition that does not contain a file system.
> **USR** is a partition that does contain a file system.
> **ALTS** contains alternate sectors to which the driver re-maps bad sectors. Currently a maximum of 62 alternate sectors is supported.
> **OTHER** is a partition that the UNIX system does not know how to handle, such as MS-DOS space.

perm = *permname*   specifies a permission type for the partition. Permissions are not mutually exclusive.
RO indicates that the partition cannot be written upon. Normally, write access is granted (standard UNIX system file permissions notwithstanding).
NOMOUNT disallows the driver from mounting the file system that may be contained in the partition.
VALID indicates that the partition contains valid data. Any partition added with the **-A** flag will be marked VALID.

start = *number*   is the starting sector number for the partition.
Note: For AT386 systems, the root file system should start at the *second* track of the cylinder which is the beginning of the active UNIX system 'fdisk' partition. This allows space for the writing of the boot code.

size = *number*   is the size, in sectors, of the partition.

When **mkpart** is run, it first attempts to read the volume label (for multibus systems) or the 'fdisk' table (for AT386 systems), the VTOC block, and the alternate sector table. If any of the structures is invalid or cannot be read, or if the **-i** flag is specified, the internal tables are initialized to default values for the device specified (taken from the device stanza in the partition file). If the **-F** flag is specified, the device is formatted. If either the **-V** or **-v** flag is specified, the appropriate surface analysis is performed. After these steps, partitions are deleted or added as required. Next, any bad sectors specified in the partition file, found during surface analysis, or specified in the command line with **-A** flags are merged into the alternate sectors table. Note that an alternate partition must exist for any bad-sector marking to occur, as bad sectors are assigned good alternates at this point. Finally, the boot program is written to track 0 of cylinder 0

(Multibus systems) or the cylinder where the active UNIX system 'fdisk' partition starts (AT386 systems). If −b was not the only parameter specified, the updated VTOC and alternates tables are written, and the disk driver is instructed to re-read the tables when the drive is opened the next time. When only −t is specified, only a listing is created and no updating occurs.

−F *interleave*   causes the entire device to be hardware formatted. This process re-writes all the sector headers on each track of the disk, enabling subsequent access using normal reads and writes. *interleave* is the distance in physical sectors between each successive logical sector. Normal values are 1 for track-cache controllers, 3–4 for standard controllers. The device for this option must be a raw UNIX system device. The −F option precludes all other options, thus should be used alone.

FILES

/etc/partitions /etc/boot /dev/rdsk/*s0

NOTES

The mkpart command will not be supported in a future release. Use prtvtoc and edvtoc instead [see prtvtoc(1M) and edvtoc(1M)].

Currently, very little consistency checking is done. No checks are made to ensure that the 'fdisk' partition table is consistent with the UNIX system partitions placed in the VTOC. If a DOS 'fdisk' partition is started at cylinder 0, DOS will happily overwrite the UNIX system VTOC.

SEE ALSO

edvtoc(1M), prtvtoc(1M)

NAME

montbl – create monetary database

SYNOPSIS

montbl [-o *outfile*] *infile*

DESCRIPTION

The **montbl** command takes as input a specification file, *infile*, that describes the formatting conventions for monetary quantities for a specific locale.

-o *outfile*   Write the output on *outfile*; otherwise, write the output on a file named **LC_MONETARY**.

The output of **montbl** is suitable for use by the **localeconv( )** function (see **localeconv**(3C)). Before *outfile* can be used by **localeconv( )**, it must be installed in the **/usr/lib/locale/***locale* directory with the name **LC_MONETARY** by someone who is super-user or a member of group **bin**. *locale* is the locale whose monetary formatting conventions are described in *infile*. This file must be readable by user, group, and other; no other permissions should be set. To use formatting conventions for monetary quantities described in this file, use **setlocale**(3C) to change the locale for category **LC_MONETARY** to *locale* [see **setlocale**(3C)].

Once installed, this file will be used by the **localeconv( )** function to initialize the monetary specific fields of a structure of type **struct lconv**. For a description of each field in this structure, see **localeconv**(3C).

```
struct      lconv      {
        char *decimal_point;       /* "." */
        char *thousands_sep;       /* "" (zero length string) */
        char *grouping;            /* "" */
        char *int_curr_symbol;     /* "" */
        char *currency_symbol;     /* "" */
        char *mon_decimal_point;   /* "" */
        char *mon_thousands_sep;   /* "" */
        char *mon_grouping;        /* "" */
        char *positive_sign;       /* "" */
        char *negative_sign;       /* "" */
        char int_frac_digits;      /* CHAR_MAX */
        char frac_digits;          /* CHAR_MAX */
        char p_cs_precedes;        /* CHAR_MAX */
        char p_sep_by_space;       /* CHAR_MAX */
        char n_cs_precedes;        /* CHAR_MAX */
        char n_sep_by_space;       /* CHAR_MAX */
        char p_sign_posn;          /* CHAR_MAX */
        char n_sign_posn;          /* CHAR_MAX */
};
```

The specification file specifies the value of each **struct lconv** member, except for the first three members, *decimal_point*, *thousands_sep*, and *grouping* which are set by the **LC_NUMERIC** category of **setlocale**(3C). Each member's value is given on a line with the following format:

> *keyword* <white space> *value*

where *keyword* is identical to the **struct lconv** field name and *value* is a quoted string for those fields that are a **char** * and an integer for those fields that are an **int**. For example,

```
int_curr_symbol        "ITL."
int_frac_digits        0
```

will set the international currency symbol and the number of fractional digits to be displayed in an internationally formatted monetary quantity to **ITL.** and **0**, respectively.

Blank lines and lines starting with a **#** are taken to be comments and are ignored. A character in a string may be in octal or hex representation. For example, **\141** or **\x61** could be used to represent the letter 'a'. If there is no specification line for a given structure member, then the default 'C' locale value for that member is used (see the values in comments in the **struct lconv** definition above).

Given below is an example of what the specification file for Italy would look like:

```
# Italy

int_curr_symbol        "ITL."
currency_symbol        "L."
mon_decimal_point      ""
mon_thousands_sep      "."
mon_grouping           "\3"
positive_sign          ""
negative_sign          "-"
int_frac_digits        0
frac_digits            0
p_cs_precedes          1
p_sep_by_space         0
n_cs_precedes          1
n_sep_by_space         0
p_sign_posn            1
n_sign_posn            1
```

FILES

    /usr/lib/locale/*locale*/LC_MONETARY
              LC_MONETARY database for *locale*

    /usr/lib/locale/C/montbl_C
              input file used to construct **LC_MONETARY** in the default locale.

SEE ALSO

    localeconv(3C), **setlocale**(3C) in the *Programmer's Reference Manual*

NAME

more, page – browse or page through a text file

SYNOPSIS

more [–cdflrsuw] [–lines] [+linenumber] [+/pattern] [filename . . .
page [–cdflrsuw] [–lines] [+linenumber] [+/pattern] [filename . . .

DESCRIPTION

more is a filter that displays the contents of a text file on the terminal, one screenful at a time. It normally pauses after each screenful, and prints --More-- at the
bottom of the screen. more provides a two-line overlap between screens for con-
tinuity. If more is reading from a file rather than a pipe, the percentage of characters displayed so far is also shown.

more scrolls up to display one more line in response to a RETURN character; it
displays another screenful in response to a SPACE character. Other commands are
listed below.

page clears the screen before displaying the next screenful of text; it only provides a one-line overlap between screens.

more sets the terminal to *noecho* mode, so that the output can be continuous.
Commands that you type do not normally show up on your terminal, except for
the / and ! commands.

If the standard output is not a terminal, more acts just like cat(1V), except that a
header is printed before each file in a series.

OPTIONS

The following options are available with more:

–c   Clear before displaying. Redrawing the screen instead of scrolling
            for faster displays. This option is ignored if the terminal does not
            have the ability to clear to the end of a line.

–d   Display error messages rather than ringing the terminal bell if an
            unrecognized command is used. This is helpful for inexperienced
            users.

–f   Do not fold long lines. This is useful when lines contain nonprint-
            ing characters or escape sequences, such as those generated when
            nroff(1) output is piped through ul(1).

–l   Do not treat FORMFEED characters (CTRL-d) as page breaks. If –l is
            not used, more pauses to accept commands after any line containing
            a ^L character (CTRL-d). Also, if a file begins with a FORMFEED, the
            screen is cleared before the file is printed.

–r   Normally, more ignores control characters that it does not interpret
            in some way. The –r option causes these to be displayed as ^C
            where C stands for any such control character.

–s   Squeeze. Replace multiple blank lines with a single blank line. This
            is helpful when viewing nroff(1) output, on the screen.

-u   Suppress generation of underlining escape sequences. Normally,
              more handles underlining, such as that produced by nroff(1), in a
              manner appropriate to the terminal. If the terminal can perform
              underlining or has a stand-out mode, more supplies appropriate
              escape sequences as called for in the text file.

-w   Normally, more exits when it comes to the end of its input. With
              -w, however, more prompts and waits for any key to be struck
              before exiting.

-*lines*   Display the indicated number of *lines* in each screenful, rather than
              the default (the number of lines in the terminal screen less two).

+*linenumber* Start up at *linenumber*.

+/*pattern*   Start up two lines above the line containing the regular expression
              pattern. Note: unlike editors, this construct should *not* end with a
              '/'. If it does, then the trailing slash is taken as a character in the
              search pattern.

USAGE
Environment

more uses the terminal's termcap(5) entry to determine its display characteristics,
and looks in the environment variable for any preset options. For instance, to
page through files using the -c mode by default, set the value of this variable to
-c. (Normally, the command sequence to set up this environment variable is
placed in the .login or .profile file).

Commands

The commands take effect immediately; it is not necessary to type a carriage
return. Up to the time when the command character itself is given, the user may
type the line kill character to cancel the numerical argument being formed. In
addition, the user may type the erase character to redisplay the '--More--(*xx*%)'
message.

In the following commands, *i* is a numerical argument (1 by default).

*i*SPACE   Display another screenful, or *i* more lines if *i* is specified.

*i*RETURN   Display another line, or *i* more lines, if specified.

i^D   (CTRL-d) Display (scroll down) 11 more lines. If *i* is given, the scroll
              size is set to *i*.

*i*d   Same as ^D.

*i*z   Same as SPACE, except that *i*, if present, becomes the new default
              number of lines per screenful.

*i*s   Skip *i* lines and then print a screenful.

*i*f   Skip *i* screenfuls and then print a screenful.

i^B   (CTRL-b) Skip back *i* screenfuls and then print a screenful.

b   Same as ^B (CTRL-d).

q
Q   Exit from **more**.

=   Display the current line number.

v   Drop into the editor indicated by the **EDITOR** environment variable, at
                     the current line of the current file. The default editor is **ed**(1).

h   Help. Give a description of all the **more** commands.

i/pattern   Search forward for the *i* th occurrence of the regular expression *pat-
                     tern*. Display the screenful starting two lines before the line that con-
                     tains the *i* th match for the regular expression *pattern*, or the end of a
                     pipe, whichever comes first. If **more** is displaying a file and there is no
                     such match, its position in the file remains unchanged. Regular
                     expressions can be edited using erase and kill characters. Erasing back
                     past the first column cancels the search command.

*i*n   Search for the *i* th occurrence of the last *pattern* entered.

´   Single quote. Go to the point from which the last search started. If no
                     search has been performed in the current file, go to the beginning of
                     the file.

!*command*   Invoke a shell to execute *command*. The characters **%** and **!**, when
                     used within *command* are replaced with the current filename and the
                     previous shell command, respectively. If there is no current filename,
                     % is not expanded. Prepend a backslash to these characters to escape
                     expansion.

i:n   Skip to the *i* th next filename given in the command line, or to the last
                     filename in the list if *i* is out of range.

i:p   Skip to the *i* th previous filename given in the command line, or to the
                     first filename if *i* is out of range. If given while **more** is positioned
                     within a file, go to the beginning of the file. If **more** is reading from a
                     pipe, **more** simply rings the terminal bell.

:f   Display the current filename and line number.
:q
:Q   Exit from **more** (same as **q** or **Q**).

.   Dot. Repeat the previous command.

^\   Halt a partial display of text. **more** stops sending output, and displays
                     the usual **--More--** prompt. Unfortunately, some output is lost as a
                     result.

FILES
        /usr/share/lib/termcap   terminal data base
        /usr/lib/more.help   help file
SEE ALSO
        cat(1), csh(1), man(1), script(1), sh(1)
        environ(5V), termcap(5) in the *System Administrator's Reference Manual*
NOTES
        Skipping backwards is too slow on large files.

NAME

mount, umount (generic) – mount or unmount file systems and remote resources

SYNOPSIS

```
mount [-v |-p]
mount [-F FSType] [-v] [current_options] [-o specific_options] {special | mount_point}
mount [-F FSType] [-v] [current_options] [-o specific_options] special mount_point
umount [-v] [-o specific_options] {special | mount_point}
```

DESCRIPTION

File systems other than **root** (**/**) are considered removable in the sense that they can be either available to users or unavailable. **mount** notifies the system that *special*, a block special device or a remote resource, is available to users from the *mount_point* which must already exist; it becomes the name of the root of the newly mounted *special* or resource.

mount, when entered with arguments, validates all arguments except for the device name and invokes an *FSType* specific **mount** module. If invoked with no arguments, **mount** lists all the mounted file systems from the mount table. If invoked with any of the following partial argument lists, for example, one of *special* or *mount_point* or when both arguments are specified but no *FSType* is specified **mount** will search **/etc/vfstab** to fill in the missing arguments: *FSType*, *special*, *mount_point*, and *specific_options*. It will then invoke the *FSType*-specific **mount** module.

Most *FSTypes* do not have a **umount** specific module. If one exists it is executed; otherwise the generic module unmounts the file systems. If the **-o** option is specified the **umount** specific module is always executed.

current_options are options supported by the **s5**-specific module of **mount** and **umount**. Other *FSTypes* do not necessarily support these options. *specific_options* indicate suboptions specified in a comma-separated list of suboptions and/or keyword-attribute pairs for interpretation by the *FSType*-specific module of the command.

The options are:

-v	Print the output in a new style. The new output has the *FSType* and flags displayed in addition to the old output. The *mount_point* and *special* fields are reversed.
-p	Print the list of mounted file systems in the **/etc/vfstab** format.
-F	used to specify the *FSType* on which to operate. The *FSType* must be specified or must be determinable from **/etc/vfstab** while mounting a file system.
-V	Echo the complete command line, but do not execute the command. The command line is generated by using the options and arguments provided by the user and adding to them information derived from **/etc/vfstab**. This option should be used to verify and validate the command line.

      −o   used to specify *FSType*-specific options.

mount can be used by any user to list mounted file systems and resources. Only a super-user can mount or unmount file systems.

NOTES

mount will not prevent you from mounting a file system on a directory that's not empty.

The old output format will be phased out in a future release and all output will be in the new −v format. The most significant changes are the addition of two new fields to show the *FSType* and flags and the reversal of the *mount_point* and *special* name.

mount adds an entry to the mount table /etc/mnttab; umount removes an entry from the table.

FILES

    /etc/mnttab   mount table

    /etc/vfstab   list of default parameters for each file system.

SEE ALSO

    setmnt(1M), mountfsys(1M), umountfsys(1M), mnttab(4), vfstab(4)

    Manual pages for the *FSType*-specific modules of mount

NAME

mount (bfs) - mount **bfs** file systems

SYNOPSIS

mount [-F bfs] [*generic_options*] [-r] [-o *specific_options*] {*special* | *mount_point*}
mount [-F bfs] [*generic_options*] [-r] [-o *specific_options*] *special mount_point*

DESCRIPTION

generic_options are options supported by the generic **mount** command.

mount attaches a **bfs** file system, referenced by *special,* to the file system hierarchy at the pathname location *mount_point*, which must already exist. If *mount_point* has any contents prior to the **mount** operation, these are hidden until the file system is unmounted.

The options are:

-F bfs   Specify the **bfs**-FSType

-r   Mount the file system read-only

-o   Specify the options specific to the **bfs** file system. Available options are:

        rw | **ro**   Read/write or read-only. Default is read/write.

Only a privileged user can mount file systems.

FILES

/etc/mnttab   mount table

SEE ALSO

generic **mount**(1M), **mountfsys**(1M), **mnttab**(4)
mount(2) in the *Programmer's Reference Manual*

NAME

mount – mount remote NFS resources

SYNOPSIS

mount [-F nfs] [-r] [-o *specific_options*] {*resource* | *mountpoint*}
mount [-F nfs] [-r] [-o *specific_options*] *resource mountpoint*

DESCRIPTION

The **mount** command attaches a named *resource* to the file system hierarchy at the pathname location *mountpoint*, which must already exist. If *mountpoint* has any contents prior to the **mount** operation, the contents remain hidden until the *resource* is once again unmounted.

If the resource is listed in the **vfstab** file, the command line can specify either *resource* or *mountpoint*, and **mount** will consult **vfstab** for more information. If the **-F** option is omitted, **mount** will take the file system type from **vfstab**.

mount maintains a table of mounted file systems in **/etc/mnttab**, described in **mnttab**(4).

The following options are available to the **mount** command:

-r   Mount the specified file system read-only.

-o   Specify the **nfs** file-specific options in a comma-separated list. The available options are:

  rw| ro   *resource* is mounted read-write or read-only. The default is **rw**.

  suid| nosuid Setuid execution allowed or disallowed. The default is **suid**.

  remount   If a file system is mounted read-only, remounts the file system read-write.

  bg| fg   If the first attempt fails, retry in the background, or, in the foreground. The default is **fg**.

  retry=*n*   The number of times to retry the mount operation. The default is 10000.

  port=*n*   The server IP port number. The default is **NFS_PORT**.

  grpid   Create a file with its GID set to the effective GID of the calling process. This behavior may be overridden on a per-directory basis by setting the set-GID bit of the parent directory; in this case, the GID is set to the GID of the parent directory [see **open**(2) and **mkdir**(2)]. Files created on file systems that are *not* mounted with the **grpid** option will obey BSD semantics; that is, the GID is unconditionally inherited from that of the parent directory.

  rsize=*n*   Set the read buffer size to *n* bytes.

  wsize=*n*   Set the write buffer size to *n* bytes.

  timeo=*n*   Set the NFS timeout to *n* tenths of a second.

  retrans=*n* Set the number of NFS retransmissions to *n*.

  soft| hard Return an error if the server does not respond, or continue the retry request until the server responds.

`intr`	Allow keyboard interrupts to kill a process that is hung while waiting for a response on a hard-mounted file system.
`secure`	Use a more secure protocol for NFS transactions.
`noac`	Suppress attribute caching.
`acregmin=`n	Hold cached attributes for at least n seconds after file modification.
`acregmax=`n	Hold cached attributes for no more than n seconds after file modification.
`acdirmin=`n	Hold cached attributes for at least n seconds after directory update.
`acdirmax=`n	Hold cached attributes for no more than n seconds after directory update.
`actimeo=`n	Set *min* and *max* times for regular files and directories to n seconds.

NFS FILE SYSTEMS

Background vs. Foreground

File systems mounted with the **bg** option indicate that **mount** is to retry in the background if the server's mount daemon [**mountd**(1M)] does not respond. **mount** retries the request up to the count specified in the **retry=**n option. Once the file system is mounted, each NFS request made in the kernel waits **timeo=**n tenths of a second for a response. If no response arrives, the time-out is multiplied by 2 and the request is retransmitted. When the number of retransmissions has reached the number specified in the **retrans=**n option, a file system mounted with the **soft** option returns an error on the request; one mounted with the **hard** option prints a warning message and continues to retry the request.

Read-Write vs. Read-Only

File systems that are mounted **rw** (read-write) should use the **hard** option.

Secure File Systems

The **secure** option must be given if the server requires secure mounting for the file system.

File Attributes

The attribute cache retains file attributes on the client. Attributes for a file are assigned a time to be flushed. If the file is modified before the flush time, then the flush time is extended by the time since the last modification (under the assumption that files that changed recently are likely to change soon). There is a minimum and maximum flush time extension for regular files and for directories. Setting **actimeo=**n extends flush time by n seconds for both regular files and directories.

EXAMPLES

To mount a remote file system: **mount -F nfs serv:/usr/src /usr/src**
To hard mount a remote file system: **mount -o hard serv:/usr/src /usr/src**

FILES

`/etc/mnttab`	mount table
`/etc/dfs/fstypes`	default distributed file system type
`/etc/vfstab`	table of automatically mounted resources

SEE ALSO

mountall(1M), mount(2), umount(2), mnttab(4)

NOTES

If the directory on which a file system is to be mounted is a symbolic link, the file system is mounted on *the directory to which the symbolic link refers*, rather than being mounted on top of the symbolic link itself.

NAME

mount – mount remote resources

SYNOPSIS

mount [-F rfs] [-cr] [-o *specific_options*] *resource directory*

DESCRIPTION

The **mount** command makes a remote *resource* available to users from the mount point *directory*. The command adds an entry to the table of mounted devices, **/etc/mnttab**.

If multiple transport providers are installed and administrators attempt to mount a resource over them, the transport providers should be specified as network IDs in the **/etc/netconfig** file. The NETPATH environment variable can be used to specify the sequence of transport providers **mount** will use to attempt a connection to a server machine (**NETPATH=tcp:starlan**). If only one transport provider is installed and **/etc/netconfig** has not been set up, all resources will be mounted over this transport provider by default.

The following options are available:

-F rfs   Specifies the **rfs**-FSType.

-c   Disable client caching. This is the same as **-o nocaching**.

-r   *resource* is to be mounted read-only. If the *resource* is write-protected, this flag or the **-o ro** specific option must be used.

-o   Specify the **rfs** file system specific options in a comma-separated list. The available options are:

        nocaching   Disable client caching.

        rw|ro   *resource* is to be mounted read/write or read-only. The default is read/write.

        suid|nosuid   Set-uid bits are to be obeyed or ignored, respectively, on execution. The default is **nosuid**.

        Note that mounting a resource from an untrusted server introduces possible security risks. While the use of **nosuid** protects against some risks, it is not completely effective. The best defense against such security risks is to avoid such mounts.

FILES

/etc/mnttab   mount table
/etc/netconfig   network configuration database
/etc/vfstab   table of automatically mounted resources

SEE ALSO

dfmounts(1M),   **dfshares**(1M),   **fuser**(1M),   **share**(1M),   **umount**(1M), **unshare**(1M), **vfstab**(1M), **mnttab**(4), **netconfig**(4)

NAME

mount (s5) – mount an **s5** file system

SYNOPSIS

mount [**-F s5**] [*generic_options*] [**-r**] [**-o** *specific_options*] {*special | mount_point*}
mount [**-F s5**] [*generic_options*] [**-r**] [**-o** *specific_options*] *special mount_point*

DESCRIPTION

generic_options are options supported by the generic **mount** command.

mount notifies the system that *special*, an **s5** block special device, is available to users from the *mount_point* which must exist before **mount** is called; it becomes the name of the root of the newly mounted *special*.

The options are:

-F s5   Specify an **s5** FSType.

-r   Mount the file system read-only.

-o   Specify **s5** file-specific options in a comma-separated list. The avilable options are:

    rw | ro   Read/write or read-only. Default is **rw**.

    suid | nosuid

        Setuid is honored or ignored on execution Default is **suid**.

        Note that a **mount** of an unprotected medium (such as a floppy disk) introduces possible security risks. While the use of **nosuid** protects against some risks, it is not completely effective. The best defense against such security risks is to avoid mounting unprotected media.

    remount   Used in conjunction with **rw**. A file system mounted read-only can be *remounted* read-write. Fails if the file system is not currently mounted or if the file system is mounted **rw**. Option is in force only when specified.

Only a privileged user can mount file systems.

FILES

/etc/mnttab   mount table

SEE ALSO

generic **mount**(1M), **mountfsys**(1M), **setmnt**(1M)
mount(2), **setuid**(2), in the *Programmer's Reference Manual*
mnttab(4) in the *System Administrator's Reference Manual*

NAME

    mount (ufs) – mount **ufs** file systems

SYNOPSIS

    mount [**-F ufs**] [*generic_options*] [**-r**] [**-o** *specific_options*] { *special| mount_point* }

    mount [**-F ufs**] [*generic_options*] [**-r**] [**-o** *specific_options*] *special mount_point*

DESCRIPTION

    generic_options are options supported by the generic **mount** command. **mount** attaches a **ufs** file system, referenced by *special*, to the file system hierarchy at the pathname location *mount_point*, which must already exist. If *mount_point* has any contents prior to the **mount** operation, these remain hidden until the file system is once again unmounted.

    The options are:

    -F ufs Specifies the **ufs**-FSType.

    -r   Mount the file system read-only.

    -o   Specify the **ufs** file system specific options in a comma-separated list. If invalid options are specified, a warning message is printed and the invalid options are ignored. The following options are available:

        f   Fake an **/etc/mnttab** entry, but do not actually mount any file systems. Parameters are not verified.

        n   Mount the file system without making an entry in **/etc/mnttab**.

        rw| ro   Read/write or read-only. Default is **rw**.

        nosuid   By default the file system is mounted with setuid execution allowed. Specifying **nosuid** overrides the default and causes the file system to be mounted with setuid execution disallowed.

        remount Used in conjunction with **rw**. A file system mounted read-only can be *remounted* read-write. Fails if the file system is not currently mounted or if the file system is mounted **rw**.

NOTES

    If the directory on which a file system is to be mounted is a symbolic link, the file system is mounted on the directory to which the symbolic link refers, rather than on top of the symbolic link itself.

FILES

    /etc/mnttab   mount table

SEE ALSO

    generic **mount**(1M), **mountfsys**(1M), **umountfsys**(1M), **mkdir**(2), **mount**(2), **open**(2), **unmount**(2), **mnttab**(4)

NAME

mountall, umountall – mount, unmount multiple file systems

SYNOPSIS

mountall [–F *FSType*] [–l | –r] [*file_system_table*]
umountall [–F *FSType*] [–k] [–l | –r]

DESCRIPTION

These commands may be executed only by a privileged user.

mountall is used to mount file systems according to a *file_system_table*.
(/etc/vfstab is the default file system table.) The special file name "–" reads
from the standard input. If the dash is specified, then the standard input must be
in the same format as /etc/vfstab. With no arguments mountall restricts the
mount to all systems with automnt field set to yes in the *file_system_table*.

Before each file system is mounted, a sanity check is done using fsck [see
fsck(1M)] to see if it appears mountable. If the file system does not appear
mountable, it is fixed, using fsck, before the mount is attempted.

umountall causes all mounted file systems except root, /proc, /stand, and
/dev/fd to be unmounted. If the *FSType* is specified mountall and umountall
limit their actions to the *FSType* specified.

The options are:

–F   Specify the File System type to be mounted or unmounted. If *FSType*
          is specified the action is limited to file systems of this *FSType*.

–l   Limit the action to local file systems.

–r   Limit the action to remote file system types.

–k   Send a *SIGKILL* signal to processes that have files opened.

DIAGNOSTICS

No messages are printed if the file systems are mountable and clean.

Error and warning messages come from fsck(1M) and mount(1M).

SEE ALSO

fsck(1M), fuser(1M), mount(1M), mnttab(4), vfstab(4)
signal(2) in the *Programmer's Reference Manual*

NAME

    mountd – NFS mount request server

SYNOPSIS

    mountd [-n]

DESCRIPTION

    mountd is an RPC server that answers file system mount requests. It reads the file /etc/dfs/sharetab, described in sharetab(4), to determine which file systems are available for mounting by which machines. It also provides information as to what file systems are mounted by which clients. This information can be printed using the dfmounts(1M) command.

    The mountd daemon is automatically invoked in run level 3.

    With the -n option, mountd does not check that the clients are root users. Though this option makes things slightly less secure, it does allow older versions (pre-3.0) of client NFS to work.

FILES

    /etc/dfs/sharetab

SEE ALSO

    dfmounts(1M), sharetab(4)

NAME

mountfsys, umountfsys – mount, unmount a file system

SYNOPSIS

mountfsys

umountfsys

DESCRIPTION

The mountfsys command mounts a file system so that users can read from it and write to it. The umountfsys command unmounts the file system.

The command invokes a visual interface (the **mount** or **unmount** tasks available through the sysadm command).

The initial prompt for both commands allows you to select the device on which to mount/unmount the file system.

For the mountfsys command, you are asked to select how the file system is to be mounted; for example, read-only or read/write.

The identical functions are available under the sysadm menu:

sysadm mount

sysadm unmount

DIAGNOSTICS

Both mountfsys and umountfsys exit with one of the following values:

0   Normal exit.

2   Invalid command syntax. A usage message is displayed.

7   The visual interface for this command is not available because it cannot invoke fmli. (The fmli package is not installed or is corrupt.)

NOTES

For a removable medium, once the disk is mounted it must not be removed from the disk drive until it has been unmounted. Removing the disk while it is still mounted can cause severe damage to the data on the disk.

SEE ALSO

checkfsys(1M), labelit(1M), makefsys(1M), mkfs(1M), mount(1M), sysadm(1M)

NAME

mouseadmin - mouse administration

SYNOPSIS

mouseadmin [-nbl] [-d *terminal*] [-a *terminal mouse*]

DESCRIPTION

mouseadmin allows any user with system administrator privileges to add or delete mouse devices. Users without "superuser" privileges will only be allowed to list the current mouse/display assignments. The mouseadmin command issued without arguments will execute in menu mode, providing the user with a listing of current assignments and a selection menu of operations.

OPTIONS

The command line arguments are defined as follows:

-n   build mouse/display pair table without downloading to driver. (This option should only be used within install scripts.)

-b   do not validate for BUS mouse in system configuration. (This option should only be used within install scripts.)

-l   list mouse/display assignments.

-d   delete terminal assignment.

-a   assign mouse device (PS2, BUS, tty00, s0tty0, etc.) to terminal (console, s0vt00, etc.).

When using the -a option, the mouseadmin command format is:

mouseadmin -a *terminal mouse_device*

For example:

```
mouseadmin -a console PS2
mouseadmin -a console BUS
mouseadmin -a s0vt00 tty00
mouseadmin -a s0vt00 tty01
```

FILES

/usr/bin/mouseadmin
/usr/lib/mousemgr

SEE ALSO

mouse(7)
Mouse Driver Administrator's Guide

NAME
mt – magnetic tape control

SYNOPSIS
/usr/ucb/mt [−f *tapename*] *command* [*count*]

DESCRIPTION
mt sends commands to a magnetic tape drive. If *tapename* is not specified, the environment variable **TAPE** is used. If **TAPE** does not exist, mt uses the device /dev/rmt12. *tapename* must refer to a raw (not block) tape device. By default, mt performs the requested operation once; multiple operations may be performed by specifying *count*.

The available commands are listed below. Only as many characters as are required to uniquely identify a command need be specified.

mt returns a 0 exit status when the operation(s) were successful, 1 if the command was unrecognized or if mt was unable to open the specified tape drive, and 2 if an operation failed.

the following commands are available to mt:

eof, weof   Write *count* EOF marks at the current position on the tape.

fsf   Forward space *count* files.

fsr   Forward space *count* records.

bsf   Back space *count* files.

bsr   Back space *count* records.

asf   Absolute space to *count* file number. This is equivalent to a **rewind** followed by a **fsf** *count*.

For the following commands, *count* is ignored:

eom   Space to the end of recorded media on the tape (SCSI only). This is useful for appending files onto previously written tapes.

rewind   Rewind the tape.

offline, rewoffl
    Rewind, unload, and place the tape drive unit off-line.

status   Print status information about the tape unit.

retension   Wind the tape to the end of the reel and then rewind it, smoothing out the tape tension.

erase   Erase the entire tape.

FILES
/dev/rmt*	raw magnetic tape interface
/dev/rar*	raw Archive cartridge tape interface
/dev/rst*	raw SCSI tape interface
/dev/rmt*	raw Xylogics® tape interface

SEE ALSO

    dd(1M), **ar**(4), **environ**(5), **xt**(7) in the *System Administrator's Reference Manual*

NOTES

    Not all devices support all options. For example, **ar** currently does not support the **fsr**, **bsf**, or **bsr** options. The half-inch tape driver, **/dev/rmt***, does not support the **retension** option.

NAME

mv – move files

SYNOPSIS

mv [-f] [-i] *file1* [*file2* ...] *target*

DESCRIPTION

The **mv** command moves *filen* to *target*. *filen* and *target* may not have the same name. (Care must be taken when using **sh**(1) metacharacters). If *target* is not a directory, only one file may be specified before it; if it is a directory, more than one file may be specified. If *target* does not exist, **mv** creates a file named *target*. If *target* exists and is not a directory, its contents are overwritten. If *target* is a directory the file(s) are moved to that directory. *target* and *filen* do not have to share the same parent directory.

If **mv** determines that the mode of *target* forbids writing, it will print the mode [see **chmod**(2)], ask for a response, and read the standard input for one line. If the line begins with **y**, the **mv** occurs, if permissible; otherwise, the command exits. When the parent directory of *filen* is writable and has the sticky bit set, one or more of the following conditions must be true:

> the user must own the file
> the user must own the directory
> the file must be writable by the user
> the user must be a privileged user

The following options are recognized:

-i   **mv** will prompt for confirmation whenever the move would overwrite an existing *target*. A **y** answer means that the move should proceed. Any other answer prevents **mv** from overwriting the *target*.

-f   **mv** will move the file(s) without prompting even if it is writing over an existing *target*. This option overrides the –i option. Note that this is the default if the standard input is not a terminal.

You can use **mv** to move directories as well as files. If *filen* is a directory, *target* must be a directory in the same physical file system.

If *filen* is a file and *target* is a link to another file with links, the other links remain and *target* becomes a new file.

NOTES

If *filen* and *target* are on different file systems, **mv** copies the file and deletes the original; any links to other files are lost.

A –– permits the user to mark explicitly the end of any command line options, allowing **mv** to recognize filename arguments that begin with a –. As an aid to BSD migration, **mv** will accept – as a synonym for ––. This migration aid may disappear in a future release. If a –– and a – both appear on the same command line, the second will be interpreted as a filename.

SEE ALSO

chmod(1), cp(1), cpio(1), ln(1), rm(1)

NAME

mvdir – move a directory

SYNOPSIS

/usr/sbin/mvdir *dirname name*

DESCRIPTION

mvdir moves directories within a file system. *dirname* must be a directory. If *name* does not exist, it will be created as a directory. If *name* does exist, and is a directory, *dirname* will be created as *name/dirname*. *dirname* and *name* may not be on the same path; that is, one may not be subordinate to the other. For example:

      mvdir x/y x/z

is legal, but

      mvdir x/y x/y/z

is not.

SEE ALSO

mkdir(1), mv(1) in the *User's Reference Manual*

NOTE

Only the super-user can use **mvdir**.

NAME

named, in.named – Internet domain name server

SYNOPSIS

in.named [–d *level*] [–p *port*] [[–b] *bootfile*]

DESCRIPTION

named is the Internet domain name server. It is used by hosts on the Internet to provide access to the Internet distributed naming database. See RFC 1034 and RFC 1035 for more details. With no arguments **named** reads /etc/named.boot for any initial data, and listens for queries on a privileged port.

The following options are available:

–d *level*   Print debugging information. *level* is a number indicating the level of messages printed.

–p *port*   Use a different *port* number.

–b *bootfile*   Use *bootfile* rather than /etc/named.boot.

EXAMPLE

```
;
;       boot file for name server
;
; type            domain               source file or host
;
domain            berkeley.edu
primary           berkeley.edu    named.db
secondary         cc.berkeley.edu 10.2.0.78 128.32.0.10
cache             .               named.ca
```

The **domain** line specifies that **berkeley.edu** is the domain of the given server.

The **primary** line states that the file **named.db** contains authoritative data for **berkeley.edu**. The file **named.db** contains data in the master file format, described in RFC 1035, except that all domain names are relative to the origin; in this case, **berkeley.edu** (see below for a more detailed description).

The **secondary** line specifies that all authoritative data under **cc.berkeley.edu** is to be transferred from the name server at **10.2.0.78**. If the transfer fails it will try **128.32.0.10**, and continue for up to 10 tries at that address. The secondary copy is also authoritative for the domain.

The **cache** line specifies that data in **named.ca** is to be placed in the cache (typically such data as the locations of root domain servers). The file **named.ca** is in the same format as **named.db**.

The master file consists of entries of the form:

```
$INCLUDE < filename >
$ORIGIN < domain >
< domain > < opt_ttl > < opt_class > < type > < resource_record_data >
```

where *domain* is "." for the root, "@" for the current origin, or a standard domain name. If *domain* is a standard domain name that does not end with ".", the current origin is appended to the domain. Domain names ending with "." are unmodified.

The *opt_ttl* field is an optional integer number for the time-to-live field. It defaults to zero.

The *opt_class* field is currently one token, **IN** for the Internet.

The *type* field is one of the following tokens; the data expected in the *resource_record_data* field is in parentheses.

A	A host address (dotted quad).
NS	An authoritative name server (domain).
MX	A mail exchanger (domain).
CNAME	The canonical name for an alias (domain).
SOA	Marks the start of a zone of authority (5 numbers). See RFC 1035.
MB	A mailbox domain name (domain).
MG	A mail group member (domain).
MR	A mail rename domain name (domain).
NULL	A null resource record (no format or data).
WKS	A well know service description (not implemented yet).
PTR	A domain name pointer (domain).
HINFO	Host information (cpu_type OS_type).
MINFO	Mailbox or mail list information (request_domain error_domain).

FILES

/etc/named.boot	name server configuration boot file
/etc/named.pid	the process ID
/var/tmp/named.run	debug output
/var/tmp/named_dump.db	dump of the name servers database

SEE ALSO

kill(1), signal(3), resolver(3N), resolve.conf(4)

Mockapetris, Paul, *Domain Names - Concepts and Facilities*, RFC 1034, Network Information Center, SRI International, Menlo Park, Calif., November 1987

Mockapetris, Paul, *Domain Names - Implementation and Specification*, RFC 1035, Network Information Center, SRI International, Menlo Park, Calif., November 1987

Mockapetris, Paul, *Domain System Changes and Observations*, RFC 973, Network Information Center, SRI International, Menlo Park, Calif., January 1986

Partridge, Craig, *Mail Routing and the Domain System*, RFC 974, Network Information Center, SRI International, Menlo Park, Calif., January 1986

NOTES

The following signals have the specified effect when sent to the server process using the **kill**(1) command.

SIGHUP	Reads **/etc/named.boot** and reloads database.
SIGINT	Dumps the current database and cache to **/var/tmp/named_dump.db**.
SIGUSR1	Turns on debugging; each subsequent **SIGUSR1** increments debug level.
SIGUSR2	Turns off debugging completely.

NAME

nawk – pattern scanning and processing language

SYNOPSIS

nawk [-**F** *re*] [-**v** *var=value*] ['*prog*'] [*file* . . .]

nawk [-**F** *re*] [-**v** *var=value*] [-**f** *progfile*] [*file* . . .]

DESCRIPTION

nawk scans each input *file* for lines that match any of a set of patterns specified in *prog*. The *prog* string must be enclosed in single quotes (') to protect it from the shell. For each pattern in *prog* there may be an associated action performed when a line of a *file* matches the pattern. The set of pattern-action statements may appear literally as *prog* or in a file specified with the -**f** *progfile* option. Input files are read in order; if there are no files, the standard input is read. The file name – means the standard input.

Each input line is matched against the pattern portion of every pattern-action statement; the associated action is performed for each matched pattern. Any *file* of the form **var**=*value* is treated as an assignment, not a filename, and is executed at the time it would have been opened if it were a filename, and is executed at the time it would have been opened if it were a filename. The option -**v** followed by **var**=*value* is an assignment to be done before *prog* is executed; any number of -**v** options may be present.

An input line is normally made up of fields separated by white space. (This default can be changed by using the **FS** built-in variable or the -**F** *re* option.) The fields are denoted **$1**, **$2**, . . . ; **$0** refers to the entire line.

A pattern-action statement has the form:

> *pattern* { *action* }

Either pattern or action may be omitted. If there is no action with a pattern, the matching line is printed. If there is no pattern with an action, the action is performed on every input line. Pattern-action statements are separated by newlines or semicolons.

Patterns are arbitrary Boolean combinations (**!**, **||**, **&&**, and parentheses) of relational expressions and regular expressions. A relational expression is one of the following:

> *expression relop expression*
> *expression* **matchop** *regular_expression*
> *expression* **in** *array-name*
> (*expression*,*expression*, . . .) **in** *array-name*

where a *relop* is any of the six relational operators in C, and a *matchop* is either ~ (contains) or **!~** (does not contain). An *expression* is an arithmetic expression, a relational expression, the special expression

> *var* **in** *array*

or a Boolean combination of these.

Regular expressions are as in **egrep**(1). In patterns they must be surrounded by slashes. Isolated regular expressions in a pattern apply to the entire line. Regular expressions may also occur in relational expressions. A pattern may consist of two patterns separated by a comma; in this case, the action is performed for all lines between an occurrence of the first pattern and the next occurrence of the second pattern.

The special patterns **BEGIN** and **END** may be used to capture control before the first input line has been read and after the last input line has been read respectively. These keywords do not combine with any other patterns.

A regular expression may be used to separate fields by using the **-F** *re* option or by assigning the expression to the built-in variable FS. The default is to ignore leading blanks and to separate fields by blanks and/or tab characters. However, if FS is assigned a value, leading blanks are no longer ignored.

Other built-in variables include:

ARGC	command line argument count
ARGV	command line argument array
ENVIRON	array of environment variables; subscripts are names
FILENAME	name of the current input file
FNR	ordinal number of the current record in the current file
FS	input field separator regular expression (default blank and tab)
NF	number of fields in the current record
NR	ordinal number of the current record
OFMT	output format for numbers (default **%.6g**)
OFS	output field separator (default blank)
ORS	output record separator (default new-line)
RS	input record separator (default new-line)
SUBSEP	separates multiple subscripts (default is 034)

An action is a sequence of statements. A statement may be one of the following:

```
if ( expression ) statement [ else statement ]
while ( expression ) statement
do statement while ( expression )
for ( expression ; expression ; expression ) statement
for ( var in array ) statement
delete array[subscript] #delete an array element
break
continue
{ [ statement ] ... }
expression     # commonly variable = expression
print [ expression-list ] [ >expression ]
printf format [ , expression-list ] [ >expression ]
next           # skip remaining patterns on this input line
```

> **exit** [**expr**] # skip the rest of the input; exit status is expr
> **return** [**expr**]

Statements are terminated by semicolons, new-lines, or right braces. An empty expression-list stands for the whole input line. Expressions take on string or numeric values as appropriate, and are built using the operators **+, -, *, /, %, ^** and concatenation (indicated by a blank). The operators **++ -- += -= *= /= %= ^= > >= < <= == != ?:** are also available in expressions. Variables may be scalars, array elements (denoted x[i]), or fields. Variables are initialized to the null string or zero. Array subscripts may be any string, not necessarily numeric; this allows for a form of associative memory. Multiple subscripts such as **[i,j,k]** are permitted; the constituents are concatenated, separated by the value of **SUBSEP**. String constants are quoted (**""**), with the usual C escapes recognized within.

The **print** statement prints its arguments on the standard output, or on a file if *>expression* is present, or on a pipe if | *cmd* is present. The arguments are separated by the current output field separator and terminated by the output record separator. The **printf** statement formats its expression list according to the format [see **printf**(3S) in the *Programmer's Reference Manual*]. The built-in function **close**(*expr*) closes the file or pipe *expr*.

The mathematical functions: **atan2, cos, exp, log, sin, sqrt**, are built-in.

Other built-in functions include:

gsub(*for, repl, in*)
behaves like **sub** (see below), except that it replaces successive occurrences of the regular expression (like the **ed** global substitute command).

index(*s, t*)　　returns the position in string *s* where string *t* first occurs, or 0 if it does not occur at all.

int　　truncates to an integer value.

length(*s*)　　returns the length of its argument taken as a string, or of the whole line if there is no argument.

match(*s, re*)　　returns the position in string *s* where the regular expression *re* occurs, or 0 if it does not occur at all. **RSTART** is set to the starting position (which is the same as the returned value), and **RLENGTH** is set to the length of the matched string.

rand　　random number on (0, 1).

split(*s, a, fs*)　　splits the string *s* into array elements *a*[1], *a*[2], . . ., *a*[*n*], and returns *n*. The separation is done with the regular expression *fs* or with the field separator **FS** if *fs* is not given.

srand　　sets the seed for **rand**

sprintf(*fmt, expr, expr,* ...)
formats the expressions according to the **printf**(3S) format given by *fmt* and returns the resulting string.

sub(*for, repl, in*)   substitutes the string *repl* in place of the first instance of the regular expression *for* in string *in* and returns the number of substitutions. If *in* is omitted, **nawk** substitutes in the current record (**$0**).

substr(*s, m, n*)   returns the *n*-character substring of *s* that begins at position *m*.

The input/output built-in functions are:

close(*filename*)   closes the file or pipe named *filename*.

cmd **| getline**   pipes the output of *cmd* into **getline**; each successive call to *getline* returns the next line of output from *cmd*.

getline   sets **$0** to the next input record from the current input file.

getline *<file*   sets **$0** to the next record from *file*.

getline *x*   sets variable *x* instead.

getline *x <file*   sets *x* from the next record of *file*.

system(*cmd*)   executes *cmd* and returns its exit status.

All forms of **getline** return 1 for successful input, 0 for end of file, and −1 for an error.

nawk also provides user-defined functions. Such functions may be defined (in the pattern position of a pattern-action statement) as

     function *name*(*args*, . . .) **{** *stmts* **}**

Function arguments are passed by value if scalar and by reference if array name. Argument names are local to the function; all other variable names are global. Function calls may be nested and functions may be recursive. The **return** statement may be used to return a value.

EXAMPLES

Print lines longer than 72 characters:

     length > 72

Print first two fields in opposite order:

     { print $2, $1 }

Same, with input fields separated by comma and/or blanks and tabs:

     BEGIN { FS = ",[\t]*|[\t]+" }
          { print $2, $1 }

Add up first column, print sum and average:

         { s += $1 }
     END { print "sum is", s, " average is", s/NR }

Print fields in reverse order:

     { for (i = NF; i > 0; --i) print $i }

Print all lines between start/stop pairs:

/start/, /stop/

Print all lines whose first field is different from previous one:

```
$1 != prev { print; prev = $1 }
```

Simulate **echo**(1):

```
BEGIN {
        for (i = 1; i < ARGC; i++)
                printf "%s", ARGV[i]
        printf "\n"
        exit
        }
```

Print a file, filling in page numbers starting at 5:

```
/Page/      { $2 = n++; }
            { print }
```

Assuming this program is in a file named **prog**, the following command line prints the file **input** numbering its pages starting at 5: **nawk -f prog n=5 input**.

SEE ALSO

egrep(1), **grep**(1), **sed**(1)
lex(1), **printf**(3S) in the *Programmer's Reference Manual*
The **awk** chapter in the *User's Guide*
A. V. Aho, B. W. Kernighan, P. J. Weinberger, *The AWK Programming Language* Addison-Wesley, 1988

NOTES

nawk is a new version of **awk** that provides capabilities unavailable in previous versions. This version will become the default version of **awk** in the next major UNIX system release.

Input white space is not preserved on output if fields are involved.

There are no explicit conversions between numbers and strings. To force an expression to be treated as a number add 0 to it; to force it to be treated as a string concatenate the null string (" ") to it.

NAME

ncheck (generic) – generate a list of path names vs i-numbers

SYNOPSIS

ncheck [-**F** *FSType*] [-**V**] [*current_options*] [-**o** *specific_options*] [*special* . . .]

DESCRIPTION

ncheck with no options generates a path-name vs. i-number list of all files on *special*. If *special* is not specified on the command line the list is generated for all *specials* in **/etc/vfstab** for entries which have a numeric *fsckpass*. *special* is a block special device on which the file system exists.

current_options are options supported by the **s5**-specific module of **ncheck**. Other *FSTypes* do not necessarily support these options. *specific_options* indicate suboptions specified in a comma-separated list of suboptions and/or keyword-attribute pairs for interpretation by the *FSType*-specific module of the command.

The options are:

-**F**   Specify the *FSType* on which to operate. The *FSType* should either be specified here or be determinable from **/etc/vfstab** by finding an entry in the table that has a numeric *fsckpass* field and a matching *special* if specified.

-**V**   Echo the complete command line, but do not execute the command. The command line is generated by using the options and arguments provided by the user and adding to them information derived from **/etc/vfstab**. This option should be used to verify and validate the command line.

-**o**   used to specify *FSType* specific options if any.

FILES

/etc/vfstab   list of default parameters for each file system

SEE ALSO

vfstab(4)

Manual pages for the *FSType*-specific modules of **ncheck**

NOTES

This command may not be supported for all *FSTypes*.

NAME

ncheck (s5) – generate path names versus i-numbers for **s5** file systems

SYNOPSIS

ncheck [**-F s5**] [*generic_options*] [**-i** *i-number* . . .] [**-a**] [**-s**] [*special* . . .]

DESCRIPTION

generic_options are options supported by the generic **ncheck** command.

ncheck generates a path-name vs. i-number list of all files on the specified *special* device(s). Names of directory files are followed by "**/.**" .

The options are:

-F s5   Specifies the **s5**-FSType.

-i *i-number*
          Limits the report to those files whose i-numbers follow. The *i-number*s must be separated by commas without spaces.

-a   Allows printing of the names "**.**" and "**..**", which are ordinarily suppressed.

-s   Limits the report to special files and files with set-user-ID mode. This option may be used to detect violations of security policy.

DIAGNOSTICS

If the file system structure is not consistent, **??** denotes the parent of a parentless file and a path-name beginning with . . . denotes a loop.

SEE ALSO

generic **ncheck**(1M)

NAME

ncheck (ufs) – generate pathnames versus i-numbers for **ufs** file systems

SYNOPSIS

ncheck [**–F ufs**] [*generic_options*] [**–i** *i-list*] [**–a**] [**–s**] [**–o m**] [*special* . . .]

DESCRIPTION

generic_options are options supported by the generic **ncheck** command.

ncheck generates a pathname versus i-number list of files for the **ufs** file system. Names of directory files are followed by "**/. **".

The options are:

–F ufs   Specifies the **ufs**-FSType.

–i *i-list*   Limits the report to the files on the i-list that follows. The i-list must be separated by commas without spaces.

–a   Allows printing of the names "." and "..", which are ordinarily suppressed.

–s   Limits the report to special files and files with set-user-ID mode. This option may be used to detect violations of security policy.

–o   Specify **ufs** file system specific options. The available option is:

            m   Print mode information.

DIAGNOSTICS

When the file system structure is improper, **??** denotes the parent of a parentless file and a pathname beginning with . . . denotes a loop.

SEE ALSO

generic **ncheck**(1M)

NAME

netstat – show network status

SYNOPSIS

netstat [-aAn] [-f *addr_family*] [**system**] [**core**]

netstat [-n] [-s] [-i | -r] [-f *addr_family*] [**system**] [**core**]

netstat [-n] [-I *interface*] *interval* [**system**] [**core**]

DESCRIPTION

netstat displays the contents of various network-related data structures in various formats, depending on the options you select.

The first form of the command displays a list of active sockets for each protocol. The second form selects one from among various other network data structures. The third form displays running statistics of packet traffic on configured network interfaces; the *interval* argument indicates the number of seconds in which to gather statistics between displays.

The default value for the **system** argument is **/unix**; for *core*, the default is **/dev/kmem**.

The following options are available:

-a   Show the state of all sockets; normally sockets used by server processes are not shown.

-A   Show the address of any protocol control blocks associated with sockets; used for debugging.

-i   Show the state of interfaces that have been auto-configured. Interfaces that are statically configured into a system, but not located at boot time, are not shown.

-n   Show network addresses as numbers. **netstat** normally displays addresses as symbols. This option may be used with any of the display formats.

-r   Show the routing tables. When used with the **-s** option, show routing statistics instead.

-s   Show per-protocol statistics. When used with the **-r** option, show routing statistics.

-f *addr_family*
     Limit statistics or address control block reports to those of the specified *addr_family*, which can be one of:

         inet   For the AF_INET address family, or
         unix   For the AF_UNIX family.

-I *interface*
     Highlight information about the indicated *interface* in a separate column; the default (for the third form of the command) is the interface with the most traffic since the system was last rebooted. *interface* can be any valid interface listed in the system configuration file, such as **emd1** or **lo0**.

DISPLAYS

Active Sockets (First Form)

The display for each active socket shows the local and remote address, the send and receive queue sizes (in bytes), the protocol, and the internal state of the protocol.

The symbolic format normally used to display socket addresses is either:

> *hostname*.*port*

when the name of the host is specified, or:

> *network*.*port*

if a socket address specifies a network but no specific host. Each **hostname** and *network* is shown according to its entry in the **/etc/hosts** or the **/etc/networks** file, as appropriate.

If the network or hostname for an address is not known (or if the **-n** option is specified), the numerical network address is shown. Unspecified, or wildcard, addresses and ports appear as *. For more information regarding the Internet naming conventions, refer to **inet**(7).

TCP Sockets

The possible state values for TCP sockets are as follows:

CLOSED	Closed. The socket is not being used.
LISTEN	Listening for incoming connections.
SYN_SENT	Actively trying to establish connection.
SYN_RECEIVED	Initial synchronization of the connection under way.
ESTABLISHED	Connection has been established.
CLOSE_WAIT	Remote shut down; waiting for the socket to close.
FIN_WAIT_1	Socket closed; shutting down connection.
CLOSING	Closed, then remote shutdown; awaiting acknowledgement.
LAST_ACK	Remote shut down, then closed; awaiting acknowledgement.
FIN_WAIT_2	Socket closed; waiting for shutdown from remote.
TIME_WAIT	Wait after close for remote shutdown retransmission.

Network Data Structures (Second Form)

The form of the display depends upon which of the **-i** or **-r** options you select. If you specify more than one of these options, **netstat** selects one in the order listed here.

Routing Table Display

The routing table display lists the available routes and the status of each. Each route consists of a destination host or network, and a gateway to use in forwarding packets. The *flags* column shows the status of the route (**U** if up), whether the route is to a gateway (**G**), and whether the route was created dynamically by a redirect (**D**).

Direct routes are created for each interface attached to the local host; the gateway field for such entries shows the address of the outgoing interface.

The **refcnt** column gives the current number of active uses per route. Connection-oriented protocols normally hold on to a single route for the duration of a connection, whereas connectionless protocols obtain a route while sending to the same destination.

The **use** column displays the number of packets sent per route.

The *interface* entry indicates the network interface utilized for the route.

Cumulative Traffic Statistics (Third Form)

When the *interval* argument is given, **netstat** displays a table of cumulative statistics regarding packets transferred, errors and collisions, the network addresses for the interface, and the maximum transmission unit (mtu). The first line of data displayed, and every 24th line thereafter, contains cumulative statistics from the time the system was last rebooted. Each subsequent line shows incremental statistics for the *interval* (specified on the command line) since the previous display.

SEE ALSO

iostat(1M), **trpt**(1M), **vmstat**(1M), **hosts**(4), **networks**(4), **protocols**(4), **services**(4)

NOTES

The notion of errors is ill-defined.

The kernel's tables can change while **netstat** is examining them, creating incorrect or partial displays.

NAME

newaliases – rebuild the data base for the mail aliases file

SYNOPSIS

/usr/ucb/newaliases

DESCRIPTION

newaliases rebuilds the random access data base for the mail aliases file /etc/aliases. newaliases should be run whenever the /etc/aliases file is updated.

FILES

/etc/aliases
/etc/aliases.dir
/etc/aliases.pag

SEE ALSO

sendmail(1M), aliases(4)

NAME

newform – change the format of a text file

SYNOPSIS

newform [-s] [-itabspec] [-otabspec] [-bn] [-en] [-pn] [-an] [-f] [-cchar] [-1n]
[*files*]

DESCRIPTION

newform reads lines from the named *files*, or the standard input if no input file is
named, and reproduces the lines on the standard output. Lines are reformatted
in accordance with command line options in effect.

Except for **-s**, command line options may appear in any order, may be repeated,
and may be intermingled with the optional *files*. Command line options are processed in the order specified. This means that option sequences like "-e15 -160"
will yield results different from "-160 -e15". Options are applied to all *files* on
the command line.

-s   Shears off leading characters on each line up to the first tab and places
            up to 8 of the sheared characters at the end of the line. If more than 8
            characters (not counting the first tab) are sheared, the eighth character
            is replaced by a * and any characters to the right of it are discarded.
            The first tab is always discarded.

            An error message and program exit will occur if this option is used on
            a file without a tab on each line. The characters sheared off are saved
            internally until all other options specified are applied to that line. The
            characters are then added at the end of the processed line.

            For example, to convert a file with leading digits, one or more tabs,
            and text on each line, to a file beginning with the text, all tabs after the
            first expanded to spaces, padded with spaces out to column 72 (or
            truncated to column 72), and the leading digits placed starting at
            column 73, the command would be:
                   newform -s -i -1 -a -e *file*

-i*tabspec* Input tab specification: expands tabs to spaces, according to the tab
            specifications given. *tabspec* accepts four types of tab specifications:
            canned, repetitive, arbitrary and file. $-n$ represents the repetitive tab
            specification. This format can be used to replace each tab in a file with
            n spaces. For example,
                   newform -i-4 *file*
            replaces tabs with 4 spaces. For more information about the *tabspec*
            formats see **tabs**(1). In addition, *tabspec* may be --, in which **newform**
            assumes that the tab specification is to be found in the first line read
            from the standard input (see **fspec**(4)). If no *tabspec* is given, *tabspec*
            defaults to -8. A *tabspec* of -0 expects no tabs; if any are found, they
            are treated as -1.

-o*tabspec* Output tab specification: replaces spaces by tabs, according to the tab
            specifications given. The tab specifications are the same as for
            -i*tabspec*. If no *tabspec* is given, *tabspec* defaults to -8. A *tabspec* of -0
            means that no spaces will be converted to tabs on output.

−b*n*   Truncate *n* characters from the beginning of the line when the line length is greater than the effective line length (see **−l***n*). Default is to truncate the number of characters necessary to obtain the effective line length. The default value is used when **−b** with no *n* is used. This option can be used to delete the sequence numbers from a COBOL program as follows:

           newform −l1 −b7 *file*

−e*n*   Same as **−b***n* except that characters are truncated from the end of the line.

−p*n*   Prefix *n* characters (see **−c***k*) to the beginning of a line when the line length is less than the effective line length. Default is to prefix the number of characters necessary to obtain the effective line length.

−a*n*   Same as **−p***n* except characters are appended to the end of a line.

−f   Write the tab specification format line on the standard output before any other lines are output. The tab specification format line which is printed will correspond to the format specified in the *last* **−o** option. If no **−o** option is specified, the line which is printed will contain the default specification of **−8**.

−c*k*   Change the prefix/append character to *k*. Default character for *k* is a space.

−l*n*   Set the effective line length to *n* characters. If *n* is not entered, **−l** defaults to 72. The default line length without the **−l** option is 80 characters. Note that tabs and backspaces are considered to be one character (use **−i** to expand tabs to spaces).

        The **−l1** must be used to set the effective line length shorter than any existing line in the file so that the **−b** option is activated.

DIAGNOSTICS
All diagnostics are fatal.

usage: **...**	**newform** was called with a bad option.
"not −s format"	There was no tab on one line.
"can't open file"	Self-explanatory.
"internal line too long"	

                      A line exceeds 512 characters after being expanded in the internal work buffer.

"tabspec in error"   A tab specification is incorrectly formatted, or specified tab stops are not ascending.

"tabspec indirection illegal"

                      A *tabspec* read from a file (or standard input) may not contain a *tabspec* referencing another file (or standard input).

0 − normal execution

1 − for any error

SEE ALSO

csplit(1), **tabs**(1)

fspec(4) in the *System Administrator's Reference Manual*

NOTES

newform normally only keeps track of physical characters; however, for the **−i** and **−o** options, **newform** will keep track of backspaces in order to line up tabs in the appropriate logical columns.

newform will not prompt the user if a *tabspec* is to be read from the standard input (by use of **−i−−** or **−o−−**).

If the **−f** option is used, and the last **−o** option specified was **−o−−**, and was preceded by either a **−o−−** or a **−i−−**, the tab specification format line will be incorrect.

NAME

newgrp – log in to a new group

SYNOPSIS

newgrp [–] [group]

DESCRIPTION

newgrp changes a user's real and effective group ID. The user remains logged in and the current directory is unchanged. The user is always given a new shell, replacing the current shell, by newgrp, regardless of whether it terminated successfully or due to an error condition (i.e., unknown group).

Exported variables retain their values after invoking newgrp; however, all unexported variables are either reset to their default value or set to null. System variables (such as PS1, PS2, PATH, MAIL, and HOME), unless exported by the system or explicitly exported by the user, are reset to default values. For example, a user has a primary prompt string (PS1) other than $ (default) and has not exported PS1. After an invocation of newgrp, successful or not, the user's PS1 will now be set to the default prompt string $. Note that the shell command export [see the sh(1) manual page] is the method to export variables so that they retain their assigned value when invoking new shells.

With no arguments, newgrp changes the user's group IDs (real and effective) back to the group specified in the user's password file entry. This is a way to exit the effect of an earlier newgrp command.

If the first argument to newgrp is a –, the environment is changed to what would be expected if the user actually logged in again as a member of the new group.

A password is demanded if the group has a password and the user is not listed in /etc/group as being a member of that group.

FILES

/etc/group   system's group file

/etc/passwd   system's password file

NOTES

The ability of the user to enter a password when using this command will be removed in a future release.

SEE ALSO

login(1), sh(1) in the *User's Reference Manual*
group(4), passwd(4), environ(5) in the *System Administrator's Reference Manual*
see intro(2) "Effective User ID and Effective Group ID" in *Programmer's Reference Manual*

NAME

newkey – create a new key in the publickey database

SYNOPSIS

newkey **-h** *hostname*

newkey **-u** *username*

DESCRIPTION

The **newkey** command is normally run by the RPC administrator on the machine that contains the **publickey**(4) database, to establish public keys for users and privileged users on the network. These keys are needed when using secure RPC or secure NFS.

newkey will prompt for a password for the given *username* or *hostname* and then create a new public/secret key pair for the user or host in **/etc/publickey**, encrypted with the given password.

The following options are available:

-h *hostname*   Create a new public/secret key pair for the privileged user at the given *hostname*. Prompts for a password for the given *hostname*.

-u *username*   Create a new public/secret key pair for the given *username*. Prompts for a password for the given *username*.

SEE ALSO

chkey(1), **keylogin**(1), **keylogout**(1), **keyserv**(1M), **publickey**(4)

NAME

news – print news items

SYNOPSIS

news [–a] [–n] [–s] [*items*]

DESCRIPTION

news is used to keep the user informed of current events. By convention, these events are described by files in the directory /var/news.

When invoked without arguments, news prints the contents of all current files in /var/news, most recent first, with each preceded by an appropriate header. news stores the "currency" time as the modification date of a file named .news_time in the user's home directory (the identity of this directory is determined by the environment variable $HOME); only files more recent than this currency time are considered "current."

–a   option causes news to print all items, regardless of currency. In this case, the stored time is not changed.

–n   option causes news to report the names of the current items without printing their contents, and without changing the stored time.

–s   option causes news to report how many current items exist, without printing their names or contents, and without changing the stored time. It is useful to include such an invocation of news in one's .profile file, or in the system's /etc/profile.

All other arguments are assumed to be specific news items that are to be printed.

If a *delete* is typed during the printing of a news item, printing stops and the next item is started. Another *delete* within one second of the first causes the program to terminate.

FILES

/etc/profile
/var/news/*
$HOME/.news_time

SEE ALSO

profile(4), environ(5) in the *System Administrator's Reference Manual*

NAME
newvt – opens virtual terminals.

SYNOPSIS
newvt [-e *prog*] [-n *vt_number*]

DESCRIPTION
Use the **newvt** command to open a new virtual terminal. The newly opened virtual terminal will inherit your environment.

-e   Specifies a program (*prog*) to execute in the new virtual terminal. Without the **-e** option, the program pointed to by the **$SHELL** environment variable is started in the new virtual terminal. If **$SHELL** is NULL or points to a nonexecutable program, then **/bin/sh** is invoked.

-n   Specifies a particular virtual terminal (*vt_number*) to open. If the **-n** option is not specified, then the next available virtual terminal is opened. Close virtual terminals by pressing CTRL-d (control d). Repeat CTRL-d until all open virtual terminals are closed.

DIAGNOSTICS
The **newvt** command will fail under the following conditions:

If an illegal option is specified.
If the device cannot be opened.
If **newvt** is invoked from a remote terminal.
If no virtual terminals are available (**-n** option not specified).
If the requested virtual terminal is not available (**-n** option specified).
If the requested virtual terminal cannot be opened.
If the specified command cannot be executed (**-e** option specified).
If the **$SHELL** program cannot be executed (**$SHELL** set and **-e** option not specified).
If **/dev/vtmon** cannot be opened.

SEE ALSO
vtlmgr(1)
vtgetty(1M) in the *System Administrator's Reference Manual*

NAME

nfsd – NFS daemon

SYNOPSIS

nfsd [**-a**] [**-p** *protocol*] [**-t** *device*] [*nservers*]

DESCRIPTION

nfsd starts the daemons that handle client file system requests.

The following options are recognized:

-a   start **nfsd**'s over all available connectionless transports

-p *protocol* start **nfsd**'s over the specified protocol

-t *device* start **nfsd**'s for the transport specified by the given device

nservers the number of file system request daemons to start.

nservers should be based on the load expected on this server. Four is the usual number of *nservers*.

The **nfsd** daemons are automatically invoked in run level 3.

FILES

.**nfs**XXX   client machine pointer to an open-but-unlinked file

SEE ALSO

biod(1M), **mountd**(1M), **sharetab**(4).

NAME
nfsstat – Network File System statistics

SYNOPSIS
nfsstat [-csnrz]

DESCRIPTION
nfsstat displays statistical information about the NFS (Network File System) and RPC (Remote Procedure Call), interfaces to the kernel. It can also be used to reinitialize this information. If no options are given the default is

    nfsstat -csnr

That is, display everything, but reinitialize nothing.

Options
The options for nfsstat are as follows:

-c   Display client information. Only the client side NFS and RPC information will be printed. Can be combined with the -n and -r options to print client NFS or client RPC information only.

-s   Display server information.

-n   Display NFS information. NFS information for both the client and server side will be printed. Can be combined with the -c and -s options to print client or server NFS information only.

-r   Display RPC information.

-z   Zero (reinitialize) statistics. This option is for use by the super-user only, and can be combined with any of the above options to zero particular sets of statistics after printing them.

Displays
The server RPC display includes the fields:

         calls   total number of RPC calls received

         badcalls total number of calls rejected

         nullrecv number of times no RPC packet was available when trying to receive

         badlen   number of packets that were too short

         xdrcall   number of packets that had a malformed header

The server NFS display shows the number of NFS calls received (calls) and rejected (badcalls), and the counts and percentages for the various calls that were made.

The client RPC display includes the following fields:

         calls   total number of RPC calls sent

         badcalls total of calls rejected by a server

         retrans   number of times a call had to be retransmitted

`badxid`   number of times a reply did not match the call

`timeout`   number of times a call timed out

`wait`   number of times a call had to wait on a busy **CLIENT** handle

`newcred`   number of times authentication information had to be refreshed

The client NFS display shows the number of calls sent and rejected, as well as the number of times a **CLIENT** handle was received (`nclget`), the number of times a call had to sleep while awaiting a handle (`nclsleep`), as well as a count of the various calls and their respective percentages.

FILES

`/vmunix`   system namelist
`/dev/kmem`   kernel memory

NAME

nice – run a command at low priority

SYNOPSIS

nice [–increment] command [arguments]

DESCRIPTION

nice executes command with a lower CPU scheduling priority. The **priocntl** command is a more general interface to scheduler functions.

The invoking process (generally the user's shell) must be in the time-sharing scheduling class. The command is executed in the time-sharing class.

If the increment argument (in the range 1–19) is given, it is used; if not, an increment of 10 is assumed.

The super-user may run commands with priority higher than normal by using a negative increment, e.g., **--10**.

SEE ALSO

nohup(1), **priocntl**(1)
nice(2) in the Programmer's Reference Manual

DIAGNOSTICS

nice returns the exit status of command.

NOTES

An increment larger than 19 is equivalent to 19.

NAME

nl – line numbering filter

SYNOPSIS

nl [−**b**type] [−**f**type] [−**h**type] [−**v**start#] [−**i**incr] [−**p**] [−**l**num] [−**s**sep] [−**w**width]
[−**n**format] [−**d**delim] [file]

DESCRIPTION

nl reads lines from the named file, or the standard input if no file is named, and reproduces the lines on the standard output. Lines are numbered on the left in accordance with the command options in effect.

nl views the text it reads in terms of logical pages. Line numbering is reset at the start of each logical page. A logical page consists of a header, a body, and a footer section. Empty sections are valid. Different line numbering options are independently available for header, body, and footer. For example, −**bt** (the default) numbers non-blank lines in the body section and does not number any lines in the header and footer sections.

The start of logical page sections are signaled by input lines containing nothing but the following delimiter character(s):

Line contents	Start of
\:\:\:	header
\:\:	body
\:	footer

Unless optioned otherwise, **nl** assumes the text being read is in a single logical page body.

Command options may appear in any order and may be intermingled with an optional file name. Only one file may be named. The options are:

−**b**type   Specifies which logical page body lines are to be numbered. Recognized types and their meanings are:

>   **a**   number all lines
>   **t**   number lines with printable text only
>   **n**   number lines with printable text only
>   **p**exp   number only lines that contain the regular expression specified in exp (see **ed**(1))

Default type for logical page body is **t** (text lines numbered).

−**f**type   Same as −**b**type except for footer. Default type for logical page footer is **n** (no lines numbered).

−**h**type   Same as −**b**type except for header. Default type for logical page header is **n** (no lines numbered).

−**v**start#   start# is the initial value used to number logical page lines. Default start# is 1.

−i*incr*	*incr* is the increment value used to number logical page lines. Default *incr* is 1.
−p	Do not restart numbering at logical page delimiters.
−l*num*	*num* is the number of blank lines to be considered as one. For example, **−l2** results in only the second adjacent blank being numbered (if the appropriate **−ha**, **−ba**, and/or **−fa** option is set). Default *num* is 1.
−s*sep*	*sep* is the character(s) used in separating the line number and the corresponding text line. Default *sep* is a tab.
−w*width*	*width* is the number of characters to be used for the line number. The default for *width* is 6. The maximum for *width* is 100. If a number greater than the maximum is specified for *width*, the maximum is automatically used.
−n*format*	*format* is the line numbering format. Recognized values are: **ln**, left justified, leading zeroes suppressed; **rn**, right justified, leading zeroes suppressed; **rz**, right justified, leading zeroes kept. Default *format* is **rn** (right justified).
−d*delim*	The two delimiter characters specifying the start of a logical page section may be changed from the default characters (\:) to two user-specified characters. If only one character is entered, the second character remains the default character (:). No space should appear between the **−d** and the delimiter characters. To enter a backslash, use two backslashes.

EXAMPLE

The command:

```
nl −v10 −i10 −d!+ file1
```

will cause the first line of the page body to be numbered 10, the second line of the page body to be numbered 20, the third 30, and so forth. The logical page delimiters are !+.

SEE ALSO

    pr(1), **ed**(1)

NAME

nlsadmin – network listener service administration

SYNOPSIS

/usr/sbin/nlsadmin –x
/usr/sbin/nlsadmin [*options*] *net_spec*
/usr/sbin/nlsadmin [*options*] **–N** *port_monitor_tag*
/usr/sbin/nlsadmin –V
/usr/sbin/nlsadmin –c *cmd* | **–o** *streamname* [**–p** *modules*] \
   [**–A** *address* | **–D**] [**–R** *prognum:versnum*]

DESCRIPTION

nlsadmin is the administrative command for the network listener process(es) on a machine. Each network has at least one instance of the network listener process associated with it; each instance (and thus, each network) is configured separately. The listener process "listens" to the network for service requests, accepts requests when they arrive, and invokes servers in response to those service requests. The network listener process may be used with any network (more precisely, with any connection-oriented transport provider) that conforms to the transport provider specification.

nlsadmin can establish a listener process for a given network, configure the specific attributes of that listener, and start and kill the listener process for that network. **nlsadmin** can also report on the listener processes on a machine, either individually (per network) or collectively.

The list below shows how to use **nlsadmin**. In this list, *net_spec* represents a particular listener process. Specifically, *net_spec* is the relative path name of the entry under **/dev** for a given network (that is, a transport provider). *address* is a transport address on which to listen and is interpreted using a syntax that allows for a variety of address formats. By default, *address* is interpreted as the symbolic ASCII representation of the transport address. An *address* preceded by a **\x** will let you enter an address in hexadecimal notation. Note that *address* must appear as a single word to the shell and thus must be quoted if it contains any blanks.

Changes to the list of services provided by the listener or the addresses of those services are put into effect immediately.

nlsadmin may be used with the following combinations of options and arguments:

nlsadmin   gives a brief usage message.

nlsadmin –x reports the status of all of the listener processes installed on this machine.

nlsadmin *net_spec*
    prints the status of the listener process for *net_spec*.

nlsadmin –q *net_spec*
    queries the status of the listener process for the specified network, and reflects the result of that query in its exit code. If a listener process is active, **nlsadmin** will exit with a status of 0; if no process is active, the exit code will be 1; the exit code will be greater than 1 in case of error.

nlsadmin **-v** *net_spec*

prints a verbose report on the servers associated with *net_spec*, giv-ing the service code, status, command, and comment for each. It also specifies the **uid** the server will run as and the list of modules to be pushed, if any, before the server is started.

nlsadmin **-z** *service_code net_spec*

prints a report on the server associated with *net_spec* that has ser-vice code *service_code*, giving the same information as in the **-v** option.

nlsadmin **-q -z** *service_code net_spec*

queries the status of the service with service code *service_code* on network *net_spec*, and exits with a status of 0 if that service is enabled, 1 if that service is disabled, and greater than 1 in case of error.

nlsadmin **-l** *address net_spec*

changes or set the transport address on which the listener listens (the general listener service). This address can be used by remote processes to access the servers available through this listener (see the **-a** option, below).

If *address* is just a dash ("-"), **nlsadmin** will report the address currently configured, instead of changing it.

A change of address takes effect immediately.

nlsadmin **-t** *address net_spec*

changes or sets the address on which the listener listens for requests for terminal service but is otherwise similar to the **-l** option above. A terminal service address should not be defined unless the appropriate remote login software is available; if such software is available, it must be configured as service code 1 (see the **-a** option, below).

nlsadmin **-i** *net_spec*

initializes an instance of the listener for the network specified by *net_spec*; that is, creates and initializes the files required by the listener as well as starting that instance of the listener. Note that a particular instance of the listener should be initialized only once. The listener must be initialized before assigning addresses or ser-vices.

nlsadmin **-a** *service_code* [**-p** *modules*] [**-w** *name*] **-c** *cmd* **-y** *comment net_spec*

adds a new service to the list of services available through the indicated listener. *service_code* is the code for the service, *cmd* is the command to be invoked in response to that service code, comprised of the full path name of the server and its arguments, and *comment* is a brief (free-form) description of the service for use in various reports. Note that *cmd* must appear as a single word to the shell; if arguments are required the *cmd* and its arguments must be enclosed in quotation marks. The *comment* must also appear as a single word to the shell. When a service is added, it is initially enabled (see the **-e** and **-d** options, below).

Service codes are alphanumeric strings, and are administered by AT&T. The numeric service codes 0 through 100 are reserved for internal use by the listener. Service code 0 is assigned to the nlps server, which is the service invoked on the general listening address. In particular, code 1 is assigned to the remote login service, which is the service automatically invoked for connections to the terminal login address.

If the **-p** option is specified, then *modules* will be interpreted as a list of STREAMS modules for the listener to push before starting the service being added. The modules are pushed in the order they are specified. *modules* should be a comma-separated list of modules, with no white space included.

If the **-w** option is specified, then *name* is interpreted as the user name from **/etc/passwd** that the listener should look up. From the user name, the listener obtains the user ID, the group ID(s), and the home directory for use by the server. If **-w** is not specified, the default is to use the user name **listen**.

A service must explicitly be added to the listener for each network on which that service is to be available. This operation will normally be performed only when the service is installed on a machine, or when populating the list of services for a new network.

nlsadmin -r *service_code net_spec*

> removes the entry for the *service_code* from that listener's list of services. This is normally done only in conjunction with the deinstallation of a service from a machine.

nlsadmin -e *service_code net_spec*
nlsadmin -d *service_code net_spec*

> enables or disables (respectively) the service indicated by *service_code* for the specified network. The service must previously have been added to the listener for that network (see the **-a** option, above). Disabling a service will cause subsequent service requests for that service to be denied, but the processes from any prior service requests that are still running will continue unaffected.

nlsadmin -s *net_spec*
nlsadmin -k *net_spec*

> starts and kills (respectively) the listener process for the indicated network. These operations will normally be performed as part of the system startup and shutdown procedures. Before a listener can be started for a particular network, it must first have been initialized (see the **-i** option, above). When a listener is killed, processes that are still running as a result of prior service requests will continue unaffected.

Under the Service Access Facility, it is possible to have multiple instances of the listener on a single *net_spec*. In any of the above commands, the option −N *port_monitor_tag* may be used in place of the *net_spec* argument. This argument specifies the tag by which an instance of the listener is identified by the Service Access Facility. If the −N option is not specified (i.e., the *net_spec* is specified in the invocation), then it will be assumed that the last component of the *net_spec* represents the tag of the listener for which the operation is destined. In other words, it is assumed that there is at least one listener on a designated *net_spec*, and that its tag is identical to the last component of the *net_spec*. This listener may be thought of as the primary, or default, listener for a particular *net_spec*.

nlsadmin is also used in conjunction with the Service Access Facility commands. In that capacity, the following combinations of options can be used:

nlsadmin −V

> writes the current version number of the listener's administrative file to the standard output. It is used as part of the **sacadm** command line when **sacadm** add a port monitor to the system.

nlsadmin −c *cmd* | **−o** *streamname* [**−p** *modules*] [**−A** *address* | **−D**] \
[**−R** *prognum:versnum*]

> formats the port monitor-specific information to be used as an argument to **pmadm**(1M).

> The −c option specifies the full path name of the server and its arguments. *cmd* must appear as a single word to the shell, and its arguments must therefor be surrounded by quotes.

> The −o option specifies the full path name of a FIFO or named STREAM through which a standing server is actually receiving the connection.

> If the −p option is specified, then *modules* will be interpreted as a list of STREAMS modules for the listener to push before starting the service being added. The modules are pushed in the order in which they are specified. *modules* must be a comma-separated list, with no white space included.

> If the −A option is specified, then *address* will be interpreted as the server's private address. The listener will monitor this address on behalf of the service and will dispatch all calls arriving on this address directly to the designated service. This option may not be used in conjunction with the −D option.

> If the −D option is specified, then the service is assigned a private address dynamically, that is, the listener will have the transport provider select the address each time the listener begins listening on behalf of this service. For RPC services, this option will be often be used in conjunction with the −R option to register the dynamically assigned address with the rpcbinder. This option may not be used in conjunction with the −A option.

> When the −R option is specified, the service is an RPC service whose address, program number, and version number should be registered with the rpcbinder for this transport provider. This registration is performed each time the listener begins listening on behalf of the service. *prognum* and *versnum* are the program number and version number, respectively, of the RPC service.

nlsadmin may be invoked by any user to generate reports but all operations that affect a listener's status or configuration are restricted to privileged users.

The options specific to the Service Access Facility may not be mixed with any other options.

SEE ALSO

listen(1M), **pmadm**(1M), **rpcbind**(1M), **sacadm**(1M)

Network Programmer's Guide

NOTES

Dynamically assigned addresses are not displayed in reports as statically assigned addresses are.

NAME

nm – print name list of an object file

SYNOPSIS

nm [-oxhvnefurplVT] *files*

DESCRIPTION

The **nm** command displays the symbol table of each ELF or COFF object file, specified by *file(s)*. The file may be a relocatable or absolute ELF or COFF object file; or it may be an archive of relocatable or absolute ELF or COFF object files. For each symbol, the following information will be printed:

Index   The index of the symbol. (The index appears in brackets.)

Value   The value of the symbol is one of the following: a section offset for defined symbols in a relocatable file; alignment constraints for symbols whose section index is **SHN_COMMON**; a virtual address in executable and dynamic library files.

Size   The size in bytes of the associated object.

Type   A symbol is of one of the following types: **NOTYPE** (no type was specified), **OBJECT** (a data object such as an array or variable), **FUNC** (a function or other executable code), **SECTION** (a section symbol), or **FILE** (name of the source file).

Bind   The symbol's binding attributes. **LOCAL** symbols have a scope limited to the object file containing their definition; **GLOBAL** symbols are visible to all object files being combined; and **WEAK** symbols are essentially global symbols with a lower precedence than **GLOBAL**.

Other   A field reserved for future use, currently containing 0.

Shndx   Except for three special values, this is the section header table index in relation to which the symbol is defined. The following special values exist: **ABS** indicates the symbol's value will not change through relocation; **COMMON** indicates an unallocated block and the value provides alignment constraints; and **UNDEF** indicates an undefined symbol.

Name   The name of the symbol.

The output of **nm** may be controlled using the following options:

-o   Print the value and size of a symbol in octal instead of decimal.

-x   Print the value and size of a symbol in hexadecimal instead of decimal.

-h   Do not display the output heading data.

-v   Sort external symbols by value before they are printed.

-n   Sort external symbols by name before they are printed.

-e   See NOTES below.

-f   See NOTES below.

-u   Print undefined symbols only.

-r   Prepend the name of the object file or archive to each output line.

-p   Produce easily parsable, terse output. Each symbol name is preceded
            by its value (blanks if undefined) and one of the letters U (undefined), N
            (symbol has no type), D (data object symbol), T (text symbol), S (section
            symbol), or F (file symbol). If the symbol's binding attribute is LOCAL,
            the key letter is lower case; if the symbol's binding attribute is WEAK,
            the key letter is upper case; if the -1 modifier is specified, the upper
            case key letter is followed by a *; if the symbol's binding attribute is
            GLOBAL, the key letter is upper case.

-1   Distinguish between WEAK and GLOBAL symbols by appending a * to the
            key letter for WEAK symbols.

-V   Print the version of the nm command executing on the standard error
            output.

-T   See NOTES below.

Options may be used in any order, either singly or in combination, and may
appear anywhere in the command line. When conflicting options are specified
(such as nm -v -n) the first is taken and the second ignored with a warning message to the user.

SEE ALSO
as(1), cc(1), dump(1), ld(1), a.out(4), ar(4)

NOTES
The following options are obsolete because of changes to the object file format
and will be deleted in a future release.

-e   Print only external and static symbols. The symbol table now contains
            only static and external symbols. Automatic symbols no longer appear
            in the symbol table. They do appear in the debugging information pro-
            duced by cc -g, which may be examined using dump(1).

-f   Produce full output. Redundant symbols (such as .text, .data, and so
            on) which existed previously do not exist and producing full output
            will be identical to the default output.

-T   By default, nm prints the entire name of the symbols listed. Since sym-
            bol names have been moved to the last column, the problem of
            overflow is removed and it is no longer necessary to truncate the sym-
            bol name.

NAME

nohup – run a command immune to hangups and quits

SYNOPSIS

nohup *command* [*arguments*]

DESCRIPTION

nohup executes *command* with hangups and quits ignored. If output is not re-directed by the user, both standard output and standard error are sent to **nohup.out**. If **nohup.out** is not writable in the current directory, output is redirected to $HOME/**nohup.out**.

EXAMPLE

It is frequently desirable to apply **nohup** to pipelines or lists of commands. This can be done only by placing pipelines and command lists in a single file, called a shell procedure. One can then issue:

    nohup sh *file*

and the **nohup** applies to everything in *file*. If the shell procedure *file* is to be executed often, then the need to type **sh** can be eliminated by giving *file* execute permission. Add an ampersand and the contents of *file* are run in the background with interrupts also ignored (see **sh**(1)):

    nohup *file* &

An example of what the contents of *file* could be is:

    sort ofile > nfile

SEE ALSO

chmod(1), nice(1), sh(1)
signal(2) in the *Programmer's Reference Manual*

NOTES

In the case of the following command

    nohup command1; command2

nohup applies only to **command1**. The command

    nohup (command1; command2)

is syntactically incorrect.

NAME

notify – notify user of the arrival of new mail

SYNOPSIS

notify -y [-m *mailfile*]

notify [-n]

DESCRIPTION

When a new mail message arrives, the **mail** command first checks if the recipient's mailbox indicates that the message is to be forwarded elsewhere (to some other recipient or as the input to some command). **notify** is used to set up forwarding on the user's mailbox so that the new message is saved into an alternative mailbox and, if the user is currently logged in, he or she is notified immediately of the arrival of new mail.

Command-line options are:

-m *mailfile*   File to save mail messages into while automatic notification is activated. If not specified, it defaults to *$HOME/.mailfile*.

-n   Remove mail notification facility

-y   Install mail notification facility

If invoked with no arguments, **notify** reports whether automatic mail notification is activated or not.

The notification is done by looking in **/var/adm/utmp** to determine if the recipient is currently logged in, and if so, on which terminal device. Then the terminal device is opened for writing and the user is notified about the new message. The notification will indicate who the message is from. If the message contains a **Subject:** header line it will be included. (For security, all unprintable characters within the header will be converted to an exclamation point.)

If the user is logged in multiple times he or she will get multiple notifications, one per terminal. To disable notifications to a particular login session, the **mesg**(1) command can be used to disable writing to that terminal.

If there are multiple machines connected together via RFS or NFS, **notify** will look up the **/var/adm/utmp** files on the other systems as well. To do this, the file **/etc/mail/notify.sys** will be consulted, which will contain two columns, the first being the name of a system and the second being a path to find the root filesystem for that machine.

If **notify** has troubles delivering the mail to the specified mailfile, **notify** will look up the directory of the mailfile in **/etc/mail/notify.fsys**. If the file's directory is found in the first column of the file, the mail will be forwarded to the system listed in the second column instead of being returned to the sender.

FILES

/tmp/notif*	temporary file
/var/mail/*	users' standard mailboxes
/usr/lib/mail/notify2	program that performs the notification
/etc/mail/notify.fsys	list of file systems and home systems

/etc/mail/notify.sys	list of machines and paths to their root filesystems
/var/adm/utmp	list of users who are logged in

SEE ALSO

mail(1), mesg(1)

User's Guide

NOTES

Because **notify** uses the "**Forward to** |*command*" facility of **mail** to implement notifications, **/var/mail/***username* should not be specified as the place to put newly arrived messages via the **−m** invocation option. The **mail** command uses **/var/mail/***username* to hold either mail messages, **or** indications of mail forwarding, but not both simultaneously.

If the user is using **layers**(1), the notification will **only** appear in the **login** window.

NAME

nroff – format documents for display or line-printer

SYNOPSIS

/usr/ucb/nroff [-ehiqz] [-F*dir*] [-m*name*] [-n*N*] [-o*pagelist*] [-ra*N*]
    [-s*N*] [-T*name*] [-u*N*] [*filename* . . .]

DESCRIPTION

nroff formats text in the named *filename* for typewriter-like devices. See also
troff.

If no *filename* argument is present, nroff reads the standard input. An argument
consisting of a '–' is taken to be a file name corresponding to the standard input.

The following options may appear in any order, but must appear *before* the files.

-e	Produce equally-spaced words in adjusted lines, using full terminal resolution.
-h	Use output TAB characters during horizontal spacing to speed output and reduce output character count. TAB settings are assumed to be every 8 nominal character widths.
-i	Read the standard input after the input files are exhausted.
-q	Invoke the simultaneous input-output mode of the rd request.
-F*dir*	Search directory *dir* for font tables instead of the system-dependent default.
-m*name*	Prepend the macro file /usr/share/lib/tmac/tmac.*name* to the input files.
-n*N*	Number first generated page *N* .
-o*pagelist*	Print only pages whose page numbers appear in the comma-separated *list* of numbers and ranges. A range *N*– M means pages *N* through *M*; an initial –*N* means from the beginning to page *N*; and a final *N*– means from *N* to the end.
-ra*N*	Set register *a* (one-character) to *N*.
-s*N*	Stop every *N* pages. nroff will halt prior to every *N* pages (default *N*=1) to allow paper loading or changing, and will resume upon receipt of a NEWLINE.
-T*name*	Prepare output for a device of the specified name. Known names are:

	37	Teletype Corporation Model 37 terminal — this is the default.
	crt | lpr | tn300	
		GE TermiNet 300, or any line printer or terminal without half-line capability.
	300	DASI-300.
	300-12	DASI-300 — 12-pitch.

```
300S | 302 | dtc
```
　　　　　　DASI-300S.

```
300S-12 | 302-12 | dtc12
```
　　　　　　DASI-300S.

`382`　　　　　DASI-382 (fancy DTC 382).

`382-12`　　　DASI-82 (fancy DTC 382 — 12-pitch).

`450 | ipsi`　DASI-450 (Diablo Hyterm).

```
450-12 | ipsi12
```
　　　　　　DASI-450 (Diablo Hyterm) — 12-pitch.

`450-12-8`　DASI-450 (Diablo Hyterm) — 12-pitch and 8 lines-per-inch.

`450X`　　　　DASI-450X (Diablo Hyterm).

`832`　　　　　AJ 832.

`833`　　　　　AJ 833.

`832-12`　　　AJ 832 — 12-pitch.

`833-12`　　　AJ 833 — 12-pitch.

`epson`　　　Epson FX80.

`itoh`　　　　C:ITOH Prowriter.

`itoh-12`　　C:ITOH Prowriter — 12-pitch.

`nec`　　　　　NEC 55?0s0 or NEC 77?0s0 Spinwriter.

`nec12`　　　NEC 55?0 or NEC 77?0 Spinwriter — 12-pitch.

`nec-t`　　　NEC 55?0/77?0 Spinwriter — Tech-Math/Times-Roman thimble.

`qume`　　　　Qume Sprint — 5 or 9.

`qume12`　　　Qume Sprint — 5 or 9,12-pitch.

`xerox`　　　Xerox 17?0 or Diablo 16?0.

`xerox12`　　Xerox 17?0 or Diablo 16?0 — 12-pitch.

`x-ecs`　　　Xerox/Diablo 1730/630 — Extended Character Set.

`x-ecs12`　　Xerox/Diablo 1730/630 — Extended Character Set, 12-pitch.

−uN　　　Set emboldening factor for the font mounted on position 3 to **N**. Emboldening is accomplished by overstriking the specified number of times.

−z　　　　Suppress formatted output. The only output will consist of diagnostic messages from **nroff** and messages output with the `.tm` request.

EXAMPLE

The following command:

```
nroff -s4 -me users.guide
```

formats **users.guide** using the **-me** macro package, and stopping every 4 pages.

FILES

`/tmp/ta*`	temporary file
`/usr/ucblib/doctools/tmac/tmac.*`	standard macro files
`/usr/ucblib/doctools/term/*`	terminal driving tables for **nroff**
`/usr/ucblib/doctools/term/README`	index to terminal description files

SEE ALSO

checknr(1), eqn(1), tbl(1), troff(1), man(7), me(7), ms(7)

col(1) in the *User's Reference Manual*
term(4) in the *System Administrator's Reference Manual*

NAME

nslookup – query name servers interactively

SYNOPSIS

nslookup [-l] [*address*]

DESCRIPTION

nslookup is an interactive program to query ARPA Internet domain name servers. The user can contact servers to request information about a specific host or print a list of hosts in the domain.

OPTIONS

-l   Use the local host's name server instead of the servers in /etc/resolve.conf. (If /etc/resolve.conf does not exist or does not contain server information, the -l option does not have any effect).

address   Use the name server on the host machine with the given Internet address.

USAGE

Overview

The Internet domain name-space is tree-structured, with four top-level domains at present:

COM   commercial establishments

EDU   educational institutions

GOV   government agencies

MIL   MILNET hosts

If you are looking for a specific host, you need to know something about the host's organization in order to determine the top-level domain it belongs to. For instance, if you want to find the Internet address of a machine at UCLA , do the following:

- Connect with the root server using the **root** command. The root server of the name space has knowledge of the top-level domains.

- Since UCLA is a university, its domain name is **ucla.edu**. Connect with a server for the **ucla.edu** domain with the command **server ucla.edu**. The response will print the names of hosts that act as servers for that domain. Note: the root server does not have information about **ucla.edu**, but knows the names and addresses of hosts that do. Once located by the root server, all future queries will be sent to the UCLA name server.

- To request information about a particular host in the domain (for instance, **locus**), just type the host name. To request a listing of hosts in the UCLA domain, use the **ls** command. The **ls** command requires a domain name (in this case, **ucla.edu**) as an argument.

If you are connected with a name server that handles more than one domain, all lookups for host names must be fully specified with its domain. For instance, the domain **harvard.edu** is served by **seismo.css.gov**, which also services the

css.gov and **cornell.edu** domains. A lookup request for the host **aiken** in the **harvard.edu** domain must be specified as **aiken.harvard.edu**. However, the

>   **set domain** = *name*

and

>   **set defname**

commands can be used to automatically append a domain name to each request.

After a successful lookup of a host, use the **finger** command to see who is on the system, or to finger a specific person. To get other information about the host, use the

>   **set querytype** = *value*

command to change the type of information desired and request another lookup. (**finger** requires the type to be A.)

Commands

To exit, type Ctrl-D (EOF). The command line length must be less than 80 characters. An unrecognized command will be interpreted as a host name.

host [*server*]
> Look up information for *host* using the current default server or using *server* if it is specified.

server *domain*
lserver *domain*
> Change the default server to *domain*. **lserver** uses the initial server to look up information about *domain* while **server** uses the current default server. If an authoritative answer can't be found, the names of servers that might have the answer are returned.

root Changes the default server to the server for the root of the domain name space. Currently, the host **sri-nic.arpa** is used; this command is a synonym for **lserver sri-nic.arpa**.) The name of the root server can be changed with the **set root** command.

finger [*name*]
> Connect with the finger server on the current host, which is defined by a previous successful lookup for a host's address information (see the **set** *querytype* =**A** command). As with the shell, output can be redirected to a named file using > and >>.

ls [–ah]
> List the information available for *domain*. The default output contains host names and their Internet addresses. The –**a** option lists aliases of hosts in the domain. The –**h** option lists CPU and operating system information for the domain. As with the shell, output can be redirected to a named file using > and >>. When output is directed to a file, hash marks are printed for every 50 records received from the server.

view *filename*
> Sort and list the output of the **ls** command with **more**(1).

```
help
?
```
         Print a brief summary of commands.

set *keyword* [= *value*] This command is used to change state information that affects the lookups. Valid keywords are:

     all   Prints the current values of the various options to **set**. Information about the current default server and host is also printed.

     [**no**] **deb**[**ug**]
         Turn debugging mode on. A lot more information is printed about the packet sent to the server and the resulting answer. The default is **nodebug**.

     [**no**] **def**[*name*]
         Append the default domain name to every lookup. The default is **nodefname**.

     do [**main**] = *filename*
         Change the default domain name to *filename*. The default domain name is appended to all lookup requests if **defname** option has been set. The default is the value in **/etc/resolve.conf**.

     q [**querytype**] = *value*
         Change the type of information returned from a query to one of:

         A   The host's Internet address (the default).
         CNAME   The canonical name for an alias.
         HINFO   The host CPU and operating system type.
         MD   The mail destination.
         MX   The mail exchanger.
         MB   The mailbox domain name.
         MG   The mail group member.
         MINFO   The mailbox or mail list information.

         (Other types specified in the RFC883 document are valid, but are not very useful.)

     [**no**] **recurse**
         Tell the name server to query other servers if it does not have the information. The default is **recurse**.

     ret [**ry**] = *count*
         Set the number of times to retry a request before giving up to *count*. When a reply to a request is not received within a certain amount of time (changed with **set timeout**), the request is resent. The default is *count* is **2**.

     ro [**ot**] = *host*
         Change the name of the root server to *host*. This affects the **root** command. The default root server is **sri-nic.arpa**.

t [**timeout**] = *interval*

>   Change the time-out for a reply to *interval* seconds. The default *interval* is **10** seconds.

[**no**] **v**[**c**]

>   Always use a virtual circuit when sending requests to the server. The default is **novc**.

FILES

>   **/etc/resolve.conf**   initial domain name and name server addresses.

SEE ALSO

>   **named**(1M), **resolver**(3N), **resolve.conf**(4), RFC 882, RFC 883

DIAGNOSTICS

>   If the lookup request was not successful, an error message is printed. Possible errors are:

Time-out

>   The server did not respond to a request after a certain amount of time (changed with **set timeout** = *value*) and a certain number of retries (changed with **set retry** = *value*).

No information

>   Depending on the query type set with the **set querytype** command, no information about the host was available, though the host name is valid.

Non-existent domain

>   The host or domain name does not exist.

Connection refused
Network is unreachable

>   The connection to the name or finger server could not be made at the current time. This error commonly occurs with **finger** requests.

Server failure

>   The name server found an internal inconsistency in its database and could not return a valid answer.

Refused

>   The name server refused to service the request.

>   The following error should not occur and it indicates a bug in the program.

Format error

>   The name server found that the request packet was not in the proper format.

NAME

nsquery – Remote File Sharing name server query

SYNOPSIS

nsquery [–h] [*name*]

DESCRIPTION

nsquery provides information about resources available to the host from both the local domain and from other domains. All resources are reported, regardless of whether the host is authorized to access them. When used with no options, nsquery identifies all resources in the domain that have been advertised as sharable. A report on selected resources can be obtained by specifying *name*, where *name* is:

nodename   The report will include only those resources available from *nodename*.

domain.   The report will include only those resources available from *domain*.

domain.nodename   The report will include only those resources available from *domain.nodename*.

When the name does not include the delimiter ".", it will be interpreted as a *nodename* within the local domain. If the name ends with a delimiter ".", it will be interpreted as a domain name.

The information contained in the report on each resource includes its advertised name (*domain.resource*), the read/write permissions, the server (*nodename.domain*) that advertised the resource, and a brief textual description.

When –h is used, the header is not printed.

A remote domain must be listed in your **rfmaster** file in order to query that domain.

EXIT STATUS

If no entries are found when **nsquery** is executed, the report header is printed.

SEE ALSO

adv(1M), unadv(1M), rfmaster(4)

NOTES

If your host cannot contact the domain name server, an error message will be sent to standard error.

NAME

od – octal dump

SYNOPSIS

od [**–bcDdFfOoSsvXx**] [*file*] [[**+**]*offset*[**.** | **b**]]

DESCRIPTION

od displays *file* in one or more formats, as selected by the first argument. If the first argument is missing, **–o** is default. If no *file* is specified, the standard input is used. For the purposes of this description, "word" refers to a 16-bit unit, independent of the word size of the machine; "long word" refers to a 32-bit unit, and "double long word" refers to a 64-bit unit. The meanings of the format options are:

–b   Interpret bytes in octal.

–c   Interpret bytes as single-byte characters. Certain non-graphic characters appear as C-language escapes: null=\0, backspace=\b, form-feed=\f, new-line=\n, return=\r, tab=\t; others appear as 3-digit octal numbers. For example:

```
echo "hello world" | od -c
0000000   h   e   l   l   o       w   o   r   l   d  \n
0000014
```

–D   Interpret long words in unsigned decimal.

–d   Interpret words in unsigned decimal.

–F   Interpret double long words in extended precision.

–f   Interpret long words in floating point.

–O   Interpret long words in unsigned octal.

–o   Interpret words in octal.

–S   Interpret long words in signed decimal.

–s   Interpret words in signed decimal.

–v   Show all data (verbose).

–X   Interpret long words in hex.

–x   Interpret words in hex.

offset specifies an offset from the beginning of *file* where the display will begin. *offset* is normally interpreted as octal bytes. If **.** is appended, *offset* is interpreted in decimal. If **x** is appended, *offset* is interpreted in hexadecimal. If **b** is appended, *offset* is interpreted in blocks of 512 bytes. If *file* is omitted, *offset* must be preceded by **+**.

The display continues until an end-of-file is reached.

NAME

offline – take a processor offline

SYNOPSIS

offline [-v] [*processor-id* . . .]

DESCRIPTION

offline takes each processor that is specified on the command line offline. If no processors are specified, all processors in the system are taken offline. In either case, some processors may not be taken offline because of hardware restrictions. At least one processor must remain online at all times. Processors that have bound processes can not be taken offline. If the -v flag is specified, the status of the processor is displayed before and after the attempt to take it offline.

SEE ALSO

online(1M), p_online(2)

NOTES

This command may not be supported in future releases.

NAME

　　online – bring a processor online

SYNOPSIS

　　online [-v] [*processor-id* . . .]

DESCRIPTION

　　online brings each processor that is specified on the command line online. If no
　　processors are listed, all processors are brought online. If the **-v** flag is specified,
　　the status of the processor is displayed before and after the attempt to turn it on.

SEE ALSO

　　offline(1M), **p_online**(2)

NOTES

　　This command may not be supported in future releases.

NAME

　　pack, pcat, unpack – compress and expand files

SYNOPSIS

　　pack [–] [–f] *name* . . .

　　pcat *name* . . .

　　unpack *name* . . .

DESCRIPTION

　　pack attempts to store the specified files in a compressed form. Wherever possible (and useful), each input file *name* is replaced by a packed file *name*.z with the same access modes, access and modified dates, and owner as those of *name*. The –f option will force packing of *name*. This is useful for causing an entire directory to be packed even if some of the files will not benefit. If pack is successful, *name* will be removed. Packed files can be restored to their original form using unpack or pcat.

　　pack uses Huffman (minimum redundancy) codes on a byte-by-byte basis. If the – argument is used, an internal flag is set that causes the number of times each byte is used, its relative frequency, and the code for the byte to be printed on the standard output. Additional occurrences of – in place of *name* will cause the internal flag to be set and reset.

　　The amount of compression obtained depends on the size of the input file and the character frequency distribution. Because a decoding tree forms the first part of each .z file, it is usually not worthwhile to pack files smaller than three blocks, unless the character frequency distribution is very skewed, which may occur with printer plots or pictures.

　　Typically, text files are reduced to 60-75% of their original size. Load modules, which use a larger character set and have a more uniform distribution of characters, show little compression, the packed versions being about 90% of the original size.

　　pack returns a value that is the number of files that it failed to compress.

　　No packing will occur if:

　　　　the file appears to be already packed;
　　　　the file name has more than 12 characters;
　　　　the file has links;
　　　　the file is a directory;
　　　　the file cannot be opened;
　　　　no disk storage blocks will be saved by packing;
　　　　a file called *name*.z already exists;
　　　　the .z file cannot be created;
　　　　an I/O error occurred during processing;
　　　　the file size is over 16 MB.

　　The last segment of the file name must contain no more than 12 characters to allow space for the appended .z extension. Directories cannot be compressed.

pcat does for packed files what cat(1) does for ordinary files, except that pcat cannot be used as a filter. The specified files are unpacked and written to the standard output. Thus to view a packed file named name.z use:

    pcat name.z

or just:

    pcat name

To make an unpacked copy, say nnn, of a packed file named name.z (without destroying name.z) use the command:

    pcat name >nnn

pcat returns the number of files it was unable to unpack. Failure may occur if:

    the file name (exclusive of the .z) has more than 12 characters;
    the file cannot be opened;
    the file does not appear to be the output of pack.

unpack expands files created by pack. For each file *name* specified in the command, a search is made for a file called *name*.z (or just *name*, if *name* ends in .z). If this file appears to be a packed file, it is replaced by its expanded version. The new file has the .z suffix stripped from its name, and has the same access modes, access and modification dates, and owner as those of the packed file.

Unpack returns a value that is the number of files it was unable to unpack. Failure may occur for the same reasons that it may in pcat, as well as for the following:

    a file with the "unpacked" name already exists;
    if the unpacked file cannot be created.

SEE ALSO

cat(1), compress(1)

NAME

pagesize – display the size of a page of memory

SYNOPSIS

/usr/ucb/pagesize

DESCRIPTION

pagesize prints the size of a page of memory in bytes, as returned by get-pagesize. This program is useful in constructing portable shell scripts.

SEE ALSO

getpagesize(3)

NAME

partsize – returns the size of the active UNIX System partition

SYNOPSIS

partsize *raw-device*

DESCRIPTION

The function of **partsize** is to print the size of the active UNIX System partition for the raw-device disk drive. The size value returned is in megabytes (MB = 2^20 bytes). This command is intended for use with the installation scripts, but is available for general use. If the system cannot retrieve a valid partition table, there will be a non-zero exit value. If a valid partition table is found, but no active UNIX system partition is found, it will display a value of zero.

raw-device   the required raw-device argument is the character special device for the disk drive to be accessed. It should be the slice 0 device to represent the entire device (for example, **/dev/rdsk/0s0** or **/dev/rdsk/c0t0d0s0**).

FILES

/dev/dsk/0s0
/dev/rdsk/1s0
/dev/rdsk/c?t?d?s0

SEE ALSO

fdisk(1M)

NAME
passmgmt – password files management

SYNOPSIS
passmgmt **-a** *options name*
passmgmt **-m** *options name*
passmgmt **-d** *name*

DESCRIPTION
The **passmgmt** command updates information in the password files. This command works with both **/etc/passwd** and **/etc/shadow**.

passmgmt -a adds an entry for user *name* to the password files. This command does not create any directory for the new user and the new login remains locked (with the string ***LK*** in the password field) until the **passwd**(1) command is executed to set the password.

passmgmt -m modifies the entry for user *name* in the password files. The name field in the **/etc/shadow** entry and all the fields (except the password field) in the **/etc/passwd** entry can be modified by this command. Only fields entered on the command line will be modified.

passmgmt -d deletes the entry for user *name* from the password files. It will not remove any files that the user owns on the system; they must be removed manually.

The following options are available:

-c *comment* A short description of the login. It is limited to a maximum of 128 characters and defaults to an empty field.

-h *homedir* Home directory of *name*. It is limited to a maximum of 256 characters and defaults to **/usr/**name.

-u *uid* UID of the *name*. This number must range from 0 to the maximum non-negative value for the system. It defaults to the next available UID greater than 99. Without the **-o** option, it enforces the uniqueness of a UID.

-o This option allows a UID to be non-unique. It is used only with the **-u** option.

-g *gid* GID of the *name*. This number must range from 0 to the maximum non-negative value for the system. The default is 1.

-s *shell* Login shell for *name*. It should be the full pathname of the program that will be executed when the user logs in. The maximum size of *shell* is 256 characters. The default is for this field to be empty and to be interpreted as **/usr/bin/sh**.

-l logname
This option changes the *name* to **logname**. It is used only with the **-m** option.

The total size of each login entry is limited to a maximum of 511 bytes in each of the password files.

FILES

/etc/passwd,
/etc/shadow,
/etc/opasswd,
/etc/oshadow

SEE ALSO

useradd(1M), userdel(1M), usermod(1M), passwd(4), and shadow(4) in the *System Administrator's Reference Manual*
passwd(1) in the *User's Reference Manual*

DIAGNOSTICS

The **passmgmt** command exits with one of the following values:

0   Success.

1   Permission denied.

2   Invalid command syntax. Usage message of the **passmgmt** command will be displayed.

3   Invalid argument provided to option.

4   UID in use.

5   Inconsistent password files (e.g., *name* is in the **/etc/passwd** file and not in the **/etc/shadow** file, or vice versa).

6   Unexpected failure. Password files unchanged.

7   Unexpected failure. Password file(s) missing.

8   Password file(s) busy. Try again later.

9   *name* does not exist (if −m or −d is specified), already exists (if −a is specified), or **logname** already exists (if −m −l is specified).

NOTES

You cannot use a colon or carriage return as part of an argument because it is interpreted as a field separator in the password file.

This command will be removed in a future release. Its functionality has been replaced and enhanced by **useradd**, **userdel**, and **usermod**. These commands are currently available.

NAME

passwd – change login password and password attributes

SYNOPSIS

passwd [*name*]

passwd [-l | -d] [-f] [-n *min*] [-x *max*] [-w *warn*] *name*

passwd -s [-a]

passwd -s [*name*]

DESCRIPTION

The **passwd** command changes the password or lists password attributes associated with the user's login *name*. Additionally, privileged-users may use **passwd** to install or change passwords and attributes associated with any login *name*.

When used to change a password, **passwd** prompts ordinary users for their old password, if any. It then prompts for the new password twice. When the old password is entered, **passwd** checks to see if it has aged sufficiently. If aging is insufficient, **passwd** terminates; see **shadow**(4).

If the user's password aging has not been turned on, then password aging is turned on for the user using the **MAXWEEKS** and **MINWEEKS** parameters in **/etc/default/passwd.** If password aging is turned on the password aging information in **/etc/shadow** remains unmodified.

Assuming aging is sufficient, a check is made to ensure that the new password meets construction requirements. When the new password is entered a second time, the two copies of the new password are compared. If the two copies are not identical the cycle of prompting for the new password is repeated for at most two more times.

Passwords must be constructed to meet the following requirements:

Each password must have at least **PASSLENGTH** characters as set in **/etc/default/passwd. PASSLENGTH** must contain a minimum of six characters, but only the first eight characters are significant.

Each password must contain at least two alphabetic characters and at least one numeric or special character. In this case, alphabetic refers to all upper or lower case letters.

Each password must differ from the user's login *name* and any reverse or circular shift of that login *name*. For comparison purposes, an upper case letter and its corresponding lower case letter are equivalent.

New passwords must differ from the old by at least three characters. For comparison purposes, an upper case letter and its corresponding lower case letter are equivalent.

Privileged users (for example, real and effective **uid** equal to zero, see **id**(1M) and **su**(1M) may change any password; hence, **passwd** does not prompt privileged users for the old password. Privileged users are not forced to comply with password aging and password construction requirements. A privileged-user can create a null password by entering a carriage return in response to the prompt for a new password. (This differs from **passwd** -d because the **password** prompt will still be displayed.)

Any user may use the **-s** option to show password attributes for his or her own login *name*.

The format of the display will be:

> *name status mm/dd/yy min max warn*

or, if password aging information is not present,

> *name status*

where

name   The login ID of the user.

status   The password status of *name*: **PS** stands for passworded or locked, **LK** stands for locked, and **NP** stands for no password.

mm/dd/yy   The date password was last changed for *name*. (Note that all password aging dates are determined using Greenwich Mean Time and, therefore, may differ by as much as a day in other time zones.)

min   The minimum number of days required between password changes for *name*. **MINWEEKS** is found in **/etc/default/passwd** and is set to 0.

max   The maximum number of days the password is valid for *name*. **MAXWEEKS** is found in **/etc/default/passwd** and is set to 0

warn   The number of days relative to *max* before the password expires that the *name* will be warned.

Only a privileged user can use the following options:

-1   Lock password entry for *name*.

-d   Delete password for *name*. The login *name* will not be prompted for password.

-n   Set minimum field for *name*. The *min* field contains the minimum number of days between password changes for *name*. If *min* is greater than *max*, the user may not change the password. Always use this option with the **-x** option, unless *max* is set to −1 (aging turned off). In that case, *min* need not be set.

-x   Set maximum field for *name*. The *max* field contains the number of days that the password is valid for *name*. The aging for *name* will be turned off immediately if *max* is set to −1. (Aging will be turned on again if the password is changed.) If it is set to 0, then aging is turned off.

-w   Set warn field for *name*. The *warn* field contains the number of days before the password expires that the user will be warned.

-a   Show password attributes for all entries. Use only with **-s** option; *name* must not be provided.

-f   Force the user to change password at the next login by expiring the password for *name*.

FILES

/etc/shadow, /etc/passwd, /etc/oshadow

SEE ALSO

`login`(1)

`crypt`(3C) in the *Programmer's Reference Manual*

`useradd`(1M), `usermod`(1M), `userdel`(1M), `id`(1M), `passmgmt`(1M), `pwconv`(1M), `su`(1M), `passwd`(4), `shadow`(4) in the *System Administrator's Reference Manual*

DIAGNOSTICS

The **passwd** command exits with one of the following values:

0   SUCCESS.

1   Permission denied.

2   Invalid combination of options.

3   Unexpected failure. Password file unchanged.

4   Unexpected failure. Password file(s) missing.

5   Password file(s) busy. Try again later.

6   Invalid argument to option.

WARNING

If root deletes a password for a user with the **passwd -d** command and password aging is in effect for that user, the user will not be allowed to add a new password until the null password has been aged. This is true even if the **PASSREQ** flag in **/etc/default/login** is set to **YES**. This results in a user without a password. It is recommended that the **-f** option be used whenever the **-d** (delete) option is used. This will force a user to change the password at the next login.

If a user is to be set up without a password, the password entry of the user must be absent from the **/etc/shadow** file. (When a user has no password, **passwd -s** *user* should return **NP**.)

NAME

paste – merge same lines of several files or subsequent lines of one file

SYNOPSIS

paste –| *file1* –| *file2* . . .

paste –**d** *list* –| *file1* –| *file2* . . .

paste –**s** [–**d** *list*] –| *file1* . . .

DESCRIPTION

In the first two forms, **paste** concatenates corresponding lines of the given input files *file1*, *file2*, etc. It treats each file as a column or columns of a table and pastes them together horizontally (parallel merging). If you will, it is the counterpart of **cat**(1) which concatenates vertically, that is, one file after the other. In the last form above, **paste** replaces the function of an older command with the same name by combining subsequent lines of the input file (serial merging). If more than one file is specified with the –**s** option, **paste**(1) concatenates the merged files one below the other. In all cases, lines are glued together with the *tab* character, or with characters from an optionally specified *list*. Output is to the standard output, so it can be used as the start of a pipe, or as a filter, if – is used in place of a file name.

The meanings of the options are:

–**d**   Without this option, the new-line characters of each but the last file (or last line in case of the –**s** option) are replaced by a *tab* character. This option allows replacing the *tab* character by one or more alternate characters (see below).

list   One or more characters immediately following –**d** replace the default *tab* as the line concatenation character. The list is used sequentially and circularly: first, the first element on the list is used to concatenate the lines, then the next, and so on; when all elements have been used, the list is reused starting from the first element. In parallel merging (that is, no –**s** option), the lines from the last file are always terminated with a new-line character, not from the *list*. The list may contain the special escape sequences: \n (new-line), \t (tab), \\ (backslash), and \0 (empty string, not a null character). Quoting may be necessary, if characters have special meaning to the shell (e.g., to get one backslash, use –*d* \\\\"").

–**s**   Merge subsequent lines rather than one from each input file. Use *tab* for concatenation, unless a *list* is specified with –**d** option. Regardless of the *list*, the very last character of the file is forced to be a new-line.

–   May be used in place of any file name, to read a line from the standard input. (There is no prompting).

EXAMPLES

**ls	paste –d" " –**	Lists directory in one column
**ls	paste – – – –**	Lists directory in four columns
paste –d"\t\n" *file1 file2*	Lists *file1* in column 1 and *file2* in column 2. The columns are separated by a tab.

`paste -s -d"\t\n"` *file1 file2*   Merges pairs of subsequent lines first in *file1*, then in *file2*. Concatenates the merged *file2* below *file1*.

DIAGNOSTICS

`"line too long"`   Output lines are restricted to 511 characters.

`"too many files"`   Except for −s option, no more than 12 input files may be specified.

SEE ALSO

cut(1), grep(1), pr(1)

NAME

pathconv – search FMLI criteria for filename

SYNOPSIS

pathconv [–f] [–v *alias*]
pathconv [–t] [–1] [–n*num*] [–v *string*]

DESCRIPTION

The **pathconv** function converts an alias to its pathname. By default, it takes the alias as a string from *stdin*.

–f   If –f is specified, the full path will be returned (this is the default).

–t   If –t is specified, **pathconv** will truncate a pathname specified in *string* in a format suitable for display as a frame title. This format is a shortened version of the full pathname, created by deleting components of the path from the middle of the string until it is under **DISPLAYW** – 6 characters in length, and then inserting ellipses (**. . .**) between the remaining pieces. Ellipses are also used to show truncation at the ends of the strings if necessary, unless the –1 option is given.

  –1   If –1 is specified, **<** and **>** will be used instead of ellipses (**. . .**) to indicate truncation at the ends of the string generated by the –t option. Truncation in the middle of the string is still indicated with ellipses. Using –1 allows display of the longest possible string while still notifying users it has been truncated.

  –n*num* If –n is specified, *num* is the maximum length of the string (in characters) generated by the –t option. The argument *num* can be any integer from 1 to 255.

–v *arg* If the **–v option is used, then** *alias* or *string* can be specified when **pathconv** is called. The argument *alias* must be an alias defined in the *alias_file* named when **fmli** was invoked. The argument *string* can only be used with the –t option and must be a pathname.

EXAMPLES

Here is a menu descriptor that uses **pathconv** to construct the menu title. It searches for **MYPATH** in the *alias_file* named when **fmli** was invoked:

        menu=`pathconv –v MYPATH/ls`
        .
        .
        .

where there is a line in *alias_file* that defines **MYPATH**. For example, **MYPATH=$HOME/bin:/usr/bin**.

Here is a menu descriptor that takes *alias* from *stdin*.

        menu=`echo MYPATH/ls | pathconv`
        .
        .
        .

SEE ALSO
     fmli(1)

NAME

pbind – bind a process to a processor

SYNOPSIS

pbind -b *processor-id pid* . . .

pbind -u *pid* . . .

pbind -q [*pid* . . .]

DESCRIPTION

If the **-b** option is specified, **pbind** binds the processes specified by the process ID (*pid*) arguments to the processor specified by *processor-id*. Processes that are bound to a processor will run only on that processor, except briefly when the process requires a resource that only another processor can provide. The processor may run other processes in addition to those which are bound to it.

If there are already processes exclusively bound to the specified processor (for example, by **pexbind**), the **pbind** command will fail.

If a process specified by *pid* is already bound to a different processor, the binding for that process shall be changed to the specified processor. If, however, a process specified by *pid* is bound exclusively (for example, by **pexbind**) the **pbind** command will fail.

If the **-u** option is specified, any binding will be removed for the specified processes.

Users can control only those processes they own unless the user is a super-user.

If the **-q** option is specified, **pbind** displays binding information for the specified *pid*s. If no *pid*s are specified, **pbind** displays binding information for the entire system.

NOTES

The format of the output displayed by **pbind -q** may change significantly in a future release. Applications and shell scripts should not depend on this format.

SEE ALSO

pexbind(1M)

processor_bind(2) in the *Programmer's Supplement*

NAME

pexbind – exclusively bind processes to a processor

SYNOPSIS

pexbind -b *processor-id pid* . . .

pexbind -u *pid* . . .

pexbind -q [*pid* . . .]

DESCRIPTION

If the **-b** option is specified **pexbind** exclusively binds the process(es) specified by the *pid* arguments to the processor specified by *processor-id*. Processes that are exclusively bound to a processor will execute only on that processor. However, an exclusively bound process will execute briefly on another processor if the process requires a resource that only that other processor can provide. In general, the processor will execute only those processes that are exclusively bound to it. However, the processor can briefly execute other processes in the system if it must provide a resource to the other processes that no other processor can provide.

If there are already processes bound to the specified processor, either exclusively or non-exclusively, the **pexbind(1M)** command will fail. Note, to exclusively bind several processes to a processor, all processes must be specified in one invocation of **pexbind**.

If a process specified by *pid* is already exclusively bound to a different processor, the exclusive binding for that process will be changed to the specified processor. If, however, a process specified by *pid* is bound non-exclusively (for example, with **pbind**) the previous non-exclusive binding will remain in effect for that process (the **pexbind** call will have no effect on that process).

If the **-u** option is specified, any exclusive binding will be removed for the specified processes.

Only the super-user can change the exclusive binding of processes using the **pexbind** command.

If the **-q** option is specified, **pexbind** displays exclusive binding information for the specified *pids*. If no *pids* are specified, **pexbind** displays exclusive binding information for the entire system.

NOTES

This command may not be supported in future releases. The format of the output displayed by **pexbind** **-q** may change significantly in a future release. Applications and shell scripts should not depend on this format.

SEE ALSO

pbind(1M)
processor_bind(2) in the *Programmer's Supplement*

NAME

pg – file perusal filter for CRTs

SYNOPSIS

pg [−*number*] [−p *string*] [−cefnrs] [+*linenumber*] [+/*pattern*/] [*file* . . .]

DESCRIPTION

The **pg** command is a filter that allows the examination of *files* one screenful at a time on a CRT. (If no *file* is specified or if it encounters the file name −, **pg** reads from standard input.) Each screenful is followed by a prompt. If the user types a carriage return, another page is displayed; other possibilities are listed below.

This command is different from previous paginators in that it allows you to back up and review something that has already passed. The method for doing this is explained below.

To determine terminal attributes, **pg** scans the **terminfo**(4) data base for the terminal type specified by the environment variable **TERM**. If **TERM** is not defined, the terminal type **dumb** is assumed.

The command line options are:

−*number*   An integer specifying the size (in lines) of the window that **pg** is to use instead of the default. (On a terminal containing 24 lines, the default window size is 23).

−c   Home the cursor and clear the screen before displaying each page. This option is ignored if **clear_screen** is not defined for this terminal type in the **terminfo**(4) data base.

−e   Causes **pg** *not* to pause at the end of each file.

−f   Normally, **pg** splits lines longer than the screen width, but some sequences of characters in the text being displayed (for example, escape sequences for underlining) generate undesirable results. The −f option inhibits **pg** from splitting lines.

−n   Normally, commands must be terminated by a <*newline*> character. This option causes an automatic end of command as soon as a command letter is entered.

−p *string*   Causes **pg** to use *string* as the prompt. If the prompt string contains a **%d**, the first occurrence of **%d**' in the prompt will be replaced by the current page number when the prompt is issued. The default prompt string is ":".

−r   Restricted mode. The shell escape is disallowed. **pg** will print an error message but does not exit.

−s   Causes **pg** to print all messages and prompts in standout mode (usually inverse video).

+*linenumber*   Start up at *linenumber*.

+/*pattern*/   Start up at the first line containing the regular expression pattern.

The responses that may be typed when **pg** pauses can be divided into three categories: those causing further perusal, those that search, and those that modify the perusal environment.

Commands that cause further perusal normally take a preceding *address*, an optionally signed number indicating the point from which further text should be displayed. This *address* is interpreted in either pages or lines depending on the command. A signed *address* specifies a point relative to the current page or line, and an unsigned *address* specifies an address relative to the beginning of the file. Each command has a default address that is used if none is provided.

The perusal commands and their defaults are as follows:

(+1)<*newline*> or <*blank*>
> This causes one page to be displayed. The address is specified in pages.

(+1) **l**
> With a relative address this causes **pg** to simulate scrolling the screen, forward or backward, the number of lines specified. With an absolute address this command prints a screenful beginning at the specified line.

(+1) **d** or **^D** Simulates scrolling half a screen forward or backward.

*i***f**   Skip *i* screens of text.

*i***z**   Same as <*newline*> except that *i*, if present, becomes the new default number of lines per screenful.

The following perusal commands take no *address*.

. or **^L**   Typing a single period causes the current page of text to be redisplayed.

$ Displays the last windowful in the file. Use with caution when the input is a pipe.

The following commands are available for searching for text patterns in the text. The regular expressions described in **ed**(1) are available. They must always be terminated by a <*newline*>, even if the −*n* option is specified.

i/*pattern*/   Search forward for the *i*th (default *i*=1) occurrence of *pattern*. Searching begins immediately after the current page and continues to the end of the current file, without wrap-around.

i^*pattern*^
i?*pattern*?   Search backwards for the *i*th (default *i*=1) occurrence of *pattern*. Searching begins immediately before the current page and continues to the beginning of the current file, without wrap-around. The ^ notation is useful for Adds 100 terminals which will not properly handle the ?.

After searching, **pg** will normally display the line found at the top of the screen. This can be modified by appending **m** or **b** to the search command to leave the line found in the middle or at the bottom of the window from now on. The suffix **t** can be used to restore the original situation.

The user of **pg** can modify the environment of perusal with the following commands:

*i***n**   Begin perusing the *i*th next file in the command line. The *i* is an unsigned number, default value is 1.

*i***p**   Begin perusing the *i*th previous file in the command line. *i* is an unsigned number, default is 1.

*i***w**   Display another window of text. If *i* is present, set the window size to *i*.

s *filename*

       Save the input in the named file. Only the current file being perused is saved. The white space between the **s** and *filename* is optional. This command must always be terminated by a *<newline>*, even if the *−n* option is specified.

h   Help by displaying an abbreviated summary of available commands.

q or **Q**   Quit **pg**.

! *command*

       Command is passed to the shell, whose name is taken from the **SHELL** environment variable. If this is not available, the default shell is used. This command must always be terminated by a *<newline>*, even if the *−n* option is specified.

At any time when output is being sent to the terminal, the user can hit the quit key (normally CTRL-\) or the interrupt (break) key. This causes **pg** to stop sending output, and display the prompt. The user may then enter one of the above commands in the normal manner. Unfortunately, some output is lost when this is done, because any characters waiting in the terminal's output queue are flushed when the quit signal occurs.

If the standard output is not a terminal, then **pg** acts just like **cat**(1), except that a header is printed before each file (if there is more than one).

EXAMPLE

       The following command line uses **pg** to read the system news:

```
news | pg -p "(Page %d):"
```

FILES

       /usr/share/lib/terminfo/?/*   terminal information database

       /tmp/pg*   temporary file when input is from a pipe

SEE ALSO

       ed(1), **grep**(1), **more**(1)

       terminfo(4) in the *System Administrator's Reference Manual*

NOTES

       While waiting for terminal input, **pg** responds to BREAK, DEL, and CTRL-\ by terminating execution. Between prompts, however, these signals interrupt **pg**'s current task and place the user in prompt mode. These should be used with caution when input is being read from a pipe, since an interrupt is likely to terminate the other commands in the pipeline.

The terminal **/**, **^**, or **?** may be omitted from the searching commands.

If terminal tabs are not set every eight positions, undesirable results may occur.

When using **pg** as a filter with another command that changes the terminal I/O options, terminal settings may not be restored correctly.

NAME

pinfo – get information about processors

SYNOPSIS

pinfo [-v] [*processor-id* . . .]

DESCRIPTION

pinfo displays information about the processors named in the command line by their *processor-id*s. If no processors are specified, information is displayed about all processors in the system. The online/offline status of the processor is displayed. If the processor is online and the **-v** flag is specified, the type of the processor is also displayed, along with the clock rate (in megahertz) of the processor, and the types of any floating point units attached to the processor.

SEE ALSO

processor_info(2) in the *Programmer's Supplement*

NOTES

This command may not be supported in future releases.

NAME

ping – send ICMP **ECHO_REQUEST** packets to network hosts

SYNOPSIS

/usr/sbin/ping *host* [*timeout*]

/usr/sbin/ping –s [**–lrRv**] *host* [*packetsize*] [*count*]

DESCRIPTION

ping utilizes the ICMP protocol's **ECHO_REQUEST** datagram to elicit an ICMP **ECHO_RESPONSE** from the specified *host* or network gateway. If *host* responds, **ping** will print *host* **is alive** on the standard output and exit. Otherwise after *timeout* seconds, it will write **no answer from** *host*. The default value of *timeout* is 20 seconds.

When the **–s** flag is specified, **ping** sends one datagram per second, and prints one line of output for every **ECHO_RESPONSE** that it receives. No output is produced if there is no response. In this second form, **ping** computes round trip times and packet loss statistics; it displays a summary of this information upon termination or timeout. The default datagram packet size is 64 bytes, or you can specify a size with the *packetsize* command-line argument. If an optional *count* is given, **ping** sends only that number of requests.

When using **ping** for fault isolation, first ping the local host to verify that the local network interface is running.

OPTIONS

–l   Loose source route. Use this option in the IP header to send the packet to the given host and back again. Usually specified with the **–R** option.

–r   Bypass the normal routing tables and send directly to a host on an attached network. If the host is not on a directly-attached network, an error is returned. This option can be used to **ping** a local host through an interface that has been dropped by the router daemon [see **routed**(1M)].

–R   Record route. Sets the IP record route option, which will store the route of the packet inside the IP header. The contents of the record route will only be printed if the **–v** option is given, and only be set on return packets if the target host preserves the record route option across echos, or the **–l** option is given.

–v   Verbose output. List any ICMP packets, other than **ECHO_RESPONSE**, that are received.

SEE ALSO

ifconfig(1M), **netstat**(1M), **rpcinfo**(1M), **icmp**(7)

NAME

pkgadd – transfer software package to the system

SYNOPSIS

pkgadd [-d *device*] [-r *response*] [-n] [-a *admin*] [*pkginst1*
[*pkginst2*[. . .]]]

pkgadd -s *spool* [-d *device*] [*pkginst1* [*pkginst2*[. . .]]]

DESCRIPTION

pkgadd transfers the contents of a software package from the distribution
medium or directory to install it onto the system. Used without the -d option,
pkgadd looks in the default spool directory for the package (/var/spool/pkg).
Used with the -s option, it reads the package to a spool directory instead of installing it.

-d *device*   Installs or copies a package from *device*. *device* can be (a) the full pathname to a directory (such as /var/tmp), (b) the full pathname to a
device (such as /dev/rmt/c0s0 or /dev/dsk/f0t), or (c) a device
alias. An alias is the unique name by which a device is known. (For
example, the alias for a cartridge tape drive might be ctape1.) The
name must be limited in length to 64 characters (DDB_MAXALIAS) and
may contain only alphanumeric characters and/or any of the following
special characters: underscore (_), dollar sign ($), hyphen (-), and
period (.). No two devices in the database may share the same alias.

-r *response*

Identifies a file or directory, *response*, which contains the answers to
questions posed by a "request script" during a previous pkgask session conducted in interactive mode. (For a complete description of
request scripts and response files, see the *Programmer's Guide: Application Development*.) *response* must be a full pathname.

-n   Installation occurs in non-interactive mode. The default mode is
interactive.

-a *admin*   Defines an installation administration file, *admin*, to be used in place of
the default administration file to specify whether installation checks
(such as the check on the amount of space, the system state, and so
on) are done. [For a description of the format of an "admin" file, see
admin(4).] The token none overrides the use of any *admin* file, and
thus forces interaction with the user. Unless a full pathname is given,
pkgadd looks in the /var/sadm/install/admin directory for the file.

pkginst   A short string used to designate a package. It is composed of one or
two parts: *pkg* (an abbreviation for the package name) or, if more than
one instance of that package exists, *pkg* plus *inst* (an instance
identifier). (The term "package instance" is used loosely: it refers to
all instantiations of *pkginst*, even those that do not include instance
identifiers.)

The package name abbreviation (*pkg*) is the mandatory part of *pkginst*.
To create such an abbreviation, assign it with the PKG parameter. For
example, to assign the abbreviation sds to the Software Distribution
Service package, enter PKG=sds.

The second part (*inst*), which is required only if you have more than one instance of the package in question, is a suffix that identifies the instance. This suffix is either a number (preceded by a period) or any short mnemonic string you choose. If you don't assign your own instance identifier when one is required, the system assigns a numeric one by default. For example, if you have three instances of the Software Distribution Service package and you don't create your own mnemonic identifiers (such as **old** and **beta**), the system adds the suffixes **.2** and **.3** to the second and third packages, automatically.

To indicate all instances of a package, specify **inst.***. (When using this format, enclose the command line in single quotes to prevent the shell from interpreting the * character.) Use the token **all** to refer to all packages available on the source medium.

-**s** *spool*　　Reads the package into the directory *spool* instead of installing it.

When executed without options, **pkgadd** uses **/var/spool/pkg** (the default spool directory).

NOTES

When transferring a package to a spool directory, the -**r**, -**n**, and -**a** options cannot be used.

The -**r** option can be used to indicate a directory name as well as a filename. The directory can contain numerous *response* files, each sharing the name of the package with which it should be associated. This would be used, for example, when adding multiple interactive packages with one invocation of **pkgadd**. Each package would need a *response* file. If you create response files with the same name as the package (for example, *package1* and *package2*) then, after the -**r** option, name the directory in which these files reside.

The -**n** option will cause the installation to halt if any interaction is needed to complete it.

SEE ALSO

admin(4), **compver**(4), **copyright**(4), **depend**(4), **installf**(1M), **pkgask**(1M), **pkgchk**(1M), **pkginfo**(1), **pkginfo**(4), **pkgmap**(4), **pkgparam**(1), **pkgrm**(1M), **putdev**(1M), **removef**(1), **space**(4)

NAME

pkgask – stores answers to a request script

SYNOPSIS

/usr/sbin/pkgask [–d *device*] –r *response* [*pkginst* [*pkginst* [. . .]]]

DESCRIPTION

pkgask allows the administrator to store answers to an interactive package (one with a request script). Invoking this command generates a *response* file that is then used as input at installation time. The use of this *response* file prevents any interaction from occurring during installation since the file already contains all of the information the package needs.

–d   Runs the request script for a package on *device*. *device* can be a full pathname to a directory or the identifiers for tape, floppy disk or removable disk (for example, **/var/tmp**, **/dev/dsk/0s2**, and **/dev/dsk/f0t**). The default device is the installation spool directory.

–r   Identifies a file or directory, which should be created to contain the responses to interaction with the package. The name must be a full pathname. The file, or directory of files, can later be used as input to the **pkgadd** command.

pkginst   Specifies the package instance or list of instances for which request scripts will be created. The token **all** may be used to refer to all packages available on the source medium. The format *pkginst*.* can be used to indicate all instances of a package. When using this format, enclose the command line in single quotes to prevent the shell from interpreting the * character.

NOTES

The –r option can be used to indicate a directory name as well as a filename. The directory name is used to create numerous *response* files, each sharing the name of the package with which it should be associated. This would be used, for example, when you will be adding multiple interactive packages with one invocation of **pkgadd**. Each package would need a *response* file. To create multiple response files with the same name as the package instance, name the directory in which the files should be created and supply multiple instance names with the **pkgask** command. When installing the packages, you will be able to identify this directory to the **pkgadd** command.

SEE ALSO

installf(1M), pkgadd(1M), pkgchk(1), pkgmk(1), pkginfo(1), pkgparam(1), pkgproto(1), pkgtrans(1), pkgrm(1M), removef(1M)

NAME

pkgchk – check accuracy of installation

SYNOPSIS

/usr/sbin/pkgchk [-1 | -acfqv] [-nx] [-p *path1*[,*path2* . . .] [-i *file*] [*pkginst* . . .]

/usr/sbin/pkgchk -d *device* [-1 | v] [-p *path1*[,*path2* . . .] [-i *file*] [*pkginst* . . .]

/usr/sbin/pkgchk -m *pkgmap* [-e *envfile*] [-1 | -acfqv] [-nx] [-i *file*]
　　　[-p *path1*[,*path2* . . .]]

DESCRIPTION

pkgchk checks the accuracy of installed files or, by use of the -1 option, displays information about package files. The command checks the integrity of directory structures and the files. Discrepancies are reported on **stderr** along with a detailed explanation of the problem.

The first synopsis defined above is used to list or check the contents and/or attributes of objects that are currently installed on the system. Package names may be listed on the command line, or by default the entire contents of a machine will be checked.

The second synopsis is used to list or check the contents of a package which has been spooled on the specified device, but not installed. Note that attributes cannot be checked for spooled packages.

The third synopsis is used to list or check the contents and/or attributes of objects which are described in the indicated *pkgmap*.

The option definitions are:

-1　　　Lists information on the selected files that make up a package. It is not compatible with the **a**, **c**, **f**, **g**, and **v** options.

-a　　　Audits the file attributes only, does not check file contents. Default is to check both.

-c　　　Audits the file contents only, does not check file attributes. Default is to check both.

-f　　　Corrects file attributes if possible. When **pkgchk** is invoked with this option it creates directories, named pipes, links and special devices if they do not already exist.

-q　　　Quiet mode. Does not give messages about missing files.

-v　　　Verbose mode. Files are listed as processed.

-n　　　Does not check volatile or editable files. This should be used for most post-installation checking.

-x　　　Searches exclusive directories only, looking for files which exist that are not in the installation software database or the indicated *pkgmap* file. If used with the -f option, hidden files are removed; no other checking is done.

-p   Only checks the accuracy of the pathname or pathnames listed. *pathname* can be one or more pathnames separated by commas (or by white space, if the list is quoted).

-i   Reads a list of pathnames from *file* and compares this list against the installation software database or the indicated *pkgmap* file. Pathnames which are not contained in *inputfile* are not checked.

-d   Specifies the device on which a spooled package resides. *device* can be a directory pathname or the identifiers for tape, floppy disk or removable disk (for example, **/var/tmp** or **/dev/diskette**).

-m   Requests that the package be checked against the pkgmap file *pkgmap*.

-e   Requests that the pkginfo file named as *envfile* be used to resolve parameters noted in the specified pkgmap file.

pkginst   Specifies the package instance or instances to be checked. The format *pkginst.** can be used to check all instances of a package. When using this format, enclose the command line in single quotes to prevent the shell from interpreting the * character. The default is to display all information about all installed packages.

NOTES

To remove hidden files only, use the **-f** and **-x** options together. To remove hidden files and check attributes and contents of files, use the **-f**, **-x**, **-c**, and **-a** options together.

SEE ALSO

pkgadd(1M), **pkgask**(1M), **pkginfo**(1), **pkgrm**(1M), **pkgtrans**(1)

NAME

pkginfo – display software package information

SYNOPSIS

pkginfo [-q| x| l] [-p| i] [-a *arch*] [-v *version*]
      [-c *category1*, [*category2*[, . . .]]] [*pkginst*[, *pkginst*[, . . .]]]

pkginfo [-d *device* [-q| x| l] [-a *arch*] [-v *version*]
      [-c *category1*, [*category2*[, . . .]]] [*pkginst*[, *pkginst*[, . . .]]]

DESCRIPTION

pkginfo displays information about software packages which are installed on the system (with the first synopsis) or which reside on a particular device or directory (with the second synopsis). Only the package name and abbreviation for pre-System V Release 4 packages will be included in the display.

The options for this command are:

-q   Does not list any information, but can be used from a program to check (that is, query) whether or not a package has been installed.

-x   Designates an extracted listing of package information. It contains the package abbreviation, package name, package architecture (if available) and package version (if available).

-l   Designates long format, which includes all available information about the designated package(s).

-p   Designates that information should be presented only for partially installed packages.

-i   Designates that information should be presented only for fully installed packages.

-a   Specifies the architecture of the package as *arch*.

-v   Specifies the version of the package as *version*. All compatible versions can be requested by preceding the version name with a tilde (~). The list produced by -v will include pre-Release 4 packages (with which no version numbers are associated). Multiple white spaces are replaced with a single space during version comparison.

-c   Selects packages to be display based on the category *category*. (Categories are defined in the category field of the pkginfo file.) If more than one category is supplied, the package must only match one of the list of categories. The match is not case specific.

pkginst   Designates a package by its instance. An instance can be the package abbreviation or a specific instance (for example, inst.1 or inst.beta). All instances of package can be requested by inst.*. When using this format, enclose the command line in single quotes to prevent the shell from interpreting the * character.

-d   Defines a device, *device*, on which the software resides. *device* can be a full pathname to a directory or the identifiers for tape, floppy disk, removable disk, and so on. The special token "spool" may be used to indicate the default installation spool directory.

NOTES

Without options, **pkginfo** lists the primary category, package instance, and name of all completely installed and partially installed packages. One line per package selected is produced.

The **-p** and **-i** options are meaningless if used in conjunction with the **-d** option.

The options **-q**, **-x**, and **-l** are mutually exclusive.

pkginfo cannot tell if a pre-Release 4 package is only partially installed. It is assumed that all pre-Release 4 packages are fully installed.

SEE ALSO

pkgadd(1M), **pkgask**(1M), **pkgchk**(1M), **pkgrm**(1M), **pkgtrans**(1)

NAME

pkgmk – produce an installable package

SYNOPSIS

pkgmk [-o] [-d *device*] [-r *rootpath*] [-b *basedir*] [-1 *limit*] [-a *arch*]
    [-v *version*] [-p *pstamp*] [-f *prototype*] [*variable=value* . . .] [*pkginst*]

DESCRIPTION

pkgmk produces an installable package to be used as input to the pkgadd command. The package contents will be in directory structure format.

The command uses the package **prototype** file as input and creates a **pkgmap** file. The contents for each entry in the **prototype** file is copied to the appropriate output location. Information concerning the contents (checksum, file size, modification date) is computed and stored in the **pkgmap** file, along with attribute information specified in the **prototype** file.

-o	Overwrites the same instance, package instance will be overwritten if it already exists.
-d *device*	Creates the package on *device*. *device* can be a full pathname to a directory or the identifiers for a floppy disk or removable disk (for example, **/dev/diskette**). The default device is the installation spool directory.
-r *rootpath*	Ignores destination paths in the **prototype** file. Instead, uses the indicated *rootpath* with the source pathname appended to locate objects on the source machine.
-b *basedir*	Prepends the indicated *basedir* to locate relocatable objects on the source machine.
-1 *limit*	Specifies the maximum size in 512 byte blocks of the output device as *limit*. By default, if the output file is a directory or a mountable device, **pkgmk** will employ the **df** command to dynamically calculate the amount of available space on the output device. Useful in conjunction with **pkgtrans** to create package with datastream format.
-a *arch*	Overrides the architecture information provided in the **pkginfo** file with *arch*.
-v *version*	Overrides version information provided in the **pkginfo** file with *version*.
-p *pstamp*	Overrides the production stamp definition in the **pkginfo** file with *pstamp*.
-f *prototype*	Uses the file *prototype* as input to the command. The default name for this file is either **Prototype** or **prototype**.
variable=value	Places the indicated variable in the packaging environment. [See **prototype**(4) for definitions of packaging variables.]
pkginst	Specifies the package by its instance. **pkgmk** will automatically create a new instance if the version and/or architecture is different. A user should specify only a package abbreviation; a particular instance should not be specified unless the user is overwriting it.

NOTES

Architecture information is provided on the command line with the **-a** option or in the **prototype** file. If no architecture information is supplied at all, the output of **uname -m** will be used.

Version information is provided on the command line with the **-v** option or in the **prototype** file. If no version information is supplied, a default based on the current date will be provided.

Command line definitions for both architecture and version override the **prototype** definitions.

SEE ALSO

pkgparam(1), pkgproto(1), pkgtrans(1)

NAME

pkgparam – displays package parameter values

SYNOPSIS

pkgparam [-v][-d *device*] *pkginst* [*param*[. . .]]

pkgparam -f *file* [-v] [*param*[. . .]]

DESCRIPTION

pkgparam displays the value associated with the parameter or parameters requested on the command line. The values are located in either the pkginfo file for *pkginst* or from the specific file named with the -f option.

One parameter value is shown per line. Only the value of a parameter is given unless the -v option is used. With this option, the output of the command is in this format:

> *parameter1='value1'*
> *parameter2='value2'*
> *parameter3='value3'*

If no parameters are specified on the command line, values for all parameters associated with the package are shown.

Options and arguments for this command are:

-v   Specifies verbose mode. Displays name of parameter and its value.

-d   Specifies the *device* on which a *pkginst* is stored. It can be a full pathname to a directory or the identifiers for tape, floppy disk or removable disk (for example, **/var/tmp**, **/dev/dsk/f0t**, and **/dev/dsk/0s2**). The default device is the installation spool directory. If no instance name is given, parameter information for all packages residing in *device* is shown.

-f   Requests that the command read *file* for parameter values.

pkginst   Defines a specific package instance for which parameter values should be displayed. The format *pkginst.** can be used to indicate all instances of a package. When using this format, enclose the command line in single quotes to prevent the shell from interpreting the * character.

param   Defines a specific parameter whose value should be displayed.

ERRORS

If parameter information is not available for the indicated package, the command exits with a non-zero status.

NOTES

The -f synopsis allows you to specify the file from which parameter values should be extracted. This file should be in the same format as a pkginfo file. As an example, such a file might be created during package development and used while testing software during this stage.

SEE ALSO

installf(1M), pkgmk(1), pkgparam(3x), pkgproto(1), pgktrans(1)

NAME
pkgproto – generate a **prototype** file

SYNOPSIS
pkgproto [-i] [-c *class*] [*path1*[=*path2*] . . .]

DESCRIPTION
pkgproto scans the indicated paths and generates a **prototype** file that may be used as input to the **pkgmk** command.

-i　　　　Ignores symbolic links and records the paths as **ftype=f** (a file) versus **ftype=s**(symbolic link)

-c　　　　Maps the class of all paths to *class*.

path1　　Path of directory where objects are located.

path2　　Path that should be substituted on output for *path1*.

If no paths are specified on the command line, standard input is assumed to be a list of paths. If the path listed on the command line is a directory, the contents of the directory are searched. However, if input is read from **stdin**, a directory specified as a path will not be searched.

NOTES
By default, **pkgproto** creates symbolic link entries for any symbolic link encountered (**ftype=s**). When you use the **-i** option, **pkgproto** creates a file entry for symbolic links (**ftype=f**). The **prototype** file would have to be edited to assign such file types as **v** (volatile), **e** (editable), or **x** (exclusive directory). **pkgproto** detects linked files. If multiple files are linked together, the first path encountered is considered the source of the link.

EXAMPLE
The following two examples show uses of **pkgproto** and a partial listing of the output produced.

Example 1:
```
$ pkgproto /usr/bin=bin /usr/usr/bin=usrbin /etc=etc
f none bin/sed=/bin/sed 0775 bin bin
f none bin/sh=/bin/sh 0755 bin daemon
f none bin/sort=/bin/sort 0755 bin bin
f none usrbin/sdb=/usr/bin/sdb 0775 bin bin
f none usrbin/shl=/usr/bin/shl 4755 bin bin
d none etc/master.d 0755 root daemon
f none etc/master.d/kernel=/etc/master.d/kernel 0644 root daemon
f none etc/rc=/etc/rc 0744 root daemon
```

Example 2:
```
$ find / -type d -print | pkgproto
d none / 755 root root
d none /usr/bin 755 bin bin
d none /usr 755 root root
d none /usr/bin 775 bin bin
d none /etc 755 root root
d none /tmp 777 root root
```

SEE ALSO
     installf(1M), pkgmk(1), pkgparam(1), pkgtrans(1)

NAME

pkgrm – removes a package from the system

SYNOPSIS

pkgrm [-n] [-a *admin*] [*pkginst1* [*pkginst2*[. . .]]]

pkgrm -s *spool* [*pkginst*]

DESCRIPTION

pkgrm will remove a previously installed or partially installed package from the system. A check is made to determine if any other packages depend on the one being removed. The action taken if a dependency exists is defined in the **admin** file.

The default state for the command is interactive mode, meaning that prompt messages are given during processing to allow the administrator to confirm the actions being taken. Non-interactive mode can be requested with the **-n** option.

The **-s** option can be used to specify the directory from which spooled packages should be removed.

The options and arguments for this command are:

-n   Non-interactive mode. If there is a need for interaction, the command will exit. Use of this option requires that at least one package instance be named upon invocation of the command.

-a *admin*   Defines an installation administration file, *admin*, to be used in place of the default *admin* file.

-s *spool*   Removes the specified package(s) from the directory *spool*.

pkginst   A short string used to designate a package. It is composed of one or two parts: *pkg* (an abbreviation for the package name) or, if more than one instance of that package exists, *pkg* plus *inst* (an instance identifier). (The term "package instance" is used loosely: it refers to all instantiations of *pkginst*, even those that do not include instance identifiers.)

The package name abbreviation (*pkg*) is the mandatory part of *pkginst*. To create such an abbreviation, assign it with the **PKG** parameter. For example, to assign the abbreviation **sds** to the Software Distribution Service package, enter **PKG=sds**.

The second part (*inst*), which is required only if you have more than one instance of the package in question, is a suffix that identifies the instance. This suffix is either a number (preceded by a period) or any short mnemonic string you choose. If you don't assign your own instance identifier when one is required, the system assigns a numeric one by default. For example, if you have three instances of the Software Distribution Service package and you don't create your own mnemonic identifiers (such as **old** and **beta**), the system adds the suffixes **.2** and **.3** to the second and third packages, automatically.

To indicate all instances of a package, specify **inst.**∗. (When using this format, enclose the command line in single quotes to prevent the shell from interpreting the ∗ character.) Use the token **all** to refer to all packages available on the source medium.

SEE ALSO

compver(4), copyright(4), depend(4), installf(1M), pkgadd(1M), pkgask(1M), pkgchk(1M), pkginfo(1), pkginfo(4), pkgmap(4), pkgmk(1), pkgparam(1), pkgproto(1), pkgtrans(1), removef(1M), space(4)

NAME

pkgtrans – translate package format

SYNOPSIS

pkgtrans [**-ions**] *device1* *device2* [*pkginst1* [*pkginst2* [. . .]]]

DESCRIPTION

pkgtrans translates an installable package from one format to another. It translates:

— a file system format to a datastream

— a datastream to a file system format

— a file system format to another file system format

The options and arguments for this command are:

-i   Copies only the **pkginfo** and **pkgmap** files.

-o   Overwrites the same instance on the destination device, package instance will be overwritten if it already exists.

-n   Creates a new instance if any instance of this package already exists.

-s   Indicates that the package should be written to *device2* as a datastream rather than as a file system. The default behavior is to write a file system format on devices that support both formats.

device1 Indicates the source device. The package or packages on this device will be translated and placed on *device2*.

device2 Indicates the destination device. Translated packages will be placed on this device.

pkginst A short string used to designate a package. It is composed of one or two parts: *pkg* (an abbreviation for the package name) or, if more than one instance of that package exists, *pkg* plus *inst* (an instance identifier). (The term "package instance" is used loosely: it refers to all instantiations of *pkginst*, even those that do not include instance identifiers.)

      The package name abbreviation (*pkg*) is the mandatory part of *pkginst*. To create such an abbreviation, assign it with the **PKG** parameter. For example, to assign the abbreviation **sds** to the Software Distribution Service package, enter **PKG=sds**.

      The second part (*inst*), which is required only if you have more than one instance of the package in question, is a suffix that identifies the instance. This suffix is either a number (preceded by a period) or any short mnemonic string you choose. If you don't assign your own instance identifier when one is required, the system assigns a numeric one by default. For example, if you have three instances of the Software Distribution Service package and you don't create your own mnemonic identifiers (such as **old** and **beta**), the system adds the suffixes **.2** and **.3** to the second and third packages, automatically.

To indicate all instances of a package, specify **inst.**∗. (When using this format, enclose the command line in single quotes to prevent the shell from interpreting the ∗ character.) Use the token **all** to refer to all packages available on the source medium.

NOTES

Device specifications can be either the special node name (**/dev/rmt/ctape**) or the device alias (**ctape1**). The device **spool** indicates the default spool directory. Source and destination devices may not be the same.

By default, **pkgtrans** will not transfer any instance of a package if any instance of that package already exists on the destination device. Use of the **-n** option will create a new instance if an instance of this package already exists. Use of the **-o** option will overwrite the same instance if it already exists. Neither of these options are useful if the destination device is a datastream.

pkgtrans depends on the integrity of the **/etc/device.tab** file to determine whether a device can support a datastream and/or file system formats. Problems in transferring a device in a particular format could mean corruption of **/etc/device.tab**.

EXAMPLE

The following example translates all packages on the tape drive **/dev/rmt/ctape** and places the translations on **/tmp**.

        pkgtrans /dev/rmt/ctape /tmp all

The next example translates packages **pkg1** and **pkg2** on **/tmp** and places their translations (that is, a datastream) on the **9track1** output device.

        pkgtrans /tmp 9track1 pkg1 pkg2

The next example translates **pkg1** and **pkg2** on **/tmp** and places them on the tape in a datastream format.

        pkgtrans -s /tmp /dev/rmt/ctape pkg1 pkg2

SEE ALSO

installf(1M), pkgadd(1M), pkgask(1M), pkginfo(1), pkgmk(1), pkgparam(1), pkgproto(1), pkgrm(1M), putdev(1M), removef(1M)

NAME

plot, aedplot, atoplot, bgplot, crtplot, dumbplot, gigiplot, hpplot, implot, plottoa, t300, t300s, t4013, t450, tek – graphics filters for various plotters

SYNOPSIS

/usr/ucb/plot [−T*terminal*]

DESCRIPTION

plot reads plotting instructions [see plot(4)] from the standard input and produces plotting instructions suitable for a particular *terminal* on the standard output.

If no *terminal* is specified, the environment variable TERM is used. The default *terminal* is tek.

ENVIRONMENT

Except for **ver**, the following terminal-types can be used with 'lpr −g' (see lpr) to produce plotted output:

2648 | 2648a | h8 | hp2648 | hp2648a
  Hewlett Packard® 2648 graphics terminal.

300   DASI 300 or GSI terminal (Diablo® mechanism).

300s | 300S
  DASI 300s terminal (Diablo mechanism).

450   DASI Hyterm 450 terminal (Diablo mechanism).

4013   Tektronix® 4013 storage scope.

4014 | tek Tektronix 4014 and 4015 storage scope with Enhanced Graphics Module. (Use 4013 for Tektronix 4014 or 4015 without the Enhanced Graphics Module).

aed   AED 512 color graphics terminal.

bgplot | bitgraph
  BBN bitgraph graphics terminal.

crt   Any crt terminal capable of running **vi**(1).

dumb | un | unknown
  Dumb terminals without cursor addressing or line printers.

gigi | vt125
  DEC® vt125 terminal.

h7 | hp7 | hp7221
  Hewlett Packard 7221 graphics terminal.

implot   Imagen plotter.

var   Benson Varian printer-plotter

ver   Versatec® D1200A printer-plotter. The output is scan-converted and suitable input to 'lpr −v'.

FILES

```
/usr/ucb/aedplot
/usr/ucb/atoplot
/usr/ucb/bgplot
/usr/ucb/crtplot
/usr/ucb/dumbplot
/usr/ucb/gigiplot
/usr/ucb/hpplot
/usr/ucb/implot
/usr/ucb/plot
/usr/ucb/plottoa
/usr/ucb/t300
/usr/ucb/t300s
/usr/ucb/t4013
/usr/ucb/t450
/usr/ucb/tek
/usr/ucb/vplot
/var/ucb/vplot*nnnnnn*
```

SEE ALSO

lpr(1)

vi(1) in the *User's Reference Manual*
plot(3X), **plot**(4) in the *Programmer's Reference Manual*

NAME

pmadm – port monitor administration

SYNOPSIS

pmadm −a [−p *pmtag* | −t *type*] −s *svctag* −i id −m *pmspecific*
    −v *ver* [−f xu] [−y *comment*] [−z *script*]

pmadm −r −p *pmtag* −s *svctag*

pmadm −e −p *pmtag* −s *svctag*

pmadm −d −p *pmtag* −s *svctag*

pmadm −l [−t *type* | −p *pmtag*] [−s *svctag*]

pmadm −L [−t *type* | −p *pmtag*] [−s *svctag*]

pmadm −g −p *pmtag* −s *svctag* [−z *script*]

pmadm −g −s *svctag* −t *type* −z *script*

DESCRIPTION

pmadm is the administrative command for the lower level of the Service Access
Facility hierarchy, that is, for service administration. A port may have only one
service associated with it although the same service may be available through
more than one port. In order to uniquely identify an instance of a service the
pmadm command must identify both the port monitor or port monitors through
which the service is available (−p or −t) and the service (−s). See the option
descriptions below.

pmadm performs the following functions:

        – add or remove a service
        – enable or disable a service
        – install or replace a per-service configuration script
        – print requested service information

Any user on the system may invoke pmadm to request service status (−l or −L) or
to print per-service configuration scripts (−g without the −z option). pmadm with
other options may be executed only by a privileged user.

The options have the following meanings:

−a   Add a service. pmadm adds an entry for the new service to the port
        monitor's administrative file. Because of the complexity of the options
        and arguments that follow the −a option, it may be convenient to use a
        command script or the menu system to add services. If you use the
        menu system, enter sysadm ports, then choose the port_services
        option.

−d   Disable a service. Add x to the flag field in the entry for the service
        svctag in the port monitor's administrative file. This is the entry used by
        port monitor *pmtag*. See the −f option, below, for a description of the
        flags available.

−e Enable a service. Remove **x** from the flag field in the entry for the service *svctag* in the port monitor administrative file. This is the entry used by port monitor *pmtag*. See the **−f** option, below, for a description of the flags available.

−f xu The **−f** option specifies one or both of the following two flags which are then included in the flag field of the entry for the new service in the port monitor's administrative file. If the **−f** option is not included, no flags are set and the default conditions prevail. By default, a new service is enabled and no **utmp** entry is created for it. A **−f** option without a following argument is illegal.

> **x** Do not enable the service *svctag* available through port monitor *pmtag*.
>
> **u** Create a **utmp** entry for service *svctag* available through port monitor *pmtag*.

−g Print, install, or replace a per-service configuration script. The **−g** option with a **−p** option and a **−s** option prints the per-service configuration script for service *svctag* available through port monitor *pmtag*. The **−g** option with a **−p** option, a **−s** option, and a **−z** option installs the per-service configuration script contained in the file *script* as the per-service configuration script for service *svctag* available through port monitor *pmtag*. The **−g** option with a **−s** option, a **−t** option, and a **−z** option installs the file *script* as the per-service configuration script for service *svctag* available through any port monitor of type *type*. Other combinations of options with **−g** are invalid.

−i id **id** is the identity that is to be assigned to service *svctag* when it is started. **id** must be an entry in **/etc/passwd**.

−l The **−l** option requests service information. Used by itself and with the options described below it provides a filter for extracting information in several different groupings.

> **−l**   By itself, the **−l** option lists all services on the system.
>
> **−l −p** *pmtag* Lists all services available through port monitor *pmtag*.
>
> **−l −s** *svctag* Lists all services with tag *svctag*.
>
> **−l −p** *pmtag* **−s** *svctag*
>   Lists service *svctag*.
>
> **−l −t** *type* Lists all services available through port monitors of type *type*.
>
> **−l −t** *type* **−s** *svctag*
>   Lists all services with tag *svctag* available through a port monitor of type *type*.

Other combinations of options with **−l** are invalid.

-L   The -L option is identical to the -1 option except that output is printed in a condensed format.

-m *pmspecific*
            pmspecific is the port monitor-specific portion of the port monitor administrative file entry for the service.

-p *pmtag*
            Specifies the tag associated with the port monitor through which a service (specified as -s *svctag*) is available.

-r   Remove a service. When **pmadm** removes a service, the entry for the service is removed from the port monitor's administrative file.

-s *svctag*
            Specifies the service tag associated with a given service. The service tag is assigned by the system administrator and is part of the entry for the service in the port monitor's administrative file.

-t *type*   Specifies the the port monitor type.

-v *ver*   Specifies the version number of the port monitor administrative file. The version number may be given as

                    -v `pmspec -V`

            where *pmspec* is the special administrative command for port monitor *pmtag*. This special command is **ttyadm** for **ttymon** and **nlsadmin** for **listen**. The version stamp of the port monitor is known by the command and is returned when *pmspec* is invoked with a -V option.

-y *comment*
            Associate *comment* with the service entry in the port monitor administrative file.

-z *script*
            Used with the -g option to specify the name of the file that contains the per-service configuration script. Modifying a configuration script is a three-step procedure. First a copy of the existing script is made (-g alone). Then the copy is edited. Finally, the copy is put in place over the existing script (-g with -z).

OUTPUT

If successful, **pmadm** will exit with a status of 0. If it fails for any reason, it will exit with a nonzero status.

Options that request information write the requested information to the standard output. A request for information using the -1 option prints column headers and aligns the information under the appropriate headings. In this format, a missing field is indicated by a hyphen. A request for information in the condensed format using the -L option prints the information in colon-separated fields; missing fields are indicated by two successive colons. # is the comment character.

EXAMPLES

Add a service to a port monitor with tag **pmtag**. Give the service the tag **svctag**. Port monitor-specific information is generated by **specpm**. The service defined by **svctag** will be invoked with identity **root**.

```
pmadm -a -p pmtag -s svctag -i root -m `specpm -a arg1 -b arg2` \
   -v `specpm -V`
```

Add a service with service tag **svctag**, identity **guest**, and port monitor-specific information generated by **specpm** to all port monitors of type **type**:

```
pmadm -a -s svctag -i guest -t type -m `specpm -a arg1 -b arg2` \
   -v `specpm -V`
```

Remove the service **svctag** from port monitor **pmtag**:

```
pmadm -r -p pmtag -s svctag
```

Enable the service **svctag** available through port monitor **pmtag**:

```
pmadm -e -p pmtag -s svctag
```

Disable the service **svctag** available through port monitor **pmtag**:

```
pmadm -d -p pmtag -s svctag
```

List status information for all services:

```
pmadm -l
```

List status information for all services available through the port monitor with tag **ports**:

```
pmadm -l -p ports
```

List the same information in condensed format:

```
pmadm -L -p ports
```

List status information for all services available through port monitors of type **listen**:

```
pmadm -l -t listen
```

Print the per-service configuration script associated with the service **svctag** available through port monitor **pmtag**:

```
pmadm -g -p pmtag -s svctag
```

FILES

```
/etc/saf/pmtag/_config
/etc/saf/pmtag/svctag
/var/saf/pmtag/*
```

SEE ALSO

doconfig(3n), sacadm(1M), sac(1M).

NAME

　　　`postdaisy` – PostScript translator for Diablo 630 files

SYNOPSIS

　　　`/usr/lib/lp/postscript/postdaisy` [*options*] [*files*]

DESCRIPTION

　　　The `postdaisy` filter translates Diablo 630 daisy-wheel *files* into PostScript and writes the results on the standard output. If no *files* are specified, or if – is one of the input *files*, the standard input is read. The following *options* are understood:

–c *num*	Print *num* copies of each page. By default only one copy is printed.
–f *name*	Print *files* using font *name*. Any PostScript font can be used, although the best results will be obtained only with constant-width fonts. The default font is Courier.
–h *num*	Set the initial horizontal motion index to *num*. Determines the character advance and the default point size, unless the **–s** option is used. The default is 12.
–m *num*	Magnify each logical page by the factor *num*. Pages are scaled uniformly about the origin, which is located near the upper left corner of each page. The default magnification is 1.0.
–n *num*	Print *num* logical pages on each piece of paper, where *num* can be any positive integer. By default, *num* is set to 1.
–o *list*	Print pages whose numbers are given in the comma-separated *list*. The list contains single numbers N and ranges N1 – N2. A missing N1 means the lowest numbered page, a missing N2 means the highest.
–p *mode*	Print *files* in either portrait or landscape *mode*. Only the first character of *mode* is significant. The default *mode* is portrait.
–r *num*	Selects carriage return and line feed behavior. If *num* is 1, a line feed generates a carriage return. If *num* is 2, a carriage return generates a line feed. Setting *num* to 3 enables both modes.
–s *num*	Use point size *num* instead of the default value set by the initial horizontal motion index.
–v *num*	Set the initial vertical motion index to *num*. The default is 8.
–x *num*	Translate the origin *num* inches along the positive x axis. The default coordinate system has the origin fixed near the upper left corner of the page, with positive x to the right and positive y down the page. Positive *num* moves everything right. The default offset is 0.25 inches.
–y *num*	Translate the origin *num* inches along the positive y axis. Positive *num* moves text up the page. The default offset is −0.25 inches.

DIAGNOSTICS

An exit status of 0 is returned if *files* were successfully processed.

FILES

```
/usr/lib/lp/postscript/postdaisy.ps
/usr/lib/lp/postscript/forms.ps
/usr/lib/lp/postscript/ps.requests
```

SEE ALSO

download(1), dpost(1), postdmd(1), postio(1), postmd(1), postprint(1), postreverse(1), posttek(1)

NAME

postdmd – PostScript translator for DMD bitmap files

SYNOPSIS

`/usr/lib/lp/postscript/postdmd` [*options*] [*files*]

DESCRIPTION

postdmd translates DMD bitmap *files*, as produced by *dmdps*, or *files* written in the Ninth Edition **bitfile**(9.5) format into PostScript and writes the results on the standard output. If no *files* are specified, or if – is one of the input *files*, the standard input is read. The following *options* are understood:

-b *num*	Pack the bitmap in the output file using *num* byte patterns. A value of 0 turns off all packing of the output file. By default, *num* is 6.
-c *num*	Print *num* copies of each page. By default only one copy is printed.
-f	Flip the sense of the bits in *files* before printing the bitmaps.
-m *num*	Magnify each logical page by the factor *num*. Pages are scaled uniformly about the origin, which by default is located at the center of each page. The default magnification is 1.0.
-n *num*	Print *num* logical pages on each piece of paper, where *num* can be any positive integer. By default *num* is set to 1.
-o *list*	Print pages whose numbers are given in the comma-separated *list*. The list contains single numbers N and ranges N1 – N2. A missing N1 means the lowest numbered page, a missing N2 means the highest.
-p *mode*	Print *files* in either portrait or landscape *mode*. Only the first character of *mode* is significant. The default *mode* is portrait.
-x *num*	Translate the origin *num* inches along the positive x axis. The default coordinate system has the origin fixed at the center of the page, with positive x to the right and positive y up the page. Positive *num* moves everything right. The default offset is 0 inches.
-y *num*	Translate the origin *num* inches along the positive y axis. Positive *num* moves everything up the page. The default offset is 0.

Only one bitmap is printed on each logical page, and each of the input *files* must contain complete descriptions of at least one bitmap. Decreasing the pattern size using the **-b** option may help throughput on printers with fast processors (such as PS-810s), while increasing the pattern size will often be the right move on older models (such as PS-800s).

DIAGNOSTICS

An exit status of 0 is returned if *files* were successfully processed.

FILES

```
/usr/lib/lp/postscript/postdmd.ps
/usr/lib/lp/postscript/forms.ps
/usr/lib/lp/postscript/ps.requests
```

SEE ALSO

download(1), dpost(1), postdaisy(1), postio(1), postmd(1), postprint(1), postreverse(1), posttek(1)

NAME

postio – serial interface for PostScript printers

SYNOPSIS

postio −1 *line* [*options*] [*files*]

DESCRIPTION

postio sends *files* to the PostScript printer attached to *line*. If no *files* are specified the standard input is sent. The first group of *options* should be sufficient for most applications:

−b *speed*　　　Transmit data over *line* at baud rate *speed*. Recognized baud rates are 1200, 2400, 4800, 9600, and 19200. The default *speed* is 9600 baud.

−1 *line*　　　Connect to the printer attached to *line*. In most cases there is no default and **postio** must be able to read and write *line*. If the *line* doesn't begin with a / it may be treated as a Datakit destination.

−q　　　Prevents status queries while *files* are being sent to the printer. When status queries are disabled a dummy message is appended to the log file before each block is transmitted.

−B *num*　　　Set the internal buffer size for reading and writing *files* to *num* bytes. By default *num* is 2048 bytes.

−D　　　Enable debug mode. Guarantees that everything read on *line* will be added to the log file (standard error by default).

−L *file*　　　Data received on *line* gets put in *file*. The default log *file* is standard error. Printer or status messages that don't show a change in state are not normally written to *file* but can be forced out using the −D option.

−P *string*　　　Send *string* to the printer before any of the input files. The default *string* is simple PostScript code that disables timeouts.

−R *num*　　　Run *postio* as a single process if *num* is 1 or as separate read and write processes if *num* is 2. By default **postio** runs as a single process.

The next two *options* are provided for users who expect to run **postio** on their own. Neither is suitable for use in spooler interface programs:

−i　　　Run the program in interactive mode. Any *files* are sent first and followed by the standard input. Forces separate read and write processes and overrides many other options. To exit interactive mode use your interrupt or quit character. To get a friendly interactive connection with the printer type **executive** on a line by itself.

−t　　　Data received on *line* and not recognized as printer or status information is written to the standard output. Forces separate read and write processes. Convenient if you have a PostScript program that will be returning useful data to the host.

The last option is not generally recommended and should only be used if all else fails to provide a reliable connection:

-s   Slow the transmission of data to the printer. Severely limits throughput, runs as a single process, disables the **–q** option, limits the internal buffer size to 1024 bytes, can use an excessive amount of CPU time, and does nothing in interactive mode.

The best performance will usually be obtained by using a large internal buffer (the **–B** option) and by running the program as separate read and write processes (the **–R 2** option). Inability to fork the additional process causes **postio** to continue as a single read/write process. When one process is used, only data sent to the printer is flow controlled.

The *options* are not all mutually exclusive. The **–i** option always wins, selecting its own settings for whatever is needed to run interactive mode, independent of anything else found on the command line. Interactive mode runs as separate read and write processes and few of the other *options* accomplish anything in the presence of the **–i** option. The **–t** option needs a reliable two way connection to the printer and therefore tries to force separate read and write processes. The **–s** option relies on the status query mechanism, so **–q** is disabled and the program runs as a single process.

In most cases **postio** starts by making a connection to *line* and then attempts to force the printer into the IDLE state by sending an appropriate sequence of **^T** (status query), **^C** (interrupt), and **^D** (end of job) characters. When the printer goes IDLE, *files* are transmitted along with an occasional **^T** (unless the **–q** option was used). After all the *files* are sent the program waits until it's reasonably sure the job is complete. Printer generated error messages received at any time except while establishing the initial connection (or when running interactive mode) cause **postio** to exit with a non-zero status. In addition to being added to the log file, printer error messages are also echoed to standard error.

EXAMPLES

Run as a single process at 9600 baud and send *file1* and *file2* to the printer attached to **/dev/tty01**:

     postio -1 /dev/tty01 *file1 file2*

Same as above except two processes are used, the internal buffer is set to 4096 bytes, and data returned by the printer gets put in file *log*:

     postio -R2 -B4096 -1/dev/tty01 -L*log file1 file2*

Establish an interactive connection with the printer at Datakit destination *my/printer*:

     postio -i -1 *my/printer*

Send file program to the printer connected to **/dev/tty22**, recover any data in file results, and put log messages in file *log*:

     postio -t -1 /dev/tty22 -L *log program* **>***results*

NOTES

The input *files* are handled as a single PostScript job. Sending several different jobs, each with their own internal end of job mark (^D) is not guaranteed to work properly. **postio** may quit before all the jobs have completed and could be restarted before the last one finishes.

All the capabilities described above may not be available on every machine or even across the different versions of the UNIX system that are currently supported by the program. For example, the code needed to connect to a Datakit destination may work only on System V and may require that the DKHOST software package be available at compile time.

There may be no default *line*, so using the −1 option is strongly recommended. If omitted, **postio** may attempt to connect to the printer using the standard output. If Datakit is involved, the −b option may be ineffective and attempts by **postio** to impose flow control over data in both directions may not work. The −q option can help if the printer is connected to RADIAN. The −s option is not generally recommended and should be used only if all other attempts to establish a reliable connection fail.

DIAGNOSTICS

An exit status of 0 is returned if the files ran successfully. System errors (such as an inability to open the line) set the low order bit in the exit status, while PostScript errors set bit 1. An exit status of 2 usually means the printer detected a PostScript error in the input *files*.

SEE ALSO

download(1), dpost(1), postdaisy(1), postdmd(1), postmd(1), postprint(1), postreverse(1), posttek(1)

NAME

postmd – matrix display program for PostScript printers

SYNOPSIS

/usr/lib/lp/postscript/postmd [options] [files]

DESCRIPTION

The postmd filter reads a series of floating point numbers from *files*, translates them into a PostScript gray scale image, and writes the results on the standard output. In a typical application the numbers might be the elements of a large matrix, written in row major order, while the printed image could help locate patterns in the matrix. If no *files* are specified, or if – is one of the input *files,* the standard input is read. The following *options* are understood:

-b *num*   Pack the bitmap in the output file using *num* byte patterns. A value of 0 turns off all packing of the output file. By default, *num* is 6.

-c *num*   Print *num* copies of each page. By default, only one copy is printed.

-d *dimen*   Sets the default matrix dimensions for all input *files* to *dimen*. The *dimen* string can be given as rows or rows**x**columns. If *columns* is omitted it will be set to rows. By default, postmd assumes each matrix is square and sets the number of rows and columns to the square root of the number of elements in each input file.

-g *list*   *List* is a comma or space separated string of integers, each lying between 0 and 255 inclusive, that assigns PostScript gray scales to the regions of the real line selected by the **-i** option. 255 corresponds to white, and 0, to black. The postmd filter assigns a default gray scale that omits white (that is, 255) and gets darker as the regions move from left to right along the real line.

-i *list*   *List* is a comma, space or slash(/) separated string of *N* floating point numbers that partition the real line into $2N+1$ regions. The *list* must be given in increasing numerical order. The partitions are used to map floating point numbers read from the input *files* into gray scale integers that are either assigned automatically by postmd or arbitrarily selected using the **-g** option. The default interval *list* is **-1,0,1**, which partions the real line into seven regions.

-m *num*   Magnify each logical page by the factor *num*. Pages are scaled uniformly about the origin which, by default, is located at the center of each page. The default magnification is 1.0.

-n *num*   Print *num* logical pages on each piece of paper, where *num* can be any positive integer. By default, *num* is set to 1.

-o *list*   Print pages whose numbers are given in the comma separated *list*. The list contains single numbers *N* and ranges *N1* – *N2*. A missing *N1* means the lowest numbered page, a missing *N2* means the highest.

-p *mode*	Print *files* in either portrait or landscape *mode*. Only the first character of *mode* is significant. The default *mode* is portrait.
-w *window*	*Window* is a comma or space separated list of four positive integers that select the upper left and lower right corners of a submatrix from each of the input *files*. Row and column indices start at 1 in the upper left corner and the numbers in the input *files* are assumed to be written in row major order. By default, the entire matrix is displayed.
-x *num*	Translate the origin *num* inches along the positive x axis. The default coordinate system has the origin fixed at the center of the page, with positive x to the right and positive y up the page. Positive *num* moves everything right. The default offset is 0 inches.
-y *num*	Translate the origin *num* inches along the positive y axis. Positive *num* moves everything up the page. The default offset is 0.

Only one matrix is displayed on each logical page, and each of the input *files* must contain complete descriptions of exactly one matrix. Matrix elements are floating point numbers arranged in row major order in each input file. White space, including newlines, is not used to determine matrix dimensions. By default, **postmd** assumes each matrix is square and sets the number of rows and columns to the square root of the number of elements in the input file. Supplying default dimensions on the command line with the **-d** option overrides this default behavior, and in that case the dimensions apply to all input *files*.

An optional header can be supplied with each input file and is used to set the matrix dimensions, the partition of the real line, the gray scale map, and a window into the matrix. The header consists of keyword/value pairs, each on a separate line. It begins on the first line of each input file and ends with the first unrecognized string, which should be the first matrix element. Values set in the header take precedence, but apply only to the current input file. Recognized header keywords are **dimension**, **interval**, **grayscale**, and **window**. The syntax of the value string that follows each keyword parallels what's accepted by the **-d**, **-i**, **-g**, and **-w** options.

EXAMPLES

For example, suppose file initially contains the 1000 numbers in a 20x50 matrix. Then you can produce exactly the same output by completing three steps. First, issue the following command line:

```
postmd -d20x50 -i"-100 100" -g0,128,254,128,0 file
```

Second, prepend the following header to *file*:

```
dimension 20x50
interval  -100.0 .100e+3
grayscale 0 128 254 128 0
```

Third, issue the following command line:

> **postmd** *file*

The interval list partitions the real line into five regions and the gray scale list maps numbers less than -100 or greater than 100 into 0 (that is, black), numbers equal to -100 or 100 into 128 (that is, 50 percent black), and numbers between -100 and 100 into 254 (that is, almost white).

NOTES

The largest matrix that can be adequately displayed is a function of the interval and gray scale lists, the printer resolution, and the paper size. A 600x600 matrix is an optimistic upper bound for a two element interval list (that is, five regions) using 8.5x11 inch paper on a 300 dpi printer.

Using white (that is, 255) in a gray scale list is not recommended and won't show up in the legend and bar graph that **postmd** displays below each image.

DIAGNOSTICS

An exit status of 0 is returned if *files* were successfully processed.

FILES

```
/usr/lib/lp/postscript/postmd.ps
/usr/lib/lp/postscript/forms.ps
/usr/lib/lp/postscript/ps.requests
```

SEE ALSO

dpost(1), postdaisy(1), postdmd(1), postio(1), postprint(1), postreverse(1), posttek(1)

NAME

postplot – PostScript translator for **plot** graphics files

SYNOPSIS

/usr/lib/lp/postscript/postplot [*options*] [*files*]

DESCRIPTION

The **postplot** filter translates **plot**(4) graphics *files* into PostScript and writes the results on the standard output. If no *files* are specified, or if – is one of the input *files*, the standard input is read. The following *options* are understood:

-c *num*   Print *num* copies of each page. By default, only one copy is printed.

-f *name*   Print text using font *name*. Any PostScript font can be used, although the best results will be obtained only with constant width fonts. The default font is Courier.

-m *num*   Magnify each logical page by the factor *num*. Pages are scaled uniformly about the origin which, by default, is located at the center of each page. The default magnification is 1.0.

-n *num*   Print *num* logical pages on each piece of paper, where *num* can be any positive integer. By default, *num* is set to 1.

-o *list*   Print pages whose numbers are given in the comma-separated *list*. The list contains single numbers *N* and ranges *N1* – *N2*. A missing *N1* means the lowest numbered page, a missing *N2* means the highest.

-p *mode*   Print *files* in either portrait or landscape *mode*. Only the first character of *mode* is significant. The default *mode* is landscape.

-w *num*   Set the line width used for graphics to *num* points, where a point is approximately 1/72 of an inch. By default, *num* is set to 0 points, which forces lines to be one pixel wide.

-x *num*   Translate the origin *num* inches along the positive x axis. The default coordinate system has the origin fixed at the center of the page, with positive x to the right and positive y up the page. Positive *num* moves everything right. The default offset is 0.0 inches.

-y *num*   Translate the origin *num* inches along the positive y axis. Positive *num* moves everything up the page. The default offset is 0.0.

DIAGNOSTICS

An exit status of 0 is returned if *files* were successfully processed.

NOTES

The default line width is too small for write-white print engines, such as the one used by the PS-2400.

FILES

/usr/lib/lp/postscript/postplot.ps
/usr/lib/lp/postscript/forms.ps
/usr/lib/lp/postscript/ps.requests

SEE ALSO
download(1), dpost(1), postdaisy(1), postdmd(1), postio(1), postmd(1), post-print(1), postreverse(1), plot(4)

NAME

    postprint – PostScript translator for text files

SYNOPSIS

    /usr/lib/lp/postscript/postprint [*options*] [*files*]

DESCRIPTION

    The **postprint** filter translates text *files* into PostScript and writes the results on the standard output. If no *files* are specified, or if – is one of the input *files*, the standard input is read. The following *options* are understood:

-c *num*	Print *num* copies of each page. By default, only one copy is printed.
-f *name*	Print *files* using font *name*. Any PostScript font can be used, although the best results will be obtained only with constant width fonts. The default font is Courier.
-l *num*	Set the length of a page to *num* lines. By default, *num* is 66. Setting *num* to 0 is allowed, and will cause *postprint* to guess a value, based on the point size that's being used.
-m *num*	Magnify each logical page by the factor *num*. Pages are scaled uniformly about the origin, which is located near the upper left corner of each page. The default magnification is 1.0.
-n *num*	Print *num* logical pages on each piece of paper, where *num* can be any positive integer. By default, *num* is set to 1.
-o *list*	Print pages whose numbers are given in the comma-separated *list*. The *list* contains single numbers N and ranges $N1 - N2$. A missing $N1$ means the lowest numbered page, a missing $N2$ means the highest.
-p *mode*	Print *files* in either portrait or landscape *mode*. Only the first character of *mode* is significant. The default *mode* is portrait.
-r *num*	Selects carriage return behavior. Carriage returns are ignored if *num* is 0, cause a return to column 1 if *num* is 1, and generate a newline if *num* is 2. The default *num* is 0.
-s *num*	Print *files* using point size *num*. When printing in landscape mode *num* is scaled by a factor that depends on the imaging area of the device. The default size for portrait mode is 10.
-t *num*	Assume tabs are set every *num* columns, starting with the first column. By default, tabs are set every 8 columns.
-x *num*	Translate the origin *num* inches along the positive x axis. The default coordinate system has the origin fixed near the upper left corner of the page, with positive x to the right and positive y down the page. Positive *num* moves everything right. The default offset is 0.25 inches.
-y *num*	Translate the origin *num* inches along the positive y axis. Positive *num* moves text up the page. The default offset is −0.25 inches.

A new logical page is started after 66 lines have been printed on the current page, or whenever an ASCII form feed character is read. The number of lines per page can be changed using the **-1** option. Unprintable ASCII characters are ignored, and lines that are too long are silently truncated by the printer.

EXAMPLES

To print *file1* and *file2* in landscape mode, issue the following command:

postprint -pland *file1 file2*

To print three logical pages on each physical page in portrait mode:

postprint -n3 *file*

DIAGNOSTICS

An exit status of 0 is returned if *files* were successfully processed.

FILES

/usr/lib/lp/postscript/postprint.ps
/usr/lib/lp/postscript/forms.ps
/usr/lib/lp/postscript/ps.requests

SEE ALSO

download(1), dpost(1), postdaisy(1), postdmd(1), postio(1), postmd(1), postreverse(1), posttek(1)

NAME

postreverse – reverse the page order in a PostScript file

SYNOPSIS

/usr/lib/lp/postscript/postreverse [*options*] [*file*]

DESCRIPTION

The **postreverse** filter reverses the page order in files that conform to Adobe's Version 1.0 or Version 2.0 file structuring conventions, and writes the results on the standard output. Only one input *file* is allowed and if no *file* is specified, the standard input is read. The following *options* are understood:

-o *list* Select pages whose numbers are given in the comma-separated *list*. The *list* contains single numbers *N* and ranges *N1 – N2*. A missing *N1* means the lowest numbered page, a missing *N2* means the highest.

-r Don't reverse the pages in *file*.

The **postreverse** filter can handle a limited class of files that violate page independence, provided all global definitions are bracketed by **%%BeginGlobal** and **%%EndGlobal** comments. In addition, files that mark the end of each page with **%%EndPage: label ordinal** comments will also reverse properly, provided the prologue and trailer sections can be located. If **postreverse** fails to find an **%%EndProlog** or **%%EndSetup** comment, the entire *file* is copied, unmodified, to the standard output.

Because global definitions are extracted from individual pages and put in the prologue, the output file can be minimally conforming, even if the input *file* wasn't.

EXAMPLES

To select pages 1 to 100 from *file* and reverse the pages:

  postreverse -o1-100 *file*

To print four logical pages on each physical page and reverse all the pages:

  postprint -n4 *file* **| postreverse**

To produce a minimally conforming file from output generated by **dpost** without reversing the pages:

  dpost *file* **| postreverse -r**

DIAGNOSTICS

An exit status of 0 is returned if *file* was successfully processed.

NOTES

No attempt has been made to deal with redefinitions of global variables or procedures. If standard input is used, the input *file* will be read three times before being reversed.

SEE ALSO

download(1), dpost(1), postdaisy(1), postdmd(1), postio(1), postmd(1), postprint(1), posttek(1)

NAME

posttek – PostScript translator for tektronix 4014 files

SYNOPSIS

/usr/lib/lp/postscript/posttek [*options*] [*files*]

DESCRIPTION

The posttek filter translates tektronix 4014 graphics *files* into PostScript and writes the results on the standard output. If no *files* are specified, or if – is one of the input *files*, the standard input is read. The following *options* are understood:

-c *num*   Print *num* copies of each page. By default, only one copy is printed.

-f *name*   Print text using font *name*. Any PostScript font can be used, although the best results will be obtained only with constant width fonts. The default font is Courier.

-m *num*   Magnify each logical page by the factor *num*. Pages are scaled uniformly about the origin which, by default, is located at the center of each page. The default magnification is 1.0.

-n *num*   Print *num* logical pages on each piece of paper, where *num* can be any positive integer. By default, *num* is set to 1.

-o *list*   Print pages whose numbers are given in the comma-separated *list*. The *list* contains single numbers N and ranges N1 – N2. A missing N1 means the lowest numbered page, a missing N2 means the highest.

-p *mode*   Print *files* in either portrait or landscape *mode*. Only the first character of *mode* is significant. The default *mode* is landscape.

-w *num*   Set the line width used for graphics to *num* points, where a point is approximately 1/72 of an inch. By default, *num* is set to 0 points, which forces lines to be one pixel wide.

-x *num*   Translate the origin *num* inches along the positive x axis. The default coordinate system has the origin fixed at the center of the page, with positive x to the right and positive y up the page. Positive *num* moves everything right. The default offset is 0.0 inches.

-y *num*   Translate the origin *num* inches along the positive y axis. Positive *num* moves everything up the page. The default offset is 0.0.

DIAGNOSTICS

An exit status of 0 is returned if *files* were successfully processed.

NOTES

The default line width is too small for write-white print engines, such as the one used by the PS-2400.

FILES

/usr/lib/lp/postscript/posttek.ps
/usr/lib/lp/postscript/forms.ps
/usr/lib/lp/postscript/ps.requests

SEE ALSO

download(1), dpost(1), postdaisy(1), postdmd(1), postio(1), postmd(1), post-print(1), postreverse(1)

NAME

pr – print files

SYNOPSIS

pr [[*–columns*] [*–wwidth*] [*–a*]] [*–eck*] [*–ick*] [*–drtfp*] [*+page*] [*–nck*] [*–ooffset*]
    [*–llength*] [*–sseparator*] [*–hheader*] [*–F*] [*file* ...]

pr [[*–m*] [*–wwidth*]] [*–eck*] [*–ick*] [*–drtfp*] [*+page*] [*–nck*] [*–ooffset*] [*–llength*]
    [*–sseparator*] [*–hheader*] [*–F*] [*file1 file2* ...]

DESCRIPTION

The **pr** command formats and prints the contents of a file. If *file* is **–**, or if no files are specified, **pr** assumes standard input. **pr** prints the named files on standard output.

By default, the listing is separated into pages, each headed by the page number, the date and time that the file was last modified, and the name of the file. Page length is 66 lines which includes 10 lines of header and trailer output. The header is composed of 2 blank lines, 1 line of text (can be altered with **–h**), and 2 blank lines; the trailer is 5 blank lines. For single column output, line width may not be set and is unlimited. For multicolumn output, line width may be set and the default is 72 columns. Diagnostic reports (failed options) are reported at the end of standard output associated with a terminal, rather than interspersed in the output. Pages are separated by series of line feeds rather than form feed characters.

By default, columns are of equal width, separated by at least one space; lines which do not fit are truncated. If the **–s** option is used, lines are not truncated and columns are separated by the *separator* character.

Either *–columns* or **–m** should be used to produce multi-column output. **–a** should only be used with *–columns* and not **–m**.

Command line options are

+page   Begin printing with page numbered *page* (default is 1).

–columns   Print *columns* columns of output (default is 1). Output appears as if **–e** and **–i** are on for multi-column output. May not use with **–m**.

–a   Print multi-column output across the page one line per column. *columns* must be greater than one. If a line is too long to fit in a column, it is truncated.

–m   Merge and print all files simultaneously, one per column. The maximum number of files that may be specified is eight. If a line is too long to fit in a column, it is truncated. May not use with *–column*.

–d   Double-space the output. Blank lines that result from double-spacing are dropped when they occur at the top of a page.

–eck   Expand input tabs to character positions $k+1$, $2*k+1$, $3*k+1$, etc. If k is 0 or is omitted, default tab settings at every eighth position are assumed. Tab characters in the input are expanded into the appropriate number of spaces. If c (any non-digit character) is given, it is treated as the input tab character (default for c is the tab character).

-ick	In output, replace white space wherever possible by inserting tabs to character positions $k+1$, $2*k+1$, $3*k+1$, etc. If k is 0 or is omitted, default tab settings at every eighth position are assumed. If c (any non-digit character) is given, it is treated as the output tab character (default for c is the tab character).
-nck	Provide k-digit line numbering (default for k is 5). The number occupies the first $k+1$ character positions of each column of single column output or each line of **-m** output. If c (any non-digit character) is given, it is appended to the line number to separate it from whatever follows (default for c is a tab).
-wwidth	Set the width of a line to *width* character positions (default is 72). This is effective only for multi-column output (*-column* and **-m**). There is no line limit for single column output.
-ooffset	Offset each line by *offset* character positions (default is 0). The number of character positions per line is the sum of the width and offset.
-llength	Set the length of a page to *length* lines (default is 66). A *length* of 0 specifies the default length. By default, output contains 5 lines of header and 5 lines of trailer leaving 56 lines for user-supplied text. When **-l**length is used and *length* exceeds 10, then *length*–10 lines are left per page for user supplied text. When *length* is 10 or less, header and trailer output is omitted to make room for user supplied text; see the **-t** option.
-h *header*	Use *header* as the text line of the header to be printed instead of the file name. **-h** is ignored when **-t** is specified or **-l**length is specified and the value of *length* is 10 or less. (**-h** is the only **pr** option requiring space between the option and argument.)
-p	Pause before beginning each page if the output device is a terminal. **pr** rings the terminal bell and waits for a carriage return.
-f	Use a single form-feed character for new pages (default is to use a sequence of line feeds). Pause before beginning the first page if the standard output is associated with a terminal.
-r	Print no diagnostic reports on files that cannot be opened.
-t	Print neither the five-line identifying header nor the five-line trailer normally supplied for each page. Quit printing after the last line of each file without spacing to the end of the page. Use of **-t** overrides the **-h** option.
-sseparator	Separate columns by the single character *separator* instead of by the appropriate number of spaces (default for *separator* is a tab). Prevents truncation of lines on multicolumn output unless **-w** is specified.
-F	Fold the lines of the input file. When used in multi-column mode (with the **-a** or **-m** options) lines will be folded to fit the current column's width, otherwise they will be folded to fit the current line width (80 columns).

EXAMPLES

Print **file1** and **file2** as a double-spaced, three-column listing headed by "**file list**":

        pr -3dh "file list" file1 file2

Copy **file1** to **file2**, expanding tabs to columns 10, 19, 28, 37, ... :

        pr -e9 -t < file1 > file2

Print **file1** and **file2** simultaneously in a two-column listing with no header or trailer where both columns have line numbers:

        pr -t -n file1 | pr -t -m -n file2 -

FILES

> **/dev/tty**∗   If standard output is directed to one of the special files **/dev/tty**∗, then other output directed to this terminal is delayed until standard output is completed. This prevents error messages from being interspersed throughout the output.

SEE ALSO

cat(1), fold(1), more(1), pg(1), page(1)

NAME

printenv – display environment variables currently set

SYNOPSIS

/usr/ucb/printenv [*variable*]

DESCRIPTION

printenv prints out the values of the variables in the environment. If a *variable* is specified, only its value is printed.

SEE ALSO

tset(1)

csh(1), echo(1), sh(1), stty(1) in the *User's Reference Manual*
environ(5) in the *System Administrator's Reference Manual*

DIAGNOSTICS

If a *variable* is specified and it is not defined in the environment, **printenv** returns an exit status of **1**.

NAME

printf – print formatted output

SYNOPSIS

printf *format* [*arg* . . .]

DESCRIPTION

The **printf** command converts, formats, and prints its *args* under control of the *format*. It fully supports conversion specifications for strings (**%s** descriptor); however, the results are undefined for the other conversion specifications supported by **printf**(3S).

format   a character string that contains three types of objects: 1) plain characters, which are simply copied to the output stream; 2) conversion specifications, each of which results in fetching zero or more *args*; and 3) C-language escape sequences, which are translated into the corresponding characters.

arg   string(s) to be printed under the control of *format*. The results are undefined if there are insufficient *args* for the format. If the format is exhausted while *args* remain, the excess *args* are simply ignored.

Each conversion specification is introduced by the character **%**. After the **%**, the following appear in sequence:

An optional field, consisting of a decimal digit string followed by a **$**, specifying the next *arg* to be converted. If this field is not provided, the *arg* following the last *arg* converted is used.

An optional decimal digit string specifying a minimum *field width*. If the converted value has fewer characters than the field width, it is padded on the left (or right, if the left-adjustment flag '–' has been given) to the field width. The padding is with blanks unless the field width digit string starts with a zero, in which case the padding is with zeros.

An optional *precision* that gives the maximum number of characters to be printed from a string in **%s** conversion. The precision takes the form of a period (**.**) followed by a decimal digit string; a null digit string is treated as zero (nothing is printed). Padding specified by the precision overrides the padding specified by the field width. That is, if *precision* is specified, its value is used to control the number of characters printed.

A field width or precision or both may be indicated by an asterisk (∗) instead of a digit string. In this case, an integer *arg* supplies the field width or precision. The *arg* that is actually converted is not fetched until the conversion letter is seen, so the *args* specifying field width or precision must appear *before* the *arg* (if any) to be converted. A negative field width argument is taken as a '–' (left-adjustment) flag followed by a positive field width. If the precision argument is negative, it is changed to zero (nothing is printed). In no case does a non-existent or small field width cause truncation of a field; if the result of a conversion is wider than the field width, the field is simply expanded to contain the conversion result.

The conversion characters and their meanings are:

%s   The *arg* is taken to be a string and characters from the string are printed until a null character (\0) is encountered or the number of characters indicated by the precision specification is reached. If the precision is missing, it is taken to be infinite, so all characters up to the first null character are printed. A null value for *arg* yields undefined results.

%%   Print a %; no argument is converted.

EXAMPLES

The command

        printf '%s %s %s\n' Good Morning World

results in the output:

        Good Morning World

The following command produces the same output.

        printf '%2$s %s %1$s\n' World Good Morning

Here is an example that prints the first 6 characters of $PATH left-adjusted in a 10-character field:

        printf 'First 6 chars of %s are %-10.6s.\n' $PATH $PATH

If $PATH has the value /usr/bin:/usr/local/bin, then the above command would print the following output:

        First 6 chars of /usr/bin:/usr/local/bin are /usr/b   .

SEE ALSO

printf(3S) in the *Programmer's Reference Manual*

NAME

priocntl – process scheduler control

SYNOPSIS

priocntl -l
priocntl -d [-i *idtype*] [*idlist*]
priocntl -s [-c *class*] [*class-specific options*] [-i *idtype*] [*idlist*]
priocntl -e [-c *class*] [*class-specific options*] *command* [*argument(s)*]

DESCRIPTION

The priocntl command displays or sets scheduling parameters of the specified
process(es). It can also be used to display the current configuration information
for the system's process scheduler or execute a command with specified scheduling parameters.

Processes fall into distinct classes with a separate scheduling policy applied to
each class. The two process classes currently supported are the real-time class
and the time-sharing class. The characteristics of these two classes and the class-
specific options they accept are described below under the headings REAL-TIME
CLASS and TIME-SHARING CLASS. With appropriate permissions, the priocntl
command can change the class and other scheduling parameters associated with a
running process.

In the default configuration, a runnable real-time process runs before any other
process. Therefore, inappropriate use of real-time processes can have a dramatic
negative impact on system performance.

The command

        priocntl -l

displays a list of classes currently configured in the system along with class-
specific information about each class. The format of the class-specific information
displayed is described under the appropriate heading below.

The -d and -s options to priocntl allow the user to display or set the scheduling parameters associated with a set of processes. The -i option and its associated *idtype* argument, together with the *idlist* arguments to priocntl (if any),
specify one or more processes to which the priocntl command is to apply. The
interpretation of *idlist* depends on the value of *idtype*. The valid *idtype* arguments
and corresponding interpretations of *idlist* are as follows:

-i pid   *idlist* is a list of process IDs. The priocntl command applies to
          the specified processes.

-i ppid   *idlist* is a list of parent process IDs. The priocntl command
          applies to all processes whose parent process ID is in the list.

-i pgid   *idlist* is a list of process group IDs. The priocntl command
          applies to all processes in the specified process groups.

-i sid   *idlist* is a list of session IDs. The priocntl command applies to all
          processes in the specified sessions.

-i class   *idlist* consists of a single class name (**RT** for real-time or **TS** for time-sharing). The **priocntl** command applies to all processes in the specified class.

-i uid   *idlist* is a list of user IDs. The **priocntl** command applies to all processes with an effective user ID equal to an ID from the list.

-i gid   *idlist* is a list of group IDs. The **priocntl** command applies to all processes with an effective group ID equal to an ID from the list.

-i all   The **priocntl** command applies to all existing processes. No *idlist* should be specified (if one is it is ignored). The permission restrictions described below still apply.

If the **-i** *idtype* option is omitted when using the **-d** or **-s** options the default *idtype* of **pid** is assumed.

If an *idlist* is present it must appear last on the command line and the elements of the list must be separated by white space. If no *idlist* is present an *idtype* argument of **pid**, **ppid**, **pgid**, **sid**, **class**, **uid**, or **gid** specifies the process ID, parent process ID, process group ID, session ID, class, user ID, or group ID respectively of the **priocntl** command itself.

The command

    priocntl **-d** [**-i** *idtype*] [*idlist*]

displays the class and class-specific scheduling parameters of the process(es) specified by *idtype* and *idlist*.

The command

    priocntl **-s** [**-c** *class*] [*class-specific options*] [**-i** *idtype*] [*idlist*]

sets the class and class-specific parameters of the specified processes to the values given on the command line. The **-c** *class* option specifies the class to be set. (The valid *class* arguments are **RT** for real-time or **TS** for time-sharing). The class-specific parameters to be set are specified by the class-specific options as explained under the appropriate heading below. If the **-c** *class* option is omitted, *idtype* and *idlist* must specify a set of processes which are all in the same class, otherwise an error results. If no class-specific options are specified the process's class-specific parameters are set to the default values for the class specified by **-c** *class* (or to the default parameter values for the process's current class if the **-c** *class* option is also omitted).

In order to change the scheduling parameters of a process using **priocntl** the real or effective user ID of the user invoking **priocntl** must match the real or effective user ID of the receiving process or the effective user ID of the user must be super-user. These are the minimum permission requirements enforced for all classes. An individual class may impose additional permissions requirements when setting processes to that class or when setting class-specific scheduling parameters.

When *idtype* and *idlist* specify a set of processes, **priocntl** acts on the processes in the set in an implementation-specific order. If **priocntl** encounters an error for one or more of the target processes, it may or may not continue through the set of processes, depending on the nature of the error. If the error is related to permissions, **priocntl** prints an error message and then continue through the process set, resetting the parameters for all target processes for which the user has appropriate permissions. If **priocntl** encounters an error other than permissions, it does not continue through the process set but prints an error message and exits immediately.

A special **sys** scheduling class exists for the purpose of scheduling the execution of certain special system processes (such as the swapper process). It is not possible to change the class of any process to **sys**. In addition, any processes in the **sys** class that are included in the set of processes specified by *idtype* and *idlist* are disregarded by **priocntl**. For example, if *idtype* were **uid**, an *idlist* consisting of a zero would specify all processes with a UID of zero except processes in the **sys** class and (if changing the parameters using the **-s** option) the **init** process.

The **init** process may be assigned to any class configured on the system, but the time-sharing class is almost always the appropriate choice. (Other choices may be highly undesirable; see the *System Administrator's Guide* for more information.)

The command

> **priocntl -e** [**-c** *class*] [*class-specific options*] *command* [*argument(s)*]

executes the specified command with the class and scheduling parameters specified on the command line (*arguments* are the arguments to the command). If the **-c** *class* option is omitted the command is run in the user's current class.

REAL-TIME CLASS

The real-time class provides a fixed priority preemptive scheduling policy for those processes requiring fast and deterministic response and absolute user/application control of scheduling priorities. If the real-time class is configured in the system it should have exclusive control of the highest range of scheduling priorities on the system. This ensures that a runnable real-time process is given CPU service before any process belonging to any other class.

The real-time class has a range of real-time priority (*rtpri*) values that may be assigned to processes within the class. Real-time priorities range from 0 to x, where the value of x is configurable and can be displayed for a specific installation by using the command

> **priocntl -l**

The real-time scheduling policy is a fixed priority policy. The scheduling priority of a real-time process never changes except as the result of an explicit request by the user/application to change the *rtpri* value of the process.

For processes in the real-time class, the *rtpri* value is, for all practical purposes, equivalent to the scheduling priority of the process. The *rtpri* value completely determines the scheduling priority of a real-time process relative to other processes within its class. Numerically higher *rtpri* values represent higher priorities. Since the real-time class controls the highest range of scheduling priorities in the system it is guaranteed that the runnable real-time process with the highest *rtpri* value is always selected to run before any other process in the system.

In addition to providing control over priority, **priocntl** provides for control over the length of the time quantum allotted to processes in the real-time class. The time quantum value specifies the maximum amount of time a process may run assuming that it does not complete or enter a resource or event wait state (**sleep**). Note that if another process becomes runnable at a higher priority the currently running process may be preempted before receiving its full time quantum.

The command

   priocntl −d [**−i** *idtype*] [*idlist*]

displays the real-time priority and time quantum (in millisecond resolution) for each real-time process in the set specified by *idtype* and *idlist*.

The valid class-specific options for setting real-time parameters are:

   −p *rtpri*   Set the real-time priority of the specified process(es) to *rtpri*.

   −t *tqntm* [**−r** *res*]   Set the time quantum of the specified process(es) to *tqntm*. You may optionally specify a resolution as explained below.

Any combination of the **−p** and **−t** options may be used with **priocntl −s** or **priocntl −e** for the real-time class. If an option is omitted and the process is currently real-time the associated parameter is unaffected. If an option is omitted when changing the class of a process to real-time from some other class, the associated parameter is set to a default value. The default value for *rtpri* is 0 and the default for time quantum is dependent on the value of *rtpri* and on the system configuration; see **rt_dptbl**(4).

When using the **−t** *tqntm* option you may optionally specify a resolution using the **−r** *res* option. (If no resolution is specified, millisecond resolution is assumed.) If *res* is specified it must be a positive integer between 1 and 1,000,000,000 inclusive and the resolution used is the reciprocal of *res* in seconds. For example, specifying **−t 10 −r 100** would set the resolution to hundredths of a second and the resulting time quantum length would be 10/100 seconds (one tenth of a second). Although very fine (nanosecond) resolution may be specified, the time quantum length is rounded up by the system to the next integral multiple of the system clock's resolution. For example the finest resolution currently available on the 3B2 is 10 milliseconds (1 "tick"). If the **−t** and **−r** options are used to specify a time quantum of 34 milliseconds, it is rounded up to 4 ticks (40 milliseconds) on the 3B2. Requests for time quantums of zero or quantums greater than the (typically very large) implementation-specific maximum quantum result in an error.

In order to change the class of a process to real-time (from any other class) the user invoking **priocntl** must have super-user privileges. In order to change the *rtpri* value or time quantum of a real-time process the user invoking **priocntl** must either be super-user, or must currently be in the real-time class (shell running as a real-time process) with a real or effective user ID matching the real or effective user ID of the target process.

The real-time priority and time quantum are inherited across the **fork**(2) and **exec**(2) system calls.

Examples

    `priocntl -s -c RT -t 1 -r 10 -i` *idtype idlist*

sets the class of any non-real-time processes selected by *idtype* and *idlist* to real-time and sets their real-time priority to the default value of 0. The real-time priorities of any processes currently in the real-time class are unaffected. The time quantums of all of the specified processes are set to 1/10 seconds.

    `priocntl -e -c RT -p 15 -t 20` *command*

executes *command* in the real-time class with a real-time priority of 15 and a time quantum of 20 milliseconds.

TIME-SHARING CLASS

The time-sharing scheduling policy provides for a fair and effective allocation of the CPU resource among processes with varying CPU consumption characteristics. The objectives of the time-sharing policy are to provide good response time to interactive processes and good throughput to CPU-bound jobs while providing a degree of user/application control over scheduling.

The time-sharing class has a range of time-sharing user priority (*tsupri*) values that may be assigned to processes within the class. User priorities range from $-x$ to $+x$, where the value of x is configurable. The range for a specific installation can be displayed by using the command

    `priocntl -l`

The purpose of the user priority is to provide some degree of user/application control over the scheduling of processes in the time-sharing class. Raising or lowering the *tsupri* value of a process in the time-sharing class raises or lowers the scheduling priority of the process. It is not guaranteed, however, that a time-sharing process with a higher *tsupri* value will run before one with a lower *tsupri* value. This is because the *tsupri* value is just one factor used to determine the scheduling priority of a time-sharing process. The system may dynamically adjust the internal scheduling priority of a time-sharing process based on other factors such as recent CPU usage.

In addition to the system-wide limits on user priority (displayed with **priocntl** **-l**), there is a per process user priority limit (*tsuprilim*), which specifies the maximum *tsupri* value that may be set for a given process.

The command

    `priocntl -d [-i` *idtype*`]` *[idlist]*

displays the user priority and user priority limit for each time-sharing process in the set specified by *idtype* and *idlist*.

The valid class-specific options for setting time-sharing parameters are:

    -m *tsuprilim*   Set the user priority limit of the specified process(es) to *tsuprilim*.

    -p *tsupri*   Set the user priority of the specified process(es) to *tsupri*.

Any time-sharing process may lower its own *tsuprilim* (or that of another process with the same user ID). Only a time-sharing process with super-user privileges may raise a *tsuprilim*. When changing the class of a process to time-sharing from some other class, super-user privileges are required in order to set the initial *tsuprilim* to a value greater than zero.

Any time-sharing process may set its own *tsupri* (or that of another process with the same user ID) to any value less than or equal to the process's *tsuprilim*. Attempts to set the *tsupri* above the *tsuprilim* (and/or set the *tsuprilim* below the *tsupri*) result in the *tsupri* being set equal to the *tsuprilim*.

Any combination of the **-l** and **-p** options may be used with **priocntl -s** or **priocntl -e** for the time-sharing class. If an option is omitted and the process is currently time-sharing the associated parameter is normally unaffected. The exception is when the **-p** option is omitted and **-l** is used to set a *tsuprilim* below the current *tsupri*. In this case the *tsupri* is set equal to the *tsuprilim* which is being set. If an option is omitted when changing the class of a process to time-sharing from some other class, the associated parameter is set to a default value. The default value for *tsuprilim* is 0 and the default for *tsupri* is to set it equal to the *tsuprilim* value which is being set.

The time-sharing user priority and user priority limit are inherited across the **fork**(2) and **exec**(2) system calls.

Examples

    priocntl -s -c TS -i *idtype idlist*

sets the class of any non-time-sharing processes selected by *idtype* and *idlist* to time-sharing and sets both their user priority limit and user priority to 0. Processes already in the time-sharing class are unaffected.

    priocntl -e -c TS -l 0 -p -15 *command* [*arguments*]

executes *command* with the arguments *arguments* in the time-sharing class with a user priority limit of 0 and a user priority of −15.

SEE ALSO

    ps(1), **nice**(1), **priocntl**(2), rt_dptbl(4)

DIAGNOSTICS

    priocntl prints the following error messages:

    Process(es) not found: None of the specified processes exists.

    Specified processes from different classes: The **-s** option is being used to set parameters, the **-c** *class* option is not present, and processes from more than one class are specified.

    Invalid option or argument: An unrecognized or invalid option or option argument is used.

NAME

prof – display profile data

SYNOPSIS

prof [-t | c | a | n] [-o | x] [-g | l] [-z] [-h] [-s] [-m *mdata*] -V [*prog*]

DESCRIPTION

The **prof** command interprets a profile file produced by the **monitor** function. The symbol table in the object file *prog* (**a.out** by default) is read and correlated with a profile file (**mon.out** by default). For each external text symbol the percentage of time spent executing between the address of that symbol and the address of the next is printed, together with the number of times that function was called and the average number of milliseconds per call.

The mutually exclusive options –t, –c, –a, and –n determine the type of sorting of the output lines:

-t   Sort by decreasing percentage of total time (default).

-c   Sort by decreasing number of calls.

-a   Sort by increasing symbol address.

-n   Sort lexically by symbol name.

The mutually exclusive options –o and –x specify the printing of the address of each symbol monitored:

-o   Print each symbol address (in octal) along with the symbol name.

-x   Print each symbol address (in hexadecimal) along with the symbol name.

The mutually exclusive options –g and –l control the type of symbols to be reported. The –l option must be used with care; it applies the time spent in a static function to the preceding (in memory) global function, instead of giving the static function a separate entry in the report. If all static functions are properly located (see example below), this feature can be very useful. If not, the resulting report may be misleading.

Assume that **A** and **B** are global functions and only **A** calls static function **S**. If **S** is located immediately after **A** in the source code (that is, if **S** is properly located), then, with the –l option, the amount of time spent in **A** can easily be determined, including the time spent in **S**. If, however, both **A** and **B** call **S**, then, if the –l option is used, the report will be misleading; the time spent during **B**'s call to **S** will be attributed to **A**, making it appear as if more time had been spent in **A** than really had. In this case, function **S** cannot be properly located.

-g   Include static (non-global) functions.

-l   Do not include static (non-global) functions (default).

The following options may be used in any combination:

-z   Include all symbols in the profile range, even if associated with zero number of calls and zero time.

  -h Suppress the heading normally printed on the report. (This is useful if the report is to be processed further.)

  -s Print a summary of several of the monitoring parameters and statistics on the standard error output.

 -m *mdata*

    Use file *mdata* instead of **mon.out** as the input profile file.

  -V Print **prof** version information on the standard error output.

A program creates a profile file if it has been link edited with the **-p** option of **cc**. This option to the **cc** command arranges for calls to **monitor** at the beginning and end of execution. It is the call to **monitor** at the end of execution that causes the system to write a profile file. The number of calls to a function is tallied if the **-p** option was used when the file containing the function was compiled.

The name of the file created by a profiled program is controlled by the environmental variable **PROFDIR**. If **PROFDIR** is not set, **mon.out** is produced in the directory current when the program terminates. If **PROFDIR**=*string*, *string*/*pid.progname* is produced, where *progname* consists of **argv[0]** with any path prefix removed, and *pid* is the process ID of the program. If **PROFDIR** is set, but null, no profiling output are produced.

A single function may be split into subfunctions for profiling by means of the **MARK** macro [see **prof**(5)].

FILES

  mon.out default profile file
  a.out   default namelist (object) file

SEE ALSO

  cc(1), **lprof**(1), **exit**(2), **profil**(2), **monitor**(3C), **prof**(5)
  The "**lprof**" chapter in the *Programmer's Guide: ANSI C and Programming Support Tools*

NOTES

  The times reported in successive identical runs may show variances because of varying cache-hit ratios that result from sharing the cache with other processes. Even if a program seems to be the only one using the machine, hidden background or asynchronous processes may blur the data. In rare cases, the clock ticks initiating recording of the program counter may "beat" with loops in a program, grossly distorting measurements. Call counts are always recorded precisely, however.

  Only programs that call **exit** or return from **main** are guaranteed to produce a profile file, unless a final call to **monitor** is explicitly coded.

  The times for static functions are attributed to the preceding external text symbol if the **-g** option is not used. However, the call counts for the preceding function are still correct; that is, the static function call counts are not added to the call counts of the external function.

If more than one of the options −t, −c, −a, and −n is specified, the last option specified is used and the user is warned.

Profiling may be used with dynamically linked executables, but care must be applied. Currently, shared objects cannot be profiled with **prof**. Thus, when a profiled, dynamically linked program is executed, only the "main" portion of the image is sampled. This means that all time spent outside of the "main" object, that is, time spent in a shared object, will not be included in the profile summary; the total time reported for the program may be less than the total time used by the program.

Because the time spent in a shared object cannot be accounted for, the use of shared objects should be minimized whenever a program is profiled with **prof**. If possible, the program should be linked statically before being profiled.

Consider an extreme case. A profiled program dynamically linked with the shared C library spends 100 units of time in some **libc** routine, say, **malloc**. Suppose **malloc** is called only from routine **B** and **B** consumes only 1 unit of time. Suppose further that routine **A** consumes 10 units of time, more than any other routine in the "main" (profiled) portion of the image. In this case, **prof** will conclude that most of the time is being spent in **A** and almost no time is being spent in **B**. From this it will be almost impossible to tell that the greatest improvement can be made by looking at routine **B** and not routine **A**. The value of the profiler in this case is severely degraded; the solution is to use archives as much as possible for profiling.

NAME

profiler: **prfld, prfstat, prfdc, prfsnap, prfpr** – UNIX system profiler

SYNOPSIS

/usr/sbin/prfld [*system_namelist*]
/usr/sbin/prfstat on
/usr/sbin/prfstat off
/usr/sbin/prfdc *file* [*period* [*off_hour*]]
/usr/sbin/prfsnap *file*
/usr/sbin/prfpr *file* [*cutoff* [*system_namelist*]]

DESCRIPTION

prfld, prfstat, prfdc, prfsnap, and **prfpr** form a system of programs to facilitate an activity study of the UNIX operating system.

prfld is used to initialize the recording mechanism in the system. It generates a table containing the starting address of each system subroutine as extracted from *system_namelist*.

prfstat is used to enable or disable the sampling mechanism. Profiler overhead is less than 1% as calculated for 500 text addresses. **prfstat** will also reveal the number of text addresses being measured.

prfdc and **prfsnap** perform the data collection function of the profiler by copying the current value of all the text address counters to a file where the data can be analyzed. **prfdc** will store the counters into *file* every *period* minutes and will turn off at *off_hour* (valid values for *off_hour* are **0–24**). **prfsnap** collects data at the time of invocation only, appending the counter values to *file*.

prfpr formats the data collected by **prfdc** or **prfsnap**. Each text address is converted to the nearest text symbol (as found in *system_namelist*) and is printed if the percent activity for that range is greater than *cutoff*.

FILES

/dev/prf   interface to profile data and text addresses

/stand/unix   default for system namelist file

NAME

profiler: **prfld**, **prfstat**, **prfdc**, **prfsnap**, **prfpr** – UNIX system profiler

SYNOPSIS

/usr/sbin/prfld [*system_namelist*]
/usr/sbin/prfstat on
/usr/sbin/prfstat off
/usr/sbin/prfdc *file* [*period* [*off_hour*]]
/usr/sbin/prfsnap *file*
/usr/sbin/prfpr [**-P**] *file* [*cutoff* [*system_namelist*]]

DESCRIPTION

prfld, **prfstat**, **prfdc**, **prfsnap**, and **prfpr** form a system of programs to facilitate an activity study of the UNIX operating system.

prfld is used to initialize the recording mechanism in the system. It generates a table containing the starting address of each system subroutine as extracted from *system_namelist*.

prfstat is used to enable or disable the sampling mechanism. Profiler overhead is less than 1% as calculated for 500 text addresses. **prfstat** will also reveal the number of text addresses being measured.

prfdc and **prfsnap** perform the data collection function of the profiler by copying the current value of all the text address counters to a file where the data can be analyzed. **prfdc** will store the counters into *file* every *period* minutes and will turn off at *off_hour* (valid values for *off_hour* are **0–24**). **prfsnap** collects data at the time of invocation only, appending the counter values to *file*.

prfpr formats the data collected by **prfdc** or **prfsnap**. Each text address is converted to the nearest text symbol (as found in *system_namelist*) and is printed if the percent activity for that range is greater than *cutoff*. By default, system-wide totals are printed.

Specifying the **-P** option prints the per-processor total.

FILES

/dev/prf   interface to profile data and text addresses

/stand/unix   default for system namelist file

NAME

prs – print an SCCS file

SYNOPSIS

prs [–**d**[*dataspec*]] [–**r**[*SID*]] [–**e**] [–**l**] [–**c**[*date–time*]] [–**a**] *files*

DESCRIPTION

prs prints, on the standard output, parts or all of an SCCS file [see **sccsfile**(4)] in a user-supplied format. If a directory is named, **prs** prints the files in that directory, except the non-SCCS files (last component of the path name does not begin with **s.**) and unreadable files. If a name of – is given, the standard input is read; each line of the standard input is taken to be the name of an SCCS file or directory to be processed. **prs** silently ignores non-SCCS files and unreadable files.

Arguments to **prs**, which may appear in any order, consist of keyletter arguments and file names.

The keyletter arguments apply independently to each named file:

    –**d**[*dataspec*]   Specifies the output data specification. The *dataspec* is a string consisting of SCCS file data keywords (see the DATA KEYWORDS section) interspersed with optional user-supplied text.

    –**r**[*SID*]   Specifies the SCCS identification (SID) string of a delta for which information is desired. The default is the top delta.

    –**e**   Requests information for all deltas created earlier than and including the delta designated via the –**r** keyletter or the date given by the –**c** option.

    –**l**   Requests information for all deltas created later than and including the delta designated via the –**r** keyletter or the date given by the –**c** option.

    –**c**[*date–time*]   The cutoff date–time in the form:

                    YY[*MM*[*DD*[*HH*[*MM*[*SS*]]]]]]

                  Units omitted from the date–time default to their maximum possible values; for example, –**c7502** is equivalent to –**c750228235959**. Any number of non-numeric characters may separate the fields of the cutoff date; for example, "–**c77/2/2 9:22:25**".

    –**a**   Requests printing of information for both removed, that is, delta type = R, [see **rmdel**(1)] and existing, that is, delta type = D, deltas. If the –**a** keyletter is not specified, information for existing deltas only is provided.

DATA KEYWORDS

Data keywords specify those parts of an SCCS file that are to be retrieved and output. All parts of an SCCS file [see **sccsfile**(4)] have an associated data keyword. There is no limit on the number of times a data keyword may appear in a *dataspec*.

The information printed by **prs** consists of: (1) the user-supplied text; and (2) appropriate values (extracted from the SCCS file) substituted for the recognized data keywords in the order of appearance in the *dataspec*. The format of a data keyword value is either "Simple" (S), in which keyword substitution is direct, or "Multi-line" (M), in which keyword substitution is followed by a carriage return.

User-supplied text is any text other than recognized data keywords. A tab is specified by \t and carriage return/new-line is specified by \n. The default data keywords are:

```
":Dt:\t:DL:\nMRs:\n:MR:COMMENTS:\n:C:"
```

Keyword	Data Item	File Section	Value	Format
:Dt:	Delta information	Delta Table	See below*	S
:DL:	Delta line statistics	"	:Li:/:Ld:/:Lu:	S
:Li:	Lines inserted by Delta	"	*nnnnn*	S
:Ld:	Lines deleted by Delta	"	*nnnnn*	S
:Lu:	Lines unchanged by Delta	"	*nnnnn*	S
:DT:	Delta type	"	D *or* R	S
:I:	SCCS ID string (SID)	"	:R:.:L:.:B:.:S:	S
:R:	Release number	"	*nnnn*	S
:L:	Level number	"	*nnnn*	S
:B:	Branch number	"	*nnnn*	S
:S:	Sequence number	"	*nnnn*	S
:D:	Date Delta created	"	:Dy:/:Dm:/:Dd:	S
:Dy:	Year Delta created	"	*nn*	S
:Dm:	Month Delta created	"	*nn*	S
:Dd:	Day Delta created	"	*nn*	S
:T:	Time Delta created	"	:Th:::Tm:::Ts:	S
:Th:	Hour Delta created	"	*nn*	S
:Tm:	Minutes Delta created	"	*nn*	S
:Ts:	Seconds Delta created	"	*nn*	S
:P:	Programmer who created Delta	"	*logname*	S
:DS:	Delta sequence number	"	*nnnn*	S
:DP:	Predecessor Delta seq-no.	"	*nnnn*	S
:DI:	Seq-no. of deltas incl., excl., ignored	"	:Dn:/:Dx:/:Dg:	S
:Dn:	Deltas included (seq #)	"	:DS: :DS:...	S
:Dx:	Deltas excluded (seq #)	"	:DS: :DS:...	S
:Dg:	Deltas ignored (seq #)	"	:DS: :DS:...	S
:MR:	MR numbers for delta	"	*text*	M
:C:	Comments for delta	"	*text*	M
:UN:	User names	User Names	*text*	M
:FL:	Flag list	Flags	*text*	M

Keyword	Data Item	File Section	Value	Format
:Y:	Module type flag	"	*text*	S
:MF:	MR validation flag	"	**yes** or **no**	S
:MP:	MR validation pgm name	"	*text*	S
:KF:	Keyword error/warning flag	"	**yes** or **no**	S
:KV:	Keyword validation string	"	*text*	S
:BF:	Branch flag	"	**yes** or **no**	S
:J:	Joint edit flag	"	**yes** or **no**	S
:LK:	Locked releases	"	:R: ...	S
:Q:	User-defined keyword	"	*text*	S
:M:	Module name	"	*text*	S
:FB:	Floor boundary	"	:R:	S
:CB:	Ceiling boundary	"	:R:	S
:Ds:	Default SID	"	:I:	S
:ND:	Null delta flag	"	**yes** or **no**	S
:FD:	File descriptive text	Comments	*text*	M
:BD:	Body	Body	*text*	M
:GB:	Gotten body	"	*text*	M
:W:	A form of what(1) string	N/A	:Z::M:\t:I:	S
:A:	A form of what(1) string	N/A	:Z::Y: :M: :I::Z:	S
:Z:	what(1) string delimiter	N/A	@(#)	S
:F:	SCCS file name	N/A	*text*	S
:PN:	SCCS file path name	N/A	*text*	S

* :Dt: = :DT: :I: :D: :T: :P: :DS: :DP:

EXAMPLES

The command

```
prs -d"Users and/or user IDs for :F: are:\n:UN:" s.file
```

may produce on the standard output:

```
Users and/or user IDs for s.file are:
xyz
131
abc
```

The command

```
prs -d"Newest delta for pgm :M:: :I: Created :D: By :P:" -r
s.file
```

may produce on the standard output:

```
Newest delta for pgm main.c: 3.7 Created 77/12/1 By cas
```

The default case:

```
prs s.file
```

produces on the standard output:

```
D 1.1 77/12/1 00:00:00 cas 1 000000/00000/00000
MRs:
bl78-12345
bl79-54321
COMMENTS:
this is the comment line for s.file initial delta
```

for each delta table entry of the "D" type. The only keyletter argument allowed to be used with the "special case" is the −a keyletter.

FILES

/var/tmp/pr?????

SEE ALSO

admin(1), delta(1), get(1), help(1), sccsfile(4)

DIAGNOSTICS

Use help(1) for explanations.

NAME

prt – display the delta and commentary history of an SCCS file

SYNOPSIS

/usr/ucb/prt [–abdefistu] [–y[SID]] [–c[cutoff]] [–r[rev-cutoff]] filename . . .

DESCRIPTION

Note: the **prt** command is an older version of **prs**(1) that in most circumstances is more convenient to use, but is less flexible than **prs**.

prt prints part or all of an SCCS file in a useful format. If a directory is named, **prt** behaves as though each file in the directory were specified as a named file, except that non-SCCS files (last component of the pathname does not begin with **s.**) and unreadable files are silently ignored. If a name of '–' is given, the standard input is read; each line of the standard input is taken to be the name of an SCCS file to be processed. Again, non-SCCS files and unreadable files are silently ignored.

The following options are available with **prt** :

–a   Print those types of deltas normally not printed by the **d** keyletter. These are types **R** (removed). This keyletter is effective only if the **d** keyletter is also specified (or assumed).

–b   Print the body of the SCCS file.

–d   This keyletter normally prints delta table entries of the **D** type.

–e   This keyletter implies the **d, i, u, f,** and **t** keyletters and is provided for convenience.

–f   Print the flags of the named file.

–i   Print the serial numbers of those deltas included, excluded, and ignored. This keyletter is effective only if the **d** keyletter is also specified (or assumed).

The following format is used to print those portions of the SCCS file as specified by the above keyletters. The printing of each delta table entry is preceded by a NEWLINE.

- Type of delta (**D** or **R**).
- SPACE.
- SCCS identification string (SID).
- TAB.
- Date and time of creation (in the form YY/MM/DD HH:MM:SS).
- SPACE.
- Creator.
- TAB.
- Serial number.
- SPACE.
- Predecessor delta's serial number.
- TAB.

- Statistics (in the form inserted/deleted/unchanged).
- NEWLINE.
- "Included:TAB", followed by SID's of deltas included, followed by NEWLINE (only if there were any such deltas and if **i** keyletter was supplied).
- "Excluded:TAB", followed by SID's of deltas excluded, followed by NEWLINE (see note above).
- "Ignored:TAB", followed by SID's of deltas ignored, followed by NEWLINE (see note above).
- "MRs:TAB", followed by MR numbers related to the delta, followed by NEWLINE (only if any MR numbers were supplied).
- Lines of comments (delta commentary), followed by newline (if any were supplied).

−s   Print only the first line of the delta table entries; that is, only up to the statistics. This keyletter is effective only if the **d** keyletter is also specified (or assumed).

−t   Print the descriptive text contained in the file.

−u   Print the login-names and/or numerical group IDs of those users allowed to make deltas.

−y[*SID*]

Print the delta table entries to stop when the delta just printed has the specified SID. If no delta in the table has the specified SID, the entire table is printed. If no SID is specified, the first delta in the delta table is printed. This keyletter will print the entire delta table entry for each delta as a single line (the NEWLINE in the normal multi-line format of the **d** keyletter are replaced by SPACE characters) preceded by the name of the SCCS file being processed, followed by a **:**, followed by a TAB. This keyletter is effective only if the **d** keyletter is also specified (or assumed).

−c[*cutoff*]

Stop printing the delta table entries if the delta about to be printed is older than the specified cutoff date-time (see **get**(1) for the format of date-time). If no date-time is supplied, the epoch 0000 GMT Jan. 1, 1970 is used. As with the **y** keyletter, this keyletter will cause the entire delta table entry to be printed as a single line and to be preceded by the name of the SCCS file being processed, followed by a **:**, followed by a tab. This keyletter is effective only if the **d** keyletter is also specified (or assumed).

−r[*rev-cutoff*]

Begin printing the delta table entries when the delta about to be printed is older than or equal to the specified cutoff date-time (see **get**(1) for the format of date-time). If no date-time is supplied, the epoch 0000 GMT Jan. 1, 1970 is used. (In this case, nothing will be printed). As with the **y** keyletter, this keyletter will cause the entire delta table entry to be printed as a single line and to be preceded by the name of the SCCS file being processed, followed by a **:**, followed by a tab. This keyletter is effective only if the **d** keyletter is also specified (or assumed).

If any keyletter but **y**, **c**, or **r** is supplied, the name of the file being processed (preceded by one NEWLINE and followed by two NEWLINE characters) is printed before its contents.

If none of the **u**, **f**, **t**, or **b** keyletters is supplied, the **d** keyletter is assumed.

Note: the **s** and **i** keyletters, and the **c** and **r** keyletters are mutually exclusive; therefore, they may not be specified together on the same **prt** command.

The form of the delta table as produced by the **y**, **c**, and **r** keyletters makes it easy to sort multiple delta tables in chronological order.

When both the **y** and **c** or the **y** and **r** keyletters are supplied, **prt** will stop printing when the first of the two conditions is met.

SEE ALSO

admin(1), get(1), delta(1), prs(1), what(1), sccs(1)

sccsfile(5) in the *System Administrator's Reference Manual*

NAME

prtvtoc – disk information display utility

SYNOPSIS

prtvtoc [-aep] [-f *vtoc-file*] *raw-device*

DESCRIPTION

The default and primary function of **prtvtoc** is to display the contents of the VTOC (Volume Table Of Contents). The information displayed for each valid slice includes slice number, slice tag, slice flag/permissions, slice start sector, slice size (in sectors).

When editing the VTOC, the following entries are the valid slice tags and slice permission flags.

Slice Tags

#define V_BOOT	0x01	/* Boot slice */
#define V_ROOT	0x02	/* Root filesystem */
#define V_SWAP	0x03	/* Swap filesystem */
#define V_USR	0x04	/* Usr filesystem */
#define V_BACKUP	0x05	/* full disk */
#define V_ALTS	0x06	/* alternate sector space */
#define V_OTHER	0x07	/* non-unix space */
#define V_ALTTRK	0x08	/* alternate track space */
#define V_STAND	0x09	/* Stand slice */
#define V_VAR	0x0a	/* Var slice */
#define V_HOME	0x0b	/* Home slice */
#define V_DUMP	0x0c	/* dump slice */

Slice Permission Flags

#define V_UNMNT	0x01	/* Unmountable partition */
#define V_RONLY	0x10	/* Read only */
#define V_VALID	0x200	/* Partition is valid to use */

The start and size value are in absolute sector numbers where the first sector on the drive is 0 (which is reserved for the partition table). Slices should start and end on a cylinder boundary if possible. The head, cylinder and sectors/track information provided by **prtvtoc -p** will assist in the calculations. Slices should not overlap (slice 0 is the exception, it describes the entire UNIX partition).

OPTIONS

-a   prints the alternates tables (bad tracks and bad sectors).

-e   creates or adds information to the **/etc/partitions** file. This option is provided to allow support for **mkpart**[see **mkpart**(1M)]. Dependence on this feature is not suggested since it will not be supported in a future release.

-p   prints the information contained in the **pdinfo** structure.

-f *vtoc-file*

       writes the current contents of the VTOC into the *vtoc-file* in a condensed format. The format of the file is slice number, slice tag value, slice flag value, slice start sector, slice size (in sectors). The purpose of this file is to be input for the **edvtoc** command.

raw-device

raw-device is the character special device for the disk drive to be accessed. It must be the slice 0 device to represent the entire device (for example, **/dev/rdsk/0s0** or **/dev/rdsk/c0t0d0s0**).

FILES

/dev/dsk/0s0
/dev/rdsk/1s0
/dev/rdsk/c?t?d?s0

SEE ALSO

edvtoc(1M)

NAME

ps – report process status

SYNOPSIS

ps [*options*]

DESCRIPTION

ps prints information about active processes. Without *options,* **ps** prints information about processes associated with the controlling terminal. The output contains only the process ID, terminal identifier, cumulative execution time, and the command name. Otherwise, the information that is displayed is controlled by the *options*.

Some options accept lists as arguments. Items in a list can be either separated by commas or else enclosed in double quotes and separated by commas or spaces. Values for *proclist* and *grplist* must be numeric.

The *options* are:

-e	Print information about **e**very process now running.
-d	Print information about all processes except session leaders.
-a	Print information about **a**ll processes most frequently requested: all those except session leaders and processes not associated with a terminal.
-j	Print session ID and process group ID.
-f	Generate a **f**ull listing. (See below for significance of columns in a full listing.)
-l	Generate a **l**ong listing. (See below.)
-c	Print information in a format that reflects scheduler properties as described in **priocntl**(1). The **-c** option affects the output of the **-f** and **-l** options, as described below.
-t *termlist*	List only process data associated with the terminal given in *termlist.* Terminal identifiers may be specified in one of two forms: the device's file name (e.g., **tty04**) or, if the device's file name starts with **tty**, just the digit identifier (e.g., **04**).
-p *proclist*	List only process data whose process ID numbers are given in *proclist*.
-u *uidlist*	List only process data whose user ID number or login name is given in *uidlist*. In the listing, the numerical user ID will be printed unless you give the **-f** option, which prints the login name.
-g *grplist*	List only process data whose group leader's ID number(s) appears in *grplist*. (A group leader is a process whose process ID number is identical to its process group ID number.
-s *sesslist*	List information on all session leaders whose IDs appear in *sesslist*.

Under the **-f** option, **ps** tries to determine the command name and arguments given when the process was created by examining the user block. Failing this, the command name is printed, as it would have appeared without the **-f** option, in square brackets.

The column headings and the meaning of the columns in a **ps** listing are given below; the letters **f** and **l** indicate the option (**f**ull or **l**ong, respectively) that causes the corresponding heading to appear; **all** means that the heading always appears. Note that these two options determine only what information is provided for a process; they do not determine which processes will be listed.

F   (l)   Flags (hexadecimal and additive) associated with the process

           00   Process has terminated: process table entry now available.

           01   A system process: always in primary memory.

           02   Parent is tracing process.

           04   Tracing parent's signal has stopped process: parent is waiting [**ptrace**(2)].

           08   Process is currently in primary memory.

           10   Process currently in primary memory: locked until an event completes.

S   (l)   The state of the process:

           O   Process is running on a processor.

           S   Sleeping: process is waiting for an event to complete.

           R   Runnable: process is on run queue.

           I   Idle: process is being created.

           Z   Zombie state: process terminated and parent not waiting.

           T   Traced: process stopped by a signal because parent is tracing it.

           X   SXBRK state: process is waiting for more primary memory.

UID   (f,l)   The user ID number of the process owner (the login name is printed under the **-f** option).

PID   (all)   The process ID of the process (this datum is necessary in order to kill a process).

PPID   (f,l)   The process ID of the parent process.

C   (f,l)   Processor utilization for scheduling. Not printed when the **-c** option is used.

CLS   (f,l)   Scheduling class. Printed only when the **-c** option is used.

PRI   (l)   The priority of the process. Without the **-c** option, higher numbers mean lower priority. With the **-c** option, higher numbers mean higher priority.

NI   (l)   Nice value, used in priority computation. Not printed when the **-c** option is used. Only processes in the time-sharing class have a nice value.

ADDR   (l)   The memory address of the process.

SZ	(l)	The size (in pages or clicks) of the swappable process's image in main memory.
WCHAN	(l)	The address of an event for which the process is sleeping, or in SXBRK state, (if blank, the process is running).
STIME	(f)	The starting time of the process, given in hours, minutes, and seconds. (A process begun more than twenty-four hours before the **ps** inquiry is executed is given in months and days.)
TTY	(all)	The controlling terminal for the process (the message, **?**, is printed when there is no controlling terminal).
TIME	(all)	The cumulative execution time for the process.
COMMAND	(all)	The command name (the full command name and its arguments are printed under the **−f** option).

A process that has exited and has a parent, but has not yet been waited for by the parent, is marked **<defunct>**.

FILES

```
/dev
/dev/sxt/*
/dev/tty*
/dev/xt/*        terminal ("tty") names searcher files
/dev/kmem        kernel virtual memory
/dev/swap        the default swap device
/dev/mem         memory
/etc/passwd      UID information supplier
/etc/ps_data     internal data structure
```

SEE ALSO

kill(1), nice(1), priocntl(1).

getty(1M) in the *System Administrator's Reference Manual*.

NOTES

Things can change while **ps** is running; the snap-shot it gives is true only for a split-second, and it may not be accurate by the time you see it. Some data printed for defunct processes is irrelevant.

If no *termlist, proclist, uidlist,* or *grplist* is specified, **ps** checks **stdin**, **stdout**, and **stderr** in that order, looking for the controlling terminal and will attempt to report on processes associated with the controlling terminal. In this situation, if **stdin**, **stdout**, and **stderr** are all redirected, **ps** will not find a controlling terminal, so there will be no report.

On a heavily loaded system, **ps** may report an **lseek** error and exit. **ps** may seek to an invalid user area address: having obtained the address of a process' user area, **ps** may not be able to seek to that address before the process exits and the address becomes invalid.

ps −ef may not report the actual start of a tty login session, but rather an earlier time, when a getty was last respawned on the tty line.

NAME

ps – report process status

SYNOPSIS

ps [-Pedajflc] [-t *termlist*] [-p *proclist*] [-u *uidlist*] [-g *grplist*] [-s *sesslist*]

DESCRIPTION

ps prints information about active processes. Without *options*, ps prints information about processes associated with the controlling terminal. The output contains only the process ID, terminal identifier, cumulative execution time, and the
command name. Otherwise, the information that is displayed is controlled by the
options.

Some options accept lists as arguments. Items in a list can be either separated by
commas or else enclosed in double quotes and separated by commas or spaces.
Values for *proclist* and *grplist* must be numeric.

The *options* are:

-P   Print the processor ID number of the processor on which a process is exe-
        cuting, in the case of processor binding. The processor ID number
        appears under the PSR column heading. If the process is not bound to a
        specific processor, a dash appears in the field.

-e   Print information about every process now running.

-d   Print information about all processes except session leaders.

-a   Print information about all processes most frequently requested: all those
        except session leaders and processes not associated with a terminal.

-j   Print session ID and process group ID.

-f   Generate a full listing. (See below for significance of columns in a full
        listing.)

-l   Generate a long listing. (See below.)

-c   Print information in a format that reflects scheduler properties as
        described in priocntl(1). The –c option affects the output of the –f and
        –l options, as described below.

-t *termlist*
        List only process data associated with the terminal given in *termlist*. Ter-
        minal identifiers may be specified in one of two forms: the device's file
        name (for example, term/04) or, if the device's file name starts with term,
        just the digit identifier (for example, 04).

-p *proclist*
        List only process data whose process ID numbers are given in *proclist*.

-u *uidlist*
        List only the process data for those user IDs or login names given in
        uidlist. In the listing, the numerical user ID will be printed unless you
        give the –f option, which prints the login name.

−**g** *grplist*

List only process data whose group leader's ID number(s) appears in *grplist*. (A group leader is a process whose process ID number is identical to its process group ID number.)

−**s** *sesslist*

List information on all session leaders whose IDs appear in *sesslist*.

Under the −**f** option, **ps** tries to determine the command name and arguments given when the process was created by examining the user block. Failing this, the command name is printed, as it would have appeared without the −**f** option, in square brackets.

The column headings and the meaning of the columns in a **ps** listing are given below; the letters **f** and **l** indicate the option (**f**ull or **l**ong, respectively) that causes the corresponding heading to appear; **all** means that the heading always appears. Note that these two options determine only what information is provided for a process; they do not determine which processes will be listed.

F   (1)   Flags (hexadecimal and additive) associated with the process:

      00   Process has terminated: process table entry now available.

      01   A system process: always in primary memory.

      02   Parent is tracing process.

      04   Tracing parent's signal has stopped process: parent is waiting [**ptrace**(2)].

      08   Process is currently in primary memory.

      10   Process currently in primary memory: locked until an event completes.

S   (1)   The state of the process:

      O   Process is running on a processor.

      S   Sleeping: process is waiting for an event to complete.

      R   Runnable: process is on run queue.

      I   Idle: process is being created.

      Z   Zombie state: process terminated and parent not waiting.

      T   Traced: process stopped by a signal because parent is tracing it.

      X   SXBRK state: process is waiting for more primary memory.

UID   (f,l)   The user ID number of the process owner (the login name is printed under the −**f** option).

PID   (all)   The process ID of the process (the PID is necessary in order to kill a process).

PPID   (f,l)   The process ID of the parent process.

C   (f,l)   Processor utilization for scheduling. Not printed when the −**c** option is used.

CLS	(f,1)	Scheduling class. Printed only when the –c option is used.
PRI	(1)	The priority of the process. Without the –c option, higher numbers mean lower priority. With the –c option, higher numbers mean higher priority.
NI	(1)	Nice value, used in priority computation. Not printed when the –c option is used. Only processes in the time-sharing class have a nice value.
ADDR	(1)	The memory address of the process.
SZ	(1)	The size (in pages or clicks) of the virtual address space of the process.
WCHAN	(1)	The address of an event for which the process is sleeping, or in SXBRK state, (if blank, the process is running).
STIME	(f)	The starting time of the process, given in hours, minutes, and seconds. (A process begun more than twenty-four hours before the ps inquiry is executed is given in months and days.)
TTY	(all)	The controlling terminal for the process (the message, ?, is printed when there is no controlling terminal).
TIME	(all)	The cumulative execution time for the process.
COMMAND	(all)	The command name (the full command name and its arguments are printed under the –f option).

A process that has exited and has a parent, but has not yet been waited for by the parent, is marked <defunct>.

FILES

/dev	
/dev/sxt/*	
/dev/term*	
/dev/xt/*	terminal ("tty") names searcher files
/dev/kmem	kernel virtual memory
/dev/swap	the default swap device
/dev/mem	memory
/etc/passwd	UID information supplier
/etc/ps_data	internal data structure

SEE ALSO

kill(1), nice(1), priocntl(1)
getty(1M) in the *System Administrator's Reference Manual*
ps(1) in the *User's Reference Manual*

NOTES

Things can change while ps is running; the snap-shot it gives is true only for a split second, and it may not be accurate by the time you see it. Some data printed for defunct processes is irrelevant.

If no *termlist*, *proclist*, *uidlist*, or *grplist* is specified, **ps** checks **stdin**, **stdout**, and **stderr** in that order, looking for the controlling terminal, and will attempt to report on processes associated with the controlling terminal. In this situation, if **stdin**, **stdout**, and **stderr** are all redirected, **ps** will not find a controlling terminal, so there will be no report.

ps may report an **lseek** error and exit. **ps** may seek to an invalid user area address: having obtained the address of a process' user area, **ps** may not be able to seek to that address before the process exits and the address becomes invalid.

ps -ef may not report the actual start of a tty login session, but rather an earlier time, when a **getty** was last respawned on the tty line.

NAME

ps – display the status of current processes

SYNOPSIS

/usr/ucb/ps [–acglnrSuUvwx] [–t*term*] [*num*]

DESCRIPTION

The **ps** command displays information about processes. Normally, only those processes that are running with your effective user ID and are attached to a controlling terminal (see **termio**(4)) are shown. Additional categories of processes can be added to the display using various options. In particular, the **–a** option allows you to include processes that are not owned by you (that do not have your user ID), and the **–x** option allows you to include processes without control terminals. When you specify both **–a** and **–x**, you get processes owned by anyone, with or without a control terminal. The **–r** option restricts the list of processes printed to running and runnable processes.

ps displays the process ID, under PID; the control terminal (if any), under TT; the cpu time used by the process so far, including both user and system time, under TIME; the state of the process, under S; and finally, an indication of the COMMAND that is running.

The state is given by a single letter from the following:

O	Process is running on a processor.
S	Sleeping. Process is waiting for an event to complete.
R	Runnable. Process is on run queue.
I	Idle. Process is being created.
Z	Zombie state. Process terminated and parent not waiting.
T	Traced. Process stopped by a signal because parent is tracing it.
X	**SXBRK** state. Process is waiting for more primary memory.

The following options must all be combined to form the first argument:

–a	Include information about processes owned by others.
–c	Display the command name, as stored internally in the system for purposes of accounting, rather than the command arguments, which are kept in the process' address space. This is more reliable, if less informative, since the process is free to destroy the latter information.
–g	Display all processes. Without this option, **ps** only prints interesting processes. Processes are deemed to be uninteresting if they are process group leaders. This normally eliminates top-level command interpreters and processes waiting for users to login on free terminals.
–l	Display a long listing, with fields **F**, **PPID**, **CP**, **PRI**, **NI**, **SZ**, **RSS** and **WCHAN** as described below.
–n	Produce numerical output for some fields. In a user listing, the **USER** field is replaced by a **UID** field.
–r	Restrict output to running and runnable processes.

-S   Display accumulated CPU time used by this process and all of its reaped children.

-u   Display user-oriented output. This includes fields **USER**, **SZ**, **RSS** and **START** as described below.

-U   Update a private database where **ps** keeps system information.

-v   Display a version of the output containing virtual memory. This includes fields **SIZE** and **RSS**, described below.

-w   Use a wide output format (132 columns rather than 80); if repeated, that is, **-ww**, use arbitrarily wide output. This information is used to decide how much of long commands to print.

-x   Include processes with no controlling terminal.

-t*term*   List only process data associated with the terminal, *term*. Terminal identifiers may be specified in one of two forms: the device's file name (for example, **tty04** or **term/14**) or, if the device's file name starts with **tty**, just the digit identifier (for example, **04**).

num   A process number may be given, in which case the output is restricted to that process. This option must be supplied last.

DISPLAY FORMATS

Fields that are not common to all output formats:

USER   Name of the owner of the process.

NI   Process scheduling increment [see **getpriority**(3) and **nice**(3C)].

SIZE
SZ   The combined size of the data and stack segments (in kilobyte units)

RSS   Real memory (resident set) size of the process (in kilobyte units).

UID   Numerical user-ID of process owner.

PPID   Numerical ID of parent of process.

CP   Short-term CPU utilization factor (used in scheduling).

PRI   The priority of the process (higher numbers mean lower priority).

START   The starting time of the process, given in hours, minutes, and seconds. A process begun more than 24 hours before the **ps** inquiry is executed is given in months and days.

WCHAN   The address of an event for which the process is sleeping, or in **SXBRK** state (if blank, the process is running).

F   Flags (hexadecimal and additive) associated with the process:
        00   Process has terminated. Process table now available.
        01   A system process, always in primary memory.
        02   Parent is tracing process.
        04   Tracing parent's signal has stopped process. Parent is waiting, see **ptrace**(2).

08   Process is currently in primary memory.
10   Process currently in primary memory, locked until an event is
        completed.

A process that has exited and has a parent, but has not yet been waited for by the
parent is marked <defunct>; otherwise, **ps** tries to determine the command name
and arguments given when the process was created by examining the user block.

FILES

/dev
/dev/sxt/*
/dev/tty*
/dev/xt/*   terminal (**tty**) names searcher files
/dev/kmem   kernel virtual memory
/dev/swap   default swap device
/dev/mem   memory
/etc/passwd   UID information supplier
/etc/ps_data   internal data structure

SEE ALSO

getpriority(3), nice(3C)

kill(1) in the *User's Reference Manual*
whodo(1) in the *System Administrator's Reference Manual*
lseek(2) in the *Programmer's Reference Manual*

NOTES

Things can change while **ps** is running; the picture it gives is only a close approximation to the current state. Some data printed for defunct processes is
irrelevant.

If no *term* or *num* is specified, **ps** checks the standard input, the standard output,
and the standard error in that order, looking for the controlling terminal and will
attempt to report on processes associated with the controlling terminal. In this
situation, if the standard input, the standard output, and the standard error are
all redirected, **ps** will not find a controlling terminal, so there will be no report.

On a heavily loaded system, **ps** may report an **lseek**(2) error and exit. **ps** may
seek to an invalid user area address, having obtained the address of process' user
area, **ps** may not be able to seek to that address before the process exits and the
address becomes invalid.

NAME

     putdev – edits device table

SYNOPSIS

     putdev -a *alias* [*attribute=value* [. . .]]

     putdev -m *device attribute=value* [*attribute=value* [. . .]]

     putdev -d *device* [*attribute* [. . .]]

DESCRIPTION

     putdev can add a new device to the device table, modify an existing device description or remove a device entry from the table. The first synopsis is used to add a device. The second synopsis is used to modify existing entries by adding or changing attributes. If a specified attribute is not defined, this option adds that attribute to the device definition. If it is already defined, it modifies the attribute definition. The third synopsis is used to delete either an entire device entry or, if the attribute argument is used, to delete an attribute assignment for a device.

     The options and arguments for this command are:

     -a   Adds a device to the device table using the specified attributes. The device must be referenced by its *alias*.

     -m   Modifies a device entry in the device table. If an entry already exists, it adds any specified attributes that are not defined. It also modifies any attributes which already have a value with the value specified with this command.

     -d   Removes a device from the device table, when executed without the *attributes* argument. Used with the *attribute* argument, it deletes the given attribute specification for *device* from the table.

     alias   Designates the alias of the device to be added.

     device   Designates the pathname or alias of the device whose attribute is to be added, modified, or removed.

     attribute Designates a device attribute to be added or modified. Can be any of the device attributes described under NOTES except alias. This prevents an accidental modification or deletion of a device's alias from the table.

     value   Designates the value to be assigned to a device's attribute.

NOTES

     The following list shows all of the attributes which can be defined for a device:

     alias   The unique name by which a device is known. No two devices in the database may share the same alias name. The name is limited in length to 14 characters and should contain only alphanumeric characters and also the following special characters if they are escaped with a backslash: underscore (_), dollar sign ($), hyphen (-), and period (.).

bdevice	The pathname to the block special device node associated with the device, if any. The associated major/minor combination should be unique within the database and should match that associated with the **cdevice** field, if any. (It is the administrator's responsibility to ensure that these **major/minor** numbers are unique in the database.)
capacity	The capacity of the device or of the typical volume, if removable.
cdevice	The pathname to the character special device node associated with the device, if any. The associated major/minor combination should be unique within the database and should match that associated with the **bdevice** field, if any. (It is the administrator's responsibility to ensure that these **major/minor** numbers are unique in the database.)
cyl	Used by the command specified in the **mkfscmd** attribute.
desc	A description of any instance of a volume associated with this device (such as floppy diskette).
dpartlist	The list of disk partitions associated with this device. Used only if **type=disk**. The list should contain device aliases, each of which must have **type=dpart**.
dparttype	The type of disk partition represented by this device. Used only if **type=dpart**. It should be either **fs** (for filesystem) or **dp** (for data partition).
erasecmd	The command string that, when executed, erases the device.
fmtcmd	The command string that, when executed, formats the device.
fsname	The filesystem name on the file system administered on this partition, as supplied to the **/usr/sbin/labelit** command. This attribute is specified only if **type=dpart** and **dparttype=fs**.
gap	Used by the command specified in the **mkfscmd** attribute.
mkfscmd	The command string that, when executed, places a file system on a previously formatted device.
mountpt	The default mount point to use for the device. Used only if the device is mountable. For disk partitions where **type=dpart** and **dparttype=fs**, this attribute should specify the location where the partition is normally mounted.
nblocks	The number of blocks in the filesystem administered on this partition. Used only if **type=dpart** and **dparttype=fs**.
ninodes	The number of inodes in the filesystem administered on this partition. Used only if **type=dpart** and **dparttype=fs**.
norewind	The name of the character special device node that allows access to the serial device without rewinding when the device is closed.
pathname	Defines the pathname to an i-node describing the device (used for non-block or character device pathnames, such as directories).

    type   A token that represents inherent qualities of the device. Standard types include: 9-track, ctape, disk, directory, diskette, dpart, and qtape.

    volname   The volume name on the filesystem administered on this partition, as supplied to the **/usr/sbin/labelit** command. Used only if **type=dpart** and **dparttype=fs**.

    volume   A text string used to describe any instance of a volume associated with this device. This attribute should not be defined for devices which are not removable.

ERRORS

The command will exit with one of the following values:

0 =   successful completion of the task.

1 =   command syntax incorrect, invalid option used, or internal error occurred.

2 =   device table could not be opened for reading or new device table could not be created.

3 =   if executed with the **-a** option, indicates that an entry in the device table with the alias *alias* already exits. If executed with the **-m** or **-d** options, indicates that no entry exists for device *device*.

4 =   indicates that **-d** was requested and one or more of the specified attributes were not defined for the device.

FILES

    /etc/device.tab

SEE ALSO

    devattr(1), **putdgrp**(1M)

NAME

putdgrp – edits device group table

SYNOPSIS

putdgrp [**-d**] *dgroup* [*device* [...]]

DESCRIPTION

putdgrp modifies the device group table. It performs two kinds of modification. It can modify the table by creating a new device group or removing a device group. It can also change group definitions by adding or removing a device from the group definition.

When the command is invoked with only a *dgroup* specification, the command adds the specified group name to the device group table if it does not already exist. If the **-d** option is also used with only the *dgroup* specification, the command deletes the group from the table.

When the command is invoked with both a *dgroup* and a *device* specification, it adds the given device name (or names) to the group definition. When invoked with both arguments and the **-d** option, the command deletes the device name (or names) from the group definition.

When the command is invoked with both a *dgroup* and a *device* specification and the device group does not exist, it creates the group and adds the specified devices to that new group.

The options and arguments for this command are:

-d   Deletes the group or, if used with *device*, the device from a group definition.

dgroup   Specifies a device group name.

device   Specifies the pathname or alias of the device that is to added to or deleted from the device group.

ERRORS

The command will exit with one of the following values:

0 = successful completion of the task.

1 = command syntax incorrect, invalid option used, or internal error occurred.

2 = device group table could not be opened for reading or a new device group table could not be created.

3 = if executed with the **-d** option, indicates that an entry in the device group table for the device group *dgroup* does not exist and so cannot be deleted. Otherwise, indicates that the device group *dgroup* already exists and cannot be added.

4 = if executed with the **-d** option, indicates that the device group *dgroup* does not have as members one or more of the specified devices. Otherwise, indicates that the device group *dgroup* already has one or more of the specified devices as members.

EXAMPLE

To add a new device group:

        putdgrp floppies

To add a device to a device group:

        putdgrp floppies diskette2

To delete a device group:

        putdgrp -d floppies

To delete a device from a device group:

        putdgrp -d floppies diskette2

FILES

/etc/dgroup.tab

SEE ALSO

listdgrp(1), putdev(1M)

NAME

pwck, grpck – password/group file checkers

SYNOPSIS

/usr/sbin/pwck [*file*]

/usr/sbin/grpck [*file*]

DESCRIPTION

pwck scans the password file and notes any inconsistencies. The checks include validation of the number of fields, login name, user ID, group ID, and whether the login directory and the program-to-use-as-shell exist. The default password file is /etc/passwd.

grpck verifies all entries in the group file. This verification includes a check of the number of fields, group name, group ID, whether any login names belong to more than NGROUPS_MAX groups and that all login names appear in the password file. The default group file is /etc/group.

FILES

/etc/group

/etc/passwd

SEE ALSO

group(4), passwd(4)

DIAGNOSTICS

Group entries in /etc/group with no login names are flagged.

NAME
pwck – check password database entries

SYNOPSIS
/usr/ucb/pwck [*filename*]

DESCRIPTION
pwck checks a password file for errors. If specified, *filename* is checked, otherwise /etc/passwd is checked.

This command differs from /usr/sbin/pwck in its ability to correctly parse YP entries in /etc/passwd.

DIAGNOSTICS

Too many/few fields
> An entry in the password file does not have the proper number of fields.

No login name
> The login name field of an entry is empty.

Bad character(s) in login name
> The login name in an entry contains characters other than lower-case letters and digits.

First char in login name not lower case alpha
> The login name in an entry does not begin with a lower-case letter.

Login name too long
> The login name in an entry has more than 8 characters.

Invalid UID
> The user ID field in an entry is not numeric or is greater than 65535.

Invalid GID
> The group ID field in an entry is not numeric or is greater than 65535.

No login directory
> The login directory field in an entry is empty.

Login directory not found
> The login directory field in an entry refers to a directory that does not exist.

Optional shell file not found.
> The login shell field in an entry refers to a program or shell script that does not exist.

No netgroup name
> The entry is a Yellow Pages entry referring to a netgroup, but no netgroup is present.

Bad character(s) in netgroup name
> The netgroup name in a Yellow Pages entry contains characters other than lower-case letters and digits.

First char in netgroup name not lower case alpha
> The netgroup name in a Yellow pages entry does not begin with a lower-case letter.

FILES

/etc/passwd

SEE ALSO

group(4), passwd(4) in the *System Administrator's Reference Manual*

NAME

　　pwconv – install and update **/etc/shadow** with information from **/etc/passwd**

SYNOPSIS

　　pwconv

DESCRIPTION

　　The **pwconv** command creates and updates **/etc/shadow** with information from **/etc/passwd**.

　　If the **/etc/shadow** file does not exist, **pwconv** creates **/etc/shadow** with information from **/etc/passwd**. The command populates **/etc/shadow** with the user's login name, password, and password aging information. If password aging information does not exist in **/etc/passwd** for a given user, none is added to **/etc/shadow**. However, the last changed information is always updated.

　　If the **/etc/shadow** file does exist, the following tasks are performed:

　　　　Entries that are in the **/etc/passwd** file and not in the **/etc/shadow** file are added to the **/etc/shadow** file.

　　　　Entries that are in the **/etc/shadow** file and not in the **/etc/passwd** file are removed from **/etc/shadow**.

　　　　Password attributes (for example, password and aging information) in an **/etc/passwd** entry are moved to the corresponding entry in **/etc/shadow**.

　　The **pwconv** program is a privileged system command that cannot be executed by ordinary users.

FILES

　　/etc/passwd, /etc/shadow, /etc/opasswd, /etc/oshadow

SEE ALSO

　　passwd(1), passmgmt(1M)

DIAGNOSTICS

　　The **pwconv** command exits with one of the following values:

　　　　0　　Success.
　　　　1　　Permission denied.
　　　　2　　Invalid command syntax.
　　　　3　　Unexpected failure. Conversion not done.
　　　　4　　Unexpected failure. Password file(s) missing.
　　　　5　　Password file(s) busy. Try again later.

NAME

    pwd – working directory name

SYNOPSIS

    pwd

DESCRIPTION

    pwd prints the path name of the working (current) directory.

SEE ALSO

    cd(1)

DIAGNOSTICS

    "Cannot open .." and "Read error in .." indicate possible file system trouble and should be referred to a UNIX system administrator.

NOTES

    If you move the current directory or one above it, **pwd** may not give the correct response. Use the **cd**(1) command with a full path name to correct this situation.

NAME

quot – summarize file system ownership

SYNOPSIS

quot [–acfhnv] [*filesystem*]

DESCRIPTION

quot displays the number of blocks (1024 bytes) in the named *filesystem* currently owned by each user. There is a limit of 2048 blocks. Files larger than this will be counted as a 2048 block file, but the total blocks count will be correct.

The options are:

–a   Generate a report for all mounted file systems.

–c   Display three columns giving a file size in blocks, the number of files of that size, and a cumulative total of blocks containing files of that size or a smaller size. Files exceeding 499 blocks are listed as 499 blocks. The last line always lists 499 blocks, even if there are no files of that size.

–f   Display count of number of files as well as space owned by each user. This option is incompatible with the –c and –v options.

–h   Estimate the number of blocks in the file — this does not account for files with holes in them.

–n   Attach names to the list of files read from standard input. quot –n cannot be used alone, because it expects data from standard input. For example, the pipeline

      ncheck filesystem | sort +0n | quot –n filesystem

will produce a list of all files and their owners. This option is incompatible with all other options.

–v   In addition to the default output, display three columns containing the number of blocks not accessed in the last 30, 60, and 90 days.

NOTES

This command may only be used by a privileged user.

FILES

/etc/mnttab   mounted file systems
/etc/passwd   to get user names

SEE ALSO

du(1M)

NAME

quota – display a user's disk quota and usage

SYNOPSIS

quota [−v] [*username*]

DESCRIPTION

quota displays users' disk usage and limits. Only a privileged user may use the optional *username* argument to view the limits of other users.

quota without options displays only warnings about mounted file systems where usage is over quota. Remotely mounted file systems which do not have quotas turned on are ignored.

username can be numeric, corresponding to the uid of a user.

The −v option displays user's quotas on all mounted file systems where quotas exist.

FILES

/etc/mnttab   list of currently mounted filesystems

SEE ALSO

edquota(1M), quotaon(1M)

NAME

quotacheck – file system quota consistency checker

SYNOPSIS

quotacheck [-v] [-p] *filesystem* . . .

quotacheck [-apv]

DESCRIPTION

quotacheck examines each file system, builds a table of current disk usage, and compares this table against that stored in the disk quota file for the file system. If any inconsistencies are detected, both the quota file and the current system copy of the incorrect quotas are updated (the latter only occurs if an active file system is checked).

quotacheck expects each file system to be checked to have a quota file named quotas in the root directory. If none is present, quotacheck will ignore the file system.

quotacheck accesses the character special device in calculating the actual disk usage for each user. Thus, the file systems checked should be quiescent while quotacheck is running.

The options are:

-v   Indicate the calculated disk quotas for each user on a particular file system. quotacheck normally reports only those quotas modified.

-a   Check the file systems indicated in /etc/mnttab to be read-write with disk quotas. Only those file systems that have "rq" in the mntopts field of the /etc/vfstab file are checked.

-p   Run parallel passes on the required file systems.

FILES

/etc/mnttab   mounted file systems
/etc/vfstab   list of default parameters for each file system

SEE ALSO

quotaon(1M)

NAME

quotaon, quotaoff – turn file system quotas on and off

SYNOPSIS

quotaon [–v] *filesystem* . . .

quotaoff [–v] *filesystem* . . .

DESCRIPTION

quotaon announces to the system that disk quotas should be enabled on one or more file systems. The file systems specified must be mounted at the time. The file system quota files must be present in the root directory of the specified file system and be named **quotas**.

quotaoff announces to the system that file systems specified should have any disk quotas turned off.

The option for **quotaon**:

–v   Displays a message for each file system where quotas are turned on.

The option for **quotaoff**:

–v   Displays a message for each file system affected.

These commands update the status field of devices located in **/etc/mnttab** to indicate when quotas are on or off for each file system.

FILES

/etc/mnttab	mounted file systems
/etc/vfstab	list of default parameters for each file system

SEE ALSO

mnttab(4), vfstab(4)

NAME

random – generate a random number

SYNOPSIS

random [**-s**] [*scale*]

DESCRIPTION

random generates a random number on the standard output, and returns the number as its exit value. By default, this number is either 0 or 1. If *scale* is given a value between 1 and 255, then the range of the random value is from 0 to *scale*. If *scale* is greater than 255, an error message is printed.

When the **-s** (silent) option is given, then the random number is returned as an exit value, but is not printed on the standard output. If an error occurs, **random** returns an exit value of zero.

SEE ALSO

rand(3C)

NOTES

This command does not perform any floating point computations. **random** uses the time of day as a seed.

NAME

rarpd – DARPA Reverse Address Resolution Protocol server

SYNOPSIS

rarpd *interface* [*hostname*]

/usr/sbin/rarpd -a

DESCRIPTION

rarpd starts a daemon that responds to Reverse Address Resolution Protocol (RARP) requests. The daemon forks a copy of itself that runs in background. It must be run as root.

RARP is used by machines at boot time to discover their Internet Protocol (IP) address. The booting machine provides its Ethernet Address in a RARP request message. Using the ethers and hosts databases, rarpd maps this Ethernet Address into the corresponding IP address which it returns to the booting machine in an RARP reply message. The booting machine must be listed in both databases for rarpd to locate its IP address. rarpd issues no reply when it fails to locate an IP address.

In the first synopsis, the *interface* parameter names the network interface upon which rarpd is to listen for requests. The *interface* parameter takes the "name unit" form used by ifconfig(1M). The second argument, *hostname*, is used to obtain the IP address of that interface. An IP address in "decimal dot" notation may be used for *hostname*. If *hostname* is omitted, the address of the interface will be obtained from the kernel. When the first form of the command is used, rarpd must be run separately for each interface on which RARP service is to be supported. A machine that is a router may invoke rarpd multiple times, for example:

```
/usr/sbin/rarpd emd1 host
/usr/sbin/rarpd emd2 host-backbone
```

In the second synopsis, rarpd locates all of the network interfaces present on the system and starts a daemon process for each one that supports RARP.

FILES

/etc/ethers
/etc/hosts

SEE ALSO

boot(1M), ifconfig(1M), ethers(4), hosts(4), netconfig(4)

Finlayson, Ross, Timothy Mann, Jeffrey Mogul, and Marvin Theimer, *A Reverse Address Resolution Protocol*, RFC 903, Network Information Center, SRI International, Menlo Park, Calif., June 1984

NAME

rc0 – run commands performed to stop the operating system

SYNOPSIS

/sbin/rc0

DESCRIPTION

This file is executed at each system state change that needs to have the system in an inactive state. It is responsible for those actions that bring the system to a quiescent state, traditionally called "shutdown".

There are three system states that require this procedure. They are state **0** (the system halt state), state **5** (the firmware state), and state **6** (the reboot state). Whenever a change to one of these states occurs, the **rc0** procedure is run. The entry in /etc/inittab, which may vary slightly on different machine types, might read:

        r0:056:wait:/sbin/rc0 >/dev/sysmsg 2>&1 </dev/console

Some of the actions performed by **rc0** are carried out by files beginning with **K** in /etc/rc0.d. These files are executed in ASCII order (see FILES below for more information), terminating some system service. The combination of commands in **rc0** and files in /etc/rc0.d determines how the system is shut down.

The recommended sequence for **rc0** is:

Stop System Services and Daemons.

> Various system services (such as a Local Area Network or LP Spooler) are gracefully terminated.

> When new services are added that should be terminated when the system is shut down, the appropriate files are installed in and /etc/rc0.d.

Terminate Processes

> **SIGTERM** signals are sent to all running processes by **killall**(1M). Processes stop themselves cleanly if sent **SIGTERM**.

Kill Processes

> **SIGKILL** signals are sent to all remaining processes; no process can resist **SIGKILL**.

> At this point the only processes left are those associated with **rc0** and processes **0** and **1**, which are special to the operating system.

Unmount All File Systems

> Only the root file system (/) remains mounted.

Depending on which system state the systems end up in (**0**, **5**, or **6**), the entries in /etc/inittab will direct what happens next. If the /etc/inittab has not defined any other actions to be performed as in the case of system state **0**, then the operating system will have nothing to do. It should not be possible to get the system's attention. The only thing that can be done is to turn off the power or possibly get the attention of a firmware monitor. The command can be used only by a privileged user.

FILES

The execution by **/usr/bin/sh** of any files in **/etc/rc0.d** occurs in ASCII sort-sequence order. See **rc2**(1M) for more information.

SEE ALSO

killall(1M), **rc2**(1M), **shutdown**(1M).

NAME

rc2 – run commands performed for multi-user environment

SYNOPSIS

/sbin/rc2

DESCRIPTION

This file is executed via an entry in /etc/inittab and is responsible for those initializations that bring the system to a ready-to-use state, traditionally state 2, called the "multi-user" state.

The actions performed by rc2 are found in files in the directory /etc/rc.d and files beginning with S in /etc/rc2.d. These files are executed by /usr/bin/sh in ASCII sort–sequence order (see FILES for more information). When functions are added that need to be initialized when the system goes multi-user, an appropriate file should be added in /etc/rc2.d.

The functions done by the rc2 command and associated /etc/rc2.d files include:

> Setting and exporting the TIMEZONE variable.
>
> Setting-up and mounting the user (/usr) file system.
>
> Cleaning up (remaking) the /tmp and /var/tmp directories.
>
> Loading the network interface and ports cards with program data and starting the associated processes.
>
> Starting the cron daemon by executing /usr/sbin/cron.
>
> Cleaning up (deleting) uucp locks status, and temporary files in the /var/spool/uucp directory.

Other functions can be added, as required, to support the addition of hardware and software features.

EXAMPLES

The following are prototypical files found in /etc/rc2.d. These files are prefixed by an S and a number indicating the execution order of the files.

MOUNTFILESYS

```
#     Set up and mount file systems
cd /
/sbin/mountall /etc/fstab
```

RMTMPFILES

```
# clean up /tmp
rm -rf /tmp
mkdir /tmp
chmod 777 /tmp
chgrp sys /tmp
chown sys /tmp
```

uucp

```
#     clean-up uucp locks, status, and temporary files
rm -rf /var/spool/locks/*
```

The file /etc/TIMEZONE is included early in rc2, thus establishing the default time zone for all commands that follow.

FILES

Here are some hints about files in /etc/rc.d:

The order in which files are executed is important. Since they are executed in ASCII sort–sequence order, using the first character of the file name as a sequence indicator will help keep the proper order. Thus, files starting with the following characters would be:

[0-9].	very early
[A-Z].	early
[a-n].	later
[o-z].	last

Files in /etc/rc.d that begin with a dot (.) will not be executed. This feature can be used to hide files that are not to be executed for the time being without removing them. The command can be used only by a privileged user.

Files in /etc/rc2.d must begin with an S or a K followed by a number and the rest of the file name. Upon entering run level 2, files beginning with S are executed with the start option; files beginning with K, are executed with the stop option. Files beginning with other characters are ignored.

SEE ALSO

shutdown(1M).

NAME

rc6 – run commands performed to stop and reboot the operating system

SYNOPSIS

/sbin/rc6

DESCRIPTION

The shell script **rc6** is run whenever a transition to run state 6 is requested either through **init 6** or **shutdown −i6**.

The sequence of events in **rc6** is as follows:

Check to see if a new bootable operating system (**/stand/unix**) needs to be built; if so, build one by running the **buildsys** command.

Unmount all file systems.

Then **init** executes the **initdefault** entry in the **/etc/inittab** file to bring the system to the operating state defined by that entry.

Note that if an error occurs while **buildsys** is building a new bootable operating system, a shell is spawned that will exit only to firmware state; [see **buildsys**(1M)].

SEE ALSO

buildsys(1M), cunix(1M), init(1M), rc0(1M), rc2(1M), shutdown(1M), inittab(4)

System Administrator's Guide

NAME

rcp – remote file copy

SYNOPSIS

rcp [**-p**] *filename1 filename2*

rcp [**-pr**] *filename...directory*

DESCRIPTION

The **rcp** command copies files between machines. Each *filename* or *directory* argument is either a remote file name of the form:

> *hostname:path*

or a local file name (containing no **:** characters, or a **/** before any **:** characters).

If a *filename* is not a full path name, it is interpreted relative to your home directory on *hostname*. A *path* on a remote host may be quoted (using \ , " , or ') so that the metacharacters are interpreted remotely.

rcp does not prompt for passwords; your current local user name must exist on *hostname* and allow remote command execution by **rsh**(1).

rcp handles third party copies, where neither source nor target files are on the current machine. Hostnames may also take the form

> *username@hostname:filename*

to use *username* rather than your current local user name as the user name on the remote host. **rcp** also supports Internet domain addressing of the remote host, so that:

> *username@host.domain:filename*

specifies the username to be used, the hostname, and the domain in which that host resides. Filenames that are not full path names will be interpreted relative to the home directory of the user named *username*, on the remote host.

The destination hostname may also take the form *hostname.username:filename* to support destination machines that are running older versions of **rcp**.

The following options are available:

-p　　Attempt to give each copy the same modification times, access times, and modes as the original file.

-r　　Copy each subtree rooted at *filename*; in this case the destination must be a directory.

SEE ALSO

ftp(1), rlogin(1), rsh(1), hosts.equiv(4)

NOTES

rcp is meant to copy between different hosts; attempting to rcp a file onto itself, as with:

```
rcp tmp/file myhost:/tmp/file
```

results in a severely corrupted file.

rcp does not detect all cases where the target of a copy might be a file in cases where only a directory should be legal.

rcp requires that the source host have permission to execute commands on the remote host when doing third-party copies.

If you forget to quote metacharacters intended for the remote host you get an incomprehensible error message.

NAME

    rdate – set system date from a remote host

SYNOPSIS

    rdate *hostname*

DESCRIPTION

    rdate sets the local date and time from the *hostname* given as an argument. You must be super-user on the local system. Typically **rdate** can be inserted as part of a startup script.

NAME

readfile, `longline` – reads file, gets longest line

SYNOPSIS

readfile *file*

`longline` [*file*]

DESCRIPTION

The `readfile` function reads *file* and copies it to *stdout*. No translation of NEW-LINE is done. It keeps track of the longest line it reads and if there is a subsequent call to `longline`, the length of that line, including the NEWLINE character, is returned.

The `longline` function returns the length, including the NEWLINE character, of the longest line in *file*. If *file* is not specified, it uses the file named in the last call to `readfile`.

EXAMPLES

Here is a typical use of **readfile** and **longline** in a text frame definition file:

```
        .
        .
        .

    text="`readfile myfile`"
    columns=`longline`
        .
        .
        .
```

DIAGNOSTICS

If *file* does not exist, **readfile** will return FALSE (that is, the expression will have an error return).

longline returns 0 if a **readfile** has not previously been issued.

NOTES

More than one descriptor can call **readfile** in the same frame definition file. In text frames, if one of those calls is made from the **text** descriptor, then a subsequent use of **longline** will always get the longest line of the file read by the **readfile** associated with the **text** descriptor, even if it was not the most recent use of **readfile**.

SEE ALSO

cat(1)

NAME

reboot – restart the operating system

SYNOPSIS

/usr/ucb/reboot [-dnq] [*boot arguments*]

DESCRIPTION

reboot restarts the kernel. The kernel is loaded into memory by the PROM monitor, which transfers control to it.

Although reboot can be run by the privileged user at any time, shutdown(1M) is normally used first to warn all users logged in of the impending loss of service. See shutdown(1M) for details.

reboot performs a sync(1) operation on the disks, and then a multiuser reboot is initiated. See init(1M) for details.

reboot normally logs the reboot to the system log daemon, syslogd(1M), and places a shutdown record in the login accounting file /var/adm/wtmp. These actions are inhibited if the -n or -q options are present.

The following options are available:

-d   Dump system core before rebooting. This option is provided for compatibility, but is not supported by the underlying reboot(3) call.

-n   Avoid the sync(1). It can be used if a disk or the processor is on fire.

-q   Quick. Reboots quickly and ungracefully, without first shutting down running processes.

boot arguments
     These arguments are accepted for compatibility, but are ignored by reboot. See boot(1M) for details.

Power Fail and Crash Recovery

Normally, the system will reboot itself at power-up or after crashes.

FILES

/var/adm/wtmp   login accounting file

SEE ALSO

halt(1M), syslogd(1M), reboot(3)

boot(1M), crash(1M), fsck(1M), init(1M), shutdown(1M), sync(1M), in the *System Administrator's Reference Manual*

NAME

refer – expand and insert references from a bibliographic database

SYNOPSIS

/usr/ucb/refer [–b] [–e] [–n] [–a*r*] [–c*string*] [–k*x*] [–l*m,n*]
[–p *filename*] [–s*keys*] *filename* . . .

DESCRIPTION

refer is a preprocessor for **nroff**(1), or **troff**(1), that finds and formats references. The input files (standard input by default) are copied to the standard output, except for lines between '**. [**' and '**.]**' command lines. Such lines are assumed to contain keywords as for **lookbib**(1), and are replaced by information from a bibliographic data base. The user can avoid the search, override fields from it, or add new fields. The reference data, from whatever source, is assigned to a set of **troff** strings. Macro packages such as **ms**(7) print the finished reference text from these strings. A flag is placed in the text at the point of reference. By default, the references are indicated by numbers.

When **refer** is used with **eqn**(1), **neqn**, or **tbl**(1), **refer** should be used first in the sequence, to minimize the volume of data passed through pipes.

The following options are available:

–b   Bare mode — do not put any flags in text (neither numbers or labels).

–e   Accumulate references instead of leaving the references where encountered, until a sequence of the form:

```
.[
$LIST$
.]
```

is encountered, and then write out all references collected so far. Collapse references to the same source.

–n   Do not search the default file.

–a*r*   Reverse the first *r* author names (Jones, J. A. instead of J. A. Jones). If *r* is omitted, all author names are reversed.

–c*string*
Capitalize (with SMALL CAPS) the fields whose key-letters are in *string*.

–k*x*   Instead of numbering references, use key labels as specified in a reference data line beginning with the characters %*x*; By default, %*x* is %L.

–l*m,n* Instead of numbering references, use labels from the senior author's last name and the year of publication. Only the first *m* letters of the last name and the last *n* digits of the date are used. If either of *m* or *n* is omitted, the entire name or date, respectively, is used.

–p *filename*
Take the next argument as a file of references to be searched. The default file is searched last.

    −s*keys* Sort references by fields whose key-letters are in the *keys* string, and per-
        mute reference numbers in the text accordingly. Using this option implies
        the **−e** option. The key-letters in *keys* may be followed by a number indi-
        cating how many such fields are used, with a + sign taken as a very large
        number. The default is **AD**, which sorts on the senior author and date. To
        sort on all authors and then the date, for instance, use the options '**−sA+T**'.

FILES

    /usr/ucblib/reftools/papers　　default publication lists and indexes
    /usr/ucblib/reftools　　　　　　programs

SEE ALSO

    addbib(1), **eqn**(1), **indxbib**(1), **lookbib**(1), **nroff**(1), **roffbib**(1), **sortbib**(1),
    tbl(1), **troff**(1)

NAME

       `regcmp` – regular expression compile

SYNOPSIS

       `regcmp` [–] *file* . . .

DESCRIPTION

       The `regcmp` command performs a function similar to `regcmp` and, in most cases, precludes the need for calling `regcmp` from C programs. Bypassing `regcmp` saves on both execution time and program size. The command `regcmp` compiles the regular expressions in *file* and places the output in *file*`.i`. If the – option is used, the output is placed in *file*`.c`. The format of entries in *file* is a name (C variable) followed by one or more blanks followed by one or more regular expressions enclosed in double quotes. The output of `regcmp` is C source code. Compiled regular expressions are represented as **extern char** vectors. *file*`.i` files may thus be `#include`d in C programs, or *file*`.c` files may be compiled and later loaded. In the C program that uses the `regcmp` output, `regex(abc,line)` applies the regular expression named **abc** to **line**. Diagnostics are self-explanatory.

EXAMPLES

       `name`   `"([A-Za-z][A-Za-z0-9_]*)$0"`

       `telno`   `"\({0,1}([2-9][01][1-9])$0\){0,1} *"`
                   `"([2-9][0-9]{2})$1[ -]{0,1}"`
                   `"([0-9]{4})$2"`

       The three arguments to **telno** shown above must all be entered on one line.

       In the C program that uses the `regcmp` output,

            `regex(telno, line, area, exch, rest)`

       applies the regular expression named **telno** to **line**.

SEE ALSO

       `regcmp`(3G)

NAME

 regex – match patterns against a string

SYNOPSIS

 regex [−**e**] [−**v** "*string*"] [*pattern template*] ... *pattern* [*template*]

DESCRIPTION

 The **regex** command takes a string from *stdin*, and a list of *pattern/template* pairs, and runs **regex**(3X) to compare the string against each *pattern* until there is a match. When a match occurs, **regex** writes the corresponding *template* to *stdout* and returns TRUE. The last (or only) *pattern* does not need a template. If that is the pattern that matches the string, the function simply returns TRUE. If no match is found, **regex** returns FALSE.

 −**e**   means **regex** will evaluate the corresponding template and write the result to *stdout*.

 −**v** "*string*"   If −**v** is specified, *string* will be used instead of *stdin* to match against patterns.

 The argument *pattern* is a regular expression of the form described in **regex**(3X). In most cases *pattern* should be enclosed in single quotes to turn off special meanings of characters. Note that only the final *pattern* in the list may lack a *template*.

 The argument *template* may contain the strings **$m0** through **$m9**, which will be expanded to the part of *pattern* enclosed in (. . .)**$0** through (. . .)**$9** constructs (see examples below). Note that if you use this feature, you must be sure to enclose *template* in single quotes so that FMLI doesn't expand **$m0** through **$m9** at parse time. This feature gives **regex** much of the power of **cut**(1), **paste**(1), and **grep**(1), and some of the capabilities of **sed**(1). If there is no *template*, the default is "**$m0$m1$m2$m3$m4$m5$m6$m7$m8$m9**".

EXAMPLES

 To cut the 4th through 8th letters out of a string (this example will output **strin** and return TRUE):

  `` `regex -v "my string is nice" '^.{3}(.{5})$0' '$m0'` ``

 In a form, to validate input to field 5 as an integer:

  `` valid=`regex -v "$F5" '^[0-9]+$'` ``

 In a form, to translate an environment variable which contains one of the numbers **1**, **2**, **3**, **4**, **5** to the letters **a**, **b**, **c**, **d**, **e**:

  `` value=`regex -v "$VAR1" 1 a 2 b 3 c 4 d 5 e '.*' 'Error'` ``

 Note the use of the pattern **'.*'** to mean "anything else."

 In the example below, all three lines constitute a single backquoted expression. This expression, by itself, could be put in a menu definition file. Since backquoted expressions are expanded as they are parsed, and output from a backquoted expression (the **cat** command, in this example) becomes part of the definition file being parsed, this expression would read **/etc/passwd** and make a dynamic menu of all the login ids on the system.

```
`cat /etc/passwd | regex '^([^:]*)$0.*$' '
name=$m0
action=`message "$m0 is a user"`'`
```

DIAGNOSTICS

If none of the patterns matches, **regex** returns FALSE, otherwise TRUE.

NOTES

Patterns and templates must often be enclosed in single quotes to turn off the special meanings of characters. Especially if you use the $m0 through $m9 variables in the template, since FMLI will expand the variables (usually to "") before **regex** even sees them.

Single characters in character classes (inside [ ]) must be listed before character ranges, otherwise they will not be recognized. For example, [a-zA-Z_/] will not find underscores (_) or slashes (/), but [_/a-zA-Z] will.

The regular expressions accepted by **regcmp** differ slightly from other utilities (that is, **sed**, **grep**, **awk**, **ed**, and so on).

regex with the −e option forces subsequent commands to be ignored. In other words if a backquoted statement appears as follows:

```
`regex -e ...; command1; command2`
```

command1 and *command2* would never be executed. However, dividing the expression into two:

```
`regex -e ...``command1; command2`
```

would yield the desired result.

SEE ALSO

regcmp(3), **regex**(3X) in the *UNIX System V Programmer's Reference Manual*

awk(1), **cut**(1), **grep**(1), **paste**(1), **sed**(1) in the *UNIX System V User's Reference Manual*

NAME

reinit – runs an initialization file

SYNOPSIS

reinit *file*

DESCRIPTION

The **reinit** command is used to change the values of descriptors defined in the initialization file that was named when **fmli** was invoked and/or define additional descriptors. FMLI will parse and evaluate the descriptors in *file*, and then continue running the current application. The argument *file* must be the name of a valid FMLI initialization file.

The **reinit** command does not re-display the introductory frame or change the layout of screen labels for function keys.

NAME
relogin – rename login entry to show current layer

SYNOPSIS
/usr/lib/layersys/relogin [-s] [*line*]

DESCRIPTION
The **relogin** command changes the terminal *line* field of a user's **utmp** entry to the name of the windowing terminal layer attached to standard input. **write** messages sent to this user are directed to this layer. In addition, the **who** command will show the user associated with this layer. **relogin** may only be invoked under **layers**.

relogin is invoked automatically by **layers** to set the **utmp** entry to the terminal line of the first layer created upon startup, and to reset the **utmp** entry to the real line on termination. It may be invoked by a user to designate a different layer to receive **write** messages.

-s   Suppress error messages.

line   Specifies which **utmp** entry to change. The **utmp** file is searched for an entry with the specified *line* field. That field is changed to the line associated with the standard input. (To learn what lines are associated with a given user, say jdoe, type **ps -f -u jdoe** and note the values shown in the **TTY** field [see **ps**(1)]).

FILES
/var/adm/utmp   database of users versus terminals

SEE ALSO
layers(1), **mesg**(1), **ps**(1), **who**(1), **write**(1), in the *User's Reference Manual*
utmp(4)

DIAGNOSTICS
Returns 0 upon successful completion, 1 otherwise.

NOTES
relogin will fail, if *line* does not belong to the user issuing the **relogin** command or standard input is not associated with a terminal.

NAME

    removef – remove a file from software database

SYNOPSIS

    removef pkginst path1 [path2 ...]

    removef -f pkginst

DESCRIPTION

    removef informs the system that the user, or software, intends to remove a path-
name. Output from removef is the list of input pathnames that may be safely
removed (no other packages have a dependency on them).

    After all files have been processed, removef should be invoked with the -f
option to indicate that the removal phase is complete.

EXAMPLE

    The following shows the use of removef in an optional pre-install script:

```
echo "The following files are no longer part of this package
    and are being removed."
removef $PKGINST /dev/xt[0-9][0-9][0-9] |
while read pathname
do
    echo "$pathname"
    rm -f $pathname
done
removef -f $PKGINST || exit 2
```

SEE ALSO

    installf(1M), pkgadd(1M), pkgask(1M), pkgchk(1), pkginfo(1), pkgmk(1),
pkgproto(1), pkgtrans(1), pkgparam(3X)

NAME

rename – change the name of a file

SYNOPSIS

rename *old new*

DESCRIPTION

rename renames a file. *old* is the pathname of the file or directory to be renamed. *new* is the new pathname of the file or directory. Both *old* and *new* must be of the same type (either both files, or both directories) and must reside on the same file system.

If *new* already exists, it is removed. Thus, if *new* names an existing directory, the directory must not have any entries other than, possibly, ".” and "..". When renaming directories, the *new* pathname must not name a descendant of *old*. The implementation of **rename** ensures that upon successful completion a link named *new* will always exist.

If the final component of *old* is a symbolic link, the symbolic link is renamed, not the file or directory to which it points.

Write permission is required for both the directory containing *old* and the directory containing *new*.

NOTES

The system can deadlock if there is a loop in the file system graph. Such a loop takes the form of an entry in directory *a*, say *a/foo*, being a hard link to directory *b*, and an entry in directory *b*, say *b/bar*, being a hard link to directory *a*. When such a loop exists and two separate processes attempt to perform **rename** *a/foo b/bar* and **rename** *b/bar a/foo*, respectively, the system may deadlock attempting to lock both directories for modification. The system administrator should replace hard links to directories by symbolic links.

SEE ALSO

link(2), **rename**(2), **unlink**(2) in the *Programmer's Reference Manual*

NAME

renice – alter priority of running processes

SYNOPSIS

/usr/ucb/renice *priority pid* ...

/usr/ucb/renice *priority* [-p *pid* ...] [-g *pgrp* ...] [-u *username* ...]

DESCRIPTION

The **renice** command alters the scheduling priority of one or more running processes. By default, the processes to be affected are specified by their process IDs. *priority* is the new priority value.

The following options are available:

-p *pid* ...   Specify a list of process IDs.

-g *pgrp* ...   Specify a list of process group IDs. The processes in the specified process groups have their scheduling priority altered.

-u *user* ...   Specify a list of user IDs or usernames. All processes owned by each *user* have their scheduling altered.

Users other than the privileged user may only alter the priority of processes they own, and can only monotonically increase their nice value within the range 0 to 20. This prevents overriding administrative fiats. The privileged user may alter the priority of any process and set the priority to any value in the range -20 to 20. Useful priorities are: 19 (the affected processes will run only when nothing else in the system wants to), 0 (the base scheduling priority) and any negative value (to make things go very fast).

If only the priority is specified, the current process (alternatively, process group or user) is used.

FILES

/etc/passwd   map user names to user ID's

SEE ALSO

priocntl(1) in the *User's Reference Manual*

NOTES

If you make the priority very negative, then the process cannot be interrupted.

To regain control you must make the priority greater than zero.

Users other than the privileged user cannot increase scheduling priorities of their own processes, even if they were the ones that decreased the priorities in the first place.

The **priocntl** command subsumes the function of **renice**.

NAME

repquota – summarize quotas for a file system

SYNOPSIS

repquota [**-v**] *filesystem* . . .
repquota [**-av**]

DESCRIPTION

repquota prints a summary of the disk usage and quotas for the specified file systems. For each user the current number of files and amount of space (in kilobytes) is printed, along with any quotas created with **edquota**.

The options are:

-a   Report on all file systems that have "rq" in the **mntopts** field of the **/etc/vfstab** file.

-v   Report all quotas, even if there is no usage.

Only privileged users may view quotas which are not their own.

SEE ALSO

edquota(1M), **quota**(1M), **quotacheck**(1M), **quotaon**(1M)

NAME

   reset – reset the current form field to its default values

SYNOPSIS

   reset

DESCRIPTION

   The **reset** function causes the **value** descriptor of the current field to be re-
   evaluated, restoring the default value of the field if the current value is different.
   The descriptor is re-evaluated even if it has been modified by **const**.

NAME

restore – initiate restores of filesystems, data partitions, or disks

SYNOPSIS

restore [–o *target*] [–d *date*] [–mn] [–s|v] –P *partdev*

restore [–o *target*] [–d *date*] [–mn] [–s|v] –S *odevice*

restore [–o *target*] [–d *date*] [–mn] [–s|v] –A *partdev*

DESCRIPTION

restore posts requests for the restore of a data partition, a filesystem partition, or a disk from system-maintained archives. If the appropriate archive containing the required partition is online, the partition is restored immediately. If not, a request to restore the specified archive of the partition is posted to a restore status table. The restore status table is **/etc/bkup/rsstatus.tab**. The restore request is assigned a **restore** jobid that can be used to monitor the progress of the restore or to cancel it. A restore request that has been posted must later be resolved by an operator (see **rsoper**(1M)).

restore may be executed only by a privileged user.

If **restore** –**A** *partdev* is issued, the **fdisk**(1M) (full disk recovery) method is used to repartition and repopulate disk *partdev*. *partdev* is the name of the device that refers to the entire disk. For example, the name might be **/dev/rdsk/***, where the value of * is machine specific.

Options

–**d** *date*   Restores the partition as of *date*. This may or may not be the latest archive. See **getdate**(1M) for valid date formats.

–**m**   If the restore cannot be carried out immediately, this option notifies the invoking user (via **mail**(1M)) when the request has been completed.

–**n**   Displays a list of all archived versions of the object contained in the backup history log, but does not attempt to restore the object.

–**o** *target*   Instead of restoring directly to the specified object (*partdev* or *fsdev*), this option restores the archive to *target*. *target* is of the form:

   [*oname*][:*odev*]

   where *oname* is the name of the filesystem to be restored to (for –**S** archives) and *odev* is the name of the partition to be restored to (for –**P** and –**A** archives).

–**s**   While a restore operation is occurring, displays a "." for each 100 (512-byte) blocks transferred from the destination device.

–**v**   Displays the name of each object as it is restored. Only those archiving methods that restore named directories and files (**incfile, ffile**) support this option.

–**A** *partdev*   Initiates restore of the entire disk *partdev*.

     -P *partdev*   Initiates restore of the data partition *partdev*.

     -S *odevice*   Initiates restore of the filesystem partition *odevice*.

DIAGNOSTICS

The exit codes for **restore** are the following:

0 = the task completed successfully
1 = one or more parameters to **restore** are invalid
2 = an error has occurred, causing **restore** to fail to
    complete *all* portions of its task

EXAMPLES

Example 1:

```
restore -m -S /usr
```

posts a request to restore the most current archived version of **/usr**. If the restore cannot be carried out immediately, notify the invoking user when the request has been completed.

Example 2:

```
restore -o /dev/rdsk/* -P /dev/rdsk/y
```

posts a request that the archived data partition **/dev/rdsk/**y be restored to the target device partition **/dev/rdsk/***, where the value of * and y are machine specific.

Example 3:

```
restore -d "december 1, 1987" -A /dev/rdsk/*
```

posts a request for the restore of the entire disk **/dev/rdsk/***, where the value of * is machine specific. The restore should be made as of December 1, 1987.

Example 4:

```
restore -n -P /dev/rdsk/*
```

requests the system to display the backup date and an **ls -1** listing from the backup history log of all archived versions of the data partition **/dev/rdsk/***, where the value of * is machine specific. The data partition is not restored.

FILES

/etc/bkup/bkhist.tab	lists the labels of all volumes that have been used for backup operations
/etc/bkup/rsstatus.tab	lists the status of all restore requests from users
/etc/bkup/rsnotify.tab	lists the email address of the operator to be notified whenever restore requests require operator intervention

SEE ALSO

fdisk(1M), **mail**(1M), **rsnotify**(1M), **rsoper**(1M), **rsstatus**(1M),
urestore(1M), **ursstatus**(1M).
getdate(3C) in the *Programmer's Reference Manual*.

NAME

restore – restore file to original directory

SYNOPSIS

restore [–c] [–i] [–o] [–t] [–d *device*] | [*pattern* [*pattern*]. . .]

DESCRIPTION

-c   complete restore. All files on the tape are restored.

-i   gets the index file off of the medium. This only works when the archive was created using **backup**. The output is a list of all the files on the medium. No files are actually restored.

-o   overwrite existing files. If the file being restored already exists it will not be restored unless this option is specified.

-t   indicates that the tape device is to be used. Must be used with the –d option when restoring from tape.

-d   *device* is the raw device to be used. It defaults to **dev/SA/diskette**

When doing a restore, one or more patterns can be specified. These patterns are matched against the files on the tape. When a match is found, the file is restored. Since backups are done using full pathnames, the file is restored to its original directory. Metacharacters can be used to match multiple files. The patterns should be in quotes to prevent the characters from being expanded before they are passed to the command. If no patterns are specified, it defaults to restoring all files. If a pattern does not match any file on the tape, a message is printed.

When end of medium is reached, the user is prompted for the next media. The user can exit at this point by typing **q**. (This may cause files to be corrupted if a file happens to span a medium.) In general, quitting in the middle is not a good idea.

If the file already exists and an attempt is made to restore it without the –o option, the file name will be printed on the screen followed by a question mark. This file will not be retored.

In order for multi-volume restores to work correctly, the raw device must be used.

SEE ALSO

sh(1)

NAME

rexecd – remote execution server

SYNOPSIS

in.rexecd *host.port*

DESCRIPTION

rexecd is the server for the **rexec**(3N) routine. The server provides remote execution facilities with authentication based on user names and encrypted passwords. It is invoked automatically as needed by **inetd**(1M), and then executes the following protocol:

1) The server reads characters from the socket up to a null (**\0**) byte. The resultant string is interpreted as an ASCII number, base 10.

2) If the number received in step 1 is non-zero, it is interpreted as the port number of a secondary stream to be used for the **stderr**. A second connection is then created to the specified port on the client's machine.

3) A null terminated user name of at most 16 characters is retrieved on the initial socket.

4) A null terminated, encrypted, password of at most 16 characters is retrieved on the initial socket.

5) A null terminated command to be passed to a shell is retrieved on the initial socket. The length of the command is limited by the upper bound on the size of the system's argument list.

6) **rexecd** then validates the user as is done at login time and, if the authentication was successful, changes to the user's home directory, and establishes the user and group protections of the user. If any of these steps fail the connection is aborted with a diagnostic message returned.

7) A null byte is returned on the connection associated with the **stderr** and the command line is passed to the normal login shell of the user. The shell inherits the network connections established by **rexecd**.

SEE ALSO

inetd(1M)

DIAGNOSTICS

All diagnostic messages are returned on the connection associated with the **stderr**, after which any network connections are closed. An error is indicated by a leading byte with a value of 1 (0 is returned in step 7 above upon successful completion of all the steps prior to the command execution).

username too long
    The name is longer than 16 characters.

password too long
    The password is longer than 16 characters.

command too long
    The command line passed exceeds the size of the argument list (as configured into the system).

Login incorrect.
> No password file entry for the user name existed.

Password incorrect.
> The wrong password was supplied.

No remote directory.
> The **chdir** command to the home directory failed.

Try again.
> A **fork** by the server failed.

/usr/bin/sh: ...
> The user's login shell could not be started.

NOTES

Indicating **Login incorrect** as opposed to **Password incorrect** is a security breach which allows people to probe a system for users with null passwords.

A facility to allow all data exchanges to be encrypted should be present.

NAME

    rfadmin – Remote File Sharing domain administration

SYNOPSIS

    rfadmin

    rfadmin **–a** *hostname*

    rfadmin **–r** *hostname*

    rfadmin **–p** [–t *transport1,transport2, . . .*]

    rfadmin **–q**

    rfadmin **–o** *option*

DESCRIPTION

    rfadmin is used to add and remove hosts, and their associated authentication
    information, from a *domain*/**passwd** file on a Remote File Sharing primary domain
    name server. It is also used to transfer domain name server responsibilities from
    one machine to another. Used with no options, **rfadmin** returns the *hostname* of
    the current domain name server for the local domain on each of the transport
    providers that span the domain.

    rfadmin can only be used to modify domain files on the primary domain name
    server (**–a** and **–r** options). If domain name server responsibilities are tem-
    porarily passed to a secondary domain name server, that computer can use the **–p**
    option to pass domain name server responsibility back to the primary. The com-
    mand can be directed to a specific set of transport providers by using the **–t**
    option with a comma-separated list of transport providers. Any host can use
    rfadmin with no options to print information about the domain. The user must
    have **root** permissions to use this command, except in the case when the **–q**
    option is used.

    –a *hostname*   Add a host to a domain that is served by this domain name server.
                     hostname must be of the form *domain.nodename*. It creates an entry
                     for *hostname* in the *domain*/**passwd** file and prompts for an initial
                     authentication password; the password prompting process con-
                     forms with that of **passwd**(1).

    –r *hostname*   Remove a host, *hostname*, from its domain by removing it from the
                     domain/**passwd file.**

    –p   Used to pass the domain name server responsibilities back to a pri-
                     mary or to a secondary name server.

    –t *transport1, transport2 . . .*
                     Select transport provider(s). The **–t** option is used only with the
                     –p option.

    –q   Tells if RFS is running.

    –o *option*   Sets RFS system option. *option* is one of the following:

                     loopback   Enable loop back facility. This allows a resource
                                   advertised by a computer to be mounted by the same
                                   computer. **loopback** is off by default.

noloopback   Turn off the loop back facility. `noloopback` is the default.

loopmode   Check if the loop back facility is on or off.

ERRORS

When used with the −a option, if *hostname* is not unique in the domain, an error message will be sent to standard error.

When used with the −r option, if (1) *hostname* does not exist in the domain, (2) *hostname* is defined as a domain name server, or (3) there are resources advertised by *hostname*, an error message will be sent to standard error.

When used with the −p option to change the domain name server, if there are no backup name servers defined for *domain*, an error message will be sent to standard error.

FILES

/etc/rfs/auth.info/*domain*/passwd

For each *domain*, this file is created on the primary, copied to all secondaries, and copied to all hosts that want to do password verification of hosts in the *domain*.

SEE ALSO

passwd(1), dname(1M), rfstart(1M), rfstop(1M), umount(1M)

NAME

    `rfpasswd` – change Remote File Sharing host password

SYNOPSIS

    `rfpasswd`

DESCRIPTION

    `rfpasswd` updates the Remote File Sharing authentication password for a host; processing of the new password follows the same criteria as `passwd`(1). The updated password is registered at the domain name server (`/etc/dfs/rfs/auth.info/`*domain*`/passwd`) and replaces the password stored at the local host (`/etc/dfs/rfs/loc.passwd` file).

    This command is restricted to the super-user.

    NOTE: If you change your host password, make sure that hosts that validate your password are notified of this change. To receive the new password, hosts must obtain a copy of the *domain/***passwd** file from the domain's primary name server. If this is not done, attempts to mount remote resources may fail!

ERRORS

    If (1) the old password entered from this command does not match the existing password for this machine, (2) the two new passwords entered from this command do not match, (3) the new password does not satisfy the security criteria in `passwd`(1), (4) the domain name server does not know about this machine, or (5) the command is not run with super-user privileges, an error message will be sent to standard error. Also, Remote File Sharing must be running on your host and your domain's primary name server. A new password cannot be logged if a secondary is acting as the domain name server.

FILES

    `/etc/dfs/rfs/auth.info/`*domain*`/passwd`
    `/etc/dfs/rfs/loc.passwd`

SEE ALSO

    `rfstart`(1M), `rfadmin`(1M)
    `passwd`(1) in the *User's Reference Manual*

NAME

rfstart – start Remote File Sharing

SYNOPSIS

rfstart [**–v**] [**–p** *primary_addr*]

DESCRIPTION

rfstart starts Remote File Sharing and defines an authentication level for incoming requests. [This command can only be used after the domain name server is set up and your computer's domain name and network specification have been defined using **dname**(1M).]

–v   Specifies that verification of all clients is required in response to initial incoming mount requests; any host not in the file **/etc/rfs/auth.info/***domain*/passwd for the **domain** they belong to, will not be allowed to mount resources from your host. If **–v** is not specified, hosts named in *domain*/passwd will be verified. Other hosts will be allowed to connect without verification.

–p *primary_addr*
        Indicates the primary domain name server for your domain. *primary_addr* can specify any of the following: the network address of the primary name server for a domain (*addr*); a list of address tuples when RFS is used over multiple transport providers (*transport1:addr1,transport2:addr2, . . .*). An example of each type of specification follows:

        –p *addr*
        –p *transport1:addr1,transport2:addr2, . . .*

If the **–p** option is not specified, the address of the domain name server is taken from the associated **rfmaster** files. The **–p** *addr* specification is valid only when one transport provider is being used. See the **rfmaster**(1M) manual page for a description of the valid address syntax.

If the host password has not been set, **rfstart** will prompt for a password. The password prompting process must match the password entered for your machine at the primary domain name server [see **rfadmin**(1M)]. If you remove the **loc.passwd** file or change domains, you will also have to reenter the password.

Also, when **rfstart** is run on a domain name server, entries in the **rfmaster**(4) file are syntactically validated.

This command is restricted to the super-user.

ERRORS

If syntax errors are found when validating an **rfmaster**(4) file, a warning describing each error will be sent to standard error.

An error message will be sent to standard error if any of the following conditions are true:

1. remote file sharing is already running
2. there is no communications network
3. a domain name server cannot be found
4. a domain name server does not recognize the machine

5. the command is run without super-user privileges

Remote file sharing will not start if a host password in `/etc/rfs/<transport>/loc.passwd` is corrupted. If you suspect this has happened, remove the file and run **rfstart** again to reenter your password.

Note: **rfstart** will not fail if your host password does not match the password on the domain name server. You will simply receive a warning message. However, if you try to mount a resource from the primary, or any other host that validates your password, the mount will fail if your password does not match the one that the host has listed for your machine.

FILES
      `/etc/rfs/<transport>/rfmaster`
      `/etc/rfs/<transport>/loc.passwd`

SEE ALSO
      share(1M), **dname**(1M), **idload**(1M), **mount**(1M), **rfadmin**(1M), **rfstop**(1M), **unshare**(1M)
      rfmaster(4) in the *Programmer's Reference Manual*

NOTES
      You must run **idload**(1M) to put any non-default user and group mappings into place.

NAME

    rfstop – stop the Remote File Sharing environment

SYNOPSIS

    rfstop

DESCRIPTION

    rfstop disconnects a host from the Remote File Sharing environment until another rfstart(1M) is executed.

    When executed on the domain name server, the domain name server responsibility is moved to a secondary name server as designated in the rfmaster(4) file. If there is no designated secondary name server rfstop will issue a warning message, Remote File Sharing will be stopped, and name service will no longer be available to the domain.

    This command is restricted to the super-user.

ERRORS

    If (1) there are resources currently advertised by this host, (2) resources from this machine are still remotely mounted by other hosts, (3) there are still remotely mounted resources in the local file system tree, (4) rfstart(1M) had not previously been executed, or (5) the command is not run with super-user privileges, an error message will be sent to standard error and Remote File Sharing will not be stopped.

SEE ALSO

    adv(1M), mount(1M), rfadmin(1M), rfstart(1M), unadv(1M), rfmaster(4)

NAME

rfuadmin – Remote File Sharing notification shell script

SYNOPSIS

/etc/rfs/rfuadmin *message remote_resource* [*seconds*]

DESCRIPTION

The **rfuadmin** administrative shell script responds to unexpected Remote File Sharing events, such as broken network connections and forced unmounts, picked up by the **rfudaemon** process. This command is not intended to be run directly from the shell.

The response to messages received by **rfudaemon** can be tailored to suit the particular system by editing the **rfuadmin** script. The following paragraphs describe the arguments passed to **rfuadmin** and the responses.

disconnect *remote_resource*

> A link to a remote resource has been cut. **rfudaemon** executes **rfuadmin**, passing it the message **disconnect** and the name of the disconnected resource. **rfuadmin** sends this message to all terminals using **wall**(1):

> *Remote_resource* **has been disconnected from the system.**

> Then it executes **fuser**(1M) to kill all processes using the resource, unmounts the resource [**umount**(1M)] to clean up the kernel, and starts **rmount** to try to remount the resource.

fumount *remote_resource*

> A remote server machine has forced an unmount of a resource a local machine has mounted. The processing is similar to processing for a disconnect.

fuwarn *remote_resource seconds*

> This message notifies **rfuadmin** that a resource is about to be unmounted. **rfudaemon** sends this script the **fuwarn** message, the resource name, and the number of seconds in which the forced unmount will occur. **rfuadmin** sends this message to all terminals:

> *Remote_resource* **is being removed from the system in # seconds.**

SEE ALSO

fumount(1M), **rmount**(1M), **rfudaemon**(1M), **rfstart**(1M)
wall(1) in the *User's Reference Manual*

NOTES

The console must be on when Remote File Sharing is running. If it's not, **rfuadmin** will hang when it tries to write to the console (**wall**) and recovery from disconnected resources will not complete.

NAME

rfudaemon – Remote File Sharing daemon process

SYNOPSIS

/etc/rfs/rfudaemon

DESCRIPTION

The **rfudaemon** command is started automatically by **rfstart**(1M) and runs as a daemon process as long as Remote File Sharing is active. Its function is to listen for unexpected events, such as broken network connections and forced unmounts, and execute appropriate administrative procedures.

When such an event occurs, **rfudaemon** executes the administrative shell script **rfuadmin**, with arguments that identify the event. This command is not intended to be run from the shell. Here are the events:

DISCONNECT   A link to a remote resource has been cut. **rfudaemon** executes **rfuadmin**, with two arguments: **disconnect** and the name of the disconnected resource.

FUMOUNT   A remote server machine has forced an unmount of a resource a local machine has mounted. **rfudaemon** executes **rfuadmin**, with two arguments: **fumount** and the name of the disconnected resource.

GETUMSG   A remote user-level program has sent a message to the local **rfudaemon**. Currently the only message sent is *fuwarn*, which notifies **rfuadmin** that a resource is about to be unmounted. It sends **rfuadmin** the *fuwarn*, the resource name, and the number of seconds in which the forced unmount will occur.

LASTUMSG   The local machine wants to stop the **rfudaemon** [**rfstop**(1M)]. This causes **rfudaemon** to exit.

SEE ALSO

rfstart(1M), rfuadmin(1M)

NAME

rlogin – remote login

SYNOPSIS

rlogin [-L] [-8] [-e c] [-l *username*] *hostname*

DESCRIPTION

rlogin establishes a remote login session from your terminal to the remote machine named *hostname*.

Hostnames are listed in the *hosts* database, which may be contained in the /etc/hosts file, the Internet domain name server, or in both. Each host has one official name (the first name in the database entry), and optionally one or more nicknames. Either official hostnames or nicknames may be specified in *hostname*.

Each remote machine may have a file named /etc/hosts.equiv containing a list of trusted hostnames with which it shares usernames. Users with the same username on both the local and remote machine may rlogin from the machines listed in the remote machine's /etc/hosts.equiv file without supplying a password. Individual users may set up a similar private equivalence list with the file .rhosts in their home directories. Each line in this file contains two names: a *hostname* and a *username* separated by a space. An entry in a remote user's .rhosts file permits the user named *username* who is logged into *hostname* to log in to the remote machine as the remote user without supplying a password. If the name of the local host is not found in the /etc/hosts.equiv file on the remote machine, and the local username and hostname are not found in the remote user's .rhosts file, then the remote machine will prompt for a password. Hostnames listed in /etc/hosts.equiv and .rhosts files must be the official hostnames listed in the hosts database; nicknames may not be used in either of these files.

To counter security problems, the .rhosts file must be owned by either the remote user or by root.

The remote terminal type is the same as your local terminal type (as given in your environment **TERM** variable). The terminal or window size is also copied to the remote system if the server supports the option, and changes in size are reflected as well. All echoing takes place at the remote site, so that (except for delays) the remote login is transparent. Flow control using **CTRL-S** and **CTRL-Q** and flushing of input and output on interrupts are handled properly.

The following options are available:

-L   Allow the rlogin session to be run in litout mode.

-8   Pass eight-bit data across the net instead of seven-bit data.

-e *c*   Specify a different escape character, *c*, for the line used to disconnect from the remote host.

-l *username*
        Specify a different *username* for the remote login. If you do not use this option, the remote username used is the same as your local username.

Escape Sequences

Lines that you type which start with the tilde character are escape sequences (the escape character can be changed using the **-e** options):

~.   Disconnect from the remote host — this is not the same as a logout, because the local host breaks the connection with no warning to the remote end.

susp   Suspend the login session (only if you are using a shell with Job Control). **susp** is your suspend character, usually see **tty**(1).

FILES

```
/etc/passwd
/usr/hosts/*         for hostname version of the command
/etc/hosts.equiv     list of trusted hostnames with shared usernames
$HOME/.rhosts        private list of trusted hostname/username combinations
```

SEE ALSO

rsh(1), **stty**(1), **tty**(1), **named**(1M), **hosts**(4), **hosts.equiv**(4)

NOTES

When a system is listed in **hosts.equiv**, its security must be as good as local security. One insecure system listed in **hosts.equiv** can compromise the security of the entire system.

When a line of the form *hostname username* appears in **hosts.equiv**, the user named may log in as anyone in the local password file by using the command

          rlogin -l *username hostname*

where *username* is any valid username in the **passwd** file.

If you use a windowing terminal and you intend to run **layers**(1) on the remote system, then you must invoke **rlogin** with the **-8** option.

This implementation can only use the TCP network service.

NAME

`rlogind` – remote login server

SYNOPSIS

`in.rlogind`

DESCRIPTION

`rlogind` is the server for the `rlogin`(1) program. The server provides a remote login facility with authentication based on privileged port numbers.

`rlogind` is invoked by `inetd`(1M) when a remote login connection is established, and executes the following protocol:

1)   The server checks the remote client's source port. If the port is not in the range 0-1023, the server aborts the connection.

2)   The server checks the remote client's source address. If an entry for the client exists in both `/etc/hosts` and `/etc/hosts.equiv`, a user logging in from the client is not prompted for a password. If the address is associated with a host for which no corresponding entry exists in `/etc/hosts`, the user is prompted for a password, regardless of whether or not an entry for the remote client is present in `/etc/hosts.equiv` [see `hosts`(4) and `hosts.equiv`(4)].

Once the source port and address have been checked, `rlogind` allocates a pseudo-terminal and manipulates file descriptors so that the slave half of the pseudo-terminal becomes the `stdin`, `stdout`, and `stderr` for a login process.

The login process is an instance of the `in.login` program, which is based on `login`(1). The login process is invoked with the `-r` option to indicate that it is originated by `rlogind`. The login process proceeds with the authentication process as described in `rshd`(1M), but if automatic authentication fails, it reprompts the user to login as one finds on a standard terminal line.

`rlogind` manipulates the master side of the pseudo-terminal, operating as an intermediary between the login process and the remote client's `rlogin` program. In normal operation, a packet protocol is invoked to provide `Ctrl-S` / `Ctrl-Q` type facilities and propagate interrupt signals to the remote programs. The login process propagates the client terminal's baud rate and terminal type, as found in the environment variable, `TERM`; see `environ`(4).

SEE ALSO

`inetd`(1M), `hosts`(4), `hosts.equiv`(4)

DIAGNOSTICS

All diagnostic messages are returned on the connection associated with the `stderr`, after which any network connections are closed. An error is indicated by a leading byte with a value of 1.

`Hostname for your address unknown.`
         No entry in the host name database existed for the client's machine.

`Try again.`
         A *fork* by the server failed.

`/usr/bin/sh:` ...
> The user's login shell could not be started.

NOTES

The authentication procedure used here assumes the integrity of each client machine and the connecting medium. This is insecure, but is useful in an "open" environment.

A facility to allow all data exchanges to be encrypted should be present.

NAME

    rm, rmdir – remove files or directories

SYNOPSIS

    rm [–f] [–i] *file* . . .

    rm –r [–f] [–i] dirname . . . [*file* . . .]

    rmdir [–p] [–s] dirname . . .

DESCRIPTION

    rm removes the entries for one or more files from a directory. If a file has no write permission and the standard input is a terminal, the full set of permissions (in octal) for the file are printed followed by a question mark. This is a prompt for confirmation. If the answer begins with **y** (for yes), the file is deleted, otherwise the file remains.

    If *file* is a symbolic link, the link will be removed, but the file or directory to which it refers will not be deleted. A user does not need write permission on a symbolic link to remove it, provided they have write permissions in the directory.

    Note that if the standard input is not a terminal, the command will operate as if the –f option is in effect.

    Three options apply to rm:

–f   This option causes the removal of all files (whether write-protected or not) in a directory without prompting the user. In a write-protected directory, however, files are never removed (whatever their permissions are), but no messages are displayed. If the removal of a write-protected directory is attempted, this option will not suppress an error message.

–r   This option causes the recursive removal of any directories and subdirectories in the argument list. The directory will be emptied of files and removed. Note that the user is normally prompted for removal of any write-protected files which the directory contains. The write-protected files are removed without prompting, however, if the –f option is used, or if the standard input is not a terminal and the –i option is not used.

       Symbolic links that are encountered with this option will not be traversed.

       If the removal of a non-empty, write-protected directory is attempted, the command will always fail (even if the –f option is used), resulting in an error message.

–i   With this option, confirmation of removal of any write-protected file occurs interactively. It overrides the –f option and remains in effect even if the standard input is not a terminal.

    Two options apply to rmdir:

–p   This option allows users to remove the directory *dirname* and its parent directories which become empty. A message is printed on standard output about whether the whole path is removed or part of the path remains for some reason.

-s   This option is used to suppress the message printed on standard error when
        -p is in effect.

DIAGNOSTICS

All messages are generally self-explanatory.

It is forbidden to remove the files "." and ".." in order to avoid the conse-
quences of inadvertently doing something like the following:

        rm -r .*

Both **rm** and **rmdir** return exit codes of 0 if all the specified directories are
removed successfully. Otherwise, they return a non-zero exit code.

SEE ALSO

unlink(2), **rmdir**(2) in the *Programmer's Reference Manual*

NOTES

A -- permits the user to mark explicitly the end of any command line options,
allowing **rm** to recognize filename arguments that begin with a -. As an aid to
BSD migration, **rm** will accept - as a synonym for --. This migration aid may
disappear in a future release. If a -- and a - both appear on the same command
line, the second will be interpreted as a filename.

NAME

rmdel – remove a delta from an SCCS file

SYNOPSIS

rmdel −r*SID files*

DESCRIPTION

rmdel removes the delta specified by the *SID* (SCCS identification string) from each named SCCS file. The delta to be removed must be the newest (most recent) delta in its branch in the delta chain of each named SCCS file. In addition, the delta specified must not be that of a version being edited for the purpose of making a delta; that is, if a p-file exists for the named SCCS file [see get(1)], the delta specified must not appear in any entry of the p-file.

The −r option specifies the *SID* level of the delta to be removed.

If a directory is named, rmdel behaves as though each file in the directory were specified as a named file, except that non-SCCS files (last component of the path name does not begin with s.) and unreadable files are silently ignored. If a name of − is given, the standard input is read; each line of the standard input is taken to be the name of an SCCS file to be processed; non-SCCS files and unreadable files are silently ignored.

The rules governing the removal of a delta are as follows: if you make a delta and have appropriate file permissions, you can remove it; if you own the file and directory in which a new delta file resides, you can remove the delta.

FILES

x.file   [See delta(1)]
z.file   [See delta(1)]

SEE ALSO

delta(1), get(1), help(1), prs(1), sccsfile(4)

DIAGNOSTICS

Use help(1) for explanations.

NAME

rmntstat – display mounted resource information

SYNOPSIS

rmntstat [–h] [*resource*]

DESCRIPTION

When used with no options, rmntstat displays a list of all local Remote File Sharing resources that are remotely mounted, the local path name, and the corresponding clients. rmntstat returns the remote mount data regardless of whether a resource is currently advertised; this ensures that resources that have been unadvertised but are still remotely mounted are included in the report. When a *resource* is specified, rmntstat displays the remote mount information only for that resource. The –h option causes header information to be omitted from the display.

EXIT STATUS

If no local resources are remotely mounted, rmntstat will return a successful exit status.

ERRORS

If *resource* (1) does not physically reside on the local machine or (2) is an invalid resource name, an error message will be sent to standard error.

SEE ALSO

mount(1M), fumount(1M), unadv(1M).

NAME

    rmnttry – attempt to mount queued remote resources

SYNOPSIS

    /etc/rfs/rmnttry [*resource* . . .]

DESCRIPTION

    rmnttry sequences through the pending mount requests stored in **/etc/rfs/rmnttab**, trying to mount each resource. If a mount succeeds, the resource entry is removed from the **/etc/rfs/rmnttab** file.

    If one or more resource names are supplied, mounts are attempted only for those resources, rather than for all pending mounts. Mounts are not attempted for resources not present in the **/etc/rfs/rmnttab** file (see **rmount**(1M)). If a mount invoked from **rmnttry** takes over 3 minutes to complete, **rmnttry** aborts the mount and issues a warning message.

    rmnttry is typically invoked from a cron entry in **/var/spool/cron/crontabs/root** to attempt mounting queued resources at periodic intervals. The default strategy is to attempt mounts at 15 minute intervals. The cron entry for this is:

        10,25,40,55 * * * * /etc/rfs/rmnttry >/dev/null

FILES

    /etc/rfs/rmnttab pending mount requests

SEE ALSO

    mount(1M), **rmount**(1M), **rumount**(1M), **mnttab**(4)
    crontab(1) in the *User's Reference Manual*

DIAGNOSTICS

    An exit code of 0 is returned if all requested mounts succeeded, 1 is returned if one or more mounts failed, and 2 is returned for bad usage.

NAME

rmount – queue remote resource mounts

SYNOPSIS

/usr/sbin/rmount [**–d**[**r**] *resource directory*]

DESCRIPTION

rmount queues a remote resource for mounting. The command enters the resource request into **/etc/rfs/rmnttab**, which is formatted identically to **mnttab**(4). **rmnttry**(1M) is used to poll entries in this file.

When used without arguments, **rmount** prints a list of resources with pending mounts along with their destined directories, modes, and date of request. The resources are listed chronologically, with the oldest resource request appearing first.

The following options are available:

–d   indicates that the *resource* is a remote resource to be mounted on **directory**.

–r   indicates that the *resource* is to be mounted read-only. If the *resource* is write-protected, this flag must be used.

FILES

/etc/rfs/rmnttab   pending mount requests

SEE ALSO

mount(1M), rmnttry(1M), rumount(1M), rmountall(1M), mnttab(4).

DIAGNOSTICS

An exit code of 0 is returned upon successful completion of **rmount**. Otherwise, a non-zero value is returned.

NAME
rmountall, **rumountall** – mount, unmount Remote File Sharing resources

SYNOPSIS
/usr/sbin/rmountall [–] " *file-system-table* " [. . .]
/usr/sbin/rumountall [**–k**]

DESCRIPTION
rmountall is a Remote File Sharing command used to mount remote resources according to a *file-system-table*. (**/etc/vfstab** is the recommended *file-system-table*.) **rmountall** also invokes the **rmnttry** command, which attempts to mount queued resources. The special file name "–" reads from the standard input.

rumountall causes all mounted remote resources to be unmounted and deletes all resources that were queued from **rmount**. The **–k** option sends a **SIGKILL** signal, via **fuser**, to processes that have files open.

Only a privileged user can execute these commands.

The format of the *file-system-table* is as follows:

column 1   block special file name of file system

column 2   file system name for **fsck** (ignored)

column 3   mount-point directory

column 4   file system type (must be **rfs**)

column 5   file system check option (ignored)

column 6   automount option (must be **yes**)

column 7   mount flags (**ro** for read-only, **rw** for read-write, – for read-write)

Columns are separated by white space. Lines beginning with a pound sign (**#**) are comments. Empty lines are ignored.

SEE ALSO
fuser(1M), **mount**(1M), **rfstart**(1M), **rmnttry**(1M), **rmount**(1M)
sysadm(1) in the *User's Reference Manual*
signal(2) in the *Programmer's Reference Manual*

DIAGNOSTICS
No messages are printed if the remote resources are mounted successfully.

Error and warning messages come from **mount**(1M).

NAME

roffbib – format and print a bibliographic database

SYNOPSIS

/usr/ucb/roffbib [–e] [–h] [–Q] [–x] [–m *filename*] [–n*p*] [–o*list*]
[–r*aN*] [–s*N*] [–T*term*] [*filename*] . . .

DESCRIPTION

The **roffbib** command prints out all records in a bibliographic database, in bibliography format rather than as footnotes or endnotes. Generally it is used in conjunction with **sortbib**(1):

        example% sortbib database | roffbib

If abstracts or comments are entered following the **%X** field key, **roffbib** will format them into paragraphs for an annotated bibliography. Several **%X** fields may be given if several annotation paragraphs are desired.

roffbib accepts all options understood by **nroff**(1) except **–i** and **–q**, as well as those listed below:

–e   Produce equally-spaced words in adjusted lines using full terminal resolution.

–h   Use output tabs during horizontal spacing to speed output and reduce output character count. TAB settings are assumed to be every 8 nominal character widths.

–Q   Queue output for the phototypesetter. Page offset is set to 1 inch.

–x   Suppress printing of abstracts.

–m *filename*   Prepend the macro file /usr/ucblib/doctools/tmac/tmac.name to the input files. There should be a space between the **–m** and the macro filename. This set of macros will replace the ones defined in /usr/ucblib/doctools/tmac/tmac.bib.

–n*p*   Number first generated page *p*.

–o*list*   Print only page numbers that appear in the comma-separated *list* of numbers and ranges. A range *N–M* means pages *N* through *M*; an initial *–N* means from the beginning to page *N*; a final *N–* means from page *N* to end.

–r*aN*   Set register *a* (one-character) to *N*. The command-line argument **–rN1** will number the references starting at 1.

              Four command-line registers control formatting style of the bibliography, much like the number registers of **ms**(7). The flag **–rV2** will double space the bibliography, while **–rV1** will double space references but single space annotation paragraphs. The line length can be changed from the default 6.5 inches to 6 inches with the **–rL6i** argument, and the page offset can be set from the default of 0 to one inch by specifying **–rO1i** (capital O, not zero).

      −s*N*   Halt prior to every *N* pages for paper loading or changing (default *N* =1). To resume, enter NEWLINE or RETURN.

      −T*term*   Specify *term* as the terminal type.

FILES

    `/usr/ucblib/doctools/tmac/tmac.bib`   file of macros used by **nroff/troff**

SEE ALSO

    addbib(1), **indxbib**(1), **lookbib**(1), **nroff**(1) **refer**(1), **sortbib**(1), **troff**(1)

NOTES

    Users have to rewrite macros to create customized formats.

NAME

route – manually manipulate the routing tables

SYNOPSIS

route [–fn] { add | delete } { *destination* | default } [host | net] [*gateway* [*metric*]]

DESCRIPTION

route manually manipulates the network routing tables normally maintained by the system routing daemon, routed(1M), or through default routes and redirect messages from routers. route allows the super-user to operate directly on the routing table for the specific host or network indicated by *destination*. default is available for gateways to use after all other routes have been attempted. The *gateway* argument, if present, indicates the network gateway to which packets should be addressed. The *metric* argument indicates the number of hops to the *destination*. The *metric* is required for *add* commands; it must be zero if the destination is on a directly-attached network, and nonzero if the route utilizes one or more gateways.

The add command instructs route to add a route to *destination*. delete deletes a route.

Routes to a particular host must be distinguished from those to a network. The optional keywords net and host force the destination to be interpreted as a network or a host, respectively. Otherwise, if the destination has a local address part of INADDR_ANY, then the route is assumed to be to a network; otherwise, it is presumed to be a route to a host. If the route is to a destination connected by a gateway, the *metric* parameter should be greater than 0. If adding a route with metric 0, the gateway given is the address of this host on the common network, indicating the interface to be used directly for transmission. All symbolic names specified for a *destination* (except default) or *gateway* are looked up in the hosts database using gethostbyname(3N). If this lookup fails, then the name is looked up in the networks database using getnetbyname(3N).

OPTIONS

–f   Flush the routing tables of all gateway entries. If this is used in conjunction with one of the commands described above, route flushes the gateways before performing the command.

–n   Prevents attempts to print host and network names symbolically when reporting actions. This is useful, for example, when all name servers are down on your local net, so you need a route before you can contact the name server.

FILES

/etc/hosts
/etc/networks

SEE ALSO

ioctl(2), gethostbyname(3N), getnetbyname(3N), routing(4N), routed(1M)

DIAGNOSTICS

add [**host** | **net**] *destination*:*gateway*
> The specified route is being added to the tables. The values printed are from the routing table entry supplied in the **ioctl**(2) call.

delete [**host** | **net**] *destination*:*gateway*
> The specified route is being deleted.

destination **done**
> When the **−f** flag is specified, each routing table entry deleted is indicated with a message of this form.

Network is unreachable
> An attempt to add a route failed because the gateway listed was not on a directly-connected network. Give the next-hop gateway instead.

not in table
> A delete operation was attempted for an entry that is not in the table.

routing table overflow
> An add operation was attempted, but the system was unable to allocate memory to create the new entry.

NAME

routed – network routing daemon

SYNOPSIS

in.routed [–qstv] [*logfile*]

DESCRIPTION

routed is invoked at boot time to manage the network routing tables. The routing daemon uses a variant of the Xerox NS Routing Information Protocol in maintaining up to date kernel routing table entries.

In normal operation routed listens on udp(4P) socket 520 (decimal) for routing information packets. If the host is an internetwork router, it periodically supplies copies of its routing tables to any directly connected hosts and networks.

When routed is started, it uses the SIOCGIFCONF ioctl(2) to find those directly connected interfaces configured into the system and marked up (the software loopback interface is ignored). If multiple interfaces are present, it is assumed the host will forward packets between networks. routed then transmits a *request* packet on each interface (using a broadcast packet if the interface supports it) and enters a loop, listening for *request* and *response* packets from other hosts.

When a *request* packet is received, routed formulates a reply based on the information maintained in its internal tables. The *response* packet generated contains a list of known routes, each marked with a hop count metric (a count of 16, or greater, is considered infinite). The metric associated with each route returned provides a metric relative to the sender.

request packets received by routed are used to update the routing tables if one of the following conditions is satisfied:

(1)   No routing table entry exists for the destination network or host, and the metric indicates the destination is reachable (that is, the hop count is not infinite).

(2)   The source host of the packet is the same as the router in the existing routing table entry. That is, updated information is being received from the very internetwork router through which packets for the destination are being routed.

(3)   The existing entry in the routing table has not been updated for some time (defined to be 90 seconds) and the route is at least as cost effective as the current route.

(4)   The new route describes a shorter route to the destination than the one currently stored in the routing tables; the metric of the new route is compared against the one stored in the table to decide this.

When an update is applied, routed records the change in its internal tables and generates a *response* packet to all directly connected hosts and networks. routed waits a short period of time (no more than 30 seconds) before modifying the kernel's routing tables to allow possible unstable situations to settle.

In addition to processing incoming packets, **routed** also periodically checks the routing table entries. If an entry has not been updated for 3 minutes, the entry's metric is set to infinity and marked for deletion. Deletions are delayed an additional 60 seconds to insure the invalidation is propagated throughout the internet.

Hosts acting as internetwork routers gratuitously supply their routing tables every 30 seconds to all directly connected hosts and networks.

Supplying the **-s** option forces **routed** to supply routing information whether it is acting as an internetwork router or not. The **-q** option is the opposite of the **-s** option. If the **-t** option is specified, all packets sent or received are printed on the standard output. In addition, **routed** will not divorce itself from the controlling terminal so that interrupts from the keyboard will kill the process. Any other argument supplied is interpreted as the name of file in which **routed**'s actions should be logged. This log contains information about any changes to the routing tables and a history of recent messages sent and received which are related to the changed route. The **-v** option allows a logfile to be created showing the changes made to the routing tables with a timestamp.

In addition to the facilities described above, **routed** supports the notion of distant *passive* and *active* gateways. When **routed** is started up, it reads the file **gateways** to find gateways which may not be identified using the **SIOGIFCONF ioctl**. Gateways specified in this manner should be marked passive if they are not expected to exchange routing information, while gateways marked active should be willing to exchange routing information (that is, they should have a **routed** process running on the machine). Passive gateways are maintained in the routing tables forever and information regarding their existence is included in any routing information transmitted. Active gateways are treated equally to network interfaces. Routing information is distributed to the gateway and if no routing information is received for a period of the time, the associated route is deleted.

The **gateways** is comprised of a series of lines, each in the following format:

> < **net** | **host** > *filename1* **gateway** *filename2* **metric** *value* < **passive** |
> **active** >

The **net** or **host** keyword indicates if the route is to a network or specific host.

filename1 is the name of the destination network or host. This may be a symbolic name located in **networks** or **hosts**, or an Internet address specified in dot notation; see **inet**(3N).

filename2 is the name or address of the gateway to which messages should be forwarded.

value is a metric indicating the hop count to the destination host or network.

The keyword **passive** or **active** indicates if the gateway should be treated as passive or active (as described above).

FILES

/etc/gateways   for distant gateways
/etc/networks
/etc/hosts

SEE ALSO

ioctl(2), inet(7), udp(7)

NOTES

The kernel's routing tables may not correspond to those of **routed** for short periods of time while processes utilizing existing routes exit; the only remedy for this is to place the routing process in the kernel.

routed should listen to intelligent interfaces, such as an IMP, and to error protocols, such as ICMP, to gather more information.

NAME
rpcbind – universal addresses to RPC program number mapper

SYNOPSIS
rpcbind

DESCRIPTION
rpcbind is a server that converts RPC program numbers into universal addresses. It must be running to make RPC calls.

When an RPC service is started, it will tell rpcbind at what address it is listening, and what RPC program numbers it is prepared to serve. When a client wishes to make an RPC call to a given program number, it will first contact rpcbind on the server machine to determine the address where RPC packets should be sent.

Normally, standard RPC servers are started by port monitors, so rpcbind must be started before port monitors are invoked.

rpcbind is restricted to users with appropriate privileges.

NOTES
If rpcbind crashes, all RPC servers must be restarted.

SEE ALSO
rpcinfo(1M)

NAME
rpcgen – an RPC protocol compiler

SYNOPSIS
rpcgen *infile*

rpcgen [-D*name*[=*value*]] [-**T**] [-**K** *secs*] *infile*

rpcgen -c|-h|-l|-m|-t [-o *outfile*] *infile*

rpcgen -s *nettype* [-o *outfile*] *infile*

rpcgen -n *netid* [-o *outfile*] *infile*

DESCRIPTION
rpcgen is a tool that generates C code to implement an RPC protocol. The input to **rpcgen** is a language similar to C known as RPC Language (Remote Procedure Call Language).

rpcgen is normally used as in the first synopsis where it takes an input file and generates up to four output files. If the *infile* is named **proto.x**, then **rpcgen** will generate a header file in **proto.h**, XDR routines in **proto_xdr.c**, server-side stubs in **proto_svc.c**, and client-side stubs in **proto_clnt.c**. With the -**T** option, it will also generate the RPC dispatch table in **proto_tbl.i**.

The server created can be started both by the port monitors (for example, **inetd** or **listen**) or by itself. When it is started by a port monitor, it creates servers only for the transport for which the file descriptor **0** was passed. The name of the transport must be specified by setting up the environment variable **PM_TRANSPORT**. When the server generated by **rpcgen** is executed, it creates server handles for all the transports specified in **NETPATH** environment variable, or if it is not set, it creates server handles for all the visible transports from **/etc/netconfig** file. Note: the transports are chosen at run time and not at compile time. When the server is self-started, it backgrounds itself by default. A special symbol, **RPC_SVC_FG**, can be defined at compilation time to make the server process run in foreground.

The second synopsis provides special features which allow for the creation of more sophisticated RPC servers. These features include support for user provided **#defines** and RPC dispatch tables. The entries in the RPC dispatch table contain:

- pointers to the service routine corresponding to that procedure,
- a pointer to the input and output arguments
- the size of these routines

A server can use the dispatch table to check authorization and then to execute the service routine; a client library may use it to deal with the details of storage management and XDR data conversion.

The other three synopses shown above are used when one does not want to generate all the output files, but only a particular one. Some examples of their usage is described in the EXAMPLE section below. When **rpcgen** is executed with the -**s** option, it creates servers for that particular class of transports. When executed with the -**n** option, it creates a server for the transport specified by *netid*. If *infile* is not specified, **rpcgen** accepts the standard input.

The C preprocessor, **cc -E** [see **cc**(1)], is run on the input file before it is actually interpreted by **rpcgen**. For each type of output file, **rpcgen** defines a special preprocessor symbol for use by the **rpcgen** programmer:

RPC_HDR	defined when compiling into header files
RPC_XDR	defined when compiling into XDR routines
RPC_SVC	defined when compiling into server-side stubs
RPC_CLNT	defined when compiling into client-side stubs
RPC_TBL	defined when compiling into RPC dispatch tables

Any line beginning with '**%**' is passed directly into the output file, uninterpreted by **rpcgen**.

For every data type referred to in *infile*, **rpcgen** assumes that there exists a routine with the string **xdr_** prepended to the name of the data type. If this routine does not exist in the RPC/XDR library, it must be provided. Providing an undefined data type allows customization of XDR routines.

The following options are available:

-c   Compile into XDR routines.

-D*name*[*=value*]

Define a symbol *name*. Equivalent to the **#define** directive in the source. If no *value* is given, *value* is defined as **1**. This option may be specified more than once.

-h   Compile into **C** data-definitions (a header file). **-T** option can be used in conjunction to produce a header file which supports RPC dispatch tables.

-K *secs*

By default, services created using **rpcgen** wait **120** seconds after servicing a request before exiting. That interval can be changed using the **-K** flag. To create a server that exits immediately upon servicing a request, **-K 0** can be used. To create a server that never exits, the appropriate argument is **-K -1**.

When monitoring for a server, some portmonitors, like **listen**(1M), *always* spawn a new process in response to a service request. If it is known that a server will be used with such a monitor, the server should exit immediately on completion. For such servers, **rpcgen** should be used with **-K -1**.

-l   Compile into client-side stubs.

-m   Compile into server-side stubs, but do not generate a main routine. This option is useful for doing callback-routines and for users who need to write their own main routine to do initialization.

-n *netid*

Compile into server-side stubs for the transport specified by *netid*. There should be an entry for *netid* in the netconfig database. This option may be specified more than once, so as to compile a server that serves multiple transports.

    −o *outfile*

        Specify the name of the output file. If none is specified, standard output is used (**−c**, **−h**, **−l**, **−m**, **−n**, **−s** and **−t** modes only).

    −s *nettype*

        Compile into server-side stubs for all the transports belonging to the class *nettype*. The supported classes are **netpath**, **visible**, **circuit_n**, **circuit_v**, **datagram_n**, **datagram_v**, **tcp**, and **udp** [see **rpc**(3N) for the meanings associated with these classes]. This option may be specified more than once. Note: the transports are chosen at run time and not at compile time.

    −t   Compile into RPC dispatch table.

    −T   Generate the code to support RPC dispatch tables.

    The options **−c**, **−h**, **−l**, **−m**, **−s** and **−t** are used exclusively to generate a particular type of file, while the options **−D** and **−T** are global and can be used with the other options.

NOTES

    The RPC Language does not support nesting of structures. As a work-around, structures can be declared at the top-level, and their name used inside other structures in order to achieve the same effect.

    Name clashes can occur when using program definitions, since the apparent scoping does not really apply. Most of these can be avoided by giving unique names for programs, versions, procedures and types.

    The server code generated with **−n** option refers to the transport indicated by *netid* and hence is very site specific.

EXAMPLE

    The following example:

        `$ rpcgen −T prot.x`

    generates all the five files: **prot.h**, **prot_clnt.c**, **prot_svc.c**, **prot_xdr.c** and **prot_tbl.i**.

    The following example sends the C data-definitions (header file) to the standard output.

        `$ rpcgen −h prot.x`

    To send the test version of the **−DTEST**, server side stubs for all the transport belonging to the class **datagram_n** to standard output, use:

        `$ rpcgen −s datagram_n −DTEST prot.x`

    To create the server side stubs for the transport indicated by *netid* **tcp**, use:

        `$ rpcgen −n tcp −o prot_svc.c prot.x`

SEE ALSO

    cc(1)

NAME

rpcinfo – report RPC information

SYNOPSIS

rpcinfo [*host*]

rpcinfo -p [*host*]

rpcinfo -T *transport host program version*

rpcinfo [-n *portnum*] -u *host program version*

rpcinfo [-n *portnum*] -t *host program version*

rpcinfo -a *serv_address* -T *transport program* [*version*]

rpcinfo -b [-T *transport*] *program version*

rpcinfo -d [-T *transport*] *program version*

DESCRIPTION

rpcinfo makes an RPC call to an RPC server and reports what it finds.

In the first synopsis, it lists all the registered RPC services with **rpcbind** on *host*. If *host* is not specified, it defaults to the local host.

In the second synopsis, it lists all the RPC services registered with **portmapper**. Also note that the format of the information is different in the first and the second synopsis; this is because in the first case, **rpcbind** (version 3) is contacted, while in the second case **portmap** (version 2) is contacted for information.

The third synopsis makes an RPC call to procedure 0 of *program* and *version* on the specified *host* and reports whether a response was received. *transport* is the transport which has to be used for contacting the given service. The remote address of the service is obtained by making a call to remote **rpcbind**.

The other ways of using **rpcinfo** are described below. See EXAMPLES.

The following options are available:

-T *transport* Specify the transport on which the service is required. If this option is not specified, **rpcinfo** uses the transport specified in the **NETPATH** environment variable, or if that is unset or null, in the netconfig database. This is a generic option, and can be used in conjunction with any other option, except the -b option.

-a *serv_address* Use *serv_address* as the (universal) address for the service on *transport*, to ping procedure 0 of the specified *program* and report whether a response was received. The use of -T option is required with -a option.

If version number is not specified, **rpcinfo** tries to ping all the available version numbers for that program number. This option avoids calls to remote **rpcbind** to find the address of the service. The *serv_address* is specified in universal address format of the given transport.

-b Make an RPC broadcast to procedure 0 of the specified *program* and *version* and report all hosts that respond. If *transport* is specified, it broadcasts its request only on the transport specified through *transport*. If broadcasting is not supported by any transport, an error message is printed. Only UDP transports support broadcasting.

-d   Delete registration for the RPC service of the specified *program*
            and *version*. If *transport* is specified, unregister the service on
            only that transport, otherwise unregister the services on all the
            transports on which it was registered. This option can be exer-
            cised only by the privileged user.

-n   Use *portnum* as the port number for the −t and −u options
            instead of the port number given by the portmapper. Use of this
            option avoids a call to the remote portmapper to find out the
            address of the service.

-p   Probe the portmapper on *host*, and print a list of all registered
            RPC programs. If *host* is not specified, it defaults to the local
            host.

-t   Make an RPC call to procedure 0 of *program* on the specified *host*
            using TCP, and report whether a response was received.

-u   Make an RPC call to procedure 0 of *program* on the specified *host*
            using UDP, and report whether a response was received.

The *program* argument is a number.

If a *version* is specified, **rpcinfo** attempts to call that version of the specified *program*. Otherwise, **rpcinfo** attempts to find all the registered version numbers for
the specified *program* by calling version 0, which is presumed not to exist; if it
does exist, **rpcinfo** attempts to obtain this information by calling an extremely
high version number instead, and attempts to call each registered version. Note:
the version number is required for −b and −d options.

EXAMPLES

To show all of the RPC services registered on the local machine use:

         $ **rpcinfo**

To show all of the RPC services registered with rpcbind on the machine named
klaxon use:

         $ **rpcinfo klaxon**

To show if the RPC service with program number *prog_no* and version *vers* is
registered on the machine named **klaxon** for the transport **tcp** use:

         $ **rpcinfo −T tcp klaxon** *prog_no vers*

To show all of the RPC services registered with the portmapper on the local
machine use:

         $ **rpcinfo −p**

To ping version 2 of **rpcbind** (program number **100000**) on host **sparky**:

         $ **rpcinfo −t sparky 100000 2**

To delete the registration for version 1 of the **walld** (program number 100008) service for all transports use:

> `# rpcinfo -d 100008 1`

SEE ALSO

> rpcbind(1M), rpc(4)

NAME

rsh – remote shell

SYNOPSIS

rsh [**-n**] [**-l** *username*] *hostname command*

rsh *hostname* [**-n**] [**-l** *username*] *command*

hostname [**-n**] [**-l** *username*] *command*

DESCRIPTION

rsh connects to the specified *hostname* and executes the specified *command*. rsh copies its standard input to the remote command, the standard output of the remote command to its standard output, and the standard error of the remote command to its standard error. Interrupt, quit and terminate signals are propagated to the remote command; rsh normally terminates when the remote command does.

If you omit *command*, instead of executing a single command, rsh logs you in on the remote host using rlogin(1). Shell metacharacters which are not quoted are interpreted on the local machine, while quoted metacharacters are interpreted on the remote machine. See EXAMPLES.

Hostnames are given in the *hosts* database, which may be contained in the /etc/hosts file, the Internet domain name database, or both. Each host has one official name (the first name in the database entry) and optionally one or more nicknames. Official hostnames or nicknames may be given as *hostname*.

If the name of the file from which rsh is executed is anything other than rsh, rsh takes this name as its *hostname* argument. This allows you to create a symbolic link to rsh in the name of a host which, when executed, will invoke a remote shell on that host. By creating a directory and populating it with symbolic links in the names of commonly used hosts, then including the directory in your shell's search path, you can run rsh by typing *hostname* to your shell.

Each remote machine may have a file named /etc/hosts.equiv containing a list of trusted hostnames with which it shares usernames. Users with the same username on both the local and remote machine may rsh from the machines listed in the remote machine's /etc/hosts file. Individual users may set up a similar private equivalence list with the file .rhosts in their home directories. Each line in this file contains two names: a *hostname* and a *username* separated by a space. The entry permits the user named *username* who is logged into *hostname* to use rsh to access the remote machine as the remote user. If the name of the local host is not found in the /etc/hosts.equiv file on the remote machine, and the local username and hostname are not found in the remote user's .rhosts file, then the access is denied. The hostnames listed in the /etc/hosts.equiv and .rhosts files must be the official hostnames listed in the hosts database; nicknames may not be used in either of these files.

rsh will not prompt for a password if access is denied on the remote machine unless the *command* argument is omitted.

OPTIONS

−l *username*
    Use *username* as the remote username instead of your local username. In the absence of this option, the remote username is the same as your local username.

−n
    Redirect the input of **rsh** to **/dev/null**. You sometimes need this option to avoid unfortunate interactions between **rsh** and the shell which invokes it. For example, if you are running **rsh** and invoke a **rsh** in the background without redirecting its input away from the terminal, it will block even if no reads are posted by the remote command. The −**n** option will prevent this.

The type of remote shell (**sh**, the restricted shell—**/usr/lib/rsh**, or other) is determined by the user's entry in the file **/etc/passwd** on the remote system.

EXAMPLES

The command:

```
rsh lizard cat lizard.file >> example.file
```

appends the remote file **lizard.file** from the machine called "lizard" to the file called **example.file** on the local machine, while the command:

```
rsh lizard cat lizard.file ">>" lizard.file2
```

appends the file **lizard.file** on the machine called "lizard" to the file **lizard.file2** which also resides on the machine called "lizard."

FILES

```
/etc/hosts
/etc/passwd
```

SEE ALSO

rlogin(1), **vi**(1), **named**(1M), **hosts**(4), **hosts.equiv**(4)

NOTES

When a system is listed in **hosts.equiv**, its security must be as good as local security. One insecure system listed in **hosts.equiv** can compromise the security of the entire system.

You cannot run an interactive command [such as **vi**(1)]; use **rlogin** if you want to do so.

Stop signals stop the local **rsh** process only; this is arguably wrong, but currently hard to fix for reasons too complicated to explain here.

The current local environment is not passed to the remote shell.

Sometimes the −**n** option is needed for reasons that are less than obvious. For example, the command:

```
rsh somehost dd if=/dev/nrmt0 bs=20b | tar xvpBf -
```

will put your shell into a strange state. Evidently, what happens is that the **tar** terminates before the **rsh**. The **rsh** then tries to write into the "broken pipe" and, instead of terminating neatly, proceeds to compete with your shell for its standard input. Invoking **rsh** with the −**n** option avoids such incidents.

This bug occurs only when **rsh** is at the beginning of a pipeline and is not reading standard input. Do not use the **−n** if **rsh** actually needs to read standard input. For example,

        tar cf − . | rsh sundial dd of=/dev/rmt0 obs=20b

does not produce the bug. If you were to use the **−n** in a case like this, **rsh** would incorrectly read from **/dev/null** instead of from the pipe.

Prior to Release 4, the **rsh** command invoked the restricted shell. This restricted shell command is **/usr/lib/rsh** and can be executed by using the full pathname.

NAME

rshd – remote shell server

SYNOPSIS

in.rshd *host.port*

DESCRIPTION

rshd is the server for the rsh(1) program. The server provides remote execution facilities with authentication based on privileged port numbers.

rshd is invoked by inetd(1M) each time a shell service is requested, and executes the following protocol:

1)   The server checks the client's source port. If the port is not in the range 0-1023, the server aborts the connection. The clients host address (in hex) and port number (in decimal) are the argument passed to rshd.

2)   The server reads characters from the socket up to a null (\0) byte. The resultant string is interpreted as an ASCII number, base 10.

3)   If the number received in step 1 is non-zero, it is interpreted as the port number of a secondary stream to be used for the stderr. A second connection is then created to the specified port on the client's machine. The source port of this second connection is also in the range 0-1023.

4)   The server checks the client's source address. If the address is associated with a host for which no corresponding entry exists in the host name data base [see hosts(4)], the server aborts the connection.

5)   A null terminated user name of at most 16 characters is retrieved on the initial socket. This user name is interpreted as a user identity to use on the server's machine.

6)   A null terminated user name of at most 16 characters is retrieved on the initial socket. This user name is interpreted as the user identity on the client's machine.

7)   A null terminated command to be passed to a shell is retrieved on the initial socket. The length of the command is limited by the upper bound on the size of the system's argument list.

8)   rshd then validates the user according to the following steps. The remote user name is looked up in the password file and a chdir is performed to the user's home directory. If the lookup or fails, the connection is terminated. If the chdir fails, it does a chdir to / (root). If the user is not the super-user, (user ID 0), the file /etc/hosts.equiv is consulted for a list of hosts considered equivalent. If the client's host name is present in this file, the authentication is considered successful. If the lookup fails, or the user is the super-user, then the file .rhosts in the home directory of the remote user is checked for the machine name and identity of the user on the client's machine. If this lookup fails, the connection is terminated.

9)   A null byte is returned on the connection associated with the stderr and the command line is passed to the normal login shell of the user. The shell inherits the network connections established by rshd.

FILES

/etc/hosts.equiv

SEE ALSO

rsh(1)

DIAGNOSTICS

The following diagnostic messages are returned on the connection associated with the **stderr**, after which any network connections are closed. An error is indicated by a leading byte with a value of 1 (0 is returned in step 9 above upon successful completion of all the steps prior to the command execution).

locuser too long

The name of the user on the client's machine is longer than 16 characters.

remuser too long

The name of the user on the remote machine is longer than 16 characters.

command too long

The command line passed exceeds the size of the argument list (as configured into the system).

Hostname for your address unknown.

No entry in the host name database existed for the client's machine.

Login incorrect.

No password file entry for the user name existed.

Permission denied.

The authentication procedure described above failed.

Can't make pipe.

The pipe needed for the **stderr** was not created.

Try again.

A *fork* by the server failed.

NOTES

The authentication procedure used here assumes the integrity of each client machine and the connecting medium. This is insecure, but is useful in an open environment.

A facility to allow all data exchanges to be encrypted should be present.

NAME

rsoper – service pending restore requests and service media insertion prompts

SYNOPSIS

rsoper −d *ddev* [−j *jobids*] [−u *user*] [−m *method*] [−n] [−s|v] [−t]
          [−o *oname*[:*odevice*]]

rsoper −r *jobid*

rsoper −c *jobid*

DESCRIPTION

rsoper −d identifies media containing backup archives of file systems and data partitions, and allows an operator to complete pending restore(1M) and urestore(1M) requests. rsoper takes information about the archive entered on the command line and matches it against pending restore or urestore requests in the restore status table. rsoper then invokes the proper archiving method to read the archive and extract requested files, directories, and data partitions. As subsequent archive volumes are needed, the operator is requested to insert or mount the appropriate archive volumes. See getvol(1M).

Depending on the information available in bkhist.tab and the volume labeling technique (internal or external), all options and arguments listed below may not be required. If required fields are omitted, rsoper issues an error message indicating the information that is needed. The command can then be reissued with the appropriate fields specified.

rsoper may be executed only by a user with superuser privileges.

rsoper −r removes a pending restore job from the restore status table (see rsstatus(1M) and ursstatus(1M)) and notifies the requesting user that the job has been marked complete.

rsoper −c removes a pending restore job from the restore status table (see rsstatus(1M) and ursstatus(1M)) and notifies the requesting user that the job has been canceled.

Options

−c *jobid* Cancels a pending restore request and notifies the originating user that the request has been canceled.

−d *ddev* Describes the device that will be used to read the archive containing the required file system or data partition. *ddev* is of the form:

  ddevice[:[*dchar*][:[*dmnames*]]]

ddevice is the device name for the device; see device.tab(4). *dchar* describes characteristics associated with the device. *dchar* is of the form:

  [density=*density*] [blk_fac=*blockingfactor*] [mntpt=*dir*]

If mntpt=*dir* is specified, *ddevice* is assumed to be a file system partition and *dir* is the place in the UNIX directory structure where *ddevice* will be mounted. This is valid only for fimage(1M) archives. *dmnames* is a list of volume labels, separated by either commas or blanks. If the list is blank separated, the entire *ddev* argument must be surrounded by quotes.

−j *jobids*   Limits the scope of the request to the jobs specified. *jobids* is a list of restore job IDs (either comma separated or blank separated and surrounded by quotes).

−m *method*   Assumes the archive on the first volume in the destination device was created by the *method* archiving operation. Valid *methods* are: **incfile**, **ffile**, **fimage**, **fdp**, **fdisk**, and any customized methods in the **/etc/bkup/method** directory. This option is required if the backup history log is not available, if the log does not include information about the specified archive or if **rsoper** cannot determine the format of the archive.

−n   Displays attributes of the specified destination device but does not attempt to service pending restore requests.

−o *oname*[: *odevice*]
              Specifies the originating file system partition or data partition to be restored. *oname* is the name of the the originating file system. It may be null. *odevice* is the device name of the originating file system or data partition. This option is required if the backup history log is not available or does not include information about the specified archive.

−r *jobid*   Removes the restore request for the specified job.

−s   While a restore operation is occurring, this option displays a period (.) for each 100 (512-byte) blocks transferred from the destination device.

−t   Assumes that the volume inserted in the destination device contains a table of contents for an archive. This option is required if the backup history log is not available, if the log does not include information about the specified archive, or if **rsoper** cannot determine the format of the volume.

−u *user*   Restricts restores to those requested by the user specified.

−v   Displays the name of each object as it is restored. Only those archiving methods that restore named directories and files (**incfile** and **ffile**) support this option.

DIAGNOSTICS

The exit codes for **rsoper** are the following:

0 = the task completed successfully
1 = one or more parameters to **rsoper** are invalid
2 = an error has occurred, causing **rsoper** to fail to
     complete all portions of its task

If a method reports that no part of a restore request was completed, **rsoper** reports this fact to the user.

EXAMPLES

Example 1:

> **rsoper –d /dev/tape/c4d0s2**

asks the restore service to read the archive volume that has been inserted into the device **/dev/tape/c4d0s2**. The service will attempt to resolve any restore requests that can be satisfied by the archive volume.

Example 2:

The following example assumes that the backup history table contains a record of backups performed and that the restore status table contains a record of the restore requests. The command line

> **rsoper –d /dev/ctape:density=1600:USRLBL1 –v –u clerk1**

instructs the restore service to perform only pending restore requests from the **rsstatus.tab** table issued by **clerk1**. The restore procedures are to be done from the cartridge tape labeled USRLBL1, with a density of 1600 bps. The restore service will display on the operator terminal the names of the files and directories as they are successfully restored.

Example 3:

The following example assumes that the backup history table no longer contains a log of the requested backup operations. With that assumption:

rsoper –d /dev/diskette2:blk_fac=2400:arc.dec79 –m incfile –o /usr2

instructs the restore service to perform a restore of the **/usr2** file system using the incremental restore method. The **/usr2** file system is to be restored from archived diskettes with a blocking factor of 2400. The diskettes containing the archive are labeled ''arc.dec79.a,'' ''arc.dec79.b,'' and ''arc.dec79.c.''

Example 4:

> **rsoper –c rest-737b**

cancels the restore request with the job ID **rest-737b**.

FILES

/etc/bkup/bkhist.tab	–	lists the labels of all volumes that have been used for backup operations
/etc/bkup/rsstatus.tab	–	lists the status of all restore requests from users
/etc/bkup/rsnotify.tab	–	lists the electronic mail address of the operator to be notified whenever restore requests require operator intervention
/etc/bkup/method	–	a directory that contains the programs used for various backup methods

SEE ALSO

fdisk(1M), fdp(1M), ffile(1M), fimage(1M), getvol(1M), incfile(1M), restore(1M), rsnotify(1M), rsstatus(1M), urestore(1M), ursstatus(1M)
mail(1) in the *User's Reference Manual*
getdate(3C), device.tab(4) in the *Programmer's Reference Manual*

NAME

rumount – cancel queued remote resource request

SYNOPSIS

/etc/rfs/rumount *resource* . . .

DESCRIPTION

rumount cancels a request for one or more resources that are queued for mount. The entries for the resources are deleted from **/etc/rfs/rmnttab**.

FILES

/etc/rfs/rmnttab — pending mount requests

SEE ALSO

mount(1M), rmnttry(1M), rmount(1M), rumountall(1M), mnttab(4)

DIAGNOSTICS

An exit code of 0 is returned if rumount completes successfully. A 1 is returned if the resource requested for dequeuing is not in **/etc/rfs/rmnttab**. A 2 is returned for bad usage or an error in reading or writing **/etc/rfs/rmnttab**.

NAME

run – run an executable

SYNOPSIS

run [–s] [–e] [–n] [–t *string*] *program*

DESCRIPTION

The **run** function runs *program*, using the PATH variable to find it. By default, when *program* has completed, the user is prompted (**Press ENTER to con-tinue:**), before being returned to FMLI. The argument *program* is a UNIX system executable followed by its options (if any).

–e   If **–e** is specified the user will be prompted before returning to FMLI only if there is an error condition

–n   If **–n** is specified the user will never be prompted before returning to FMLI (useful for programs like **vi**, in which the user must do some specific action to exit in the first place).

–s   The **–s** option means "silent", implying that the screen will not have to be repainted when *program* has completed. NOTE: The **–s** option should only be used when *program* does not write to the terminal. In addition, when **–s** is used, *program* cannot be interrupted, even if it recognizes interrupts.

–t *string*   If **–t** is specified, *string* is the name this process will have in the pop-up menu generated by the **frm-list** command. This feature requires the executable **facesuspend**, (currently only available with the FACE product), to suspend the UNIX system process and return to the FMLI application.

EXAMPLE

Here is a menu that uses **run**:

```
menu="Edit special System files"

name="Password file"
action=`run -e vi /etc/passwd`

name="Group file"
action=`run -e vi /etc/group`

name="My .profile"
action=`run -n vi $HOME/.profile`
```

NAME

runacct – run daily accounting

SYNOPSIS

/usr/lib/acct/runacct [mmdd [state]]

DESCRIPTION

runacct is the main daily accounting shell procedure. It is normally initiated via cron. runacct processes connect, fee, disk, and process accounting files. It also prepares summary files for prdaily or billing purposes. runacct is distributed only to source code licensees.

runacct takes care not to damage active accounting files or summary files in the event of errors. It records its progress by writing descriptive diagnostic messages into *active*. When an error is detected, a message is written to /dev/console, mail [see mail(1)] is sent to root and adm, and runacct terminates. runacct uses a series of lock files to protect against re-invocation. The files lock and lock1 are used to prevent simultaneous invocation, and lastdate is used to prevent more than one invocation per day.

runacct breaks its processing into separate, restartable *states* using *statefile* to remember the last *state* completed. It accomplishes this by writing the *state* name into *statefile*. runacct then looks in *statefile* to see what it has done and to determine what to process next. *states* are executed in the following order:

SETUP　　　　Move active accounting files into working files.

WTMPFIX　　　Verify integrity of wtmp file, correcting date changes if necessary.

CONNECT　　　Produce connect session records in tacct.h format.

PROCESS　　　Convert process accounting records into tacct.h format.

MERGE　　　　Merge the connect and process accounting records.

FEES　　　　　Convert output of chargefee into tacct.h format and merge with connect and process accounting records.

DISK　　　　　Merge disk accounting records with connect, process, and fee accounting records.

MERGETACCT

　　　　　　　Merge the daily total accounting records in daytacct with the summary total accounting records in /var/adm/acct/sum/tacct.

CMS　　　　　Produce command summaries.

USEREXIT　　　Any installation dependent accounting programs can be included here.

CLEANUP　　　Clean up temporary files and exit.

To restart runacct after a failure, first check the *active* file for diagnostics, then fix any corrupted data files, such as pacct or wtmp. The lock, lock1, and lastdate files must be removed before runacct can be restarted. The argument *mmdd* is necessary if runacct is being restarted, and specifies the month and day for which runacct will rerun the accounting. The entry point for processing is based on the contents of *statefile*; to override this, include the desired *state* on the command line to designate where processing should begin.

EXAMPLES

To start **runacct**:

    nohup runacct 2> /var/adm/acct/nite/fd2log &

To restart **runacct**:

    nohup runacct 0601 2>> /var/adm/acct/nite/fd2log &

To restart **runacct** at a specific *state*:

    nohup runacct 0601 MERGE 2>> /var/adm/acct/nite/fd2log &

FILES

/var/adm/wtmp
/var/adm/pacct*incr*
/usr/src/cmd/acct/tacct.h
/usr/src/cmd/acct/ctmp.h
/var/adm/acct/nite/active
/var/adm/acct/nite/daytacct
/var/adm/acct/nite/lock
/var/adm/acct/nite/lock1
/var/adm/acct/nite/lastdate
/var/adm/acct/nite/statefile

SEE ALSO

acct(1M),   acctcms(1M),   acctcon(1M),   acctmerg(1M),   acctprc(1M),
acctsh(1M), cron(1M), fwtmp(1M), acct(4), utmp(4)
acctcom(1), mail(1) in the *User's Reference Manual*
acct(2) in the *Programmer's Reference Manual*

NOTES

Normally it is not a good idea to restart **runacct** in the SETUP *state*. Run SETUP manually and restart via:

    runacct *mmdd* WTMPFIX

If **runacct** failed in the PROCESS *state*, remove the last **ptacct** file because it will not be complete.

NAME

ruptime – show host status of local machines

SYNOPSIS

ruptime [-alrtu]

DESCRIPTION

ruptime gives a status line like uptime for each machine on the local network; these are formed from packets broadcast by each host on the network once a minute.

Machines for which no status report has been received for 5 minutes are shown as being down.

Normally, the listing is sorted by host name, but this order can be changed by specifying one of the options listed below.

The following options are available:

-a   Count even those users who have been idle for an hour or more.

-l   Sort the display by load average.

-r   Reverse the sorting order.

-t   Sort the display by up time.

-u   Sort the display by number of users.

FILES

/var/spool/rwho/whod.*   data files

SEE ALSO

rwho(1), rwhod(1M)

NAME

rusers – who's logged in on local machines

SYNOPSIS

rusers [-ahilu] *host* . . .

DESCRIPTION

The **rusers** command produces output similar to **who**(1), but for remote machines. The listing is in the order that responses are received, but this order can be changed by specifying one of the options listed below.

The default is to print out the names of the users logged in. When the **-1** flag is given, additional information is printed for each user, including idle time, when user logged in, and tty.

A remote host will only respond if it is running the **rusersd**(1M) daemon, which may be started up from **inetd**(1M) or **listen**(1M).

The following options are available:

-a   Give a report for a machine even if no users are logged on.

-h   Sort alphabetically by host name.

-i   Sort by idle time.

-1   Give a longer listing in the style of **who**(1).

-u   Sort by number of users.

SEE ALSO

inetd(1M), **listen**(1M), **pmadm**(1M), **rusersd**(1M), **sacadm**(1M), **who**(1)

NAME

    rpc.rusersd – network username server

SYNOPSIS

    /usr/lib/netsvc/rusers/rpc.rusersd

DESCRIPTION

    rusersd is a server that returns a list of users on the host. The **rusersd** daemon
    may be started by **inetd**(1M) or **listen**(1M).

SEE ALSO

    inetd(1M), **listen**(1M), **pmadm**(1M), **sacadm**(1M)

NAME

rwall – write to all users over a network

SYNOPSIS

/usr/sbin/rwall *hostname* . . .

DESCRIPTION

rwall reads a message from standard input until EOF. It then sends this message, preceded by the line:

    Broadcast Message ...

to all users logged in on the specified host machines.

A machine can only receive such a message if it is running **rwalld**(1M), which may be started by **inetd**(1M) or **listen**(1M).

NOTES

The timeout is fairly short to allow transmission to a large group of machines (some of which may be down) in a reasonable amount of time. Thus the message may not get through to a heavily loaded machine.

SEE ALSO

inetd(1M), listen(1M), pmadm(1M), rwalld(1M), sacadm(1M), wall(1)

NAME

 rpc.rwalld – network rwall server

SYNOPSIS

 /usr/lib/netsvc/rwall/rpc.rwalld

DESCRIPTION

 rwalld is a server that handles rwall(1M) requests. It is implemented by calling wall(1M) on all the appropriate network machines. The rwalld daemon may be started by inetd(1M) or listen(1M).

SEE ALSO

 inetd(1M), listen(1M), rwall(1M), wall(1M)

NAME

rwho – who's logged in on local machines

SYNOPSIS

rwho [–a]

DESCRIPTION

The **rwho** command produces output similar to **who**(1), but for all machines on your network. If no report has been received from a machine for 5 minutes, **rwho** assumes the machine is down, and does not report users last known to be logged into that machine.

If a user has not typed to the system for a minute or more, **rwho** reports this idle time. If a user has not typed to the system for an hour or more, the user is omitted from the output of **rwho** unless the **–a** flag is given.

The **–a** option reports all users whether or not they have typed to the system in the past hour.

FILES

/var/spool/rwho/whod.*   information about other machines

SEE ALSO

finger(1), ruptime(1), who(1), rwhod(1M)

NOTES

Does not work through gateways.

This is unwieldy when the number of machines on the local net is large.

The **rwho** service daemon, **rwhod**(1M), must be enabled for this command to return useful results.

NAME

rwhod, in.rwhod – system status server

SYNOPSIS

in.rwhod

DESCRIPTION

rwhod is the server which maintains the database used by the rwho(1) and ruptime(1) programs. Its operation is predicated on the ability to broadcast messages on a network.

rwhod operates as both a producer and consumer of status information. As a producer of information it periodically queries the state of the system and constructs status messages which are broadcast on a network. As a consumer of information, it listens for other rwhod servers' status messages, validating them, then recording them in a collection of files located in the directory /var/spool/rwho.

The rwho server transmits and receives messages at the port indicated in the rwho service specification, see services(4). The messages sent and received, are of the form:

```
struct     outmp {
       char out_line[8];     /* tty name */
       char out_name[8];     /* user id */
       long out_time;  /* time on */
};

struct     whod {
       char wd_vers;
       char wd_type;
       char wd_fill[2];
       int  wd_sendtime;
       int  wd_recvtime;
       char wd_hostname[32];
       int  wd_loadav[3];
       int  wd_boottime;
          struct     whoent {
          struct       outmp we_utmp;
          int  we_idle;
       } wd_we[1024 / sizeof (struct whoent)];
};
```

All fields are converted to network byte order prior to transmission. The load averages are as calculated by the w(1) program, and represent load averages over the 5, 10, and 15 minute intervals prior to a server's transmission. The host name included is that returned by the gethostname(2) system call. The array at the end of the message contains information about the users logged in to the sending machine. This information includes the contents of the utmp(4) entry for each non-idle terminal line and a value indicating the time since a character was last received on the terminal line.

Messages received by the **rwho** server are discarded unless they originated at a **rwho** server's port. In addition, if the host's name, as specified in the message, contains any unprintable ASCII characters, the message is discarded. Valid messages received by **rwhod** are placed in files named **whod.**_hostname_ in the directory **/var/spool/rwho**. These files contain only the most recent message, in the format described above.

Status messages are generated approximately once every 60 seconds. **rwhod** performs an **nlist**(3) on **/stand/unix** every 10 minutes to guard against the possibility that this file is not the system image currently operating.

FILES

> **/var/spool/rwho**

SEE ALSO

> **rwho**(1), **ruptime**(1), **w**(1), **gethostname**(3), **nlist**(3), **utmp**(4)

NOTES

This service takes up progressively more network bandwidth as the number of hosts on the local net increases. For large networks, the cost becomes prohibitive.

rwhod should relay status information between networks. People often interpret the server dying as a machine going down.

For **rwho** to work properly, the directory **/var/spool/rwho** must exist on the system.

NAME

sac – service access controller

SYNOPSIS

sac −t *sanity_interval*

DESCRIPTION

The Service Access Controller (SAC) is the overseer of the server machine. It is started when the server machine enters multiuser mode. The SAC performs several important functions as explained below.

Customizing the SAC environment. When sac is invoked, it first looks for the per-system configuration script /etc/saf/_sysconfig. sac interprets _sysconfig to customize its own environment. The modifications made to the SAC environment by _sysconfig are inherited by all the children of the SAC. This inherited environment may be modified by the children.

Starting port monitors. After it has interpreted the _sysconfig file, the sac reads its administrative file /etc/saf/_sactab. _sactab specifies which port monitors are to be started. For each port monitor to be started, sac forks a child [fork(2)] and creates a utmp entry with the *type* field set to LOGIN_PROCESS. Each child then interprets its per-port monitor configuration script /etc/saf/*pmtag*/_config, if the file exists. These modifications to the environment affect the port monitor and will be inherited by all its children. Finally, the child process execs the port monitor, using the command found in the _sactab entry. (See sacadm; this is the command given with the −c option when the port monitor is added to the system.)

Polling port monitors to detect failure. The −t option sets the frequency with which sac polls the port monitors on the system. This time may also be thought of as half of the maximum latency required to detect that a port monitor has failed and that recovery action is necessary.

Administrative functions. The Service Access Controller represents the administrative point of control for port monitors. Its administrative tasks are explained below.

When queried (sacadm with either −l or −L), the Service Access Controller returns the status of the port monitors specified, which sacadm prints on the standard output. A port monitor may be in one of six states:

ENABLED   The port monitor is currently running and is accepting connections. See sacadm(1M) with the −e option.

DISABLED   The port monitor is currently running and is not accepting connections. See sacadm with the −d option, and see NOTRUNNING, below.

STARTING   The port monitor is in the process of starting up. STARTING is an intermediate state on the way to ENABLED or DISABLED.

FAILED   The port monitor was unable to start and remain running.

STOPPING   The port monitor has been manually terminated but has not completed its shutdown procedure. STOPPING is an intermediate state on the way to NOTRUNNING.

NOTRUNNING   The port monitor is not currently running. (See sacadm with −k.) This is the normal "not running" state. When a port monitor is killed, all ports it was monitoring are inaccessible. It is not possible for an external user to tell whether a port is not being monitored or the system is down. If the port monitor is not killed but is in the DISABLED state, it may be possible (depending on the port monitor being used) to write a message on the inaccessible port telling the user who is trying to access the port that it is disabled. This is the advantage of having a DISABLED state as well as the NOTRUNNING state.

When a port monitor terminates, the SAC removes the utmp entry for that port monitor.

The SAC receives all requests to enable, disable, start, or stop port monitors and takes the appropriate action.

The SAC is responsible for restarting port monitors that terminate. Whether or not the SAC will restart a given port monitor depends on two things:

  − the restart count specified for the port monitor when the port monitor was added by sacadm; this information is included in /etc/saf/*pmtag*/_sactab

  − the number of times the port monitor has already been restarted

SEE ALSO

sacadm(1M), pmadm(1M).

FILES

/etc/saf/_sactab
/etc/saf/_sysconfig
/var/adm/utmp
/var/saf/_log

NAME

sacadm – service access controller administration

SYNOPSIS

sacadm -a -p *pmtag* -t *type* -c *cmd* -v *ver* [-f dx] [-n *count*] \
    [-y *comment*] [-z script]

sacadm -r -p *pmtag*

sacadm -s -p *pmtag*

sacadm -k -p *pmtag*

sacadm -e -p *pmtag*

sacadm -d -p *pmtag*

sacadm -l [-p *pmtag* | -t *type*]

sacadm -L [-p *pmtag* | -t *type*]

sacadm -g -p *pmtag* [-z script]

sacadm -G [-z script]

sacadm -x [-p *pmtag*]

DESCRIPTION

sacadm is the administrative command for the upper level of the Service Access Facility hierarchy, that is, for port monitor administration. sacadm performs the following functions:

- adds or removes a port monitor
- starts or stops a port monitor
- enables or disables a port monitor
- installs or replaces a per-system configuration script
- installs or replaces a per-port monitor configuration script
- prints requested port monitor information

Requests about the status of port monitors (-l and -L) and requests to print per-port monitor and per-system configuration scripts (-g and -G without the -z option) may be executed by any user on the system. Other sacadm commands may be executed only by a privileged user.

The options have the following meanings:

-a   Add a port monitor. When adding a port monitor, sacadm creates the supporting directory structure in /etc/saf and /var/saf and adds an entry for the new port monitor to /etc/saf/_sactab. The file _sactab already exists on the delivered system. Initially, it is empty except for a single line, which contains the version number of the Service Access Controller.

Unless the command line that adds the new port monitor includes a -f option with the argument x, the new port monitor will be started. Because of the complexity of the options and arguments that follow the -a option, it may be convenient to use a command script or the menu system to add port monitors. If you use the menu system, enter **sysadm ports** and then choose the **port_monitors** option.

-c *cmd*   Execute the command string *cmd* to start a port monitor. The −c option may be used only with a −a. A −a option requires a −c.

−d   Disable the port monitor *pmtag*.

−e   Enable the port monitor *pmtag*.

−f **dx**   The −f option specifies one or both of the following two flags which are then included in the flags field of the _sactab entry for the new port monitor. If the −f option is not included on the command line, no flags are set and the default conditions prevail. By default, a port monitor is started. A −f option with no following argument is illegal.

      d   Do not enable the new port monitor.

      x   Do not start the new port monitor.

−g   The −g option is used to request output or to install or replace the per-port monitor configuration script /etc/saf/*pmtag*/_config. −g requires a −p option. The −g option with only a −p option prints the per-port monitor configuration script for port monitor *pmtag*. The −g option with a −p option and a −z option installs the file **script** as the per-port monitor configuration script for port monitor *pmtag*. Other combinations of options with −g are invalid.

−G   The −G option is used to request output or to install or replace the per-system configuration script /etc/saf/_sysconfig. The −G option by itself prints the per-system configuration script. The −G option in combination with a −z option installs the file **script** as the per-system configuration script. Other combinations of options with a −G option are invalid.

−k   Stop port monitor *pmtag*.

−l   The −l option is used to request port monitor information. The −l by itself lists all port monitors on the system. The −l option in combination with the −p option lists only the port monitor specified by *pmtag*. A −l in combination with the −t option lists all port monitors of type *type*. Any other combination of options with the −l option is invalid.

−L   The −L option is identical to the −l option except that the output appears in a condensed format.

−n *count*

Set the restart count to *count*. If a restart count is not specified, count is set to 0. A count of 0 indicates that the port monitor is not to be restarted if it fails.

−p *pmtag*

Specifies the tag associated with a port monitor.

-r   Remove port monitor *pmtag*. **sacadm** removes the port monitor entry from /etc/saf/_sactab. If the removed port monitor is not running, then no further action is taken. If the removed port monitor is running, the Service Access Controller (SAC) sends it **SIGTERM** to indicate that it should shut down. Note that the port monitor's directory structure remains intact.

-s   Start a port monitor. The SAC starts the port monitor *pmtag*.

-t *type*   Specifies the port monitor type.

-v *ver*   Specifies the version number of the port monitor. This version number may be given as

$$-v \text{ `}pmspec -V\text{`}$$

where *pmspec* is the special administrative command for port monitor *pmtag*. This special command is **ttyadm** for **ttymon** and **nlsadmin** for **listen**. The version stamp of the port monitor is known by the command and is returned when *pmspec* is invoked with a **-v** option.

-x   The **-x** option by itself tells the SAC to read its database file (_sactab). The **-x** option with the **-p** option tells port monitor *pmtag* to read its administrative file.

-y *comment*

       Include *comment* in the _sactab entry for port monitor *pmtag*.

-z script

       Used with the **-g** and **-G** options to specify the name of a file that contains a configuration script. With the **-g** option, **script** is a per-port monitor configuration script; with **-G** it is a per-system configuration script. Modifying a configuration script is a three-step procedure. First a copy of the existing script is made (**-g** or **-G**). Then the copy is edited. Finally, the copy is put in place over the existing script (**-g** or **-G** with **-z**).

OUTPUT

If successful, **sacadm** will exit with a status of **0**. If **sacadm** fails for any reason, it will exit with a nonzero status. Options that request information will write the information on the standard output. In the condensed format (**-L**), port monitor information is printed as a sequence of colon-separated fields; empty fields are indicated by two successive colons. The standard format (**-l**) prints a header identifying the columns, and port monitor information is aligned under the appropriate headings. In this format, an empty field is indicated by a hyphen. The comment character is **#**.

EXAMPLES

The following command line adds a port monitor. The port monitor tag is **npack**; its type is **listen**; if necessary, it will restart three times before failing; its administrative command is **nlsadmin**; and the configuration script to be read is in the file **script**:

```
sacadm -a -p npack -t listen -c /usr/lib/saf/listen npack \
    -v `nlsadmin -V` -n 3 -z script
```

Remove a port monitor whose tag is **pmtag**:

    sacadm -r -p pmtag

Start the port monitor whose tag is **pmtag**:

    sacadm -s -p pmtag

Stop the port monitor whose tag is **pmtag**:

    sacadm -k -p pmtag

Enable the port monitor whose tag is **pmtag**:

    sacadm -e -p pmtag

Disable the port monitor whose tag is **pmtag**:

    sacadm -d -p pmtag

List status information for all port monitors:

    sacadm -l

List status information for the port monitor whose tag is **pmtag**:

    sacadm -l -p pmtag

List the same information in condensed format:

    sacadm -L -p pmtag

List status information for all port monitors whose type is **listen**:

    sacadm -l -t listen

Replace the per-port monitor configuration script associated with the port monitor whose tag is **pmtag** with the contents of the file **file.config**:

    sacadm -g -p pmtag -z file.config

SEE ALSO

doconfig(3N), pmadm(1M), sac(1M)

FILES

    /etc/saf/_sactab
    /etc/saf/_sysconfig
    /etc/saf/pmtag/_config

NAME

sact – print current SCCS file editing activity

SYNOPSIS

sact *files*

DESCRIPTION

sact informs the user of any impending deltas to a named SCCS file. This situation occurs when **get** with the **-e** option has been previously executed without a subsequent execution of **delta**. If a directory is named on the command line, sact behaves as though each file in the directory were specified as a named file, except that non-SCCS files and unreadable files are silently ignored. If a name of – is given, the standard input is read with each line being taken as the name of an SCCS file to be processed.

The output for each named file consists of five fields separated by spaces.

Field 1	specifies the SID of a delta that currently exists in the SCCS file to which changes will be made to make the new delta.
Field 2	specifies the SID for the new delta to be created.
Field 3	contains the logname of the user who will make the delta (that is, executed a **get** for editing).
Field 4	contains the date that **get** **-e** was executed.
Field 5	contains the time that **get** **-e** was executed.

SEE ALSO

delta(1), diff(1), get(1), help(1), unget(1)

DIAGNOSTICS

Use help(1) for explanations.

NAME

sadc, sa1, sa2 – system activity report package

SYNOPSIS

/usr/lib/sa/sadc [*t n*] [*ofile*]

/usr/lib/sa/sa1 [*t n*]

/usr/lib/sa/sa2 [-ubdycwaqvmpgrkxDSAC] [-s *time*] [-e *time*] [-i *sec*]

DESCRIPTION

System activity data can be accessed at the special request of a user [see **sar**(1M)] and automatically, on a routine basis, as described here. The operating system contains several counters that are incremented as various system actions occur. These include counters for CPU utilization, buffer usage, disk and tape I/O activity, TTY device activity, switching and system-call activity, file-access, queue activity, inter-process communications, paging, and Remote File Sharing.

sadc and two shell procedures, **sa1** and **sa2**, are used to sample, save, and process this data.

sadc, the data collector, samples system data *n* times, with an interval of *t* seconds between samples, and writes in binary format to *ofile* or to standard output. The sampling interval *t* should be greater than 5 seconds; otherwise, the activity of **sadc** itself may affect the sample. If *t* and *n* are omitted, a special record is written. This facility is used at system boot time, when booting to a multiuser state, to mark the time at which the counters restart from zero. For example, the **/etc/init.d/perf** file writes the restart mark to the daily data by the command entry:

```
su sys -c "$TFADMIN /usr/lib/sa/sadc /var/adm/sa/sa`date +%d`"
```

The shell script **sa1**, a variant of **sadc**, is used to collect and store data in the binary file **/var/adm/sa/sa***dd*, where *dd* is the current day. The arguments *t* and *n* cause records to be written *n* times at an interval of *t* seconds, or once if omitted. The following entries in **/var/spool/cron/crontabs/sys** produce records every 20 minutes during working hours and hourly otherwise:

```
0 * * * 0-6 $TFADMIN /usr/lib/sa/sa1
20,40 8-17 * * 1-5 $TFADMIN /usr/lib/sa/sa1
```

See **crontab**(1) for details.

The shell script **sa2**, a variant of **sar**, writes a daily report in the file **/var/adm/sa/sar***dd*. The options are explained in **sar**(1M). The following entry in **/var/spool/cron/crontabs/sys** reports important activities hourly during the working day:

```
5 18 * * 1-5 $TFADMIN /usr/lib/sa/sa2 -s 8:00 -e 18:01 -i 1200 -A
```

FILES

/var/adm/sa/sa*dd* daily data file
/var/adm/sa/sar*dd*   daily report file
/tmp/sa.adrfl   address file

SEE ALSO

crontab(1), sag(1M), sar(1M), timex(1).

NAME

sadc sa1, sa2 – system activity report package

SYNOPSIS

/usr/lib/sa/sadc [*t n*] [*ofile*]

/usr/lib/sa/sa1 [*t n*]

/usr/lib/sa/sa2 [–ubdycwaqvmpgrkxDSAC] [–s *time*] [–e *time*] [–i *sec*] [–P
processor-id]

DESCRIPTION

System activity data can be accessed at the special request of a user (see sar(1M))
and automatically on a routine basis. The operating system contains several
counters that are incremented as various system actions occur. These include
counters for processor utilization, buffer usage, disk and tape I/O activity, TTY
device activity, switching and system-call activity, file-access, queue activity,
inter-process communications, paging and Remote File Sharing.

Some of these counters (those in the si member of the binary activity record produced by sadc) are maintained separately for each processor that is or has been
online in the system. For each separately maintained counter, the system also
maintains a corresponding aggregate counter. The per-processor counters are a
measure of the actions performed by each processor in the system. The
corresponding aggregate counters represent a measure of the same actions performed by the system as a whole.

sadc and shell procedures, sa1 and sa2, are used to sample, save, and process
this data.

sadc, the data collector, samples system data *n* times, with an interval of *t*
seconds between samples. The sampling interval *t* should be greater than 5
seconds; otherwise, the activity of sadc itself may affect the sample. If *t* and *n*
are omitted, a special record is written. This facility is used at system boot time,
when booting to a multiuser state, to mark the time at which the counters restart
from zero. For example, the /etc/init.d/perf file writes the restart mark to
the daily data by the command entry:

```
su sys -c "/usr/lib/sa/sadc /var/adm/sa/sadate +%d"
```

sadc writes system activity records in binary format. If *ofile* is not specified, sadc
writes records that pertain to the system as a whole to standard output.

If *ofile* is specified, sadc writes records that pertain to the system as a whole to
ofile. In addition, for each processor online in the system, sadc writes system
activity records to *ofile.***cpu***processor*. Each such system activity record contains the
counters maintained for the processor in question instead of the aggregate
counters.

If the -P option is used, sa2 reports system activity information that applies to
the processor specified by *processor-id* to standard output.

The shell script **sa1**, a variant of **sadc**, is used to collect and store data in binary file **/var/adm/sa/sa**_dd_ **where** _dd_ is the current day. The arguments _t_ and _n_ cause records to be written _n_ times at an interval of _t_ seconds, or once if omitted. The following entries in **/var/spool/cron/crontabs/sys** will produce records every 20 minutes during working hours and hourly otherwise:

```
0 * * * 0-6 /usr/lib/sa/sa1
20,40 8-17 * * 1-5 /usr/lib/sa/sa1
```

See **crontab**(1) for details.

EXAMPLE

The shell script **sa2**, a variant of **sar**, writes a daily report in the file **/var/adm/sa/sar**_dd_. The options are explained in **sar**(1). The following entry in **/var/spool/cron/crontabs/sys** will report important activities hourly during the working day:

```
5 18 * * 1-5 /usr/lib/sa/sa2 -s 8:00 -e 18:01 -i 1200 -A
```

FILES

/var/adm/sa/sa_dd_
      daily data file for system as a whole
/var/adm/sa/sa_dd_**.cpu**_processor-id_
      daily data file for each online processor
/var/adm/sa/sar_dd_
      daily report file
/tmp/sa.adrfl
      address file

SEE ALSO

sar(1M)
crontab(1) and **timex**(1) in the _User's Reference Manual_

NAME

sag – system activity graph

SYNOPSIS

sag [*options*]

DESCRIPTION

sag graphically displays the system activity data stored in a binary data file by a previous **sar**(1M) run. Any of the **sar** data items may be plotted singly, or in combination; as cross plots, or versus time. Simple arithmetic combinations of data may be specified. **sag** invokes **sar** and finds the desired data by string-matching the data column header (run **sar** to see what is available). These *options* are passed through to **sar**:

-s *time*   Select data later than *time* in the form *hh*[:*mm*]. The default is 08:00.

-e *time*   Select data up to *time*. The default is 18:00.

-i *sec*   Select data at intervals as close as possible to *sec* seconds.

-f *file*   Use *file* as the data source for **sar**. The default value is the current daily data file (**/usr/adm/sa/sa**dd).

Other *options*:

-T *term*   Produce output suitable for terminal *term*. The default value is $TERM. The following known terminals are available:

300	DASI 300.
300S	DASI 300s.
450	DASI 450.
4014	Tektronix 4014.

-x *spec*   x axis specification with *spec* in the form:
"*name* [*op name*] . . . [*lo hi*]"

-y *spec*   y axis specification with *spec* in the same form as above.

Name is either a string that will match a column header in the **sar** report, with an optional device name in square brackets, (such as **r+w/s[dsk-1]**, or an integer value. *Op* is one of four characters ("**+**", "**-**", "*****", or "**/**"), surrounded by blanks. (Parentheses are not recognized.) Up to five names may be specified. Contrary to custom, **+** and **-** have precedence over ***** and **/**". Evaluation is done from left to right. Thus A / A + B * **100** is evaluated $(A/(A+B))*$**100,** and A + B / C + D is $(A+B)/(C+D)$. *Lo* and *hi* are optional numeric scale limits. If unspecified, they are deduced from the data.

A single *spec* is permitted for the x axis; if unspecified, *time* is used. For the **y** axis, specify up to five *specs*, separated by semi-colons (**;**). If you specify more than one argument to **-x** or **-y**, and leave one or more blank spaces between list items, enclose the list in double quotes (**""**). The default value for the **-y** option is

```
-y "%usr 0 100; %usr + %sys 0 100; %usr + %sys + %wio 0 100"
```

EXAMPLES

For a report on today's CPU utilization:

    sag

For a report on the activity of all disk drives over a 15-minute period:

    TS=*date* +%*H*:%*M*
    sar -o *tempfile* 60 15
    TE=*date* +%*H*:%*M*
    sag -f *tempfile* -s $TS -e $TE -y "r+w/s[*dsk*]"

FILES

    /usr/adm/sa/sa*dd*   daily data file for day *dd*

SEE ALSO

    sar(1M)

NAME

sar – system activity reporter

SYNOPSIS

sar [–ubdycwaqvmpgrkxDSAC] [–o *file*] *t* [*n*]

sar [–ubdycwaqvmpgrkxDSAC] [–s *time*] [–e *time*] [–i *sec*] [–f *file*]

DESCRIPTION

In the first instance, **sar** samples cumulative activity counters in the operating system at *n* intervals of *t* seconds, where *t* should be 5 or greater. If *t* is specified with more than one option, all headers are printed together and the output may be difficult to read. (If the sampling interval is less than 5, the activity of **sar** itself may affect the sample.) If the –o option is specified, it saves the samples in *file* in binary format. The default value of *n* is 1. In the second instance, with no sampling interval specified, **sar** extracts data from a previously recorded *file*, either the one specified by the –f option or, by default, the standard system activity daily data file **/var/adm/sa/sa***dd* for the current day *dd*. The starting and ending times of the report can be bounded via the –s and –e *time* arguments of the form *hh*[:*mm*[:*ss*]]. The –i option selects records at *sec* second intervals. Otherwise, all intervals found in the data file are reported.

In either case, subsets of data to be printed are specified by option:

–u   Report CPU utilization (the default):
       %usr, %sys, %wio, %idle – portion of time running in user mode, running in system mode, idle with some process waiting for block I/O, and otherwise idle. When used with –D, **%sys** is split into percent of time servicing requests from remote machines (**%sys** remote) and all other system time (**%sys** local). If you are using an AT&T 3B2 Computer with a co-processor, the CPU utilization (default) report will contain the following fields:
       %usr, %sys, %idle, scall/s – where **scalls/s** is the number of system calls, of all types, encountered on the co-processor per second.

–b   Report buffer activity:
       bread/s, bwrit/s – transfers per second of data between system buffers and disk or other block devices;
       lread/s, lwrit/s – accesses of system buffers;
       %rcache, %wcache – cache hit ratios, that is, (**1–bread/lread**) as a percentage;
       pread/s, pwrit/s – transfers via raw (physical) device mechanism. When used with –D, buffer caching is reported for locally-mounted remote resources.

–d   Report activity for each block device, for example, disk or tape drive, with the exception of XDC disks and tape drives. When data is displayed, the device specification *dsk–* is generally used to represent a disk drive. The device specification used to represent a tape drive is machine dependent. The activity data reported is:
       %busy, avque – portion of time device was busy servicing a transfer request, ratio of total time for all requests to complete to total time device was busy servicing these requests.
       r+w/s, blks/s – number of data transfers from or to device, number of

bytes transferred in 512-byte units;
avwait, avserv – average time in milliseconds that transfer requests wait idly on queue, and average time to be serviced (which for disks includes seek, rotational latency and data transfer times).

-y　Report TTY device activity:
rawch/s, canch/s, outch/s – input character rate, input character rate processed by canon, output character rate;
rcvin/s, xmtin/s, mdmin/s – receive, transmit and modem interrupt rates.

-c　Report system calls:
scall/s – system calls of all types;
sread/s, swrit/s, fork/s, exec/s – specific system calls;
rchar/s, wchar/s – characters transferred by read and write system calls. When used with **-D**, the system calls are split into incoming, outgoing, and strictly local calls. No incoming or outgoing fork or exec calls are reported.

-w　Report system swapping and switching activity:
swpin/s, swpot/s, pswin/s, pswot/s – number of transfers and number of 512-byte units transferred for swapins and swapouts (including initial loading of some programs);
pswch/s – process switches.

-a　Report use of file access system routines:
iget/s, namei/s, dirblk/s.

-q　Report average queue length while occupied, and % of time occupied:
runq-sz, %runocc – run queue of processes in memory and runnable;
swpq-sz, %swpocc – these are no longer reported by sar.

-v　Report status of process, i-node, file tables:
proc-sz, inod-sz, file-sz, lock-sz – entries/size for each table, evaluated once at sampling point;
ov – overflows that occur between sampling points for each table.

-m　Report message and semaphore activities:
msg/s, sema/s – primitives per second.

-p　Report paging activities:
atch/s – page faults per second that are satisfied by reclaiming a page currently in memory (attaches per second);
pgin/s – page-in requests per second;
ppgin/s – pages paged-in per second;
pflt/s – page faults from protection errors per second (illegal access to page) or "copy-on-writes"
vflt/s – address translation page faults per second (valid page not in memory);
slock/s – faults per second caused by software lock requests requiring physical I/O.

-g　Report paging activities:
pgout/s – page-out requests per second;
ppgout/s – pages paged-out per second;
pgfree/s – pages per second placed on the free list by the page stealing daemon;

pgscan/s – pages per second scanned by the page stealing daemon.

%s5ipf – the percentage of S5 inodes taken off the freelist by **iget** which had reusable pages associated with them. These pages are flushed and cannot be reclaimed by processes. Thus this is the percentage of **iget**s with page flushes.

-r   Report unused memory pages and disk blocks:
freemem – average pages available to user processes;
freeswap – disk blocks available for page swapping.

-k   Report kernel memory allocation (KMA) activities:
sml_mem, alloc, fail – information about the memory pool reserving and allocating space for small requests: the amount of memory in bytes KMA has for the small pool, the number of bytes allocated to satisfy requests for small amounts of memory, and the number of requests for small amounts of memory that were not satisfied (failed);
lg_mem, alloc, fail – information for the large memory pool (analogous to the information for the small memory pool);
ovsz_alloc, fail – the amount of memory allocated for oversize requests and the number of oversize requests which could not be satisfied (because oversized memory is allocated dynamically, there is not a pool).

-x   Report remote file sharing (RFS) operations:
open/s, create/s, lookup/s, readdir/s, getpage/s, putpage/s, other/s – The number of open, create, lookup, readdir, getpage, putpage, and other operations made per second by clients (incoming) and by the server (outgoing).

-D   Report Remote File Sharing activity:
When used in combination with **–u**, **–b** or **–c**, it causes **sar** to produce the remote file sharing version of the corresponding report. **–Du** is assumed when only **–D** is specified.

-S   Report server and request queue status:
serv/lo-hi – average number of Remote File Sharing servers on the system (lo and hi are the minimum and maximum number of servers respectively.)
request %busy – % of time receive descriptors are on the request queue
request avg lgth – average number of receive descriptors waiting for service when queue is occupied
server %avail – % of time there are idle servers
server avg avail – average number of idle servers when idle ones exist

-A   Report all data. Equivalent to **–udqbwcayvmpgrkxSDC**.

-C   Report Remote File Sharing data caching overhead:
snd-inv/s – number of invalidation messages per second sent by your machine as a server.
snd-msg/s – total outgoing RFS messages sent per second.
rcv-inv/s – number of invalidation messages received from the remote server.
rcv-msg/s – total number of incoming RFS messages received per second.
dis-bread/s – number of read messages that would be eligible for caching

if caching had not been turned off because of an invalidation message. (Indicates the penalty incurred because of the invalidation message.) **blk-inv/s** – number of pages removed from the client cache in response to cache invalidation messages.

EXAMPLES

To see today's CPU activity so far:

    sar

To watch CPU activity evolve for ten minutes and save data:

    sar -o temp 60 10

To later review disk and tape activity from that period:

    sar -d -f temp

FILES

/var/adm/sa/sa_dd_   daily data file, where _dd_ are digits representing the day of the month.

SEE ALSO

sag(1M), **sadc**(1M)

NAME

sar – system activity reporter

SYNOPSIS

sar [**-ubdycwaqvmpgrkxDSAC**] [**-P** *processor-id*] [**-o** *file*] *t* [*n*]

sar [**-ubdycwaqvmpgrkxDSAC**] [**-P** *processor-id*] [**-s** *time*] [**-e** *time*]
[**-i** *sec*] [**-f** *file*]

DESCRIPTION

In the first synopsis line, **sar** samples cumulative activity counters in the operating system at *n* intervals of *t* seconds, where *t* should be 5 or greater and the default value of *n* is 1. (Note that if the sampling interval is less than 5, the activity of **sar** itself may affect the sample.) If the **-o** option is specified, **sar** saves the samples in *file* in binary format. The type of command shown in the first synopsis line immediately sends the output for every option specified to standard output, without organizing it into a rational format; data for different options appears in an undifferentiated jumble and is difficult to read. Therefore, when running **sar** in the format of the first synopsis line, we recommend (a) specifying only one option, and (b) avoiding the **-A** option (which is equivalent to specifying all options).

When the **-P** option is specified, **sar** reports activity that applies only to *processor-id* specifically; command line options that request information not specific to *processor-id* are silently ignored. Options that are effective with **-P** are **-abcgmuwyD**.

In the second synopsis line, with no sampling interval specified, **sar** extracts data from a previously recorded *file*, either the one specified by the **-f** option or, by default, the standard system activity daily data file **/var/adm/sa/sa***dd* for the current day *dd*. The starting and ending times of the report can be bounded using the **-s** and **-e** *time* arguments of the form *hh*[:*mm*[:*ss*]]. The **-i** option selects records at *sec* second intervals. Otherwise, all intervals found in the data file are reported.

In either case, subsets of data to be printed are specified by option:

-u   Report processor utilization (the default):

    %usr   portion of time running in user mode

    %sys   portion of time running in system mode

    %wio   portion of time idle with some process waiting for block I/O

    %idle   portion of time otherwise idle

    When used with **-D**, **%sys** is split into percentage of time servicing requests from remote machines via RFS (**%sys remote**) and all other system time (**%sys local**).

-b   Report buffer activity:

    bread/s, **bwrit/s**   transfers per second of data between system buffers and disk or other block devices.

lread/s, lwrit/s   accesses per second of system buffers.

%rcache, %wcache   cache hit ratios, such as (1-bread/lread) as a percentage.

pread/s, pwrit/s   transfers per second by means of raw (physical) device mechanism.

When used with -D, buffer caching is reported for locally-mounted RFS remote resources.

-d   Report activity for hard disks. When data is displayed, the device specification *dsk-* is generally used to represent a disk drive. The data reported is:

%busy   percentage of time disk was busy servicing a transfer request.

avque   The average number of requests outstanding during the monitored period (the number of requests being serviced). This number is the ratio of total time for all requests to complete to total time disk was busy servicing these requests minus 1.

r+w/s   number of data transfers to or from disk per second.

blks/s   number of 512-byte blocks transferred to or from the disk per second.

avwait   average time in milliseconds that transfer requests wait idly on queue.

avserv   average time in milliseconds for a transfer request to be completed by the disk (including seek, rotational latency, and data transfer times).

-y   Report TTY device activity (per second):

rawch/s   input characters.

canch/s   input characters processed by canon.

outch/s   output characters.

rcvin/s   receiver hardware interrupts.

xmtin/s   transmitter hardware interrupts.

mdmin/s   modem interrupts.

-c   Report system calls (per second):

scall/s   system calls of all types.

sread/s, swrit/s, fork/s, exec/s
   specific system calls (read, write, fork, and exec).

rchar/s   characters (bytes) transferred by read system calls.

wchar/s   characters (bytes) transferred by write system calls.

When used with -D, the system calls are split into RFS incoming, RFS outgoing, and local calls. No RFS incoming or outgoing fork and exec calls are reported.

-w   Report system swapping and switching activity (per second):

swpin/s, swpot/s
    number of transfers to and from memory

pswin/s, pswot/s
    number of 512-byte blocks transferred for swapins and swapouts.

pswch/s   process switches.

-a   Report use of file access system routines (per second):

iget/s   number of S5 and UFS files located by inode entry.

namei/s   number of file system path searches.

dirblk/s   number of S5 directory block reads issued.

-q   Report average queue length while occupied, and percentage of time occupied:

runq-sz   run queue of processes in memory and runnable.

%runocc   percentage of time run queue is occupied.

swpq-sz   The average number of processes in the swap queue when there were processes in the queue. If there were no processes in the swap queue, this field is blank.

%swpocc   The percent of time during the sample that there were processes in the swap queue. If there were no processes in the swap queue, this field is blank.

-v   Report status of process, i-node, file, and file and record locking tables:

proc-sz, inod-sz, file-sz, lock-sz
    entries/size for each table, evaluated once at sampling point.

ov   overflows that occur between sampling points for each table.

-m   Report message and semaphore activities:

msg/s, sema/s
    primitives per second.

-p   Report paging activities:

atch/s   page faults per second that are satisfied by reclaiming a page currently in memory (attaches per second).

pgin/s   page-in requests per second.

ppgin/s   pages paged-in per second.

pflt/s   page faults from protection errors per second (invalid access to page or "copy-on-writes").

vflt/s   address translation page faults per second (valid page not in memory).

      slock/s   faults per second caused by software lock requests requiring physical I/O.

-g   Report paging activities:

      pgout/s   page-out requests per second.

      ppgout/s   pages paged-out per second.

      pgfree/s   pages per second placed on the freelist by the page stealing daemon.

      pgscan/s   pages per second scanned by the page stealing daemon.

      %s5ipf   the percentage of S5 inodes taken off the freelist by **iget** that had reusable pages associated with them. These pages are flushed and cannot be reclaimed by processes. Thus, this is the percentage of **igets** with page flushes.

-r   Report unused memory pages and disk blocks:

      freemem   average pages available to user processes.

      freeswap   disk blocks available for page swapping.

-k   Report kernel memory allocation (KMA) activities:

    Information about the memory pool reserving and allocating space for small requests (less than 256 bytes):

      sml_mem   the amount of memory in bytes KMA has for the small pool.

      alloc   the number of bytes allocated to satisfy requests for small amounts of memory.

      fail   the number of requests for small amounts of memory that were not satisfied (failed).

    Information for the large memory pool:

      lg_mem, alloc, fail
            (analogous to the information for the small memory pool.)

    Information for oversized requests (because oversized memory is allocated dynamically, there is not a pool):

      ovsz_alloc
            the amount of memory allocated for oversize requests.

      fail   the number of oversize requests that could not be satisfied.

-x   Report remote file sharing (RFS) operations:

      open/s   the number of open operations made per second by clients (incoming) and by the server (outgoing).

      create/s   the number of create operations made per second by clients (incoming) and by the server (outgoing).

      lookup/s   the number of lookup operations made per second by clients (incoming) and by the server (outgoing).

readdir/s the number of readdir operations made per second by clients (incoming) and by the server (outgoing).

getpage/s the number of getpage operations made per second by clients (incoming) and by the server (outgoing).

putpage/s the number of putpage operations made per second by clients (incoming) and by the server (outgoing).

other/s the number of other operations made per second by clients (incoming) and the server (outgoing).

-D Report Remote File Sharing activity:

When used in combination with −u, −b, or −c, it causes **sar** to produce the remote file sharing version of the corresponding report. −**Du** is assumed when only −**D** is specified.

-S Report server and request queue status:

serv/*lo-hi* average number of Remote File Sharing servers on the system (*lo* and *hi* are the minimum and maximum number of servers respectively).

request %busy percentage of time receive descriptors are on the request queue.

request avg lgth
 average number of receive descriptors waiting for service when queue is occupied.

server %avail percentage of time there are idle servers.

server avg avail
 average number of idle servers when idle ones exist.

-A Without the -P option, this option reports all data (that is, it's equivalent to -udqbwcayvmpgrkxCSD). When run with -P, this option is equivalent to -ubwcaymgD.

-C Report Remote File Sharing data caching overhead:

snd-inv/s number of invalidation messages per second sent by your machine as a server.

snd-msg/s total outgoing RFS messages sent per second.

rcv-inv/s number of invalidation messages received from the remote server.

rcv-msg/s total number of incoming RFS messages received per second.

dis-bread/s number of read messages that would be eligible for caching if caching had not been turned off because of an invalidation message. (Indicates the penalty incurred because of the invalidation message).

blk-inv/s   number of pages removed from the client cache in response to cache invalidation messages.

EXAMPLES

To see today's processor activity so far:

    sar

To see the system call activity so far for processor 0:

    sar -c -P0

To watch processor activity evolve for ten minutes and save data:

    sar -o temp 60 10

To later review disk activity from that period:

    sar -d -f temp

FILES

/var/adm/sa/sa*dd*   daily data file, where *dd* are digits representing the day of the month

SEE ALSO

sadc(1M) and sag(1M) in the *System Administrator's Reference Manual*

NAME

sccs – front end for the Source Code Control System (SCCS)

SYNOPSIS

/usr/ucb/sccs [–r] [–d*prefixpath*] [–p*finalpath*] *command*
[*SCCS-flags* . . .] [*filename* . . .]

DESCRIPTION

The **sccs** command is a front end to the utility programs of the Source Code
Control System (SCCS).

sccs normally prefixes each *filename*, or the last component of each *filename*, with
the string '**SCCS/s.**', because you normally keep your SCCS database files in a
directory called **SCCS**, and each database file starts with an '**s.**' prefix. If the
environment variable PROJECTDIR is set, and is an absolute pathname (that is,
begins with a slash) **sccs** will search for SCCS files in the directory given by that
variable. If it is a relative pathname (that is, does not begin with a slash), it is
treated as the name of a user, and **sccs** will search in that user's home directory
for a directory named **src** or **source**. If that directory is found, **sccs** will search
for SCCS files in the directory given by that variable.

sccs program options must appear before the *command* argument. Flags to be
passed to the actual SCCS command (utility program) must appear after the *command* argument. These flags are specific to the *command* being used.

sccs also includes the capability to run "set user ID" to another user to provide
additional protection. Certain commands (such as **admin**(1)) cannot be run "set
user ID" by all users, since this would allow anyone to change the authorizations.
Such commands are always run as the real user.

OPTIONS

–r   Run **sccs** as the real user rather than as whatever effective user **sccs** is
            "set user ID" to.

–d*prefixpath*
            Define the prefix portion of the pathname for the SCCS database files. The
            default prefix portion of the pathname is the current directory. *prefixpath*
            is prefixed to the entire pathname. See EXAMPLE.

            This flag overrides any directory specified by the **PROJECTDIR** environment variable.

–p*finalpath*
            Define the name of a lower directory in which the SCCS files will be
            found; SCCS is the default. *finalpath* is appended before the final component of the pathname. See EXAMPLE.

USAGE

Additional sccs Commands

Several "pseudo-commands" are available in addition to the usual SCCS commands. These are:

create   **create** is used when creating new **s.** files. For example, given a C
            source language file called '**obscure.c**', **create** would perform the
            following actions: (1) create the '**s.**' file called '**s.obscure.c**' in the
            SCCS directory; (2) rename the original source file to '**,obscure.c**';

(3) do an 'sccs get' on 'obscure.c'. Compared to the SCCS admin command, create does more of the startup work for you and should be used in preference to admin.

enter   enter is just like create, except that it does not do the final 'sccs get'. It is usually used if an 'sccs edit' is to be performed immediately after the enter.

edit   Get a file for editing.

delget   Perform a delta on the named files and then get new versions. The new versions have ID keywords expanded, and so cannot be edited.

deledit   Same as delget, but produces new versions suitable for editing. deledit is useful for making a "checkpoint" of your current editing phase.

fix   Remove the named delta, but leaves you with a copy of the delta with the changes that were in it. fix must be followed by a -r flag. fix is useful for fixing small compiler bugs, etc. Since fix does not leave audit trails, use it carefully.

clean   Remove everything from the current directory that can be recreated from SCCS files. clean checks for and does not remove any files being edited. If 'clean -b' is used, branches are **not** checked to see if they are currently being edited. Note: -b is dangerous if you are keeping the branches in the same directory.

unedit   "Undo" the last edit or 'get -e' and return a file to its previous condition. If you unedit a file being edited, all changes made since the beginning of the editing session are lost.

info   Display a list of all files being edited. If the -b flag is given, branches (that is, SID's with two or fewer components) are ignored. If the -u flag is given (with an optional argument), only files being edited by you (or the named user) are listed.

check   Check for files currently being edited, like info, but returns an exit code rather than a listing: nothing is printed if nothing is being edited, and a non-zero exit status is returned if anything is being edited. check may thus be included in an "install" entry in a makefile, to ensure that everything is included in an SCCS file before a version is installed.

tell   Display a list of files being edited on the standard output. Filenames are separated by NEWLINE characters. Take the -b and -u flags like info and check.

diffs   Compare (in diff-like format) the current version of the program you have out for editing and the versions in SCCS format. diffs accepts the same arguments as diff, except that the -c flag must be specified as -C instead, because the -c flag is taken as a flag to get indicating which version is to be compared with the current version.

> print   Print verbose information about the named files. **print** does an
> 'sccs prs -e' followed by an 'sccs get -p -m' on each file.

EXAMPLE

The command:

```
sccs  -d/usr/include  get sys/inode.h
```

converts to:

```
get  /usr/include/sys/SCCS/s.inode.h
```

The intent here is to create aliases such as:

```
alias  syssccs  sccs  -d/usr/src
```

which will be used as:

```
syssccs  get  cmd/who.c
```

The command:

```
sccs  -pprivate  get  usr/include/stdio.h
```

converts to:

```
get  usr/include/private/s.stdio.h
```

To put a file called **myprogram.c** into SCCS format for the first time, assuming
also that there is no SCCS directory already existing:

```
$ mkdir SCCS
$ sccs create myprogram.c
$ myprogram.c:
1.1
14 lines
```
after you have verified that everything is all right
you remove the version of the file that starts with a comma:
```
$ rm myprogram.c
$
```

To get a copy of **myprogram.c** for editing, edit that file, then place it back in the
SCCS database:

```
$ sccs edit myprogram.c
1.1
new delta 1.2
14 lines
$ vi myprogram.c
```
your editing session
```
$ sccs delget myprogram.c
comments? Added abusive responses for compatibility
1.2
7 inserted
7 deleted
7 unchanged
1.2
14 lines
$
```

To get a file from another directory:

        sccs -p/usr/src/sccs/ get cc.c

or:

        sccs get /usr/src/sccs/cc.c

To make a delta of a large number of files in the current directory:

        sccs delta *.c

To get a list of files being edited that are not on branches:

        sccs info -b

To delta everything that you are editing:

        $ sccs delta `sccs tell -u`

In a makefile, to get source files from an SCCS file if it does not already exist:

        SRCS = <list of source files>
        $(SRCS):
                sccs get $(REL) $@

Regular sccs Commands

The "regular" SCCS commands are described very briefly below. It is unlikely that you ever need to use these commands because the user interface is so complicated, and the **sccs** front end command does 99.9% of the interesting tasks for you.

admin   Create new SCCS files and changes parameters of existing SCCS files. You can use '**sccs create**' to create new SCCS files, or use '**sccs admin**' to do other things.

cdc   Change the commentary material in an SCCS delta.

comb   Combine SCCS deltas and reconstructs the SCCS files.

delta   Permanently introduces changes that were made to a file previously retrieved using '**sccs get**'. You can use '**sccs delget**' as the more useful version of this command since '**sccs delget**' does all of the useful work and more.

get   Extract a file from the SCCS database, either for compilation, or for editing when the **-e** option is used. Use '**sccs get**' if you really need it, but '**sccs delget**' will normally have done this job for you. Use **sccs edit** instead of **get** with the **-e** option.

help   Supposed to help you interpret SCCS error messages.

prs   Display information about what is happening in an SCCS file.

rmdel   Remove a delta from an SCCS file.

sccsdiff Compare two versions of an SCCS file and generates the differences between the two versions.

val   Determine if a given SCCS file meets specified criteria. If you use the **sccs** command, you should not need to use **val**, because its user interface is unbelievable.

what   Display SCCS identification information.

FILES

/usr/sccs/*

SEE ALSO

admin(1), cdc(1), comb(1), delta(1), get(1), help(1), prs(1), rmdel(1), sact(1), sccsdiff(1), unget(1), val(1), what(1), sccsfile(5) in the *Programmer's Reference Manual*

NOTES

The **help** command usually just parrots SCCS error messages and is generally not considered very helpful.

NAME

sccsdiff – compare two versions of an SCCS file

SYNOPSIS

sccsdiff **−r**_SID1_ **−r**_SID2_ [**−p**] [**−s**_n_] _files_

DESCRIPTION

sccsdiff compares two versions of an SCCS file and generates the differences between the two versions. Any number of SCCS files may be specified, but arguments apply to all files.

−r_SID1_ **−r**_SID2_	_SID1_ and _SID2_ specify the deltas of an SCCS file that are to be compared. Versions are passed to **bdiff** in the order given.
−p	pipe output for each file through **pr**.
−s_n_	_n_ is the file segment size that **bdiff** will pass to **diff**. This option is useful when **diff** fails due to a high system load.

FILES

/var/tmp/get?????   temporary files

SEE ALSO

get(1), help(1)

diff(1), bdiff(1), pr(1) in the _User's Reference Manual_

NAME

scompat – set up compatibility environment for console applications

SYNOPSIS

scompat [-r *interpretnumber*] [*UNIX System command line*]

DESCRIPTION

COFF- or ELF-based applications developed for SCO UNIX System V/386 3.2 (or later releases) that use graphics may not work correctly on the system VGA/EGA/CGA console or Fiber Optic Workstations, which are now STREAMS-based in UNIX System V/386 Release 4.

The scompat command sets up the workstation environment so that these applications may function correctly. While the environment is in effect, access to the workstation as a STREAMS device will not work correctly unless the **-r** option is used with the argument **4** (see below).

OPTIONS

For COFF or ELF executables, scompat may be invoked with no arguments to give you XENIX ioctl interpretation [see ioctl(2) in the *Programmer's Reference Manual*]. In this case, a sub-shell is created. For the lifetime of the shell, the compatibility environment is in effect on the workstation.

scompat may also be invoked with the **-r** *interpretnumber* option, where *interpretnumber* is:

3   UNIX System V/386 Release 3.2 ioctl interpretation for XENIX applications

4   STREAMS ioctl interpretation for COFF executables or XENIX applications

scompat also accepts as arguments a shell command line (that is, **scompat ls -l**). This results in the command line being executed with the compatibility environment in effect. When the command completes execution, the compatibility environment is restored to its previous state.

NOTES

For computers based on Intel microprocessors, if **SCOMPAT** is set to **3.2**, **uname -a** gives a value of **3.2** for *release* and a value of **2** for *version*.

To set **SCOMPAT** to any other version, use the syntax

        SCOMPAT=*release*:*version*

To return to the beginning state, unset **SCOMPAT**.

In all cases, when **SCOMPAT** is set, it must be exported [see **sh**(1) in the *User's Reference Manual*].

SEE ALSO

ioctl(2) in the *Programmer's Reference Manual*

sh(1) and uname(1) in the *User's Reference Manual*

NAME

script – make typescript of a terminal session

SYNOPSIS

script [-a] [*filename*]

DESCRIPTION

script makes a typescript of everything printed on your terminal. The typescript is written to *filename*, or appended to *filename* if the -a option is given. If no file name is given, the typescript is saved in the file typescript.

The script ends when the forked shell exits or when ctrl-D is typed.

NOTES

script places *everything* that appears on the screen in the log file, including prompts.

NAME

sdb – symbolic debugger

SYNOPSIS

sdb [–e] [–s *signo*] [–V] [–W] [–w] [*objfile* [*corfile* [*directory-list*]]]

DESCRIPTION

sdb is the symbolic debugger for C and assembly programs. sdb may be used to examine executable program files and core files. It may also be used to examine live processes in a controlled execution environment.

The *objfile* argument is the name of an executable program file. To take full advantage of the symbolic capabilities of sdb, this file should be compiled with the –g (debug) option. If it has not been compiled with the –g option, the symbolic capabilities of sdb will be limited, but the file can still be examined and the program debugged. *objfile* may also be a path name in the /proc directory, in which case the currently executing process denoted by that path name is controlled by sdb.

The *corfile* argument is the name of a core image file. A core image file is produced by the abnormal termination of *objfile* or by the use of gcore. A core image file contains a copy of the segments of a program. The default for *corfile* is core. A core image file need not be present to use sdb. Using a hyphen (–) instead of *corfile* forces sdb to ignore an existing core image file.

The *directory-list* argument is a colon-separated list of directories that is used by sdb to locate source files used to build *objfile*. If no directory list is specified, sdb will look in the current directory.

The following options are recognized by sdb:

–e Ignore symbolic information and treat nonsymbolic addresses as file offsets.

–s *signo*

 Where *signo* is a decimal number that corresponds to a signal number [see signal(2)], do not stop live processes under control of sdb that receive the signal. This option may be used more than once on the sdb command line.

–V Print version information. If no *objfile* argument is specified on the command line, sdb will exit after printing the version information.

–W Suppress warnings about *corfile* being older than *objfile* or about source files that are older than *objfile*.

–w Allow user to write to *objfile* or *corfile*.

sdb recognizes a current line and a current file. When sdb is examining an executable program file without a core file, the current line and current file are initially set to the line and file containing the first line of main. If *corfile* exists, then current line and current file are initially set to the line and file containing the source statement where the process terminated. The current line and current file change automatically as a live process executes. They may also be changed with the source file examination commands.

Names of variables are written as in C. Variables local to a procedure may be accessed using the form *procedure:variable*. If no procedure name is given, the procedure containing the current line is used by default.

Structure members may be referred to as *variable.member*, pointers to structure members as *variable–>member*, and array elements as *variable[number]*. Pointers may also be dereferenced by using the form *pointer[number]*. Combinations of these forms may also be used. The form *number–>member* may be used where *number* is the address of a pointer, and *number.member* where *number* is interpreted as the address of a structure instance. The template of the structure type used in this case will be the last structure type referenced. When **sdb** displays the value of a structure, it does so by displaying the value of all elements of the structure. The address of a structure is displayed by displaying the address of the structure instance rather than the addresses of individual elements.

Elements of a multidimensional array may be referred to as *variable [number] [number]...*, or as *variable [number,number,...]*. In place of *number*, the form *number;number* may be used to indicate a range of values, * may be used to indicate all legitimate values for that subscript, or subscripts may be omitted entirely if they are the last subscripts and the full range of values is desired. If no subscripts are specified, **sdb** will display the value of all elements of the array.

A particular instance of a variable on the stack is referred to as *procedure:variable,number*. The *number* is the occurrence of the specified procedure on the stack, with the topmost occurrence being 1. The default procedure is the one containing the current line.

Addresses may be used in **sdb** commands as well. Addresses are specified by decimal, octal, or hexadecimal numbers.

Line numbers in the source program are specified by the form *filename:number* or *procedure:number*. In either case, the *number* is relative to the beginning of the file and corresponds to the line number used by text editors or the output of **pr**. A number used by itself implies a line in the current file.

While a live process is running under **sdb**, all addresses and identifiers refer to the live process. When **sdb** is not examining a live process, the addresses and identifiers refer to *objfile* or *corfile*.

Commands

The commands for examining data in the program are:

t   Prints a stack trace of the terminated or halted program. The function invoked most recently is at the top of the stack. For C programs, the stack ends with **_start**, which is the startup routine that invokes **main**.

T   Prints the top line of the stack trace.

variable/clm

Print the value of *variable* according to length *l* and format *m*. The numeric count *c* indicates that a region of memory, beginning at the address implied by *variable*, is to be displayed. The length specifiers are:

b   one byte

h   two bytes (half word)

l   four bytes (long word)

Legal values for *m* are:

c   character

d   signed decimal

u   unsigned decimal

o   octal

x   hexadecimal

f   32-bit single precision floating point

g   64-bit double precision floating point

s   Assumes that *variable* is a string pointer and prints characters starting at the address pointed to by the variable.

a   Prints characters starting at the variable's address. Do not use this with register variables.

p   pointer to procedure

i   Disassembles machine-language instruction with addresses printed numerically and symbolically.

I   Disassembles machine-language instruction with addresses printed numerically only.

Length specifiers are effective with formats **c, d, u, o, x.** The length specifier determines the output length of the value to be displayed. This value may be truncated. The count specifier *c* displays that many units of memory, starting at the address of the *variable.* The number of bytes in the unit of memory is determined by *l* or by the size associated with the variable. If the specifiers *c*, *l*, and *m* are omitted, **sdb** uses defaults. If a count specifier is used with the **s** or **a** command, then that many characters are printed. Otherwise, successive characters are printed until either a null byte is reached or 128 characters are printed. The last variable may be redisplayed with the **./** command.

For a limited form of pattern matching, use the **sh** metacharacters ∗ and **?** within procedure and variable names. (**sdb** does not accept these metacharacters in file names, as the function name in a line number when setting a breakpoint, in the function call command, or as the argument to the **e** command.) If no procedure name is supplied, **sdb** matches both local and global variables. If the procedure name is specified, then **sdb** matches only local variables. To match global variables only, use **:***pattern.* To print all variables, use ∗**:**∗.

linenumber?*lm*
variable : ?*lm*

> Prints the value at the address from the executable or text space given by *linenumber* or *variable* (procedure name), according to the format *lm*. The default format is **i**.

variable=*lm*
linenumber=*lm*
number=*lm*

> Prints the address of *variable* or *linenumber*, or the value of *number*. *l* specifies length and *m* specifies the format. If no format is specified, then **sdb** uses **1x** (four-byte hex). *m* allows you to convert between decimal, octal, and hexadecimal.

variable ! *value*

> Sets *variable* to the given *value*. The value may be a number, a character constant, or a variable. The value must be well-defined; structures are allowed only if assigning to another structure variable of the same type. Character constants are denoted ´*character*. Numbers are viewed as integers unless a decimal point or exponent is used. In this case, they are treated as having the type **double**. Registers, except the floating point registers, are viewed as integers. Register names are identical to those used by the assembler (for example, %*regname* where *regname* is the name of a register). If the address of a variable is given, it is regarded as the address of a variable of type **int**. C conventions are used in any type conversions necessary to perform the indicated assignment.

x   Prints the machine registers and the current machine-language instruction.

X   Prints the current machine-language instruction.

The commands for examining source files are:

e
e *procedure*
e *filename*
e *directory*/

> **e**, without arguments, prints the name of the current file. The second form sets the current file to the file containing the procedure. The third form sets the current file to *filename*. The current line is set to the first line in the named procedure or file. Source files are assumed to be in the directories in the directory list. The fourth form adds *directory* to the end of the directory list.

/*regular expression*/

> Searches forward from the current line for a line containing a string matching *regular expression*, as in **ed**. The trailing / may be omitted, except when associated with a breakpoint.

?*regular expression*?

> Searches backward from the current line for a line containing a string matching *regular expression*, as in **ed**. The trailing ? may be omitted, except when associated with a breakpoint.

p   Prints the current line.

z   Prints the current line and the following nine lines. Sets the current line to the last line printed.

w   Prints the 10 lines (the window) around the current line.

number
Specifies the current line. Prints the new current line.

count+
Advances the current line by *count* lines. Prints the new current line.

count−
Resets the current line by *count* lines back. Prints the new current line.

The commands for controlling the execution of the source program are:

count **r** *args*
count **R**
Runs the program with the given arguments. The **r** command with no arguments reuses the previous arguments to the program. The **R** command runs the program with no arguments. An argument beginning with **<** or **>** redirects the standard input or output, respectively. Full **sh** syntax is accepted. If *count* is given, it specifies the number of breakpoints to be ignored.

linenumber **c** *count*
linenumber **C** *count*
Continues execution. **sdb** stops when it encounters *count* breakpoints. The signal that stopped the program is reactivated with the **C** command and ignored with the **c** command. If a line number is specified, then a temporary breakpoint is placed at the line and execution continues. The breakpoint is deleted when the command finishes.

linenumber **g** *count*
Continues with execution resumed at the given line. If *count* is given, it specifies the number of breakpoints to be ignored.

s *count*
S *count*
s single steps the program through *count* lines or if no *count* is given, then the program runs for one line. **s** will step from one function into a called function. **S** also steps a program, but it will not step into a called function. It steps over the function called.

i *count*
I *count*
Single steps by *count* machine-language instructions. The signal that caused the program to stop is reactivated with the **I** command and ignored with the **i** command.

*variable***$m** *count*
*address***:m** *count*

Single steps (as with **s**) until the specified location is modified with a new value. If *count* is omitted, it is, in effect, infinity. *Variable* must be accessible from the current procedure. This command can be very slow.

level **v**

Toggles verbose mode. This is for use when single stepping with **S**, **s**, or **m**. If *level* is omitted, then just the current source file and/or function name is printed when either changes. If *level* is 1 or greater, each C source line is printed before it executes. If *level* is 2 or greater, each assembler statement is also printed. A **v** turns verbose mode off.

k   Kills the program being debugged.

procedure (*arg1,arg2,...*)
procedure (*arg1,arg2,...*) */m*

Executes the named procedure with the given arguments. Arguments can be register names, integer, character, or string constants, or names of variables accessible from the current procedure. The second form causes the value returned by the procedure to be printed according to format *m*. If no format is given, it defaults to **d**.

linenumber **b** *commands*

Sets a breakpoint at the given line. If a procedure name without a line number is given (for example, *proc***:**), a breakpoint is placed at the first line in the procedure even if it was not compiled with the **–g** option. If no *linenumber* is given, a breakpoint is placed at the current line. If no *commands* are given, execution stops at the breakpoint and control is returned to **sdb**. Otherwise the *commands* are executed when the breakpoint is encountered. Multiple commands are specified by separating them with semicolons. Nested associated commands are not permitted; setting breakpoints within the associated environments is permitted.

B   Prints a list of the currently active breakpoints.

linenumber **d**

Deletes a breakpoint at the given line. If no *linenumber* is given, then the breakpoints are deleted interactively. Each breakpoint location is printed and a line is read from the standard input. If the line begins with a **y** or **d**, then the breakpoint is deleted.

D   Deletes all breakpoints.

l   Prints the last executed line.

linenumber **a**

Announces a line number. If *linenumber* is of the form *proc***:***number*, the command effectively does a *linenumber***:b l;c**. If *linenumber* is of the form *proc***:**, the command effectively does a *proc***:b T;c**.

Miscellaneous commands:

#*rest-of-line*
>   The *rest-of-line* represents comments that are ignored by **sdb**.

!*command*
>   The *command* is interpreted by **sh**.

new-line
>   If the previous command printed a source line, then advance the current line by one line and print the new current line. If the previous command displayed a memory location, then display the next memory location. If the previous command disassembled an instruction, then disassemble the next instruction.

end-of-file character
>   Scrolls the next 10 lines of instructions, source, or data depending on which was printed last. The end-of-file character is usually **control-d**.

< *filename*
>   Read commands from *filename* until the end of file is reached, and then continue to accept commands from standard input. Commands are echoed, preceded by two asterisks, just before being executed. This command may not be nested; < may not appear as a command in a file.

M   Prints the address maps.

" *string* "
>   Prints the given string. The C escape sequences of the form *character*, *octaldigits*, or **x**hexdigits are recognized, where *character* is a nonnumeric character. The trailing quote may be omitted.

q   Exits the debugger.

v   Prints version stamping information.

SEE ALSO
cc(1), **signal**(2), **a.out**(4), **core**(4), **syms**(4)
ed(1), **gcore**(1), **sh**(1) in the *User's Reference Manual*
The "**sdb**" chapter in the *Programmer's Guide: ANSI C and Programming Support Tools*

NOTES
If *objfile* is a dynamically linked executable, variables, function names, and so on that are defined in shared objects may not be referenced until the shared object in which the variable, and so on, is defined is attached to the process. For shared objects attached at startup (for example, **libc.so.1**, the default C library), this implies that such variables may not be accessed until **main** is called.

The *objfile* argument is accessed directly for debugging information while the process is created via the **PATH** variable.

NAME

sdiff – print file differences side-by-side

SYNOPSIS

sdiff [*options*] *file1 file2*

DESCRIPTION

sdiff uses the output of the diff command to produce a side-by-side listing of two files indicating lines that are different. Lines of the two files are printed with a blank gutter between them if the lines are identical, a < in the gutter if the line appears only in *file1*, a > in the gutter if the line appears only in *file2*, and a | for lines that are different. For example:

```
        x    |    y
        a         a
        b    <
        c    <
        d         d
             >    c
```

Valid options are:

-w *n*   Use the argument *n* as the width of the output line. The default line length is 130 characters.

-l   Print only the left side of any lines that are identical.

-s   Do not print identical lines.

-o *output*   Use the argument *output* as the name of a third file that is created as a user-controlled merge of *file1* and *file2*. Identical lines of *file1* and *file2* are copied to *output*. Sets of differences, as produced by diff, are printed; where a set of differences share a common gutter character. After printing each set of differences, sdiff prompts the user with a % and waits for one of the following user-typed commands:

```
        l       Append the left column to the output file.
        r       Append the right column to the output file.
        s       Turn on silent mode; do not print identical lines.
        v       Turn off silent mode.
        e l     Call the editor with the left column.
        e r     Call the editor with the right column.
        e b     Call the editor with the concatenation of left and right.
        e       Call the editor with a zero length file.
        q       Exit from the program.
```

On exit from the editor, the resulting file is concatenated to the end of the *output* file.

SEE ALSO

diff(1), ed(1)

NAME

sed – stream editor

SYNOPSIS

sed [–n] [–e *script*] [–f *sfile*] [*file* ...]

DESCRIPTION

sed copies the named *file* (standard input default) to the standard output, edited according to a script of commands. The –f option causes the script to be taken from file *sfile*; these options accumulate. If there is just one –e option and no –f options, the flag –e may be omitted. The –n option suppresses the default output. A script consists of editing commands, one per line, of the following form:

[*address* [, *address*]] *function* [*arguments*]

In normal operation, sed cyclically copies a line of input into a *pattern space* (unless there is something left after a D command), applies in sequence all commands whose *addresses* select that pattern space, and at the end of the script copies the pattern space to the standard output (except under –n) and deletes the pattern space.

Some of the commands use a *hold space* to save all or part of the *pattern space* for subsequent retrieval.

An *address* is either a decimal number that counts input lines cumulatively across files, a $ that addresses the last line of input, or a context address, i.e., a /*regular expression*/ in the style of ed(1) modified thus:

In a context address, the construction \?*regular expression*?, where ? is any character, is identical to /*regular expression*/. Note that in the context address \xabc\xdefx, the second x stands for itself, so that the regular expression is abcxdef.

The escape sequence \n matches a new-line *embedded* in the pattern space.

A period (.) matches any character except the *terminal* new-line of the pattern space.

A command line with no addresses selects every pattern space.

A command line with one address selects each pattern space that matches the address.

A command line with two addresses selects the inclusive range from the first pattern space that matches the first address through the next pattern space that matches the second address. (If the second address is a number less than or equal to the line number selected by the first address, only the line corresponding to the first address is selected.) Thereafter the process is repeated, looking again for the first address.

Editing commands can be applied only to non-selected pattern spaces by use of the negation function ! (below).

In the following list of functions the maximum number of permissible addresses for each function is indicated in parentheses.

The *text* argument consists of one or more lines, all but the last of which end with \ to hide the new-line. Backslashes in text are treated like backslashes in the replacement string of an **s** command, and may be used to protect initial blanks and tabs against the stripping that is done on every script line. The *rfile* or *wfile* argument must terminate the command line and must be preceded by exactly one blank. Each *wfile* is created before processing begins. There can be at most 10 distinct *wfile* arguments.

(1) **a**
text   Append. Place *text* on the output before reading the next input line.

(2) **b** *label*   Branch to the **:** command bearing the *label*. If *label* is empty, branch to the end of the script.

(2) **c**
text   Change. Delete the pattern space. Place *text* on the output. Start the next cycle.

(2) **d**   Delete the pattern space. Start the next cycle.

(2) **D**   Delete the initial segment of the pattern space through the first new-line. Start the next cycle.

(2) **g**   Replace the contents of the pattern space by the contents of the hold space.

(2) **G**   Append the contents of the hold space to the pattern space.

(2) **h**   Replace the contents of the hold space by the contents of the pattern space.

(2) **H**   Append the contents of the pattern space to the hold space.

(1) **i**
text   Insert. Place *text* on the standard output.

(2) **l**   List the pattern space on the standard output in an unambiguous form. Non-printable characters are displayed in octal notation and long lines are folded.

(2) **n**   Copy the pattern space to the standard output. Replace the pattern space with the next line of input.

(2) **N**   Append the next line of input to the pattern space with an embedded new-line. (The current line number changes.)

(2) **p**   Print. Copy the pattern space to the standard output.

(2) **P**   Copy the initial segment of the pattern space through the first new-line to the standard output.

(1) **q**   Quit. Branch to the end of the script. Do not start a new cycle.

(2) **r** *rfile* Read the contents of *rfile*. Place them on the output before reading the next input line.

(2) **s** / *regular expression* / *replacement* / *flags*
                Substitute the *replacement* string for instances of the *regular expression* in the pattern space. Any character may be used instead of /. For a fuller description see **ed**(1). *flags* is zero or more of:

n	*n*= 1 - 512. Substitute for just the *n*th occurrence of the *regular expression*.
g	Global. Substitute for all nonoverlapping instances of the *regular expression* rather than just the first one.
p	Print the pattern space if a replacement was made.
w *wfile*	Write. Append the pattern space to *wfile* if a replacement was made.

(2) **t** *label*   Test. Branch to the **:** command bearing the *label* if any substitutions have been made since the most recent reading of an input line or execution of a **t**. If *label* is empty, branch to the end of the script.

(2) **w** *wfile*   Write. Append the pattern space to *wfile*. The first occurrence of **w** will cause *wfile* to be cleared. Subsequent invocations of **w** will append. Each time the **sed** command is used, *wfile* is overwritten.

(2) **x**   Exchange the contents of the pattern and hold spaces.

(2) **y** / *string1* / *string2* /

Transform. Replace all occurrences of characters in *string1* with the corresponding characters in *string2*. *string1* and *string2* must have the same number of characters.

(2) **!** *function*

Don't. Apply the *function* (or group, if *function* is **{**) only to lines *not* selected by the address(es).

(0) **:** *label*   This command does nothing; it bears a *label* for **b** and **t** commands to branch to.

(1) **=**   Place the current line number on the standard output as a line.

(2) **{**   Execute the following commands through a matching **}** only when the pattern space is selected.

(0)   An empty command is ignored.

(0) **#**   If a **#** appears as the first character on a line of a script file, then that entire line is treated as a comment, with one exception: if a **#** appears on the first line and the character after the **#** is an **n**, then the default output will be suppressed. The rest of the line after **#n** is also ignored. A script file must contain at least one non-comment line.

SEE ALSO

awk(1), ed(1), grep(1)

NAME

sendmail – send mail over the internet

SYNOPSIS

/usr/ucblib/sendmail [–ba] [–bd] [–bi] [–bm] [–bp] [–bs] [–bt] [–bv]
     [–bz] [–C*file*] [–d*X*] [–F*fullname*] [–f*name*] [–h*N*] [–n] [–o x*value*]
     [–q [*time*]] [–r*name*] [–t] [–v] [*address* . . .]

DESCRIPTION

sendmail sends a message to one or more people, routing the message over whatever networks are necessary. **sendmail** does internetwork forwarding as necessary to deliver the message to the correct place.

sendmail is not intended as a user interface routine; other programs provide user-friendly front ends; **sendmail** is used only to deliver pre-formatted messages.

With no flags, **sendmail** reads its standard input up to an EOF, or a line with a single dot and sends a copy of the letter found there to all of the addresses listed. It determines the network to use based on the syntax and contents of the addresses.

Local addresses are looked up in the local **aliases**(4) file, or by using the YP name service, and aliased appropriately. In addition, if there is a **.forward** file in a recipient's home directory, **sendmail** forwards a copy of each message to the list of recipients that file contains. Aliasing can be prevented by preceding the address with a backslash. Normally the sender is not included in alias expansions, for example, if 'john' sends to 'group', and 'group' includes 'john' in the expansion, then the letter will not be delivered to 'john'.

sendmail will also route mail directly to other known hosts in a local network. The list of hosts to which mail is directly sent is maintained in the file **/usr/lib/mailhosts**.

The following options are available:

–ba	Go into ARPANET mode. All input lines must end with a CR-LF, and all messages will be generated with a CR-LF at the end. Also, the "From:" and "Sender:" fields are examined for the name of the sender.
–bd	Run as a daemon, waiting for incoming SMTP connections.
–bi	Initialize the alias database.
–bm	Deliver mail in the usual way (default).
–bp	Print a summary of the mail queue.
–bs	Use the SMTP protocol as described in RFC 821. This flag implies all the operations of the –ba flag that are compatible with SMTP.
–bt	Run in address test mode. This mode reads addresses and shows the steps in parsing; it is used for debugging configuration tables.

-bv	Verify names only — do not try to collect or deliver a message. Verify mode is normally used for validating users or mailing lists.
-bz	Create the configuration freeze file.
-C_file_	Use alternate configuration file.
-d_X_	Set debugging value to _X_.
-F_fullname_	Set the full name of the sender.
-f_name_	Sets the name of the "from" person (that is, the sender of the mail). **-f** can only be used by "trusted" users (who are listed in the config file).
-h_N_	Set the hop count to _N_. The hop count is incremented every time the mail is processed. When it reaches a limit, the mail is returned with an error message, the victim of an aliasing loop.
-M_id_	Attempt to deliver the queued message with message-id **id**.
-n	Do not do aliasing.
-o_x value_	Set option _x_ to the specified _value_. Options are described below.
-q[_time_]	Processed saved messages in the queue at given intervals. If _time_ is omitted, process the queue once. _Time_ is given as a tagged number, with **s** being seconds, **m** being minutes, **h** being hours, **d** being days, and **w** being weeks. For example, **-q1h30m** or **-q90m** would both set the timeout to one hour thirty minutes.
-r_name_	An alternate and obsolete form of the **-f** flag.
-R_string_	Go through the queue of pending mail and attempt to deliver any message with a recipient containing the specified string. This is useful for clearing out mail directed to a machine which has been down for awhile.
-t	Read message for recipients. "To:", "Cc:", and "Bcc:" lines will be scanned for people to send to. The "Bcc:" line will be deleted before transmission. Any addresses in the argument list will be suppressed.
-v	Go into verbose mode. Alias expansions will be announced, and so on.

PROCESSING OPTIONS

There are also a number of processing options that may be set. Normally these will only be used by a system administrator. Options may be set either on the command line using the **-o** flag or in the configuration file. The options are:

A_file_	Use alternate alias file.
c	On mailers that are considered "expensive" to connect to, do not initiate immediate connection. This requires queuing.
d_x_	Set the delivery mode to _x_. Delivery modes are **i** for interactive (synchronous) delivery, **b** for background (asynchronous) delivery, and **q** for queue only — that is, actual delivery is done the next time the queue is run.

D   Run **newaliases**(1M) to automatically rebuild the alias database, if necessary.

e*x*   Set error processing to mode *x*. Valid modes are **m** to mail back the error message, **w** to "write" back the error message (or mail it back if the sender is not logged in), **p** to print the errors on the terminal (default), 'q' to throw away error messages (only exit status is returned), and 'e' to do special processing for the BerkNet. If the text of the message is not mailed back by modes **m** or **w** and if the sender is local to this machine, a copy of the message is appended to the file **dead.letter** in the sender's home directory.

F*mode*   The mode to use when creating temporary files.

f   Save UNIX-system-style "From" lines at the front of messages.

g*N*   The default group ID to use when calling mailers.

H*file*   The **SMTP** help file.

i   Do not take dots on a line by themselves as a message terminator.

L*n*   The log level.

m   Send to "me" (the sender) also if I am in an alias expansion.

o   If set, this message may have old style headers. If not set, this message is guaranteed to have new style headers (that is, commas instead of spaces between addresses). If set, an adaptive algorithm is used that will correctly determine the header format in most cases.

Q*queuedir*   Select the directory in which to queue messages.

r*timeout*   The timeout on reads; if none is set, **sendmail** will wait forever for a mailer.

S*file*   Save statistics in the named file.

s   Always instantiate the queue file, even under circumstances where it is not strictly necessary.

T*time*   Set the timeout on messages in the queue to the specified time. After sitting in the queue for this amount of time, they will be returned to the sender. The default is three days.

t*stz,dtz*   Set the name of the time zone.

u*N*   Set the default user id for mailers.

If the first character of the user name is a vertical bar, the rest of the user name is used as the name of a program to pipe the mail to. It may be necessary to quote the name of the user to keep **sendmail** from suppressing the blanks from between arguments.

sendmail returns an exit status describing what it did. The codes are defined in **sysexits.h**.

EX_OK	Successful completion on all addresses.
EX_NOUSER	User name not recognized.
EX_UNAVAILABLE	Catchall meaning necessary resources were not available.
EX_SYNTAX	Syntax error in address.
EX_SOFTWARE	Internal software error, including bad arguments.
EX_OSERR	Temporary operating system error, such as cannot fork.
EX_NOHOST	Host name not recognized.
EX_TEMPFAIL	Message could not be sent immediately, but was queued.

If invoked as **newaliases**, **sendmail** rebuilds the alias database. If invoked as *mailq*, **sendmail** prints the contents of the mail queue.

FILES

Except for **/etc/sendmail.cf**, these pathnames are all specified in **/etc/sendmail.cf**. Thus, these values are only approximations.

/usr/bin/uux	to deliver uucp mail
/usr/bin/mail	to deliver local mail
/var/spool/mqueue/*	temp files and queued mail
~/.forward	list of recipients for forwarding messages

SEE ALSO

biff(1), **mail**(1), **mailstat**(1), **newaliases**(1), **mconnect**(1M), **aliases**(4)

Su, Zaw-Sing, and Jon Postel, *The Domain Naming Convention for Internet User Applications*, RFC 819, Network Information Center, SRI International, Menlo Park, Calif., August 1982

Postel, Jon, *Simple Mail Transfer Protocol*, RFC 821, Network Information Center, SRI International, Menlo Park, Calif., August 1982

Crocker, Dave, *Standard for the Format of ARPA-Internet Text Messages*, RFC 822, Network Information Center, SRI International, Menlo Park, Calif., August 1982

NOTES

Do not use the **-bz** option if you plan to run **sendmail** as a daemon, that is, with the **-bd** option.

If the frozen configuration file, **/usr/ucblib/sendmail.fc**, was created with the **-bz** option, running **sendmail** as a daemon (with the **-bd** option) fails with a core dump.

NAME
set, unset – set and unset local or global environment variables

SYNOPSIS
set [-l *variable*[=*value*]] . . .
set [-e *variable*[=*value*]] . . .
set [-f*file variable*[=*value*]] . . .

unset -l *variable* . . .
unset -f*file variable* . . .

DESCRIPTION
The **set** command sets *variable* in the environment, or adds *variable=value* to *file*.
If *variable* is not equated it to a value, **set** expects the value to be on standard
input. The **unset** command removes *variable*. Note that the FMLI predefined,
read-only variables (such as **ARG1**), may not be set or unset.

FMLI inherits the UNIX environment when invoked:

-l   sets or unsets the specified variable in the local environment. Variables set
      with **-l** will not be inherited by processes invoked from FMLI.

-e   sets the specified variable in the UNIX environment. Variables set with **-e**
      will be inherited by any processes started from FMLI. Note that these
      variables cannot be **unset**.

-f*file* sets or unsets the specified variable in the global environment. The argu-
      ment *file* is the name, or pathname, of a file containing lines of the form
      variable=value. *file* will be created if it does not already exist. Note that no
      space intervenes between **-f** and *file*.

Note that at least one of the above options must be used for each variable being
set or unset. If you set a variable with the *-ffilename* option, you must thereafter
include *filename* in references to that variable. For example, **${** (*file*) *VARIABLE***}**.

EXAMPLE
Storing a selection made in a menu:

```
name=Selection 2
action=`set -l SELECTION=2`close
```

NOTES
Variables set to be available to the UNIX environment (those set using the **-e**
option) can only be set for the current **fmli** process and the processes it calls.

When using the **-f** option, unless *file* is unique to the process, other users of
FMLI on the same machine will be able to expand these variables, depending on
the read/write permissions on *file*.

A variable set in one frame may be referenced or unset in any other frame. This
includes local variables.

SEE ALSO
env(1), **sh**(1) in the *UNIX System V User's Reference Manual*

NAME

setclk – set system time from hardware clock

SYNOPSIS

/sbin/setclk

DESCRIPTION

setclk is used to set the internal system time from the hardware time-of-day clock. The command can be used only by the super-user. It is normally executed by an entry in the /etc/inittab file when the system is initialized at boot time. Note that setclk checks the Nonvolatile Random Access Memory (NVRAM) only for the date. If the date is set, setclk runs silently. If the date is not set, setclk prompts the user to use sysadm datetime [see sysadm(1)] for the proper setting of the hardware clock.

SEE ALSO

sysadm(1) in the *User's Reference Manual*.

NAME

setcolor, setcolour – set screen color

SYNOPSIS

setcolor [-nbrgopc] *argument* [*argument*]
setcolour [-nbrgopc] *argument* [*argument*]

DESCRIPTION

setcolor and setcolour allow the user to set the screen to a specific color. Both foreground and background colors can be set independently in a range of 16 colors. setcolor can also set the reverse video and graphics character colors. setcolor with no arguments produces a usage message that displays all available colors, then resets the screen to its previous state.

For example, the following strings are possible colors:

blue	magenta	brown	black
lt_blue	lt_magenta	yellow	gray
cyan	white	green	red
lt_cyan	hi_white	lt_green	lt_red

OPTIONS

The following options are available for setcolor and setcolour. In the arguments below, *color* is taken from the above list.

-n	Sets the screen to normal white characters on black background.
color [*color*]	Sets the foreground to the first color. Sets background to second color if a second color choice is specified.
-b *color*	Sets the background to the specified color.
-r *color color*	Set the foreground reverse video characters to the first color. Set reverse video characters' background to second color.
-g *color color*	Set the foreground graphics characters to the first color. Set graphics characters' background to second color.
-o *color*	Sets the color of the screen border (over scan region). To reset border color, use -o black.
-p *pitch duration*	Set the pitch and duration of the bell. Pitch is the period in microseconds, and duration is measured in fifths of a second. When using this option, a control-G (bell) must be echoed to the screen for the command to work. For example:

```
setcolor -p 2500 2
echo ^G
```

-c*first last*	Set the first and last scan lines of the cursor.

NOTES

The ability of setcolor to set any of these described functions is ultimately dependent on the ability of devices to support them. For example, the -o option does not work on the Color Graphics Adapter (CGA).

setcolor emits an escape sequence that may or may not have an effect on mono-chrome devices.

Occasionally changing the screen color can help prolong the life of your monitor.

NAME

    setcolor – redefine or create a color

SYNOPSIS

    setcolor *color red_level green_level blue_level*

DESCRIPTION

    The **setcolor** command takes four arguments: *color*, which must be a string naming the color; and the arguments *red_level*, *green_level*, and *blue_level*, which must be integer values defining, respectively, the intensity of the red, green, and blue components of *color*. Intensities must be in the range of 0 to 1000. If you are redefining an existing color, you must use its current name (default color names are: **black, blue, green, cyan, red, magenta, yellow,** and **white**). **setcolor** returns the color's name string.

EXAMPLE

        `` `setcolor blue 100 24 300` ``

NAME

setkey – assigns the function keys

SYNOPSIS

setkey *keynum string*

DESCRIPTION

The **setkey** command assigns the given ANSI *string* to be the output of the computer function key given by *keynum*. For example, the command:

        setkey 1 date

assigns the string **date** as the output of function key 1. The *string* can contain control characters, such as a newline character, and should be quoted to protect it from processing by the shell. For example, the command:

        setkey 2 "pwd ; lc\n"

assigns the command sequence **pwd ; lc** to function key 2. Notice how the newline character is embedded in the quoted string. This causes the commands to be carried out when function key 2 is pressed. Otherwise, the Enter key would have to be pressed after pressing the function key, as in the previous example.

setkey translates ^ into ^^, which, when passed to the screen driver, is interpreted as a right angle bracket (>), or greater than key.

NOTES

setkey works only on the console keyboard.

The string mapping table is where the function keys are defined. It is an array of 512 bytes (**typedef strmap_t**) where null terminated strings can be put to redefine the function keys. The first null terminated string is assigned to the first string key, the second to the second string key, and so on. There is one string mapping table per multiscreen.

Although the size of the **setkey** string mapping table is 512 bytes, there is a limit of 30 characters that can be assigned to any individual function key.

Assigning more than 512 characters to the string mapping table causes the function key buffer to overflow. When this happens, the sequences sent by the arrow keys are overwritten, effectively disabling them. Once the function key buffer overflows, the only way to enable the arrow keys is to reboot the system.

The table below lists the *keynum* values for the function keys:

Function key	_keynum_	Function key	_keynum_
F1	1	Ctrl-F10	34
F2	2	Ctrl-F11	35
F3	3	Ctrl-F12	36
F4	4	Ctrl-Shift-F1	37
F5	5	Ctrl-Shift-F2	38
F6	6	Ctrl-Shift-F3	39
F7	7	Ctrl-Shift-F4	40
F8	8	Ctrl-Shift-F5	41
F9	9	Ctrl-Shift-F6	42
F10	10	Ctrl-Shift-F7	43
F11	11	Ctrl-Shift-F8	44
F12	12	Ctrl-Shift-F9	45
Shift-F1	13	Ctrl-Shift-F10	46
Shift-F2	14	Ctrl-Shift-F11	47
Shift-F3	15	Ctrl-Shift-F12	48
Shift-F4	16		
Shift-F5	17	Numeric Key-Pad	_keynum_
Shift-F6	18		
Shift-F7	19	7	49
Shift-F8	20	8	50
Shift-F9	21	9	51
Shift-F10	22	-	52
Shift-F11	23	4	53
Shift-F12	24	5	54
Ctrl-F1	25	6	55
Ctrl-F2	26	+	56
Ctrl-F3	27	1	57
Ctrl-F4	28	2	58
Ctrl-F5	29	3	59
Ctrl-F6	30	0	60
Ctrl-F7	31		
Ctrl-F8	32		
Ctrl-F9	33		

For a table of the escape sequences, see **keyboard**(7) in the _System Administrator's Guide_.

FILES

     `/bin/setkey`

SEE ALSO

     keyboard(7)

NAME

setmnt – establish mount table

SYNOPSIS

/sbin/setmnt

DESCRIPTION

setmnt creates the /etc/mnttab table which is needed for both the mount and umount commands. setmnt reads standard input and creates a mnttab entry for each line. Input lines have the format:

filesys node

where *filesys* is the name of the file system's "special file" (such as /dev/dsk/c?d?s?) and *node* is the root name of that file system. Thus *filesys* and *node* become the first two strings in the mount table entry.

FILES

/etc/mnttab

SEE ALSO

mount(1M)

NOTES

Problems may occur if *filesys* or *node* are longer than 32 characters.

setmnt silently enforces an upper limit on the maximum number of mnttab entries.

NAME

settime – change the access and modification dates of files

SYNOPSIS

settime *mmddhhmm*[*yy*] [-f *fname*] *name*. . .

DESCRIPTION

settime sets the access and modification dates for one or more files. The dates are set to the specified date, or to the access and modification dates of the file specified via -f. Exactly one of these methods must be used to specify the new date(s). The first *mm* is the month number; *dd* is the day number in the month; *hh* is the hour number (24 hour system); the second *mm* is the minute number; *yy* is the last two digits of the year and is optional. For example:

settime 1008004583 ralph pete

sets the access and modification dates of files **ralph** and **pete** to Oct. 8, 12:45 AM, 1983. Another example:

settime -f ralph john

This sets the access and modification dates of the file **john** to those of the file **ralph**.

NOTES

Use of **touch** in place of **settime** is encouraged.

NAME

setuname – changes machine information

SYNOPSIS

setuname [-s *name*] [-n *node*] [-t]

DESCRIPTION

setuname changes the parameter value for the system name and node name. Each parameter can be changed using **setuname** and the appropriate option.

The options and arguments for this command are:

-s   Changes the system name. *name* specifies new system name and can consist of alphanumeric characters and the special characters dash, underbar, and dollar sign.

-n   Changes the node name. *node* specifies the new network node name and can consist of alphanumeric characters and the special characters dash, underbar, and dollar sign.

-t   Temporary change. No attempt will be made to create a permanent change.

Either or both the -s and -n options must be given when invoking **setuname**.

The system architecture may place requirements on the size of the system and network node name. The command will issue a fatal warning message and an error message if the name entered is incompatible with the system requirements.

NOTES

setuname attempts to change the parameter values in two places: the running kernel and, as necessary per implementation, to cross system reboots. A temporary change changes only the running kernel.

NAME

setup – initialize system for first user

SYNOPSIS

setup

DESCRIPTION

The **setup** command, which is also accessible as a login by the same name, allows the first user to be established as the "owner" of the machine.

The user can then set the date, time and time zone of the machine.

The user can then set the node name of the machine.

The user can then protect the system from unauthorized modification of the machine configuration and software by giving passwords to the administrative and maintenance functions. Normally, the first user of the machine enters this command through the setup login, which initially has no password, and then gives passwords to the various functions in the system. Any that the user leaves without password protection can be exercised by anyone.

The user can then give passwords to system logins such as "root", "bin", etc. (*provided they do not already have passwords*). Once given a password, each login can only be changed by that login or "root".

Finally, the user is permitted to add the first logins to the system, usually starting with his or her own.

SEE ALSO

passwd(1)

DIAGNOSTICS

The **passwd**(1) command complains if the password provided does not meet its standards.

NOTES

If the setup login is not under password control, anyone can put passwords on the other functions.

NAME

sh, jsh, rsh – command interpreters: standard shell, job control shell, restricted shell

SYNOPSIS

sh [–acefhiknprstuvx] [*args*]

jsh [–acefhiknprstuvx] [*args*]

/usr/lib/rsh [–acefhiknprstuvx] [*args*]

DESCRIPTION

sh is a command programming language that executes commands read from a terminal or a file. The command jsh is an interface to the shell which provides all of the functionality of sh and enables Job Control (see ''Job Control,'' below). /usr/lib/rsh is a restricted version of the standard command interpreter sh; It is used to restrict logins to execution environments whose capabilities are more controlled than those of the standard shell. See ''Invocation,'' below for the meaning of arguments to the shell.

Definitions

A *blank* is a tab or a space. A *name* is a sequence of ASCII letters, digits, or underscores, beginning with a letter or an underscore. A *parameter* is a name, a digit, or any of the following characters: *, @, #, ?, –, $, and !

Commands

A *simple-command* is a sequence of non-blank *word*s separated by *blank*s. The first *word* specifies the name of the command to be executed. Except as specified below, the remaining *word*s are passed as arguments to the invoked command. The command name is passed as argument 0 [see exec(2)]. The *value* of a *simple-command* is its exit status if it terminates normally, or (octal) **200**+*status* if it terminates abnormally; see signal(5) for a list of status values.

A *pipeline* is a sequence of one or more *command*s separated by |. The standard output of each *command* but the last is connected by a pipe(2) to the standard input of the next *command*. Each *command* is run as a separate process; the shell waits for the last *command* to terminate. The exit status of a *pipeline* is the exit status of the last command in the *pipeline*.

A *list* is a sequence of one or more *pipeline*s separated by ;, &, &&, or | |, and optionally terminated by ; or &. Of these four symbols, ; and & have equal precedence, which is lower than that of && and | |. The symbols && and | | also have equal precedence. A semicolon (;) causes sequential execution of the preceding *pipeline* (that is, the shell waits for the *pipeline* to finish before executing any commands following the semicolon); an ampersand (&) causes asynchronous execution of the preceding pipeline (that is, the shell does *not* wait for that pipeline to finish). The symbol && (| |) causes the *list* following it to be executed only if the preceding pipeline returns a zero (non-zero) exit status. An arbitrary number of newlines may appear in a *list*, instead of semicolons, to delimit commands.

A *command* is either a *simple-command* or one of the following. Unless otherwise stated, the value returned by a command is that of the last *simple-command* executed in the command.

for *name* [**in** *word* . . .] **do** *list* **done**
> Each time a **for** command is executed, *name* is set to the next *word* taken from the **in** *word* list. If **in** *word* . . . is omitted, then the **for** command executes the **do** *list* once for each positional parameter that is set (see "Parameter Substitution," below). Execution ends when there are no more words in the list.

case *word* **in** [*pattern* [| *pattern*] . . .) *list* ;;] . . . **esac**
> A **case** command executes the *list* associated with the first *pattern* that matches *word*. The form of the patterns is the same as that used for file-name generation (see "Filename Generation") except that a slash, a leading dot, or a dot immediately following a slash need not be matched explicitly.

if *list* **then** *list* [**elif** *list* **then** *list*] . . . [**else** *list*] **fi**
> The *list* following **if** is executed and, if it returns a zero exit status, the *list* following the first **then** is executed. Otherwise, the *list* following **elif** is executed and, if its value is zero, the *list* following the next **then** is executed. Failing that, the **else** *list* is executed. If no **else** *list* or **then** *list* is executed, then the **if** command returns a zero exit status.

while *list* **do** *list* **done**
> A **while** command repeatedly executes the **while** *list* and, if the exit status of the last command in the list is zero, executes the **do** *list*; otherwise the loop terminates. If no commands in the **do** *list* are executed, then the **while** command returns a zero exit status; **until** may be used in place of **while** to negate the loop termination test.

(*list*)
> Execute *list* in a sub-shell.

{ *list*; }
> *list* is executed in the current (that is, parent) shell. The { must be followed by a space.

name () { *list*; }
> Define a function that is referenced by *name*. The body of the function is the *list* of commands between { and }. The *list* may appear on the same line as the {. If it does, the { and *list* must be separated by a space. The } may not be on the same line as *list*; it must be on a newline. Execution of functions is described below (see "Execution"). The { and } are unnecessary if the body of the function is a *command* as defined above, under "Commands."

The following words are recognized only as the first word of a command and when not quoted:

```
    if   then   else   elif   fi   case   esac   for   while   until   do
    done   {   }
```

Comments
A word beginning with **#** causes that word and all the following characters up to a newline to be ignored.

Command Substitution

The shell reads commands from the string between two back quotes (` `) and the standard output from these commands may be used as all or part of a word. Trailing newlines from the standard output are removed.

No interpretation is done on the string before the string is read, except to remove backslashes (\) used to escape other characters. Backslashes may be used to escape a back quote (` ) or another backslash (\) and are removed before the command string is read. Escaping back quotes allows nested command substitution. If the command substitution lies within a pair of double quotes (" . . . ` . . . ` . . . "), a backslash used to escape a double quote (\") will be removed; otherwise, it will be left intact.

If a backslash is used to escape a newline character (\newline), both the backslash and the newline are removed (see the later section on "Quoting"). In addition, backslashes used to escape dollar signs (\$) are removed. Because no parameter substitution is done on the command string before it is read, inserting a backslash to escape a dollar sign has no effect. Backslashes that precede characters other than \, ` , ", newline, and $ are left intact when the command string is read.

Parameter Substitution

The character $ is used to introduce substitutable *parameters*. There are two types of parameters, positional and keyword. If *parameter* is a digit, it is a positional parameter. Positional parameters may be assigned values by **set**. Keyword parameters (also known as variables) may be assigned values by writing:

> *name=value* [*name=value*] . . .

Pattern-matching is not performed on *value*. There cannot be a function and a variable with the same *name*.

${*parameter*}
> The value, if any, of the parameter is substituted. The braces are required only when *parameter* is followed by a letter, digit, or underscore that is not to be interpreted as part of its name. If *parameter* is * or @, all the positional parameters, starting with $1, are substituted (separated by spaces). Parameter $0 is set from argument zero when the shell is invoked.

${*parameter*:-*word*}
> If *parameter* is set and is non-null, substitute its value; otherwise substitute *word*.

${*parameter*:=*word*}
> If *parameter* is not set or is null set it to *word*; the value of the parameter is substituted. Positional parameters may not be assigned in this way.

${*parameter*:?*word*}
> If *parameter* is set and is non-null, substitute its value; otherwise, print *word* and exit from the shell. If *word* is omitted, the message "parameter null or not set" is printed.

${*parameter*:+*word*}
> If *parameter* is set and is non-null, substitute *word*; otherwise substitute nothing.

In the above, *word* is not evaluated unless it is to be used as the substituted string, so that, in the following example, **pwd** is executed only if **d** is not set or is null:

   echo ${d:-` pwd ` }

If the colon (:) is omitted from the above expressions, the shell only checks whether *parameter* is set or not.

The following parameters are automatically set by the shell.

     *   Expands to the positional parameters, beginning with 1.

     @   Expands to the positional parameters, beginning with 1, except when expanded within double quotes, in which case each positional parameter expands as a separate field.

     #   The number of positional parameters in decimal.

     –   Flags supplied to the shell on invocation or by the **set** command.

     ?   The decimal value returned by the last synchronously executed command.

     $ The process number of this shell. **$** reports the process ID of the parent shell in all shell constructs, including pipelines, and in parenthesized sub-shells.

     !   The process number of the last background command invoked.

The following parameters are used by the shell. The parameters in this section are also referred to as environment variables.

    HOME   The default argument (home directory) for the **cd** command, set to the user's login directory by **login**(1) from the password file [see **passwd**(4)].

    PATH   The search path for commands (see "Execution," below). The user may not change **PATH** if executing under **/usr/lib/rsh**.

    CDPATH
           The search path for the **cd** command.

    MAIL   If this parameter is set to the name of a mail file *and* the **MAILPATH** parameter is not set, the shell informs the user of the arrival of mail in the specified file.

    MAILCHECK
           This parameter specifies how often (in seconds) the shell will check for the arrival of mail in the files specified by the **MAILPATH** or **MAIL** parameters. The default value is **600** seconds (10 minutes). If set to **0**, the shell will check before each prompt.

    MAILPATH
           A colon (:) separated list of filenames. If this parameter is set, the shell informs the user of the arrival of mail in any of the specified files. Each filename can be followed by **%** and a message that will be printed when the modification time changes. The default message is **you have mail**.

PS1	Primary prompt string, by default "**$**".
PS2	Secondary prompt string, by default "**>**".
IFS	Internal field separators, normally space, tab, and newline (see "Blank Interpretation"). The user can modify **IFS** to allow additional field separators, but space, tab and newline are always included in the list of field separators.
LANG	If this parameter is set, the shell will use it to determine the current locale; see **environ**(5), **setlocale**(3C).
SHACCT	

> If this parameter is set to the name of a file writable by the user, the shell will write an accounting record in the file for each shell procedure executed.

SHELL   When the shell is invoked, it scans the environment (see "Environment," below) for this name. If it is found and **rsh** is the filename part of its value, the shell becomes a restricted shell.

The shell gives default values to **PATH**, **PS1**, **PS2**, **MAILCHECK**, and **IFS**. **HOME** and **MAIL** are set by **login**(1).

Blank Interpretation

After parameter and command substitution, the results of substitution are scanned for internal field separator characters (those found in **IFS**) and split into distinct arguments where such characters are found. Explicit null arguments (**" "** or ´ ´) are retained. Implicit null arguments (those resulting from *parameters* that have no values) are removed. The original whitespace characters (space, tab, and newline) are always considered internal field separators.

Input/Output

A command's input and output may be redirected using a special notation interpreted by the shell. The following may appear anywhere in a *simple-command* or may precede or follow a *command* and are *not* passed on as arguments to the invoked command. Note that parameter and command substitution occurs before *word* or *digit* is used.

<*word*	Use file *word* as standard input (file descriptor 0).
>*word*	Use file *word* as standard output (file descriptor 1). If the file does not exist, it is created; otherwise, it is truncated to zero length.
>>*word*	Use file *word* as standard output. If the file exists, output is appended to it (by first seeking to the end-of-file); otherwise, the file is created.
<<[–]*word*	After parameter and command substitution is done on *word*, the shell input is read up to the first line that literally matches the resulting *word*, or to an end-of-file. If, however, – is appended to <<:

> 1) leading tabs are stripped from *word* before the shell input is read (but after parameter and command substitution is done on *word*),

2)   leading tabs are stripped from the shell input as it is read and before each line is compared with *word*, and

3)   shell input is read up to the first line that literally matches the resulting *word*, or to an end-of-file.

If any character of *word* is quoted (see "Quoting," later), no additional processing is done to the shell input. If no characters of *word* are quoted:

1)   parameter and command substitution occurs,

2)   (escaped) \newlines are removed, and

3)   \ must be used to quote the characters \, $, and ` .

The resulting document becomes the standard input.

<&*digit*   Use the file associated with file descriptor *digit* as standard input. Similarly for the standard output using >&*digit*.

<&–   The standard input is closed. Similarly for the standard output using >&–.

If any of the above is preceded by a digit, the file descriptor which will be associated with the file is that specified by the digit (instead of the default 0 or 1). For example:

     . . . 2>&1

associates file descriptor 2 with the file currently associated with file descriptor 1.

The order in which redirections are specified is significant. The shell evaluates redirections left-to-right. For example:

     . . . 1>*xxx* 2>&1

first associates file descriptor 1 with file *xxx*. It associates file descriptor 2 with the file associated with file descriptor 1 (that is, *xxx*). If the order of redirections were reversed, file descriptor 2 would be associated with the terminal (assuming file descriptor 1 had been) and file descriptor 1 would be associated with file *xxx*.

Using the terminology introduced on the first page, under "Commands," if a *command* is composed of several *simple commands*, redirection will be evaluated for the entire *command* before it is evaluated for each *simple command*. That is, the shell evaluates redirection for the entire *list*, then each *pipeline* within the *list*, then each *command* within each *pipeline*, then each *list* within each *command*.

If a command is followed by & the default standard input for the command is the empty file **/dev/null**. Otherwise, the environment for the execution of a command contains the file descriptors of the invoking shell as modified by input/output specifications.

Redirection of output is not allowed in the restricted shell.

Filename Generation

Before a command is executed, each command *word* is scanned for the characters *, ?, and [. If one of these characters appears the word is regarded as a *pattern*. The word is replaced with alphabetically sorted filenames that match the pattern. If no filename is found that matches the pattern, the word is left unchanged. The character . at the start of a filename or immediately following a /, as well as the character **/** itself, must be matched explicitly.

     *   Matches any string, including the null string.

     ?   Matches any single character.

     [. . .]

            Matches any one of the enclosed characters. A pair of characters separated by – matches any character lexically between the pair, *inclusive. If the first character following the opening [is a !, any* character not enclosed is matched.

Note that all quoted characters (see below) must be matched explicitly in a filename.

Quoting

The following characters have a special meaning to the shell and cause termination of a word unless quoted:

     ; & ( ) | ^ < > **newline** **space** **tab**

A character may be *quoted* (that is, made to stand for itself) by preceding it with a backslash (\) or inserting it between a pair of quote marks (´ ´ or **" "**). During processing, the shell may quote certain characters to prevent them from taking on a special meaning. Backslashes used to quote a single character are removed from the word before the command is executed. The pair **\newline** is removed from a word before command and parameter substitution.

All characters enclosed between a pair of single quote marks (´ ´), except a single quote, are quoted by the shell. Backslash has no special meaning inside a pair of single quotes. A single quote may be quoted inside a pair of double quote marks (for example, **" ´ "**), but a single quote can not be quoted inside a pair of single quotes.

Inside a pair of double quote marks (**" "**), parameter and command substitution occurs and the shell quotes the results to avoid blank interpretation and filename generation. If **$*** is within a pair of double quotes, the positional parameters are substituted and quoted, separated by quoted spaces (**"$1 $2 . . . "**); however, if **$@** is within a pair of double quotes, the positional parameters are substituted and quoted, separated by unquoted spaces (**"$1" "$2" . . .)**. \ quotes the characters \, ´, ", and $. The pair **\newline** is removed before parameter and command substitution. If a backslash precedes characters other than \, ´, ", $, and newline, then the backslash itself is quoted by the shell.

Prompting

When used interactively, the shell prompts with the value of **PS1** before reading a command. If at any time a newline is typed and further input is needed to complete a command, the secondary prompt (that is, the value of **PS2**) is issued.

Environment

The *environment* [see **environ**(5)] is a list of name-value pairs that is passed to an executed program in the same way as a normal argument list. The shell interacts with the environment in several ways. On invocation, the shell scans the environment and creates a parameter for each name found, giving it the corresponding value. If the user modifies the value of any of these parameters or creates new parameters, none of these affects the environment unless the **export** command is used to bind the shell's parameter to the environment (see also **set −a**). A parameter may be removed from the environment with the **unset** command. The environment seen by any executed command is thus composed of any unmodified name-value pairs originally inherited by the shell, minus any pairs removed by **unset**, plus any modifications or additions, all of which must be noted in **export** commands.

The environment for any *simple-command* may be augmented by prefixing it with one or more assignments to parameters. Thus:

>   **TERM=450** *cmd*   and
>   **(export TERM; TERM=450;** *cmd***)**

are equivalent as far as the execution of *cmd* is concerned if *cmd* is not a Special Command. If *cmd* is a Special Command, then

>   **TERM=450** *cmd*

will modify the **TERM** variable in the current shell.

If the **−k** flag is set, *all* keyword arguments are placed in the environment, even if they occur after the command name. The following first prints **a=b c** and **c**:

>   **echo a=b c**
>   **set −k**
>   **echo a=b c**

Signals

When a command is run in the background (*cmd &*) under **sh**, it can receive INTERRUPT and QUIT signals but ignores them by default. [A background process can override this default behavior via trap or signal. For details, see the description of **trap**, below, or **signal**(2).] When a command is run in the background under **jsh**, however, it does not receive INTERRUPT or QUIT signals. Otherwise signals have the values inherited by the shell from its parent, with the exception of three signals: **11** (**SIGSEV**), **14** (**SIGALARM**), and **18** (**SIGCHILD**).

Execution

Each time a command is executed, the command substitution, parameter substitution, blank interpretation, input/output redirection, and filename generation listed above are carried out. If the command name matches the name of a defined function, the function is executed in the shell process (note how this differs from the execution of shell procedures). If the command name does not match the name of a defined function, but matches one of the *Special Commands* listed below, it is executed in the shell process. The positional parameters **$1**, **$2**, . . . are set to the arguments of the function. If the command name matches neither a *Special Command* nor the name of a defined function, a new process is created and an attempt is made to execute the command via **exec**(2).

The shell parameter **PATH** defines the search path for the directory containing the command. Alternative directory names are separated by a colon (**:**). The default path is **/usr/bin**. The current directory is specified by a null path name, which can appear immediately after the equal sign, between two colon delimiters anywhere in the path list, or at the end of the path list. If the command name contains a **/** the search path is not used; such commands will not be executed by the restricted shell. Otherwise, each directory in the path is searched for an executable file. If the file has execute permission but is not an **a.out** file, it is assumed to be a file containing shell commands (that is, a shell script). A sub-shell is spawned to read it. A parenthesized command is also executed in a sub-shell.

For shell script files, in order for the "set user ID on execution" and/or the "set group ID on execution" mode to be effective, the first line of the file must be

    #! /sbin/sh

The location in the search path where a command was found is remembered by the shell (to help avoid unnecessary *execs* later). If the command was found in a relative directory, its location must be re-determined whenever the current directory changes. The shell forgets all remembered locations whenever the **PATH** variable is changed or the **hash -r** command is executed (see below).

Special Commands

Input/output redirection is now permitted for these commands. File descriptor 1 is the default output location. When Job Control is enabled, additional *Special Commands* are added to the shell's environment (see "Job Control").

:   No effect; the command does nothing. A zero exit code is returned.

. *file*   Read and execute commands from *file* and return. The search path specified by **PATH** is used to find the directory containing *file*.

break [*n*]
    Exit from the enclosing **for** or **while** loop, if any. If *n* is specified, break *n* levels.

continue [*n*]
    Resume the next iteration of the enclosing **for** or **while** loop. If *n* is specified, resume at the *n*-th enclosing loop.

cd [*arg*]
    Change the current directory to *arg*. The shell parameter **HOME** is the default *arg*. The shell parameter **CDPATH** defines the search path for the directory containing *arg*. Alternative directory names are separated by a colon (**:**). The default path is **<null>** (specifying the current directory). Note that the current directory is specified by a null path name, which can appear immediately after the equal sign or between the colon delimiters anywhere else in the path list. If *arg* begins with a **/** the search path is not used. Otherwise, each directory in the path is searched for *arg*. The **cd** command may not be executed by **/usr/lib/rsh**.

echo [*arg* . . .]
    Echo arguments. See **echo**(1) for usage and description.

eval [*arg* . . .]
    The arguments are read as input to the shell and the resulting command(s) executed.

exec [*arg* . . .]
    The command specified by the arguments is executed in place of this shell without creating a new process. Input/output arguments may appear and, if no other arguments are given, cause the shell input/output to be modified.

exit [*n*]
>   Causes a shell to exit with the exit status specified by *n*. If *n* is omitted the exit status is that of the last command executed (an end-of-file will also cause the shell to exit.)

export [*name* . . .]
>   The given *name*s are marked for automatic export to the *environment* of subsequently executed commands. If no arguments are given, variable names that have been marked for export during the current shell's execution are listed. (Variable names exported from a parent shell are listed only if they have been exported again during the current shell's execution.) Function names are *not* exported.

getopts
>   Use in shell scripts to support command syntax standards [see **intro**(1)]; it parses positional parameters and checks for legal options. See **getopts**(1) for usage and description.

hash [**-r**] [*name* . . .]
>   For each *name*, the location in the search path of the command specified by *name* is determined and remembered by the shell. The **-r** option causes the shell to forget all remembered locations. If no arguments are given, information about remembered commands is presented. *Hits* is the number of times a command has been invoked by the shell process. *Cost* is a measure of the work required to locate a command in the search path. If a command is found in a "relative" directory in the search path, after changing to that directory, the stored location of that command is recalculated. Commands for which this will be done are indicated by an asterisk (∗) adjacent to the *hits* information. *Cost* will be incremented when the recalculation is done.

newgrp [*arg*]
>   Equivalent to **exec newgrp** *arg*. See **newgrp**(1M) for usage and description.

pwd   Print the current working directory. See **pwd**(1) for usage and description.

read *name* . . .
>   One line is read from the standard input and, using the internal field separator, **IFS** (normally space or tab), to delimit word boundaries, the first word is assigned to the first *name*, the second word to the second *name*, and so on, with leftover words assigned to the last *name*. Lines can be continued using **\newline**. Characters other than newline can be quoted by preceding them with a backslash. These backslashes are removed before words are assigned to *names*, and no interpretation is done on the character that follows the backslash. The return code is **0**, unless an end-of-file is encountered.

readonly [*name* . . .]
>   The given *name*s are marked *readonly* and the values of the these *name*s may not be changed by subsequent assignment. If no arguments are given, a list of all *readonly* names is printed.

return [*n*]

Causes a function to exit with the return value specified by *n*. If *n* is omitted, the return status is that of the last command executed.

set [**--aefhkntuvx** [*arg* . . .]]

-a   Mark variables which are modified or created for export.

-e   Exit immediately if a command exits with a non-zero exit status.

-f   Disable filename generation

-h   Locate and remember function commands as functions are defined (function commands are normally located when the function is executed).

-k   All keyword arguments are placed in the environment for a command, not just those that precede the command name.

-n   Read commands but do not execute them.

-t   Exit after reading and executing one command.

-u   Treat unset variables as an error when substituting.

-v   Print shell input lines as they are read.

-x   Print commands and their arguments as they are executed.

--   Do not change any of the flags; useful in setting $1 to -.

Using + rather than - causes these flags to be turned off. These flags can also be used upon invocation of the shell. The current set of flags may be found in $-. The remaining arguments are positional parameters and are assigned, in order, to $1, $2, . . . If no arguments are given the values of all names are printed.

shift [*n*]

The positional parameters from $*n*+1 . . . are renamed $1 . . . If *n* is not given, it is assumed to be 1.

test

Evaluate conditional expressions. See **test**(1) for usage and description.

times

Print the accumulated user and system times for processes run from the shell.

trap [*arg*] [*n*] . . .

The command *arg* is to be read and executed when the shell receives numeric or symbolic signal(s) (*n*). (Note that *arg* is scanned once when the trap is set and once when the trap is taken.) Trap commands are executed in order of signal number or corresponding symbolic names. Any attempt to set a trap on a signal that was ignored on entry to the current shell is ineffective. An error results when an attempt is made to trap on any of the following three signals: (1) signal 11 (SIGSEV—segmentation fault); (2) signal 14 (SIGALRM—alarm clock); and (3) signal 18 (SIGCHILD—child status changed). If *arg* is absent all trap(s) *n* are reset to their original values. If *arg* is the null string this signal is ignored by the shell and by the commands it invokes. If *n* is 0 the command *arg* is executed on exit from the shell. The **trap** command with no arguments prints a list of commands associated with each signal number.

type [*name* . . .]

For each *name*, indicate how it would be interpreted if used as a command name.

ulimit [−[**HS**][**a** | **cdfnstv**]]

ulimit [−[**HS**][**c** | **d** | **f** | **n** | **s** | **t** | **v**]] *limit*

ulimit prints or sets hard or soft resource limits. These limits are described in **getrlimit**(2).

If *limit* is not present, **ulimit** prints the specified limits. Any number of limits may be printed at one time. The −**a** option prints all limits.

If *limit* is present, **ulimit** sets the specified limit to *limit*. The string **unlimited** requests the largest valid limit. Limits may be set for only one resource at a time. Any user may set a soft limit to any value below the hard limit. Any user may lower a hard limit. Only a super-user may raise a hard limit; see **su**(1).

The −**H** option specifies a hard limit. The −**S** option specifies a soft limit. If neither option is specified, **ulimit** will set both limits and print the soft limit.

The following options specify the resource whose limits are to be printed or set. If no option is specified, the file size limit is printed or set.

−**c**	maximum core file size (in 512-byte blocks)
−**d**	maximum size of data segment or heap (in kbytes)
−**f**	maximum file size (in 512-byte blocks)
−**n**	maximum file descriptor plus 1
−**s**	maximum size of stack segment (in kbytes)
−**t**	maximum CPU time (in seconds)
−**v**	maximum size of virtual memory (in kbytes)

umask [*nnn*]

The user file-creation mask is set to *nnn* [see **umask**(1)]. If *nnn* is omitted, the current value of the mask is printed.

unset [*name* . . .]

For each *name*, remove the corresponding variable or function value. The variables **PATH**, **PS1**, **PS2**, **MAILCHECK**, and **IFS** cannot be unset.

wait [*n*]

Wait for your background process whose process id is *n* and report its termination status. If *n* is omitted, all your shell's currently active background processes are waited for and the return code will be zero.

Invocation

If the shell is invoked through **exec**(2) and the first character of argument zero is −, commands are initially read from **/etc/profile** and from **$HOME/.profile**, if such files exist. Thereafter, commands are read as described below, which is also the case when the shell is invoked as **/usr/bin/sh**. The flags below are interpreted by the shell on invocation only. Note that unless the −**c** or −**s** flag is specified, the first argument is assumed to be the name of a file containing commands, and the remaining arguments are passed as positional parameters to that command file:

-c *string*   If the –c flag is present commands are read from *string*.

-i   If the –i flag is present or if the shell input and output are attached to a terminal, this shell is *interactive*. In this case TERMINATE is ignored (so that **kill 0** does not kill an interactive shell) and INTERRUPT is caught and ignored (so that **wait** is interruptible). In all cases, QUIT is ignored by the shell.

-p   If the –p flag is present, the shell will not set the effective user and group IDs to the real user and group IDs.

-r   If the –r flag is present the shell is a restricted shell.

-s   If the –s flag is present or if no arguments remain, commands are read from the standard input. Any remaining arguments specify the positional parameters. Shell output (except for *Special Commands*) is written to file descriptor 2.

The remaining flags and arguments are described under the **set** command above.

Job Control (jsh)

When the shell is invoked as **jsh**, Job Control is enabled in addition to all of the functionality described previously for **sh**. Typically Job Control is enabled for the interactive shell only. Non-interactive shells typically do not benefit from the added functionality of Job Control.

With Job Control enabled every command or pipeline the user enters at the terminal is called a *job*. All jobs exist in one of the following states: foreground, background or stopped. These terms are defined as follows: 1) a job in the foreground has read and write access to the controlling terminal; 2) a job in the background is denied read access and has conditional write access to the controlling terminal [see **stty**(1)]; 3) a stopped job is a job that has been placed in a suspended state, usually as a result of a **SIGTSTP** signal [see **signal**(5)]. Jobs in the foreground can be stopped by INTERRUPT or QUIT signals from the keyboard; background jobs cannot be stopped by these signals.

Every job that the shell starts is assigned a positive integer, called a *job number* which is tracked by the shell and will be used as an identifier to indicate a specific job. Additionally the shell keeps track of the *current* and *previous* jobs. The *current job* is the most recent job to be started or restarted. The *previous job* is the first non-current job.

The acceptable syntax for a Job Identifier is of the form:

   %*jobid*

where, *jobid* may be specified in any of the following formats:

   % or +   for the current job

   –   for the previous job

   ?<*string*>   specify the job for which the command line uniquely contains *string*.

n　　　　　　　for job number *n*, where *n* is a job number

pref　　　　　　where *pref* is a unique prefix of the command name (for example, if the command **ls -l foo** were running in the background, it could be referred to as **%ls**); *pref* cannot contain
blanks unless it is quoted.

When Job Control is enabled, the following commands are added to the user's
environment to manipulate jobs:

bg [*%jobid . . .*]
　　　Resumes the execution of a stopped job in the background. If *%jobid* is
　　　omitted the current job is assumed.

fg [*%jobid . . .*]
　　　Resumes the execution of a stopped job in the foreground, also moves an
　　　executing background job into the foreground. If *%jobid* is omitted the
　　　current job is assumed.

jobs [**-p|-1**] [*%jobid . . .*]

jobs -x *command* [*arguments*]
　　　Reports all jobs that are stopped or executing in the background. If *%jobid*
　　　is omitted, all jobs that are stopped or running in the background will be
　　　reported. The following options will modify/enhance the output of **jobs**:

　　　-1　　Report the process group ID and working directory of the jobs.

　　　-p　　Report only the process group ID of the jobs.

　　　-x　　Replace any *jobid* found in *command* or *arguments* with the
　　　　　　corresponding process group ID, and then execute *command* pass-
　　　　　　ing it *arguments*.

kill [*-signal*] *%jobid*
　　　Builtin version of **kill** to provide the functionality of the **kill** command
　　　for processes identified with a *jobid*.

stop *%jobid . . .*
　　　Stops the execution of a background job(s).

suspend
　　　Stops the execution of the current shell (but not if it is the login shell).

wait [*%jobid . . .*]
　　　wait builtin accepts a job identifier. If *%jobid* is omitted **wait** behaves as
　　　described above under **Special Commands**.

Restricted Shell (/usr/lib/rsh) Only

/usr/lib/rsh is used to set up login names and execution environments whose
capabilities are more controlled than those of the standard shell. The actions of
/usr/lib/rsh are identical to those of **sh**, except that the following are disallowed:

　　　changing directory [see **cd**(1)],
　　　setting the value of *$PATH*,
　　　specifying path or command names containing **/**,
　　　redirecting output (**>** and **>>**).

The restrictions above are enforced after .profile is interpreted.

A restricted shell can be invoked in one of the following ways: (1) rsh is the filename part of the last entry in the /etc/passwd file [see passwd(4)]; (2) the environment variable SHELL exists and rsh is the filename part of its value; (3) the shell is invoked and rsh is the filename part of argument 0; (4) the shell is invoked with the −r option.

When a command to be executed is found to be a shell procedure, /usr/lib/rsh invokes sh to execute it. Thus, it is possible to provide to the end-user shell procedures that have access to the full power of the standard shell, while imposing a limited menu of commands; this scheme assumes that the end-user does not have write and execute permissions in the same directory.

The net effect of these rules is that the writer of the .profile [see profile(4)] has complete control over user actions by performing guaranteed setup actions and leaving the user in an appropriate directory (probably *not* the login directory).

The system administrator often sets up a directory of commands (that is, /usr/rbin) that can be safely invoked by a restricted shell. Some systems also provide a restricted editor, red.

EXIT STATUS

Errors detected by the shell, such as syntax errors, cause the shell to return a non-zero exit status. If the shell is being used non-interactively execution of the shell file is abandoned. Otherwise, the shell returns the exit status of the last command executed (see also the exit command above).

jsh Only

If the shell is invoked as jsh and an attempt is made to exit the shell while there are stopped jobs, the shell issues one warning:

        There are stopped jobs.

This is the only message. If another exit attempt is made, and there are still stopped jobs they will be sent a SIGHUP signal from the kernel and the shell is exited.

FILES

        /etc/profile
        $HOME/.profile
        /tmp/sh*
        /dev/null

SEE ALSO

        cd(1), csh(1), echo(1), getopts(1), intro(1), ksh(1), login(1), pwd(1), stty(1), test(1), umask(1), wait(1)
        dup(2), exec(2), fork(2), getrlimit(2), pipe(2), ulimit(2), setlocale(3C) in the *Programmer's Reference Manual*
        newgrp(1M), profile(4), environ(5), signal(5) in the *System Administrator's Reference Manual*
        rsh(1) in the *Network User's and Administrator's Guide*

NOTES

Words used for filenames in input/output redirection are not interpreted for filename generation (see "Filename Generation," above). For example, **cat file1 >a*** will create a filenamed **a***.

Because commands in pipelines are run as separate processes, variables set in a pipeline have no effect on the parent shell.

If you get the error message

```
cannot fork, too many processes
```

try using the **wait**(1) command to clean up your background processes. If this doesn't help, the system process table is probably full or you have too many active foreground processes. (There is a limit to the number of process ids associated with your login, and to the number the system can keep track of.)

Only the last process in a pipeline can be waited for.

If a command is executed, and a command with the same name is installed in a directory in the search path before the directory where the original command was found, the shell will continue to **exec** the original command. Use the **hash** command to correct this situation.

Prior to Release 4, the **rsh** command invoked the restricted shell. This restricted shell command is **/usr/lib/rsh** and it can be executed by using the full pathname. Beginning with Release 4, the **rsh** command is the remote shell. See **rsh**(1) in the *Network User's and Administrator's Guide*.

NAME

share – make local resource available for mounting by remote systems

SYNOPSIS

share [**-F** *fstype*] [**-o** *specific_options*] [**-d** *description*] [*pathname* [*resourcename*]]

DESCRIPTION

The **share** command makes a resource available for mounting through a remote file system of type *fstype*. If the option **-F** *fstype* is omitted, the first file system type listed in file **/etc/dfs/fstypes** will be used as the default. *Specific_options* as well as the semantics of *resourcename* are specific to particular distributed file systems. When invoked with only a file system type, **share** displays all resources shared by the given file system to the local system. When invoked with no arguments, **share** displays all resources shared by the local system.

The *access_spec* is used to control access of the shared resource. It may be one of the following:

> **rw** *pathname* is shared read/write to all clients. This is also the default behavior.

> **rw=***client*[*:client*]
> *pathname* is shared read/write only to the listed clients. No other systems can access *resourcename*.

> **ro** *pathname* is shared read-only to all clients.

> **ro=***client*[*:client*]
> *pathname* is shared read-only only to the listed clients. No other systems can access *pathname*.

The **-d** flag may be used to provide a description of the resource being shared.

FILES

/etc/dfs/dfstab
/etc/dfs/sharetab
/etc/dfs/fstypes

SEE ALSO

unshare(1M)

NAME

share – make local NFS resource available for mounting by remote systems

SYNOPSIS

share [**-F nfs**] [**-o** *specific_options*] [**-d** *description*] *pathname*

DESCRIPTION

The **share** command makes local resources available for mounting by remote systems.

If no argument is specified, then **share** displays all resources currently shared, including NFS resources and resources shared through other distributed file system packages.

The following options are recognized:

-o *specific_options*

Specify options in a comma-separated list of keywords and attribute-value-assertions for interpretation by the file-system-type-specific command.

specific_options can be any combination of the following:

rw   Sharing will be read-write to all clients.

rw=client[**:**client]. . .

Sharing will be read-write to the listed clients; overrides the **ro** suboption for the clients specified.

ro   Sharing will be read-only to all clients.

ro=client[**:**client]...

Sharing will be read-only to the listed clients; overrides the **rw** suboption for the clients specified.

anon=uid

Set *uid* to be the effective user ID of unauthenticated users if AUTH_DES authentication is used, or to be root if AUTH_UNIX authentication is used. By default, unknown users are given the effective user ID **UID_NOBODY**. If *uid* is set to **-1**, access is denied.

root=host[**:**host]. . .

Only root users from the specified hosts will have root access. By default, no host has root access.

secure

Clients must use the AUTH_DES authentication of RPC. AUTH_UNIX authentication is the default.

If *specific_options* is not specified, then by default sharing will be read-write to all clients.

-d *description*

Provide a comment that describes the resource to be shared.

pathname   Specify the pathname of the resource to be shared.

FILES

    /etc/dfs/fstypes
    /etc/dfs/sharetab

SEE ALSO

    unshare(1M)

NOTES

The command will fail if both **ro** and **rw** are specified. If the same client name exists in both the **ro=** and **rw=** lists, the **rw** will override the **ro**, giving read/write access to the client specified.

ro=, **rw=**, and **root=** are guaranteed to work over UDP but may not work over other transport providers.

If a resource is shared with a **ro=** list and a **root=** list, any host that is on the **root=** list will be given only read-only access, regardless of whether that host is specified in the **ro=** list, unless **rw** is declared as the default, or the host is mentioned in a **rw=** list. The same is true if the resource is shared with **ro** as the default. For example, the following **share** commands will give read-only permissions to **hostb**:

        share -F nfs -oro=hosta,root=hostb /var

        share -F nfs -oro,root=hostb /var

While the following will give read/write permissions to hostb:

        share -F nfs -oro=hosta,rw=hostb,root=hostb /var

        share -F nfs -oroot=hostb /var

NAME

share – make local RFS resource available for mounting by remote systems

SYNOPSIS

share [–F rfs] [–o *access_spec*] [–d *description*] [*pathname resourcename*]

DESCRIPTION

The **share** command makes a resource available for mounting through Remote File Sharing. The **–F** flag may be omitted if rfs is the first file system type listed in the file **/etc/dfs/fstypes**. When invoked with only a file system type (or no arguments), **share** displays all local resources shared through Remote File Sharing.

The *access_spec* is used to control client access of the shared resource. Clients may be specified in any of the following forms:

> *domain.*
> *domain.system*
> *system*

The *access_spec* can be one of the following:

rw   *resourcename* is shared read/write to all clients. This is also the default behavior.

rw=*client*[*:client*]...
                     resourcename is shared read/write only to the listed clients. No other systems can access *resourcename*.

ro   *resourcename* is shared read-only to all clients.

ro=*client*[*:client*]...
                     resourcename is shared read-only only to the listed clients. No other systems can access *resourcename*.

The **–d** flag may be used to provide a description of the resource being shared.

ERRORS

If the network is not up and running or *pathname* is not a full path, an error message will be sent to standard error. If *pathname* isn't on a file system mounted locally or the *client* is specified but syntactically incorrect, an error message will be sent to standard error. If the same *resource* name in the network over the same transport provider is to be shared more than once, an error message will be sent to standard error.

FILES

/etc/dfs/dfstab
/etc/dfs/sharetab
/etc/dfs/fstypes

SEE ALSO

unshare(1M)

NAME
shareall, unshareall – share, unshare multiple resources

SYNOPSIS
shareall [–F *fstype*[,*fstype*...]] [– | *file*]
unshareall [–F *fstype*[,*fstype*...]]

DESCRIPTION
When used with no arguments, **shareall** shares all resources from *file*, which contains a list of **share** command lines. If the operand is a hyphen (–), then the **share** command lines are obtained from the standard input. Otherwise, if neither a *file* nor a hyphen is specified, then the file **/etc/dfs/dfstab** is used as the default.

Resources may be shared to specific file systems by specifying the file systems in a comma-separated list as an argument to **–F**.

unshareall unshares all currently shared resources. Without a **–F** flag, it unshares resources for all distributed file system types.

FILES
/etc/dfs/dfstab

SEE ALSO
share(1M), unshare(1M).

NAME

shell – run a command using shell

SYNOPSIS

shell *command* [*command*] . . .

DESCRIPTION

The **shell** function concatenates its arguments, separating each by a space, and passes this string to the UNIX system shell (**$SHELL** if set, otherwise **/usr/bin/sh**).

EXAMPLES

Since the Form and Menu Language does not directly support background processing, the **shell** function can be used instead.

'shell "build prog > /dev/null &"'

If you want the user to continue to be able to interact with the application while the background job is running, the output of an executable run by **shell** in the background must be redirected: to a file if you want to save the output, or to **/dev/null** if you don't want to save it (or if there is no output), otherwise your application may appear to be hung until the background job finishes processing.

shell can also be used to execute a command that has the same name as an FMLI built-in function.

NOTES

The arguments to **shell** will be concatenated using spaces, which may or may not do what is expected. The variables set in local environments will not be expanded by the shell because "local" means "local to the current process."

SEE ALSO

sh(1)

NAME

shl – shell layer manager

SYNOPSIS

shl

DESCRIPTION

shl allows a user to interact with more than one shell from a single terminal. The user controls these shells, known as **layers**, using the commands described below.

The *current layer* is the layer which can receive input from the keyboard. Other layers attempting to read from the keyboard are blocked. Output from multiple layers is multiplexed onto the terminal. To have the output of a layer blocked when it is not current, the **stty** option **loblk** may be set within the layer.

The **stty** character **swtch** (set to ^Z if NUL) is used to switch control to **shl** from a layer. **shl** has its own prompt, >>>, to help distinguish it from a layer.

A *layer* is a shell which has been bound to a virtual tty device (**/dev/sxt???**). The virtual device can be manipulated like a real tty device using **stty**(1) and **ioctl**(2). Each layer has its own process group id.

Definitions

A *name* is a sequence of characters delimited by a blank, tab or new-line. Only the first eight characters are significant. The *name*s (**1**) through (**7**) cannot be used when creating a layer. They are used by **shl** when no name is supplied. They may be abbreviated to just the digit.

Commands

The following commands may be issued from the **shl** prompt level. Any unique prefix is accepted.

create [*name*]

> Create a layer called *name* and make it the current layer. If no argument is given, a layer will be created with a name of the form *(#)* where # is the last digit of the virtual device bound to the layer. The shell prompt variable **PS1** is set to the name of the layer followed by a space. A maximum of seven layers can be created.

block *name* [*name* . . .]

> For each *name*, block the output of the corresponding layer when it is not the current layer. This is equivalent to setting the **stty** option **-loblk** within the layer.

delete *name* [*name* . . .]

> For each *name*, delete the corresponding layer. All processes in the process group of the layer are sent the SIGHUP signal (see **signal**(2)).

help (or ?)

> Print the syntax of the **shl** commands.

layers [**-l**] [*name* . . .]

> For each *name*, list the layer name and its process group. The **-l** option produces a **ps**(1)-like listing. If no arguments are given, information is presented for all existing layers.

resume [*name*]
> Make the layer referenced by *name* the current layer. If no argument is given, the last existing current layer will be resumed.

toggle
> Resume the layer that was current before the last current layer.

unblock *name* [*name* . . .]
> For each *name*, do not block the output of the corresponding layer when it is not the current layer. This is equivalent to setting the **stty** option −**loblk** within the layer.

quit   Exit **shl**. All layers are sent the SIGHUP signal.

name   Make the layer referenced by *name* the current layer.

FILES

/dev/sxt???	Virtual tty devices
$SHELL	Variable containing path name of the shell to use (default is **/bin/sh**).

SEE ALSO
> **sh**(1), **stty**(1)
> **ioctl**(2), **signal**(2) in the *Programmer's Reference Manual*
> **sxt**(7) in the *System Administrator's Reference Manual*

NOTES
> To avoid disabling the suspend character when in the job control environment, the *swtch* character must be redefined.

NAME

shutdown – shut down system, change system state

SYNOPSIS

shutdown [**–y**] [**–g***grace_period* [**–i***init_state*]

DESCRIPTION

This command is executed by the super-user to change the state of the machine. In most cases, it is used to change from the multi-user state (state 2) to another state (see below).

By default, it brings the system to a state where only the console has access to the UNIX system. This state is called single-user (see below).

The command sends a warning message and a final message before it starts actual shutdown activities. By default, the command asks for confirmation before it starts shutting down daemons and killing processes. The options are used as follows:

–y   pre-answers the confirmation question so the command can be run without user intervention. A default of 60 seconds is allowed between the warning message and the final message. Another 60 seconds is allowed between the final message and the confirmation.

–g*grace_period*
          allows the super-user to change the number of seconds from the 60-second default.

–i*init_state*
          specifies the state that **init** is to be put in following the warnings, if any. By default, system state "**s**" is used.

Other recommended system state definitions are:

state 0   Shut the machine down so it is safe to remove the power. Have the machine remove power if it can. The **rc0** procedure is called to do this work.

state 1   State 1 is referred to as the administrative state. In state 1 filesystems required for multi-user operations are mounted, and logins requiring access to multi-user filesystems can be used. When the system comes up from firmware mode into state 1, only the console is active and other multi-user (state 2) services are unavailable. Note that not all user processes are stopped when transitioning from multi-user state to state 1.

state s, S   State s (or S) is referred to as the single-user state. All user processes are stopped on transitions to this state. In the single-user state, filesystems required for multi-user logins are unmounted and the system can only be accessed through the console. Logins requiring access to multi-user file systems cannot be used.

state 5   Stop the UNIX system and go to firmware mode.

state 6　　　Stop the UNIX system and reboot to the state defined by the **initde-fault** entry in **/etc/inittab**; configure a new bootable operating system, if necessary, before the reboot. The **rc6** procedure is called to do this work.

NOTES

shutdown(1M) behaves differently depending on the number of users logged in. If several users are logged in, three messages are displayed, warning, final and confirmation, with grace period between each message. If only the user issuing **shutdown**(1M) is logged in, two messages are displayed, the final and confirmation message, with grace period between them.

SEE ALSO

init(1M), **rc0**(1M), **rc2**(1M), **rc6**(1M), **inittab**(4)

NAME

shutdown – close down the system at a given time

SYNOPSIS

/usr/ucb/shutdown [–fhknr] *time* [*warning-message* ...]

DESCRIPTION

shutdown provides an automated procedure to notify users when the system is to be shut down. *time* specifies when shutdown will bring the system down; it may be the word now (indicating an immediate shutdown), or it may specify a future time in one of two formats: +*number* and *hour*:*min*. The first form brings the system down in *number* minutes, and the second brings the system down at the time of day indicated in 24-hour notation.

At intervals that get closer as the apocalypse approaches, warning messages are displayed at terminals of all logged-in users, and of users who have remote mounts on that machine. Five minutes before shutdown, or immediately if shutdown is in less than 5 minutes, logins are disabled by creating /etc/nologin and writing a message there. If this file exists when a user attempts to log in, login(1M) prints its contents and exits. The file is removed just before shutdown exits.

At shutdown time a message is written to the system log daemon, syslogd(1M), containing the time of shutdown, the instigator of the shutdown, and the reason. Then a terminate signal is sent to init, which brings the system down to single-user mode.

The time of the shutdown and the warning message are placed in /etc/nologin, which should be used to inform the users as to when the system will be back up, and why it is going down (or anything else).

OPTIONS

As an alternative to the above procedure, these options can be specified:

–f   Arrange, in the manner of fastboot(1M), that when the system is rebooted, the file systems will not be checked.

–h   Execute halt(1M).

–k   Simulate shutdown of the system. Do not actually shut down the system.

–n   Prevent the normal sync(2) before stopping.

–r   Execute reboot(1M).

FILES

/etc/nologin   tells login not to let anyone log in
/etc/xtab   list of remote hosts that have mounted this host

SEE ALSO

fastboot(1M), halt(1M), reboot(1M), syslogd(1M)

login(1) in the *User's Reference Manual*
sync(2) in the *Programmer's Reference Manual*

NOTES

Only allows you to bring the system down between **now** and 23:59 if you use the absolute time for shutdown.

NAME

size – print section sizes in bytes of object files

SYNOPSIS

size [−F −f −n −o −V −x] *files*

DESCRIPTION

The **size** command produces segment or section size information in bytes for each loaded section in ELF or COFF object files. **size** prints out the size of the text, data, and bss (uninitialized data) segments (or sections) and their total.

size processes ELF and COFF object files entered on the command line. If an archive file is input to the **size** command, the information for each object file in the archive is displayed.

When calculating segment information, the **size** command prints out the total file size of the non-writable segments, the total file size of the writable segments, and the total memory size of the writable segments minus the total file size of the writable segments.

If it cannot calculate segment information, **size** calculates section information. When calculating section information, it prints out the total size of sections that are allocatable, non-writable, and not NOBITS, the total size of the sections that are allocatable, writable, and not NOBITS, and the total size of the writable sections of type NOBITS. (NOBITS sections do not actually take up space in the *file*.)

If **size** cannot calculate either segment or section information, it prints an error message and stops processing the file.

−F Prints out the size of each loadable segment, the permission flags of the segment, then the total of the loadable segment sizes. If there is no segment data, **size** prints an error message and stops processing the file.

−f Prints out the size of each allocatable section, the name of the section, and the total of the section sizes. If there is no section data, **size** prints out an error message and stops processing the file.

−n Prints out non-loadable segment or non-allocatable section sizes. If segment data exists, **size** prints out the memory size of each loadable segment or file size of each non-loadable segment, the permission flags, and the total size of the segments. If there is no segment data, **size** prints out, for each allocatable and non-allocatable section, the memory size, the section name, and the total size of the sections. If there is no segment or section data, **size** prints an error message and stops processing.

−o Prints numbers in octal, not decimal.

−V Prints the version information for the **size** command on the standard error output.

−x Prints numbers in hexadecimal; not decimal.

EXAMPLES

The examples below are typical **size** output.

size *file*	`2724 + 88 + 0 =  2812`
size –f *file*	`26(.text) + 5(.init) + 5(.fini)  = 36`
size –F *file*	`2724(r-x) + 88(rwx) + 0(rwx) = 2812`

SEE ALSO

as(1), cc(1), ld(1), a.out(4), ar(4)

NOTES

Since the size of bss sections is not known until link-edit time, the **size** command does not give the true total size of pre-linked objects.

NAME

    sleep – suspend execution for an interval

SYNOPSIS

    sleep *time*

DESCRIPTION

    sleep suspends execution for *time* seconds. It is used to execute a command after a certain amount of time, as in:

```
(sleep 105; command)&
```

or to execute a command every so often, as in:

```
while true
do
        command
        sleep 37
done
```

SEE ALSO

    alarm(2), **sleep**(3C) in the *Programmer's Reference Manual.*

NAME

　　　slink – streams linker

SYNOPSIS

　　　slink [-v] [-p] [-u] [-f] [-c *file*] [func [*arg1 arg2* . . .]]

DESCRIPTION

　　　slink is a STREAMS configuration utility which is used to link together the various STREAMS modules and drivers required for STREAMS TCP/IP. Input to slink is in the form of a script specifying the STREAMS operations to be performed. Input is normally taken from the file /etc/strcf.

　　　The following options may be specified on the slink command line:

　　　-c *file*　　Use *file* instead of /etc/strcf.

　　　-v　　　　Verbose mode (each operation is logged to stderr).

　　　-p　　　　Don't use persistent links (i.e., slink will remain in the background).

　　　-f　　　　Don't use persistent links and don't fork (i.e., slink will remain in foreground).

　　　-u　　　　Unlink persistent links (i.e., shut down network).

　　　The configuration file contains a list of *functions*, each of which is composed of a list of *commands*. Each command is a call to one of the functions defined in the configuration file or to one of a set of built-in functions. Among the built-in functions are the basic STREAMS operations **open**, **link**, and **push**, along with several TCP/IP-specific functions.

　　　slink processing consists of parsing the input file, then calling the user-defined function **boot**, which is normally used to set up the standard configuration at boot time. If a function is specified on the slink command line, that function will be called instead of **boot**.

　　　By default, slink establishes streams with persistent links (I_PLINK) and exits following the execution of the specified function. If the -p flag is specified, slink establishes streams with regular links (I_LINK) and remains idle in the background, holding open whatever file descriptors have been opened by the configuration commands. If the -f flag is specified, slink establishes streams with regular links (I_LINK) and remains in the foreground, holding open whatever file descriptors have been opened by the configuration commands.

　　　A function definition has the following form:

```
        function-name {
            command1
            command2
            ...
        }
```

　　　The syntax for commands is:

　　　　　function arg1 arg2 arg3 . . .

　　　or

　　　　　var = *function arg1 arg2 arg3* . . .

The placement of newlines is important: a newline must follow the left and right braces and every command. Extra newlines are allowed, i.e. where one newline is required, more than one may be used. A backslash (\) followed immediately by a newline is considered equivalent to a space, i.e. may be used to continue a command on a new line. The use of other white space characters (spaces and tabs) is at the discretion of the user, except that there must be white space separating the function name and the arguments of a command.

Comments are delimited by # and newline, and are considered equivalent to a newline.

Function and variable names may be any string of characters taken from A-Z, a-z, 0-9, and _, except that the first character cannot be a digit. Function names and variable names occupy separate name spaces. All functions are global and may be forward referenced. All variables are local to the functions in which they occur.

Variables are defined when they appear to the left of an equals (=) on a command line; for example,

```
tcp = open /dev/tcp
```

The variable acquires the value returned by the command. In the above example, the value of the variable **tcp** will be the file descriptor returned by the **open** call.

Arguments to a command may be either variables, parameters, or strings.

A variable that appears as an argument must have been assigned a value on a previous command line in that function.

Parameters take the form of a dollar sign ($) followed by one or two decimal digits, and are replaced with the corresponding argument from the function call. If a given parameter was not specified in the function call, an error results (e.g. if a command references $3 and only two arguments were passed to the function, an execution error will occur).

Strings are sequences of characters optionally enclosed in double quotes ("). Quotes may be used to prevent a string from being interpreted as a variable name or a parameter, and to allow the inclusion of spaces, tabs, and the special characters {, }, =, and #. The backslash (\) may also be used to quote the characters {, }, =, #, ", and \ individually.

The following built-in functions are provided by **slink**:

open *path*	Open the device specified by pathname *path*. Returns a file descriptor referencing the open stream.
link *fd1 fd2*	Link the stream referenced by *fd2* beneath the stream referenced by *fd1*. Returns the link identifier associated with the link. Unless the **-f** or **-p** flag is specified on the command line, the streams will be linked with persistent links. Note: *fd2* cannot be used after this operation.
push *fd module*	Push the module *module* onto the stream referenced by *fd*.

sifname *fd link name* Send a **SIOCSIFNAME** (set interface name) ioctl down the stream referenced by *fd* for the link associated with link identifier *link* specifying the name *name*.

unitsel *fd unit* Send a **IF_UNITSEL** (unit select) ioctl down the stream referenced by *fd* specifying unit *unit*.

dlattach *fd unit* Send a **DL_ATTACH_REQ** message down the stream referenced by *fd* specifying unit *unit*.

initqp *path qname lowat hiwat ...*
Send an **INITQPARMS** (initialize queue parameters) ioctl to the driver corresponding to pathname *path*. *qname* specifies the queue for which the low and high water marks will be set, and must be one of:

hd	stream head
rq	read queue
wq	write queue
muxrq	multiplexor read queue
muxwq	multiplexor write queue

lowat and *hiwat* specify the new low and high water marks for the queue. Both *lowat* and *hiwat* must be present. To change only one of these parameters, the other may be replaced with a dash (–). Up to five *qname lowat hiwat* triplets may be present.

strcat *str1 str2* Concatenate strings *str1* and *str2* and return the resulting string.

return *val* Set the return value for the current function to *val*.
Note: executing a **return** command does not terminate execution of the current function.

FILES
/etc/strcf

SEE ALSO
strcf(4)

NAME

smtp – send SMTP mail to a remote host using Simple Mail Transfer Protocol

SYNOPSIS

smtp [-D] [-d *domain*] [-H *helohost*] [-N] *sender host recip ...*

DESCRIPTION

smtp sends a message to a remote host *host* using the Simple Mail Transfer Proto-col (SMTP). The message is read from standard input. *sender* is used to identify the sender of the message and the *recip*s are used as the recipients.

When establishing a connection, smtp will use the first transport for which netdir_getbyname(3) returns an address, based on hostname, transport [returned from getnetpath(3)], and service smtp. Normally, this will be the "tcp" transport.

The options to smtp and their meanings are as follows:

-D   This option turns on debugging. Debugging information is printed on standard error.

-H *helohost*   This option can be used to set the hostname used in SMTP HELO message (this defaults to the system's name).

-d *domain*   This option can be used to set the domain name to be used for this host.

-N   This option disables the sending of MX records. It should not be used on systems that run the Domain Name Server.

smtp is normally run by the smtpsched process to deliver mail queued in /var/spool/smtpq.

FILES

/var/spool/smtpq   where messages are queued

SEE ALSO

named(1M) smtpsched(1M)
RFC821 – Simple Mail Transfer Protocol

NAME
smtpd – receive incoming SMTP messages

SYNOPSIS
smtpd [−n] [−H *helohost*] [−h *thishost*] [−L *loadlim*] [−l *maxprocs*]

DESCRIPTION
smtpd is a daemon that normally runs while in multi-user mode, waiting for requests from remote hosts to send mail. smtpd listens for these requests on any TLI-based network for which the SMTP service is defined (to netdir_getbyname(3)). Normally, this will only be the "tcp" network. As requests are received, smtpd will fork off child smtpd processes to handle each individual SMTP transaction.

The options to smtpd and their meanings are as follows:

−n   Do not create smtpsched processes to process the incoming mail. Rely on the hourly cron(1) invocation of smtpsched instead.

−H *helohost*   This option can be used to specify the name to be used for the host in the initial SMTP HELO message. If it is not specified, the name used in the HELO message defaults to the system node name.

−h *thishost*   Specify the network name to be prepended onto the sender path in the From line of the message. This option is passed through to the fromsmtp program.

−L *loadlim*   Specify the maximum load at which smtpd will create children. If this option is not specified, there is no limit to the load at which children may run. The load is determined by reading the kernel variable avenrun.

−l *maxprocs*   This option is used to specify the maximum number of children of smtpd that can be running at once. Each child handles one SMTP conversation. If this option is not specified, there is no limit to the number of children that may run.

Mail that is successfully received is piped to the fromsmtp command, which in turn delivers the mail by piping it to rmail. A log of all smtpd's activities is kept in the file /var/spool/smtpq/LOG.

FILES
/dev/kmem	To get the current machine load (avenrun)
/etc/services	List of TCP/UDP services (SMTP should be 25/tcp)
/etc/net/*/services	List of other TLI networks' services
/usr/lib/mail/surrcmd/fromsmtp	
	Where incoming mail is piped to
/var/spool/smtpq/LOG	Log of smtpd transactions

SEE ALSO
cron(1M), fromsmtp(1M), smtp(1M)

NAME

smtpqer – queue mail for delivery by SMTP

SYNOPSIS

smtpqer [–nu] [–a *toaddr*] [–d *domain*] [–H *helohost*] *sender host recip* ...

DESCRIPTION

smtpqer queues the mail message it reads from standard input for eventual delivery by smtp. The message is queued for delivery to the host specified in the *to* address.

smtpqer should normally be invoked by the **mail** command by placing the following line in /etc/mail/mailsurr:

´.+´ ´([^!@]+)!(.+)´ ´< /usr/lib/mail/surrcmd/smtpqer %R \\1 \\2´

smtpqer will check the host name in the *to* address. If it is one that can be reached (i.e., if **netdir_getbyname**(3) can find it on at least one TLI network), the message will be queued, and smtpqer will exit with a return code of 0 (which means the mail was successfully queued). Otherwise, it will return with an exit code of 1, and the message will not be queued.

Messages that are queued are stored in a file under the SMTP queue directory (/var/spool/smtpq). If the –u option is not used, they are first converted to RFC822 format, by filtering them through the program **tosmtp**. Finally, smtpqer invokes the **smtpsched** program to deliver the mail.

The –H option is used to specify the host name that should be used in the SMTP HELO message. This option is passed to both the **tosmtp** and **smtp** programs.

The –d option is used to specify the domain name that should be used for your host. This option is passed to the **tosmtp** program. If this option is not used, and a domain has been specified in the mail configuration file *mailcnfg*, that domain will be used instead.

The –a option is used to specify the "to address" that is passed to the **smtp** program. Finally, the –n option is used to prevent smtpqer from starting an **smtpsched** process to deliver the mail.

FILES

/usr/bin/rmail	where mail originates from
/etc/hosts	database of remote hosts (for TCP/IP)
/etc/mail/mailcnfg	mail configuration file
/etc/net/*/hosts	database of remote hosts (for other TLI networks)
/etc/mail/mailsurr	control file containing rule to invoke smtpqer

/usr/lib/mail/surrcmd/smtpsched
      program to process message queues

/usr/lib/mail/surrcmd/smtp
      program that passes message to remote host

/usr/lib/mail/surrcmd/tosmtp
         filter to convert to RFC822 format

/var/spool/smtpq   where messages are queued

SEE ALSO

rmail(1M), smtpsched(1M), smtp(1M), tosmtp(1M)
getdomainname(3) in the *Programmer's Reference Manual.*
RFC822 – Standard for the Format of ARPA Internet Text Messages

NAME
  smtpsched – process messages queued in the SMTP mail queue

SYNOPSIS
  smtpsched [-c] [-v] [-t] [-s *scheds*] [-r *days*] [-w *days*] [*qnames*]

DESCRIPTION
  smtpsched is used to process the messages queued up in the SMTP mail queue
  /var/spool/smtpq. It is invoked automatically by the SMTP mail surrogate
  smtpqer, whenever mail is queued for SMTP delivery to a remote host, and by
  smtpd whenever incoming mail arrives. It should also be run once per hour
  (from **cron**) to attempt delivery of any mail that cannot be delivered immediately.

  smtpsched will normally attempt to send all messages queued under all subdirectories of **/var/spool/smtpq**. However, if *qnames* are specified, only those listed
  subdirectories of **/var/spool/smtpq** will be searched for messages to deliver.
  The subdirectories each refer to a different remote host.

  The options to **smtpsched** are as follows:

  -c   Causes empty queue directories to be removed.

  -v   Causes verbose logging to occur.

  -t   Test mode. The actions **smtpsched** would take are logged but not
              performed.

  -s *scheds* Specifies the maximum number of concurrent **smtpsched**s that may
              be running at once. If more than this number is running,
              smtpsched will exit.

  -r *days*   Causes mail older than *days* days to be returned.

  -w *days*   Any mail older than *days* days will trigger a warning message,
              which is sent to the originator.

FILES

/usr/lib/mail/surrcmd/smtp	delivers the mail
/usr/lib/mail/surrcmd/smtpqer	queues the mail
/var/spool/smtpq	queued mail messages
/var/spool/smtpq/LOG*	log files
/var/spool/smtpq/_host_	mail messages queued for *host*

SEE ALSO
  cron(1M), smtp(1M), smtpqer(1M)

NAME

soelim – resolve and eliminate .so requests from nroff or troff input

SYNOPSIS

/usr/ucb/soelim [*filename* . . .]

DESCRIPTION

The **soelim** command reads the specified files or the standard input and performs the textual inclusion implied by the **nroff**(1) directives of the form

.**so** *somefile*

when they appear at the beginning of input lines. This is useful since programs such as **tbl**(1) do not normally do this; it allows the placement of individual tables in separate files to be run as a part of a large document.

An argument consisting of '–' is taken to be a file name corresponding to the standard input.

Note: inclusion can be suppressed by using ' ´ ' instead of ' . ', that is,

´ **so /usr/ucblib/doctools/tmac/tmac.s**

EXAMPLE

A sample usage of **soelim** would be

soelim exum?.n | tbl | nroff –ms | col | lpr

SEE ALSO

nroff(1), tbl(1)

more(1) in the *User's Reference Manual*

NAME

sort – sort and/or merge files

SYNOPSIS

sort [-cmu] [-o*output*] [-y*kmem*] [-z*recsz*] [-dfiMnr] [-btx] [+*pos1* [-*pos2*]] [*files*]

DESCRIPTION

The **sort** command sorts lines of all the named files together and writes the result on the standard output. The standard input is read if – is used as a file name or no input files are named.

Comparisons are based on one or more sort keys extracted from each line of input. By default, there is one sort key, the entire input line, and ordering is lexicographic by bytes in machine collating sequence.

The following options alter the default behavior:

-c   Check that the input file is sorted according to the ordering rules; give no output unless the file is out of sort.

-m   Merge only, the input files are already sorted.

-u   Unique: suppress all but one in each set of lines having equal keys.

-o*output*
   The argument given is the name of an output file to use instead of the standard output. This file may be the same as one of the inputs. There may be optional blanks between –o and *output*.

-y*kmem*
   The amount of main memory used by **sort** has a large impact on its performance. Sorting a small file in a large amount of memory is a waste. If this option is omitted, **sort** begins using a system default memory size, and continues to use more space as needed. If this option is presented with a value, **kmem**, **sort** will start using that number of kilobytes of memory, unless the administrative minimum or maximum is violated, in which case the corresponding extremum will be used. Thus, –y0 is guaranteed to start with minimum memory. By convention, –y (with no argument) starts with maximum memory.

-z*recsz*
   The size of the longest line read is recorded in the sort phase so buffers can be allocated during the merge phase. If the sort phase is omitted via the –c or –m options, a popular system default size will be used. Lines longer than the buffer size will cause **sort** to terminate abnormally. Supplying the actual number of bytes in the longest line to be merged (or some larger value) will prevent abnormal termination.

The following options override the default ordering rules.

-d   "Dictionary" order: only letters, digits, and blanks (spaces and tabs) are significant in comparisons.

-f   Fold lower-case letters into upper case.

-i   Ignore non-printable characters.

-M   Compare as months. The first three non-blank characters of the field are folded to upper case and compared. For example, in English the sorting order is "JAN" < "FEB" < . . . < "DEC". Invalid fields compare low to "JAN". The -M option implies the -b option (see below).

-n   An initial numeric string, consisting of optional blanks, optional minus sign, and zero or more digits with optional decimal point, is sorted by arithmetic value. The -n option implies the -b option (see below). Note that the -b option is only effective when restricted sort key specifications are in effect.

-r   Reverse the sense of comparisons.

When ordering options appear before restricted sort key specifications, the requested ordering rules are applied globally to all sort keys. When attached to a specific sort key (described below), the specified ordering options override all global ordering options for that key.

The notation +*pos1* −*pos2* restricts a sort key to one beginning at *pos1* and ending just before *pos2*. The characters at position *pos1* and just before *pos2* are included in the sort key (provided that *pos2* does not precede *pos1*). A missing −*pos2* means the end of the line.

Specifying *pos1* and *pos2* involves the notion of a field, a minimal sequence of characters followed by a field separator or a new-line. By default, the first blank (space or tab) of a sequence of blanks acts as the field separator. All blanks in a sequence of blanks are considered to be part of the next field; for example, all blanks at the beginning of a line are considered to be part of the first field. The treatment of field separators can be altered using the options:

-b   Ignore leading blanks when determining the starting and ending positions of a restricted sort key. If the -b option is specified before the first +*pos1* argument, it will be applied to all +*pos1* arguments. Otherwise, the **b** flag may be attached independently to each +*pos1* or −*pos2* argument (see below).

-t*x*   Use *x* as the field separator character; *x* is not considered to be part of a field (although it may be included in a sort key). Each occurrence of *x* is significant (for example, *xx* delimits an empty field).

pos1 and *pos2* each have the form *m.n* optionally followed by one or more of the flags **bdfiMnr**. A starting position specified by +*m.n* is interpreted to mean the *n*+1st character in the *m*+1st field. A missing *.n* means *.0*, indicating the first character of the *m*+1st field. If the **b** flag is in effect *n* is counted from the first non-blank in the *m*+1st field; +*m.0***b** refers to the first non-blank character in the *m*+1st field.

A last position specified by −*m.n* is interpreted to mean the *n*th character (including separators) after the last character of the *m th* field. A missing *.n* means *.0*, indicating the last character of the *m*th field. If the **b** flag is in effect *n* is counted from the last leading blank in the *m*+1st field; −*m.1***b** refers to the first non-blank in the *m*+1st field.

When there are multiple sort keys, later keys are compared only after all earlier keys compare equal. Lines that otherwise compare equal are ordered with all bytes significant.

EXAMPLES

Sort the contents of *infile* with the second field as the sort key:

    sort +1 −2 *infile*

Sort, in reverse order, the contents of *infile1* and *infile2*, placing the output in *outfile* and using the first character of the second field as the sort key:

    sort −r −o *outfile* +1.0 −1.2 *infile1 infile2*

Sort, in reverse order, the contents of *infile1* and *infile2* using the first non-blank character of the second field as the sort key:

    sort −r +1.0b −1.1b *infile1 infile2*

Print the password file [**passwd**(4)] sorted by the numeric user ID (the third colon-separated field):

    sort −t: +2n −3 /etc/passwd

Sort the contents of the password file using the group ID (third field) as the primary sort key and the user ID (second field) as the secondary sort key:

    sort −t: +3 −4 +2 −3 /etc/passwd

Print the lines of the already sorted file *infile*, suppressing all but the first occurrence of lines having the same third field (the options −**um** with just one input file make the choice of a unique representative from a set of equal lines predictable):

    sort −um +2 −3 *infile*

FILES

/var/tmp/stm???

SEE ALSO

comm(1), join(1), uniq(1)

NOTES

Comments and exits with non-zero status for various trouble conditions (for example, when input lines are too long), and for disorder discovered under the −c option.

When the last line of an input file is missing a **new-line** character, **sort** appends one, prints a warning message, and continues.

sort does not guarantee preservation of relative line ordering on equal keys.

NAME

sortbib – sort a bibliographic database

SYNOPSIS

/usr/ucb/sortbib [–s*key-letters*] *database* . . .

DESCRIPTION

The **sortbib** command sorts files of records containing **refer** key-letters by user-specified keys. Records may be separated by blank lines, or by '.[' and '.]' delimiters, but the two styles may not be mixed together. This program reads through each *database* and pulls out key fields, which are sorted separately. The sorted key fields contain the file pointer, byte offset, and length of corresponding records. These records are delivered using disk seeks and reads, so **sortbib** may not be used in a pipeline to read standard input.

By default, **sortbib** alphabetizes by the first **%A** and the **%D** fields, which contain the senior author and date. The **–s** option is used to specify new *key-letters*. See **addbib** for a list of the most common key letters. For instance, **–sATD** will sort by author, title, and date, while **–sA+D** will sort by all authors, and date. Sort keys past the fourth are not meaningful. No more than 16 databases may be sorted together at one time. Records longer than 4096 characters will be truncated.

sortbib sorts on the last word on the **%A** line, which is assumed to be the author's last name. A word in the final position, such as 'jr.' or 'ed.', will be ignored if the name beforehand ends with a comma. Authors with two-word last names or unusual constructions can be sorted correctly by using the **nroff** convention '\0' in place of a blank. A **%Q** field is considered to be the same as **%A**, except sorting begins with the first, not the last, word. **sortbib** sorts on the last word of the **%D** line, usually the year. It also ignores leading articles (like 'A' or 'The') when sorting by titles in the **%T** or **%J** fields; it will ignore articles of any modern European language. If a sort-significant field is absent from a record, **sortbib** places that record before other records containing that field.

SEE ALSO

addbib(1), indxbib(1), lookbib(1), refer(1), roffbib(1)

NOTES

Records with missing author fields should probably be sorted by title.

NAME

spell, hashmake, spellin, hashcheck, compress – find spelling errors

SYNOPSIS

spell [–v] [–b] [–x] [–l] [+*local_file*] [*files*]

/usr/lib/spell/hashmake

/usr/lib/spell/spellin *n*

/usr/lib/spell/hashcheck *spelling_list*

/usr/lib/spell/compress

DESCRIPTION

spell collects words from the named *files* and looks them up in a spelling list. Words that neither occur among nor are derivable (by applying certain inflections, prefixes, and/or suffixes) from words in the spelling list are printed on the standard output. If no *files* are named, words are collected from the standard input.

spell ignores most troff(1), tbl(1), and eqn(1) constructions.

–v   All words not literally in the spelling list are printed, and plausible derivations from the words in the spelling list are indicated.

–b   British spelling is checked. Besides preferring centre, colour, programme, speciality, travelled, etc., this option insists upon -*ise* in words like standardise, Fowler and the OED (Oxford English Dictionary) to the contrary notwithstanding.

–x   Every plausible stem is displayed, one per line, with = preceding each word.

–l   Follow the chains of *all* included files. By default, spell (like der-off(1)) follows chains of included files (.so and .nx troff(1) requests), *unless* the names of such included files begin with /usr/lib.

+*local_file*   Words found in *local_file* are removed from spell's output. *local_file* is the name of a user-provided file that contains a sorted list of words, one per line. The list must be sorted with the ordering used by sort(1) (e.g. upper case preceding lower case). If this ordering is not followed, some entries in *local_file* may be ignored. With this option, the user can specify a set of words that are correct spellings (in addition to spell's own spelling list) for each job.

The spelling list is based on many sources, and while more haphazard than an ordinary dictionary, is also more effective with respect to proper names and popular technical words. Coverage of the specialized vocabularies of biology, medicine, and chemistry is light.

Alternate auxiliary files (spelling lists, stop list, history file) may be specified on the command line by using environment variables. These variables and their default settings are shown in the FILES section. Copies of all misspellings and entries that specify the login, tty, and time of each invocation of spell are accumulated in the *history* file. The *stop list* filters out misspellings (e.g., thier=thy–y+ier) that would otherwise pass.

Three routines help maintain and check the hash lists used by **spell**:

hashmake Reads a list of words from the standard input and writes the corresponding nine-digit hash code on the standard output. This is the first step in creating a new spelling list or adding words to an existing list; it must be used prior to using **spellin**.

spellin Reads *n* hash codes (created by **hashmake**) from the standard input and writes a compressed spelling list on the standard output. Use **spellin** to add words to an existing spelling list or create a new spelling list.

hashcheck Reads a compressed *spelling_list* and recreates the nine-digit hash codes for all the words in it; it writes these codes on the standard output. It takes as input an existing spelling list (**hlista** or **hlistb**) or a list created or modified by **spellin**. By using **hashcheck** on an existing compressed *spelling_list* and **hashmake** on a file of selected words, you can compare the two output files to determine if the selected words are present in the existing *spelling_list*.

compress When **spell** is executed, the misspelled words are added to a file called **spellhist**. This file may contain identical entries since the same word may be misspelled during different executions of **spell**. The **compress** program deletes redundant misspelled words in the **spellhist** file, thereby reducing the size of the file, making it easier to analyze.

FILES

`D_SPELL=/usr/share/lib/spell/hlist[ab]`	hashed spelling lists, American & British
`S_SPELL=/usr/share/lib/spell/hstop`	hashed stop list
`H_SPELL=/var/adm/spellhist`	history file
`/usr/lib/spell/spellprog`	program

SEE ALSO

deroff(1), sed(1), sort(1), tee(1)
eqn(1), tbl(1), troff(1) in the *DOCUMENTER'S WORKBENCH Software Technical Discussion and Reference Manual*

NOTES

The spelling list's coverage is uneven; new installations will probably wish to monitor the output for several months to gather local additions; typically, these are kept in a separate local file that is added to the hashed *spelling_list* via - **spellin**.

NAME

    split – split a file into pieces

SYNOPSIS

    split [*-n*] [*file* [*name*]]

DESCRIPTION

    split reads *file* and writes it in *n*-line pieces (default 1000 lines) onto a set of output files. The name of the first output file is *name* with **aa** appended, and so on lexicographically, up to **zz** (a maximum of 676 files). The maximum length of *name* is 2 characters less than the maximum filename length allowed by the filesystem. See **statvfs**(2). If no output name is given, **x** is default.

    If no input file is given, or if – is given in its stead, then the standard input file is used.

SEE ALSO

    bfs(1), **csplit**(1)

    statvfs(2) in the *Programmer's Reference Manual*

NAME

spray – spray packets

SYNOPSIS

/usr/sbin/spray [-c count] [-d delay] [-l length] [-t nettype host]

DESCRIPTION

spray sends a one-way stream of packets to *host* using RPC, and reports how
many were received, as well as the the transfer rate. The *host* argument can be
either a name or an Internet address.

The following options are available:

-c *count*　　　　Specify how many packets to send. The default value of *count* is
　　　　　　　　the number of packets required to make the total stream size
　　　　　　　　100000 bytes.

-d *delay*　　　　Specify how many microseconds to pause between sending each
　　　　　　　　packet. The default is 0.

-l *length*　　　　The *length* parameter is the numbers of bytes in the Ethernet
　　　　　　　　packet that holds the RPC call message. Since the data is
　　　　　　　　encoded using XDR, and XDR only deals with 32 bit quantities,
　　　　　　　　not all values of *length* are possible, and spray rounds up to the
　　　　　　　　nearest possible value. When *length* is greater than 1514, then the
　　　　　　　　RPC call can no longer be encapsulated in one Ethernet packet, so
　　　　　　　　the *length* field no longer has a simple correspondence to Ether-
　　　　　　　　net packet size. The default value of *length* is 86 bytes (the size
　　　　　　　　of the RPC and UDP headers).

-t *nettype*　　　Specify class of transports. Defaults to **netpath**. See **rpc**(3N)
　　　　　　　　for a description of supported classes.

SEE ALSO

sprayd(1M), rpc(3N)

NAME

rpc.sprayd – spray server

SYNOPSIS

/usr/lib/netsvc/spray/rpc.sprayd

DESCRIPTION

rpc.sprayd is a server which records the packets sent by spray(1M). The
rpc.sprayd daemon may be started by inetd(1M) or listen(1M).

SEE ALSO

inetd(1M) listen(1M), pmadm(1M), sacadm(1M), spray(1M)

NAME

srchtxt – display contents of, or search for a text string in, message data bases

SYNOPSIS

srchtxt [**-s**] [**-l** *locale*] [**-m** *msgfile*, ...] [*text*]

DESCRIPTION

The **srchtxt** utility is used to display all the text strings in message data bases, or to search for a text string in message data bases (see **mkmsgs**(1)). These data bases are files in the directory **/usr/lib/locale/***locale***/LC_MESSAGES** (see **setlocale**(3C)), unless a file name given with the **-m** option contains a **/**. The directory *locale* can be viewed as the name of the language in which the text strings are written. If the **-l** option is not specified, the files accessed will be determined by the value of the environment variable **LC_MESSAGES**. If **LC_MESSAGES** is not set, the files accessed will be determined by the value of the environment variable **LANG**. If **LANG** is not set, the files accessed will be in the directory **/usr/lib/locale/C/LC_MESSAGES**, which contains default strings.

If no *text* argument is present, then all the text strings in the files accessed will be displayed.

The meanings of the options are as follows:

-s　　　　　　　suppress printing of the message sequence numbers of the messages being displayed

-l *locale*　　　access files in the directory **/usr/lib/locale/***locale***/LC_MESSAGES**. If **-m** *msgfile* is also supplied, *locale* is ignored for *msgfile*s containing a **/**.

-m *msgfile*　　access file(s) specified by one or more *msgfile*s. If *msgfile* contains a **/** character, then *msgfile is* interpreted as a pathname; otherwise, it will be assumed to be in the directory determined as described above. To specify more than one *msgfile*, separate the file names using commas.

text　　　　　　search for the text string specified by *text* and display each one that matches. *text* can take the form of a regular expression (see **ed**(1)).

If the **-s** option is not specified, the displayed text is prefixed by message sequence numbers. The message sequence numbers are enclosed in angle brackets: **<***msgfile***:***msgnum***>**.

msgfile　　　　name of the file where the displayed text occurred

msgnum　　　 sequence number in *msgfile* where the displayed text occurred

This display is in the format used by **gettxt**(1) and **gettxt**(3C).

EXAMPLES

The following examples show uses of **srchtxt**.

Example 1:

> If message files have been installed in a locale named **french** by using **mkmsgs**(1), then you could display the entire set of text strings in the **french** locale (**/usr/lib/locale/french/LC_MESSAGES/**∗) by typing:

```
srchtxt -l french
```

Example 2:

If a set of error messages associated with the UNIX operating system have been installed in the file **UX** in the **french** locale (`/usr/lib/locale/french/LC_MESSAGES/UX`), then, using the value of the **LANG** environment variable to determine the locale to be searched, you could search that file in that locale for all error messages dealing with files by typing:

```
LANG=french; export LANG
srchtxt -m UX "[Ff]ichier"
```

If `/usr/lib/locale/french/LC_MESSAGES/UX` contained the following strings:

```
Erreur E/S\n
Liste d'arguments trop longue\n
Fichier inexistant\n
Argument invalide\n
Trop de fichiers ouverts\n
Fichier trop long\n
Trop de liens\n
Argument hors du domaine\n
Identificateur supprim\n
Etreinte fatale\n
     .
     .
     .
```

then the following strings would be displayed:

```
<UX:3>Fichier inexistant\n
<UX:5>Trop de fichiers ouverts\n
<UX:6>Fichier trop long\n
```

Example 3:

If a set of error messages associated with the UNIX operating system have been installed in the file **UX** and a set of error messages associated with the INGRESS data base product have been installed in the file **ingress**, both in the **german** locale, then you could search for the pattern **[Dd]atei** in both the files **UX** and **ingress** in the **german** locale by typing:

```
srchtxt -l german -m UX,ingress "[Dd]atei"
```

FILES

`/usr/lib/locale/C/LC_MESSAGES/*`   default files created by **mkmsgs**(1)

`/usr/lib/locale/`*locale*`/LC_MESSAGES/*`   message files created by **mkmsgs**(1)

SEE ALSO

ed(1), **exstr**(1), **gettxt**(1), **mkmsgs**(1)
gettxt(3C), **setlocale**(3C) in the *Programmer's Reference Manual*

DIAGNOSTICS

The error messages produced by **srchtxt** are intended to be self-explanatory. They indicate an error in the command line or errors encountered while searching for a particular locale and/or message file.

NAME

statd – network status monitor

SYNOPSIS

/usr/lib/nfs/statd

DESCRIPTION

statd is an intermediate version of the status monitor. It interacts with lockd(1M) to provide the crash and recovery functions for the locking services on NFS.

FILES

/etc/sm
/etc/sm.bak
/etc/state

SEE ALSO

lockd(1M)

NOTES

The crash of a site is only detected upon its recovery.

NAME

strace – print STREAMS trace messages

SYNOPSIS

strace [*mid sid level*] . . .

DESCRIPTION

strace without arguments writes all STREAMS event trace messages from all drivers and modules to its standard output. These messages are obtained from the STREAMS log driver [log(7)]. If arguments are provided they must be in triplets of the form *mid, sid, level*, where *mid* is a STREAMS module ID number, *sid* is a sub-ID number, and *level* is a tracing priority level. Each triplet indicates that tracing messages are to be received from the given module/driver, sub-ID (usually indicating minor device), and priority level equal to or less than the given level. The token **all** may be used for any member to indicate no restriction for that attribute.

The format of each trace message output is:

<seq> <time> <ticks> <level> <flags> <mid> <sid> <text>

<seq>	trace sequence number
<time>	time of message in *hh:mm:ss*
<ticks>	time of message in machine ticks since boot
<level>	tracing priority level
<flags>	**E** : message is also in the error log **F** : indicates a fatal error **N** : mail was sent to the system administrator
<mid>	module ID number of source
<sid>	sub-ID number of source
<text>	formatted text of the trace message

Once initiated, strace will continue to execute until terminated by the user.

EXAMPLES

Output all trace messages from the module or driver whose module ID is 41:

    strace 41 all all

Output those trace messages from driver/module ID 41 with sub-IDs 0, 1, or 2:

    strace 41 0 1 41 1 1 41 2 0

Messages from sub-IDs 0 and 1 must have a tracing level less than or equal to 1. Those from sub-ID 2 must have a tracing level of 0.

SEE ALSO

log(7)

Programmer's Guide: STREAMS

NOTES

Due to performance considerations, only one strace process is permitted to open the STREAMS log driver at a time. The log driver has a list of the triplets specified in the command invocation, and compares each potential trace message against this list to decide if it should be formatted and sent up to the **strace** process. Hence, long lists of triplets will have a greater impact on overall STREAMS performance. Running **strace** will have the most impact on the timing of the modules and drivers generating the trace messages that are sent to the **strace** process. If trace messages are generated faster than the **strace** process can handle them, then some of the messages will be lost. This last case can be determined by examining the sequence numbers on the trace messages output.

NAME

strchg, strconf – change or query stream configuration

SYNOPSIS

strchg -h *module1*[, *module2* ...]
strchg -p [-a | -u *module*]
strchg -f *file*
strconf [-t | -m *module*]

DESCRIPTION

These commands are used to alter or query the configuration of the stream associated with the user's standard input. The **strchg** command pushes modules on
and/or pops modules off the stream. The **strconf** command queries the
configuration of the stream. Only the super-user or owner of a STREAMS device
may alter the configuration of that stream.

With the **-h** option, **strchg** pushes modules onto a stream; it takes as arguments
the names of one or more pushable streams modules. These modules are pushed
in order; that is, *module1* is pushed first, *module2* is pushed second, etc.

The **-p** option pops modules off the stream. With the **-p** option alone, **strchg**
pops the topmost module from the stream. With the **-p** and **-a** options, all the
modules above the topmost driver are popped. When the **-p** option is followed
by **-u** *module*, then all modules above but not including *module* are popped off the
stream. The **-a** and **-u** options are mutually exclusive.

With the **-f** option, the user can specify a *file* that contains a list of modules
representing the desired configuration of the stream. Each module name must
appear on a separate line where the first name represents the topmost module
and the last name represents the module that should be closest to the driver. The
strchg command will determine the current configuration of the stream and pop
and push the necessary modules in order to end up with the desired
configuration.

The **-h**, **-f** and **-p** options are mutually exclusive.

Invoked without any arguments, **strconf** prints a list of all the modules in the
stream as well as the topmost driver. The list is printed with one name per line
where the first name printed is the topmost module on the stream (if one exists)
and the last item printed is the name of the driver. With the **-t** option, only the
topmost module (if one exists) is printed. The **-m** option determines if the named
module is present on a stream. If it is, **strconf** prints the message **yes** and
returns zero. If not, **strconf** prints the message **no** and returns a non-zero value.
The **-t** and **-m** options are mutually exclusive.

EXAMPLES

The following command pushes the module **ldterm** on the stream associated
with the user's standard input:

        strchg -h ldterm

The following command pops the topmost module from the stream associated with **/dev/term/24**. The user must be the owner of this device or the super-user.

        `strchg -p < /dev/term/24`

If the file **fileconf** contains the following:

        `compat`
        `ldterm`
        `ptem`

then the command

        `strchg -f fileconf`

will configure the user's standard input stream so that the module **ptem** is pushed over the driver, followed by **ldterm** and **compat** closest to the stream head.

The **strconf** command with no arguments lists the modules and topmost driver on the stream; for a stream that has only the module **ldterm** pushed above the **ports** driver, it would produce the following output:

        `ldterm`
        `ports`

The following command asks if **ldterm** is on the stream

        `strconf -m ldterm`

and produces the following output while returning an exit status of 0:

        `yes`

SEE ALSO
streamio(7) in the *Programmer's Guide: STREAMS*

DIAGNOSTICS
strchg returns zero on success. It prints an error message and returns non-zero status for various error conditions, including usage error, bad module name, too many modules to push, failure of an ioctl on the stream, or failure to open *file* from the **–f** option.

strconf returns zero on success (for the **–m** or **–t** option, "success" means the named or topmost module is present). It returns a non-zero status if invoked with the **–m** or **–t** option and the module is not present. It prints an error message and returns non-zero status for various error conditions, including usage error or failure of an **ioctl** on the stream.

NOTES
If the user is neither the owner of the stream nor the super-user, the **strchg** command will fail. If the user does not have read permissions on the stream and is not the super-user, the **strconf** command will fail.

If modules are pushed in the wrong order, one could end up with a stream that does not function as expected. For ttys, if the line discipline module is not pushed in the correct place, one could have a terminal that does not respond to any commands.

NAME

strclean – STREAMS error logger cleanup program

SYNOPSIS

strclean [-d *logdir*] [-a *age*]

DESCRIPTION

strclean is used to clean up the STREAMS error logger directory on a regular basis (for example, by using cron). By default, all files with names matching error.* in /var/adm/streams that have not been modified in the last three days are removed. A directory other than /var/adm/streams can be specified using the −d option. The maximum age in days for a log file can be changed using the −a option.

EXAMPLE

strclean −d /var/adm/streams −a 3

has the same result as running strclean with no arguments.

FILES

/var/adm/streams/error.*

SEE ALSO

cron(1M), strerr(1M)
Programmer's Guide: STREAMS

NOTES

strclean is typically run from cron on a daily or weekly basis.

NAME

strerr – STREAMS error logger daemon

SYNOPSIS

strerr

DESCRIPTION

strerr receives error log messages from the STREAMS log driver [log(7)] and appends them to a log file. The error log files produced reside in the directory **/var/adm/streams**, and are named **error.***mm-dd*, where *mm* is the month and *dd* is the day of the messages contained in each log file.

The format of an error log message is:

<seq> <time> <ticks> <flags> <mid> <sid> <text>

<seq>	error sequence number
<time>	time of message in hh:mm:ss
<ticks>	time of message in machine ticks since boot priority level
<flags>	**T** : the message was also sent to a tracing process **F** : indicates a fatal error **N** : send mail to the system administrator
<mid>	module ID number of source
<sid>	sub-ID number of source
<text>	formatted text of the error message

Messages that appear in the error log are intended to report exceptional conditions that require the attention of the system administrator. Those messages which indicate the total failure of a STREAMS driver or module should have the **F** flag set. Those messages requiring the immediate attention of the administrator will have the **N** flag set, which causes the error logger to send the message to the system administrator via **mail**. The priority level usually has no meaning in the error log but will have meaning if the message is also sent to a tracer process.

Once initiated, **strerr** continues to execute until terminated by the user. It is commonly executed asynchronously.

FILES

/var/adm/streams/error.*mm-dd*

SEE ALSO

log(7)
Programmer's Guide: STREAMS

NOTES

Only one **strerr** process at a time is permitted to open the STREAMS log driver.

If a module or driver is generating a large number of error messages, running the error logger will cause a degradation in STREAMS performance. If a large burst of messages are generated in a short time, the log driver may not be able to deliver some of the messages. This situation is indicated by gaps in the sequence numbering of the messages in the log files.

NAME

strings – find printable strings in an object file or binary

SYNOPSIS

strings [**-a**] [**-o**] [**-n** *number* | *-number*] *filename* . . .

DESCRIPTION

The **strings** command looks for ASCII strings in a binary file. A string is any sequence of 4 or more printing characters ending with a newline or a null character.

strings is useful for identifying random object files and many other things.

The following options are available:

-a　　　　Look everywhere in the file for strings. If this flag is omitted, **strings** only looks in the initialized data space of object files.

-o　　　　Precede each string by its offset in the file.

-n *number*　Use *number* as the minimum string length rather than 4.

SEE ALSO

od(1)

NOTES

The algorithm for identifying strings is extremely primitive.

For backwards compatibility, *-number* can be used in place of **-n** *number*. Similarly, the **-a** and a **-** option are interchangeable. The **-** and the *-number* variations are obsolescent.

NAME

strip – strip symbol table, debugging and line number information from an object file.

SYNOPSIS

strip [-blrVx] *file* . . .

DESCRIPTION

The **strip** command strips the symbol table, debugging information, and line number information from **ELF** object files; **COFF** object files can no longer be stripped. Once this stripping process has been done, no symbolic debugging access will be available for that file; therefore, this command is normally run only on production modules that have been debugged and tested.

If **strip** is executed on a common archive file [see **ar**(4)] in addition to processing the members, **strip** will remove the archive symbol table. The archive symbol table must be restored by executing the **ar**(1) command with the **-s** option before the archive can be linked by the **ld**(1) command. **strip** will produce appropriate warning messages when this situation arises.

The amount of information stripped from the **ELF** object file can be controlled by using any of the following options:

-b   Same effect as the default behavior. This option is obsolete and will be removed in the next release.

-l   Strip line number information only; do not strip the symbol table or debugging information.

-r   Same effect as the default behavior. This option is obsolete and will be removed in the next release.

-V   Print, on standard error, the version number of **strip**.

-x   Do not strip the symbol table; debugging and line number information may be stripped.

strip is used to reduce the file storage overhead taken by the object file.

FILES

TMPDIR/strp*   temporary files

TMPDIR   usually **/var/tmp** but can be redefined by setting the environment variable **TMPDIR** [see **tempnam**() in **tmpnam**(3S)].

SEE ALSO

ar(1), **as**(1), **cc**(1), **ld**(1), **tmpnam**(3S), **a.out**(4), **ar**(4)

NOTES

The symbol table section will not be removed if it is contained within a segment, or the file is either a relocatable or dynamic shared object.

The line number and debugging sections will not be removed if they are contained within a segment, or their associated relocation section is contained within a segment.

NAME

stty – set the options for a terminal

SYNOPSIS

stty [-a] [-g] [*options*]

DESCRIPTION

stty sets certain terminal I/O options for the device that is the current standard input; without arguments, it reports the settings of certain options.

In this report, if a character is preceded by a caret (ˆ), then the value of that option is the corresponding control character (e.g., "**ˆh**" is CTRL-h; in this case, recall that CTRL-h is the same as the "back-space" key.) The sequence "**ˆ '**" means that an option has a null value.

-a   reports all of the option settings;

-g   reports current settings in a form that can be used as an argument to another **stty** command.

For detailed information about the modes listed from Control Modes through Local Modes, below, see **termio**(7). For detailed information about the modes listed under Hardware Flow Control Modes and Clock Modes, below, see **termiox**(7). Options described in the Combination Modes section are implemented using options in the earlier sections. Note that many combinations of options make no sense, but no sanity checking is performed. Hardware flow control and clock modes options may not be supported by all hardware interfaces. The options are selected from the following:

Control Modes

parenb (-parenb)   enable (disable) parity generation and detection.

parext (-parext)   enable (disable) extended parity generation and detection for mark and space parity.

parodd (-parodd)   select odd (even) parity, or mark (space) parity if **parext** is enabled.

cs5 cs6 cs7 cs8   select character size [see **termio**(7)].

0   hang up line immediately.

110 300 600 1200 1800 2400 4800 9600 19200 38400
                        Set terminal baud rate to the number given, if possible. (All speeds are not supported by all hardware interfaces.)

ispeed 0 110 300 600 1200 1800 2400 4800 9600 19200 38400
                        Set terminal input baud rate to the number given, if possible. (Not all hardware supports split baud rates.) If the input baud rate is set to zero, the input baud rate will be specified by the value of the output baud rate.

ospeed 0 110 300 600 1200 1800 2400 4800 9600 19200 38400
                        Set terminal output baud rate to the number given, if possible. (Not all hardware supports split baud rates.) If the output baud rate is set to zero, the line will be hung up immediately.

hupcl (-hupcl)	hang up (do not hang up) connection on last close.
hup (-hup)	same as **hupcl** (**-hupcl**).
cstopb (-cstopb)	use two (one) stop bits per character.
cread (-cread)	enable (disable) the receiver.
clocal (-clocal)	n assume a line without (with) modem control.
loblk (-loblk)	block (do not block) output from a non-current layer.

Input Modes

ignbrk (-ignbrk)	ignore (do not ignore) break on input.
brkint (-brkint)	signal (do not signal) INTR on break.
ignpar (-ignpar)	ignore (do not ignore) parity errors.
parmrk (-parmrk)	mark (do not mark) parity errors [see **termio**(7)].
inpck (-inpck)	enable (disable) input parity checking.
istrip (-istrip)	strip (do not strip) input characters to seven bits.
inlcr (-inlcr)	map (do not map) NL to CR on input.
igncr (-igncr)	ignore (do not ignore) CR on input.
icrnl (-icrnl)	map (do not map) CR to NL on input.
iuclc (-iuclc)	map (do not map) upper-case alphabetics to lower case on input.
ixon (-ixon)	enable (disable) START/STOP output control. Output is stopped by sending STOP control character and started by sending the START control character.
ixany (-ixany)	allow any character (only DC1) to restart output.
ixoff (-ixoff)	request that the system send (not send) START/STOP characters when the input queue is nearly empty/full.
imaxbel (-imaxbel)	echo (do not echo) BEL when the input line is too long.
KB_ENABLE	performs a TIOCKBON which allows extended characters to be transmitted to the user's program. Extended characters are transmitted as a null byte followed by a second byte containing the character's extended code. [see **keyboard**(7)].
DB_DISABLE	performs a TIOCKBON which disables the transmission of extended characters. This is the default. [see **keyboard**]

Output Modes

opost (-opost)	post-process output (do not post-process output; ignore all other output modes).

olcuc (-olcuc)	map (do not map) lower-case alphabetics to upper case on output.
onlcr (-onlcr)	map (do not map) NL to CR-NL on output.
ocrnl (-ocrnl)	map (do not map) CR to NL on output.
onocr (-onocr)	do not (do) output CRs at column zero.
onlret (-onlret)	on the terminal NL performs (does not perform) the CR function.
ofill (-ofill)	use fill characters (use timing) for delays.
ofdel (-ofdel)	fill characters are DELs (NULs).
cr0 cr1 cr2 cr3	select style of delay for carriage returns [see **termio**(7)].
nl0 nl1	select style of delay for line-feeds [see **termio**(7)].
tab0 tab1 tab2 tab3	
	select style of delay for horizontal tabs [see **termio**(7)].
bs0 bs1	select style of delay for backspaces [see **termio**(7)].
ff0 ff1	select style of delay for form-feeds [see **termio**(7)].
vt0 vt1	select style of delay for vertical tabs [see **termio**(7)].

Local Modes

isig (-isig)	enable (disable) the checking of characters against the special control characters INTR, QUIT, and SWTCH.
icanon (-icanon)	enable (disable) canonical input (ERASE and KILL processing).
xcase (-xcase)	canonical (unprocessed) upper/lower-case presentation.
echo (-echo)	echo back (do not echo back) every character typed.
echoe (-echoe)	echo (do not echo) ERASE character as a backspace-space-backspace string. Note: this mode will erase the ERASEed character on many CRT terminals; however, it does not keep track of column position and, as a result, may be confusing on escaped characters, tabs, and backspaces.
echok (-echok)	echo (do not echo) NL after KILL character.
lfkc (-lfkc)	the same as **echok (-echok)**; obsolete.
echonl (-echonl)	echo (do not echo) NL.
noflsh (-noflsh)	disable (enable) flush after INTR, QUIT, or SWTCH.
stwrap (-stwrap)	disable (enable) truncation of lines longer than 79 characters on a synchronous line. (Does not apply to the 3B2.)
tostop (-tostop)	send (do not send) SIGTTOU when background processes write to the terminal.

echoctl (-echoctl)
: echo (do not echo) control characters as ^*char*, delete as ^?

echoprt (-echoprt)
: echo (do not echo) erase character as character is "erased".

echoke (-echoke)
: BS-SP-BS erase (do not BS-SP-BS erase) entire line on line kill.

flusho (-flusho)
: output is (is not) being flushed.

pendin (-pendin)
: retype (do not retype) pending input at next read or input character.

iexten (-iexten)
: enable (disable) extended (implementation-defined) functions for input data.

stflush (-stflush)
: enable (disable) flush on a synchronous line after every **write**(2).

stappl (-stappl)
: use application mode (use line mode) on a synchronous line.

Hardware Flow Control Modes

rtsxoff (-rtsxoff)
: enable (disable) RTS hardware flow control on input.

ctsxon (-ctsxon)
: enable (disable) CTS hardware flow control on output.

dtrxoff (-dtrxoff)
: enable (disable) DTR hardware flow control on input.

cdxon (-cdxon)
: enable (disable) CD hardware flow control on output.

isxoff (-isxoff)
: enable (disable) isochronous hardware flow control on input.

Clock Modes

xcibrg
: get transmit clock from internal baud rate generator.

xctset
: get the transmit clock from transmitter signal element timing (DCE source) lead, CCITT V.24 circuit 114, EIA-232-D pin 15.

xcrset
: get transmit clock from receiver signal element timing (DCE source) lead, CCITT V.24 circuit 115, EIA-232-D pin 17.

rcibrg
: get receive clock from internal baud rate generator.

rctset
: get receive clock from transmitter signal element timing (DCE source) lead, CCITT V.24 circuit 114, EIA-232-D pin 15.

rcrset
: get receive clock from receiver signal element timing (DCE source) lead, CCITT V.24 circuit 115, EIA-232-D pin 17.

tsetcoff
: transmitter signal element timing clock not provided.

`tsetcrbrg`	output receive baud rate generator on transmitter signal element timing (DTE source) lead, CCITT V.24 circuit 113, EIA-232-D pin 24.
`tsetctbrg`	output transmit baud rate generator on transmitter signal element timing (DTE source) lead, CCITT V.24 circuit 113, EIA-232-D pin 24.
`tsetctset`	output transmitter signal element timing (DCE source) on transmitter signal element timing (DTE source) lead, CCITT V.24 circuit 113, EIA-232-D pin 24.
`tsetcrset`	output receiver signal element timing (DCE source) on transmitter signal element timing (DTE source) lead, CCITT V.24 circuit 113, EIA-232-D pin 24.
`rsetcoff`	receiver signal element timing clock not provided.
`rsetcrbrg`	output receive baud rate generator on receiver signal element timing (DTE source) lead, CCITT V.24 circuit 128, no EIA-232-D pin.
`rsetctbrg`	output transmit baud rate generator on receiver signal element timing (DTE source) lead, CCITT V.24 circuit 128, no EIA-232-D pin.
`rsetctset`	output transmitter signal element timing (DCE source) on receiver signal element timing (DTE source) lead, CCITT V.24 circuit 128, no EIA-232-D pin.
`rsetcrset`	output receiver signal element timing (DCE source) on receiver signal element timing (DTE source) lead, CCITT V.24 circuit 128, no EIA-232-D pin.

Control Assignments

control-character c	set *control-character* to *c*, where *control-character* is `ctab`, `discard`, `dsusp`, `eof`, `eol`, `eol2`, `erase`, `intr`, `kill`, `lnext`, `quit`, `reprint`, `start`, `stop`, `susp`, `swtch`, or `werase`. [`ctab` is used with `-stappl` [see `termio`(7)]. If *c* is preceded by a caret (^) indicating an escape from the shell, then the value used is the corresponding control character (e.g., "^d" is a CTRL-d). "^?" is interpreted as DEL and "^-" is interpreted as undefined.
min, time number	Set the value of *min* or *time* to *number*. *min* and *time* are used in Non-Canonical mode input processing (`-icanon`).

Combination Modes

`evenp` or `parity`	enable `parenb` and `cs7`.
`oddp`	enable `parenb`, `cs7`, and `parodd`.

spacep	enable **parenb**, **cs7**, and **parext**.
markp	enable **parenb**, **cs7**, **parodd**, and **parext**.
-parity, or -evenp	disable **parenb**, and set **cs8**.
-oddp	disable **parenb** and **parodd**, and set **cs8**.
-spacep	disable **parenb** and **parext**, and set **cs8**.
-markp	disable **parenb**, **parodd**, and **parext**, and set **cs8**.
raw (-raw or cooked)	enable (disable) raw input and output (no ERASE, KILL, INTR, QUIT, SWTCH, EOT, or output post processing).
nl (-nl)	unset (set) **icrnl**, **onlcr**. In addition -nl unsets **inlcr**, **igncr**, **ocrnl**, and **onlret**.
lcase (-lcase)	set (unset) **xcase**, **iuclc**, and **olcuc**.
LCASE (-LCASE)	same as **lcase** (-lcase).
tabs (-tabs or tab3)	preserve (expand to spaces) tabs when printing.
ek	reset ERASE and KILL characters back to normal # and @.
sane	resets all modes to some reasonable values.
term	set all modes suitable for the terminal type *term*, where *term* is one of **tty33**, **tty37**, **vt05**, **tn300**, **ti700**, or **tek**.
async	set normal asynchronous communications where clock settings are **xcibrg**, **rcibrg**, **tsetcoff** and **rsetcoff**.

Window Size

rows *n*	set window size to *n* rows.
columns *n*	set window size to *n* columns.
ypixels *n*	set vertical window size to *n* pixels.
xpixels *n*	set horizontal window size to *n* pixels.

Control Modes for the Video Monitor

mono   Selects the monochrome display as the output device for the console screen. This mode is valid if a standard monochrome adapter is present or if a standard enhanced graphics adapter (EGA) is present and the EGA is currently in one of the monochrome display modes.

color   Selects a standard regular color display as the output device for the console screen. This mode is valid if a color graphics adapter is present or if a standard EGA is present and is currently in one of the color graphics compatibility modes.

enhanced   Selects the enhanced color display as the output device for the console screen. This mode is valid if an EGA is present and is currently in a non-monochrome display mode.

pro   Selects the professional graphics adapter as the output device for the
           system console. This mode is valid if a VGA is present.

Control Modes for the Attached Display Devices

The **stty** command supports mode changes for the monochrome display adapter
(MDA), color graphics adapter (CGA), and enhanced graphics adapter (EGA).
Support for the video graphics array (VGA) is not provided by the **stty** com-
mand.

B40x25 Selects 40x25 (40 columns x 25 rows) black and white text display mode.

C40x25 Selects 40x25 color text display mode.

B80x25 Selects 80x25 black and white text display mode.

C80x25 Selects 80x25 color display text mode.

BG320 Selects 320x200 black and white graphics display mode.

CG320 Selects 320x200 color graphics display mode.

BG640 Selects 640x200 black and white graphics display mode.

The keyboard and display control modes above are valid for the following
configurations: standard color graphics adapter (CGA) attached to an standard
regular color display; standard enhanced graphics adapter (EGA) (modes 0-6)
attached to a standard regular color display or standard enhanced color display.

CG320_D
           Selects EGA support for 320x200 graphics display mode (EGA mode D).

CG640_E
           Selects EGA support for 640x200 graphics display mode (EGA mode E).

The two options above are only valid when an EGA is attached to a standard regular color display or an enhanced color display.

EGAMONO80x25
           Selects EGA Mode 7 as the display mode. Emulates the support pro-
           vided by the standard monochrome display adapter.

EGAMONOAPA
           Selects EGA support for 640x350 graphics display mode (EGA mode F).

ENHMONOAPA2
           Selects EGA mode F*.

The three options above are only valid when a standard EGA is attached to an
IBM monochrome display.

ENH_B40x25
           Selects enhanced EGA support for 40x25 black and white text display
           mode (EGA mode 0*).

ENH_C40x25
           Selects enhanced EGA support for 40x25 color text display mode (EGA
           mode 1*).

ENH_B80x25
> Selects enhanced EGA support for 80x25 black and white text display mode (EGA mode 2*).

ENH_C80x25
> Selects enhanced EGA support for 80x25 color text display mode (EGA mode 3*).

ENH_B80x43
> Selects enhanced EGA support for 80x43 black and white text display mode.

ENH_C80x43
> Selects enhanced EGA support for 80x43 color text display mode.

CG640x350
> Selects EGA support for 640x350 graphics display mode (EGA mode 10).

ENH_CG640
> Selects EGA mode 10*.

The options above are only valid when a standard EGA is attached to a standard enhanced color display.

MCAMODE
> Reinitializes the monochrome graphics adapter.

ENH_CGA
> Selects CGA hardware emulation, when an AT&T Super-Vu video controller is attached.

SEE ALSO
> **tabs**(1) in the *User's Reference Manual*.
> **ioctl**(2).
> **termio**(7), **termiox**(7) in the *System Administrator's Reference Manual*.

NAME

stty – set the options for a terminal

SYNOPSIS

/usr/ucb/stty [-a] [-g] [-h] [*options*]

DESCRIPTION

stty sets certain terminal I/O options for the device that is the current standard input; without arguments, it reports the settings of certain options.

In this report, if a character is preceded by a caret (^), then the value of that option is the corresponding CTRL character (for example, "^h" is CTRL-h; in this case, recall that CTRL-h is the same as the "back-space" key.) The sequence "^´" means that an option has a null value.

-a　　　reports all of the option settings;

-g　　　reports current settings in a form that can be used as an argument to another *stty* command.

-h　　　reports all the option settings with the control characters in an easy to read column format.

Options in the last group are implemented using options in the previous groups. Note that many combinations of options make no sense, but no sanity checking is performed. Hardware flow control and clock modes options may not be supported by all hardware interfaces. The options are selected from the following:

Special Requests

all　　　　　　　　Reports the same option settings as **stty** without arguments, but with the control characters in column format.

everything　　　Everything **stty** knows about is printed. Same as -h option.

speed　　　　　　The terminal speed alone is reported on the standard output.

size　　　　　　　The terminal (window) sizes are printed on the standard output, first rows and then columns. This option is only appropriate if currently running a window system.

　　　　　　　　　　size and speed always report on the settings of /dev/tty, and always report the settings to the standard output.

Control Modes

parenb (-parenb)　　enable (disable) parity generation and detection.

parext (-parext)　　enable (disable) extended parity generation and detection for mark and space parity.

parodd (-parodd)　　select odd (even) parity, or mark (space) parity if **parext** is enabled.

cs5 cs6 cs7 cs8　　select character size [see termio(7)].

0   hang up line immediately.

110 300 600 1200 1800 2400 4800 9600 19200 **exta** 38400 **extb**
                           Set terminal baud rate to the number given, if possible.
                           (All speeds are not supported by all hardware interfaces.)

ispeed 0 110 300 600 1200 1800 2400 4800 9600 19200 **exta** 38400 **extb**
                           Set terminal input baud rate to the number given, if possi-
                           ble. (Not all hardware supports split baud rates.) If the
                           input baud rate is set to zero, the input baud rate will be
                           specified by the value of the output baud rate.

ospeed 0 110 300 600 1200 1800 2400 4800 9600 19200 **exta** 38400 **extb**
                           Set terminal output baud rate to the number given, if possi-
                           ble. (Not all hardware supports split baud rates.) If the
                           baud rate is set to zero, the line will be hung up immedi-
                           ately.

hupcl (–hupcl)   hang up (do not hang up) connection on last close.

hup (–hup)   same as **hupcl** (**–hupcl**).

cstopb (–cstopb)   use two (one) stop bits per character.

cread (–cread)   enable (disable) the receiver.

clocal (–clocal)   assume a line without (with) modem control.

loblk (–loblk)   block (do not block) output from a non-current layer.

Input Modes

ignbrk (–ignbrk)   ignore (do not ignore) break on input.

brkint (–brkint)   signal (do not signal) INTR on break.

ignpar (–ignpar)   ignore (do not ignore) parity errors.

parmrk (–parmrk)   mark (do not mark) parity errors [see **termio**(7)].

inpck (–inpck)   enable (disable) input parity checking.

istrip (–istrip)   strip (do not strip) input characters to seven bits.

inlcr (–inlcr)   map (do not map) NL to CR on input.

igncr (–igncr)   ignore (do not ignore) CR on input.

icrnl (–icrnl)   map (do not map) CR to NL on input.

iuclc (–iuclc)   map (do not map) upper-case alphabetics to lower case on
                           input.

ixon (–ixon)   enable (disable) START/STOP output control. Output is
                           stopped by sending an STOP and started by sending an
                           START.

ixany (–ixany)   allow any character (only START) to restart output.

decctlq (–decctlq)   Same as **–ixany**.

ixoff (–ixoff)	request that the system send (not send) START/STOP characters when the input queue is nearly empty/full.
tandem (–tandem)	Same as **ixoff**.
imaxbel (–imaxbel)	
	echo (do not echo) BEL when the input line is too long.
iexten (–iexten)	enable (disable) extended (implementation-defined) functions for input data.

Output Modes

opost (–opost)	post-process output (do not post-process output; ignore all other output modes).
olcuc (–olcuc)	map (do not map) lower-case alphabetics to upper case on output.
onlcr (–onlcr)	map (do not map) NL to CR-NL on output.
ocrnl (–ocrnl)	map (do not map) CR to NL on output.
onocr (–onocr)	do not (do) output CRs at column zero.
onlret (–onlret)	on the terminal NL performs (does not perform) the CR function.
ofill (–ofill)	use fill characters (use timing) for delays.
ofdel (–ofdel)	fill characters are DELs (NULs).
cr0 cr1 cr2 cr3	select style of delay for carriage returns [see **termio**(7)].
nl0 nl1	select style of delay for line-feeds [see **termio**(7)].
tab0 tab1 tab2 tab3	
	select style of delay for horizontal tabs [see **termio**(7)].
bs0 bs1	select style of delay for backspaces [see **termio**(7)].
ff0 ff1	select style of delay for form-feeds [see **termio**(7)].
vt0 vt1	select style of delay for vertical tabs [see **termio**(7)].

Local Modes

isig (–isig)	enable (disable) the checking of characters against the special control characters INTR, QUIT, and SWTCH.
icanon (–icanon)	enable (disable) canonical input (ERASE and KILL processing).
cbreak (–cbreak)	Same as **–icanon**.
xcase (–xcase)	canonical (unprocessed) upper/lower-case presentation.
echo (–echo)	echo back (do not echo back) every character typed.
echoe (–echoe)	echo (do not echo) ERASE character as a backspace-space-backspace string. Note: this mode will erase the ERASEed character on many CRT terminals; however, it does *not* keep track of column position and, as a result, may be confusing on escaped characters, tabs, and backspaces.

crterase (-crterase)
　　　　　　　　　　　　Same as **echoe**.

echok (-echok)　　　echo (do not echo) NL after KILL character.

lfkc (-lfkc)　　　　the same as **echok** (**-echok**); obsolete.

echonl (-echonl)　　echo (do not echo) NL.

noflsh (-noflsh)　　disable (enable) flush after INTR, QUIT, or SWTCH.

stwrap (-stwrap)　　disable (enable) truncation of lines longer than 79 characters on a synchronous line. (Does not apply to the 3B2.)

tostop (-tostop)　　send (do not send) SIGTTOU for background processes.

echoctl (-echoctl)
　　　　　　　　　　　　echo (do not echo) control characters as *^char*, delete as *^?*

ctlecho (-ctlecho)
　　　　　　　　　　　　Same as **echoctl**.

echoprt (-echoprt)
　　　　　　　　　　　　echo (do not echo) erase character as character is "erased".

prterase (-prterase)
　　　　　　　　　　　　Same as **echoprt**.

echoke (-echoke)　　BS-SP-BS erase (do not BS-SP-BS erase) entire line on line kill.

crtkill (-crtkill)　Same as **echoke**.

flusho (-flusho)　　output is (is not) being flushed.

pendin (-pendin)　　retype (do not retype) pending input at next read or input character.

stflush (-stflush)　enable (disable) flush on a synchronous line after every *write*(2). (Does not apply to the 3B2.)

stappl (-stappl)　　use application mode (use line mode) on a synchronous line. (Does not apply to the 3B2.)

Hardware Flow Control Modes

rtsxoff (-rtsxoff)　enable (disable) RTS hardware flow control on input.

ctsxon (-ctsxon)　　enable (disable) CTS hardware flow control on output.

dterxoff (-dterxoff)
　　　　　　　　　　　　enable (disable) DTER hardware flow control on input.

rlsdxon (-rlsdxon)　enable (disable) RLSD hardware flow control on output.

isxoff (-isxoff)　　enable (disable) isochronous hardware flow control on input.

Clock Modes

`xcibrg`	get transmit clock from internal baud rate generator.
`xctset`	get the transmit clock from transmitter signal element timing (DCE source) lead, CCITT V.24 circuit 114, EIA-232-D pin 15.
`xcrset`	get transmit clock from receiver signal element timing (DCE source) lead, CCITT V.24 circuit 115, EIA-232-D pin 17.
`rcibrg`	get receive clock from internal baud rate generator.
`rctset`	get receive clock from transmitter signal element timing (DCE source) lead, CCITT V.24 circuit 114, EIA-232-D pin 15.
`rcrset`	get receive clock from receiver signal element timing (DCE source) lead, CCITT V.24 circuit 115, EIA-232-D pin 17.
`tsetcoff`	transmitter signal element timing clock not provided.
`tsetcrc`	output receive clock on transmitter signal element timing (DTE source) lead, CCITT V.24 circuit 113, EIA-232-D pin 24, clock source.
`tsetcxc`	output transmit clock on transmitter signal element timing (DTE source) lead, CCITT V.24 circuit 113, EIA-232-D pin 24, clock source.
`rsetcoff`	receiver signal element timing clock not provided.
`rsetcrc`	output receive clock on receiver signal element timing (DTE source) lead, CCITT V.24 circuit 128, no EIA-232-D pin, clock source.
`rsetcxc`	output transmit clock on receiver signal element timing (DTE source) lead, CCITT V.24 circuit 128, no EIA-232-D pin, clock source.

Control Assignments

control-character c	set *control-character* to *c*, where *control-character* is **intr**, **quit**, **erase**, **kill**, **eof**, **eol**, **eol2**, **swtch**, **start**, **stop**, **susp**, **dsusp**, **rprnt**, **flush**, **werase**, **lnext min**, **ctab**, **time**, or **brk**) [**ctab** is used with **-stappl**; **min** and **time** are used with **-icanon**; see **termio**(7)]. If *c* is preceded by an (escaped from the shell) caret (^), then the value used is the corresponding CTRL character (for example, "^d" is a CTRL-**d**); "^?" is interpreted as DEL and "^-" is interpreted as undefined.
`line` *i*	set line discipline to *i* (0 < *i* < 127).

Combination Modes

evenp or **parity**	enable **parenb** and **cs7**.
-evenp, or **-parity**	disable **parenb**, and set **cs8**.
even (**-even**)	Same as **evenp** (**-evenp**).
oddp	enable **parenb**, **cs7**, and **parodd**.
-oddp	disable **parenb** and **parodd**, and set **cs8**.
odd (**-odd**)	Same as **oddp** (**-oddp**).
spacep	enable **parenb**, **cs7**, and **parext**.
-spacep	disable **parenb** and **parext**, and set **cs8**.
markp	enable **parenb**, **cs7**, **parodd**, and **parext**.
-markp	disable **parenb**, **parodd**, and **parext**, and set **cs8**.
raw (**-raw** or **cooked**)	
	enable (disable) raw input and output (no ERASE, KILL, INTR, QUIT, SWTCH, EOT, or output post processing).
nl (**-nl**)	unset (set) **icrnl**, **onlcr**. In addition **-nl** unsets **inlcr**, **igncr**, **ocrnl**, and **onlret**.
lcase (**-lcase**)	set (unset) **xcase**, **iuclc**, and **olcuc**.
LCASE (**-LCASE**)	same as **lcase** (**-lcase**).
tabs (**-tabs** or **tab3**)	
	preserve (expand to spaces) tabs when printing.
ek	reset ERASE and KILL characters back to normal **#** and **@**.
sane	resets all modes to some reasonable values.
term	set all modes suitable for the terminal type *term*, where *term* is one of **tty33**, **tty37**, **vt05**, **tn300**, **ti700**, or **tek**.
async	set normal asynchronous communications where clock settings are **xcibrg**, **rcibrg**, **tsetcoff** and **rsetcoff**.
litout (**-litout**)	Disable (enable) **parenb**, **istrip**, and **opost**, and set **cs8** (**cs7**).
pass8 (**-pass8**)	Disable (enable) **parenb** and **istrip**, and set **cs8** (**cs7**).
crt	Set options for a CRT (**echoe**, **echoctl**, and, if >= 1200 baud, **echoke**.)
dec	Set all modes suitable for Digital Equipment Corp. operating systems users (**ERASE**, **KILL**, and **INTR** characters to **^?**, **^U**, and **^C**, **decctlq**, and **crt**.)

Window Size

rows *n*	set window size to *n* rows.
columns *n*	set window size to *n* columns.
cols *n*	An alias for **columns** *n*.
ypixels *n*	set vertical window size to *n* pixels.
xpixels *n*	set horizontal window size to *n* pixels.

SEE ALSO

tabs(1)

ioctl(2) in the *Programmer's Reference Manual*

termio(7), **termiox**(7) in the *System Administrator's Reference Manual*

NAME

sttydefs – maintain line settings and hunt sequences for TTY ports

SYNOPSIS

/usr/sbin/sttydefs –a *ttylabel* [–b] [–n *nextlabel*] [–i *initial-flags*] [–f *final-flags*]

/usr/sbin/sttydefs –l [*ttylabel*]

/usr/sbin/sttydefs –r *ttylabel*

DESCRIPTION

sttydefs is an administrative command that maintains the line settings and hunt sequences for the system's TTY ports by making entries in and deleting entries from the /etc/ttydefs file.

sttydefs with a –a or –r option may be invoked only by a privileged user. sttydefs with –l may be invoked by any user on the system.

The options have the following meanings:

–l   If a *ttylabel* is specified, sttydefs will display the record from /etc/ttydefs whose TTY label matches the specified *ttylabel*. If no *ttylabel* is specified, sttydefs will display the entire contents of /etc/ttydefs. sttydefs will verify that each entry it displays is correct and that the entry's *nextlabel* field references an existing *ttylabel*.

–a *ttylabel* Adds a record to the ttydefs file, using *ttylabel* as its label. The following describes the effect of the –b, –n, –i, or –f options when used in conjunction with the –a option:

–b   Specifies that autobaud should be enabled. Autobaud allows the system to set the line speed of a given TTY port to the line speed of the device connected to the port without the user's intervention.

–n *nextlabel* Specifies the value to be used in the *nextlabel* field in /etc/ttydefs. If this option is not specified, sttydefs will set *nextlabel* equal to *ttylabel*.

–i *initial-flags* Specifies the value to be used in the *initial-flags* field in /etc/ttydefs. *initial-flags* must be in a format recognized by the stty command. These flags are used by ttymon when searching for the correct baud rate. They are set prior to writing the prompt.

               If this option is not specified, sttydefs will set *initial-flags* equal to the termio(7) flag 9600.

–f *final-flags* Specifies the value to be used in the *final-flags* field in /etc/ttydefs. *final-flags* must be in a format recognized by the stty command. *final-flags* are the termio(7) settings used by ttymon after receiving a successful connection request and immediately before invoking the service on the port. If this option is not specified, sttydefs will set *final-flags* equal to the termio(7) flags 9600 and sane.

-r *ttylabel*   Removes any record in the **ttydefs** file that has *ttylabel* as its
                  label.

OUTPUT

If successful, **sttydefs** will exit with a status of 0. **sttydefs -l** will generate
the requested information and send it to the standard output.

EXAMPLES

The following command will list all the entries in the **ttydefs** file and print an
error message for each invalid entry that is detected.

```
sttydefs -l
```

The following shows a command that requests information for a single label and
its output:

```
# sttydefs -l 9600

------------------------------------------------------------------
9600:9600 hupcl erase ^h:9600 sane ixany tab3 hupcl erase ^h::4800
------------------------------------------------------------------

ttylabel:       9600
initial flags:  9600 hupcl erase ^h
final flags:    9600 sane ixany tab3 hupcl erase ^h
autobaud:       no
nextlabel:      4800
```

The following sequence of commands will add the labels **1200**, **2400**, **4800**, and
9600 and put them in a circular list:

```
sttydefs -a 1200 -n 2400 -i 1200 -f "1200 sane"
sttydefs -a 2400 -n 4800 -i 2400 -f "2400 sane"
sttydefs -a 4800 -n 9600 -i 4800 -f "4800 sane"
sttydefs -a 9600 -n 1200 -i 9600 -f "9600 sane"
```

FILES

/etc/ttydefs

SEE ALSO

System Administrator's Guide, "Terminal Line Settings."

NAME

su – become super-user or another user

SYNOPSIS

su [–] [*name* [*arg* ...]]

DESCRIPTION

su allows one to become another user without logging off. The default user *name* is root (that is, super-user).

To use su, the appropriate password must be supplied (unless one is already root). If the password is correct, su will execute a new shell with the real and effective user and group IDs and supplementary group list set to that of the specified user. The new shell will be the optional program named in the shell field of the specified user's password file entry [see passwd(4)] or /usr/bin/sh if none is specified [see sh(1)]. To restore normal user ID privileges, type an EOF character (CTRL-d) to the new shell.

Any additional arguments given on the command line are passed to the program invoked as the shell. When using programs such as sh, an *arg* of the form –c *string* executes *string* via the shell and an arg of –r gives the user a restricted shell.

The following statements are true only if the optional program named in the shell field of the specified user's password file entry is like sh. If the first argument to su is a –, the environment will be changed to what would be expected if the user actually logged in as the specified user. This is done by invoking the program used as the shell with an *arg0* value whose first character is –, thus causing first the system's profile (/etc/profile) and then the specified user's profile (.profile in the new HOME directory) to be executed. Otherwise, the environment is passed along with the possible exception of $PATH, which is set to /sbin:/usr/sbin:/usr/bin:/etc for root. Note that if the optional program used as the shell is /usr/bin/sh, the user's .profile can check *arg0* for –sh or –su to determine if it was invoked by login or su, respectively. If the user's program is other than /usr/bin/sh, then .profile is invoked with an *arg0* of –*program* by both login and su.

All attempts to become another user using su are logged in the log file /var/adm/sulog.

EXAMPLES

To become user bin while retaining your previously exported environment, execute:

        su bin

To become user bin but change the environment to what would be expected if bin had originally logged in, execute:

        su – bin

To execute *command* with the temporary environment and permissions of user bin, type:

        su – bin –c "*command args*"

FILES

`/etc/passwd`	system's password file
`/etc/profile`	system's profile
`$HOME/.profile`	user's profile
`/var/adm/sulog`	log file
`/etc/default/su`	the default parameters that live here are:

           SULOG: If defined, all attempts to **su** to
                         another user are logged in the indicated file.

           CONSOLE: If defined, all attempts to **suroot**
                         are logged on the console.

           PATH: Default path.

           SUPATH: Default path for a user invoking **suroot**.

SEE ALSO

       env(1), login(1), sh(1) in the *User's Reference Manual*.
       passwd(4), profile(4), environ(5) in the *Programmer's Reference Manual*.

NAME

    `sulogin` – access single-user mode

SYNOPSIS

    `sulogin`

DESCRIPTION

    `sulogin` is automatically invoked by **init** when the system is first started. It prompts the user to type the root password to enter system maintenance mode (single-user mode) or to type EOF (typically CTRL-d) for normal startup (multi-user mode). `sulogin` should never be directly invoked by the user.

FILES

    `/sbin/sulogin`

SEE ALSO

    init(1M) in the *System Administrator's Reference Manual.*

NAME

　　sum – print checksum and block count of a file

SYNOPSIS

　　sum [−**r**] *file*

DESCRIPTION

　　sum calculates and prints a 16-bit checksum for the named file, and also prints the number of 512 byte blocks in the file. It is typically used to look for bad spots, or to validate a file communicated over some transmission line. The option −**r** causes an alternate algorithm to be used in computing the checksum.

SEE ALSO

　　wc(1).

DIAGNOSTICS

　　''Read error'' is indistinguishable from end of file on most devices; check the block count.

NAME

sum – calculate a checksum for a file

SYNOPSIS

/usr/ucb/sum *filename*

DESCRIPTION

sum calculates and displays a 16-bit checksum for the named file, and also displays the size of the file in kilobytes. It is typically used to look for bad spots, or to validate a file communicated over some transmission line. The checksum is calculated by an algorithm which may yield different results on machines with 16-bit ints and machines with 32-bit ints, so it cannot always be used to validate that a file has been transferred between machines with different-sized ints.

SEE ALSO

wc(1), sum(1) in the *User's Reference Manual*

DIAGNOSTICS

Read error is indistinguishable from EOF on most devices; check the block count.

NOTES

Obsolescent.

NAME

swap – swap administrative interface

SYNOPSIS

/usr/sbin/swap −a *swapname swaplow swaplen*
/usr/sbin/swap −d *swapname swaplow*
/usr/sbin/swap −l [−s]
/usr/sbin/swap −s

DESCRIPTION

swap provides a method of adding, deleting, and monitoring the system swap areas used by the memory manager. The following options are recognized:

−a   Add the specified swap area. *swapname* is the name of the block special partition, e.g., /dev/dsk/*, where the value of * is machine dependent, or a regular file. *swaplow* is the offset in 512-byte blocks into the partition where the swap area should begin. *swaplen* is the length of the swap area in 512-byte blocks. This option can only be used by the super-user. If additional swap areas are added, it is normally done by a system start up routine in /etc/rc2.d when going into multi-user mode.

−d   Delete the specified swap area. *swapname* is the name of block special partition, e.g., /dev/dsk/c1d0s1 or a regular file. *swaplow* is the offset in 512-byte blocks into the swap area to be deleted. Using this option marks the swap area as "INDEL" (in the process of being deleted). The system will not allocate any new blocks from the area, and will try to free swap blocks from it. The area will remain in use until all blocks from it are freed. This option can be used only by the super-user.

−l   List the status of all the swap areas. The output has five columns:

path   The path name for the swap area.

dev   The major/minor device number in decimal if it is a block special device; zeros otherwise.

swaplo The *swaplow* value for the area in 512-byte blocks.

blocks The *swaplen* value for the area in 512-byte blocks.

free   The number of free 512-byte blocks in the area. If the swap area is being deleted, the word INDEL will be printed to the right of this number.

−s   Print the following information about total swap space usage:

allocated   The amount of swap space (in 512-byte blocks) allocated to private pages.

reserved   The number of swap space (in 512-bytes blocks) not currently allocated, but claimed by memory mappings that have not yet created private pages.

used   The total amount of swap space, in 512-byte blocks, that is either allocated or reserved.

        `available`   The total swap space, in 512-byte blocks, that is currently available for future reservation and allocation.

WARNINGS

No check is done to see if a swap area being added overlaps with an existing file system.

NAME

sync – update the super block

SYNOPSIS

sync

DESCRIPTION

sync executes the sync system primitive. If the system is to be stopped, sync must be called to insure file system integrity. It will flush all previously unwritten system buffers out to disk, thus assuring that all file modifications up to that point will be saved. See sync(2) for details.

NOTE

If you have done a write to a file on a remote machine in a Remote File Sharing environment, you cannot use sync to force buffers to be written out to disk on the remote machine. sync will only write local buffers to local disks.

SEE ALSO

sync(2) in the *Programmer's Reference Manual*

NAME

    sysadm – visual interface to perform system administration

SYNOPSIS

    sysadm [*menu name* | *task name*]

DESCRIPTION

    This command, when invoked without an argument, presents a set of menus that help you do administrative work. If you specify a menu or task on the command line, one of two things happens: if the requested menu or task is unique, it is immediately displayed; if the menu or task is not unique, a menu of choices is displayed.

    The **sysadm** command may be given a password. To assign a password, use the **password** task under the **system_setup** menu. To change a password after it is assigned, use the **password** command.

    When you invoke **sysadm** on a computer running UNIX System V Release 4, the main menu (a collection of twelve menus) appears as follows:

```
                    UNIX System V Administration

backup_service    - Backup Scheduling, Setup, and Control

diagnostics       - Diagnosing System Errors

file_systems      - File System Creation, Checking and Mounting

machine           - Machine Configuration, Display and Powerdown

network_services  - Network Services Administration

ports             - Port Access Services and Monitors

printers          - Printer Configuration and Services

restore_service   - Restore From Backup Data

software          - Software Installation and Removal

storage_devices   - Storage Device Operations and Definitions

system_setup      - System Name, Date/Time and Initial Password Setup

users             - User Login and Group Administration
```

    If you install software packages other than those delivered with UNIX System V Release 4, you will also see a menu entry called **Administration for Available Applications** (or **applications**) under which those packages are found.

    All menu items for pre-Release 4 optional add-on packages other than those listed on the main menu under **packagmgmt** now appear under **old_sysadm** on the main menu. (The entry **old_sysadm** will appear on the main menu only if pre-Release 4 packages have been installed.)

The rest of this section describes each menu listed on the main menu.

Backup Service Management

> This menu lists seven areas of administrative support for the backup services.
>
> **backup (Start Backup Jobs)**
>> This task starts the backup scheduled for the current day based on the default backup control table or the specified backup control table.
>
> **history (Backup History Management)**
>> This task lets you display reports of backup operations that have completed successfully.
>
> **reminder (Schedule Backup Reminder)**
>> This menu lets you schedule messages that will be sent to you to remind you to perform backups.
>
> **respond (Respond to Backup Job Prompts)**
>> This task lets you reply to operator prompts from backup jobs.
>
> **schedule (Schedule Automatic Backups)**
>> This menu lets you schedule backups so that they will run automatically. Because the backups are scheduled to run automatically and are not associated with a terminal, you must choose to run them in either automatic or background mode.
>
> **setup (Backup Control Table Management)**
>> This menu lets you modify or display backup registers.
>
> **status (Backup Status Management)**
>> This menu lets you manage backup requests that are in progress.

Manage File Systems

> This menu provides eleven tasks that are part of file system management. These tasks include checking for and repairing errors on a specific file system, monitoring disk usage for all file systems, tracking files based on age or size, listing all file systems currently mounted on your system, creating a new file system, and mounting and unmounting file systems.
>
> **check (Check a File System)**
>> This task lets you check a file system for errors and fix them, either interactively or automatically.
>
> **defaults (Manage Defaults)**
>> This task identifies the percentage of hard disks currently occupied by files.
>
> **diskuse (Display Disk Usage)**
>> This task identifies the percentage of hard disks currently occupied by files. The information is presented as a list, organized by file system name.

`display` (Display Installed Types)
> This task displays a list of the file system types installed on your system.

`fileage` (List Files by Age)
> This task lets you print the names of old files in the directory you specify. If you do not specify an age, files older than 90 days are listed.

`filesize` (List Files by Size)
> This task lets you print the names of the largest files in a specific directory. If you do not request a particular number of files, the ten largest files are listed.

`identify` (Identify File System Type)
> This task tries to determine the type of any unmounted file system without damaging the data or the medium of the file system.

`list` (List Mounted File Systems)
> This task lets you list all file systems mounted on your computer.

`make` (Create a File System)
> This task lets you create a new file system on a removable medium which can then store data you do not want to keep on hard disk. When mounted, the file system has all the properties of a file kept on hard disk.

`mount` (Mount a File System)
> This task lets you mount a file system located on a removable medium and make it available to users on your system. The file system may be unmounted using the **unmount** task.
>
> WARNING: (1) **mount** does not prevent you from mounting a file system on a directory that's not empty. (2) Do not remove the medium while the file system is still mounted.

`unmount` (Unmount a File System)
> This task lets you unmount a file system and thus lets you remove the medium on which it resides. Both **/** and **/usr** are excluded because unmounting these file systems would cause a system crash. Once a file system has been unmounted, you may remove the medium on which it resided.

Machine Configuration Display and Powerdown

This menu provides seven tasks for functions such as turning off the computer, rebooting it, and changing to firmware mode.

`configuration` (System Configuration Display)
> This task allows you to check the current configuration of the system.

`shutdown` (Stops All Running Programs and Turns Off Machine)
> This task lets you stop all running programs, close any open files, write out information (such as directory information) to disk, and then bring the system down.

reboot (Stops All Running Programs and Reboots Machine)
> This task lets you reboot the computer after all running programs have been stopped, any open files have been closed, and any necessary information (such as directory information) has been written out to disk, This procedure can be used to resolve some types of system trouble, such as a process that cannot be killed.

whos on (Displays List of Users Logged onto Machine)
> This task prints the login ID, terminal device number, and sign-on time of all users who are currently using the computer.

Network Services Management

This menu provides four functions for managing networks.

basic_networking (Basic Networking Utilities Management)
> This menu allows you to set up administrative files for UUCP utilities.

remote_files (Distributed File System Management)
> This menu allows you to set up administrative files for the Remote File Sharing (RFS) Utilities or the Network File Sharing (NFS) Utilities.

selection (Network Selection Management)
> This menu allows you to set up administrative files for Network Selection; that is, for dynamically selecting a transport protocol.

name_to_address (Machine and Service Address Management)
> This menu allows you to define machine addresses and service port information for the protocols that exist on the machine.

Peripheral Setup

This menu allows you to setup peripherals that were supported in pre-SVR4.0

Service Access Management

This menu provides functions for managing service access to the system.

port_monitors (Port Monitor Management)
> This menu provides functions for managing port monitors under the Service Access Facility. Specifically, it allows you to add, disable, enable, list, modify, remove, start, and stop port monitors.

port_services (Port Service Management)
> This menu provides functions for managing port services provides by port monitors. Specifically, it allows you to add, disable, enable, list, modify, and remove port services.

quick-terminal
> (Quick terminal Setup) This menu allows a user to easily setup a terminal and its speed.

`tty_settings` (Terminal Line Setting Management)
> This menu provides functions for managing tty line settings. Specifically, it allows you to create new tty settings and hunt sequences, and to display (on your screen) and remove those settings. To modify an existing tty line setting, remove the entry for it and then recreate it, including the modifications.

Line Printer Services Configuration and Operation

This menu provides functions for managing the printers and print services you can make available to your users through the LP print service. Specifically, this menu can help you do the following: set up and control the LP print service; start and stop the print service, check the status of the print service and, if necessary, stop and start it; add new printers to your system, and change the configuration of existing printers; add, change, and mount forms, add, change, and change filters, and monitor users' print requests.

`classes` (Manage Classes of Related Printers)
> This menu allows you to add new classes and to display a list of the current classes.

`filters` (Manage Filters for Special Processing)
> This menu allows you to manage filters for special processing.

`forms` (Manage Pre-Printed Forms)
> This menu allows you to manage pre-printed forms.

`operations` (Perform Daily Printer Service Operations)
> This menu allows you to perform daily printer operations such as enabling printers, starting the print service, and mounting forms.

`printers` (Configure Printers for the Printer Service)
> This menu allows you to configure printers for the LP print service.

`priorities` (Assign Print Queue Priorities to Users)
> This menu allows you to assign priority in the queue for print requests.

`requests` (Manage Active Print Requests)
> This menu allows you to hold and release pending print requests, to move print requests to new destinations, and to cancel print requests.

`status` (Display Status of Printer Service)
> This menu allows you to display the current status of the LP print service.

`systems` (Configure Connections to Remote Systems)
> This menu allows you to configure the connections between your LP print service system and any other LP print service.

Restore Service Management

This menu provides tasks for restoring directories, files, file systems, and data partitions from archive volumes.

operator (Set/Display the Restore Operator)
> This task lets you set up and display the restore operator.

respond (Respond to Restore Job Prompts)
> This task lets you respond to restore job prompts.

restore (Restore from Backup Archives)
> This task lets you request the restoration of files, directories, file systems, and data partitions from an archived version.

status (Modify/Report Pending Restore Request Status)
> This menu lets you display and change the status of pending restore requests.

Schedule Automatic Task

This menu permits users to modify the **cron** file. The **cron** file allows users to request jobs to be run at specific times.

add   Allows a user to add a **cron** job.

change
> Allows a user to change an existing **cron** job.

delete
> Allows a user to delete cron job.

display
> Allows a user to display **cron** jobs.

Software Installation and Information Management

The tasks in this menu provide functions for software package installation, removal, and management of information pertaining to software packages. They include the ability to install and remove packages, and to check the accuracy of package installation. In addition, they include the ability to set installation defaults, store interactions with a particular package, store a package without actually installing it, and to list all installed packages.

check (Checks Accuracy of Installation)
> This task lets you check installed software packages for consistency, correct for inconsistencies, check for hidden files, and check the contents of files which are likely to have changed.

defaults (Sets Installation Defaults)
> This task allows you to decide, ahead of time, the way that the system should respond to an installation problem.

install (Installs Software Packages)
> This task lets you install software packages onto a spool, a hard disk, or a floppy diskette, and select the method that the system will use to respond to installation problems.

interact (Stores Interactions with Package)
> This task allows you to interact with the software installation process.

list (Displays Information about Packages)
> This task shows you the software packages that are installed on your system and tells you the name, location, and category of each.

read_in (Stores Packages Without Installing)
> This task lets you read in software packages without installing them.

remove (Removes Packages)
> This task lets you remove installed software packages.

Storage Device Operations and Definitions

This menu contains tasks for getting descriptions of device aliases and attributes and for assigning device groups.

descriptions (Device Alias and Attribute Management)
> This menu contains tasks for listing, adding, removing, and modifying device descriptions and attributes. This menu also provides access to device reservation services.

groups (Device Group Management)
> This menu provides access to tasks that let you list and administer device groups and their membership lists.

System Name, Date Time and Initial Password Setup

This menu lets you set up your machine. The tasks in this menu include setting the system date and time, setting the node name of your system, doing initial system setup, and assigning passwords to administrative logins on the system.

datetime (System Date and Time Information)
> This task lets you tell the computer the date, time, time zone, and whether you observe Daylight Savings Time (DST). It is normally run once when the machine is first set up. If you observe DST, the computer automatically starts to observe it in the spring and returns to standard time in the fall. The machine must be turned off and turned back on again to guarantee that ALL times are reported correctly. Most times are correct the next time a user logs in.

nodename (System Name and Network Node Name of the Machine)
> This task lets you change the node name and system name of this machine. These names are used by various communications networks to identify this machine.

password (Assigns Administrative Login Passwords)
> This task lets you assign passwords to administrative logins.

setup (Sets up System Information for First Time)
> This task lets you define the first login, set the initial passwords on administration logins, and set the time zone for your location.

User Login and Group Administration

This menu lets you manage the user IDs and groups on your machine. Tasks include the ability to add, modify, and delete users or groups defined on your machine. You can place users in groups so that they can share access to files belonging to members of the group but protect these files from access by members of other groups. In addition, you can set defaults that are used for subsequent user definitions on your machine, and you can define or redefine user password information.

add (Adds Users or Groups)
> This task lets you define either a new user or a new group on your system.

defaults (Defines Defaults for Adding Users)
> This task lets you change some of the default values used when the **add user** task creates a new login. Changing the default values does not affect any existing logins; it affects only those added subsequently.

list (Lists Users or Groups)
> This task lets you examine the attributes of the users and groups on your system.

modify (Modifies Attributes of Users or Groups)
> This task lets you modify either a user definition or a group definition on your system.

password ((Re-)defines User Password Information)
> This task lets you define or change a user's password.

remove (Removes Users or Groups)
> This task lets you remove a user from your system.

DIAGNOSTICS

The **sysadm** command exits with one of the following values:

0　　Normal exit.

2　　Invalid command syntax. Usage message of the **sysadm** command is displayed.

4　　The menu or task name given as an argument does not exist.

5　　The menu name given as an argument is an empty placeholder menu, and therefore not available for use.

7　　The **sysadm** command is not available because it cannot invoke **fmli**. (The FMLI package may be corrupt or it may not have been installed.)

EXAMPLES

sysadm nodename

NOTES

The Release 3 version of the **sysadm** command scrolled menus down the terminal screen. The Release 4 version of **sysadm**, however, displays menus in "pop-up" windows.

Pre-Release 4 add-on packages other than those listed under `packagmgmt` are listed under `old_sysadm`.

SEE ALSO

`checkfsys`(1M), `delsysadm`(1M), `edsysadm`(1M), `makefsys`(1M), `mountfsys`(1M), `powerdown`(1M), `setup`(1M), `umountfsys`(1M)

NAME

syslogd – log system messages

SYNOPSIS

/usr/sbin/syslogd [–d] [–f*configfile*] [–m *interval*]

DESCRIPTION

syslogd reads and forwards system messages to the appropriate log files and/or
users, depending upon the priority of a message and the system facility from
which it originates. The configuration file /etc/syslog.conf [see
syslog.conf(5)] controls where messages are forwarded. syslogd logs a mark
(timestamp) message every *interval* minutes (default 20) at priority LOG_INFO to
the facility whose name is given as mark in the syslog.conf file.

A system message consists of a single line of text, which may be prefixed with a
priority code number enclosed in angle-brackets (< >); priorities are defined in
sys/syslog.h.

syslogd reads from the STREAMS log driver, /dev/log, from any transport provider specified in /etc/netconfig, /etc/net/*transport*/hosts, and
/etc/net/*transport*/services, and from the special device /dev/klog (for kernel
messages).

syslogd reads the configuration file when it starts up, and again whenever it receives a HUP signal, at which time it also closes all files it has open, re-reads its
configuration file, and then opens only the log files that are listed in that file.
syslogd exits when it receives a TERM signal.

As it starts up, syslogd creates the file /etc/syslog.pid, if possible, containing
its process ID (PID).

The following options are available:

–d   Turn on debugging.

–f*configfile*   Specify an alternate configuration file.

–m *interval*   Specify an interval, in minutes, between mark messages.

FILES

/etc/syslog.conf   configuration file
/etc/syslog.pid   process ID
/dev/log   STREAMS log driver
/etc/netconfig   specifies the transport providers available on the system
/etc/net/*transport*/hosts
                    network hosts for each transport
/etc/net/*transport*/services
                    network services for each transport

SEE ALSO

logger(1), syslog(3), syslog.conf(4)

log(7) in the *System Administrator's Reference Manual*

NAME

tabs – set tabs on a terminal

SYNOPSIS

tabs [*tabspec*] [-T*type*] [+m*n*]

DESCRIPTION

tabs sets the tab stops on the user's terminal according to the tab specification *tabspec*, after clearing any previous settings. The user's terminal must have remotely settable hardware tabs.

tabspec   Four types of tab specification are accepted for *tabspec*. They are described below: canned (*–code*), repetitive (*–n*), arbitrary (*n1,n2, . . .*), and file (*––file*). If no *tabspec* is given, the default value is **–8**, that is, UNIX system "standard" tabs. The lowest column number is 1. Note that for **tabs**, column 1 always refers to the leftmost column on a terminal, even one whose column markers begin at 0, for example, the DASI 300, DASI 300s, and DASI 450.

–code   Use one of the codes listed below to select a *canned* set of tabs. The legal codes and their meanings are as follows:

-a   1,10,16,36,72
      Assembler, IBM S/370, first format

-a2   1,10,16,40,72
       Assembler, IBM S/370, second format

-c   1,8,12,16,20,55
      COBOL, normal format

-c2   1,6,10,14,49
       COBOL compact format (columns 1-6 omitted). Using this code, the first typed character corresponds to card column 7, one space gets you to column 8, and a tab reaches column 12. Files using this tab setup should include a format specification as follows (see **fspec**(4)):

              <:t–c2 m6 s66 d:>

-c3   1,6,10,14,18,22,26,30,34,38,42,46,50,54,58,62,67
       COBOL compact format (columns 1-6 omitted), with more tabs than **–c2**. This is the recommended format for COBOL. The appropriate format specification is [see **fspec**(4)]:

              <:t–c3 m6 s66 d:>

-f   1,7,11,15,19,23
      FORTRAN

-p   1,5,9,13,17,21,25,29,33,37,41,45,49,53,57,61
      PL/I

-s   1,10,55
      SNOBOL

-u   1,12,20,44
            UNIVAC 1100 Assembler

-n   A *repetitive* specification requests tabs at columns 1+n, 1+2∗n, etc. Of particular importance is the value **8**: this represents the UNIX system "standard" tab setting, and is the most likely tab setting to be found at a terminal. Another special case is the value **0**, implying no tabs at all.

n1 , n2 , . . .
            The *arbitrary* format permits the user to type any chosen set of numbers, separated by commas, in ascending order. Up to 40 numbers are allowed. If any number (except the first one) is preceded by a plus sign, it is taken as an increment to be added to the previous value. Thus, the formats **1,10,20,30**, and **1,10,+10,+10** are considered identical.

--*file*   If the name of a *file* is given, **tabs** reads the first line of the file, searching for a format specification [see **fspec**(4)]. If it finds one there, it sets the tab stops according to it, otherwise it sets them as **-8**. This type of specification may be used to make sure that a tabbed file is printed with correct tab settings, and would be used with the **pr** command:

            tabs -- *file*; **pr** *file*

Any of the following also may be used; if a given flag occurs more than once, the last value given takes effect:

-T*type*   **tabs** usually needs to know the type of terminal in order to set tabs and always needs to know the type to set margins. *type* is a name listed in **term**(5). If no **-T** flag is supplied, **tabs** uses the value of the environment variable **TERM**. If **TERM** is not defined in the *environment* [see **environ**(5)], **tabs** tries a sequence that will work for many terminals.

+m*n*   The margin argument may be used for some terminals. It causes all tabs to be moved over n columns by making column $n+1$ the left margin. If **+m** is given without a value of n, the value assumed is **10**. For a TermiNet, the first value in the tab list should be **1**, or the margin will move even further to the right. The normal (leftmost) margin on most terminals is obtained by **+m0**. The margin for most terminals is reset only when the **+m** flag is given explicitly.

Tab and margin setting is performed via the standard output.

EXAMPLES

tabs -a   example using *–code* (*canned* specification) to set tabs to the settings required by the IBM assembler: columns 1, 10, 16, 36, 72.

tabs -8   example of using *–n* (*repetitive* specification), where n is **8**, causes tabs to be set every eighth position:
                  1+(1∗8), 1+(2∗8), . . . which evaluate to columns 9, 17, . . .

tabs 1,8,36   example of using *n1 , n2 , . . .* (*arbitrary* specification) to set tabs at columns 1, 8, and 36.

tabs --$HOME/fspec.list/att4425
> example of using --*file* (*file* specification) to indicate that tabs should be set according to the first line of $HOME/fspec.list/att4425 [see fspec(4)].

DIAGNOSTICS

illegal tabs	when arbitrary tabs are ordered incorrectly
illegal increment	when a zero or missing increment is found in an arbitrary specification
unknown tab code	when a *canned* code cannot be found
can't open	if --*file* option used, and file can't be opened
file indirection	if --*file* option used and the specification in that file points to yet another file. Indirection of this form is not permitted

SEE ALSO

newform(1), pr(1), tput(1)

fspec(4), terminfo(4), environ(5), term(5) in the *System Administrator's Reference Manual*

NOTES

There is no consistency among different terminals regarding ways of clearing tabs and setting the left margin.

tabs clears only 20 tabs (on terminals requiring a long sequence), but is willing to set 64.

The *tabspec* used with the **tabs** command is different from the one used with the **newform** command. For example, **tabs -8** sets every eighth position; whereas **newform -i-8** indicates that tabs are set every eighth position.

NAME

tail – deliver the last part of a file

SYNOPSIS

tail [± *number* **lbcr**] [*file*]
tail [**-lbcr**] [*file*]
tail [± *number* **lbcf**] [*file*]
tail [**-lbcf**] [*file*]

DESCRIPTION

tail copies the named file to the standard output beginning at a designated place. If no file is named, the standard input is used.

Copying begins at distance +*number* from the beginning, or –*number* from the end of the input (if *number* is null, the value 10 is assumed). *Number* is counted in units of lines, blocks, or characters, according to the appended option **l**, **b**, or **c**. When no units are specified, counting is by lines.

With the **-f** (follow) option, if the input file is not a pipe, the program will not terminate after the line of the input file has been copied, but will enter an endless loop, wherein it sleeps for a second and then attempts to read and copy further records from the input file. Thus it may be used to monitor the growth of a file that is being written by some other process. For example, the command:

```
tail -f fred
```

will print the last ten lines of the file **fred**, followed by any lines that are appended to **fred** between the time **tail** is initiated and killed. As another example, the command:

```
tail -15cf fred
```

will print the last 15 characters of the file **fred**, followed by any lines that are appended to **fred** between the time **tail** is initiated and killed.

The **r** option copies lines from the specified starting point in the file in reverse order. The default for **r** is to print the entire file in reverse order.

The **r** and **f** options are mutually exclusive.

SEE ALSO

cat(1), head(1), more(1), pg(1), tail(1).

dd(1M) in the *System Administrator's Reference Manual*.

NOTES

Tails relative to the end of the file are stored in a buffer, and thus are limited in length. Various kinds of anomalous behavior may happen with character special files.

The **tail** command will only tail the last 4096 bytes of a file regardless of its line count.

NAME

talk – talk to another user

SYNOPSIS

talk *username* [*ttyname*]

DESCRIPTION

talk is a visual communication program that copies lines from your terminal to that of a user on the same or on another host. *username* is that user's login name.

The program is architecture dependent; it works only between machines of the same architecture.

If you want to talk to a user who is logged in more than once, the *ttyname* argument may be used to indicate the appropriate terminal name.

When first called, talk sends the message:

    Message from TalkDaemon@ *her_machine* at *time* ...
    talk: connection requested by *your_name@your_machine*
    talk: respond with: talk *your_name@your_machine*

to the user you want to talk to. At this point, the recipient of the message should reply by typing:

    talk *your_name@your_machine*

It does not matter from which machine the recipient replies, as long as the login name is the same. Once communication is established, the two parties may type simultaneously, with their output appearing in separate windows. Typing CTRL-l redraws the screen, while your erase, kill, and word kill characters will work in talk as normal. To exit, just type your interrupt character; talk then moves the cursor to the bottom of the screen and restores the terminal.

Permission to talk may be denied or granted by use of the **mesg**(1) command. At the outset talking is allowed. Certain commands, such as **pr**(1), disallow messages in order to prevent messy output.

FILES

/etc/hosts   to find the recipient's machine
/var/adm/utmp   to find the recipient's tty

SEE ALSO

mail(1), **mesg**(1), **pr**(1), **who**(1), **write**(1), **talkd**(1M)

NAME

   talkd, in.talkd – server for talk program

SYNOPSIS

   in.talkd

DESCRIPTION

   talkd is a server used by the talk(1) program. It listens at the UDP port indicated in the "talk" service description; see services(4). The actual conversation
   takes place on a TCP connection that is established by negotiation between the
   two machines involved.

SEE ALSO

   talk(1), inetd(1M), services(4)

NOTES

   The protocol is architecture dependent.

NAME

tape – magnetic tape maintenance

SYNOPSIS

tape [-csf8i] [-a *arg*] *command* [*device*]

DESCRIPTION

tape sends commands to and receives status from the tape subsystem. tape can communicate with QIC-24/QIC-02 cartridge tape drives and SCSI tape drives.

tape reads /etc/default/tape to find the default device name for sending commands and receiving status. For example, the following line in /etc/default/tape will cause tape to communicate with the QIC-24/QIC-02 cartridge tape device:

device = /dev/rmt/c0s0

If a device name is specified on the command line, it overrides the default device. tape queries the device to determine its device type. If the device does not respond to the query, for example if the cartridge tape driver is from an earlier release, tape will print a warning message and assume the device is a QIC-24/QIC-02 cartridge tape.

OPTIONS

You can explicitly specify the type of the device by using the device type flags, as follows:

-c   QIC-24/QIC-02 cartridge tape
-s   SCSI tape

COMMANDS

The following commands can be used with the various tape drivers supported under UNIX. The letters following each description indicate which drivers support each command:

A   All drivers
C   QIC-24/QIC-02 cartridge tape driver
S   SCSI tape driver

erase   Erase and retension the tape cartridge. (C,S)

reset   Reset tape controller and tape drive. Clears error conditions and returns tape subsystem to power-up state. (C,S)

reten   Retension tape cartridge. Should be used periodically to remedy slack tape problems. Tape slack can cause an unusually large number of tape errors. (A)

rewind   Rewind to beginning of tape. (A)

rfm   Wind tape forward to the next file mark. (C,S)

FILES
Devices:

> /dev/rmt/c0s0
> /dev/rmt/c0s0n
> /dev/rmt/c0s0r
> /dev/rmt/c0s0nr
> /dev/rmt/c0t3d0s0
>
> /etc/default/tape

Include files:

> /usr/include/sys/tape.h

SEE ALSO
cpio(1), dd(1), tar(1)

backup(1M), qt(7) restore(1M), xrestore(1M) in the *System Administrator's Reference Manual*

NOTES
The **reset** command can be used while the tape is busy with other operations. All other commands wait until the currently executing command has been completed before proceeding.

When you are using the non-rewinding tape device or the **tape** command **rfm**, the tape drive light remains on after the command has been completed, indicating that more operations may be performed on the tape. The **tape rewind** command may be used to clear this condition.

NAME
tapecntl – tape control for tape device

SYNOPSIS
tapecntl [–bluetrwv] [–f *arg*] [–p *arg*] [special]

DESCRIPTION
tapecntl will send the optioned commands to the tape device driver sub-device /dev/rmt/c0s0 for all options except the -e option (position), which will use sub-device /dev/rmt/c0s0n using the ioctl command function. Sub-device /dev/rmt/c0s0 provides a rewind on close capability, while /dev/rmt/c0s0n allows for closing of the device without rewind. Error messages will be written to standard error. special is the tape device, and it defaults to /dev/rmt/c0s0n if not specified.

Not all options are supported by all tape devices and tape device drivers.

The meaning of the options are:

-b   block length limits
Reads block length limits from the tape device and displays them.

-l   load tape
Loads the tape media to the tape device and positions the tape at BOT.

-u   unload tape
Unloads the tape media from the tape device. Depending on the device, unloading may include ejecting the cartridge.

-e   erase tape
Erasing the tape causes the erase bar to be activated while moving the tape from end to end, causing all data tracks to be erased in a single pass over the tape.

-t   retension tape
Retensioning the tape causes the tape to be moved from end to end, thereby repacking the tape with the proper tension across its length.

-r   reset tape device
Reset of the tape device initializes the tape controller registers and positions the tape at the beginning of the tape mark (BOT).

-w   rewind tape
Rewinding the tape will move the tape to the BOT.

-v   set variable length block mode
Sets the tape device to read and write variable length blocks.

-f[*n*]   set fixed length block mode
sets the tape device to read abd write in fixed length blocks of *n* bytes.

    −**p**[n]   position tape to "end of file" mark – n

               Positioning the tape command requires an integer argument. Positioning the tape will move the tape forward relative to its current position to the end of the specified file mark. The positioning option used with an argument of zero will be ignored. Illegal or out-of-range value arguments to the positioning command will leave the tape positioned at the end of the last valid file mark.

Options may be used individually or strung together with selected options being executed sequentially from left to right in the command line.

FILES

    `/usr/lib/tape/tapecntl`
    `/sbin/tapecntl`
    `/dev/rmt/c0s0n`
    `/dev/rmt/c0s0`

NOTES

    Exit codes and their meanings are as follows:

    exit (1)   device function could not initiate properly due to misconnected cables or poorly inserted tape cartridge.

    exit (2)   device function failed to complete properly due to unrecoverable error condition, either in the command setup or due to mechanical failure.

    exit (3)   device function failed due to the cartridge being write protected or to the lack of written data on the tape.

    exit (4)   device **/dev/rmt/c0s0n** or **/dev/rmt/c0s0** failed to open properly due to already being opened or claimed by another process.

NAME

tar – tape file archiver

SYNOPSIS

/usr/sbin/tar –c[**vwfbLkFhienAC**[#*s*]] *device block files tapesize incfile* . . .
/usr/sbin/tar –c[**vwfbLkXhienAC**[#*s*]] *device block files tapesize excfile* . . .
/usr/sbin/tar –r[**vwfbLkFhienAC**[#*s*]] *device block files tapesize incfile* . . .
/usr/sbin/tar –r[**vwfbLkXhienAC**[#*s*]] *device block files tapesize excfile* . . .
/usr/sbin/tar –t[**vfLXien**[#*s*]] *device* [*files* . . .] *excfile*
/usr/sbin/tar –u[**vwfbLkXhienAC**[#*s*]] *device block files tapesize excfile* . . .
/usr/sbin/tar –u[**vwfbLkFhienAC**[#*s*]] *device block files tapesize incfile* . . .
/usr/sbin/tar –x[**1movwfLXpienAC**[#*s*]] *device* [*files* .

DESCRIPTION

tar saves and restores files on magnetic tape. Its actions are controlled by a string of characters containing one option (**c**, **r**, **t**, **u**, or **x**), and possibly followed by one or more modifiers (**v**, **w**, **f**, **b**, **L**, **k**, **F**, **X**, **h**, **i**, **e**, **n**, **A**, **l**, **m**, **o**, **p**, and #*s*). Other arguments to the command are *files* (or directory names) specifying which files are to be dumped or restored. In all cases, appearance of a directory name refers to the files and (recursively) subdirectories of that directory.

The options are as follows:

-c   Create a new tape; writing begins at the beginning of the tape, instead of after the last file. The **-c** option implies the **-r** option.

-r   Replace. The named *files* are written on the end of the tape. The **-c** and **-u** options imply the **-r** option.

-t   Table. The names and other information for the specified files are listed each time that they occur on the tape. The listing is similar to the format produced by the **ls -l** command [see **ls**(1)]. If no *files* argument is given, all the names on the tape are listed.

-u   Update. The named *files* are added to the tape if they are not already there, or have been modified since last written on that tape. The **-u** option implies the **-r** option.

-x   Extract. The named *files* are extracted from the tape. If a named file matches a directory whose contents had been written onto the tape, this directory is (recursively) extracted. Use the file or directory's relative path when appropriate, or **tar** will not find a match. The owner, modification time, and mode are restored (if possible). If no *files* argument is given, the entire contents of the tape is extracted. Note that if several files with the same name are on the tape, the last one overwrites all earlier ones.

The modifiers below may be used in the order shown in the synopsis.

#*s*   This modifier determines the drive on which the tape is mounted (replace # with the drive number) and the speed of the drive (replace *s* with **1**, **m**, or **h** for low, medium or high). The modifier tells **tar** to use a drive other than the default drive, or the drive specified with the **-f** modifier. The defaults are listed in **/etc/default/tar**.

v   Verbose. Normally, **tar** does its work silently. The **v** (verbose) modifier causes it to print the name of each file it treats, preceded by the option. With the **-t** option, **v** gives more information about the tape entries than just the name.

w   What. This modifier causes **tar** to print the action to be taken, followed by the name of the file, and then wait for your confirmation. If a word beginning with **y** is given, the action is performed. Any other input means no. This is not valid with the **-t** option.

f   File. This causes **tar** to use the *device* argument as the name of the archive instead of the default. If the name of the file is **-**, **tar** writes to the standard output or reads from the standard input, whichever is appropriate. Thus, **tar** can be used as the head or tail of a pipeline. **tar** can also be used to move hierarchies with the command:

>   **cd** *fromdir***; tar cf - . | (cd** *todir***; tar xf -)**

b   Blocking Factor. This modifier causes **tar** to use the *block* argument as the blocking factor for tape records. The default is 20. This modifier should not be supplied when operating on regular archives or block special devices. It is mandatory however, when reading archives on raw magnetic tape archives (see **f** above). The block size is determined automatically when reading tapes created on block special devices (options **x** and **t**).

l   Link. This modifier causes **tar** to complain if it cannot resolve all of the links to the files being dumped. If the **l** modifier is not specified, no error messages are printed.

m   Modify. This modifier causes **tar** to not restore the modification times. The modification time of the file will be the time of extraction.

o   Ownership. This modifier causes extracted files to take on the user and group identifier of the user running the program, rather than those on tape. This is only valid with the **-x** option.

L   Follow symbolic links. This modifier causes symbolic links to be followed. By default, symbolic links are not followed.

k   This modifier uses the *tapesize* argument as the size in bytes per volume for non-tape devices (such as a floppy drive). A value of 0 for *tapesize* causes multi-volume mode to be disabled (interpreted as an infinite volume size). This modifier may be used with the **-c**, **-r**, and **-u** options.

F   This modifier uses the *incfile* argument as a file containing a list of named files (or directories) to be included on the tape. This modifier may only be used with the **-c**, **-r**, and **-u** options. This modifier may not be used with the **X** modifier.

X   This modifier uses the *excfile* argument as a file containing a list of named files (or directories) to be excluded. This modifier may not be used with the **F** modifier.

h   This modifier causes **tar** to follow symbolic links as if they were normal files or directories. Normally **tar** does not follow symbolic links. The **h** modifier may be used with the **-c**, **-r**, and **-u** options.

p   This modifier restores the named *file* arguments to their original modes, ignoring the present value returned by **umask** [see **umask**(2) in the *Programmer's Reference Manual*]. **setuid** and sticky bit information are also restored if the effective user ID is root. This modifier may only be used with the **-x** option.

i   This modifier causes **tar** to ignore directory checksum errors.

e   This modifier causes **tar** to quit when certain minor errors are encountered. Otherwise **tar** will continue when minor errors are encountered.

n   This modifier must be used when the *device* argument is for a non-tape device (for example, a floppy drive).

A   This modifier causes absolute pathnames for files to be suppressed, and may be used with the **-r**, **-c**, **-u**, and **-x** options. This causes all pathnames to be interpreted as relative to the current working directory.

C   This modifier, on output, sets a flag indicating that all regular files are compressed. On input, this modifier sets a flag to decompress all regular files.

FILES

/etc/default/tar

/tmp/tar*

/usr/lib/locale/*locale*/LC_MESSAGES/uxcore
        language-specific message file [See **LANG** on **environ**(5).]

SEE ALSO

ar(1), cpio(1), ls(1).
umask(2) in the *Programmer's Reference Manual*.

DIAGNOSTICS

Complains about tape read/write errors.
Complains if insufficient memory is available to hold the link tables.

NOTES

There is no way to ask for the *n*-th occurrence of a file.

The **-b** modifier should not be used with archives that are going to be updated. The current magnetic tape driver cannot backspace raw magnetic tape. If the archive is on a disk file, the **-b** modifier should not be used at all, because updating an archive stored on disk can destroy it.

The current limit on file name length is 100 characters.

You cannot restore a mulit-level archive created with UNIX System V Release 4 **tar** on a pre-Release 4 system. A false warning message that file permissions have changed will be issued.

NAME

tbl – format tables for **nroff** or **troff**

SYNOPSIS

/usr/ucb/tbl [–me] [–ms] [–mm] [–TX] [*filename*] . . .

DESCRIPTION

The **tbl** command is a preprocessor for formatting tables for **nroff** or **troff**. The input *filenames* are copied to the standard output, except that lines between .**TS** and .**TE** command lines are assumed to describe tables and are reformatted.

If no arguments are given, **tbl** reads the standard input, so **tbl** may be used as a filter. When **tbl** is used with **eqn** or **neqn** the **tbl** command should be first, to minimize the volume of data passed through pipes.

The –**me** option copies the –**me** macro package to the front of the output file.

The –**ms** option copies the –**ms** macro package to the front of the output file.

The –**mm** option copies the –**mm** macro package to the front of the output file.

The –**TX** option produces output that does not have fractional line motions in it.

EXAMPLE

As an example, letting \t represent a TAB (which should be typed as a genuine TAB) the input

```
.TS
c s s
c c s
c c c
l n n.
Household\tPopulation
Town\tHouseholds
\tNumber\tSize
Bedminster\t789\t3.26
Bernards Twp.\t3087\t3.74
Bernardsville\t2018\t3.30
.TE
```

yields

Household Population		
Town	Households	
	Number	Size
Bedminster	789	3.26
Bernards Twp.	3087	3.74
Bernardsville	2018	3.30

SEE ALSO

eqn(1), nroff(1), troff(1)

NAME

tcopy – copy a magnetic tape

SYNOPSIS

/usr/ucb/tcopy *source* [*destination*]

DESCRIPTION

tcopy copies the magnetic tape mounted on the tape drive specified by the *source* argument. The only assumption made about the contents of a tape is that there are two tape marks at the end.

When only a source drive is specified, tcopy scans the tape, and displays information about the sizes of records and tape files. If a destination is specified, tcopy makes a copies the source tape onto the *destination* tape, with blocking preserved. As it copies, tcopy produces the same output as it does when only scanning a tape.

SEE ALSO

mt(1)

ioctl(2) in the *Programmer's Reference Manual*

NOTES

tcopy will only run on systems supporting an associated set of ioctl(2) requests.

NAME

    `tee` – pipe fitting

SYNOPSIS

    `tee` [`-i`] [`-a`] [*file*] ...

DESCRIPTION

    `tee` transcribes the standard input to the standard output and makes copies in the *files*. The

    `-i`   ignore interrupts;

    `-a`   causes the output to be appended to the *files* rather than overwriting them.

NAME

telnet – user interface to a remote system using the TELNET protocol

SYNOPSIS

telnet [*host* [*port*]]

DESCRIPTION

telnet communicates with another host using the TELNET protocol. If telnet is invoked without arguments, it enters command mode, indicated by its prompt telnet>. In this mode, it accepts and executes the commands listed below. If it is invoked with arguments, it performs an open command (see "Telnet Commands" below) with those arguments.

Once a connection has been opened, telnet enters input mode. In this mode, text typed is sent to the remote host. The input mode entered will be either character at a time or line by line depending on what the remote system supports.

In character at a time mode, most text typed is immediately sent to the remote host for processing.

In line by line mode, all text is echoed locally, and (normally) only completed lines are sent to the remote host. The local echo character (initially ^E) may be used to turn off and on the local echo (this would mostly be used to enter passwords without the password being echoed).

In either mode, if the *localchars* toggle is TRUE (the default in line mode; see below), the user's **quit**, **intr**, and **flush** characters are trapped locally, and sent as TELNET protocol sequences to the remote side. There are options (see **toggle**, **autoflush**, and **toggle**, **autosynch**) which cause this action to flush subsequent output to the terminal (until the remote host acknowledges the TELNET sequence) and flush previous terminal input (in the case of **quit** and **intr**).

While connected to a remote host, telnet command mode may be entered by typing the telnet escape character (initially ^]). When in command mode, the normal terminal editing conventions are available.

USAGE

Telnet Commands

The following commands are available. Only enough of each command to uniquely identify it need be typed (this is also true for arguments to the **mode**, **set**, **toggle**, and **display** commands).

open *host* [*port*]

    Open a connection to the named host. If no port number is specified, telnet will attempt to contact a TELNET server at the default port. The host specification may be either a host name [see **hosts**(4)] or an Internet address specified in the dot notation [see **inet**(7)].

close   Close any open TELNET session and exit telnet. An EOF (in command mode) will also close a session and exit.

quit   Same as **close**, above.

z   Suspend **telnet**. This command only works when the user is using a shell that supports job control, such as **sh**(1).

mode *type*

type is either **line** (for line by line mode) or *character* (for character at a time mode). The remote host is asked for permission to go into the requested mode. If the remote host is capable of entering that mode, the requested mode will be entered.

status

Show the current status of **telnet**. This includes the peer one is connected to, as well as the current mode.

display [*argument . . .*]

Display all, or some, of the **set** and **toggle** values (see **toggle**, *arguments*).

? [*command*]

Get help. With no arguments, **telnet** print a help summary. If a command is specified, **telnet** will print the help information for just that command.

send *arguments*

Send one or more special character sequences to the remote host. The following are the arguments which may be specified (more than one argument may be specified at a time):

escape

Send the current **telnet** escape character (initially ∧]).

synch   Send the TELNET **SYNCH** sequence. This sequence discards all previously typed (but not yet read) input on the remote system. This sequence is sent as TCP urgent data (and may not work if the remote system is a 4.2 BSD system — if it does not work, a lower case r may be echoed on the terminal).

brk   Send the TELNET **BRK** (Break) sequence, which may have significance to the remote system.

ip   Send the TELNET **IP** (Interrupt Process) sequence, which aborts the currently running process on the remote system.

ao   Sends the TELNET **AO** (Abort Output) sequence, which flushes all output **from** the remote system **to** the user's terminal.

ayt   Sends the TELNET **AYT** (Are You There) sequence, to which the remote system may or may not choose to respond.

ec   Sends the TELNET **EC** (Erase Character) sequence, which erases the last character entered.

el   Sends the TELNET **EL** (Erase Line) sequence, which should cause the remote system to erase the line currently being entered.

ga   Sends the TELNET **GA** (Go Ahead) sequence, which likely has no significance to the remote system.

nop   Sends the TELNET **NOP** (No Operation) sequence.

?   Prints out help information for the **send** command.

set *argument value*

Set any one of a number of **telnet** variables to a specific value. The special value off turns off the function associated with the variable. The values of variables may be interrogated with the **display** command. The variables which may be specified are:

echo   This is the value (initially **^E**) which, when in line by line mode, toggles between doing local echoing of entered characters (for normal processing), and suppressing echoing of entered characters (for example, entering a password).

escape

This is the **telnet** escape character (initially **^]**) which enters **telnet** command mode (when connected to a remote system).

interrupt

If **telnet** is in **localchars** mode (see **toggle localchars**) and the **interrupt** character is typed, a TELNET **IP** sequence (see **send** and **ip**) is sent to the remote host. The initial value for the interrupt character is taken to be the terminal's **intr** character.

quit   If **telnet** is in **localchars** mode (see **toggle localchars**) and the **quit** character is typed, a TELNET **BRK** sequence (see **send**, **brk**) is sent to the remote host. The initial value for the quit character is taken to be the terminal's **quit** character.

flushoutput

If **telnet** is in **localchars** mode (see **toggle localchars**) and the **flushoutput** character is typed, a TELNET **AO** sequence (see **send, ao**) is sent to the remote host. The initial value for the flush character is taken to be the terminal's **flush** character.

erase If **telnet** is in **localchars** mode (see **toggle localchars**), **and** if **telnet** is operating in character at a time mode, then when this character is typed, a TELNET **EC** sequence (see **send, ec**) is sent to the remote system. The initial value for the erase character is taken to be the terminal's **erase** character.

kill   If **telnet** is in **localchars** mode (see **toggle localchars**), **and** if **telnet** is operating in character at a time mode, then when this character is typed, a TELNET **EL** sequence (see **send, el**) is sent to the remote system. The initial value for the kill character is taken to be the terminal's **kill** character.

eof   If **telnet** is operating in line by line mode, entering this character as the first character on a line sends this character to the remote system. The initial value of the eof character is taken to be the terminal's **eof** character.

toggle *arguments* . . .

> Toggle (between TRUE and FALSE) various flags that control how **telnet** responds to events. More than one argument may be specified. The state of these flags may be interrogated with the **display** command. Valid arguments are:

autoflush

> If **autoflush** and **localchars** are both TRUE, then when the **ao**, **intr**, or **quit** characters are recognized (and transformed into TELNET sequences; see **set** for details), **telnet** refuses to display any data on the user's terminal until the remote system acknowledges (using a TELNET **Timing Mark** option) that it has processed those TELNET sequences. The initial value for this toggle is TRUE if the terminal user had not done an stty noflsh, otherwise FALSE [see **stty**(1)].

autosynch

> If **autosynch** and **localchars** are both TRUE, then when either the **intr** or *quit* characters are typed (see **set** for descriptions of the **intr** and **quit** characters), the resulting TELNET sequence sent is followed by the TELNET **SYNCH** sequence. This procedure **should** cause the remote system to begin throwing away all previously typed input until both of the TELNET sequences have been read and acted upon. The initial value of this toggle is FALSE.

crmod Toggle RETURN mode. When this mode is enabled, most RETURN characters received from the remote host will be mapped into a RETURN followed by a line feed. This mode does not affect those characters typed by the user, only those received from the remote host. This mode is not very useful unless the remote host only sends RETURN, but never LINEFEED. The initial value for this toggle is FALSE.

debug Toggle socket level debugging (useful only to the super-user). The initial value for this toggle is FALSE .

localchars

> If this is TRUE , then the **flush**, **interrupt**, **quit**, **erase**, and **kill** characters (see **set**) are recognized locally, and transformed into appropriate TELNET control sequences (respectively **ao**, **ip**, **brk**, **ec**, and **el**; see **send**). The initial value for this toggle is TRUE in line by line mode, and FALSE in character at a time mode.

netdata

> Toggle the display of all network data (in hexadecimal format). The initial value for this toggle is FALSE.

options

> Toggle the display of some internal **telnet** protocol processing

(having to do with TELNET options). The initial value for this toggle is FALSE.

? Display the legal **toggle** commands.

SEE ALSO

rlogin(1), sh(1), stty(1), hosts(4), inet(7)

NOTES

Do not attempt to run **layers**(1) while using **telnet**.

There is no adequate way for dealing with flow control.

On some remote systems, echo has to be turned off manually when in line by line mode.

There is enough settable state to justify a **.telnetrc** file.

In line by line mode, the terminal's EOF character is only recognized (and sent to the remote system) when it is the first character on a line.

NAME

`telnetd` – DARPA TELNET protocol server

SYNOPSIS

`in.telnetd`

DESCRIPTION

`telnetd` is a server which supports the DARPA standard TELNET virtual terminal protocol. `telnetd` is invoked by the internet server [see `inetd`(1M)], normally for requests to connect to the TELNET port as indicated by the `/etc/services` file [see `services`(4)].

`telnetd` operates by allocating a pseudo-terminal device for a client, then creating a login process which has the slave side of the pseudo-terminal as its standard input, output, and error. The login process is an instance of the `in.login` program, which is based on `login`(1). It is invoked with the **–h** option to indicate that it is originated by `telnetd`. `telnetd` manipulates the master side of the pseudo-terminal, implementing the TELNET protocol and passing characters between the remote client and the login process.

When a **TELNET** session is started up, `telnetd` sends TELNET options to the client side indicating a willingness to do *remote echo* of characters, to *suppress go ahead*, and to receive *terminal type information* from the remote client. If the remote client is willing, the remote terminal type is propagated in the environment of the created login process. The pseudo-terminal allocated to the client is configured to operate in cooked mode, and with **XTABS**, **ICRNL**, and **ONLCR** enabled [see `termio`(4)].

`telnetd` is willing to do: *echo, binary, suppress go ahead,* and *timing mark.*

`telnetd` is willing to have the remote client do: *binary, terminal type,* and *suppress go ahead.*

SEE ALSO

`telnet`(1)

Postel, Jon, and Joyce Reynolds, "Telnet Protocol Specification," RFC 854, Network Information Center, SRI International, Menlo Park, Calif., May 1983.

NOTES

Some TELNET commands are only partially implemented.

The TELNET protocol allows for the exchange of the number of lines and columns on the user's terminal, but `telnetd` doesn't make use of them.

Binary mode has no common interpretation except between similar operating systems

The terminal type name received from the remote client is converted to lower case.

The *packet* interface to the pseudo-terminal should be used for more intelligent flushing of input and output queues.

telnetd never sends TELNET *go ahead* commands.

telnetd can only support 64 pseudo-terminals.

NAME

test – condition evaluation command

SYNOPSIS

test *expr*

[*expr*]

DESCRIPTION

test evaluates the expression *expr* and, if its value is true, sets a zero (true) exit status; otherwise, a non-zero (false) exit status is set; test also sets a non-zero exit status if there are no arguments. When permissions are tested, the effective user ID of the process is used.

All operators, flags, and brackets (brackets used as shown in the second SYNOPSIS line) must be separate arguments to the test command; normally these items are separated by spaces.

The following primitives are used to construct *expr*:

−r *file*   true if *file* exists and is readable.

−w *file*   true if *file* exists and is writable.

−x *file*   true if *file* exists and is executable.

−f *file*   true if *file* exists and is a regular file. Alternatively, if /usr/sh users specify /usr/ucb before /usr/bin in their PATH environment variable, then test will return true if *file* exists and is (not−a−directory). This is also the default for /usr/bin/csh users.

−d *file*   true if *file* exists and is a directory.

−h *file*   true if *file* exists and is a symbolic link. With all other primitives the symbolic links are followed by default.

−c *file*   true if *file* exists and is a character special file.

−b *file*   true if *file* exists and is a block special file.

−p *file*   true if *file* exists and is a named pipe (fifo).

−u *file*   true if *file* exists and its set-user-ID bit is set.

−g *file*   true if *file* exists and its set-group-ID bit is set.

−k *file*   true if *file* exists and its sticky bit is set.

−s *file*   true if *file* exists and has a size greater than zero.

−t [*fildes*]   true if the open file whose file descriptor number is *fildes* (1 by default) is associated with a terminal device.

−z *s1*   true if the length of string *s1* is zero.

−n *s1*   true if the length of the string *s1* is non-zero.

s1 = *s2*   true if strings *s1* and *s2* are identical.

$s1$!= $s2$ true if strings $s1$ and $s2$ are *not* identical.

$s1$ true if $s1$ is *not* the null string.

$n1$ **-eq** $n2$ true if the integers $n1$ and $n2$ are algebraically equal. Any of the comparisons **-ne**, **-gt**, **-ge**, **-lt**, and **-le** may be used in place of **-eq**.

These primaries may be combined with the following operators:

!   unary negation operator.

-a   binary *and* operator.

-o   binary *or* operator (**-a** has higher precedence than **-o**).

(*expr*)   parentheses for grouping. Notice also that parentheses are meaningful to the shell and, therefore, must be quoted.

SEE ALSO

find(1), **sh**(1).

NOTES

The **not-a-directory** alternative to the **-f** option is a transition aid for BSD applications and may not be supported in future releases.

If you test a file you own (the *-r*, *-w*, or *-x* tests), but the permission tested does not have the *owner* bit set, a non-zero (false) exit status will be returned even though the file may have the **group** or *other* bit set for that permission. The correct exit status will be set if you are super-user.

The = and != operators have a higher precedence than the **-r** through **-n** operators, and = and != always expect arguments; therefore, = and != cannot be used with the **-r** through **-n** operators.

If more than one argument follows the **-r** through **-n** operators, only the first argument is examined; the others are ignored, unless a **-a** or a **-o** is the second argument.

NAME

test – condition evaluation command

SYNOPSIS

test *expr*

[*expr*]

DESCRIPTION

test evaluates the expression *expr* and if its value is true, sets a zero (TRUE) exit status; otherwise, a non-zero (FALSE) exit status is set; **test** also sets a non-zero exit status if there are no arguments. When permissions are tested, the effective user ID of the process is used.

All operators, flags, and brackets (brackets used as shown in the second SYNOPSIS line) must be separate arguments to **test**. Normally these items are separated by spaces.

The following primitives are used to construct *expr*:

−r *file*	true if *file* exists and is readable.
−w *file*	true if *file* exists and is writable.
−x *file*	true if *file* exists and is executable.
−f *file*	true if *file* exists and is a regular file.
−d *file*	true if *file* exists and is a directory.
−c *file*	true if *file* exists and is a character special file.
−b *file*	true if *file* exists and is a block special file.
−p *file*	true if *file* exists and is a named pipe (fifo).
−u *file*	true if *file* exists and its set-user-ID bit is set.
−g *file*	true if *file* exists and its set-group-ID bit is set.
−k *file*	true if *file* exists and its sticky bit is set.
−s *file*	true if *file* exists and has a size greater than zero.
−t [*fildes*]	true if the open file whose file descriptor number is *fildes* (1 by default) is associated with a terminal device.
−z *s1*	true if the length of string *s1* is zero.
−n *s1*	true if the length of the string *s1* is non-zero.
s1 = *s2*	true if strings *s1* and *s2* are identical.
s1 != *s2*	true if strings *s1* and *s2* are *not* identical.
s1	true if *s1* is *not* the null string.
n1 **−eq** *n2*	true if the integers *n1* and *n2* are algebraically equal. Any of the comparisons **−ne**, **−gt**, **−ge**, **−lt**, and **−le** may be used in place of **−eq**.

These primaries may be combined with the following operators:

!   unary negation operator.

-a   binary **and** operator.

-o   binary **or** operator (-a has higher precedence than -o).

`( expr )`   parentheses for grouping. Notice also that parentheses are meaning-
                ful to the shell and, therefore, must be quoted.

NOTES

If you test a file you own (the -r, -w , or -x tests), but the permission tested does
not have the *owner* bit set, a non-zero (false) exit status will be returned even
though the file may have the *group* or *other* bit set for that permission. The
correct exit status will be set if you are super-user.

The = and != operators have a higher precedence than the -r through -n operators, and = and != always expect arguments; therefore, = and != cannot be used
with the -r through -n operators.

If more than one argument follows the -r through -n operators, only the first
argument is examined; the others are ignored, unless a -a or a -o is the second
argument.

SEE ALSO

find(1), sh(1) in the *UNIX System V User's Reference Manual*

NAME

`test` – condition evaluation command

SYNOPSIS

/usr/ucb/test *expr*

[*expr*]

DESCRIPTION

test evaluates the expression *expr* and, if its value is true, sets a zero (true) exit status; otherwise, a non-zero (false) exit status is set; *test* also sets a non-zero exit status if there are no arguments. When permissions are tested, the effective user ID of the process is used.

All operators, flags, and brackets (brackets used as shown in the second SYNOPSIS line) must be separate arguments to the *test* command; normally these items are separated by spaces.

The following primitives are used to construct *expr*:

–r *file*	true if *file* exists and is readable.
–w *file*	true if *file* exists and is writable.
–x *file*	true if *file* exists and is executable.
–f *file*	true if *file* exists and is a regular file. Alternatively, if **/usr/sh** users specify **/usr/ucb** before **/usr/bin** in their PATH environment variable, then *test* will return true if *file* exists and is **(not–a–directory)**. This is also the default for **/usr/bin/csh** users.
–d *file*	true if *file* exists and is a directory.
–c *file*	true if *file* exists and is a character special file.
–b *file*	true if *file* exists and is a block special file.
–p *file*	true if *file* exists and is a named pipe (fifo).
–u *file*	true if *file* exists and its set-user-ID bit is set.
–g *file*	true if *file* exists and its set-group-ID bit is set.
–k *file*	true if *file* exists and its sticky bit is set.
–s *file*	true if *file* exists and has a size greater than zero.
–t [*fildes*]	true if the open file whose file descriptor number is *fildes* (1 by default) is associated with a terminal device.
–z *s1*	true if the length of string *s1* is zero.
–n *s1*	true if the length of the string *s1* is non-zero.
s1 **=** *s2*	true if strings *s1* and *s2* are identical.
s1 **!=** *s2*	true if strings *s1* and *s2* are *not* identical.
s1	true if *s1* is *not* the null string.

n1 **−eq** *n2*   true if the integers *n1* and *n2* are algebraically equal. Any of the comparisons **−ne**, **−gt**, **−ge**, **−lt**, and **−le** may be used in place of **−eq**.

−L*file*   true if **file** exists and is a symbolic link. With all other primitives, the symbolic links are followed by default.

These primaries may be combined with the following operators:

!   unary negation operator.

−a   binary *and* operator.

−o   binary *or* operator (**−a** has higher precedence than **−o**).

(*expr* **)**   parentheses for grouping. Notice also that parentheses are meaningful to the shell and, therefore, must be quoted.

SEE ALSO
find(1), **sh**(1) in the *User's Reference Manual*

NOTES
The 'not−a−directory' alternative to the **−f** option is a transition aid for BSD applications and may not be supported in future releases.

The **−L** option is a migration aid for users of other shells which have similar options and may not be supported in future releases.

If you test a file you own (the *-r*, *-w*, or *-x* tests), but the permission tested does not have the *owner* bit set, a non-zero (false) exit status will be returned even though the file may have the *group* or *other* bit set for that permission. The correct exit status will be set if you are super-user.

The **=** and **!=** operators have a higher precedence than the **−r** through **−n** operators, and **=** and **!=** always expect arguments; therefore, **=** and **!=** cannot be used with the **−r** through **−n** operators.

If more than one argument follows the **−r** through **−n** operators, only the first argument is examined; the others are ignored, unless a **−a** or a **−o** is the second argument.

NAME

tftp – trivial file transfer program

SYNOPSIS

tftp [*host*]

DESCRIPTION

tftp is the user interface to the Internet TFTP (Trivial File Transfer Protocol), which allows users to transfer files to and from a remote machine. The remote *host* may be specified on the command line, in which case **tftp** uses *host* as the default host for future transfers (see the **connect** command below).

USAGE

Commands

Once **tftp** is running, it issues the prompt **tftp>** and recognizes the following commands:

connect *host-name* [*port*]

> Set the *host* (and optionally *port*) for transfers. The TFTP protocol, unlike the FTP protocol, does not maintain connections between transfers; thus, the **connect** command does not actually create a connection, but merely remembers what host is to be used for transfers. You do not have to use the **connect** command; the remote host can be specified as part of the **get** or **put** commands.

mode *transfer-mode*

> Set the mode for transfers; *transfer-mode* may be one of **ascii** or **binary**. The default is **ascii**.

put *filename*
put *localfile remotefile*
put *filename1 filename2 ... filenameN remote-directory*

> Transfer a file, or a set of files, to the specified remote file or directory. The destination can be in one of two forms: a filename on the remote host if the host has already been specified, or a string of the form

> > *host*:*filename*

> to specify both a host and filename at the same time. If the latter form is used, the specified host becomes the default for future transfers. If the remote-directory form is used, the remote host is assumed to be running the UNIX system.

get *filename*
get *remotename localname*
get *filename1 filename2 filename3 ... filenameN*

> Get a file or set of files (three or more) from the specified remote *sources*. *source* can be in one of two forms: a filename on the remote host if the host has already been specified, or a string of the form

> > *host*:*filename*

> to specify both a host and filename at the same time. If the latter form is used, the last host specified becomes the default for future transfers.

quit   Exit **tftp**. An EOF also exits.

verbose   Toggle verbose mode.

trace   Toggle packet tracing.

status   Show current status.

rexmt *retransmission-timeout*
           Set the per-packet retransmission timeout, in seconds.

timeout *total-transmission-timeout*
           Set the total transmission timeout, in seconds.

ascii   Shorthand for **mode ascii**.

binary   Shorthand for **mode binary**.

? [*command-name* . . .]
           Print help information.

NOTES

Because there is no user-login or validation within the TFTP protocol, many remote sites restrict file access in various ways. Approved methods for file access are specific to each site, and therefore cannot be documented here.

When using the **get** command to transfer multiple files from a remote host, three or more files must be specified. The command returns an error message if only two files are specified.

NAME

tftpd – DARPA Trivial File Transfer Protocol server

SYNOPSIS

in.tftpd [-s] [*homedir*]

DESCRIPTION

tftpd is a server that supports the DARPA Trivial File Transfer Protocol (TFTP). This server is normally started by inetd(1M) and operates at the port indicated in the tftp Internet service description in the /etc/inetd.conf file. By default, the entry for tftpd in etc/inetd.conf is commented out. To make tftpd operational, the comment character(s) must be deleted from the tftpd entry. See inetd.conf(4) for details.

Before responding to a request, the server attempts to change its current directory to *homedir*; the default value is /tftpboot.

OPTIONS

-s   Secure. When specified, the directory change must succeed; and the dae-
      mon also changes its root directory to *homedir*.

      The use of tftp does not require an account or password on the remote
      system. Due to the lack of authentication information, tftp will allow
      only publicly readable files to be accessed. Files may be written only if
      they already exist and are publicly writable. Note that this extends the
      concept of public to include all users on all hosts that can be reached
      through the network; this may not be appropriate on all systems, and its
      implications should be considered before enabling this service.

tftpd runs with the user ID and group ID set to [GU]ID_NOBODY. –2, under the assumption that no files exist with that owner or group. However, nothing checks this assumption or enforces this restriction.

SEE ALSO

tftp(1), inetd(1M), ipallocd(1M), netconfig(4)

Sollins, K.R., *The TFTP Protocol (Revision 2)*, RFC 783, Network Information Center, SRI International, Menlo Park, Calif., June 1981

NAME

tic – *terminfo* compiler

SYNOPSIS

tic [-**v**[*n*]] [-**c**] *file*

DESCRIPTION

The command **tic** translates a **terminfo** file from the source format into the compiled format. The results are placed in the directory **/usr/share/lib/terminfo**. The compiled format is necessary for use with the library routines in **curses**(3X).

-**v***n*　　specifies that (verbose) output be written to standard error trace information showing **tic**'s progress. The optional integer *n* is a number from 1 to 10, inclusive, indicating the desired level of detail of information. If *n* is omitted, the default level is 1. If *n* is specified and greater than 1, the level of detail is increased.

-**c**　　specifies to check only *file* for errors. Errors in **use=** links are not detected.

file　　contains one or more **terminfo** terminal descriptions in source format [see **terminfo**(4)]. Each description in the file describes the capabilities of a particular terminal. When a **use=***entry-name* field is discovered in a terminal entry currently being compiled, **tic** reads in the binary from **/usr/share/lib/terminfo** to complete the entry. (Entries created from *file* will be used first. If the environment variable **TERMINFO** is set, that directory is searched instead of **/usr/share/lib/terminfo**.) **tic** duplicates the capabilities in *entry-name* for the current entry, with the exception of those capabilities that explicitly are defined in the current entry.

If the environment variable **TERMINFO** is set, the compiled results are placed there instead of **/usr/share/lib/terminfo**.

Total compiled entries cannot exceed 4096 bytes. The name field cannot exceed 128 bytes. Terminal names exceeding 14 characters will be truncated to 14 characters and a warning message will be printed.

FILES

/usr/share/lib/terminfo/?/* 　 Compiled terminal description database.

NOTES

When an entry, e.g., **entry_name_1**, contains a **use=***entry_name_2* field, any canceled capabilities in *entry_name_2* must also appear in **entry_name_1** before **use=** for these capabilities to be canceled in **entry_name_1**.

SEE ALSO

curses(3X), **captoinfo**(1M), **infocmp**(1M), **terminfo**(4).

NAME

　　`time` – time a command

SYNOPSIS

　　`time` *command*

DESCRIPTION

　　The *command* is executed; after it is complete, `time` prints the elapsed time during the command, the time spent in the system, and the time spent in execution of the command. Times are reported in seconds.

　　The times are printed on standard error.

SEE ALSO

　　`timex`(1)

　　`time`(2) in the *Programmer's Reference Manual*

NAME

timex – time a command; report process data and system activity

SYNOPSIS

timex [*options*] *command*

DESCRIPTION

The given *command* is executed; the elapsed time, user time and system time spent in execution are reported in seconds. Optionally, process accounting data for the *command* and all its children can be listed or summarized, and total system activity during the execution interval can be reported.

The output of **timex** is written on standard error. **timex** returns an exit status of 1 if it is used incorrectly, if it is unable to fork, or if it cannot execute *command*. Otherwise, **timex** returns the exit status of *command*.

The *options* are:

-p   List process accounting records for *command* and all its children. This option works only if the process accounting software is installed. Suboptions **f**, **h**, **k**, **m**, **r**, and **t** modify the data items reported. The options are as follows:

    -f   Print the **fork**(2)/ exec(2) flag and system exit status columns in the output.

    -h   Instead of mean memory size, show the fraction of total available CPU time consumed by the process during its execution. This "hog factor" is computed as (total CPU time)/(elapsed time).

    -k   Instead of memory size, show total kcore-minutes.

    -m   Show mean core size (the default).

    -r   Show CPU factor (user time/(system-time + user-time).

    -t   Show separate system and user CPU times. The number of blocks read or written and the number of characters transferred are always reported.

-o   Report the total number of blocks read or written and total characters transferred by *command* and all its children. This option works only if the process accounting software is installed.

-s   Report total system activity (not just that due to *command*) that occurred during the execution interval of *command*. All the data items listed in **sar**(1) are reported.

SEE ALSO

time(1), **sar**(1)

times(2) in the *Programmer's Reference Manual*

NOTES

Process records associated with *command* are selected from the accounting file **/var/adm/pacct** by inference, since process genealogy is not available. Background processes having the same user ID, terminal ID, and execution time window will be spuriously included.

EXAMPLES

A simple example:

```
timex -ops sleep 60
```

A terminal session of arbitrary complexity can be measured by timing a sub-shell:

```
timex -opskmt sh
```

session commands
EOT

NAME

    tnamed, in.tnamed – DARPA trivial name server

SYNOPSIS

    in.tnamed [–v]

DESCRIPTION

    tnamed is a server that supports the DARPA Name Server Protocol. The name server operates at the port indicated in the name service description [see **services**(4)], and is invoked by **inetd**(1M) when a request is made to the name server.

OPTIONS

    –v   Invoke the daemon in verbose mode.

SEE ALSO

    uucp(1C), inetd(1M), services(4)

    Postel, Jon, *Internet Name Server*, IEN 116, SRI International, Menlo Park, California, August 1979

NOTES

    The protocol implemented by this program is obsolete. Its use should be phased out in favor of the Internet Domain Name Service (DNS) protocol. See named(1M).

NAME

   tosmtp – send mail to SMTP

SYNOPSIS

   tosmtp [-f] [-n] [-u] [-d *domain*] [-H *helohost*] *sender host recip* . . .

DESCRIPTION

   tosmtp translates a UNIX System mail message (read from standard input), into
   an RFC822 mail message, which can then be delivered with SMTP. tosmtp is normally invoked by **smtpqer** as part of the process of queuing mail for delivery.

   The options to **tosmtp** and their meanings are as follows:

   -d *domain*   Pass the specified *domain* directly to the **smtp** program.

   -f   Act as a filter. The RFC822 message is sent to the standard output.

   -H *helohost* This option can be used to specify the name to be used for the host
                 in the initial SMTP HELO message. This option is also passed to the
                 smtp program.

   -n   Do not place a **To:** line in the resulting RFC822 header.

   -u   Do no conversion. The standard input is sent directly to the stan-
                 dard output.

FILES

   /usr/lib/mail/surrcmd/smtp   Where the message is piped to

SEE ALSO

   smtp(1M), smtpqer(1M)
   RFC822 – Standard for the Format of ARPA Internet Text Messages

NAME

touch – update access and modification times of a file

SYNOPSIS

touch [–amc] [*mmddhhmm*[*yy*]] *files*

DESCRIPTION

touch causes the access and modification times of each argument to be updated. The file name is created if it does not exist. If no time is specified [see **date**(1)] the current time is used. The –a and –m options cause touch to update only the access or modification times respectively (default is –am). The –c option silently prevents **touch** from creating the file if it did not previously exist.

The return code from **touch** is the number of files for which the times could not be successfully modified (including files that did not exist and were not created).

SEE ALSO

date(1)

utime(2) in the *Programmer's Reference Manual*

NOTES

Users familiar with the BSD environment will find that the –f option is accepted, but ignored. The –f option is unnecessary since **touch** will succeed for all files owned by the user regardless of the permissions on the files.

touch assumes that an all numeric entry is a date and so will not update the times for a file when an all numeric filename is specified.

NAME

tput – initialize a terminal or query terminfo database

SYNOPSIS

tput [-T*type*] *capname* [*parms* . . .]

tput [-T*type*] init

tput [-T*type*] reset

tput [-T*type*] longname

tput-S <<

DESCRIPTION

tput uses the **terminfo** database to make the values of terminal-dependent capabilities and information available to the shell (see **sh**(1)), to initialize or reset the
terminal, or return the long name of the requested terminal type. tput outputs a
string if the attribute (*capability name*) is of type string, or an integer if the attribute is of type integer. If the attribute is of type boolean, tput simply sets the
exit code (0 for TRUE if the terminal has the capability, 1 for FALSE if it does not),
and produces no output. Before using a value returned on standard output, the
user should test the exit code [$?, see **sh**(1)] to be sure it is 0. (See the EXIT
CODES and DIAGNOSTICS sections.) For a complete list of capabilities and the
capname associated with each, see **terminfo**(4).

-T*type*   indicates the *type* of terminal. Normally this option is unnecessary,
               because the default is taken from the environment variable **TERM**. If
               -T is specified, then the shell variables **LINES** and **COLUMNS** and the
               layer size [see **layers**(1)] will not be referenced.

capname   indicates the attribute from the **terminfo** database.

parms   If the attribute is a string that takes parameters, the arguments *parms*
               will be instantiated into the string. An all numeric argument will be
               passed to the attribute as a number.

-S   allows more than one capability per invocation of **tput**. The capabil-
               ities must be passed to **tput** from the standard input instead of from
               the command line (see example). Only one *capname* is allowed per
               line. The -S option changes the meaning of the 0 and 1 boolean and
               string exit codes (see the EXIT CODES section).

init   If the **terminfo** database is present and an entry for the user's termi-
               nal exists (see -T*type*, above), the following will occur: (1) if present,
               the terminal's initialization strings will be output (**is1**, **is2**, **is3**, **if**,
               iprog), (2) any delays (for example, newline) specified in the entry
               will be set in the tty driver, (3) tabs expansion will be turned on or
               off according to the specification in the entry, and (4) if tabs are not
               expanded, standard tabs will be set (every 8 spaces). If an entry does
               not contain the information needed for any of the four above activi-
               ties, that activity will silently be skipped.

reset   Instead of putting out initialization strings, the terminal's reset strings
            will be output if present (**rs1**, **rs2**, **rs3**, **rf**). If the reset strings are
            not present, but initialization strings are, the initialization strings will
            be output. Otherwise, **reset** acts identically to **init**.

longname   If the **terminfo** database is present and an entry for the user's termi-
            nal exists (see −T*type* above), then the long name of the terminal will
            be put out. The long name is the last name in the first line of the
            terminal's description in the **terminfo** database [see **term**(5)].

EXAMPLES

tput init   Initialize the terminal according to the type of terminal in the
                   environmental variable **TERM**. This command should be
                   included in everyone's .profile after the environmental vari-
                   able **TERM** has been exported, as illustrated on the **profile**(4)
                   manual page.

tput −T5620 reset
                   Reset an AT&T 5620 terminal, overriding the type of terminal
                   in the environmental variable **TERM**.

tput cup 0 0   Send the sequence to move the cursor to row 0, column 0 (the
                   upper left corner of the screen, usually known as the "home"
                   cursor position).

tput clear   Echo the clear-screen sequence for the current terminal.

tput cols   Print the number of columns for the current terminal.

tput −T450 cols   Print the number of columns for the 450 terminal.

bold='tput smso'

offbold='tput rmso'
                   Set the shell variables **bold**, to begin stand-out mode
                   sequence, and **offbold**, to end standout mode sequence, for
                   the current terminal. This might be followed by a prompt:
                   echo   "${bold}Please   type   in   your   name:
                   ${offbold}\c"

tput hc   Set exit code to indicate if the current terminal is a hardcopy
                   terminal.

tput cup 23 4   Send the sequence to move the cursor to row 23, column 4.

tput longname   Print the long name from the **terminfo** database for the type
                   of terminal specified in the environmental variable **TERM**.

tput −S <<!   This example shows tput processing several capabilities in
> clear   one invocation. This example clears the screen, moves the
> cup 10 10   cursor to position 10, 10 and turns on bold (extra bright)
> bold   mode. The list is terminated by an exclamation mark (!) on
> !   a line by itself.

FILES

`/usr/share/lib/terminfo/?/*`	compiled terminal description database
`/usr/include/curses.h`	`curses`(3X) header file
`/usr/include/term.h`	`terminfo` header file
`/usr/lib/tabset/*`	tab settings for some terminals, in a format appropriate to be output to the terminal (escape sequences that set margins and tabs); for more information, see the "Tabs and Initialization" section of `terminfo`(4)

SEE ALSO

clear(1), stty(1), tabs(1)

profile(4), terminfo(4) in the *System Administrator's Reference Manual*

Chapter 10 of the *Programmer's Guide*

EXIT CODES

If *capname* is of type boolean, a value of **0** is set for TRUE and **1** for FALSE unless the **-S** option is used.

If *capname* is of type string, a value of **0** is set if the *capname* is defined for this terminal *type* (the value of *capname* is returned on standard output); a value of **1** is set if *capname* is not defined for this terminal *type* (a null value is returned on standard output).

If *capname* is of type boolean or string and the **-S** option is used, a value of **0** is returned to indicate that all lines were successful. No indication of which line failed can be given so exit code **1** will never appear. Exit codes **2**, **3**, and **4** retain their usual interpretation.

If *capname* is of type integer, a value of **0** is always set, whether or not *capname* is defined for this terminal *type*. To determine if *capname* is defined for this terminal *type*, the user must test the value of standard output. A value of **−1** means that *capname* is not defined for this terminal *type*.

Any other exit code indicates an error; see the DIAGNOSTICS section.

DIAGNOSTICS

tput prints the following error messages and sets the corresponding exit codes.

exit code	error message
0	−1 (*capname* is a numeric variable that is not specified in the `terminfo`(4) database for this terminal type, for example `tput -T450 lines` and `tput -T2621 xmc`)
1	no error message is printed, see the EXIT CODES section.
2	usage error
3	unknown terminal *type* or no `terminfo` database
4	unknown `terminfo` capability *capname*

NAME

tr – translate characters

SYNOPSIS

tr [–cds] [*string1* [*string2*]]

DESCRIPTION

tr copies the standard input to the standard output with substitution or deletion of selected characters. Input characters found in *string1* are mapped into the corresponding characters of *string2*. Any combination of the options –cds may be used:

–c   Complements the set of characters in *string1* with respect to the universe of characters whose ASCII codes are 001 through 377 octal.

–d   Deletes all input characters in *string1*.

–s   Squeezes all strings of repeated output characters that are in *string2* to single characters.

The following abbreviation conventions may be used to introduce ranges of characters or repeated characters into the strings:

[a–z]   Stands for the string of characters whose ASCII codes run from character **a** to character **z**, inclusive.

[a∗*n*]   Stands for *n* repetitions of **a**. If the first digit of *n* is **0**, *n* is considered octal; otherwise, *n* is taken to be decimal. A zero or missing *n* is taken to be huge; this facility is useful for padding *string2*.

The escape character \ may be used as in the shell to remove special meaning from any character in a string. In addition, \ followed by 1, 2, or 3 octal digits stands for the character whose ASCII code is given by those digits.

EXAMPLE

The following example creates a list of all the words in *file1* one per line in *file2*, where a word is taken to be a maximal string of alphabetics. The strings are quoted to protect the special characters from interpretation by the shell; 012 is the ASCII code for newline.

> tr –cs "[A–Z][a–z]" "[\012∗]" <*file1*>*file2*

SEE ALSO

ed(1), sh(1)

ascii(5) in the *System Administrator's Reference Manual*

NOTES

Will not handle ASCII **NUL** in *string1* or *string2*; always deletes **NUL** from input.

NAME

tr – translate characters

SYNOPSIS

/usr/ucb/tr [**–cds**] [*string1* [*string2*]]

DESCRIPTION

tr copies the standard input to the standard output with substitution or deletion of selected characters. The arguments *string1* and *string2* are considered sets of characters. Any input character found in *string1* is mapped into the character in the corresponding position within *string2*. When *string2* is short, it is padded to the length of *string1* by duplicating its last character.

In either string the notation:

　　a–b

denotes a range of characters from *a* to *b* in increasing ASCII order. The character \, followed by 1, 2 or 3 octal digits stands for the character whose ASCII code is given by those digits. As with the shell, the escape character \, followed by any other character, escapes any special meaning for that character.

OPTIONS

Any combination of the options **–c**, **–d**, or **–s** may be used:

–c　　Complement the set of characters in *string1* with respect to the universe of characters whose ASCII codes are 01 through 0377 octal.

–d　　Delete all input characters in *string1*.

–s　　Squeeze all strings of repeated output characters that are in *string2* to single characters.

EXAMPLE

The following example creates a list of all the words in *filename1* one per line in *filename2*, where a word is taken to be a maximal string of alphabetics. The second string is quoted to protect ′\′ from the shell. 012 is the ASCII code for NEWLINE.

　　tr –cs A–Za–z ′**\012**′ < *filename1* > *filename2*

SEE ALSO

ed(1) in the *User's Reference Manual*
ascii(5) in the *System Administrator's Reference Manual*

NOTES

Will not handle ASCII NUL in *string1* or *string2*. **tr** always deletes NUL from input.

NAME

trchan – translate character sets

SYNOPSIS

trchan [-ciko] *mapfile*

DESCRIPTION

trchan performs mapping as a filter, using the same format of *mapfile* as mapchan [see mapchan(4) for *mapfile* format]. This allows a file consisting of one internal character set to be translated to another internal character set.

trchan reads standard input, maps it, and writes to standard output. A *mapfile* must be given on the command line. Errors cause trchan to stop processing unless -c is specified.

The following options can be used with trchan:

-c   causes errors to be echoed on stderr, and processing is continued.

-i   specifies that the input section of the *mapfile* is used when translating data.

-k   specifies that the dead and compose sections of the *mapfile* are used when translating data.

-o   specifies that the output section of the *mapfile* is used when translating data.

        The -i, -k and -o options can be specified in any combination; if none are specified, trchan uses the entire *mapfile*, as if all three were specified together.

FILES

/usr/lib/mapchan/*

SEE ALSO

ascii(5), mapchan(4), mapchan(1M)

NOTES

trchan currently ignores the control sections of the *mapfile*.

NAME

troff – typeset or format documents

SYNOPSIS

/usr/ucb/troff [-afiz] [-F*dir*] [-m*name*] [-n*N*] [-o*list*] [-r*aN*] [-s*N*]
　　　　[-T*dest*] [-u*N*] [*filename*] . . .

DESCRIPTION

troff formats text in the *filenames*. Input to troff is expected to consist of text interspersed with formatting requests and macros. If no *filename* argument is present, troff reads standard input. A – as a *filename* argument indicates that standard input is to be read at that point in the list of input files; troff reads the files named ahead of the – in the arguments list, then text from the standard input, and then text from the files named after the –.

The following options may appear in any order, but they all must appear before the first *filename*.

-a　　　Send a printable approximation of the formatted output to the standard output file.

-f　　　Do not print a trailer after the final page of output or cause the postprocessor to relinquish control of the device.

-i　　　Read the standard input after the input files are exhausted.

-z　　　Suppress formatted output. Only diagnostic messages and messages output using the .tm request are output.

-F*dir*　　Search the directory *dir* for font width tables instead of the system-dependent default directory.

-m*name*　Prepend the macro file /usr/lib/tmac/tmac.*name* to the input *filenames*. Note: most references to macro packages include the leading m as part of the name; for example, the **man** macro package resides in /usr/lib/tmac/tmac.an.

-n*N*　　Number first generated page *N*.

-o*list*　　Print only pages whose page numbers appear in the comma-separated *list* of numbers and ranges. A range *N–M* means pages *N* through *M*; an initial *–N* means from the beginning to page *N*; and a final *N–* means from *N* to the end.

-r*aN*　　Set register *a* (one-character) to *N*.

-s*N*　　Stop the phototypesetter every *N* pages. On some devices, troff produces a trailer so you can change cassettes; resume by pressing the typesetter's start button.

-T*dest*　Prepare output for typesetter *dest*. The following values can be supplied for *dest*:

202	Mergenthaler Linotron 202. This is the default value.
cat	Graphics Systems C/A/T.
aps	Autologic APS-5.

−u*N*   Set the emboldening factor for the font mounted in position 3 to *N*. If *N* is missing, then set the emboldening factor to 0.

FILES

`/tmp/trtmp`	temporary file
`/usr/ucblib/doctools/tmac/tmac.*`	standard macro files
`/usr/ucblib/doctools/font/*`	font width tables for alternate mounted **troff** fonts

SEE ALSO

checknr(1), chmod(1), eqn(1), lpd(1M), lpr(1), nroff(1), tbl(1), man(7), me(7), ms(7)

chmod(1), col(1) in the *User's Reference Manual*

NAME

trpt – transliterate protocol trace

SYNOPSIS

trpt [**-afjst**] [**-p** *hex-address*] [*system* [*core*]]

DESCRIPTION

trpt interrogates the buffer of TCP trace records created when a socket is marked for debugging [see **getsockopt**(3N)], and prints a readable description of these records. When no options are supplied, trpt prints all the trace records found in the system grouped according to TCP connection protocol control block (PCB). The following options may be used to alter this behavior.

OPTIONS

-a   In addition to the normal output, print the values of the source and destination addresses for each packet recorded.

-f   Follow the trace as it occurs, waiting a short time for additional records each time the end of the log is reached.

-j   Just give a list of the protocol control block addresses for which there are trace records.

-s   In addition to the normal output, print a detailed description of the packet sequencing information.

-t   In addition to the normal output, print the values for all timers at each point in the trace.

-p *hex-address*

Show only trace records associated with the protocol control block, the address of which follows.

The recommended use of **trpt** is as follows. Isolate the problem and enable debugging on the **socket**(s) involved in the connection. Find the address of the protocol control blocks associated with the sockets using the **-A** option to **netstat**(1M). Then run **trpt** with the **-p** option, supplying the associated protocol control block addresses. The **-f** option can be used to follow the trace log once the trace is located. If there are many sockets using the debugging option, the **-j** option may be useful in checking to see if any trace records are present for the socket in question.

If debugging is being performed on a system or core file other than the default, the last two arguments may be used to supplant the defaults.

FILES

/stand/unix
/dev/kmem

SEE ALSO

netstat(1M), getsockopt(3N)

DIAGNOSTICS

no namelist

When the system image does not contain the proper symbols to find the trace buffer; others which should be self explanatory.

NOTES

Should also print the data for each input or output, but this is not saved in the trace record.

The output format is inscrutable and should be described here.

NAME

true, false – provide truth values

SYNOPSIS

true

false

DESCRIPTION

true does nothing, successfully. false does nothing, unsuccessfully. They are typically used in input to sh such as:

```
while true
do
        command
done
```

SEE ALSO

sh(1)

DIAGNOSTICS

true has exit status zero, false nonzero.

NAME

truss – trace system calls and signals

SYNOPSIS

truss [-p] [-f] [-c] [-a] [-e] [-i] [-[tvx] [!] *syscall* ...] [-s [!] *signal* ...] [-m
[!] *fault* ...] [-[rw] [!] *fd* ...] [-o *outfile*] *command*

DESCRIPTION

truss executes the specified command and produces a trace of the system calls it
performs, the signals it receives, and the machine faults it incurs. Each line of the
trace output reports either the fault or signal name or the system call name with
its arguments and return value(s). System call arguments are displayed symbolically when possible using defines from relevant system header files; for any pathname pointer argument, the pointed-to string is displayed. Error returns are
reported using the error code names described in intro(2).

The following options are recognized. For those options which take a list argument, the name all can be used as a shorthand to specify all possible members
of the list. If the list begins with a !, the meaning of the option is negated (for
example, exclude rather than trace). Multiple occurrences of the same option
may be specified. For the same name in a list, subsequent options (those to the
right) override previous ones (those to the left).

-p Interpret the arguments to truss as a list of process-ids for
existing processes (see ps(1)) rather than as a command to be
executed. truss takes control of each process and begins
tracing it provided that the userid and groupid of the process match those of the user or that the user is a privileged
user. Processes may also be specified by their names in the
/proc directory, for example, /proc/1234; this works for
remotely-mounted /proc directories as well.

-f Follow all children created by fork and include their signals,
faults, and system calls in the trace output. Normally, only
the first-level command or process is traced. When -f is
specified, the process-id is included with each line of trace
output to show which process executed the system call or
received the signal.

-c Count traced system calls, faults, and signals rather than
displaying the trace line-by-line. A summary report is produced after the traced command terminates or when truss
is interrupted. If -f is also specified, the counts include all
traced system calls, faults, and signals for child processes.

-a Show the argument strings which are passed in each exec
system call.

-e Show the environment strings which are passed in each exec
system call.

-i Don't display interruptible sleeping system calls. Certain
system calls, such as open and read on terminal devices or
pipes can sleep for indefinite periods and are interruptible.
Normally, truss reports such sleeping system calls if they

	remain asleep for more than one second. The system call is reported again a second time when it completes. The **-i** option causes such system calls to be reported only once, when they complete.
-t [!] *syscall*,...	System calls to trace or exclude. Those system calls specified in the comma-separated list are traced. If the list begins with a '!', the specified system calls are excluded from the trace output. Default is **-tall**.
-v [!] *syscall*,...	Verbose. Display the contents of any structures passed by address to the specified system calls (if traced). Input values as well as values returned by the operating system are shown. For any field used as both input and output, only the output value is shown. Default is **-v!all**.
-x [!] *syscall*,...	Display the arguments to the specified system calls (if traced) in raw form, usually hexadecimal, rather than symbolically. This is for unredeemed hackers who must see the raw bits to be happy. Default is **-x!all**.
-s [!] *signal*,...	Signals to trace or exclude. Those signals specified in the comma-separated list are traced. The trace output reports the receipt of each specified signal, even if the signal is being ignored (not blocked) by the process. (Blocked signals are not received until the process releases them.) Signals may be specified by name or number (see **sys/signal.h**). If the list begins with a '!', the specified signals are excluded from the trace output. Default is **-sall**.
-m [!] *fault*,...	Machine faults to trace or exclude. Those machine faults specified in the comma-separated list are traced. Faults may be specified by name or number (see **sys/fault.h**). If the list begins with a '!', the specified faults are excluded from the trace output. Default is **-mall -m!fltpage**.
-r [!] *fd*,...	Show the full contents of the I/O buffer for each **read** on any of the specified file descriptors. The output is formatted 32 bytes per line and shows each byte as an ascii character (preceded by one blank) or as a two-character C language escape sequence for control characters such as horizontal tab (\t) and newline (\n). If ascii interpretation is not possible, the byte is shown in two-character hexadecimal representation. (The first 16 bytes of the I/O buffer for each traced **read** are shown even in the absence of **-r**.) Default is **-r!all**.
-w [!] *fd*,...	Show the contents of the I/O buffer for each **write** on any of the specified file descriptors (see **-r**). Default is **-w!all**.
-o *outfile*	File to be used for the trace output. By default, the output goes to standard error.

See Section 2 of the *Programmer's Reference Manual* for **syscall** names accepted by the **-t**, **-v**, and **-x** options. System call numbers are also accepted.

If **truss** is used to initiate and trace a specified command and if the **-o** option is used or if standard error is redirected to a non-terminal file, then **truss** runs with hangup, interrupt, and quit signals ignored. This facilitates tracing of interactive programs which catch interrupt and quit signals from the terminal.

If the trace output remains directed to the terminal, or if existing processes are traced (the **-p** option), then **truss** responds to hangup, interrupt, and quit signals by releasing all traced processes and exiting. This enables the user to terminate excessive trace output and to release previously-existing processes. Released processes continue normally, as though they had never been touched.

EXAMPLES

This example produces a trace of the **find**(1) command on the terminal:

```
truss find . -print >find.out
```

Or, to see only a trace of the open, close, read, and write system calls:

```
truss -t open,close,read,write find . -print >find.out
```

This produces a trace of the **spell**(1) command on the file truss.out:

```
truss -f -o truss.out spell document
```

spell is a shell script, so the **-f** flag is needed to trace not only the shell but also the processes created by the shell. (The spell script runs a pipeline of eight concurrent processes.)

A particularly boring example is:

```
truss nroff -mm document >nroff.out
```

because 97% of the output reports **lseek**, **read**, and **write** system calls. To abbreviate it:

```
truss -t !lseek,read,write nroff -mm document >nroff.out
```

This example verbosely traces the activity of process #1, **init**(1M) (provided you are a privileged user):

```
truss -p -v all 1
```

Interrupting **truss** returns **init** to normal operation.

FILES

    /proc/*nnnnn*   process files

NOTES

Some of the system calls described in Section 2 of the *Programmer's Reference Manual* differ from the actual operating system interfaces. Do not be surprised by minor deviations of the trace output from the descriptions in Section 2.

Every machine fault (except a page fault) results in the posting of a signal to the process which incurred the fault. A report of a received signal will immediately follow each report of a machine fault (except a page fault) unless that signal is being blocked by the process.

The operating system enforces certain security restrictions on the tracing of processes. In particular, any command whose object file (**a.out**) cannot be read by a user cannot be traced by that user; set-uid and set-gid commands can be traced only by a privileged user. Unless it is run by a privileged user, **truss** loses control of any process which performs an **exec**(2) of a set-id or unreadable object file; such processes continue normally, though independently of **truss**, from the point of the **exec**.

To avoid collisions with other controlling processes, **truss** will not trace a process which it detects is being controlled by another process via the **/proc** interface. This allows **truss** to be applied to *proc*(4)-based debuggers as well as to another instance of itself.

The trace output contains tab characters under the assumption that standard tab stops are set (every eight positions).

The trace output for multiple processes is not produced in strict time order. For example, a **read** on a pipe may be reported before the corresponding **write**. For any one process, the output is strictly time-ordered.

The system may run out of per-user process slots when tracing of children is requested. When tracing more than one process, **truss** runs as one controlling process for each process being traced. For the example of the **spell** command shown above, **spell** itself uses nine process slots, one for the shell and eight for the eight-member pipeline, while **truss** adds another nine processes, for a total of 18. This is perilously close to the usual system-imposed limit of 25 processes per user.

truss uses shared memory and semaphores when dealing with more than one process (**-f** option or **-p** with more than one **pid**). It issues a warning message and proceeds when these are needed but not configured in the system. However, the trace output may become garbled in this case and the output of the **-c** option reports only the top-level command or first **pid** and no children are counted.

Not all possible structures passed in all possible system calls are displayed under the **-v** option.

SEE ALSO

        intro(2), **proc**(4)

NAME

tset – provide information to set terminal modes

SYNOPSIS

tset [*options*] [*type*]

DESCRIPTION

tset allows the user to set a terminal's ERASE and KILL characters, and define the terminal's type and capabilities by creating values for the TERM environment variable. tset initializes or resets the terminal with tput [see tput(1)]. If a *type* is given with the −s option, tset creates information for a terminal of the specified type. The type may be any type given in the terminfo database. If the *type* is not specified with the −s option, tset creates information for a terminal of the type defined by the value of the TERM environment variable, unless the −h or −m option is given. If the TERM variable is defined, tset uses the terminfo database entry. If these options are used, tset searches the /etc/ttytype file for the terminal type corresponding to the current serial port; it then creates information for a terminal based on this type. If the serial port is not found in /etc/ttytype, the terminal type is set to unknown.

tset displays the created information on the standard output. The information is in a form that can be used to set the current environment variables. The exact form depends on the login shell from which tset was invoked. The examples below illustrate how to use this information to change the variables.

The options are:

−e[*c*]   Sets the ERASE character to *c* on all terminals. The default setting is the BACKSPACE, or CTRL-h.

−E[*c*]   Identical to the −e command except that it only operates on terminals that can BACKSPACE.

−k[*c*]   Sets the KILL character to *c*, defaulting to CTRL-u.

−   Prints the terminal type on the standard output.

−s   Outputs the "setenv" commands [for csh(1)], or "export" and assignment commands [for sh(1)]. The type of commands are determined by the user's login shell.

−h   Forces tset to search /etc/ttytype for information and to overlook the TERM environment variable,

−S   Only outputs the strings to be placed in the environment variables, without the shell commands printed for −s.

−r   Prints the terminal type on the diagnostic output.

−Q   Suppresses the printing of the Erase set to and Kill set to messages.

−I   Suppresses printing of the terminal initialization strings, for example, spawns tput reset instead of tput init.

−m[*ident*][*test baudrate*]:*type*
         Allows a user to specify how a given serial port is is to be mapped to an actual terminal type. The option applies to any serial port in /etc/ttytype whose type is indeterminate (for example, dialup,

plugboard, and so on). The *type* specifies the terminal type to be used, and *ident* identifies the name of the indeterminate type to be matched. If no *ident* is given, all indeterminate types are matched. The *test baudrate* defines a test to be performed on the serial port before the type is assigned. The *baudrate* must be as defined in **stty** [see **stty**(1)]. The *test* may be any combination of: >, =, <, @, and !. If the *type* begins with a question mark, the user is asked if he really wants that type. A null response means to use that type; otherwise, another type can be entered which will be used instead. The question mark must be escaped to prevent filename expansion by the shell. If more than one **–m** option is given, the first correct mapping prevails.

tset is most useful when included in the **.login** [for **csh**(1)] or **.profile** [for **sh**(1)] file executed automatically at login, with **–m** mapping used to specify the terminal type you most frequently dial in on.

EXAMPLES

    tset gt42

    tset –mdialup\>300:adm3a –mdialup:dw2 –Qr –e#

    tset –m dial:ti733 –m plug:\?hp2621 –m unknown:\? –e –k^U

To use the information created by the **–s** option for the Bourne shell, (**sh**), repeat these commands:

        tset –s ... > /tmp/tset$$
        /tmp/tset$$
        rm /tmp/tset$$

To use the information created for **csh**, use:

        set noglob
        set term=('tset –S ....')
        setenv TERM $term[1]
        unset term
        unset noglob

FILES

    /etc/ttytype   Port name to terminal type map database
    /usr/lib/terminfo/*   Terminal capability database

SEE ALSO

    stty(1), **tput**(1), **tty**(1)

    termio(7) in the *System Administrator's Reference Manual*

    terminfo(4) in the *Programmer's Reference Manual*

NOTES

This utility was developed at the University of California at Berkeley and is used with permission.

NAME

tset, reset – establish or restore terminal characteristics

SYNOPSIS

tset [–InQrs] [–e*c*] [–k*c*] [–m [*port* –ID [*baudrate*] : *type*] . . .] [*type*]

reset [–] [–e*c*] [–I] [–k*c*] [–n] [–Q] [–r] [–s]
  [–m [*indent*] [*test baudrate*]: *type*] . . . [*type*]

DESCRIPTION

tset sets up your terminal, typically when you first log in. It does terminal dependent processing such as setting erase and kill characters, setting or resetting delays, sending any sequences needed to properly initialized the terminal, and the like. tset first determines the *type* of terminal involved, and then does necessary initializations and mode settings. If a port is not wired permanently to a specific terminal (not hardwired) it is given an appropriate generic identifier such as dialup.

reset clears the terminal settings by turning off CBREAK and RAW modes, output delays and parity checking, turns on NEWLINE translation, echo and TAB expansion, and restores undefined special characters to their default state. It then sets the modes as usual, based on the terminal type (which will probably override some of the above). See stty(1) for more information. All arguments to tset may be used with reset. reset also uses rs= and rf= to reset the initialization string and file. This is useful after a program dies and leaves the terminal in a funny state. Often in this situation, characters will not echo as you type them. You may have to type '<LINEFEED>reset<LINEFEED>' since '<RETURN>' may not work.

When no arguments are specified, tset reads the terminal type from the TERM environment variable and re-initializes the terminal, and performs initialization of mode, environment and other options at login time to determine the terminal type and set up terminal modes.

When used in a startup script (.profile for sh(1) users or .login for csh(1) users) it is desirable to give information about the type of terminal you will usually use on ports that are not hardwired. Any of the alternate generic names given in /etc/termcap may be used for the identifier. Refer to the –m option below for more information. If no mapping applies and a final *type* option, not preceded by a –m, is given on the command line then that type is used.

It is usually desirable to return the terminal type, as finally determined by tset, and information about the terminal's capabilities, to a shell's environment. This can be done using the –, –s, or –S options.

For the Bourne shell, put this command in your .profile file:

  eval `tset –s *options* . . .`

or using the C shell, put this command in your .login file:

  eval `tset –s *options* . . .`

With the C shell, it is also convenient to make an alias in your `.cshrc` file:

```
alias tset 'eval `tset -s \!*`'
```

This also allows the command:

```
tset 2621
```

to be invoked at any time to set the terminal and environment. It is not possible to get this aliasing effect with a Bourne shell script, because shell scripts cannot set the environment of their parent. If a process could set its parent's environment, none of this nonsense would be necessary in the first place.

Once the terminal type is known, **tset** sets the terminal driver mode. This normally involves sending an initialization sequence to the terminal, setting the single character erase (and optionally the line-kill (full line erase)) characters, and setting special character delays. TAB and NEWLINE expansion are turned off during transmission of the terminal initialization sequence.

On terminals that can backspace but not overstrike (such as a CRT), and when the erase character is '#', the erase character is changed as if **-e** had been used.

The following options are available with **tset**:

- –   The name of the terminal finally decided upon is output on the standard output. This is intended to be captured by the shell and placed in the **TERM** environment variable.

- **-e**c   Set the erase character to be the named character c on all terminals. Default is the BACKSPACE key on the keyboard, usually **^H** (CTRL-H). The character c can either be typed directly, or entered using the circumflex-character notation used here.

- **-i**c   Set the interrupt character to be the named character c on all terminals. Default is **^C** (CTRL-C). The character c can either be typed directly, or entered using the circumflex-character notation used here.

- **-I**   Suppress transmitting terminal-initialization strings.

- **-k**c   Set the line kill character to be the named character c on all terminals. Default is **^U** (CTRL-U). The kill character is left alone if **-k** is not specified. Control characters can be specified by prefixing the alphabetical character with a circumflex (as in CTRL-U) instead of entering the actual control key itself. This allows you to specify control keys that are currently assigned.

- **-n**   Specify that the new tty driver modes should be initialized for this terminal. Probably useless since **stty new** is the default.

- **-Q**   Suppress printing the '**Erase set to**' and '**Kill set to**' messages.

- **-r**   In addition to other actions, reports the terminal type.

- **-s**   Output commands to set and export **TERM**. This can be used with
  ```
  set noglob
  eval `tset -s ...`
  unset noglob
  ```

to bring the terminal information into the environment. Doing so makes programs such as **vi**(1) start up faster. If the **SHELL** environment variable ends with **csh**, C shell commands are output, otherwise Bourne shell commands are output.

−m [*port*-ID[*baudrate*]**:** *type*] . . .

Specify (map) a terminal type when connected to a generic port (such as *dialup* or *plugboard*) identified by *port-ID*. The *baudrate* argument can be used to check the baudrate of the port and set the terminal type accordingly. The target rate is prefixed by any combination of the following operators to specify the conditions under which the mapping is made:

>   Greater than
@   Equals or "at"
<   Less than
!   It is not the case that (negates the above operators)
?   Prompt for the terminal type. If no response is given, then *type* is selected by default.

In the following example, the terminal type is set to **adm3a** if the port is a dialup with a speed of greater than 300 or to **dw2** if the port is a dialup at 300 baud or less. In the third case, the question mark preceding the terminal type indicates that the user is to verify the type desired. A **NULL** response indicates that the named type is correct. Otherwise, the user's response is taken to be the type desired.

```
tset −m 'dialup>300:adm3a' −m 'dialup:dw2' −m \
      'plugboard:?adm3a'
```

To prevent interpretation as metacharacters, the entire argument to **−m** should be enclosed in single quotes. When using the C shell, exclamation points should be preceded by a backslash (\).

EXAMPLES

These examples all use the '−' option. A typical use of **tset** in a **.profile** or **.login** will also use the **−e** and **−k** options, and often the **−n** or **−Q** options as well. These options have been omitted here to keep the examples short.

To select a 2621, you might put the following sequence of commands in your **.login** file (or **.profile** for Bourne shell users).

```
set noglob
eval `tset −s 2621`
unset noglob
```

If you have a switch which connects to various ports (making it impractical to identify which port you may be connected to), and use various terminals from time to time, you can select from among those terminals according to the *speed* or baud rate. In the example below, **tset** will prompt you for a terminal type if the baud rate is greater than 1200 (say, 9600 for a terminal connected by an RS-232 line), and use a Wyse® 50 by default. If the baud rate is less than or equal to 1200, it will select a 2621. Note the placement of the question mark, and the quotes to protect the **>** and **?** from interpretation by the shell.

```
set noglob
eval `tset -s -m 'switch>1200:?wy' -m 'switch<=1200:2621'`
unset noglob
```

The following entry is appropriate if you always dial up, always at the same
baud rate, on many different kinds of terminals, and the terminal you use most
often is an **adm3a**.

```
set noglob
eval `tset -s ?adm3a`
unset noglob
```

If you want to make the selection based only on the baud rate, you might use the
following:

```
set noglob
eval `tset -s -m '>1200:wy' 2621`
unset noglob
```

The following example quietly sets the erase character to BACKSPACE, and kill to
CTRL-U. If the port is switched, it selects a Concept™ 100 for speeds less than or
equal to 1200, and asks for the terminal type otherwise (the default in this case is
a Wyse 50). If the port is a direct dialup, it selects Concept 100 as the terminal
type. If logging in over the ARPANET, the terminal type selected is a Datamedia®
2500 terminal or emulator. Note the backslash escaping the NEWLINE at the end
of the first line in the example.

```
set noglob
eval `tset -e -k^U -Q -s -m 'switch<=1200:concept100' -m \
    'switch:?wy' -m dialup:concept100 -m arpanet:dm2500`
unset noglob
```

FILES

```
.login
.profile
```

SEE ALSO

csh(1), **sh**(1), **vi**(1), **stty**(1) in the *User's Reference Manual*

ttytab(5), **termcap**(5), **environ**(5) in the *System Administrator's Reference Manual*

NOTES

The **tset** command is one of the first commands a user must master when getting started on a UNIX system. Unfortunately, it is one of the most complex,
largely because of the extra effort the user must go through to get the environment of the login shell set. Something needs to be done to make all this simpler,
either the **login** program should do this stuff, or a default shell alias should be
made, or a way to set the environment of the parent should exist.

This program cannot intuit personal choices for erase, interrupt and line kill characters, so it leaves these set to the local system standards.

It could well be argued that the shell should be responsible for ensuring that the
terminal remains in a sane state; this would eliminate the need for the **reset** program.

NAME

tset – provide information for setting terminal modes

SYNOPSIS

tset [*options*] [*type*]

DESCRIPTION

tset allows the user to set a terminal's ERASE and KILL characters, and define the terminal's type and capabilities by creating values for the **TERM** and **TERMCAP** environment variables. If a *type* is given with the -s option, tset creates information for a terminal of the specified type. The type may be any type given in /usr/share/lib/termcap. If the *type* is not specified with the -s option, tset creates information for a terminal of the type defined by the value of the environment variable, **TERM** unless the -h or -m option is given. If the **TERM** variable is undefined, tset looks in /usr/share/lib/termcap for the appropriate information. If these options are used, tset searches the /etc/ttytype file for the terminal type corresponding to the current serial port; it then creates information for a terminal based on this type. If the serial port is not found in /etc/ttytype, the terminal type is set to dumb.

tset displays the created information on the standard output. The information is in a form that can be used to set the current environment variables. The exact form depends on the login shell from which tset was invoked. The examples below illustrate how to use this information to change the variables.

The following options are valid:

-e[*c*]   Sets the ERASE character to [*c*] on all terminals. The default setting is BACKSPACE, or CTRL-H.

-E[*c*]   Identical to the -e option except that it only operates on terminals that can backspace.

-k[*c*]   Sets the KILL character to *c*, defaulting to CTRL-U.

-          Prints the terminal type on the standard output.

-s   Outputs the "**setenv**" commands [for **csh**(1)], or "**export**" and assignment commands [for **sh**(1)]. The type of commands are determined by the user's login shell.

-S   Only outputs the strings to be placed in the environment variables.

-r   Prints the terminal type on the diagnostic output.

-Q   Suppresses the printing of the "**Erase set to**" and "**Kill set to**" messages.

-I   Suppresses printing of the terminal initialization strings.

tset is most useful when included in the .login [for csh] or .profile [for sh] file executed automatically at login, with -m option is given, the first correct mapping prevails.

EXAMPLES

```
tset gt42
tset - mdialup>300:adm3a-mdialup:dw2-Qr-e#
tset -mdial:ti733-mplug:?hp2621-munknown:?-e-k^U
```

To use the information created by the **-s** option for the Bourne shell, (**sh**), repeat these commands:

```
tset -s...>/tmp/tset$$
/tmp/tset$$
rm/tmp/tset$$
```

To use the information for **csh**, use:

```
set noglob
set term=('tset-S...')
setenv TERM$term[1]
setenv TERMCAP"$term[2]"
unset term
unset noglob
```

FILES

　　　/usr/share/lib/termcap　　　　Terminal capability database.

SEE ALSO

　　　stty(1), termcap(1), tty(1)

NAME

tsort – topological sort

SYNOPSIS

tsort [*file*]

DESCRIPTION

The **tsort** command produces on the standard output a totally ordered list of items consistent with a partial ordering of items mentioned in the input *file*. If no *file* is specified, the standard input is understood.

The input consists of pairs of items (nonempty strings) separated by blanks. Pairs of different items indicate ordering. Pairs of identical items indicate presence, but not ordering.

SEE ALSO

lorder(1)

DIAGNOSTICS

Odd data: there is an odd number of fields in the input file.

NAME

tty – get the name of the terminal

SYNOPSIS

tty [–1] [–s]

DESCRIPTION

tty prints the path name of the user's terminal.

–1   prints the synchronous line number to which the user's terminal is connected, if it is on an active synchronous line.

–s   inhibits printing of the terminal path name, allowing one to test just the exit code.

EXIT CODES

2   if invalid options were specified,
0   if standard input is a terminal,
1   otherwise.

DIAGNOSTICS

''not on an active synchronous line'' if the standard input is not a synchronous terminal and –1 is specified.

''not a tty'' if the standard input is not a terminal and –s is not specified.

NAME

ttyadm – format and output port monitor-specific information

SYNOPSIS

/usr/sbin/ttyadm [-b] [-c] [-r *count*] [-h] [-i *msg*] [-m *modules*]
         -p *prompt*] [-t *timeout*] -d *device* -1 *ttylabel* -s *service*

/usr/sbin/ttyadm -V

DESCRIPTION

The **ttyadm** command is an administrative command that formats **ttymon**-specific information and writes it to the standard output. The Service Access Facility (SAF) requires each port monitor to provide such a command. Note that the port monitor administrative file is updated by the Service Access Controller's administrative commands, **sacadm** and **pmadm**. **ttyadm** provides a means of presenting formatted port monitor-specific (that is, **ttymon**-specific) data to these commands.

-b	Sets the "bidirectional port" flag. When this flag is set, the line can be used in both directions. **ttymon** will allow users to connect to the service associated with the port, but if the port is free, **uucico**, **cu**, or **ct** can use it for dialing out.
-c	Sets the connect-on-carrier flag for the port. If the –c flag is set, **ttymon** will invoke the port's associated service immediately when a connect indication is received (that is, no prompt is printed and no baud-rate searching is done).
-d *device*	*device* is the full pathname of the device file for the TTY port.
-h	Sets the hangup flag for the port. If the –h flag is not set, **ttymon** will force a hangup on the line by setting the speed to zero before setting the speed to the default or specified value.
-i *message*	Specifies the inactive (disabled) response message. This message will be sent to the TTY port if the port is disabled or the **ttymon** monitoring the port is disabled.
-1 *ttylabel*	Specifies which *ttylabel* in the /etc/ttydefs file to use as the starting point when searching for the proper baud rate.
-m *modules*	Specifies a list of pushable STREAMS modules. The modules will be pushed, in the order in which they are specified, before the service is invoked. *modules* must be a comma-separated list of modules, with no white space included. Any modules currently on the stream will be popped before these modules are pushed.
-r *count*	When the –r option is invoked, **ttymon** will wait until it receives data from the port before it displays a prompt. If *count* is equal to zero, **ttymon** will wait until it receives any character. If *count* is greater than zero, **ttymon** will wait until *count* newlines have been received.
-p *prompt*	Specifies the prompt message, for example, "**login:**."

-s *service*   *service* is the full pathname of the service to be invoked when a connection request is received. If arguments are required, the command and its arguments must be enclosed in double quotes.

-t *timeout*   Specifies that **ttymon** should close a port if the open on the port succeeds and no input data is received in *timeout* seconds.

-v   Displays the version number of the current **/usr/lib/saf/ttymon** command.

OUTPUT

If successful, **ttyadm** will generate the requested information, write it on the standard output, and exit with a status of 0. If **ttyadm** is invoked with an invalid number of arguments or invalid arguments, or if an incomplete option is specified, an error message will be written to the standard error and **ttymon** will exit with a non-zero status.

FILES

/etc/ttydefs

SEE ALSO

pmadm(1M), sacadm(1M), ttymon(1M)
System Administrator's Guide, "The Port Monitor **ttymon**"

NAME

    ttymon – port monitor for terminal ports

SYNOPSIS

    /usr/lib/saf/ttymon

    /usr/lib/saf/ttymon –g [**–h**] [**–d** *device*] [**–l** *ttylabel*] [**–t** *timeout*] \
        [**–p** *prompt*] [**–m** *modules*]

DESCRIPTION

    ttymon is a STREAMS-based TTY port monitor. Its function is to monitor ports, to set terminal modes, baud rates, and line disciplines for the ports, and to connect users or applications to services associated with the ports. Normally, **ttymon** is configured to run under the Service Access Controller, **sac**, as part of the Service Access Facility (SAF). It is configured using the **sacadm** command. Each instance of **ttymon** can monitor multiple ports. The ports monitored by an instance of **ttymon** are specified in the port monitor's administrative file. The administrative file is configured using the **pmadm** and **ttyadm** commands. When an instance of **ttymon** is invoked by the **sac** command, it starts to monitor its ports. For each port, **ttymon** first initializes the line disciplines, if they are specified, and the speed and terminal settings. The values used for initialization are taken from the appropriate entry in the TTY settings file. This file is maintained by the **sttydefs** command. Default line disciplines on ports are usually set up by the **autopush** command of the Autopush Facility.

    ttymon then writes the prompt and waits for user input. If the user indicates that the speed is inappropriate by pressing the BREAK key, **ttymon** tries the next speed and writes the prompt again. When valid input is received, **ttymon** interprets the per-service configuration file for the port, if one exists, creates a **utmp** entry if required, establishes the service environment, and then invokes the service associated with the port. Valid input consists of a string of at least one non-newline character, terminated by a carriage return. After the service terminates, **ttymon** cleans up the **utmp** entry, if one exists, and returns the port to its initial state.

    If *autobaud* is enabled for a port, **ttymon** will try to determine the baud rate on the port automatically. Users must enter a carriage return before **ttymon** can recognize the baud rate and print the prompt. Currently, the baud rates that can be determined by *autobaud* are **110**, **1200**, **2400**, **4800**, and **9600**.

    If a port is configured as a bidirectional port, **ttymon** will allow users to connect to a service, and, if the port is free, will allow **uucico**, **cu** or **ct** to use it for dialing out. If a port is bidirectional, **ttymon** will wait to read a character before it prints a prompt.

    If the *connect-on-carrier* flag is set for a port, **ttymon** will immediately invoke the port's associated service when a connection request is received. The prompt message will not be sent.

    If a port is disabled, **ttymon** will not start any service on that port. If a disabled message is specified, **ttymon** will send out the disabled message when a connection request is received. If **ttymon** is disabled, all ports under that instance of **ttymon** will also be disabled.

SERVICE INVOCATION

The service **ttymon** invokes for a port is specified in the **ttymon** administrative file. **ttymon** will scan the character string giving the service to be invoked for this port, looking for a **%d** or a **%%** two-character sequence. If **%d** is found, **ttymon** will modify the service command to be executed by replacing those two characters by the full path name of this port (the device name). If **%%** is found, they will be replaced by a single **%**.

When the service is invoked, file descriptor **0**, **1**, and **2** are opened to the port device for reading and writing. The service is invoked with the user ID, group ID and current home directory set to that of the user name under which the service was registered with **ttymon**. Two environment variables, HOME and TTYPROMPT, are added to the service's environment by **ttymon**. HOME is set to the HOME directory of the user name under which the service is invoked. TTYPROMPT is set to the prompt string configured for the service on the port. This is provided so that a service invoked by **ttymon** has a means of determining if a prompt was actually issued by **ttymon** and, if so, what that prompt actually was.

See **ttyadm**(1M) for options that can be set for ports monitored by **ttymon** under the Service Access Controller.

INVOKING A STAND-ALONE ttymon PROCESS

A special invocation of **ttymon** is provided with the **−g** option. This form of the command should only be called by applications that need to set the correct baud rate and terminal settings on a port and then connect to **login** service, but that cannot be pre-configured under the SAC. The following combinations of options can be used with **−g**:

−d *device*   *device* is the full path name of the port to which **ttymon** is to attach. If this option is not specified, file descriptor **0** must be set up by the invoking process to a TTY port.

−h   If the -h flag is not set, **ttymon** will force a hangup on the line by setting the speed to zero before setting the speed to the default or specified speed.

−t *timeout*   Specifies that **ttymon** should exit if no one types anything in *timeout* seconds after the prompt is sent.

−l *ttylabel*   *ttylabel* is a link to a speed and TTY definition in the **ttydefs** file. This definition tells **ttymon** at what speed to run initially, what the initial TTY settings are, and what speed to try next if the user indicates that the speed is inappropriate by pressing the BREAK key. The default speed is 9600 baud.

−p *prompt*   Allows the user to specify a prompt string. The default prompt is "Login: ".

−m *modules*   When initializing the port, **ttymon** will pop all modules on the port, and then push *modules* in the order specified. *modules* is a comma-separated list of pushable modules. Default modules on the ports are usually set up by the Autopush Facility.

SEE ALSO

pmadm(1M), sac(1M), sacadm(1M), ttyadm(1M)

System Administrator's Guide, "The Port Monitor **ttymon**"

NOTES

If a port is monitored by more than one **ttymon**, it is possible for the **ttymon**s to send out prompt messages in such a way that they compete for input.

NAME

tunefs – tune up an existing file system

SYNOPSIS

tunefs [-a *maxcontig*] [-d *rotdelay*] [-e *maxbpg*] [-m *minfree*] [-o [s | space | t | time]] *special* | *filesystem*

DESCRIPTION

tunefs is designed to change the dynamic parameters of a file system which affect the layout policies. The file system must be unmounted before using tunefs. The parameters which are to be changed are indicated by the options given below:

The options are:

-a *maxcontig*   Specify the maximum number of contiguous blocks that will be laid out before forcing a rotational delay (see -d below). The default value is one, since most device drivers require an interrupt per disk transfer. Device drivers that can chain several buffers together in a single transfer should set this to the maximum chain length.

-d *rotdelay*   Specify the expected time (in milliseconds) to service a transfer completion interrupt and initiate a new transfer on the same disk. It is used to decide how much rotational spacing to place between successive blocks in a file.

-e *maxbpg*   Indicate the maximum number of blocks any single file can allocate out of a cylinder group before it is forced to begin allocating blocks from another cylinder group. Typically this value is set to approximately one quarter of the total blocks in a cylinder group. The intent is to prevent any single file from using up all the blocks in a single cylinder group, thus degrading access times for all files subsequently allocated in that cylinder group. The effect of this limit is to cause big files to do long seeks more frequently than if they were allowed to allocate all the blocks in a cylinder group before seeking elsewhere. For file systems with exclusively large files, this parameter should be set higher.

-m *minfree*   Specify the percentage of space held back from normal users; the minimum free space threshold. The default value used is 10%. This value can be set to zero, however up to a factor of three in throughput will be lost over the performance obtained at a 10% threshold. Note: if the value is raised above the current usage level, users will be unable to allocate files until enough files have been deleted to get under the higher threshold.

-o [s | space | t | time]   Change optimization strategy for the file system. s and space are interchangeable, and t and time are interchangeable.

        s or space - conserve space.
        t or time - attempt to organize file layout to minimize access time.

Generally one should optimize for time unless the file system is over 90% full.

SEE ALSO
     `mkfs`(1M)

NAME

uadmin – administrative control

SYNOPSIS

/sbin/uadmin *cmd fcn*

DESCRIPTION

The **uadmin** command provides control for basic administrative functions. This command is tightly coupled to the System Administration procedures and is not intended for general use. It may be invoked only by the super-user.

The arguments *cmd* (command) and *fcn* (function) are converted to integers and passed to the **uadmin** system call.

SEE ALSO

uadmin(2) in the *Programmer's Reference Manual*

NAME

ufsdump – incremental file system dump

SYNOPSIS

ufsdump [*options* [*arguments*]] *filesystem*

DESCRIPTION

ufsdump backs up all files in *filesystem*, where *filesystem* represents a special device, or files changed after a certain date, to magnetic tape; *options* is a string that specifies ufsdump options, as shown below. Any *arguments* supplied for specific options are given as subsequent words on the command line, in the same order as that of the *options* listed.

If no *options* are given, the default is 9u.

The options are:

0–9　　The dump level. All files in the *filesystem* that have been modified since the last ufsdump at a lower dump level are copied to the volume. For instance, if you did a level 2 dump on Monday, followed by a level 4 dump on Tuesday, a subsequent level 3 dump on Wednesday would contain all files modified or added since the level 2 (Monday) backup. A level 0 dump copies the entire filesystem to the dump volume.

b *factor*

Blocking factor. Specify the blocking factor for tape writes. The default is 20 blocks per write. Note: the blocking factor is specified in terms of 512 bytes blocks, for compatibility with tar. The default blocking factor for tapes of density 6250BPI and greater is 64. The default blocking factor for cartridge tapes (c option specified) is 126. The highest blocking factor available with most tape drives is 126.

c　　　Cartridge. Use a cartridge instead of the standard half-inch reel. This sets the density to 1000BPI and the blocking factor to 126. The length is set to 425 feet. This option is incompatible with the d option, unless you specify a density of 1000BPI with that option.

d *bpi*　Tape density. The density of the tape, expressed in BPI, is taken from *bpi*. This is used to keep a running tab on the amount of tape used per reel. The default density is 1600 except for cartridge tape. Unless a higher density is specified explicitly, ufsdump uses its default density — even if the tape drive is capable of higher-density operation (for instance, 6250BPI). Note: the density specified should correspond to the density of the tape device being used, or ufsdump will not be able to handle end-of-tape properly.

f *dump-file*

Dump file. Use *dump-file* as the file to dump to, instead of /dev/rmt8. If *dump-file* is specified as –, dump to the standard output.

n　　　Notify all operators in the operator group that ufsdump requires attention by sending messages to their terminals, in a manner similar to that used by the wall command.

s *size*   Specify the *size* of the volume being dumped to. When the specified size is reached, **ufsdump** waits for you to change the volume. **ufsdump** interprets the specified size as the length in feet for tapes and cartridges, and as the number of 1024-byte blocks for diskettes. The following are defaults:

            cartridge   425 feet

            diskette   1422 blocks (Corresponds to a 1.44 Mb diskette, with one cylinder reserved for bad block information.)

t *tracks*   Specify the number of tracks for a cartridge tape. The default is 9 tracks. The **t** option is not compatible with the **D** option.

u   Update the dump record. Add an entry to the file **/etc/dumpdates,** for each filesystem successfully dumped that includes the filesystem name, date, and dump level. This file can be edited by the super-user.

w   List the file systems that need backing up. This information is gleaned from the files **/etc/dumpdates** and **/etc/vfstab**. When the **w** option is used, all other options are ignored. After reporting, **ufsdump** exits immediately.

W   Similar to the **w** option, except that the **W** option includes all file systems that appear in **/etc/dumpdates,** along with information about their most recent dump dates and levels. Filesystems that need backing up are highlighted.

NOTES

Fewer than 32 read errors on the filesystem are ignored.

Each reel requires a new process, so parent processes for reels already written just hang around until the entire tape is written.

It is recommended that incremental dumps also be performed with the system running in single-user mode.

FILES

/dev/rmt8	default unit to dump to
/etc/dumpdates	dump date record
/etc/group	to find group operator
/etc/hosts	

SEE ALSO

df(1M), **shutdown**(1M), **ufsrestore**(1M), **wall**(1M).
tar(1) in the *User's Reference Manual.*

NAME

ufsrestore – incremental file system restore

SYNOPSIS

ufsrestore *options* [*arguments*] [*filename* . . .]

DESCRIPTION

ufsrestore restores files from backup tapes created with the ufsdump command. *options* is a string of at least one of the options listed below, along with any modifiers and arguments you supply. Any *arguments* supplied for specific options are given as subsequent words on the command line, in the same order as that of the *options* listed. Remaining arguments to ufsrestore are the names of files (or directories whose files) are to be restored to disk. Unless the h modifier is in effect, a directory name refers to the files it contains, and (recursively) its sub-directories and the files they contain.

The options are:

i   Interactive. After reading in the directory information from the tape, ufsrestore invokes an interactive interface that allows you to browse through the dump tape's directory hierarchy and select individual files to be extracted. See **Interactive Commands**, below, for a description of available commands.

r   Restore the entire tape. Load the tape's full contents into the current directory. This option should be used only to restore a complete dump tape onto a clear filesystem, or to restore an incremental dump tape after a full level 0 restore.

R   Resume restoring. ufsrestore requests a particular tape of a multivolume set from which to resume a full restore (see the r option above). This allows ufsrestore to start from a checkpoint when it is interrupted in the middle of a full restore.

t   Table of contents. List each *filename* that appears on the tape. If no *filename* argument is given, the root directory is listed. This results in a list of all files on the tape, unless the h modifier is in effect.

x   Extract the named files from the tape. If a named file matches a directory whose contents were written onto the tape, and the h modifier is not in effect, the directory is recursively extracted. The owner, modification time, and mode are restored (if possible). If no *filename* argument is given, the root directory is extracted. This results in the entire tape being extracted unless the h modifier is in effect.

Some of the following modifiers take arguments that are given as separate words on the command line. When more than one such modifier appears within *options*, the arguments must appear in the same order as the modifiers that they apply to.

c   Convert the contents of the dump tape to the new filesystem format.

d   Debug. Turn on debugging output.

h   Extract the actual directory, rather than the files that it references. This prevents hierarchical restoration of complete subtrees from the tape.

m   Extract by inode numbers rather than by filename to avoid regenerating complete pathnames. This is useful if only a few files are being extracted.

v   Verbose. **ufsrestore** displays the name of each file it restores, preceded by its file type.

y   Do not ask whether to abort the restore in the event of tape errors. **ufsrestore** tries to skip over the bad tape block(s) and continue as best it can.

b *factor*
Blocking factor. Specify the blocking factor for tape reads. By default, **ufsrestore** will attempt to figure out the block size of the tape. Note: a tape block is 512 bytes.

f *dump-file*
Use *dump-file* instead of **/dev/rmt?** as the file to restore from. If *dump-file* is specified as '−', **ufsrestore** reads from the standard input. This allows, **ufsdump**(1M) and **ufsrestore** to be used in a pipeline to dump and restore a file system, as shown in the example below. (The device names on your system may differ from those shown in the example.)

       ufsdump 0f − /dev/rxy0g | (cd /mnt; ufsrestore xf −)

If the name of the file is of the form *machine*:*device* the restore is done from the specified machine over the network using **rmt**(1M). Since **ufsrestore** is normally run by root, the name of the local machine must appear in the **.rhosts** file of the remote machine. If the file is specified as *user*!*machine*:*device*, **ufsrestore** will attempt to execute as the specified user on the remote machine. The specified user must have a **.rhosts** file on the remote machine that allows root from the local machine. If **ufsrestore** is called as **ufsrrestore**, the tape defaults to **dumphost**:**/dev/rmt8**. To direct the input from a desired remote machine, set up an alias for **dumphost** in the file **/etc/hosts**.

s *n*   Skip to the *n*'th file when there are multiple dump files on the same tape, as shown in the example below. (The device names on your system may differ from those shown in the example.)

       ufsrestore xfs /dev/nrar0 5

would position you at the fifth file on the tape.

ufsrestore enters interactive mode when invoked with the **i** option. Interactive commands are reminiscent of the shell. For those commands that accept an argument, the default is the current directory.

ls [*directory*]   List files in **directory** or the current directory, represented by a '**.**' (period). Directories are appended with a '**/**' (backslash). Entries marked for extraction are prefixed with a '*****' (asterisk). If the verbose option is in effect, inode numbers are also listed.

cd *directory*	Change to directory **directory** (within the dump-tape).
pwd	Print the full pathname of the current working directory.
add [*filename*]	Add the current directory, or the named file or directory **directory** to the list of files to extract. If a directory is specified, add that directory and its files (recursively) to the extraction list (unless the **h** modifier is in effect).

delete [*filename*]

    Delete the current directory, or the named file or directory from the list of files to extract. If a directory is specified, delete that directory and all its descendents from the extraction list (unless the **h** modifier is in effect). The most expedient way to extract a majority of files from a directory is to add that directory to the extraction list, and then delete specific files to omit.

extract	Extract all files on the extraction list from the dump tape. **ufsrestore** asks which volume the user wishes to mount. The fastest way to extract a small number of files is to start with the last tape volume and work toward the first.
verbose	Toggle the status of the **v** modifier. While **v** is in effect, the **ls** command lists the inode numbers of all entries, and **ufsrestore** displays information about each file as it is extracted.
help	Display a summary of the available commands.
quit	**ufsrestore** exits immediately, even if the extraction list is not empty.

NOTES

    ufsrestore can get confused when doing incremental restores from dump tapes that were made on active file systems.

    A level **0** dump must be done after a full restore. Because **ufsrestore** runs in user mode, it has no control over inode allocation; this means that **ufsrestore** repositions the files, although it does not change their contents. Thus, a full dump must be done to get a new set of directories reflecting the new file positions, so that later incremental dumps will be correct.

DIAGNOSTICS

    ufsrestore complains about bad option characters.

    Read errors result in complaints. If **y** has been specified, or the user responds **y**, **ufsrestore** will attempt to continue.

    If the dump extends over more than one tape, **ufsrestore** asks the user to change tapes. If the **x** or **i** option has been specified, **ufsrestore** also asks which volume the user wishes to mount.

    There are numerous consistency checks that can be listed by **ufsrestore**. Most checks are self-explanatory or can never happen. Common errors are given below.

Converting to new file system format.
> A dump tape created from the old file system has been loaded. It is automatically converted to the new file system format.

filename: not found on tape
> The specified file name was listed in the tape directory, but was not found on the tape. This is caused by tape read errors while looking for the file, and from using a dump tape created on an active file system.

expected next file *inumber*, got *inumber*
> A file that was not listed in the directory showed up. This can occur when using a dump tape created on an active file system.

Incremental tape too low
> When doing an incremental restore, a tape that was written before the previous incremental tape, or that has too low an incremental level has been loaded.

Incremental tape too high
> When doing incremental restore, a tape that does not begin its coverage where the previous incremental tape left off, or one that has too high an incremental level has been loaded.

Tape read error while restoring *filename*
Tape read error while skipping over inode inumber
Tape read error while trying to resynchronize
A tape read error has occurred.
> If a file name is specified, then its contents are probably partially wrong. If an inode is being skipped or the tape is trying to resynchronize, then no extracted files have been corrupted, though files may not be found on the tape.

resync ufsrestore, skipped *num*
> After a tape read error, ufsrestore may have to resynchronize itself. This message lists the number of blocks that were skipped over.

FILES

/dev/rmt8	the default tape drive
dumphost:/dev/rmt8	
	the default tape drive if called as **ufsrrestore**
/tmp/rstdir*	file containing directories on the tape
/tmp/rstmode*	owner, mode, and timestamps for directories
./restoresymtable	information passed between incremental restores

SEE ALSO

ufsdump(1M), mkfs(1M), mount(1M)

NAME

ul – underline

SYNOPSIS

/usr/ucb/ul [–i] [–t *terminal*] [*filename* . . .]

DESCRIPTION

The **ul** command reads the named *filenames* (or the standard input if none are given) and translates occurrences of underscores to the sequence which indicates underlining for the terminal in use, as specified by the environment variable **TERM**. **ul** uses the **/usr/share/lib/termcap** file to determine the appropriate sequences for underlining. If the terminal is incapable of underlining, but is capable of a standout mode then that is used instead. If the terminal can overstrike, or handles underlining automatically, **ul** degenerates to **cat**. If the terminal cannot underline, underlining is ignored.

The following options are available:

–t *terminal*   Override the terminal kind specified in the environment. If the terminal cannot underline, underlining is ignored.

–i   Indicate underlining by a separate line containing appropriate dashes –; this is useful when you want to look at the underlining which is present in an **nroff** output stream on a CRT-terminal.

SEE ALSO

man(1), **nroff**(1)

cat(1) in the *User's Reference Manual*

NAME

umask – set file-creation mode mask

SYNOPSIS

umask [*ooo*]

DESCRIPTION

The user file-creation mode mask is set to *ooo*. The three octal digits refer to read/write/execute permissions for *owner*, **group**, and *others*, respectively (see chmod(2) and umask(2)). The value of each specified digit is subtracted from the corresponding "digit" specified by the system for the creation of a file (see creat(2)). For example, **umask 022** removes **group** and *others* write permission (files normally created with mode **777** become mode **755**; files created with mode **666** become mode **644**).

If *ooo* is omitted, the current value of the mask is printed.

umask is recognized and executed by the shell.

umask can be included in the user's **.profile** (see **profile**(4)) and invoked at login to automatically set the user's permissions on files or directories created.

SEE ALSO

chmod(1), sh(1).
chmod(2), creat(2), umask(2) in the *Programmer's Reference Manual*.
profile(4) in the *System Administrator's Reference Manual*.

NAME

uname – print name of current UNIX system

SYNOPSIS

uname [-amnprsv]

uname [-S *nodename*]

DESCRIPTION

uname prints the current system name of the UNIX system to standard output. It is mainly useful to determine which system one is using. The options cause selected information returned by uname(2) and/or sysinfo(2) to be printed:

-a Print all information. Output will in the following order:
   systemname nodename release version machine hostprocessor

-m Print the machine hardware name (*machine*).

-n Print the *nodename* (the *nodename* is the name by which the system is known to a communications network).

-p Print the current host's processor type (*hostprocessor*).

-r Print the operating system release (*release*).

-s Print the name of the operating system (*systemname*) (for example, UNIX System V). This is the default.

-v Print the operating system version (*version*).

-S Change *nodename* (see -n option above). *nodename* is restricted to SYS_NMLN characters. SYS_NMLN is an implementation specific value defined in sys/utsname.h. Only a privileged user is allowed this capability.

   For computers based on Intel microprocessors, using the -S option also changes the name of the operating system (*systemname*).

NOTES

The output of uname is affected by the environment variable SCOMPAT. SCOMPAT is part of the application compatibility features provided to support UNIX applications other than UNIX System V Release 4.

SEE ALSO

sysinfo(2), uname(2) in the *Programmer's Reference Manual*

scompat(1) in the *Migration and Compatibility Guide*

setuname(1M) in the *System Administrator's Reference Manual*

NAME

unget – undo a previous **get** of an SCCS file

SYNOPSIS

unget [-r*SID*] [-s] [-n] *files*

DESCRIPTION

unget undoes the effect of a **get** -e done prior to creating the intended new delta. If a directory is named, **unget** behaves as though each file in the directory were specified as a named file, except that non-SCCS files and unreadable files are silently ignored. If a name of – is given, the standard input is read with each line being taken as the name of an SCCS file to be processed.

Keyletter arguments apply independently to each named file.

-r*SID*   Uniquely identifies which delta is no longer intended. (This would have been specified by **get** as the "new delta"). The use of this keyletter is necessary only if two or more outstanding **gets** for editing on the same SCCS file were done by the same person (login name). A diagnostic results if the specified *SID* is ambiguous, or if it is necessary and omitted on the command line.

-s   Suppresses the printout, on the standard output, of the intended delta's *SID*.

-n   Causes the retention of the gotten file, which would normally be removed from the current directory.

unget must be performed by the same user who performed the original **get** -e.

FILES

p-file   [see **delta**(1)]

q-file   [see **delta**(1)]

z-file   [see **delta**(1)]

SEE ALSO

delta(1), **get**(1), **help**(1), **sact**(1)

DIAGNOSTICS

Use **help**(1) for explanations.

NAME

unifdef – resolve and remove `ifdef`'ed lines from C program source

SYNOPSIS

/usr/ucb/unifdef [–clt] [–D*name*] [–U*name*] [–iD*name*] [–iU*name*]
... [*filename*]

DESCRIPTION

unifdef removes `ifdef`ed lines from a file while otherwise leaving the file alone. It is smart enough to deal with the nested `ifdef`s, comments, single and double quotes of C syntax, but it does not do any including or interpretation of macros. Neither does it strip out comments, though it recognizes and ignores them. You specify which symbols you want defined with –D options, and which you want undefined with –U options. Lines within those `ifdef`s will be copied to the output, or removed, as appropriate. Any `ifdef`, `ifndef`, `else`, and `endif` lines associated with *filename* will also be removed.

`ifdef`s involving symbols you do not specify are untouched and copied out along with their associated `ifdef`, `else`, and `endif` lines.

If an `ifdef`X occurs nested inside another `ifdef`X, then the inside `ifdef` is treated as if it were an unrecognized symbol. If the same symbol appears in more than one argument, only the first occurrence is significant.

unifdef copies its output to the standard output and will take its input from the standard input if no *filename* argument is given.

The following options are available:

-c   Complement the normal operation. Lines that would have been removed or blanked are retained, and vice versa.

-l   Replace "lines removed" lines with blank lines.

-t   Plain text option. unifdef refrains from attempting to recognize comments and single and double quotes.

-iD*name*   Ignore, but print out, lines associated with the defined symbol *name*. If you use `ifdef`s to delimit non-C lines, such as comments or code which is under construction, then you must tell unifdef which symbols are used for that purpose so that it will not try to parse for quotes and comments within them.

-iU*name*   Ignore, but print out, lines associated with the undefined symbol *name*.

SEE ALSO

cc(1)

cc(1) in the *Programmer's Reference Manual*
diff(1) in the *User's Reference Manual*

DIAGNOSTICS

Premature EOF   Inappropriate `else` or `endif`.

Exit status is 0 if output is exact copy of input, 1 if not, 2 if unifdef encounters problems.

NAME

uniq – report repeated lines in a file

SYNOPSIS

uniq [-udc [+n] [-n]] [*input* [*output*]]

DESCRIPTION

uniq reads the input file comparing adjacent lines. In the normal case, the second and succeeding copies of repeated lines are removed; the remainder is written on the output file. *Input* and *output* should always be different. Note that repeated lines must be adjacent in order to be found; see **sort**(1). If the –u flag is used, just the lines that are not repeated in the original file are output. The –d option specifies that one copy of just the repeated lines is to be written. The normal mode output is the union of the –u and –d mode outputs.

The –c option supersedes –u and –d and generates an output report in default style but with each line preceded by a count of the number of times it occurred.

The *n* arguments specify skipping an initial portion of each line in the comparison:

–*n*   The first *n* fields together with any blanks before each are ignored. A field is defined as a string of non-space, non-tab characters separated by tabs and spaces from its neighbors.

+*n*   The first *n* characters are ignored. Fields are skipped before characters.

SEE ALSO

comm(1), sort(1).

NAME

units – conversion program

SYNOPSIS

`units`

DESCRIPTION

`units` converts quantities expressed in various standard scales to their equivalents in other scales. It works interactively in this fashion:

You have: `inch`
You want: `cm`
   * 2.540000e+00
   / 3.937008e−01

A quantity is specified as a multiplicative combination of units optionally preceded by a numeric multiplier. Powers are indicated by suffixed positive integers, division by the usual sign:

You have: `15 lbs force/in2`
You want: `atm`
   * 1.020689e+00
   / 9.797299e−01

`units` only does multiplicative scale changes; thus it can convert Kelvin to Rankine, but not Celsius to Fahrenheit. Most familiar units, abbreviations, and metric prefixes are recognized, together with a generous leavening of exotica and a few constants of nature including:

pi	ratio of circumference to diameter,
c	speed of light,
e	charge on an electron,
g	acceleration of gravity,
force	same as **g**,
mole	Avogadro's number,
water	pressure head per unit height of water,
au	astronomical unit.

Pound is not recognized as a unit of mass; **lb** is. Compound names are run together, (for example, **lightyear**). British units that differ from their U.S. counterparts are prefixed thus: **brgallon**. For a complete list of units, type:

`cat /usr/share/lib/unittab`

FILES

`/usr/share/lib/unittab`

NAME

unshare – make local resource unavailable for mounting by remote systems

SYNOPSIS

unshare [–**F** *fstype*] [–**o** *specific_options*] [*pathname* | *resourcename*]

DESCRIPTION

The **unshare** command makes a shared local resource unavailable to file system type *fstype*. If the option –**F** *fstype* is omitted, then the first file system type listed in file **/etc/dfs/fstypes** will be used as the default. *Specific_options*, as well as the semantics of *resourcename*, are specific to particular distributed file systems.

FILES

/etc/dfs/fstypes
/etc/dfs/sharetab

SEE ALSO

share(1M), **shareall**(1M).

NOTES

If *pathname* or *resourcename* is not found in the shared information, an error message will be sent to standard error.

NAME

unshare – make local NFS resource unavailable for mounting by remote systems

SYNOPSIS

unshare [-F nfs] *pathname*

DESCRIPTION

The **unshare** command makes local resources unavailable for mounting by remote systems. The shared resource must correspond to a line with NFS as the *fstype* in the file **/etc/dfs/sharetab**. The **-F** option may be omitted if NFS is the first file system type listed in the files **/etc/dfs/fstypes**.

FILES

/etc/dfs/fstypes
/etc/dfs/sharetab

SEE ALSO

share(1M)

NAME

unshare – make local RFS resource unavailable for mounting by remote systems

SYNOPSIS

unshare [–**F** rfs] {*pathname* | *resourcename*}

DESCRIPTION

The **unshare** command makes a shared resource unavailable through Remote File Sharing. The shared resource must correspond to a line with rfs as the *fstype* in the file **/etc/dfs/sharetab**. The **–F** flag may be omitted if RFS is the first file system type listed in the file **/etc/dfs/fstypes**.

FILES

/etc/dfs/dfstab
/etc/dfs/fstypes
/etc/dfs/sharetab

SEE ALSO

unshare(1M), share(1M)

NAME

uptime – show how long the system has been up

SYNOPSIS

/usr/ucb/uptime

DESCRIPTION

The **uptime** command prints the current time, the length of time the system has been up. It is the first line of a **w**(1) command.

EXAMPLE

Below is an example of the output **uptime** provides:

```
uptime
6:47am  up 6 days, 16:38,   1 users
```

SEE ALSO

w(1)

whodo(1) in the *System Administrator's Reference Manual*
who in the *User's Reference Manual*

NOTES

who **−b** gives the time the system was last booted.

NAME

urestore – request restore of files and directories

SYNOPSIS

urestore [-mn] [-s | v] [-o *target*] [-d *date*] -F *file* . . .

urestore [-mn] [-s | v] [-o *target*] [-d *date*] -D *dir* . . .

urestore -c *jobid*

DESCRIPTION

urestore posts requests for files or directories to be restored from system-maintained archives. If the appropriate archive containing the requested files or directories is on-line, the files or directories are restored immediately. If not, a request to restore the specified files or directories is posted to a restore status table, **/etc/bkup/rsstatus.tab**. A restore request that has been posted must later be resolved by an operator (see **rsoper**(1M)). Each file or directory to be restored is assigned a **restore** job ID that can be used to monitor the progress of the restore (see **ursstatus**(1M)) or to cancel it.

The user must have write permission for the current directory and any subdirectories to be traversed in storing the restored files or directories. Requests for restores may be made only by the user who owned the files or directories at the time the archive containing the files or directories was made, or by a user with superuser privileges.

Options

-c *jobid*   Cancels a previously issued restore request.

-d *date*   Restores the filesystem or directory as of *date*. (This may or may not be the latest archive.) See **getdate**(3C) for valid date formats.

-m   If the restore cannot be carried out immediately, this option notifies the invoking user (via **mail**) when the request has been completed.

-n   Displays a list of all archived versions of the filesystem or directory contained in the backup history log but does not attempt to restore the filesystem or directory.

-o *target*   Instead of restoring directly to the specified file or directory, this option replaces the file or directory *target* with the archive of the specified file or directory.

-s   While a restore operation is occurring, displays a "." for each 100 (512-byte) blocks transferred from the destination device.

-v   Displays the name of each object as it is restored. Only those archiving methods that restore named directories and files (**incfile**, **ffile**) support this option.

-D   Initiates a restore operation for directories.

-F   Initiates a restore operation for files.

DIAGNOSTICS

The exit codes for **urestore** are the following:

0 = the task completed successfully
1 = one or more parameters to **urestore** are invalid
2 = an error has occurred, causing **urestore** to fail to
complete *all* portions of its task.

EXAMPLES

Example 1:

        urestore -m -F bigfile

posts a request to restore the most current archived version of the file **bigfile**.
If the restore operation cannot be carried out immediately, it notifies the invoking
user when the request has been completed.

Example 2:

        urestore -c rest-256a,rest-256b

cancels restore requests with job ID numbers **rest-256a** and **rest-256b**.

Example 3:

        urestore -o /testfiles/myfile.b -F /testfiles/myfile.a

posts a request for the archived file **/testfiles/myfile.a** to be restored as
/testfiles/myfile.b

Example 4:

        urestore -d "december 1, 1987" -D /user1 -v

posts a request for the archived directory structure **/user1**, with all its files and
subdirectories, to be restored as of December 1, 1987. If the restore is done
immediately from an on-line archive, the name of each file will be displayed on
standard output while the restore is underway.

Example 5:

        urestore -n -D /pr3/reports

requests the system to display the backup dates and an **ls -l** listing from the
backup history log of all archived versions of the directory **/pr3/reports**. The
directory is not restored.

FILES

/etc/bkup/bkhist.tab	–	contains the labels of all volumes that have been used for backup operations
/etc/bkup/rsstatus.tab	–	contains status information about all restore requests from users
/etc/bkup/rsnotify.tab	–	contains the electronic mail address of the operator to be notified whenever restore requests require operator intervention

SEE ALSO

restore(1M), **ursstatus**(1M)
mail(1) in the *User's Reference Manual*
getdate(3C) in the *Programmer's Reference Manual*

NAME

useradd – administer a new user login on the system

SYNOPSIS

useradd [−u *uid* [−o]] [−g *group*] [−G *group*[,*group*...]] [−d *dir*] [−s *shell*]
    [−c *comment*] [−m [−k *skel_dir*]] [−f *inactive*] [−e *expire*] *login*
useradd −D [−g *group*] [−b *base_dir*] [−f *inactive*] [−e *expire*]

DESCRIPTION

Invoking useradd without the −D option adds a new user entry to the /etc/passwd and /etc/shadow files. It also creates supplementary group memberships for the user (−G option) and creates the home directory (−m option) for the user if requested. The new login remains locked until the passwd(1M) command is executed.

Invoking useradd −D with no additional options displays the default values for *group*, *base_dir*, *shel_dir*, *shell*, *inactive*, and *expire*. The values for *group*, *base_dir*, *inactive*, *expire*, and *shell* are used for invocations without the −D option.

Invoking useradd −D with −g, −b, −f, or −e (or any combination of these) sets the default values for the respective fields. [As installed, the default group is other (group ID of 1) and the default value of *base_dir* is /home]. Subsequent invocations of useradd without the −D option use these arguments.

The system file entries created with this command have a limit of 512 characters per line. Specifying long arguments to several options may exceed this limit.

The following options are available:

−u *uid*   The UID of the new user. This UID must be a non-negative decimal integer below MAXUID as defined in <param.h>. The UID defaults to the next available (unique) number above the highest number currently assigned. For example, if UIDs 100, 105, and 200 are assigned, the next default UID number will be 201. (UIDs from 0-99 are reserved.)

−o   This option allows a UID to be duplicated (non-unique).

−g *group*   An existing group's integer ID or character-string name. Without the −D option, it defines the new user's primary group membership and defaults to the default group. You can reset this default value by invoking useradd −D −g *group*.

−G *group*   An existing group's integer ID or character-string name. It defines the new user's supplementary group membership. Duplicates between *group* with the −g and −G options are ignored. No more than NGROUPS_MAX groups may be specified.

−d *dir*   The home directory of the new user. It defaults to *base_dir/login*, where *base_dir* is the base directory for new login home directories and *login* is the new login.

−s *shell*   Full pathname of the program used as the user's shell on login. It defaults to an empty field causing the system to use /sbin/sh as the default. The value of *shell* must be a valid executable file.

−c *comment*
> Any text string. It is generally a short description of the login, and is currently used as the field for the user's full name. This information is stored in the user's **/etc/passwd** entry.

−m
> Create the new user's home directory if it doesn't already exist. If the directory already exists, it must have read, write, and execute permissions by *group*, where *group* is the user's primary group.

−k *skel_dir*
> A directory that contains skeleton information (such as **.profile**) that can be copied into a new user's home directory. This directory must exist. The system provides a "skel" directory (**/etc/skel**) that can be used for this purpose.

−e *expire*   The date on which a login can no longer be used; after this date, no user will be able to access this login. (This option is useful for creating temporary logins.) You may type the value of the argument *expire* (which is a date) in any format you like (except a Julian date). For example, you may enter **10/6/90** or **October 6, 1990**. A value of **' ' ' '** defeats the status of the expired date.

−f *inactive*
> The maximum number of days allowed between uses of a login **ID** before that login **ID** is declared valid. Normal values are positive integers. A value of **−1** defeats the status.

login   A string of printable characters that specifies the new login name of the user. It may not contain a colon (**:**) or a newline (**\n**).

−b *base_dir*
> The default base directory for the system. If **−d** *dir* is not specified *base_dir* is concatenated with the user's login to define the home directory. *base_dir* must exist.

FILES
> /etc/passwd
> /etc/shadow
> /etc/group
> /etc/skel

SEE ALSO
> groupadd(1M),   groupdel(1M),   groupmod(1M),   logins(1M),   passwd(1),
> passwd(1M), userdel(1M), usermod(1M), users(1).

DIAGNOSTICS

The **useradd** command exits with one of the following values:

0   The command was executed successfully.

2   The command line syntax was invalid. A usage message for the **useradd** command is displayed.

3   An invalid argument was provided with an option.

4   The *uid* specified with the **–u** option is already in use.

6   The *group* specified with the **–g** option does not exist.

9   The specified *login* is not unique.

10   Cannot update **/etc/group**. The login was added to the **/etc/passwd** file but not to the **/etc/group** file.

12   Unable to create the home directory (with the **–m** option) or unable to complete the copy of *skel_dir* to the home directory.

NAME

userdel – delete a user's login from the system

SYNOPSIS

userdel [-r] *login*

DESCRIPTION

The **userdel** command deletes a user's login from the system and makes the appropriate login-related changes to the system file and file system.

The following options are available:

-r　　Remove the user's home directory from the system. This directory must exist. The files and directories under the home directory will no longer be accessible following successful execution of the command.

login　A string of printable characters that specifies an existing login on the system. It may not contain a colon (:), or a newline (\n).

FILES

/etc/passwd
/etc/shadow
/etc/group

SEE ALSO

groupadd(1M), groupdel(1M), groupmod(1M), logins(1M), passwd(1),
passwd(1M), useradd(1M), usermod(1M), users(1).

DIAGNOSTICS

The **userdel** command exits with one of the following values:

0　　Success.

2　　Invalid command syntax. A usage message for the **userdel** command is displayed.

6　　The login to be removed does not exist.

8　　The login to be removed is in use.

10　Cannot update the **/etc/group** file but the login is removed from the **/etc/passwd** file.

12　Cannot remove or otherwise modify the home directory.

NAME

usermod – modify a user's login information on the system

SYNOPSIS

usermod [–u *uid* [–o]] [–g *group*] [–G *group*[,*group*...] [–d *dir* [–m]] [–s *shell*]
[–c *comment*] [–l *new_logname*] [–f *inactive*] [–e *expire*] *login*

DESCRIPTION

The **usermod** command modifies a user's login definition on the system. It changes the definition of the specified login and makes the appropriate login-related system file and file system changes.

The system file entries created with this command have a limit of 512 characters per line. Specifying long arguments to several options may exceed this limit.

The following options are available:

–u *uid*   New UID for the user. It must be a non-negative decimal integer below **MAXUID** as defined in **<param.h>**.

–o   This option allows the specified UID to be duplicated (non-unique).

–g *group*

An existing group's integer ID or character-string name. It redefines the user's primary group membership.

–G *group*

An existing group's integer "ID" "," or character string name. It redefines the user's supplementary group membership. Duplicates between **group** with the –g and –G options are ignored. No more than **NGROUPS_UMAX** groups may be specified as defined in **<param.h>**.

–d *dir*   The new home directory of the user. It defaults to *base_dir/login*, where *base_dir* is the base directory for new login home directories, and *login* is the new login.

–m   Move the user's home directory to the new directory specified with the –d option. If the directory already exists, it must have permissions read/write/execute by *group*, where *group* is the user's primary group.

–s *shell*

Full pathname of the program that is used as the user's shell on login. The value of *shell* must be a valid executable file.

–c *comment*

Any text string. It is generally a short description of the login, and is currently used as the field for the user's full name. This information is stored in the user's **/etc/passwd** entry.

–l *new_logname*

A string of printable characters that specifies the new login name for the user. It may not contain a colon (**:**) or a newline (**\n**).

–e *expire*

The date on which a login can no longer be used; after this date, no user will be able to access this login. (This option is useful for creating temporary logins.) You may type the value of the argument *expire* (which is a date) in any format you like (except a Julian date). For example, you may enter 10/6/90 or October 6, 1990. A value of '' '' defeats the status of the expired date.

-f *inactive*
> The maximum number of days allowed between uses of a login ID before that login ID is declared valid. Normal values are positive integers. A value of −1 defeats the status.

login   A string of printable characters that specifies the existing login name of the user. It must exist and may not contain a colon (:), or a newline (\n).

FILES
/etc/passwd, /etc/shadow, /etc/group

SEE ALSO
groupadd(1M), groupdel(1M), groupmod(1M), logins(1M), passwd(1), passwd(1M), useradd(1M), userdel(1M), users(1).

DIAGNOSTICS
The usermod command exits with one of the following values:

0   The command was executed successfully.

2   The command syntax was invalid. A usage message for the usermod command is displayed.

3   An invalid argument was provided to an option.

4   The *uid* given with the −u option is already in use.

6   The login to be modified does not exist or *group* does not exist.

8   The login to be modified is in use.

9   The *new_logname* is already in use.

10   Cannot update the /etc/group file. Other update requests will be implemented.

11   Insufficient space to move the home directory (−m option). Other update requests will be implemented.

12   Unable to complete the move of the home directory to the new home directory.

NAME

users – display a compact list of users logged in

SYNOPSIS

/usr/ucb/users [*file*]

DESCRIPTION

users lists the login names of the users currently on the system in a compact, one-line format.

Specifying *file*, tells **users** where to find its information; by default it checks /var/adm/utmp.

Typing *users* is equivalent to typing who -q.

EXAMPLE

```
users
paul george ringo
```

FILES

/var/adm/utmp

SEE ALSO

who(1) in the *User's Reference Manual*.

NAME

uucheck – check the uucp directories and permissions file

SYNOPSIS

/usr/lib/uucp/uucheck [options]

DESCRIPTION

uucheck checks for the presence of the **uucp** system required files and directories. uucheck also does error checking of the *Permissions* file (/etc/uucp/**Permissions**). uucheck has the following options:

−v   Give a detailed (verbose) explanation of how the uucp programs will interpret the *Permissions* file.

−x*debug_level*

debug_level is a number from 0 to 9. Higher numbers give more detailed debugging information.

uucheck is executed during package installation. Note that **uucheck** can only be used by the super-user or **uucp**.

FILES

/etc/uucp/Systems
/etc/uucp/Permissions
/etc/uucp/Devices
/etc/uucp/Limits
/var/spool/uucp/*
/var/spool/locks/*
/var/spool/uucppublic/*

SEE ALSO

uucico(1M), uusched(1M).
uucp(1C), uustat(1C), uux(1C) in the *User's Reference Manual*.

NOTES

The program does not check file/directory modes or some errors in the *Permissions* file such as duplicate login or machine name.

NAME

uucico – file transport program for the uucp system

SYNOPSIS

/usr/lib/uucp/uucico [*options*]

DESCRIPTION

uucico is the file transport program for uucp work file transfers. The following options are available.

-c*type*   The first field in the **Devices** file is the "Type" field. The -c option forces uucico to only use entries in the "Type" field that match the user specified *type*. The specified *type* is usually the name of a local area network.

-d*spool_directory* This option specifies the directory *spool_directory* that contains the uucp work files to be transferred. The default spool directory is **/var/spool/uucp**.

-f   This option is used to "force execution" of uucico by ignoring the limit on the maximum number of uucicos defined in the **/etc/uucp/Limits** file.

-i*interface*   This option defines the *interface* used with uucico. The interface only affects slave mode. Known interfaces are UNIX (default), TLI (basic Transport Layer Interface), and TLIS (Transport Layer Interface with Streams modules, read/write).

-r*role_number* The *role_number* 1 is used for master mode. *role_number* 0 is used for slave mode (default). When uucico is started by a program or **cron**, *role_number* 1 should be used for master mode.

-s*system_name* The -s option defines the remote system (*system_name*) that uucico will try to contact. It is required when the role is master; *system_name* must be defined in the **Systems** file.

-x*debug_level* Both uux and uucp queue jobs that will be transferred by uucico. These jobs are normally started by the uusched scheduler, for debugging purposes, and can be started manually. For example, the shell Uutry starts uucico with debugging turned on. The *debug_level* is a number between 0 and 9. Higher numbers give more detailed debugging information.

FILES

/etc/uucp/Systems
/etc/uucp/Permissions
/etc/uucp/Devices
/etc/uucp/Devconfig
/etc/uucp/Sysfiles
/etc/uucp/Limits
/var/spool/uucp/*
/var/spool/locks/*
/var/spool/uucppublic/*

SEE ALSO

cron(1M), uusched(1M), Uutry(1M)

uucp(1C), uustat(1C), uux(1C) in the *User's Reference Manual*

NAME

uucleanup – uucp spool directory clean-up

SYNOPSIS

/usr/lib/uucp/uucleanup [options]

DESCRIPTION

uucleanup will scan the spool directories for old files and take appropriate action to remove them in a useful way:

Inform the requester of send/receive requests for systems that can not be reached.

Return undeliverable mail to the sender.

Deliver rnews files addressed to the local system.

Remove all other files.

In addition, there is a provision to warn users of requests that have been waiting for a given number of days (default 1). Note that uucleanup will process as if all option times were specified to the default values unless *time* is specifically set.

The following options are available.

-C*time*   Any C. files greater or equal to *time* days old will be removed with appropriate information to the requester. (default 7 days)

-D*time*   Any D. files greater or equal to *time* days old will be removed. An attempt will be made to deliver mail messages and execute rnews when appropriate. (default 7 days)

-W*time*   Any C. files equal to *time* days old will cause a mail message to be sent to the requester warning about the delay in contacting the remote. The message includes the *JOBID*, and in the case of mail, the mail message. The administrator may include a message line telling whom to call to check the problem (-m option). (default 1 day)

-X*time*   Any X. files greater or equal to *time* days old will be removed. The D. files are probably not present (if they were, the X. could get executed). But if there are D. files, they will be taken care of by D. processing. (default 2 days)

-m*string*   Include *string* in the warning message generated by the -W option.

-o*time*   Other files whose age is more than *time* days will be deleted. (default 2 days) The default line is "See your local administrator to locate the problem".

-s*system*   Execute for system spool directory only.

-x*debug_level*

The -x debug level is a single digit between 0 and 9; higher numbers give more detailed debugging information. (This option may not be available on all systems.)

This program is typically started by the shell *uudemon.cleanup*, which should be started by **cron**(1M).

FILES

    /usr/lib/uucp   directory with commands used by **uucleanup** internally

    /var/spool/uucp   spool directory

SEE ALSO

    cron(1M)
    uucp(1C), **uux**(1C) in the *User's Reference Manual*

NAME

uucp, uulog, uuname – UNIX-to-UNIX system copy

SYNOPSIS

uucp [*options*] *source-files destination-file*
uulog [*options*] *system*
uuname [*options*]

DESCRIPTION

uucp

uucp copies files named by the *source-file* arguments to the *destination-file* argument. A source file name may be a pathname on your machine or may have the form:

> *system-name*!*pathname*

where *system-name* is taken from a list of system names that **uucp** knows about. The destination *system-name* may also include a list of system names such as

> *system-name*!*system-name*!...!*system-name*!*pathname*

In this case, an attempt is made to send the file, via the specified route, to the destination. Care should be taken to ensure that intermediate nodes in the route are willing to forward information (see NOTES below for restrictions). The shell metacharacters **?**, ∗ and **[...]** appearing in *pathname* will be expanded on the appropriate system.

These utilities process supplementary code set characters according to the locale specified in the **LC_CTYPE** environment variable [see **LANG** on **environ**(5)], except that system-dependent names (for example, user names) and the *grade* given to the **uucp** **-g** option (see below) must be specified in ASCII characters. When shell metacharacters are used, the target system must also be able to process supplementary code set characters.

Pathnames may be one of:

1.   a full pathname;

2.   a pathname preceded by *~user* where *user* is a login name on the specified system and is replaced by that user's login directory;

3.   a pathname preceded by *~/destination* where *destination* is appended to **/var/spool/uucppublic**; (NOTE: This destination will be treated as a file name unless more than one file is being transferred by this request or the destination is already a directory. To ensure that it is a directory, follow the destination with a '/'. For example *~/dan/* as the destination will make the directory /var/spool/uucppublic/dan if it does not exist and put the requested file(s) in that directory).

4.   anything else is prefixed by the current directory.

If the result is an erroneous pathname for the remote system, the copy will fail. If the *destination-file* is a directory, the last part of the *source-file* name is used.

uucp removes execute permissions across the transmission and gives 0666 read and write permissions (see **chmod**(2)).

The following options are interpreted by **uucp**:

-c   Do not copy local file to the spool directory for transfer to the remote machine (default).

-C   Force the copy of local files to the spool directory for transfer.

-d   Make all necessary directories for the file copy (default).

-f   Do not make intermediate directories for the file copy.

-g*grade*   *grade* can be either a single ASCII letter/number or a string of ASCII alphanumeric characters defining a service grade. The **uuglist** command can determine whether it is appropriate to use the single letter/number or a string of alphanumeric characters as a service grade. The output from the uuglist command will be a list of service grades that are available or a message that says to use a single letter/number as a grade of service.

-j   Output the **uucp** job identification string on the standard output. This job identification can be used by **uustat** to obtain the status of a **uucp** job or to terminate a **uucp** job. It is valid as long as the job remains queued on the local system.

-m   Send mail to the requester when the copy is completed.

-n*user*   Notify *user* on the remote system that a file was sent.

-r   Do not start the file transfer, just queue the job.

-s*file*   Report status of the transfer to *file*. This option overrides the -m option.

-w   If a file exists in the target directory with the same name as the file being transferred, do not overwrite the existing file. Instead, try to create a new file. If the file is named *file*, create *file.N* where *N* is a two-digit number. The number appended to the file name will begin with 00 and will increase by 1 for each subsequent file of the same name to a maximum of 99. If another version of the file cannot be created, the user is notified by mail.

     If the length of the file name is equal to the maximum for the system, no new version is created. If the length of the file name is less than the maximum for the system but the file name and the suffix are greater than the maximum, the suffix will be truncated. It is therefore possible for files whose names are one or two characters shorter than the maximum system file name length to be overwritten.

-x*debug_level*   Produce debugging output on standard output. *debug_level* is a number between 0 and 9; as it increases to 9, more detailed debugging information is given. This option may not be available on all systems.

uulog
     uulog queries a log file of **uucp** or **uuxqt** transactions in file

/var/uucp/.Log/uucico/system or /var/uucp/.Log/uuxqt/*system*.

These options cause **uulog** to print logging information:

-s*sys*   Print information about file transfer work involving system *sys*.

-f*system* Does a "**tail -f**" of the file transfer log for **system**. (You must hit BREAK to exit this function.)

Other options used in conjunction with the above options are:

-x   Look in the **uuxqt** log file for the given system.

-number   Indicates that a "tail" command of *number* lines should be executed.

uuname

uuname lists the names of systems known to **uucp**. **uuname** recognizes the following options:

-c   Returns the names of systems known to **cu**. (The two lists are the same, unless your machine is using different *Systems* files for **cu** and **uucp**. See the *Sysfiles* file.)

-l   Return the local system name.

FILES

/var/spool/uucp   spool directories
/var/spool/uucppublic/* public directory for receiving and sending
/usr/lib/uucp/*   other program files
/etc/uucp/*   other data files

SEE ALSO

mail(1), **uuglist**(1C), **uustat**(1C), **uux**(1C), **uuxqt**(1M)
chmod(2) in the *Programmer's Reference Manual*

NOTES

For security reasons, the domain of remotely accessible files may be severely restricted. You will very likely not be able to access files by pathname; ask a responsible person on the remote system to send them to you. For the same reasons you will probably not be able to send files to arbitrary pathnames. As distributed, the remotely accessible files are those whose names begin **/var/spool/uucppublic** (equivalent to **~/**).

All files received by **uucp** will be owned by **uucp**.

The **-m** option will only work sending files or receiving a single file. Receiving multiple files specified by special shell characters **?** * **[. . .]** will not activate the **-m** option.

The forwarding of files through other systems may not be compatible with the previous version of **uucp**. If forwarding is used, all systems in the route must have compatible versions of **uucp**.

Protected files and files that are in protected directories that are owned by the requester can be sent by **uucp**. However, if the requester is root, and the directory is not searchable by "other" or the file is not readable by "other," the request will fail.

NAME

uuencode, uudecode – encode a binary file, or decode its ASCII representation

SYNOPSIS

uuencode [*source-file*] *file-label*

uudecode [*encoded-file*]

DESCRIPTION

uuencode converts a binary file into an ASCII-encoded representation that can be sent using **mail**(1). It encodes the contents of *source-file*, or the standard input if no *source-file* argument is given. The *file-label* argument is required. It is included in the encoded file's header as the name of the file into which **uudecode** is to place the binary (decoded) data. **uuencode** also includes the ownership and permission modes of *source-file,* so that *file-label* is recreated with those same ownership and permission modes.

uudecode reads an *encoded-file*, strips off any leading and trailing lines added by mailer programs, and recreates the original binary data with the filename and the mode and owner specified in the header.

The encoded file is an ordinary ASCII text file; it can be edited by any text editor. But it is best only to change the mode or file-label in the header to avoid corrupting the decoded binary.

SEE ALSO

mail(1), uucp(1C), uux(1C)

uuencode(5) in the *System Administrator's Reference Manual*

NOTES

The encoded file's size is expanded by 35% (3 bytes become 4, plus control information), causing it to take longer to transmit than the equivalent binary.

The user on the remote system who is invoking **uudecode** (typically **uucp**) must have write permission on the file specified in the *file-label*.

Since both **uuencode** and **uudecode** run with user ID set to **uucp**, **uudecode** can fail with permission denied when attempted in a directory that does not have write permission allowed for other.

NAME

uugetty – set terminal type, modes, speed, and line discipline

SYNOPSIS

/usr/lib/uucp/uugetty [-t *timeout*] [-r] *line* [*speed* [*type* [*linedisc*]]]
/usr/lib/uucp/uugetty -c *file*

DESCRIPTION

uugetty is identical to getty(1M) but changes have been made to support using the line for uucico, cu, and ct; that is, the line can be used in both directions. The uugetty allows users to login, but if the line is free, uucico, cu, or ct can use it for dialing out. The implementation depends on the fact that uucico, cu, and ct create lock files when devices are used. When the open returns (or the first character is read when -r option is used), the status of the lock file indicates whether the line is being used by uucico, cu, ct, or someone trying to login. Note that in the -r case, several RETURN characters may be required before the login message is output. uucico trying to login will have to be told by using the following login script:

　　　"" \r\d\r\d\r\d\r in:--in: . . .

where the ". . ." is whatever would normally be used for the login sequence.

If there is a uugetty on one end of a direct line, there must be a uugetty on the other end as well. Here is an /etc/inittab entry using uugetty on an intelligent modem or direct line:

　　　30:2:respawn:/usr/lib/uucp/uugetty -r -t 60 tty12 1200

The meanings of the available options are

-t *timeout*
> Specifies that uugetty should exit if the open on the line succeeds and there is no response to the login prompt in *timeout* seconds. *timeout* is replaced by an integer.

-r
> Causes uugetty to wait to read a character before it puts out the login message, thus preventing two uugettys from looping. An entry for an intelligent modem or direct line that has a uugetty on each end must use this option.

line
> Defines the name of the line to which uugetty will attach itself. The line name will point to an entry in the /dev directory. For example, /dev/tty03.

speed
> Defines the entry to use from the /usr/lib/saf/ttymondefs file. The entry defines the line speed, the login message, the initial tty setting, and the next speed to try if the user says the speed is inappropriate (by sending a *break* character). The default *speed* is 300.

type
> Defines the type of terminal connected to the line. The default terminal is none, representing a normal terminal unknown to the system.

linedisc
> Sets the line discipline to use on the line. The default is LDISC0, which is the only one currently compiled into the operating system.

-c *file* Checks the speed and tty definitions in *file* and sends the results to standard output. Unrecognized modes and improperly constructed entries are reported. For correct entries, flag values are printed. *file* is replaced by `/usr/lib/saf/ttymondefs` or a similarly structured file.

FILES

`/usr/lib/saf/ttymondefs`
`/etc/issue`

SEE ALSO

uucico(1M), **getty**(1M), **init**(1M), **gettydefs**(4), **inittab**(4), **tty**(7).

ct(1C), **cu**(1C), **login**(1) in the *User's Reference Manual*.

ioctl(2), in the *Programmer's Reference Manual*.

NOTES

ct does not work when **uugetty** is used with an intelligent modem such as Penril or Ventel.

NAME

    uuglist – list service grades available on this UNIX system

SYNOPSIS

    uuglist [**–u**] [**–x** *debug_level*]

DESCRIPTION

    uuglist prints the list of service grades that are available on the system to use
    with the **–g** option of **uucp**(1C) and **uux**(1C). The following options are available:

    –u   List the names of the service grades that the user is allowed to
                     use with the –g option of the **uucp** and **uux** commands.

    –x *debug_level*   Produce debugging output. **debug_level** is a single digit
                     between 0 and 9; higher numbers give more detailed debugging
                     information.

FILES

    /usr/lib/uucp/Grades   list of service grades

SEE ALSO

    uucp(1C), **uux**(1C)

NAME

uusched – the scheduler for the uucp file transport program

SYNOPSIS

/usr/lib/uucp/uusched [*options*]

DESCRIPTION

uusched is the uucp(1C) file transport scheduler. It is usually started by the dae-mon *uudemon.hour* that is started by cron(1M) from an entry in /var/spool/cron/crontab:

```
41,11 * * * * /usr/bin/su uucp -c "/usr/lib/uucp/uudemon.hour >
/dev/null"
```

The options are for debugging purposes only. *debug_level* are numbers between 0 and 9. Higher numbers give more detailed debugging information:

-u*debug_level*   The **-u** *debug_level* option is passed to uucico(1M) as **-x** *debug_level*.

-x*debug_level*   Outputs debugging messages from uusched(1M).

FILES

/etc/uucp/Systems
/etc/uucp/Permissions
/etc/uucp/Devices
/var/spool/uucp/*
/var/spool/locks/*
/var/spool/uucppublic/*

SEE ALSO

cron(1M), uucico(1M)
uucp(1C), uustat(1C), uux(1C) in the *User's Reference Manual*

NAME

uustat – uucp status inquiry and job control

SYNOPSIS

uustat [-q] or [-m] or [-k*jobid* [-n]] or [-r*jobid* [-n]] or [-p]
uustat [-a [-j]] [-u*user*] [-S*qric*]
uustat [-s*system* [-j]] [-u*user*] [-S*qric*]
uustat -t*system* [-d*number*] [-c]

DESCRIPTION

uustat functions in the following three areas: displays the general status of, or cancels, previously specified uucp commands; provides remote system performance information, in terms of average transfer rates or average queue times; provides general remote system-specific and user-specific status of uucp connections to other systems.

Here are the options that obtain general status of, or cancel, previously specified uucp commands; uustat allows only one of these options to appear on each uustat command line execution:

-a　　　　List all jobs in queue.

-j　　　　List the total number of jobs displayed. The -j option can only be used in conjunction with the -a or the -s option.

-k*jobid*　Kill the uucp request whose job identification is *jobid*. The killed uucp request must belong to the person issuing the uustat command unless one is the super-user or uucp administrator. If the job is killed by the super-user or uucp administrator, electronic mail is sent to the user.

-m　　　　Report the status of accessibility of all machines.

-n　　　　Suppress all standard out output, but not standard error. The -n option is used in conjunction with the -k and -r options.

-p　　　　Execute the command ps -flp for all the process-ids that are in the lock files.

-q　　　　List the jobs queued for each machine. If a status file exists for the machine, its date, time and status information are reported. In addition, if a number appears in parentheses next to the number of C or X files, it is the age in days of the oldest c./X. file for that system. The Retry field represents the number of hours until the next possible call. The Count is the number of failure attempts. NOTE: for systems with a moderate number of outstanding jobs, this could take 30 seconds or more of real-time to execute. Here is an example of the output produced by the -q option:

```
eagle     3C    04/07-11:07    NO DEVICES AVAILABLE
mh3bs3    2C    07/07-10:42    SUCCESSFUL
```

The above output tells how many command files are waiting for each system. Each command file may have zero or more files to be sent (zero means to call the system and see if work is to be done). The date and time refer to the previous interaction with the system followed by the status of the interaction.

-r*jobid*   Rejuvenate *jobid*. The files associated with *jobid* are touched so that their modification time is set to the current time. This prevents the cleanup daemon from deleting the job until the jobs' modification time reaches the limit imposed by the daemon.

Here are the options that provide remote system performance information, in terms of average transfer rates or average queue times; the −c and −d options can only be used in conjunction with the −t option:

-t*system*   Report the average transfer rate or average queue time for the past 60 minutes for the remote *system*. The following parameters can only be used with this option:

-d*number*   *number* is specified in minutes. Used to override the 60 minute default used for calculations. These calculations are based on information contained in the optional performance log and therefore may not be available. Calculations can only be made from the time that the performance log was last cleaned up.

-c   Average queue time is calculated when the −c parameter is specified and average transfer rate when −c is not specified. For example, the command

```
uustat -teagle -d50 -c
```

produces output in the following format:

```
average queue time to eagle for last 50 minutes: 5 seconds
```

The same command without the −c parameter produces output in the following format:

```
average transfer rate with eagle for last 50 minutes: 2000.88
bytes/sec
```

Here are the options that provide general remote system-specific and user-specific status of **uucp** connections to other systems. Either or both of the following options can be specified with *uustat*. The −j option can only be used in conjunction with the −s or -a option to list the total number of jobs displayed:

-s*system*   Report the status of all **uucp** requests for remote system *system*.

-u*user*   Report the status of all **uucp** requests issued by *user*.

Output for both the −s and −u options has the following format:

```
eagleN1bd7   4/07-11:07   S   eagle   dan   522    /home/dan/A
eagleC1bd8   4/07-11:07   S   eagle   dan   59     D.3b2al2ce4924
             4/07-11:07   S   eagle   dan   rmail  mike
```

With the above two options, the first field is the *jobid* of the job. This is followed by the date/time. The next field is an **S** if the job is sending a file or an **R** if the job is requesting a file. The next field is the machine where the file is to be transferred. This is followed by the user-id of the user who queued the job. The next field contains the size of the file, or in the case of a remote execution (**rmail** is the command used for remote mail), the name of the command. When the size appears in this field, the file name is also given. This can either be the name given by the user or an internal name (for example, **D.3b2alce4924**) that is created for data files associated with remote executions (**rmail** in this example).

−S*qric*   Report the job state: **q** for queued jobs, **r** for running jobs, **i** for interrupted jobs, and **c** for completed jobs.

A job is queued if the transfer has not started. A job is running when the transfer has begun. A job is interrupted if the transfer began but was terminated before the file was completely transferred. A completed job, of course, is a job that successfully transferred. The completed state information is maintained in the accounting log, which is optional and therefore may be unavailable. The parameters can be used in any combination, but at least one parameter must be specified. The **−S** option can also be used with **−s** and **−u** options. The output for this option is exactly like the output for **−s** and **−u** except that the job states are appended as the last output word. Output for a completed job has the following format:

    eagleC1bd3 completed

When no options are given, **uustat** outputs the status of all **uucp** requests issued by the current user.

FILES

/var/spool/uucp/*	spool directories
/var/uucp/.Admin/account	accounting log
/var/uucp/.Admin/perflog	performance log

SEE ALSO

uucp(1C)

DIAGNOSTICS

The **−t** option produces no message when the data needed for the calculations is not being recorded.

NOTES

After the user has issued the **uucp** request, if the file to be transferred is moved or deleted or was not copied to the spool directory with the **−C** option when the **uucp** request was made, **uustat** reports a file size of −99999. This job will eventually fail because the file(s) to be transferred can not be found.

NAME

uuto, **uupick** – public UNIX-to-UNIX system file copy

SYNOPSIS

uuto [*options*] *source-files destination*

uupick [**-s** *system*]

DESCRIPTION

uuto sends *source-files* to *destination*. uuto uses the uucp(1C) facility to send files, while it allows the local system to control the file access. A source-file name is a path name on your machine. Destination has the form:

system[**!** *system*] . . . **!** *user*

where **system** is taken from a list of system names that **uucp** knows about [see uuname(1C)]. *user* is the login name of someone on the specified system.

Two options are available:

-p   Copy the source file into the spool directory before transmission.

-m   Send mail to the sender when the copy is complete.

The files (or sub-trees if directories are specified) are sent to *PUBDIR* on **system**, where *PUBDIR* is a public directory defined in the **uucp** source. By default, this directory is **/var/spool/uucppublic**. Specifically the files are sent to

PUBDIR/receive/*user*/*mysystem*/files.

The destined recipient is notified by **mail**(1) of the arrival of files.

uupick accepts or rejects the files transmitted to the user. Specifically, **uupick** searches *PUBDIR* for files destined for the user. For each entry (file or directory) found, the following message is printed on the standard output:

from system *sysname* : [file *file-name*] [dir *dirname*] **?**

uupick then reads a line from the standard input to determine the disposition of the file:

<new-line>	Go on to next entry.
d	Delete the entry.
m [*dir*]	Move the entry to named directory *dir*. If *dir* is not specified as a complete path name (in which *$HOME* is legitimate), a destination relative to the current directory is assumed. If no destination is given, the default is the current directory.
a [*dir*]	Same as **m** except moving all the files sent from **system**.
p	Print the content of the file.
q	Stop.
EOT (CTRL-d)	Same as **q**.
! *command*	Escape to the shell to do *command*.
*	Print a command summary.

uupick invoked with the **−s** *system* option will only search the *PUBDIR* for files sent from **system.**

FILES

    PUBDIR   **/var/spool/uucppublic**   public directory

SEE ALSO

    mail(1), uucp(1C), uustat(1C), uux(1C)
    uucleanup(1M) in the *System Administrator's Reference Manual*

NOTES

In order to send files that begin with a dot (for example, .profile), the files must be qualified with a dot. For example, the following files are correct:

        .profile
        .prof*
        .profil?

The following files are incorrect:

        prof
        ?profile

NAME

Uutry – try to contact remote system with debugging on

SYNOPSIS

/usr/lib/uucp/Uutry [*options*] *system_name*

DESCRIPTION

Uutry is a shell that is used to invoke uucico to call a remote site. Debugging is initially turned on and is set to the default value of 5. The debugging output is put in file /tmp/*system_name*. Here are the options:

-c*type*   The first field in the **Devices** file is the "Type" field. The -c option forces uucico to only use entries in the "Type" field that match the user specified *type*. The specified *type* is usually the name of a local area network.

-r   This option overrides the retry time that is set in file /var/uucp/.status/*system_name*.

-x*debug_level*   *debug_level* is a number from 0 to 9. Higher numbers give more detailed debugging information.

FILES

/etc/uucp/Systems
/etc/uucp/Permissions
/etc/uucp/Devices
/etc/uucp/Limits
/var/spool/uucp/*
/var/spool/locks/*
/var/spool/uucppublic/*
/tmp/system_name

SEE ALSO

uucico(1M)
uucp(1C), uux(1C) in the *User's Reference Manual*

NAME

uux – UNIX-to-UNIX system command execution

SYNOPSIS

uux [*options*] *command-string*

DESCRIPTION

uux will gather zero or more files from various systems, execute a command on a specified system and then send standard output to a file on a specified system.

NOTE: For security reasons, most installations limit the list of commands executable on behalf of an incoming request from **uux**, permitting only the receipt of mail [see **mail**(1)]. (Remote execution permissions are defined in **/etc/uucp/Permissions**.)

The *command-string* is made up of one or more arguments that look like a shell command line, except that the command and file names may be prefixed by *system-name*!. A null *system-name* is interpreted as the local system.

File names may be one of:

    (1)   a full pathname;

    (2)   a pathname preceded by ~*xxx*, where *xxx* is a login name on the specified system and is replaced by that user's login directory;

    (3)   anything else is prefixed by the current directory.

As an example, the command

```
uux    "!diff   sys1!/home/dan/file1    sys2!/a4/dan/file2   >
!~/dan/file.diff"
```

will get the *file1* and *file2* files from the "sys1" and "sys2" machines, execute a **diff**(1) command and put the results in *file.diff* in the local *PUBDIR*/dan/ directory. *PUBDIR* is a public directory defined in the **uucp** source. By default, this directory is **/var/spool/uucppublic**.

Any special shell characters such as <, >, ;, | should be quoted either by quoting the entire *command-string*, or quoting the special characters as individual arguments.

uux will attempt to get all appropriate files to the specified system where they will be processed. For files that are output files, the file name must be escaped using parentheses. For example, the command:

```
uux "a!cut -f1 b!/usr/file > c!/usr/file"
```

gets "/usr/file" from system "b" and sends it to system "a", performs a **cut** command on that file and sends the result of the **cut** command to system "c".

uux will notify you if the requested command on the remote system was disallowed. This notification can be turned off by the **−n** option. The response comes by remote mail from the remote machine.

The following *options* are interpreted by **uux**:

–	The standard input to **uux** is made the standard input to the *command-string*.
-aname	Use *name* as the user job identification replacing the initiator user-id. (Notification will be returned to user-id *name*.)
-b	Return whatever standard input was provided to the **uux** command if the exit status is non-zero.
-c	Do not copy local file to the spool directory for transfer to the remote machine (default).
-C	Force the copy of local files to the spool directory for transfer.
-ggrade	*grade* can be either a single letter, number, or a string of alphanumeric characters defining a service grade. The *uuglist*(1C) command determines whether it is appropriate to use the single letter, number, or a string of alphanumeric characters as a service grade. The output from the *uuglist* command will be a list of service grades that are available or a message that says to use a single letter or number as a grade of service.
-j	Output the jobid string on the standard output which is the job identification. This job identification can be used by **uustat**(1C) to obtain the status or terminate a job.
-n	Do not notify the user if the command fails.
-p	Same as –: The standard input to **uux** is made the standard input to the *command-string*.
-r	Do not start the file transfer, just queue the job.
-sfile	Report status of the transfer in *file*.
-xdebug_level	
	Produce debugging output on the standard output. *debug_level* is a number between 0 and 9; as it increases to 9, more detailed debugging information is given.
-z	Send success notification to the user.

FILES

/var/spool/uucp	spool directories
/etc/uucp/Permissions	remote execution permissions
/usr/lib/uucp/ *	other programs
/etc/uucp/ *	other data and programs

NOTES

Only the first command of a shell pipeline may have a *system-name*!. All other commands are executed on the system of the first command.

The use of the shell metacharacter * will probably not do what you want it to do. The shell tokens << and >> are not implemented.

The execution of commands on remote systems takes place in an execution directory known to the **uucp** system. All files required for the execution will be put into this directory unless they already reside on that machine. Therefore, the simple file name (without path or machine reference) must be unique within the **uux** request. The following command will NOT work:

uux "a!diff b!/home/dan/xyz c!/home/dan/xyz > !xyz.diff"

but the command

uux "a!diff a!/home/dan/xyz c!/home/dan/xyz > !xyz.diff"

will work. (If **diff** is a permitted command.)

Protected files and files that are in protected directories that are owned by the requester can be sent in commands using **uux**. However, if the requester is root, and the directory is not searchable by "other", the request will fail.

SEE ALSO

cut(1), mail(1), uuglist(1C), uucp(1C), uustat(1C)

NAME

    uuxqt – execute remote command requests

SYNOPSIS

    /usr/lib/uucp/uuxqt [*options*]

DESCRIPTION

    uuxqt is the program that executes remote job requests from remote systems generated by the use of the **uux** command. (**mail** uses **uux** for remote mail requests). **uuxqt** searches the spool directories looking for execution requests. For each request, **uuxqt** checks to see if all the required data files are available, accessible, and the requested commands are permitted for the requesting system. The **Permissions** file is used to validate file accessibility and command execution permission.

    There are two environment variables that are set before the **uuxqt** command is executed:

    UU_MACHINE is the machine that sent the job (the previous one).
    UU_USER is the user that sent the job.

    These can be used in writing commands that remote systems can execute to provide information, auditing, or restrictions. **uuxqt** has the following options:

    −s*system*   Specifies the remote **system** name.

    −x*debug_level*   *debug_level* is a number from 0 to 9. Higher numbers give more detailed debugging information.

FILES

    /etc/uucp/Permissions
    /etc/uucp/Limits
    /var/spool/uucp/*
    /var/spool/locks/*

SEE ALSO

    uucico(1M)
    uucp(1C), uustat(1C), uux(1C), mail(1) in the *User's Reference Manual*

NAME

vacation – automatically respond to incoming mail messages

SYNOPSIS

vacation [-l *logfile*] [-m *mailfile*] [-M *canned_msg_file*] [-F *failsafe*]

DESCRIPTION

When a new mail message arrives, the **mail** command first checks if the recipient's mailbox indicates that the message is to be forwarded elsewhere (to some other recipient or as the input to some command). **vacation** is used to set up forwarding on the user's mailbox so that the new message is saved into an alternative mailbox and a canned response is sent to the message's originator.

Command-line options are:

-l *logfile* File to keep track of which originators have already seen the canned response. If not specified, it defaults to **$HOME/.maillog**.

-m *mailfile* Alternate mailbox to save new messages into. If not specified, it defaults to **$HOME/.mailfile**.

-M *canned_msg_file*

 File to send back as the canned response. If *canned_msg_file* is not specified, it defaults to **/usr/lib/mail/std_vac_msg**, which contains:

  Subject: AUTOANSWERED!!!

  I am on vacation. I will read (and answer if necessary) your e-mail message when I return.

  This message was generated automatically and you will receive it only once, although all messages you send me while I am away WILL be saved.

-F *failsafe* If mail has troubles delivering to the mailfile specified, it may optionally be forwarded to another login id (*failsafe*) instead of being returned to the sender.

-d The log file will have the day's date appended.

To remove the **vacation** functionality, use

  mail -F ""

FILES

/tmp/notif*   temporary file

/usr/share/lib/mail/std_vac_msg

        default canned response

/var/mail/*   users' standard mailboxes

/usr/lib/mail/vacation2 program that actually sends back the canned response

SEE ALSO

mail(1)

User's Guide.

NOTES

Because **vacation** uses the "**Forward to** |*command*" facility of **mail** to implement notifications, **/var/mail/***username* should **not** be specified as the place to put newly arrived messages via the **–m** invocation option. The **mail** command uses **/var/mail/***username* to hold either mail messages, **or** indications of mail forwarding, but not both simultaneously.

NAME
vacation – reply to mail automatically

SYNOPSIS
/usr/ucb/vacation [-I]
/usr/ucb/vacation [-j] [-a*alias*] [-t*N*] *username*

DESCRIPTION
vacation automatically replies to incoming mail. The reply is contained in the file .vacation.msg, that you create in your home directory.

This file should include a header with at least a 'Subject:' line (it should not include a 'From:' or a 'To:' line). For example:

```
Subject: I am on vacation
I am on vacation until July 22.  If you have something urgent,
please contact Joe Jones (jones@f40).
        --John
```

If the string $SUBJECT appears in the .vacation.msg file, it is replaced with the subject of the original message when the reply is sent; thus, a .vacation.msg file such as

```
Subject: I am on vacation
I am on vacation until July 22.
Your mail regarding "$SUBJECT" will be read when I return.
If you have something urgent, please contact
Joe Jones (jones@f40).
        --John
```

will include the subject of the message in the reply.

No message is sent if the 'To:' or the 'Cc:' line does not list the user to whom the original message was sent or one of a number of aliases for them, if the initial From line includes the string -REQUEST@, or if a 'Precedence: bulk' or 'Precedence: junk' line is included in the header.

The following options are available:

-I   Initialize the .vacation.pag and .vacation.dir files and start /usr/ucb/vacation.

If the -I flag is not specified, and a *user* argument is given, /usr/ucb/vacation reads the first line from the standard input (for a 'From:' line, no colon). If absent, it produces an error message. The following options may be specified:

-a*alias*   Indicate that *alias* is one of the valid aliases for the user running /usr/ucb/vacation, so that mail addressed to that alias generates a reply.

-j   Do not check whether the recipient appears in the 'To: ' or the 'Cc:' line.

-t*N*   Change the interval between repeat replies to the same sender. The default is 1 week. A trailing s, m, h, d, or w scales *N* to seconds, minutes, hours, days, or weeks respectively.

USAGE

To start **/usr/ucb/vacation**, create a **.forward** file in your home directory containing a line of the form:

username, **"|/usr/ucb/vacation** *username***"**

where *username* is your login name.

Then type in the command:

/usr/ucb/vacation -I

To stop **/usr/ucb/vacation**, remove the **.forward** file, or move it to a new name.

If **/usr/ucb/vacation** is run with no arguments, it will permit you to interactively turn **/usr/ucb/vacation** on or off. It will create a **.vacation.msg** file for you, or edit an existing one, using the editor specified by the **VISUAL** or **EDITOR** environment variable, or **vi**(1) if neither of those environment variables are set. If a **.forward** file is present in your home directory, it will ask whether you want to remove it and turn off **/usr/ucb/vacation**. If it is not present in your home directory, it creates it for you, and automatically performs a '**/usr/ucb/vacation -I**' function, turning on **/usr/ucb/vacation**.

FILES

~/.forward
~/.vacation.mesg

A list of senders is kept in the files **.vacation.pag** and **.vacation.dir** in your home directory.

SEE ALSO

sendmail(1M)

vi(1) in the *User's Reference Manual*

NAME
　　　　val – validate an SCCS file

SYNOPSIS
　　　　val –

　　　　val [–s] [–r*SID*] [–m*name*] [–y*type*] *files*

DESCRIPTION
　　　　val determines if the specified *file* is an SCCS file meeting the characteristics
　　　　specified by the optional argument list. Arguments to val may appear in any
　　　　order. The arguments consist of keyletter arguments, which begin with a –, and
　　　　named files.

　　　　val has a special argument, –, which causes reading of the standard input until
　　　　an end-of-file condition is detected. Each line read is independently processed as
　　　　if it were a command line argument list.

　　　　val generates diagnostic messages on the standard output for each command line
　　　　and file processed, and also returns a single 8-bit code on exit as described below.

　　　　The keyletter arguments are defined as follows. The effects of any keyletter argu-
　　　　ment apply independently to each named file on the command line.

　　　　–s　　　　　The presence of this argument silences the diagnostic message nor-
　　　　　　　　　　mally generated on the standard output for any error that is
　　　　　　　　　　detected while processing each named file on a given command line.

　　　　–r*SID*　　　The argument value *SID* (SCCS identification string) is an SCCS delta
　　　　　　　　　　number. A check is made to determine if the *SID* is ambiguous (for
　　　　　　　　　　example, –r1 is ambiguous because it physically does not exist but
　　　　　　　　　　implies 1.1, 1.2, and so on, which may exist) or invalid (for example,
　　　　　　　　　　r1.0 or r1.1.0 are invalid because neither can exist as a valid delta
　　　　　　　　　　number). If the *SID* is valid and not ambiguous, a check is made to
　　　　　　　　　　determine if it actually exists.

　　　　–m*name*　　The argument value *name* is compared with the SCCS %M% keyword
　　　　　　　　　　in *file*.

　　　　–y*type*　　　The argument value *type* is compared with the SCCS %Y% keyword in
　　　　　　　　　　file.

　　　　The 8-bit code returned by val is a disjunction of the possible errors; it can be
　　　　interpreted as a bit string where (moving from left to right) set bits are inter-
　　　　preted as follows:

　　　　　　　　　　bit 0 = missing file argument
　　　　　　　　　　bit 1 = unknown or duplicate keyletter argument
　　　　　　　　　　bit 2 = corrupted SCCS file
　　　　　　　　　　bit 3 = cannot open file or file not SCCS
　　　　　　　　　　bit 4 = *SID* is invalid or ambiguous
　　　　　　　　　　bit 5 = *SID* does not exist
　　　　　　　　　　bit 6 = %Y%, –y mismatch
　　　　　　　　　　bit 7 = %M%, –m mismatch

val can process two or more files on a given command line and in turn can process multiple command lines (when reading the standard input). In these cases an aggregate code is returned: a logical OR of the codes generated for each command line and file processed.

SEE ALSO

admin(1), delta(1), get(1), help(1, prs(1)

DIAGNOSTICS

Use help(1) for explanations.

NOTES

val can process up to 50 files on a single command line.

NAME

vc – version control

SYNOPSIS

vc [-a] [-t] [-c*char*] [-s] [*keyword=value* . . . keyword=value]

DESCRIPTION

This command is obsolete and will be removed in the next release.

The **vc** command copies lines from the standard input to the standard output under control of its arguments and of "control statements" encountered in the standard input. In the process of performing the copy operation, user-declared *keyword*s may be replaced by their string *value* when they appear in plain text and/or control statements.

The copying of lines from the standard input to the standard output is conditional, based on tests (in control statements) of keyword values specified in control statements or as **vc** command arguments.

A control statement is a single line beginning with a control character, except as modified by the **-t** keyletter (see below). The default control character is colon (**:**), except as modified by the **-c** keyletter (see below). Input lines beginning with a backslash (\) followed by a control character are not control lines and are copied to the standard output with the backslash removed. Lines beginning with a backslash followed by a non-control character are copied in their entirety.

A keyword is composed of 9 or less alphanumerics; the first must be alphabetic. A value is any ASCII string that can be created with **ed**; a numeric value is an unsigned string of digits. Keyword values may not contain blanks or tabs.

Replacement of keywords by values is done whenever a keyword surrounded by control characters is encountered on a version control statement. The **-a** keyletter (see below) forces replacement of keywords in all lines of text. An uninterpreted control character may be included in a value by preceding it with \. If a literal \ is desired, then it too must be preceded by \.

The following options are valid:

-a   Forces replacement of keywords surrounded by control characters with their assigned value in all text lines and not just in **vc** statements.

-t   All characters from the beginning of a line up to and including the first tab character are ignored for the purpose of detecting a control statement. If a control statement is found, all characters up to and including the tab are discarded.

-c*char*   Specifies a control character to be used in place of the "**:**" default.

-s   Silences warning messages (not error) that are normally printed on the diagnostic output.

vc recognizes the following version control statements:

:dcl *keyword*[, ..., *keyword*]

        Declare keywords. All keywords must be declared.

:asg *keyword=value*

     Assign values to keywords. An **asg** statement overrides the assignment for the corresponding keyword on the **vc** command line and all previous **asg** statements for that keyword. Keywords that are declared but are not assigned values have null values.

:if *condition*

     ...

:end

     Skip lines of the standard input. If the condition is true, all lines between the **if** statement and the matching **end** statement are copied to the standard output. If the condition is false, all intervening lines are discarded, including control statements. Note that intervening **if** statements and matching **end** statements are recognized solely for the purpose of maintaining the proper **if-end** matching.

     The syntax of a condition is:

<cond>	::=	["**not**"] *<or>*
<or>	::=	*<and>* | *<and>* "|" *<or>*
<and>	::=	*<exp>* | *<exp>* "**&**" *<and>*
<exp>	::=	"**(**" *<or>* "**)**" | *<value> <op> <value>*
<op>	::=	"**=**" | "**!=**" | "**<**" | "**>**"
<value>	::=	*<arbitrary ASCII string>* | *<numeric string>*

     The available operators and their meanings are:

=	equal
!=	not equal
&	and
|	or
>	greater than
<	less than
( )	used for logical groupings
not	may only occur immediately after the **if**, and when present, inverts the value of the entire condition

     The **>** and **<** operate only on unsigned integer values (for example, **: 012 > 12** is false). All other operators take strings as arguments (for example, **: 012 != 12** is true).

     The precedence of the operators (from highest to lowest) is:

= != > <	all of equal precedence
&	
|	

Parentheses may be used to alter the order of precedence.

Values must be separated from operators or parentheses by at least one blank or tab.

::*text*

>   Replace keywords on lines that are copied to the standard output. The two leading control characters are removed, and keywords surrounded by control characters in text are replaced by their value before the line is copied to the output file. This action is independent of the **-a** keyletter.

:on

:off   Turn on or off keyword replacement on all lines.

:ctl *char*

>   Change the control character to *char*.

:msg *message*

>   Print *message* on the diagnostic output.

:err *message*

>   Print *message* followed by:

>>   **ERROR: err statement on line ... (915)**

>   on the diagnostic output. **vc** halts execution, and returns an exit code of 1.

SEE ALSO

>   help(1)
>   ed(1) in the *User's Reference Manual*

NAME

    vi – screen-oriented (visual) display editor based on ex

SYNOPSIS

    vi [−t *tag*] [−r *file*] [−l] [−L] [−w*n*] [−R] [−x] [−C] [−c *command*] *file*...
    view [−t *tag*] [−r *file*] [−l] [−L] [−w*n*] [−R] [−x] [−C] [−c *command*] *file*...
    vedit [−t *tag*] [−r *file*] [−l] [−L] [−w*n*] [−R] [−x] [−C] [−c *command*] *file*...

DESCRIPTION

    vi (visual) is a display-oriented text editor based on an underlying line editor **ex**. It is possible to use the command mode of **ex** from within **vi** and vice-versa. The visual commands are described on this manual page; how to set options (like automatically numbering lines and automatically starting a new output line when you type carriage return) and all **ex** line editor commands are described on the **ex**(1) manual page.

    When using **vi**, changes you make to the file are reflected in what you see on your terminal screen. The position of the cursor on the screen indicates the position within the file.

Invocation Options

    The following invocation options are interpreted by **vi** (previously documented options are discussed in the NOTES section of this manual page):

−t *tag*	Edit the file containing the *tag* and position the editor at its definition.
−r *file*	Edit *file* after an editor or system crash. (Recovers the version of *file* that was in the buffer when the crash occurred.)
−l	Set up for editing LISP programs.
−L	List the name of all files saved as the result of an editor or system crash.
−w*n*	Set the default window size to *n*. This is useful when using the editor over a slow speed line.
−R	**Readonly** mode; the **readonly** flag is set, preventing accidental overwriting of the file.
−x	Encryption option; when used, **vi** simulates the **X** command of **ex** and prompts the user for a key. This key is used to encrypt and decrypt text using the algorithm of the **crypt** command. The **X** command makes an educated guess to determine whether text read in is encrypted or not. The temporary buffer file is encrypted also, using a transformed version of the key typed in for the **−x** option. See **crypt**(1). Also, see the WARNING section at the end of this manual page.
−C	Encryption option; same as the **−x** option, except that **vi** simulates the **C** command of **ex**. The **C** command is like the **X** command of **ex**, except that all text read in is assumed to have been encrypted.

−c *command*   Begin editing by executing the specified editor *command* (usually a search or positioning command).

The *file* argument indicates one or more files to be edited.

The *view* invocation is the same as **vi** except that the **readonly** flag is set.

The *vedit* invocation is intended for beginners. It is the same as **vi** except that the **report** flag is set to 1, the **showmode** and **novice** flags are set, and **magic** is turned off. These defaults make it easier to learn how to use **vi**.

vi Modes

Command   Normal and initial mode. Other modes return to command mode upon completion. **ESC** (escape) is used to cancel a partial command.

Input   Entered by setting any of the following options: **a A i I o O c C s S R** . Arbitrary text may then be entered. Input mode is normally terminated with **ESC** character, or, abnormally, with an interrupt.

Last line   Reading input for **:** **/** **?** or **!**; terminate by typing a carriage return; an interrupt cancels termination.

COMMAND SUMMARY

In the descriptions, **CR** stands for carriage return and **ESC** stands for the escape key.

Sample commands

← ↓ ↑ →	arrow keys move the cursor
h j k l	same as arrow keys
i*text*ESC	insert *text*
cw*new*ESC	change word to *new*
ea*s*ESC	pluralize word (end of word; append **s**; escape from input state)
x	delete a character
dw	delete a word
dd	delete a line
3dd	delete 3 lines
u	undo previous change
ZZ	exit **vi**, saving changes
:q!CR	quit, discarding changes
/*text*CR	search for *text*
^U ^D	scroll up or down
:*cmd*CR	any **ex** or **ed** command

Counts before vi commands

Numbers may be typed as a prefix to some commands. They are interpreted in one of these ways.

line/column number	z G	
scroll amount	^D ^U
repeat effect	most of the rest

Interrupting, canceling

ESC	end insert or incomplete cmd
DEL	(delete or rubout) interrupts

File manipulation

ZZ	if file modified, write and exit; otherwise, exit
:wCR	write back changes
:w ! CR	forced write, if permission originally not valid
:qCR	quit
:q ! CR	quit, discard changes
:e *name*CR	edit file *name*
:e ! CR	reedit, discard changes
:e + *name*CR	edit, starting at end
:e +*n*CR	edit starting at line *n*
:e #CR	edit alternate file
:e ! #CR	edit alternate file, discard changes
:w *name*CR	write file *name*
:w ! *name*CR	overwrite file *name*
:shCR	run shell, then return
: ! *cmd*CR	run *cmd*, then return
:nCR	edit next file in arglist
:n *args*CR	specify new arglist
^G	show current file and line
:ta *tag*CR	position cursor to *tag*

In general, any **ex** or **ed** command (such as *substitute* or *global*) may be typed, preceded by a colon and followed by a carriage return.

Positioning within file

^F	forward screen
^B	backward screen
^D	scroll down half screen
^U	scroll up half screen
*n*G	go to the beginning of the specified line (end default), where *n* is a line number
/*pat*	next line matching *pat*
?*pat*	previous line matching *pat*
n	repeat last / or ? command
N	reverse last / or ? command
/*pat*/+*n*	nth line after *pat*
?*pat*?−*n*	nth line before *pat*
]]	next section/function
[[	previous section/function
(	beginning of sentence
)	end of sentence

{	beginning of paragraph
}	end of paragraph
%	find matching ( ) { or }

Adjusting the screen

^L	clear and redraw window
^R	clear and redraw window if ^L is → key
zCR	redraw screen with current line at top of window
z−CR	redraw screen with current line at bottom of window
z .CR	redraw screen with current line at center of window
/pat/z−CR	move *pat* line to bottom of window
z*n* .CR	use *n*-line window
^E	scroll window down 1 line
^Y	scroll window up 1 line

Marking and returning

` `	move cursor to previous context
´ ´	move cursor to first non-white space in line
m*x*	mark current position with the ASCII lower-case letter *x*
`*x*	move cursor to mark *x*
´*x*	move cursor to first non-white space in line marked by *x*

Line positioning

H	top line on screen
L	last line on screen
M	middle line on screen
+	next line, at first non-white
−	previous line, at first non-white
CR	return, same as +
↓ or j	next line, same column
↑ or k	previous line, same column

Character positioning

^	first non white-space character
0	beginning of line
$	end of line
h or →	forward
l or ←	backward
^H	same as ← (backspace)
space	same as → (space bar)
f*x*	find next *x*
F*x*	find previous **x**
t*x*	move to character prior to next *x*
T*x*	move to character following previous *x*
;	repeat last **f F t** or **T**
,	repeat inverse of last **f F t** or **T**
n|	move to column *n*
%	find matching ({) or }

Words, sentences, paragraphs

w	forward a word
b	back a word
e	end of word
)	to next sentence
}	to next paragraph
(	back a sentence
{	back a paragraph
W	forward a blank-delimited word
B	back a blank-delimited word
E	end of a blank-delimited word

Corrections during insert

^H	erase last character (backspace)
^W	erase last word
erase	your erase character, same as ^H (backspace)
kill	your kill character, erase this line of input
\	quotes your erase and kill characters
ESC	ends insertion, back to command mode
DEL	interrupt, terminates insert mode
^D	backtab one character; reset left margin of *autoindent*
^^D	caret (^) followed by control-d (^D); backtab to beginning of line; do not reset left margin of *autoindent*
0^D	backtab to beginning of line; reset left margin of *autoindent*
^V	quote non-printable character

Insert and replace

a	append after cursor
A	append at end of line
i	insert before cursor
I	insert before first non-blank
o	open line below
O	open above
rx	replace single char with x
R*text*ESC	replace characters

Operators

Operators are followed by a cursor motion, and affect all text that would have been moved over. For example, since **w** moves over a word, **dw** deletes the word that would be moved over. Double the operator, for example, **dd** to affect whole lines.

d	delete
c	change
y	yank lines to buffer
<	left shift
>	right shift
!	filter through command

Miscellaneous Operations

C	change rest of line (c$)
D	delete rest of line (d$)
s	substitute chars (cl)
S	substitute lines (cc)
J	join lines
x	delete characters (dl)
X	delete characters before cursor (dh)
Y	yank lines (yy)

Yank and Put

Put inserts the text most recently deleted or yanked; however, if a buffer is named (using the ASCII lower-case letters **a** - **z**), the text in that buffer is put instead.

3yy	yank 3 lines
3yl	yank 3 characters
p	put back text after cursor
P	put back text before cursor
"*x*p	put from buffer *x*
"*x*y	yank to buffer *x*
"*x*d	delete into buffer *x*

Undo, Redo, Retrieve

u	undo last change
U	restore current line
.	repeat last change
"*d*p	retrieve *d*'th last delete

AUTHOR

vi and **ex** were developed by The University of California, Berkeley California, Computer Science Division, Department of Electrical Engineering and Computer Science.

FILES

/tmp   default directory where temporary work files are placed; it can be changed using the **directory** option [see the **ex**(1) **set** command]

/usr/share/lib/terminfo/?/*
     compiled terminal description database

/usr/lib/.COREterm/?/*
     subset of compiled terminal description database

NOTES

Two options, although they continue to be supported, have been replaced in the documentation by options that follow the Command Syntax Standard [see **intro**(1)]. A **-r** option that is not followed with an option-argument has been replaced by **-L** and +*command* has been replaced by **-c** *command*.

The encryption options are provided with the Security Administration Utilities package, which is available only in the United States.

Tampering with entries in **/usr/share/lib/terminfo/?/*** or **/usr/share/lib/terminfo/?/*** (for example, changing or removing an entry) can affect programs such as **vi** that expect the entry to be present and correct. In particular, removing the "dumb" terminal may cause unexpected problems.

Software tabs using **^T** work only immediately after the *autoindent.*

Left and right shifts on intelligent terminals do not make use of insert and delete character operations in the terminal.

SEE ALSO

ed(1), **edit**(1), **ex**(1)
User's Guide
Editing Guide
curses/terminfo chapter of the *Programmer's Guide*

NAME

vidi – sets the font and video mode for a video device

SYNOPSIS

vidi [–d] [–f *fontfile*] *font*

vidi *mode*

DESCRIPTION

vidi has two functions: it loads/extracts a font or sets the video mode for the current standard input device. Without arguments, it lists the all of the valid video mode and font commands.

Font Options

Some video cards support changeable character fonts. Available fonts are **font8x8**, **font8x14**, and **font8x16**. The font options are used as follows:

vidi *font*   loads *font* from **/usr/lib/vidi/***font*.

vidi –d *font*   writes *font* to the standard output.

vidi –d –f *font fontfile*   writes *font* to *fontfile*.

vidi –f *fontfile font*   loads *font* from *fontfile* instead of default directory.

Mode Options

vidi also sets the mode of the video adapter connected to the standard input. The modes are:

mono   move current screen to the monochrome adapter.

cga   move current screen to the Color Graphics adapter.

ega   move current screen to the Enhanced Graphics adapter.

vga   move current screen to the Video Graphics adapter.

Text and Graphics Modes

The following tables list the available modes.

Text Modes

Mode	Cols	Rows	Font	Adapter
c40x25	40	25	8x8	CGA (EGA VGA)
e40x25	40	25	8x14	EGA (VGA)
v40x25	40	25	8x16	VGA
m80x25	80	25	8x14	MONO (EGA_MONO VGA_MONO)
c80x25	80	25	8x8	CGA (EGA VGA)
em80x25	80	25	8x14	EGA_MONO (VGA_MONO)
e80x25	80	25	8x14	EGA (VGA)
vm80x25	80	25	8x16	VGA_MONO
v80x25	80	25	8x16	VGA
e80x43	80	43	8x14	EGA (VGA)

	Graphics Modes	
Mode	Pixel Resolution	Colors
mode5	320x200	4
mode6	640x200	2
modeD	320x200	16
modeE	640x200	16
modeF	640x350	2 (mono)
mode10	640x350	16
mode11	640x480	2
mode12	640x480	16
mode13	320x200	256
att640	640x400	16
att800x600	800x600	16
att640x400	640x400	256

NAME

volcopy (generic) – make literal copy of file system

SYNOPSIS

volcopy [**-F** *FSType*] [**-V**] [*current_options*] [**-o** *specific_options*] *operands*

DESCRIPTION

volcopy makes a literal copy of the file system.

current_options are options supported by the **s5**-specific module of **volcopy**. Other FSTypes do not necessarily support these options. *specific_options* indicate suboptions specified in a comma-separated list of suboptions and/or keyword-attribute pairs for interpretation by the *FSType*-specific module of the command.

operands generally include the device and volume names and are file system specific. A detailed description of the *operands* can be found on the *FSType*-specific man pages of **volcopy**.

The options are:

-F   Specify the *FSType* on which to operate. The *FSType* should either be specified here or be determinable from **/etc/vfstab** by matching the *operands* with an entry in the table.

-V   Echo the complete command line, but do not execute the command. The command line is generated by using the options and arguments provided by the user and adding to them information derived from **/etc/vfstab**. This option should be used to verify and validate the command line.

-o   Specify *FSType*-specific options.

NOTE

This command may not be supported for all FSTypes.

FILES

/etc/vfstab   list of default parameters for each file system

SEE ALSO

vfstab(4)

Manual pages for the FSType-specific modules of **volcopy**

NAME

volcopy (s5) – make a literal copy of an **s5** file system

SYNOPSIS

volcopy [**-F s5**] [*generic_options*] [*current_options*] *fsname srcdevice volname1 destdevice volname2*

DESCRIPTION

generic_options are options supported by the generic **volcopy** command.

volcopy makes a literal copy of the **s5** file system using a blocksize matched to the device.

The options are:

-F s5   Specify the **s5**-FSType.

-a   Invoke a verification sequence requiring a positive operator response instead of the standard 10-second delay before the copy is made.

-y   Assume a **yes** response to all questions.

Other *options* are used only with 9-track magnetic tapes:

-bpi*density*   bits per inch

-feet*size*   size of reel in feet

-reel*num*   beginning reel number for a restarted copy

-buf   use double buffered I/O

-e   process until the end of tape, then ask for the next tape in sequence.

If the **-e** option is not selected, the program requests length and density information if this is not given on the command line, or if it is not recorded on an input tape label. If the file system is too large to fit on one reel, **volcopy** prompts for additional reels. Labels of all reels are checked. Tapes may be mounted alternately on two or more drives. If **volcopy** is interrupted, it asks if the user wants to quit or escape to the command interpreter. In the latter case, the user can perform other operations (such as **labelit**) and return to **volcopy** by exiting the command interpreter. Note that the **-e** and **-feet** options are mutually exclusive.

The *fsname* argument represents the mounted name (for example, **root**, **usr**, and so on) of the file system being copied.

The *srcdevice* or *destdevice* should be the disk partition or tape. For example, **/dev/rdsk/*** or **/dev/rmt/***, where the value of * is machine specific.

The *volname* is the physical volume name. Such label names contain up to six characters. *volname* may be ''–'' to use the existing volume name.

srcdevice and *volname1* are the device and volume from which the copy of the file system is being extracted. *destdevice* and *volname2* are the target device and volume.

fsname and *volname* are recorded in the superblock.

NOTE

volcopy does not support tape-to-tape copying. Use **dd**(1M) for tape-to-tape copying.

FILES

    `/var/adm/filesave.log`   a record of file systems/volumes copied

SEE ALSO

dd(1M), **labelit**(1M), generic **volcopy**(1M); **cpio**(1) and **sh**(1) in the *User's Reference Manual*; and **cpio**(4) and **fs**(4), in the *Programmer's Reference Manual*

NAME

volcopy (ufs) – make a literal copy of a **ufs** file system

SYNOPSIS

volcopy [**-F ufs**] [*generic_options*] [*current_options*] *fsname srcdevice volname1 destdevice volname2*

DESCRIPTION

generic_options are options supported by the generic **volcopy** command. *current_options* are options supported by the s5-specific module of **volcopy**.

volcopy makes a literal copy of the **ufs** file system using a blocksize matched to the device.

The options are:

-F ufs Specify the **ufs**-FSType.

-a   Invoke a verification sequence requiring a positive operator response instead of the standard 10-second delay before the copy is made.

-y   Assume a **yes** response to all questions.

Other *options* are used only with 9-track magnetic tapes:

-bpi*density* bits per inch

-feet*size*   size of reel in feet

-reel*num*   beginning reel number for a restarted copy

-buf   use double buffered I/O

-e   process until the end of tape, then ask for the next tape in sequence.

If the **-e** option is not selected, the program requests length and density information if this is not given on the command line or if it is not recorded on an input tape label. If the file system is too large to fit on one reel, **volcopy** prompts for additional reels. Labels of all reels are checked. Tapes may be mounted alternately on two or more drives. If **volcopy** is interrupted, it asks if the user wants to quit or wants to escape to the command interpreter. In the latter case, the user can perform other operations (such as **labelit**) and return to **volcopy** by exiting the command interpreter. Note that the **-e** and **-feet** options are mutually exclusive.

The *fsname* argument represents the mounted name (for example, **root**, **usr**, and so on) of the file system being copied.

The *srcdevice* or *destdevice* should be the disk partition or tape. For example **/dev/rdsk/*** or **/dev/rmt/***, where the value of * is machine specific.

The *volname* is the physical volume name. Such label names contain up to six characters. *volname* may be "–" to use the existing volume name.

srcdevice and *volname1* are the device and volume from which the copy of the file system is being extracted. *destdevice* and *volname2* are the target device and volume.

fsname and *volname* are recorded in the superblock.

NOTE

volcopy does not support tape-to-tape copying. Use **dd**(1M) for tape-to-tape copying.

FILES

/var/adm/filesave.log   a record of file systems/volumes copied

SEE ALSO

dd(1M), **labelit**(1M), generic **volcopy**(1M); **cpio**(1) in the *User's Reference Manual*; and **cpio**(4) and **ufs**(4) in the *Programmer's Reference Manual*

NAME

vsig – synchronize a co-process with the controlling FMLI application

SYNOPSIS

vsig

DESCRIPTION

The **vsig** executable sends a **SIGUSR2** signal to the controlling FMLI process. This signal/alarm causes FMLI to execute the FMLI built-in command **checkworld** (see Chapter 2 in the *Character User Interface Programmer's Guide*), which causes all posted objects with a **reread** descriptor evaluating to **TRUE** to be reread. **vsig** takes no arguments.

EXAMPLES

The following is a segment of a shell program:

```
echo "Sending this string to an FMLI process"
vsig
```

The **vsig** executable flushes the output buffer *before* it sends the **SIGUSR2** signal to make sure the string is actually in the pipe created by the **cocreate** function.

NOTES

Because **vsig** synchronizes with FMLI, it should be used rather than **kill** to send a **SIGUSR2** signal to FMLI.

SEE ALSO

coproc(1F)
kill(1), in the *UNIX System V User's Reference Manual*
kill(2), **signal**(2), in the *UNIX System V Programmer's Reference Manual*

NAME

vtgetty – sets terminal type, modes, speed, and line discipline.

SYNOPSIS

/etc/vtgetty [-h] [-t timeout] line [[speed[type [linedisc]]]

DESCRIPTION

The vtgetty command is a program invoked by init(1M). It is the second process in the series (init-vtgetty-getty-login-shell) that passes its arguments
and executes /etc/getty. The /etc/getty process will ultimately connect a
user with the UNIX system. vtgetty can be executed only by the super-user (a
process with the user-ID of root).

The command options are identical to those of getty(1M).

Initially, vtgetty opens the device and determines if any virtual terminals (vts)
are open for that device. If there are active vts, the user will be prompted to
determine if the vts should be closed automatically or manually when the user
logs out.

If the automatic option is selected, vtgetty will send the signals, SIGHUP and
SIGTERM, to each open vt.

It will then wait 3 seconds and send a SIGKILL signal to the vts to ensure that all
the vts are terminated.

If the manual closure option is selected, the highest numbered vt will be activated
and the user can manually close the vt. This will be repeated until all open vts
are manually closed.

DIAGNOSTICS

vtgetty will fail under the following conditions:

> If there is no memory available.
> If it cannot open the device it was given.
> If it cannot convert from a file descriptor to a file pointer.
> If it cannot get the file status [stat(2)] of the device it was given.
> If an ioctl(2) call fails.

FILES

/etc/gettydefs

SEE ALSO

getty(1M), init(1M), kill(1M), tty(1M), ioctl(2), stat(2), gettydefs(4),
inittab(4) in the *Programmer's Reference Manual*.

NAME

    vtlmgr – monitors and opens virtual terminals.

SYNOPSIS

    vtlmgr [**-k**]

DESCRIPTION

When you invoke the **vtlmgr** command (usually from within your **.profile**), it places itself in the background and monitors **/dev/vtmon** for signals from the keyboard/display driver to open new virtual terminals.

Option:

-k   The **-k** option sends a **SIGHUP** signal to all open virtual terminals when you log off (by entering CTRL-d from your home virtual terminal). This automatically closes, if possible, existing virtual terminals. For virtual terminals that cannot be automatically closed, you are asked if you want to close them manually.

After running **vtlmgr**, you open new virtual terminals and then switch between them by entering a hot-key sequence, specifically:

    ALT - SYS-REQ *key*

where *key* is either a function key whose number corresponds to the number of the virtual terminal to switch to, for example, pressing F1 switches you to /dev/vt01 (virtual terminal 01), pressing F2 switches you to /dev/vt02 (virtual terminal 02), and so forth, or one of the letters in the following table:

key	Interpretation
h	home virtual terminal (/dev/vt00)
n	next virtual terminal
p	previous virtual terminal
f	force a switch to a virtual terminal

Use the **f** key only when the current virtual terminal is essentially locked up or stuck in graphics mode. This will cause the virtual terminal to be reset to a sane text state and all processes associated with the virtual terminal will be killed.

When the hot-key sequence is entered, the executable program pointed to by the **$SHELL** variable is executed in the new virtual terminal. If **$SHELL** is NULL or pointing to a program which is not executable, **/bin/sh** is executed. The newly opened virtual terminal inherits the environment in effect when the **vtlmgr** command is invoked.

You may perform setup on each new virtual terminal as it is created by **vtlmgr** through the **.vtlrc** file. This file should be in your home directory. Its contents are a shell script that will be run by **/bin/sh** before the shell prompt is displayed. In this way it is similar to your **.profile** file. However, you may not set and export environment variables to the shell for the virtual terminal because a different shell runs the **.vtlrc** shell script.

The system administrator can control how many virtual terminals are available by setting a parameter in the file **/etc/default/workstations**. Virtual terminals 0 - 8 are configured by default and the default keyboard map makes up to 13 virtual terminals available (i.e., an additional 4 virtual terminals can readily be defined within the default settings). The default virtual terminals are the home terminal and one corresponding to each function key. An application can make two more available to the end-user (by reprogramming the keyboard map), or can reserve the last two for programmatic use only, making 15 virtual terminals available in all.

Note that processes that are no longer visible may still be continuing. Standard output is directed to the current virtual terminal's screen. For example, you can issue a **cat** command on one virtual terminal, switch to another virtual terminal to start an application, and then switch to another to do an edit. The **cat** output will be lost if the virtual terminal scrolls the data off the screen unless you initially redirect the output to a file.

DIAGNOSTICS

The **vtlmgr** command will fail under the following conditions:

If an illegal option is specified.
If the device cannot be opened.
If the command is invoked from a remote terminal.
If **/dev/vtmon** cannot be opened.
If **$SHELL** is set and is not executable.
If **$SHELL** is not set and **/bin/sh** cannot be invoked.

SEE ALSO

newvt (1M)
vtgetty(1M), keyboard(7) in the *System Administrator's Reference Manual*

NAME

w – who is logged in, and what are they doing

SYNOPSIS

/usr/ucb/w [–hls] [*user*]

DESCRIPTION

The w command displays a summary of the current activity on the system, including what each user is doing. The heading line shows the current time of day, how long the system has been up, and the number of users logged into the system.

The fields displayed are: the users login name, the name of the tty the user is on, the time of day the user logged on (in *hours:minutes*), the idle time—that is, the number of minutes since the user last typed anything (in *hours:minutes*), the CPU time used by all processes and their children on that terminal (in *minutes:seconds*), the CPU time used by the currently active processes (in *minutes:seconds*), the name and arguments of the current process.

If a *user* name is included, output is restricted to that user.

The following options are available:

-h   Suppress the heading.

-l   Produce a long form of output, which is the default.

-s   Produce a short form of output. In the short form, the tty is abbreviated, the login time and CPU times are left off, as are the arguments to commands.

EXAMPLE

```
w
7:36am  up 6 days, 16:45,  1 users
User tty  login@     idle JCPU PCPU what
ralph console   7:10am        1 10:05 4:31  w
```

FILES

/var/adm/utmp
/dev/kmem
/dev/drum

SEE ALSO

ps(1), who(1) in the *User's Reference Manual*
utmp(4), whodo(1M) in the *System Administrator's Reference Manual*

NOTES

The notion of the "current process" is muddy. The current algorithm is 'the highest numbered process on the terminal that is not ignoring interrupts, or, if there is none, the highest numbered process on the terminal'. This fails, for example, in critical sections of programs like the shell and editor, or when faulty programs running in the background fork and fail to ignore interrupts. In cases where no process can be found, w prints –.

The CPU time is only an estimate, in particular, if someone leaves a background process running after logging out, the person currently on that terminal is "charged" with the time.

Background processes are not shown, even though they account for much of the load on the system.

Sometimes processes, typically those in the background, are printed with null or garbaged arguments. In these cases, the name of the command is printed in parentheses.

w does not know about the conventions for detecting background jobs. It will sometimes find a background job instead of the right one.

NAME

wait – await completion of process

SYNOPSIS

wait [n]

DESCRIPTION

Wait for your background process whose process id is n and report its termination status. If n is omitted, all your shell's currently active background processes are waited for and the return code will be zero.

The shell itself executes **wait**, without creating a new process.

SEE ALSO

sh(1)

NOTES

If you get the error message **cannot fork, too many processes**, try using the **wait** command to clean up your background processes. If this doesn't help, the system process table is probably full or you have too many active foreground processes. (There is a limit to the number of process ids associated with your login, and to the number the system can keep track of.)

Not all the processes of a 3- or more-stage pipeline are children of the shell, and thus cannot be waited for.

If n is not an active process id, all your shell's currently active background processes are waited for and the return code will be zero.

NAME

`wall` – write to all users

SYNOPSIS

`wall` [–**g** *group*] [*filename*]

DESCRIPTION

`wall` reads the named file, or if no filename appears, it reads the standard input until an end-of-file. It then sends this message to all currently logged-in users preceded by:

> `Broadcast Message from . . .`

It is used to warn all users, typically prior to shutting down the system. If the –**g** option is given, the message is only sent to the members of the specified group, instead of all users.

The sender must be super-user to override any protections the users may have invoked [see **mesg**(1)].

`wall` runs **setgid** [see **setuid**(2)] to the group ID **tty**, in order to have write permissions on other user's terminals.

`wall` will detect non-printable characters before sending them to the user's terminal. Control characters will appear as a '**^**' followed by the appropriate ASCII character; characters with the high-order bit set will appear in meta notation. For example, '\003' is displayed as '**^C**' and '\372' as '**M-z**'.

FILES

`/dev/term/*`

SEE ALSO

mesg(1), **write**(1).

NOTES

"Cannot send to ..." when the open on a user's tty file fails.

NAME

    wc – word count

SYNOPSIS

    wc [−lwc] [*filename* . . .]

DESCRIPTION

    wc counts lines, words, and characters in the named files, or in the standard input if no *filename* appears. It also keeps a total count for all named files. A word is a maximal string of characters delimited by spaces, tabs, or new-lines.

    The options 1, w, and c may be used in any combination to specify that a subset of lines, words, and characters are to be reported. The default is −lwc.

    When a *filename* is specified on the command line, it will be printed along with the counts.

NAME

what – print identification strings

SYNOPSIS

what [–s] *files*

DESCRIPTION

what searches the given files for all occurrences of the pattern that the **get** command substitutes for %Z% (this is @(#) at this printing) and prints out what follows until the first ", >, new-line, \, or null character. For example, if the C program in file **f.c** contains

#ident " @(#)*identification information* "

and **f.c** is compiled to yield **f.o** and **a.out**, then the command

what f.c f.o a.out

prints

f.c:

identification information

f.o:

identification information

a.out:

identification information

what is intended to be used in conjunction with the **get** command, which automatically inserts identifying information, but it can also be used where the information is inserted manually. Only one option exists:

–s　　　Quit after finding the first occurrence of pattern in each file.

SEE ALSO

get(1), help(1), mcs(1)

DIAGNOSTICS

Exit status is 0 if any matches are found, otherwise 1. See **help**(1) for explanations.

NAME

whatis – display a one-line summary about a keyword

SYNOPSIS

/usr/ucb/whatis *command* . . .

DESCRIPTION

whatis looks up a given *command* and displays the header line from the manual section. You can then run the man(1) command to get more information. If the line starts '*name*(*section*) ...' you can do '**man** *section name*' to get the documentation for it. Try '**whatis ed**' and then you should do '**man 1 ed**' to get the manual page for **ed**(1).

whatis is actually just the −**f** option to the **man** command.

FILES

/usr/share/man/whatis   data base

SEE ALSO

man(1), catman(1M)

NAME

which – locate a command; display its pathname or alias

SYNOPSIS

/usr/ucb/which [*filename*] . . .

DESCRIPTION

which takes a list of names and looks for the files which would be executed had these names been given as commands. Each argument is expanded if it is aliased, and searched for along the user's path. Both aliases and path are taken from the user's **.cshrc** file.

FILES

~/.cshrc   source of aliases and path values

SEE ALSO

csh(1), **ksh**(1), **sh**(1) in the *User's Reference Manual*.

DIAGNOSTICS

A diagnostic is given for names which are aliased to more than a single word, or if an executable file with the argument name was not found in the path.

NOTES

Only aliases and paths from ~/.cshrc are used; importing from the current environment is not attempted.

which must be executed by **csh**(1), since only **csh** knows about aliases. If you are using **sh** instead of **csh**, **whence** **-v** provides similar functionality.

To compensate for ~/.cshrc files in which aliases depend upon the **prompt** variable being set, **which** sets this variable. If the ~/.cshrc produces output or prompts for input when **prompt** is set, **which** may produce some strange results.

NAME

who – who is on the system

SYNOPSIS

who [-uTlHqpdbrtas] [*file*]

who -qn *x* [*file*]

who am i

who am I

DESCRIPTION

who can list the user's name, terminal line, login time, elapsed time since activity occurred on the line, and the process-ID of the command interpreter (shell) for each current UNIX system user. It examines the **/var/adm/utmp** file to obtain its information. If *file* is given, that file (which must be in **utmp**(4) format) is examined. Usually, *file* will be **/var/adm/wtmp**, which contains a history of all the logins since the file was last created.

who with the **am i** or **am I** option identifies the invoking user.

The general format for output is:

> *name* [*state*] *line time* [*idle*] [*pid*] [*comment*] [*exit*]

The *name*, *line*, and *time* information is produced by all options except –q; the *state* information is produced only by –**T**; the *idle* and *pid* information is produced only by –u and –1; and the *comment* and **exit** information is produced only by –a. The information produced for –p, –d, and –r is explained during the discussion of each option, below.

With options, who can list logins, logoffs, reboots, and changes to the system clock, as well as other processes spawned by the **init** process. These options are:

–u   This option lists only those users who are currently logged in. The *name* is the user's login name. The *line* is the name of the line as found in the directory **/dev**. The *time* is the time that the user logged in. The *idle* column contains the number of hours and minutes since activity last occurred on that particular line. A dot (.) indicates that the terminal has seen activity in the last minute and is therefore "current". If more than twenty-four hours have elapsed or the line has not been used since boot time, the entry is marked **old**. This field is useful when trying to determine whether a person is working at the terminal or not. The *pid* is the process-ID of the user's shell. The *comment* is the comment field associated with this line as found in **/etc/inittab** [see **inittab**(4)]. This can contain information about where the terminal is located, the telephone number of the dataset, type of terminal if hard-wired, etc.

–T   This option is the same as the –**s** option, except that the *state* of the terminal line is printed. The *state* describes whether someone else can write to that terminal. A + appears if the terminal is writable by anyone; a – appears if it is not. **root** can write to all lines having a + or a – in the *state* field. If a bad line is encountered, a **?** is printed.

-l   This option lists only those lines on which the system is waiting for some-one to login. The *name* field is **LOGIN** in such cases. Other fields are the same as for user entries except that the *state* field does not exist.

-H   This option will print column headings above the regular output.

-q   This is a quick **who**, displaying only the names and the number of users currently logged on. When this option is used, all other options are ignored.

-p   This option lists any other process which is currently active and has been previously spawned by **init**. The *name* field is the name of the program executed by **init** as found in **/etc/inittab**. The *state*, **line**, and *idle* fields have no meaning. The *comment* field shows the **id** field of the line from **/etc/inittab** that spawned this process. See **inittab**(4).

-d   This option displays all processes that have expired and not been respawned by **init**. The **exit** field appears for dead processes and con-tains the termination and exit values [as returned by **wait**(2)], of the dead process. This can be useful in determining why a process terminated.

-b   This option indicates the time and date of the last reboot.

-r   This option indicates the current *run-level* of the **init** process. In addition, it produces the process termination status, process id, and process exit status [see **utmp**(4)] under the *idle*, *pid*, and *comment* headings, respectively.

-t   This option indicates the last change to the system clock (via the **date** command) by **root**. See **su**(1M).

-a   This option processes **/var/adm/utmp** or the named *file* with all options turned on.

-s   This option is the default and lists only the *name*, **line**, and *time* fields.

-n *x*   This option takes a numeric argument, *x*, which specifies the number of users to display per line. *x* must be at least **1**. The −**n** option must be used with −**q**.

Note to the super-user: after a shutdown to the single-user state, **who** returns a prompt; the reason is that since **/var/adm/utmp** is updated at login time and there is no login in single-user state, **who** cannot report accurately on this state. **who am i**, however, returns the correct information.

FILES

     /var/adm/utmp
     /var/adm/wtmp
     /etc/inittab

SEE ALSO

     date(1), login(1), mesg(1), su(1M)
     init(1M), inittab(4), utmp(4) in the *System Administrator's Reference Manual*
     wait(2) in the *Programmer's Reference Manual*

NAME

whoami – display the effective current username

SYNOPSIS

/usr/ucb/whoami

DESCRIPTION

whoami displays the login name corresponding to the current effective user ID. If you have used **su** to temporarily adopt another user, **whoami** will report the login name associated with that user ID. **whoami** gets its information from the **geteuid** and **getpwuid** library routines (see **getuid** and **getpwent**, respectively).

FILES

/etc/passwd   username data base

SEE ALSO

su(1), **who**(1) in the *User's Reference Manual*
getuid(2), **getpwent**(3) in the *Programmer's Reference Manual*

NAME

whodo – who is doing what

SYNOPSIS

/usr/sbin/whodo [-h] [-l] [*user*]

DESCRIPTION

whodo produces formatted and dated output from information in the /var/adm/utmp, /etc/ps_data, and /proc/pid files.

The display is headed by the date, time, and machine name. For each user logged in, device name, user-ID and login time is shown, followed by a list of active processes associated with the user-ID. The list includes the device name, process-ID, CPU minutes and seconds used, and process name.

If *user* is specified, output is restricted to all sessions pertaining to that user.

The following options are available:

-h   Suppress the heading.

-l   Produce a long form of output. The fields displayed are: the user's login name, the name of the tty the user is on, the time of day the user logged in (in *hours*:*minutes*), the idle time — that is, the time since the user last typed anything (in *hours*:*minutes*), the CPU time used by all processes and their children on that terminal (in *minutes*:*seconds*), the CPU time used by the currently active processes (in *minutes*:*seconds*), and the name and arguments of the current process.

EXAMPLE

The command:

    whodo

produces a display like this:

```
            Tue Mar 12 15:48:03 1985
            bailey

            term/09     mcn         8:51
                term/09     28158     0:29 sh

            term/52     bdr        15:23
                term/52     21688     0:05 sh
                term/52     22788     0:01 whodo
                term/52     22017     0:03 vi
                term/52     22549     0:01 sh

            xt/162      lee        10:20
                term/08     6748      0:01 layers
                xt/162      6751      0:01 sh
                xt/163      6761      0:05 sh
                term/08     6536      0:05 sh
```

FILES

```
/etc/passwd
/etc/ps_data
/var/adm/utmp
/proc/pid
```

DIAGNOSTICS

If the PROC driver is not installed or configured or if **/proc** is not mounted, a message to that effect is issued and **whodo** will fail.

The exit status is zero on success, non-zero on failure.

SEE ALSO

ps(1), **who**(1) in the *User's Reference Manual*.

NAME

    whois – Internet user name directory service

SYNOPSIS

    whois [**-h** *host*] *identifier*

DESCRIPTION

    whois searches for an Internet directory entry for an *identifier* which is either a name (such as "Smith") or a handle (such as "SRI-NIC"). To force a name-only search, precede the name with a period; to force a handle-only search, precede the handle with an exclamation point.

    To search for a group or organization entry, precede the argument with * (an asterisk). The entire membership list of the group will be displayed with the record.

    You may of course use an exclamation point and asterisk, or a period and asterisk together.

EXAMPLES

    The command

        whois Smith

    looks for the name or handle SMITH.

    The command

        whois !SRI-NIC

    looks for the handle SRI-NIC only.

    The command

        whois .Smith, John

    looks for the name JOHN SMITH only.

    Adding . . . to the name or handle argument will match anything from that point; that is, zu . . . will match ZUL, ZUM, and so on.

NAME

write – write to another user

SYNOPSIS

write *user* [*line*]

DESCRIPTION

write copies lines from your terminal to that of another user. When first called, it sends the message:

Message from *yourname* (**term/**??) [*date*] . . .

to the person you want to talk to. When it has successfully completed the connection, it also sends two bells to your own terminal to indicate that what you are typing is being sent.

The recipient of the message should write back at this point. Communication continues until an end of file is read from the terminal, an interrupt is sent, or the recipient has executed "mesg n". At that point **write** writes **EOT** on the other terminal and exits.

If you want to write to a user who is logged in more than once, the **line** argument may be used to indicate which line or terminal to send to (for example, **term/12**); otherwise, the first writable instance of the user found in **/var/adm/utmp** is assumed and the following message posted:

user is logged on more than one place.
You are connected to "*terminal***".**
Other locations are:
terminal

Permission to write may be denied or granted by use of the **mesg** command. Writing to others is normally allowed by default. Certain commands, such as the **pr** command, disallow messages in order to prevent interference with their output. However, if the user has super-user permissions, messages can be forced onto a write-inhibited terminal.

If the character **!** is found at the beginning of a line, **write** calls the shell to execute the rest of the line as a command.

write runs **setgid( )** [see **setuid**(2)] to the group ID **tty**, in order to have write permissions on other user's terminals.

write will detect non-printable characters before sending them to the user's terminal. Control characters will appear as a '**^**' followed by the appropriate ASCII character; characters with the high-order bit set will appear in meta notation. For example, '**\003**' is displayed as '**^C**' and '**\372**' as '**M-z**'.

The following protocol is suggested for using **write**: when you first **write** to another user, wait for them to **write** back before starting to send. Each person should end a message with a distinctive signal (that is, (**o**) for "over") so that the other person knows when to reply. The signal (**oo**) (for "over and out") is suggested when conversation is to be terminated.

FILES

/var/adm/utmp to find user
/usr/bin/sh to execute !

SEE ALSO

mail(1), mesg(1), pr(1), sh(1), who(1), setuid(2)

DIAGNOSTICS

`user is not logged on`	if the person you are trying to **write** to is not logged on.
`Permission denied`	if the person you are trying to **write** to denies that permission (with **mesg**).
`Warning: cannot respond, set mesg -y`	if your terminal is set to **mesg n** and the recipient cannot respond to you.
`Can no longer write to user`	if the recipient has denied permission (**mesg n**) after you had started writing.

NAME

   wtinit – object downloader for the 5620 DMD terminal

SYNOPSIS

   /usr/lib/layersys/wtinit [**–d**] [**–p**] *file*

DESCRIPTION

   The **wtinit** utility downloads the named *file* for execution in the AT&T 5620
   DMD terminal connected to its standard output. *file* must be a DMD object file.
   wtinit performs all necessary bootstrap and protocol procedures.

   There are two options.

   –d   Prints out the sizes of the text, data, and bss portions of the downloaded
            file on standard error.

   –p   Prints the down-loading protocol statistics and a trace on standard error.

   The environment variable **JPATH** is the analog of the shell's **PATH** variable to
   define a set of directories in which to search for *file*.

   If the environment variable **DMDLOAD** has the value **hex**, **wtinit** will use a hexadecimal download protocol that uses only printable characters.

   Terminal Feature Packages for specific versions of AT&T windowing terminals
   will include terminal-specific versions of **wtinit** under those installation subdirectories. **/usr/lib/layersys/wtinit** is used for **layers**(1) initialization only
   when no Terminal Feature Package is in use (i.e., the $**DMD** shell variable is not
   set).

DIAGNOSTICS

   Returns **0** upon successful completion, **1** otherwise.

NOTES

   Standard error should be redirected when using the **–d** or **–p** options.

SEE ALSO

   layers(1) in the *User's Reference Manual*

NAME

    x286emul – emulate XENIX 80286

SYNOPSIS

    x286emul [*arg* . . .] **prog286**

DESCRIPTION

    x286emul is an emulator that allows programs from XENIX System V/286 Release 2.3 or SCO's XENIX System V/286 Release 2.3.2 on the Intel 80286 to run on the Intel 80386 processor under UNIX System V.

    The UNIX system recognizes an attempt to **exec**(2) a 286 program, and automatically **exec**'s the 286 emulator with the 286 program name as an additional argument. It is not necessary to specify the **x286emul** emulator on the command line. The 286 programs can be invoked using the same command format as on the XENIX System V/286.

    x286emul reads the 286 program's text and data into memory and maps them through the LDT [via **sysi86**(2)] as 286 text and data segments. It also fills in the jam area, which is used by XENIX programs to do system calls and signal returns. **x286emul** starts the 286 program by jumping to its entry point.

    When the 286 program attempts to do a system call, **x286emul** takes control. It does any conversions needed between the 286 system call and the equivalent 386 system call, and performs the 386 system call. The results are converted to the form the 286 program expects, and the 286 program is resumed.

    The following are some of the differences between a program running on a 286 and a 286 program using **x286emul** on a 386:

        Attempts to unlink or write on the 286 program will fail on the 286 with **ETXTBSY**. Under **x286emul**, they will not fail.

        ptrace(2) is not supported under **x286emul**.

        The 286 program must be readable for the emulator to read it.

    The emulator must have this name and be in **/bin** if it is to be automatically invoked when **exec**(2) is used on a 286 program.

NAME

xargs – construct argument list(s) and execute command

SYNOPSIS

xargs [*flags*] [*command* [*initial-arguments*]]

DESCRIPTION

xargs combines the fixed *initial-arguments* with arguments read from standard input to execute the specified *command* one or more times. The number of arguments read for each *command* invocation and the manner in which they are combined are determined by the flags specified.

command, which may be a shell file, is searched for, using one's **$PATH**. If *command* is omitted, **/usr/bin/echo** is used.

Arguments read in from standard input are defined to be contiguous strings of characters delimited by one or more blanks, tabs, or new-lines; empty lines are always discarded. Blanks and tabs may be embedded as part of an argument if escaped or quoted. Characters enclosed in quotes (single or double) are taken literally, and the delimiting quotes are removed. Outside of quoted strings a backslash (\) escapes the next character.

Each argument list is constructed starting with the *initial-arguments*, followed by some number of arguments read from standard input (Exception: see **–i** flag). Flags **–i**, **–l**, and **–n** determine how arguments are selected for each command invocation. When none of these flags are coded, the *initial-arguments* are followed by arguments read continuously from standard input until an internal buffer is full, and then *command* is executed with the accumulated args. This process is repeated until there are no more args. When there are flag conflicts (for example, **–l** vs. **–n**), the last flag has precedence. Valid *flags* are:

–l*number*   *command* is executed for each non-empty *number* lines of arguments from standard input. The last invocation of *command* will be with fewer lines of arguments if fewer than *number* remain. A line is considered to end with the first new-line *unless* the last character of the line is a blank or a tab; a trailing blank/tab signals continuation through the next non-empty line. If *number* is omitted, 1 is assumed. Option **–x** is forced.

–i*replstr*   Insert mode: *command* is executed for each line from standard input, taking the entire line as a single arg, inserting it in *initial-arguments* for each occurrence of *replstr*. A maximum of five arguments in *initial-arguments* may each contain one or more instances of *replstr*. Blanks and tabs at the beginning of each line are thrown away. Constructed arguments may not grow larger than 255 characters, and option **–x** is also forced. **{ }** is assumed for *replstr* if not specified.

–n*number*   Execute *command* using as many standard input arguments as possible, up to *number* arguments maximum. Fewer arguments are used if their total size is greater than *size* characters, and for the last invocation if there are fewer than *number* arguments remaining. If option **–x** is also coded, each *number* arguments must fit in the *size* limitation, else **xargs** terminates execution.

-t   Trace mode: The *command* and each constructed argument list are echoed to file descriptor 2 just prior to their execution.

-p   Prompt mode: The user is asked whether to execute *command* each invocation. Trace mode (-t) is turned on to print the command instance to be executed, followed by a **?. . .** prompt. A reply of **y** (optionally followed by anything) executes the command; anything else, including just a carriage return, skips that particular invocation of *command*.

-x   Causes **xargs** to terminate if any argument list would be greater than *size* characters; -x is forced by the options -i and -l. When neither of the options -i, -l, or -n are coded, the total length of all arguments must be within the *size* limit.

-s*size*   The maximum total size of each argument list is set to *size* characters; *size* must be a positive integer less than or equal to 470. If -s is not coded, 470 is taken as the default. Note that the character count for *size* includes one extra character for each argument and the count of characters in the command name.

-e*eofstr*   *eofstr* is taken as the logical end-of-file string. Underbar (_) is assumed for the logical EOF string if -e is not coded. The value -e with no *eofstr* coded turns off the logical EOF string capability (underbar is taken literally). **xargs** reads standard input until either end-of-file or the logical EOF string is encountered.

xargs terminates if either it receives a return code of -1 from, or if it cannot execute, *command*. When *command* is a shell program, it should explicitly **exit** (see **sh**(1)) with an appropriate value to avoid accidentally returning with -1.

EXAMPLES

The following examples moves all files from directory $1 to directory $2, and echo each move command just before doing it:

```
ls $1 | xargs -i -t mv $1/{ } $2/{ }
```

The following example combines the output of the parenthesized commands onto one line, which is then echoed to the end of file **log**:

```
(logname; date; echo $0 $*) | xargs >>log
```

The user is asked which files in the current directory are to be archived and archives them into **arch** (1.) one at a time, or (2.) many at a time.

```
1. ls | xargs -p -l ar r arch
2. ls | xargs -p -l | xargs ar r arch
```

The following example executes **diff**(1) with successive pairs of arguments originally typed as shell arguments:

```
echo $* | xargs -n2 diff
```

SEE ALSO

sh(1)

NAME

  xfsck – check and repair XENIX filesystems

SYNOPSIS

  /bin/xfsck [*options*] [filesystem] . . .

DESCRIPTION

  The **xfsck** command audits and interactively repairs inconsistent conditions for
  XENIX System V filesystems. If the filesystem is consistent, then **xfsck** reports
  number of files, number of blocks used, and number of blocks free. If the filesystem is inconsistent, the user is prompted whether or not **xfsck** should proceed
  with each correction. It should be noted that most corrective actions result in
  some loss of data. The amount and severity of the loss can be determined from
  the diagnostic output. If the user does not have write permission, xfsck defaults
  to the action of the **–n** option.

  The **xfsck** options are:

  –y   Assumes a response to all questions asked by **xfsck**.

  –n   Assumes a response to all questions asked by **xfsck**. This option does
           not open the filesystem for writing.

  –s *b:c*   Ignores the actual free list and unconditionally reconstructs a new one
           by rewriting the super-block of the filesystem. The filesystem *must* be
           unmounted while this is done.

           This option allows for creating an optimal free-list organization. The fol-
           lowing forms are supported:

             -s

             -sBlocks-per-cylinder:Blocks-to-skip (filesystem interleave)

           If *b:c* is not given, then the values that were used when the filesystem
           was created are used again. If these values were not specified, then the
           default value is used.

  –S   Conditionally reconstructs the free list. This option is similar to **–s** *b:c*
           above, except that the free list is rebuilt only if there are no discrepancies
           discovered in the filesystem. The **–S** option forces a ''no'' response to all
           questions asked by **xfsck**. This option is useful for forcing free-list reor-
           ganization on uncontaminated filesystems.

  –t   Causes **xfsck** to use the next argument as the scratch file, if needed. A
           scratch file is used if **xfsck** cannot obtain enough memory to keep its
           tables. Without the **–t** flag, **xfsck** prompts the user for the name of the
           scratch file. The file chosen should not be on the filesystem being
           checked. In addition, if the scratch file is not a special file or did not
           already exist, it is removed when **xfsck** completes. Note that if the sys-
           tem has a large hard disk, there may not be enough space on another
           filesystem for the scratch file. In such cases, if the system has a floppy
           disk drive, use a blank, formatted floppy disk in the floppy disk drive
           with (for example) **/dev/fd0** specified as the scratch file.

-q   Causes **xfsck** to perform a quiet check. Does not print size-check messages in Phase 1. Unreferenced **fifo5** files are selectively removed. If **xfsck** requires it, counts in the superblock are automatically fixed and the free list salvaged.

-D   Checks directories for bad blocks. Use this option after the system crashes.

-f   Causes **xfsck** to perform a fast check. **xfsck** checks block and sizes (Phase 1) and checks the free list (Phase 5). The free list is reconstructed (Phase 6), if necessary.

-rr   Recovers the root filesystem. The required *filesystem* argument must refer to the root filesystem, and preferably to the block device (normally **/dev/root**). This switch implies **-y** (yes) and overrides **-n** (no). If any modifications to the filesystem are required, the system will be automatically shutdown to ensure the integrity of the filesystem.

-c   Causes any supported filesystem to be converted to the current filesystem type. The user is prompted to verify the conversion of each filesystem, unless the **-y** option is specified. It is recommended that every filesystem be checked with this option *while unmounted* if it is to be used with the current version of XENIX. To update the active root filesystem, check it with the following command line:

                          xfsck -c -rr /dev/root

If no *filesystems* are specified, **xfsck** reads a list of default filesystems from the **/etc/checklist** file.

The following are some of the inconsistencies **xfsck** checks for:

− Blocks claimed by more than one inode or the free list

− Blocks claimed by an inode or the free list outside the range of the filesystem

− Incorrect link counts

− Size checks:
       Incorrect number of blocks
       Directory size not 16-byte aligned

− Bad inode format

− Blocks not accounted for anywhere

− Directory checks:
       File pointing to unallocated inode
       Inode number out of range

− Super block checks:
       More than 65536 inodes
       More blocks for inodes than there are in the filesystem

    −   Bad free block list format

    −   Total free block or free inode count incorrect

With the user's consent, **xfsck** reconnects orphaned (allocated, but unreferenced) files and directories by placing them in the *lost+found* directory. The file's (or directory's) inode number then becomes its name. Note that the *lost+found* directory must already exist in the root of the filesystem being checked and must have empty slots in which entries can be made. To create the *lost+found* directory, copy a few files to the directory, then remove them (before executing **xfsck**).

FILES

    /etc/checklist   Contains default list of filesystems to check
    /etc/default/boot Contains flags for automatic boot control

SEE ALSO

    fsck(1M)

NOTES

    xfsck will not run on a mounted non-raw filesystem, unless the filesystem is the root filesystem, or the **-n** option is specified and no writing out of the filesystem will take place. If any such attempt is made, **xfsck** displays a warning and no further processing of the filesystem is done for the specified device.

    xfsck does not support filesystems created under XENIX-86 version 3.0 because the word order in type *long* variables has changed. However, **xfsck** is capable of auditing and repairing XENIX version 3.0 filesystems if the word ordering is correct.

    Run **xfsck -rr /dev/root** for the root filesystem. Run **xfsck /dev/??** on the *unmounted* block device for all other filesystems.

    It is not recommended that users use **xfsck** on raw devices. Although checking a raw device is almost always faster, there is no way to tell if the filesystem is mounted. If the filesystem is mounted, cleaning it will almost certainly result in an inconsistent superblock.

NAME

xinstall – XENIX installation shell script

SYNOPSIS

/etc/xinstall [*device*]

DESCRIPTION

/etc/xinstall is the sh (1) script used to install XENIX distribution (or application program) floppies. It performs the following tasks:

prompts for insertion of floppies

extracts files using the tar(1) utility

executes /once/init.* programs on each floppy after they have been extracted

removes any /once/init.* programs when the installation is finished

The optional argument to the command specifies the device used. The default device is /dev/rfd0.

FILES

/etc/xinstall
/once/init.*

SEE ALSO

custom(1M), fixperm(1M), installpkg(1).

NOTES

xinstall is provided for use with any existing XENIX packages you may have that you wish to install on the UNIX operating system. xinstall does not work with UNIX system applications [use installpkg(1) to install UNIX system applications].

NAME
       xinstall – install commands

SYNOPSIS
       xinstall [-c *dira*] [-f *dirb*] [-n *dirc*] [-o] [-a] *file* [*dirz* . . .]

DESCRIPTION
       xinstall is a command most commonly used in "makefiles" [see make(CP)] to
       xinstall a file (updated target file) in a specific place within a file system. Each
       file is installed by copying it into the appropriate directory, thereby retaining the
       mode and owner of the original command file. The program prints messages
       telling you exactly what files it is replacing or creating and where they are going.

       If no options or directories (*dirz* . . .) are given, xinstall will search [using
       find(C)] a set of default directories (/usr/bin/usr/usr/bin, /etc, /usr/lib,
       and /usr/usr/lib, in that order) for a file with the same name as *file*. When the
       first occurrence is found, xinstall issues a message saying that it is overwriting
       that file with *file*, and proceeds to do so. If the file is not found, the program
       states this and exits without further action.

       If one or more directories (*dirz* . . .) are specified after *file*, those directories will be
       searched before the directories specified in the default list.

       The meanings of the options are:

       -c *dira*   Installs a new command file in the directory specified in *dira*. Looks
                     for *file* in *dira* and xinstalls it there if it is not found. If it is found,
                     xinstall issues a message saying that the file already exists, and exits
                     without overwriting it. May be used alone or with the -s option.

       -f *dirb*   Forces *file* to be installed in given directory, whether or not one
                     already exists. if the file being installed does not already exist, the
                     mode and owner of the new file will be set to 755 and bin, respec-
                     tively. If the file exists, the mode and owner will be that of the
                     existing file. May be used alone or with the -o or -s options.

       -1   Ignores default directory list, searching only through the given
                     directories (*dirz* . . .). May be used alone or with any other options
                     except -c and -f.

       -n *dirc*   If *file* is not found in any of the searched directories, it is put in the
                     directory specified in *dirc*. The mode and owner of the new file will
                     be set to 755 and bin, respectively. May be used alone or with any
                     other options except -c and -f.

       -o   If *file* is found, this option saves the "found" file by copying it to
                     oldfile in the directory in which is was found. May be used alone or
                     with any other options except -c.

       -s   Suppresses printing of messages other than error messages. May be
                     used alone or with any other options.

SEE ALSO
       find(1), make(1)

NAME

xrestore, xrestor – invoke XENIX incremental filesystem restorer

SYNOPSIS

xrestore *key* [*arguments*]

xrestor *key* [*arguments*]

DESCRIPTION

xrestore is used to read archive media backed up with the XENIX **backup**(C) command. The *key* specifies what is to be done. *Key* is one of the characters **rRxt**, optionally combined with **f**. **xrestor** is an alternate spelling for the same command.

f   Uses the first *argument* as the name of the archive instead of the default.

F *num*   Specifies the file number of the first volume to be restored.

k *vsize* Specifies the size of the volume to be restored.

r , R   The archive is read and loaded into the filesystem specified in *argument*. This should not be done lightly (see below). If the *key* is **R** , **xrestore** asks which archive of a multivolume set to start on. This allows **xrestore** to be interrupted and then restarted (an **fsck** must be done before the restart).

x   Each file on the archive named by an *argument* is extracted. The filename has all "mount" prefixes removed; for example, if **/usr** is a mounted filesystem, **/usr/bin/lpr** is named **/bin/lpr** on the archive. The extracted file is placed in a file with a numeric name supplied by **xrestore** (actually the inode number). In order to keep the amount of archive read to a minimum, the following procedure is recommended:

1. Mount volume 1 of the set of backup archives.

2. Type the **xrestore** command.

3. **r1restore** will announce whether or not it found the files, give the numeric name that it will assign to the file, and in the case of a tape, rewind to the start of the archive.

4. It then asks you to "mount the desired tape volume". Type the number of the volume you choose. On a multivolume backup the recommended procedure is to mount the volumes, last through first. **restore** checks to see if any of the requested files are on the mounted archive (or a later archive–thus the reverse order). If the requested files are not there, **xrestore** doesn't read through the tape. If you are working with a single-volume backup or if the number of files being restored is large, respond to the query with 1 , and **xrestore** will read the archives in sequential order.

X *files* Puts files in the directory specified by *arguments*.

t   Prints the date the archive was written and the date the filesystem was backed up.

T   This causes **xrestore** to behave like **dumpdir** (C) except that it doesn't list directories.

The **r** option should only be used to restore a complete backup archive onto a clear filesystem, or to restore an incremental backup archive onto a filesystem so created. Thus:

```
/etc/mkfs /dev/dsk/0s3 10000
xrestore r /dev/dsk/0s3
```

is a typical sequence to restore a complete backup. Another **xrestore** can be done to get an incremental backup in on top of this.

A **backup** followed by a **mkfs** and a **xrestore** is used to change the size of a filesystem.

FILES

rst*   Temporary files

/etc/default/xrestore   Name of default archive device

The default archive unit varies with installation.

NOTES

xrestore is for XENIX compatibility and should only be used to restore filesystems that were backed up under XENIX.

It is not possible to successfully restore an entire active **root** filesystem.

DIAGNOSTICS

There are various diagnostics involved with reading the archive and writing the disk. There are also diagnostics if the i-list or the free list of the filesystem is not large enough to hold the dump.

If the dump extends over more than one disk or tape, it may ask you to change disks or tapes. Reply with a NEWLINE when the next unit has been mounted.

NAME

xts – extract and print xt driver statistics

SYNOPSIS

`xts [-f]`

DESCRIPTION

The **xts** command is a debugging tool for the **xt**(7) driver. It performs an **XTIOCSTATS ioctl**(2) call on its standard input file to extract the accumulated statistics for the attached group of channels. This call will fail if the standard input is not attached to an active **xt**(7) channel. The statistics are printed one item per line on the standard output.

-f   Causes a "formfeed" character to be put out at the end of the output, for the benefit of page-display programs.

DIAGNOSTICS

Returns 0 upon successful completion, 1 otherwise.

SEE ALSO

layers(1) in the *User's Reference Manual*
xtt(1M), **ioctl**(2), **xtproto**(5)
xt(7) in the *Programmer's Guide: STREAMS*

NAME

    xtt – extract and print xt driver packet traces

SYNOPSIS

    xtt [-f] [-o]

DESCRIPTION

    The **xtt** command is a debugging tool for the **xt**(7) driver. It performs an **XTIOCTRACE ioctl**(2) call on its standard input file to turn on tracing and extract the circular packet trace buffer for the attached group of channels. This call will fail if the standard input is not attached to an active **xt**(7) channel. The packets are printed on the standard output.

    The optional flags are:

    -f   Causes a ''formfeed'' character to be put out at the end of the output, for the benefit of page-display programs.

    -o   Turns off further driver tracing.

DIAGNOSTICS

    Returns **0** upon successful completion, **1** otherwise.

NOTES

    If driver tracing has not been turned on for the terminal session by invoking **layers**(1) with the **-t** option, **xtt** will not generate any output the first time it is executed.

SEE ALSO

    layers(1) in the *User's Reference Manual*
    xts(1M), **ioctl**(2), **xtproto**(5)
    xt(7) in the *Programmer's Guide: STREAMS*

NAME

yacc – yet another compiler-compiler

SYNOPSIS

yacc [–vVdlt] [–Q[y|n]] *file*

DESCRIPTION

The **yacc** command converts a context-free grammar into a set of tables for a simple automaton that executes an LALR(1) parsing algorithm. The grammar may be ambiguous; specified precedence rules are used to break ambiguities.

The output file, **y.tab.c**, must be compiled by the C compiler to produce a program **yyparse**. This program must be loaded with the lexical analyzer program, **yylex**, as well as **main** and **yyerror**, an error handling routine. These routines must be supplied by the user; the **lex**(1) command is useful for creating lexical analyzers usable by **yacc**.

–v   Prepares the file **y.output**, which contains a description of the parsing tables and a report on conflicts generated by ambiguities in the grammar.

–d   Generates the file **y.tab.h** with the **#define** statements that associate the **yacc**-assigned "token codes" with the user-declared "token names." This association allows source files other than **y.tab.c** to access the token codes.

–l   Specifies that the code produced in **y.tab.c** will not contain any **#line** constructs. This option should only be used after the grammar and the associated actions are fully debugged.

–Q[y| n]

    The **–Qy** option puts the version stamping information in **y.tab.c**. This allows you to know what version of **yacc** built the file. The **–Qn** option (the default) writes no version information.

–t   Compiles runtime debugging code by default. Runtime debugging code is always generated in **y.tab.c** under conditional compilation control. By default, this code is not included when **y.tab.c** is compiled. Whether or not the **–t** option is used, the runtime debugging code is under the control of **YYDEBUG**, a preprocessor symbol. If **YYDEBUG** has a non-zero value, then the debugging code is included. If its value is zero, then the code will not be included. The size and execution time of a program produced without the runtime debugging code will be smaller and slightly faster.

–V   Prints on the standard error output the version information for **yacc**.

FILES

y.output
y.tab.c
y.tab.h   defines for token names
yacc.tmp,

`yacc.debug, yacc.acts`	temporary files
LIBDIR`/yaccpar`	parser prototype for C programs
LIBDIR	usually `/usr/ccs/lib`

SEE ALSO

lex(1)

The "**yacc**" chapter in the *Programmer's Guide: ANSI C and Programming Support Tools*

DIAGNOSTICS

The number of reduce-reduce and shift-reduce conflicts is reported on the standard error output; a more detailed report is found in the `y.output` file. %Similarly, if some rules are not reachable from the start symbol, this instance is also reported.

NOTES

Because file names are fixed, at most one **yacc** process can be active in a given directory at a given time.

NAME

yes – print string repeatedly

SYNOPSIS

yes [*string*]

DESCRIPTION

yes repeatedly outputs "y", or if a single string argument is given, *string* is output repeatedly. The command continues indefinitely unless aborted. yes is useful in pipes to commands that prompt for input and require a "y" response for a yes. In this case, yes terminates when the command that it pipes to terminates so that no infinite loop occurs.

NAME

ypcat – print values in a NIS data base

SYNOPSIS

ypcat [-k] [-d *ypdomain*] *mname*

DESCRIPTION

The **ypcat** command prints out values in the NIS name service map specified by *mname*, which may be either a map name or a map nickname. Since **ypcat** uses the NIS network services, no NIS server is specified.

Refer to **ypfiles**(4) and **ypserv**(1M) for an overview of the NIS name service.

The following options are available:

-d *ypdomain*   Specify a domain other that the default domain.

-k   Display the keys for those maps in which the values are null or the key is not part of the value. None of the maps derived from files that have an ASCII version in **/etc** fall into this class.

SEE ALSO

ypmatch(1), ypserv(1M), ypfiles(4)

NAME
ypinit – build and install YP database

SYNOPSIS
/usr/sbin/ypinit -c
/usr/sbin/ypinit -m
/usr/sbin/ypinit -s *master-name*

DESCRIPTION
ypinit sets up a YP name service database on a YP server. It can be used to set up a master or a slave server, or a client system. You must be the privileged user to run it. It asks a few self-explanatory questions, and reports success or failure to the terminal.

It sets up a master server using the simple model in which that server is master to all maps in the data base. This is the way to bootstrap the YP system; later if you want you can change the association of maps to masters.

All databases are built from scratch, either from information available to the program at runtime, or from the ASCII data base files in **/etc**. These files should be in their traditional form, rather than the abbreviated form used on client machines.

A YP database on a slave server is set up by copying an existing database from a running server. The *master-name* argument should be the hostname of a YP server (either the master server for all the maps, or a server on which the data base is up-to-date and stable).

To set up a client, **ypinit** prompts for a list of YP servers to bind the client to, this list should be ordered from closest to farthest server.

Read **ypfiles**(4) and **ypserv**(1M) for an overview of the YP name service.

The following options are available:

-c   Set up a client system.

-m   Indicate that the local host is to be the YP master.

-s *master-name*   Set up a slave database.

SEE ALSO
makedbm(1M), ypmake(1M), yppush(1M), ypserv(1M), ypxfr(1M), ypfiles(4)

FILES
/var/yp/binding/*domainname*/ypservers

NAME

ypmake – rebuild YP database

SYNOPSIS

cd /var/yp ; make [*map*]

DESCRIPTION

The file called Makefile in /var/yp is used by make to build the YP name service database. With no arguments, make creates dbm databases for any YP maps that are out-of-date, and then executes yppush(1M) to notify slave databases that there has been a change.

If *map* is supplied on the command line, make will update that map only.

There are three special variables used by make: DIR, which gives the directory of the source files; NOPUSH, which when non-null inhibits doing a yppush of the new database files; and DOM, used to construct a domain other than the master's default domain. The default for DIR is /etc, and the default for NOPUSH is the null string.

ypmake also creates an entry in /var/yp/aliases.

Refer to ypfiles(4) and ypserv(1M) for an overview of the YP.

FILES

/var/yp

SEE ALSO

make(1), makedbm(1M), yppush(1M), ypserv(1M), ypfiles(4)

NAME

ypmatch – print the value of one or more keys from the NIS map

SYNOPSIS

ypmatch [–d *ypdomain*] [–k] *key... mname*

DESCRIPTION

ypmatch prints the values associated with one or more keys from the NIS name services map specified by *mname*, which may be either a *mapname* or an map nickname.

Multiple keys can be specified; the same map will be searched for all keys. The keys must be exact values insofar as capitalization and length are concerned. No pattern matching is available. If a key is not matched, a diagnostic message is produced.

The following options are available:

–d *ypdomain*   Specify a domain other than the default domain.

–k   Before printing the value of a key, print the key itself, followed by a colon ("**:**"). This is useful only if the keys are not duplicated in the values, or so many keys were specified that the output could be confusing.

SEE ALSO

ypcat(1), ypfiles(4)

NAME
yppoll – return current version of the map at the NIS server host

SYNOPSIS
/usr/sbin/yppoll [–d *ypdomain*] [–h *host*] *mapname*

DESCRIPTION
The **yppoll** command asks a **ypserv**(1M) process what the order number is, and which host is the master NIS server for the named map.

The following options are available:

–d *ypdomain*   Use *ypdomain* instead of the default domain.

–h *host*   Ask the **ypserv** process at *host* about the map parameters. If *host* is not specified, the NIS server for the local host is used. That is, the default host is the one returned by **ypwhich**(1).

SEE ALSO
ypserv(1M), **ypwhich**(1), **ypfiles**(4)

NAME

yppush – force propagation of a changed NIS map

SYNOPSIS

/usr/sbin/yppush [–v] [–d *ypdomain*] *mapname*

DESCRIPTION

yppush copies a new version of the NIS name service map from the master NIS
server to the slave NIS servers. It is normally run only on the master NIS server
by the Makefile in /var/yp after the master databases are changed. It first constructs a list of NIS server hosts by reading the NIS map ypservers within the
ypdomain, or if the map is not set up, the local file is used. Keys within the map
ypservers are the ASCII names of the machines on which the NIS servers run.

A transfer map request is sent to the NIS server at each host, along with the information needed by the transfer agent (the program that actually moves the map)
to call back the yppush. When the attempt has completed (successfully or not),
and the transfer agent has sent yppush a status message, the results may be
printed to stdout. Messages are also printed when a transfer is not possible; for
instance when the request message is undeliverable, or when the timeout period
on responses has expired.

Refer to ypfiles(4) and ypserv(1M) for an overview of the NIS name service.

The following options are available:

–v   Verbose. Print messages when each server is called, and for
                    each response. If this flag is omitted, only error messages are
                    printed.

–d *ypdomain*   Specify a *ypdomain* other than the default domain.

FILES

/var/yp/*ypdomain*/ypservers.{*dir,pag*}   local file
/var/yp

SEE ALSO

ypserv(1M), ypxfr(1M), ypfiles(4)

NAME

ypserv, ypbind – NIS server and binder processes

SYNOPSIS

/usr/lib/netsvc/yp/ypserv

/usr/lib/netsvc/yp/ypbind [–ypset | –ypsetme]

DESCRIPTION

The NIS provides a simple network lookup service consisting of databases and processes. The databases are dbm(3) files in a directory tree rooted at /var/yp. These files are described in ypfiles(4). The processes are /usr/lib/netsvc/yp/ypserv, the NIS database lookup server, and /usr/lib/netsvc/yp/ypbind, the NIS binder. The programmatic interface to NIS is described in ypclnt(3N). Administrative tools are described in yppush(1M), ypxfr(1M), yppoll(1M), ypwhich(1), and ypset(1M). Tools to see the contents of NIS maps are described in ypcat(1), and ypmatch(1). Database generation and maintenance tools are described in ypinit(1M), ypmake(1M), and makedbm(1M).

Both ypserv and ypbind are daemon processes typically activated at system startup time. ypserv runs only on NIS server machines with a complete NIS database. ypbind runs on all machines using NIS services, both NIS servers and clients.

The ypserv daemon's primary function is to look up information in its local database of NIS maps. Communication to and from ypserv is by means of RPC calls. Lookup functions are described in ypclnt(3N), and are supplied as C-callable functions in the NIS library. There are four lookup functions, all of which are performed on a specified map within some NIS domain: Match, "Get_first", "Get_next", and "Get_all". The Match operation takes a key, and returns the associated value. The "Get_first" operation returns the first key-value pair from the map, and "Get_next" can be used to enumerate the remainder. "Get_all" ships the entire map to the requester as the response to a single RPC request.

Two other functions supply information about the map, rather than map entries: "Get_order_number", and "Get_master_name". In fact, both order number and master name exist in the map as key-value pairs, but the server will not return either through the normal lookup functions. If you examine the map with makedbm(1M), however, they will be visible.

The function of ypbind is to remember information that lets client processes on a single node communicate with some ypserv process. ypbind must run on every machine which has NIS client processes; ypserv may or may not be running on the same node, but must be running somewhere on the network.

The information ypbind remembers is called a binding—the association of a domain name with a NIS server.

The process of binding is driven by client requests. As a request for an unbound domain comes in, the ypbind process steps through the ypservers list (last entry first) trying to find a ypserv process that serves maps within that domain. There must be a ypserv process on at least one of the hosts in the ypservers file. Once a domain is bound by a particular ypbind, that same binding is given to every client process on the node. The ypbind process on the local node or a remote node may be queried for the binding of a particular domain by using the **ypwhich**(1) command.

If **ypbind** is unable to speak to the **ypserv** process it is bound to, it marks the domain as unbound, tells the client process that the domain is unbound, and tries to bind the domain once again. Requests received for an unbound domain will wait until the domain requested is bound. In general, a bound domain is marked as unbound when the node running **ypserv** crashes or gets overloaded. In such a case, **ypbind** will try to bind to another NIS server listed in **/var/yp/binding/**_domainname_**/ypservers**.

ypbind also accepts requests to set its binding for a particular domain. The request is usually generated by the NIS subsystem itself. **ypset**(1M) is a command to access the "_Set_domain_" facility. Note: the _Set Domain_ procedure only accepts requests from processes with appropriate privileges, and the **–ypset** or **–ypsetme** flags must have been set for **ypbind**.

The following options are available for the **ypbind** command only:

–ypset   Allow any user to call **ypset**(1M). By default, no one can call **ypset**(1M).

–ypsetme   Only allow **root** on local machines to call **ypset**(1M). By default, no one can call **ypset**(1M).

FILES

If the file **/var/yp/ypserv.log** exists when **ypserv** starts up, log information will be written to this file when error conditions arise.

/var/yp
/var/yp/binding/_ypdomain_**/ypservers**

SEE ALSO

makedbm(1M), ypcat(1), ypinit(1M), ypmake(1M), ypmatch(1), yppoll(1M), yppush(1M), ypset(1M), ypwhich(1), ypxfr(1M), dbm(3X), ypclnt(3N), ypfiles(4)

NOTES

Both **ypbind** and **ypserv** support multiple domains. The **ypserv** process determines the domains it serves by looking for directories of the same name in the directory **/var/yp**. Additionally, the **ypbind** process can maintain bindings to several domains and their servers.

NAME

ypset – point ypbind at a particular server

SYNOPSIS

/usr/sbin/ypset [**–d** *ypdomain*] [**–h** *host*] *server*

DESCRIPTION

In order to run **ypset**, **ypbind** must be initiated with the **–ypset** or **–ypsetme** options. See **ypserv**(1M). **ypset** tells **ypbind** to get NIS services for the specified *ypdomain* from the **ypserv** process running on *server*. If *server* is down, or is not running **ypserv**, this is not discovered until the NIS client process tries to get a binding for the domain. At this point, the binding set by **ypset** will be tested by **ypbind**. If the binding is invalid, **ypbind** will attempt to rebind for the same domain.

ypset is useful for binding a client node which is not on a broadcast net, or is on a broadcast net which is not running the NIS server host. It also is useful for debugging NIS client applications, for instance where the NIS map only exists at a single NIS server host.

In cases where several hosts on the local net are supplying NIS services, it is possible for **ypbind** to rebind to another host even while you attempt to find out if the **ypset** operation succeeded. For example, you can type:

```
# ypset host1
# ypwhich
host2
```

which can be confusing. This is a function of the NIS subsystem's attempt to load-balance among the available NIS servers, and occurs when *host1* does not respond to **ypbind** because it is not running **ypserv** (or is overloaded), and *host2*, running **ypserv**, gets the binding.

server indicates the NIS server to bind to, and must be specified as a name. This will work only if the node has a current valid binding for the domain in question, and **ypbind** has been set to allow use of **ypset**. In most cases, *server* should be specified as an IP address.

ypset tries to bind **ypbind** over a datagram transport first. Datagram Transports are recommended for higher performance. The NIS library calls, **yp_enum( )**, **yp_all( )**, **yp_next( )**, and **yp_first( )** use circuit transports regardless of the main transport being used.

Refer to **ypfiles**(4) and **ypserv**(1M) for an overview of the NIS name service.

The following options are available:

–h *host*   Set **ypbind**'s binding on *host*, instead of locally. *host* must be specified as a name.

–d *ypdomain*   Use *ypdomain*, instead of the default domain.

SEE ALSO

ypserv(1M), **ypwhich**(1), **ypfiles**(4)

NAME

      ypupdated – server for changing NIS information

SYNOPSIS

      /usr/lib/netsvc/yp/ypupdated [**-is**]

DESCRIPTION

      ypupdated is a daemon that updates information in the NIS name service, nor-
mally started up by **inetd**(1M). **ypupdated** consults the file **updaters**(4) in the
directory **/var/yp** to determine which NIS maps should be updated and how to
change them.

      By default, the daemon requires the most secure method of authentication avail-
able to it, either DES (secure) or UNIX (insecure).

      The following options are available:

      -i   Accept RPC calls with the insecure AUTH_UNIX credentials. This allows
programmatic updating of NIS maps in all networks.

      -s   Only accept calls authenticated using the secure RPC mechanism
(AUTH_DES authentication). This disables programmatic updating of NIS
maps unless the network supports these calls.

FILES

      /var/yp/updaters

SEE ALSO

      inetd(1M), **keyserv**(1M), **updaters**(4)

NAME

ypwhich – return name of NIS server or map master

SYNOPSIS

ypwhich [−d [*ypdomain*]] [*hostname*]
ypwhich [−d *ypdomain*] −m [*mname*]

DESCRIPTION

ypwhich tells which NIS server supplies the NIS name services to the NIS client, or which is the master for a map. If invoked without arguments, it gives the NIS server for the local machine. If *hostname* is specified, that machine is queried to find out which NIS master it is using.

Refer to ypfiles(4) and ypserv(1M) for an overview of the NIS name services.

The following options are available:

−d [*ypdomain*]   Use *ypdomain* instead of the default domain.

−m *mname*   Find the master NIS server for a map. No *hostname* can be specified with −m. *mname* can be a mapname, or a nickname for a map. When *mname* is omitted, produce a list available maps.

SEE ALSO

ypserv(1M), ypset(1M), ypfiles(4)

NAME

ypxfr – transfer YP map from a YP server to host

SYNOPSIS

/usr/sbin/ypxfr [–c] [–f] [–d *ypdomain*] [–h *host*] [–s *ypdomain*]
[–C *tid prog server*] *mapname*

DESCRIPTION

The ypxfr command moves a YP map in the default domain for the local host to
the local host by making use of normal YP services. It creates a temporary map
in the directory /var/yp/*ypdomain* (this directory must already exist; *ypdomain* is
the default domain for the local host), fills it by enumerating the map's entries,
fetches the map parameters (master and order number), and loads them. It then
deletes any old versions of the map and moves the temporary map to the real
mapname.

If run interactively, ypxfr writes its output to the terminal. However, if it is
started without a controlling terminal, and if the log file /var/yp/ypxfr.log
exists, it appends all its output to that file. Since ypxfr is most often run from the
privileged user's crontab file, or by ypserv, the log file can be used to retain a
record of what was attempted, and what the results were.

For consistency between servers, ypxfr should be run periodically for every map
in the YP data base. Different maps change at different rates: a map may not
change for months at a time, for instance, and may therefore be checked only
once a day. Some maps may change several times per day. In such a case, you
may want to check hourly for updates. A crontab(1) entry can be used to perform periodic updates automatically. Rather than having a separate crontab
entry for each map, you can group commands to update several maps in a shell
script. Examples (mnemonically named) are in /usr/sbin/yp: ypxfr_1perday,
and ypxfr_1perhour. They can serve as reasonable first cuts.

Refer to ypfiles(4) and ypserv(1M) for an overview of the YP name service.

The following options are available:

–c	Do not send a Clear current map request to the local ypserv process. Use this flag if ypserv is not running locally at the time you are running ypxfr. Otherwise, ypxfr complains that it cannot talk to the local ypserv, and the transfer fails.
–f	Force the transfer to occur even if the version at the master is not more recent than the local version.
–C *tid prog server*	This option is *only* for use by ypserv. When ypserv starts ypxfr, it specifies that ypxfr should call back a yppush process at the host *server*, registered as program number *prog*, and wait-ing for a response to transaction *tid*.
–d *ypdomain*	Specify a domain other than the default domain.
–h *host*	Get the map from *host*, regardless of what the map says the master is. If *host* is not specified, ypxfr asks the YP service for the name of the master, and try to get the map from there. *host* must be a name.

  -s *ypdomain*   Specify a source domain from which to transfer a map that
                             should be the same across domains.

FILES

  `/var/yp/ypxfr.log`   log file

  `/usr/sbin/yp/ypxfr_1perday`   cron(1M) script to run one transfer per
                                         day

  `/usr/sbin/yp/ypxfr_1perhour`   script for hourly transfers of volatile maps

  `/var/yp/ypdomain`   YP domain

  `/usr/spool/cron/crontabs/root`   privileged user's **crontab** file

SEE ALSO

  cron(1M), crontab(1), **ypserv**(1M), **yppush**(1M), **ypfiles**(4)

NAME

zdump – time zone dumper

SYNOPSIS

zdump [−v] [−c *cutoffyear*] [*zonename* . . .]

DESCRIPTION

The zdump command prints the current time in each *zonename* named on the command line.

The following options are available:

−v　　　　　　For each *zonename* on the command line, print the current time, the time at the lowest possible time value, the time one day after the lowest possible time value, the times both one second before and exactly at each time at which the rules for computing local time change, the time at the highest possible time value, and the time at one day less than the highest possible time value. Each line ends with isdst=1 if the given time is Daylight Saving Time or isdst=0 otherwise.

−c *cutoffyear*　　Cut off the verbose output near the start of the year *cutoffyear*.

FILES

/usr/lib/locale/TZ　　　standard zone information directory

SEE ALSO

zic(1M), ctime(3C)

NAME

`zic` – time zone compiler

SYNOPSIS

`zic` [`-v`] [`-d directory`] [`-l localtime`] [*filename* . . .]

DESCRIPTION

`zic` reads text from the file(s) named on the command line and creates the time conversion information files specified in this input. If a *filename* is '–', the standard input is read.

Input lines are made up of fields. Fields are separated by any number of white space characters. Leading and trailing white space on input lines is ignored. A pound sign (#) in the input introduces a comment which extends to the end of the line the pound sign appears on. White space characters and pound signs may be enclosed in double quotes (") if they're to be used as part of a field. Any line that is blank (after comment stripping) is ignored. Non-blank lines are expected to be of one of three types: rule lines, zone lines, and link lines.

A rule line has the form

    Rule *NAME   FROM   TO   TYPE   IN   ON   AT   SAVE   LETTER/S*

For example:

    Rule   USA   1969   1973   –   Apr lastSun 2:00   1:00   D

The fields that make up a rule line are:

NAME   Gives the (arbitrary) name of the set of rules this rule is part of.

FROM   Gives the first year in which the rule applies. The word **minimum** (or an abbreviation) means the minimum year with a representable time value. The word **maximum** (or an abbreviation) means the maximum year with a representable time value.

TO   Gives the final year in which the rule applies. In addition to **minimum** and **maximum** (as above), the word **only** (or an abbreviation) may be used to repeat the value of the **FROM** field.

TYPE   Gives the type of year in which the rule applies. If **TYPE** is '–' then the rule applies in all years between **FROM** and **TO** inclusive; if **TYPE** is **uspres**, the rule applies in U.S. Presidential election years; if **TYPE** is **nonpres**, the rule applies in years other than U.S. Presidential election years. If **TYPE** is something else, then `zic` executes the command

         yearistype *year type*

to check the type of a year: an exit status of zero is taken to mean that the year is of the given type; an exit status of one is taken to mean that the year is not of the given type.

IN   Names the month in which the rule takes effect. Month names may be abbreviated.

ON   Gives the day on which the rule takes effect. Recognized forms
            include:

            5   the fifth of the month

            lastSun   the last Sunday in the month

            lastMon   the last Monday in the month

            Sun>=8   first Sunday on or after the eighth

            Sun<=25   last Sunday on or before the 25th

            Names of days of the week may be abbreviated or spelled out in full.
            Note: there must be no spaces within the **ON** field.

AT   Gives the time of day at which the rule takes effect. Recognized forms
            include:

            2   time in hours

            2:00   time in hours and minutes

            15:00   24-hour format time (for times after noon)

            1:28:14   time in hours, minutes, and seconds

Any of these forms may be followed by the letter **w** if the given time is local
"wall clock" time or **s** if the given time is local "standard" time; in the absence of
w or **s**, wall clock time is assumed.

SAVE   Gives the amount of time to be added to local standard time when the
        rule is in effect. This field has the same format as the **AT** field (although,
        of course, the **w** and **s** suffixes are not used).

LETTER/S
        Gives the "variable part" (for example, the "S" or "D" in "EST" or "EDT")
        of time zone abbreviations to be used when this rule is in effect. If this
        field is '–', the variable part is null.

A zone line has the form

        Zone   *NAME*   *GMTOFF   RULES/SAVE   FORMAT   [UNTIL]*

For example:

        Zone Australia/South-west GMTOFF   RULES/SAVE   FORMAT

The fields that make up a zone line are:

NAME   The name of the time zone. This is the name used in creating the time
        conversion information file for the zone.

GMTOFF The amount of time to add to GMT to get standard time in this zone.
        This field has the same format as the **AT** and **SAVE** fields of rule lines;
        begin the field with a minus sign if time must be subtracted from GMT.

RULES/SAVE
        The name of the rule(s) that apply in the time zone or, alternately, an
        amount of time to add to local standard time. If this field is '–' then
        standard time always applies in the time zone.

FORMAT   The format for time zone abbreviations in this time zone. The pair of characters **%s** is used to show where the "variable part" of the time zone abbreviation goes. **UNTIL** The time at which the GMT offset or the rule(s) change for a location. It is specified as a year, a month, a day, and a time of day. If this is specified, the time zone information is generated from the given GMT offset and rule change until the time specified.

The next line must be a "continuation" line; this has the same form as a zone line except that the string "Zone" and the name are omitted, as the continuation line will place information starting at the time specified as the **UNTIL** field in the previous line in the file used by the previous line. Continuation lines may contain an **UNTIL** field, just as zone lines do, indicating that the next line is a further continuation.

A link line has the form

              Link   *LINK-FROM*   *LINK-TO*

For example:

              Link US/Eastern   **EST5EDT**

The **LINK-FROM** field should appear as the **NAME** field in some zone line; the **LINK-TO** field is used as an alternate name for that zone.

Except for continuation lines, lines may appear in any order in the input.

OPTIONS

-v   Complain if a year that appears in a data file is outside the range of years representable by system time values (0:00:00 AM GMT, January 1, 1970, to 3:14:07 AM GMT, January 19, 2038).

-d directory
       Create time conversion information files in the directory **directory** rather than in the standard directory **/usr/share/lib/zoneinfo**.

-l timezone
       Use the time zone **timezone** as local time. **zic** will act as if the file contained a link line of the form

       Link   *timezone*   localtime

FILES

       /usr/share/lib/zoneinfo   standard directory used for created files

SEE ALSO

       time(1), ctime(3)

NOTE

       For areas with more than two types of local time, you may need to use local standard time in the **AT** field of the earliest transition time's rule to ensure that the earliest transition time recorded in the compiled file is correct.

Section 4 – File Formats

Where To Find Section 4 Manual Pages

| NOTE | The Section 4 manual pages have been moved to another manual in this reference set. They are now located in the *System Files and Devices Reference Manual*. |

Section 5 – Miscellaneous Facilities

Where To Find Section 5 Manual Pages

NOTE

The Section 5 manual pages have been moved to another manual in this reference set. They are now located in the *System Files and Devices Reference Manual*.

Section 7 – Special Files

SECTION 7 - SPECIAL FILES

Where To Find Section 7 Manual Pages

NOTE	The Section 7 manual pages have been moved to another manual in this reference set. They are now located in the *System Files and Devices Reference Manual*.

Permuted Index

PERMUTED INDEX

tr	translate characters .... tr(1)
tr	translate characters .... tr(1)
mailalias	translate mail alias names .... mailalias(1)
pkgtrans	translate package format .... pkgtrans(1)
cof2elf COFF to ELF object file	translation .... cof2elf(1)
postdaisy PostScript	translator for Diablo 630 files .... postdaisy(1)
postdmd PostScript	translator for DMD bitmap files .... postdmd(1)
postplot PostScript	translator for plot graphics files .... postplot(1)
posttek PostScript	translator for tektronix 4014 files .... posttek(1)
postprint PostScript	translator for text files .... postprint(1)
trpt	transliterate protocol trace .... trpt(1M)
system uucico file	transport program for the uucp .... uucico(1M)
the scheduler for the uucp file	transport program uusched .... uusched(1M)
	trchan translate character sets .... trchan(1)
tftp	trivial file transfer program .... tftp(1)
server tftpd DARPA	Trivial File Transfer Protocol .... tftpd(1M)
tnamed, in.tnamed DARPA	trivial name server .... tnamed(1M)
differences between versions of a	troff input file diffmk mark .... diffmk(1)
errors checknr check nroff and	troff input files; report possible .... checknr(1)
.so requests from nroff or	troff input /resolve and eliminate .... soelim(1)
printers dpost	troff postprocessor for PostScript .... dpost(1)
deroff remove nroff,	troff, tbl and eqn constructs .... deroff(1)
tbl format tables for nroff or	troff .... tbl(1)
	troff typeset or format documents .... troff(1)
	trpt transliterate protocol trace .... trpt(1M)
	true, false provide truth values .... true(1)
signals	truss trace system calls and .... truss(1)
machid get processor type	truth value .... machid(1)
true, false provide	truth values .... true(1)
debugging on Uutry	try to contact remote system with .... Uutry(1M)
setting terminal modes	tset provide information for .... tset(1)
terminal modes	tset provide information to set .... tset(1)
terminal characteristics	tset, reset establish or restore .... tset(1)
	tsort topological sort .... tsort(1)
mapchan Configure	tty device mapping .... mapchan(1M)
	tty get the name of the terminal .... tty(1)
settings and hunt sequences for	TTY ports sttydefs maintain line .... sttydefs(1M)
monitor-specific information	ttyadm format and output port .... ttyadm(1M)
ports	ttymon port monitor for terminal .... ttymon(1M)
idtune attempts to set value of a	tunable parameter .... idtune(1M)
tunefs	tune up an existing file system .... tunefs(1M)
system	tunefs tune up an existing file .... tunefs(1M)
quotaon, quotaoff	turn file system quotas on and off .... quotaon(1M)
/runacct, shutacct, startup,	turnacct shell procedures for/ .... chargefee(1M)
file determine file	type .... file(1)
(generic) determine file system	type fstyp .... fstyp(1M)
discipline getty set terminal	type, modes, speed, and line .... getty(1M)